THE MIDDLE EASTERN FRONT
WORLD WAR I

Sarikamish

Mosul

TIGRIS RIVER

EUPHRATES RIVER

Baghdad

Kut

IRAQ
(MESOPOTAMIA)

Basra

THE MARCH ON AQABA

Jerusalem
Amman
Azraq
Gaza

Bair

WADI

Maan
Jefer

SIRHAN

JULY 6, 1917
AQABA
Aba el Lissan

EL HOUL

RED SEA

WEJH
MAY 9, 1917

PERSIAN GULF

ARABIA

Lawrence in Arabia

Also by Scott Anderson

Nonfiction
The 4 O'Clock Murders
The Man Who Tried to Save the World

With Jon Lee Anderson
Inside the League
War Zones

Fiction
Triage
Moonlight Hotel

War, Deceit, Imperial Folly and the Making of

Lawrence in Arabia

the Modern Middle East | *Scott Anderson*

SIGNAL
McCLELLAND
& STEWART

Signal is an imprint of McClelland & Stewart,
a division of Random House of Canada Limited.

Published simultaneously in the United States of American by Doubleday,
a division of Random House, Inc., New York.

Book design by Maria Carella
Frontispiece photograph copyright © Imperial War Museum (Q58838)
Endpaper maps designed by John T. Burgoyne
Front jacket photograph by Taylor S. Kennedy/
National Geographic Stock
Jacket spine photograph © Marist Archives and Special Collections,
Lowell Thomas Papers
Jacket design by John Fontana

Library and Archives Canada Cataloguing in Publication available upon request.

ISBN 978-0-7710-0766-8

PRINTED AND BOUND IN THE UNITED STATES OF AMERICA

McClelland & Stewart,
a division of Random House of Canada Limited
One Toronto Street, Suite 300
Toronto, Ontario
M5C 2V6

www.randomhouse.ca

1 2 3 4 5   17 16 15 14 13

To the two loves of my life,
Nanette and Natasha

.

Contents

| Part Three |

Author's Note

In war, language itself often becomes a weapon, and that was certainly true in the Middle Eastern theater of World War I. For example, while the Allied powers tended to use "the Ottoman Empire" and "Turkey" interchangeably, they displayed a marked preference for the latter designation as the war went on, undoubtedly to help fortify the notion that the non-Turkish populations of the Ottoman Empire were somehow "captive peoples" in need of liberation. Similarly, while early-war Allied documents often noted that Palestine and Lebanon were provinces of Ottoman Syria, that distinction tended to disappear as the British and French made plans to seize those territories in the postwar era. On a more subtle level, all the Western powers, including the Ottoman Empire's/Turkey's chief ally in the war, Germany, continued to refer to the city of "Constantinople" (its name under a Christian empire overthrown by the Muslim Ottomans in 1453) rather than the locally preferred "Istanbul."

As many Middle East historians rightly point out, the use of these Western-preferred labels—Turkey rather than the Ottoman Empire, Constantinople instead of Istanbul—is indicative of a Eurocentric perspective that, in its most pernicious form, serves to validate the European (read imperialist) view of history.

This poses a dilemma for historians focusing on the Western role in that war theater—as I do in this book—since the bulk of their research will naturally be drawn from Western sources. In such a situation, it would seem a writer must choose between clarity and political sensitivity; since I feel many readers would find it confusing if, for example, I consistently referred to "Istanbul" when virtually all cited material refers to "Constantinople," I have opted for clarity.

I was aided in this decision, however, by the fact that these language distinctions were not nearly so clear-cut at the time as some contemporary Middle East historians contend. Even the wartime leadership of the Ottoman Empire/Turkey frequently referred to the city of "Constantinople," and also tended to use "Ottoman" and "Turkey" synonymously (see the epigraph from Djemal Pasha in Chapter One). To dwell on all this too long is only to invite more complications. As Ottoman historian Mustafa Aksakal readily concedes in *The Ottoman Road to War* (pp. x–xi), "it seems anachronistic to speak of an 'Ottoman government' and an 'Ottoman cabinet' in 1914 when the major players had explicitly repudiated 'Ottomanism' and were set on constructing a government by and for the Turks . . . "

In sum, like the principals in this book, I've used "Ottoman Empire" and "Turkey" somewhat interchangeably, guided mostly by what sounds right in a particular context, while for simplicity, I refer exclusively to "Constantinople."

On a different language-related matter, Arabic names can be transliterated in a wide variety of ways. For purposes of consistency, I have adopted the spellings that appear most often in quoted material, and have standardized those spellings within quoted material. In most cases, this adheres to Egyptian Arabic pronunciation. For example, a man named Mohammed al-Faroki, whose surname appeared in different documents of the time also as Faruqi, Farogi, Farookee, Faroukhi, etc., will appear as Faroki throughout. The most notable case in point is that of T. E. Lawrence's chief Arab ally, Faisal ibn Hussein, usually referred to as Feisal by Lawrence, but as Faisal by most others, including historians. To avoid confusion, I've changed all spellings to the latter.

Also, the use of English punctuation has changed quite dramatically over the past century, and Lawrence in particular had an extremely idiosyncratic—some might say antagonistic—approach to it in his writing. In quotations where I believed the original punctuation might obscure meaning for modern readers, I have adopted the modern norm. These changes apply only to punctuation; no words have been added or deleted from quotations except where indicated by brackets or ellipses.

Finally, two versions of *Seven Pillars of Wisdom* were published in T. E. Lawrence's lifetime. The first, a handprinted edition of only eight copies, was produced in 1922 and is commonly referred to as the "Oxford Text," while a revised edition of approximately two hundred copies was produced in 1926; it is this latter version that is most commonly read today. Since Lawrence made clear that he regarded the Oxford Text as a rough draft, I have quoted almost exclusively from the 1926 version. In those few instances where I've quoted from the Oxford Text, the endnote citation is marked "(Oxford)."

Lawrence in Arabia

Introduction

On the morning of October 30, 1918, Colonel Thomas Edward Lawrence received a summons to Buckingham Palace. The king had requested his presence.

The collective mood in London that day was euphoric. For the past four years and three months, Great Britain and much of the rest of the world had been consumed by the bloodiest conflict in recorded history, one that had claimed the lives of some sixteen million people across three continents. Now, with a speed that scarcely could have been imagined mere weeks earlier, it was all coming to an end. On that same day, one of Great Britain's three principal foes, the Ottoman Empire, was accepting peace terms, and the remaining two, Germany and Austria-Hungary, would shortly follow suit. Colonel Lawrence's contribution to that war effort had been in its Middle Eastern theater, and he too was caught quite off guard by its rapid close. At the beginning of that month, he had still been in the field assisting in the capture of Damascus, an event that heralded the collapse of the Ottoman army. Back in England for less than a week, he was already consulting with those senior British statesmen and generals tasked with mapping out the postwar borders of the Middle East, a once-fanciful endeavor that had now become quite urgent. Lawrence was apparently under the impression that his audience with King George V that morning was to discuss those ongoing deliberations.

He was mistaken. Once at the palace, the thirty-year-old colonel was ushered into a ballroom where, flanked by a half dozen dignitaries and a coterie of costumed courtiers, the king and queen soon entered. A low cushioned stool had been placed just before the king's raised dais, while to the monarch's immediate right, the lord chamberlain held a velvet pillow on which an array of medals rested. After introductions were made, George V fixed his guest with a smile: "I have some presents for you."

As a student of British history, Colonel Lawrence knew precisely what was about to occur. The pedestal was an investiture stool, upon which he was to kneel as the king performed the elaborate, centuries-old ceremony—the conferring of a sash and the medals on the pillow, the tapping with a sword and the intoning of an oath—that would make him a Knight Commander of the Order of the British Empire.

It was a moment T. E. Lawrence had long dreamed of. As a boy, he was obsessed with medieval history and the tales of King Arthur's court, and his greatest ambition, he once wrote, was to be knighted by the age of thirty. On that morning, his youthful aspiration was about to be fulfilled.

A couple of details added to the honor. Over the past four years, King George had given out so many commendations and medals to his nation's soldiers that even knighthoods were now generally bestowed en masse; in the autumn of 1918, a private investiture like Lawrence's was practically unheard of. Also unusual was the presence of Queen Mary. She normally eschewed these sorts of ceremonies, but she had been so stirred by the accounts of T. E. Lawrence's wartime deeds as to make an exception in his case.

Except Lawrence didn't kneel. Instead, just as the ceremony got under way, he quietly informed the king that he was refusing the honor.

There followed a moment of confusion. Over the nine-hundred-year history of the monarchy, the refusal of knighthood was such an extraordinary event that there was no protocol for how to handle it. Eventually, King George returned to the lord chamberlain's pillow the medal he had been awkwardly holding, and under the baleful gaze of a furious Queen Mary, Colonel Lawrence turned and walked away.

TODAY, MORE THAN seven decades after his death, and nearly a century since the exploits that made him famous, Thomas Edward Lawrence—"Lawrence of Arabia," as he is better known—remains one of the most enigmatic and controversial figures of the twentieth century. Despite scores of biographies, countless scholarly studies, and at least three movies, including one considered a masterpiece, historians have never quite decided what to make of the young, bashful Oxford scholar who rode into battle at the head of an Arab army and changed history.

One reason for the contentiousness over his memory has to do with the terrain he traversed. Lawrence was both eyewitness to and participant in some of the most pivotal events leading to the creation of the modern Middle East, and this is a corner of the earth where even the simplest assertion is dissected and parsed and argued over. In the unending debates over the roots of that region's myriad fault lines, Lawrence has been alternately extolled and pilloried, sanctified, demonized, even diminished to a footnote, as political goals require.

Then there was Lawrence's own personality. A supremely private and hidden man, he seemed intent on baffling all those who would try to know him. A natural leader of men, or a charlatan? A man without fear, or both a moral and physical coward? Long before any of his biographers, it was Lawrence who first attached these contradictory characteristics—and many others—to himself. Joined to this was a mischievous streak, a storyteller's delight in twitting those who believed in and insisted on "facts." The episode at Buckingham Palace is a case in point. In subsequent years, Lawrence offered several accounts of what had transpired in the ballroom, each at slight variance with the others and at even greater variance to the recollections of eyewitnesses. Earlier than most, Lawrence seemed to embrace the modern concept that history was malleable, that truth was what people were willing to believe.

Among writers on Lawrence, these contradictions have often spurred descents into minutiae, arcane squabbles between those seeking to tarnish his reputation and those seeking to defend it. Did he truly make a particular desert crossing in forty-nine hours, as he claimed, or might it have taken a day longer? Did he really play such a signal role in Battle X, or does more credit belong to British officer Y or to Arab chieftain Z? Only slightly less tedious are those polemicists wishing to pigeonhole him for ideological ends. Lawrence, the great defender of the Jewish people or the raging anti-Semite? The enlightened progressive striving for Arab independence or the crypto-imperialist? Lawrence left behind such a large body of writing, and his views altered so dramatically over the course of his life, that it's possible with careful cherry-picking to both confirm and refute most every accolade and accusation made of him.

Beyond being tiresome, the cardinal sin of these debates is that they obscure the most beguiling riddle of Lawrence's story: *How* did he do it? How did a painfully shy Oxford archaeologist without a single day of military training become the battlefield commander of a foreign revolutionary army, the political master strategist who foretold so many of the Middle Eastern calamities to come?

The short answer might seem somewhat anticlimactic: Lawrence was able to become "Lawrence of Arabia" because no one was paying much attention.

Amid the vast slaughter occurring across the breadth of Europe in

World War I, the Middle Eastern theater of that war was of markedly secondary importance. Within that theater, the Arab Revolt to which Lawrence became affiliated was, to use his own words, "a sideshow of a sideshow." In terms of lives and money and matériel expended, in terms of the thousands of hours spent in weighty consultation between generals and kings and prime ministers, the imperial plotters of Europe were infinitely more concerned over the future status of Belgium, for example, than with what might happen in the impoverished and distant regions of the Middle East. Consequently, in the view of British war planners, if a young army officer left largely to his own devices could sufficiently organize the fractious Arab tribes to harass their Turkish enemy, all to the good. Of course, it wouldn't be very long before both the Arab Revolt and the Middle East became vastly more important to the rest of the world, but this was a possibility barely considered—indeed, it could hardly have been imagined—at the time.

But this isn't the whole story either. That's because the low regard with which British war strategists viewed events in the Middle East found reflection in the other great warring powers. As a result, these powers, too, relegated their military efforts in the region to whatever could be spared from the more important battlefields elsewhere, consigning the task of intelligence gathering and fomenting rebellion and forging alliances to men with résumés just as modest and unlikely as Lawrence's.

As with Lawrence, these other competitors in the field tended to be young, wholly untrained for the missions they were given, and largely unsupervised. And just as with their more famous British counterpart, to capitalize on their extraordinary freedom of action, these men drew upon a very particular set of personality traits—cleverness, bravery, a talent for treachery—to both forge their own destiny and alter the course of history.

Among them was a fallen American aristocrat in his twenties who, as the only American field intelligence officer in the Middle East during World War I, would strongly influence his nation's postwar policy in the region, even as he remained on the payroll of Standard Oil of New York. There was the young German scholar who, donning the camouflage of Arab robes, would seek to foment an Islamic jihad against the Western colonial powers, and who would carry his "war by revolution" ideas into the Nazi era. Along with them was a Jewish scientist who, under the cover of working for the Ottoman government, would establish an elaborate anti-Ottoman spy ring and play a crucial role in creating a Jewish homeland in Palestine.

If little remembered today, these men shared something else with their British counterpart. Like Lawrence, they were not the senior generals who charted battlefield campaigns in the Middle East, nor the elder statesmen who drew lines on maps in the war's aftermath. Instead, their roles were perhaps even more profound: it was they who created the conditions on the ground that brought those campaigns to fruition, who made those postwar policies and boundaries possible. History is always a collaborative effort, and in the case of World War I an effort that involved literally millions of players, but to a surprising degree, the subterranean and complex game these four men played, their hidden loyalties and personal duels, helped create the modern Middle East and, by inevitable extension, the world we live in today.

Yet within this small galaxy of personalities there remain at least two compelling reasons why T. E. Lawrence and his story should reside firmly at its center.

The modern Middle East was largely created by the British. It was they who carried the Allied war effort in the region during World War I and who, at its close, principally fashioned its peace. It was a peace presaged by the nickname given the region by covetous Allied leaders in wartime: "the Great Loot." As one of Britain's most important and influential agents in that arena, Lawrence was intimately connected to all, good and bad, that was to come.

Second, and as the episode at Buckingham Palace attests, this was an experience that left him utterly changed, unrecognizable in certain respects even to himself. Victory carries a moral burden the vanquished never know, and as an architect of momentous events, Lawrence would be uniquely haunted by what he saw and did during the Great Loot.

Part One

◇◇◇◇◇

Chapter 1

Playboys in the Holy Land

I consider this new crisis that has emerged to be a blessing. I believe that
it is the Turks' ultimate duty either to live like an honorable nation
or to exit the stage of history gloriously.

DJEMAL PASHA, GOVERNOR OF SYRIA,
ON TURKEY'S ENTRY INTO WORLD WAR I, NOVEMBER 2, 1914

The storm began as a mild weather disturbance, one fairly common
for that time of year. For several days in early January 1914, a hot
dry breeze had come off the Sahara Desert to pass over the winter-cooled
waters of the eastern Mediterranean. By the morning of the ninth, this
convergence had spawned a strong southwesterly wind, one that grew
in intensity as it made landfall over southern Palestine. By the time it
approached Beersheva, a small village on the edge of the Zin Desert some
twenty-five miles inland, this wind threatened to trigger a *khamsin,* or
sandstorm.

For the inexperienced, being caught out in the desert during a *khamsin* can be unsettling. While it shares some of the properties of a severe
thunderstorm—the same drop in barometric pressure beforehand, the
same prelude of buffeting wind—the fact that sand is falling rather than
water means visibility can rapidly drop to just a few feet, and the constant
raking of sand against the body, coating the nose and mouth and collecting in every crevice of clothing, can induce a feeling of suffocation. In the
grip of this sensation, the mind can easily seize upon the worst idea—to
journey on, to attempt to fight one's way out of the storm. Men routinely
become lost and die acting on this impulse.

But the three young British men waiting in Beersheva that afternoon were not inexperienced. They had lingered an extra day in the village—a lonely outpost of perhaps eight hundred inhabitants best known as a watering hole for passing camel caravans—in expectation of the arrival of an expedition party led by two Americans. By dusk, however, there was still no sign of the Americans, and what had earlier appeared no more threatening than a dull brown haze in the west had now formed up into a mile-high wall of approaching sand. Shortly after dark, the *khamsin* rolled in.

Throughout that night, the storm raged. In the small house the British men shared, sand spattered against the shuttered windows like driven rain, and all their efforts to seal the place couldn't prevent them and everything else inside from becoming coated in a fine layer of desert dust. By dawn, the winds had abated somewhat, enough that the risen sun appeared as a pale silvery orb in the eastern sky.

The *khamsin* finally died off in early afternoon, allowing the residents of Beersheva to emerge from their homes and tents and move about. It was then that the Britons received some news of the Americans. Apparently caught out by the impending storm, they had drawn camp the previous evening in the desert just a few miles east of town. The three men saddled their camels and made for the American camp.

Considering the surrounding desolation, the opulence they found there made for a rather bizarre spectacle. Along with a couple of horse-drawn carts hauling silage for the party's herd of pack animals were several more to carry its larger "field furniture." Now that the *khamsin* had passed, the native orderlies were busily breaking camp, including dismantling the two very fine and spacious Bell tents—undoubtedly purchased from one of the better expedition outfitters in London or New York—that were the habitations of the two young Americans leading the expedition. These men, both in their midtwenties and clad in Western field suits and bowler hats, were named William Yale and Rudolf McGovern. As they explained to their British visitors, they were in southern Palestine as part of a Grand Tour of the Holy Land, an adventure that when the sandstorm hit had become a bit more than they bargained for.

But there was something about the Americans that didn't quite add up. Although they were well dressed and obviously traveling in high style, there was little about the men—McGovern small and reserved, Yale barrel-chested with a boxer's rough-hewn face—that suggested them as either natural traveling companions or likely candidates for a pilgrimage tour of biblical sites. Then there was their demeanor. Encountering other foreigners in this lonely corner of Syria was such a novelty that it tended to induce a kind of instant camaraderie, but there was none of this with

Yale and McGovern. To the contrary, the Americans appeared flustered, even perturbed, by the arrival of the Britons, and it seemed that only the dictates of desert hospitality compelled Yale—clearly the dominant personality of the two—to invite their guests into the main dining tent and to dispatch one of their camp followers to prepare tea.

But if the Americans seemed peculiar, William Yale had precisely the same reaction to his British visitors. The oldest—and the leader of the group, in Yale's estimation—was a dark-haired, hawk-faced man in his midthirties clad in a well-worn British army uniform. His companions were in civilian dress and quite a bit younger, one in his midtwenties perhaps, while the third appeared to be a mere teenager. Most puzzling to Yale, the two older men barely spoke. Instead, it was the "teenager" who commandeered the conversation in the tent and chattered like a magpie. He was very slight and slender, with a heavy-featured face that Yale found almost repellent, but his most arresting feature was his eyes; they were light blue and piercingly intense.

The young visitor explained that he and his companions were in the region to conduct an archaeological survey of biblical-era ruins for a British organization called the Palestine Exploration Fund. He then proceeded to regale his American hosts with stories of his own adventures in the Near East, stories so voluble and engaging that it took Yale quite some time to realize they masked a kind of interrogation.

"His chatter was sprinkled with a stream of questions—seemingly quite innocent questions—about us and our plans. He assumed that we were tourists traveling in grand style to see the famous ruins of the Sinai and Palestine. It was not until after our visitors had left that we realized that this seemingly inexperienced, youthful enthusiast had most successfully pumped us dry."

It would be some time before he knew it, but William Yale had just had his first encounter with Thomas Edward Lawrence, soon to become better known as Lawrence of Arabia. It would also be some time before he learned that Lawrence had only feigned interest in the Americans' Holy Land tour in order to toy with them, that he had known all along their story was false.

In reality, William Yale and Rudolf McGovern were agents of the Standard Oil Company of New York, and they were in Palestine on a secret mission in search of oil. Under orders from Standard headquarters, they had spent the previous three months posing as wealthy young men of leisure—"playboys," in the parlance of the day—on the Holy Land tourist circuit. While upholding that cover story, they had quietly slipped off to excavate along the Dead Sea and to take geological soundings in the Judean foothills.

But if the playboy tale had held the ring of plausibility during their earlier wanderings—at least Judea had ruins and the Dead Sea figured prominently in the Bible—it became rather suspect once they veered off for the forlorn outpost of Beersheva. It was downright laughable when considering Yale and McGovern's ultimate destination: a desolate massif of stone rising up out of the desert some twenty miles southeast of Beersheva known as Kornub.

In fact, it was not the *khamsin* but the growing improbability of their cover story that had kept the Americans out of Beersheva the night before. As they had approached the village, the oilmen had been alerted to the presence of the three Britons. Anxious to avoid a meeting and the awkward questions likely to arise, they had chosen to pitch camp in the desert instead, with the intention of slipping into Beersheva at first light, quickly gathering up supplies for their onward journey, and stealing away before being detected. The slow-moving *khamsin* had obviously put an end to that plan, and as he'd waited out the storm that morning, Yale had feared it was only a matter of time before the foreigners in Beersheva learned of their desert campsite and put in an appearance—an apprehension confirmed when the three men rode up.

But what Yale also couldn't have known was that his efforts at concealment were quite pointless, that this seemingly impromptu meeting in the desert was anything but. The previous day, Lawrence and his colleagues on the archaeological expedition had received a cable from the British consulate in Jerusalem alerting them to the presence of the American oilmen in the area, and they had lingered in Beersheva for the express purpose of intercepting Yale and McGovern and learning what they were up to.

If this seemed an odd mission for an archaeological survey team to undertake, there was rather more to that story, too. Although it was technically true that Lawrence and Leonard Woolley—the other civilian in the tent, and a respected archaeologist—were in southern Palestine in search of biblical ruins, that project was merely a fig leaf for a far more sensitive one, an elaborate covert operation being run by the British military. Ottoman government officials certainly knew of the Palestine Exploration Fund survey in the Zin Desert—they had approved it, after all—but they knew nothing of the five British military survey teams operating under the PEF banner who at that very moment were scattered across the desert quietly mapping the Ottoman Empire's southwestern frontier. Overseeing that covert operation was the uniformed third visitor to the American camp, Captain Stewart Francis Newcombe of the Royal Engineers.

What had taken place outside Beersheva, then, was a rather complex game of bluff, one in which one side had rummaged about for the truth behind the other's fiction, even as it sought to uphold its own framework of fiction.

LAWRENCE AND YALE weren't the only young foreigners with suspect agendas wandering about the Holy Land that mid-January. Just fifty miles to the north of Beersheva, in the city of Jerusalem, a thirty-three-year-old German scholar named Curt Prüfer was also plotting his future.

In Prüfer's physical appearance were few clues to suggest him as an intriguing figure. Quite to the contrary. The German stood just five foot eight, with narrow, sloping shoulders, and his thin thatch of brownish blond hair framed a bland, thin face most noteworthy for its lack of distinguishing characteristics, the sort of face that naturally blends into a crowd. Adding to this air of innocuousness was Prüfer's voice. He spoke in a permanent soft, feathery whisper, as if he'd spent his entire life in a library, although this condition was actually the result of a botched throat operation in childhood that had scarred his vocal cords. To many who met the young German scholar, his modest frame together with that voice conveyed an aura of effeminacy, an estimation likely to be fortified should they happen to learn the subject of the dissertation that had earned him his doctorate: a learned study on the Egyptian dramatic form known as shadow plays. In mid-January 1914, Prüfer was waiting in Jerusalem for the arrival of a friend, a Bavarian landscape painter of middling repute, with whom he'd made plans to conduct an extended tour of the Upper Nile aboard a luxury dhow.

But just as with the men gathered in the tent outside Beersheva, there was an altogether different side to Dr. Curt Prüfer. For the previous several years, he had served as the Oriental secretary to the German embassy in Cairo, a position ideally suited to both his appearance and demeanor. Removed from the policymaking deliberations of the senior diplomatic staff, the Oriental secretary was tasked to quietly keep tabs on the social and political undercurrents of the country, to maintain a low profile and report back. In that capacity, Prüfer's life in Cairo had been a never-ending social whirl, a perpetual roster of meetings and teas and dinners with Egypt's most prominent journalists, businessmen, and politicians.

His social circle had included more controversial figures, too. With Germany vying with its rival, Great Britain, for influence in the region, Prüfer had surreptitiously cultivated alliances with a wide array of Egyptian dissidents seeking to end British control of their homeland: nationalists, royalists, religious zealots. Fluent in Arabic as well as a half dozen other languages, in 1911 the German Oriental secretary had traveled across Egypt and Syria disguised as a Bedouin to foment anti-British sentiment among the tribes. The following year, he had attempted to recruit Egyptian mujahideen to join their Arab brethren in Libya against an invading Italian army.

In these varied efforts, Curt Prüfer had eventually fallen foul of the first rule of his position: to stay in the background. Alerted to his agent provocateur activities, the British secret police in Egypt had quietly compiled a lengthy dossier on the Oriental secretary, and bided their time on when to use it. When finally they did, Prüfer was effectively persona non grata. After enduring the ignominy for as long as he could, he had tendered his resignation from the German diplomatic service in late 1913. It was this that had brought him to Jerusalem that January. Once his friend, the artist Richard von Below, arrived from Germany, the two would depart for Egypt and their luxury cruise up the Nile. That journey was scheduled to last some five months, and while von Below painted, Prüfer intended to busy himself composing travelogue articles for magazines back in Germany, along with updating entries for the famous German travel guide, Baedeker's. It was to mark something of a return to Prüfer's academic roots, his extended foray into the messy arena of international politics consigned to the past.

Or maybe not. Maybe his spying activities were just put on hiatus, for on his upcoming cruise, Curt Prüfer would be traveling along the very lifeline of British-ruled Egypt, would be given the opportunity to glimpse firsthand its defensive fortifications and port facilities, to quietly take the pulse of Egyptian public opinion. And while it might appear that the exposed and disgraced former Oriental secretary was sailing into an unsettled future that January of 1914, he now held at least one conviction that gave his life a strong sense of direction: it was the British who had destroyed his diplomatic career; it was the British upon whom he would take his revenge.

Toward achieving this, he could draw on another rather surprising aspect of his personality. His aura of innocuousness notwithstanding, Curt Prüfer was a consummate charmer, and had a reputation as a notorious seducer of women. In Cairo, whatever affections he felt for his wife, a doughty American woman thirteen years his senior, had been shared between a string of mistresses. Since arriving in Jerusalem, he had taken up with a young and beautiful Russian Jewish émigré doctor named Minna Weizmann, better known to her friends and family as Fanny. In just a little over a year's time, as Germany's counterintelligence chief in wartime Syria, Prüfer would come up with the idea of recruiting Jewish émigrés to infiltrate British-held Egypt and spy for the Fatherland. Among the first spies Prüfer would send into enemy territory would be his lover, Fanny Weizmann.

. . .

JUST SEVENTY MILES to the north of Jerusalem that January, there was another man about to embark on a double life. His name was Aaron Aaronsohn. A thirty-eight-year-old Jewish émigré from Romania, Aaronsohn was already recognized as one of the preeminent agricultural scientists, or agronomists, in the Middle East, a reputation cemented by his 1906 discovery of the genetic forebear to wheat. With funding from American Jewish philanthropists, in 1909 he had established the Jewish Agricultural Experiment Station outside the village of Athlit, and for the past five years had tirelessly experimented with all manner of plants and trees in hopes of returning the arid Palestinian region of Syria to the verdant garden it had once been.

This ambition had a political component. A committed Zionist, as early as 1911 Aaronsohn had begun to articulate a scheme whereby a vast swath of Palestine might be wrested away from the Ottoman Empire and reconstituted as a Jewish homeland. Other Zionists had expressed this vision before, of course, but it was Aaronsohn, with his encyclopedic knowledge of the region's flora and soil conditions and aquifers, who first appreciated how it might practically be accomplished, how the Jewish diaspora might return to its ancestral homeland and prosper by making the desert bloom.

In the near future, Aaronsohn would perceive the chance to bring this dream closer to fruition, and he would seize it. Under the cover of advising the local government on agricultural matters, he would establish an extensive spy ring across the breadth of Palestine, and provide the Ottomans' British enemies with some of their most invaluable battlefield intelligence. The agronomist would then go on to play a signal role in promoting the cause of a Jewish homeland in the capitals of Europe. Somewhat ironically, his chief confederate in that endeavor would be the older brother of Curt Prüfer's lover-spy, Fanny Weizmann, and the future first president of Israel: Chaim Weizmann.

THE LURE OF the East: whether to conquer or explore or exploit, it has exerted its pull on the West for a thousand years. That lure brought wave after wave of Christian Crusaders to the Near East over a three-hundred-year span in the Middle Ages. More recently, it brought a conquering French general with pharaonic fantasies named Napoleon Bonaparte to Egypt in the 1790s, Europe's greatest archaeologists in the 1830s, and hordes of Western oil barons, wildcatters, and con men to the shores of the Caspian Sea in the 1870s. For a similar variety of reasons, in the early years of the twentieth century it brought together four young men of adventure: Thomas Edward Lawrence, William Yale, Curt Prüfer, and Aaron Aaronsohn.

At the time, the regions these men traveled were still a part of the Ottoman Empire, one of the greatest imperial powers the world had ever known. From its birthplace in a tiny corner of the mountainous region of Anatolia in modern-day Turkey, that empire had steadily expanded until by the early 1600s it encompassed an area rivaling that of the Roman imperium at its height: from the gates of Vienna in the north to the southern tip of the Arabian Peninsula, from the shores of the western Mediterranean clear across to the port of Basra in modern-day Iraq.

But that had been then. By the second decade of the twentieth century, the Ottoman Empire had long been in a state of seemingly terminal decline. The proverbial "sick man of Europe," its epitaph had begun to be written as far back as the 1850s, and in the intervening years no fewer than five of the imperial powers of Europe had taken turns snatching away great swaths of its territory. That the Ottomans had managed to avoid complete destruction thus far was due both to their skill at playing off those competing European powers and to no small measure of improbable good luck. In 1914, however, all that was about to change. By guessing wrong—very wrong—in the calamitous war just then descending, the Ottomans would not only bring on their own doom but unleash forces of such massive disintegration that the world is still dealing with the repercussions a century later.

Chapter 2

A Very Unusual Type

Can you make room on your excavations next winter for a young
Oxford graduate, T. Lawrence, who has been with me at Carchemish?
He is a very unusual type, and a man whom I feel quite sure you would
approve of and like.... I may add that he is extremely indifferent
to what he eats or how he lives.

DAVID HOGARTH TO EGYPTOLOGIST FLINDERS PETRIE, 1911

I think it time I dedicated a letter to you," Thomas Edward Lawrence
wrote his father on August 20, 1906, "although it does not make the
least difference in style, since all my letters are equally bare of personal
information. The buildings I try to describe will last longer than we will,
so it is only fitting that they should have the greater space."

True to his word, Lawrence spent the rest of that letter imparting
absolutely no information about himself, not even bothering to mention
how he had spent his eighteenth birthday four days earlier. Instead, he
used the space to describe in minute detail the structural peculiarities of
a fourteenth-century castle he had just visited.

Lawrence, on recess from the Oxford High School for Boys, was
spending that summer bicycling through northwestern France. The bicycle had only recently become widely available to the European general
public, a result of design innovations and mass production, and it had
sparked something of a craze among the British middle class for cycling
tours of the European countryside. Lawrence's trip was on a wholly different scale, however: a nearly thousand-mile trek that took him to most
every notable castle and cathedral in the Normandy region.

The notes he took of these places formed the basis of Lawrence's letters to his family back in Oxford. While he often prefaced them with brief expressions of concern for his mother's purportedly frail health, the chief characteristic of most of his correspondence was its utter impersonality, the same disquisitional tone as adopted in that to his father.

In some respects, this element of emotional constriction was probably not unusual for a member of a British middle-class family at the end of the Victorian age. It may have been heightened in the Lawrence household by its male preponderance—a family of five boys and no girls—but this was a segment of society that prized self-control and understatement, where children were expected to be studious and respectful, and where a parent's greatest gift to those children was not an indulgent affection but rather a sober religious grounding and a good education. It was also a segment of society that held to a simple and comfortable worldview. While radical political ideas were starting to find flower among the working class, the British middle class still adhered to a social hierarchy based less on attained wealth than on ancestry and accent, a caste system that rigidly dictated nearly every aspect of social life—in some respects, even more rigidly than a half century before. If stultifying, this stratification also meant that everyone knew his place, the station in life to which he might reasonably aspire. To the degree possible, social and economic advancement was obtained through the "godly virtues" of modesty, self-reliance, diligence, and thrift.

Perhaps the least questioned tenet of the time was the notion that the British Empire now stood at the very apex of modern civilization, and that it was the special burden of this empire to spread its enlightenment—whether through commerce, the Bible, the gun, or some combination of all three—to the world's less fortunate cultures and races. While this conviction extended to all segments of British society, it had special resonance for the middle class, since it was from precisely this social stratum that the chief custodians of empire—its midlevel military field officers and colonial administrators—were drawn. This, too, undoubtedly contributed to an emotional distance in such families; from the time of their children's birth, parents had to steel themselves to the likelihood that some of their offspring, especially the males, might ship out to a remote outpost of empire, not to be seen again for decades, if ever.

It is perhaps not surprising, then, that the British middle-class generation coming of age in the early 1900s was marked by a certain blitheness, so much so that in recalling their growing up many years later, one of Lawrence's brothers could write without a hint of irony, "We had a very happy childhood, which was never marred by a single quarrel between any of us."

But in at least one respect, there was something altogether unusual about the Lawrence family on Oxford's Polstead Road, and it undoubtedly added to the emotional austerity in that household. Quite unbeknownst to the neighbors and to most of their own children, Thomas and Sarah Lawrence were harboring a scandalous secret: they were essentially living as fugitives. The key to that secret began with the family surname, which wasn't really Lawrence.

Thomas Lawrence's real name was Thomas Robert Tighe Chapman, and in his prior incarnation he had been a prominent member of the Anglo-Irish landed aristocracy. After being educated at Eton, the future baronet had returned to Ireland and, in the early 1870s, took up the pleasant role of gentleman farmer of his family's estate in County Westmeath. He married a woman from another wealthy Anglo-Irish family, with whom he soon had four daughters.

But Chapman's gilded existence began to unravel when he started an affair with the governess to his young daughters, a twenty-four-year-old Scottish woman named Sarah Junner. By the time Chapman's wife learned of the affair in early 1888, Sarah already had one child with Thomas—an infant son secreted in a rented apartment in Dublin—and a second was on the way. Refused a divorce by his wife, the aristocrat was forced to choose between his two families.

Given the laws and moral strictures of the Victorian era, the consequences of that choice could hardly have been more profound. If he opted to stay with Sarah Junner, Thomas Chapman would not only be stripped of most of his family inheritance, but his four daughters would have great difficulty ever marrying due to the taint of family scandal. Worse was what would lie in store for his and Sarah's offspring. As illegitimates, they would be effectively barred from many of the better schools and higher professions that, had they been legally born to the Chapman name, would be their birthright. Certainly, the most prudent course was for Thomas to bundle Sarah back to her native Scotland with a supporting stipend for herself and her children, a rather common arrangement of the day when servant girls got "into trouble" with their masters. Instead, Chapman chose to stay with Sarah.

After renouncing his claim to the family fortune in favor of his younger brother, Thomas left Ireland with Sarah in mid-1888 for the anonymity of a small village in northern Wales called Tremadoc. There, the couple assumed the alias of Sarah's mother's maiden name, Lawrence, and in August of that year Sarah gave birth to their second child, a son they named Thomas Edward.

But Wales brought the couple no peace of mind. Getting by on a modest annuity from the Chapman family estate but living in constant fear that they might one day encounter someone who knew them from their former lives, the Lawrences began a furtive, peripatetic existence: Tremadoc was soon given up for an even more remote village in northern Scotland, then it was on to the Isle of Man, followed by a couple of years in a small French town, followed by two more years in a secluded hunting lodge on the south coast of England. Compounding the isolation in these places—in each, the Lawrences rented homes on village outskirts or surrounded by high stone walls—Thomas severed ties to nearly all his former friends, while Sarah rarely left the security and anonymity of the family home.

"You can imagine how your mother and I have suffered all these years," Thomas Lawrence would confide in a posthumous letter to his sons, "not knowing what day we might be recognized by some one and our sad history published far and wide."

In light of this driving fear, the Lawrences' decision to move to Oxford in 1896 must have been a downright harrowing one. For the first time, the couple would not only be living in the center of a large town but, given Thomas's aristocratic and educational background, in a place where it was very likely they *would* cross paths with someone from their past. But against this was the opportunity for their sons—now grown to four in number, with a fifth on the way—to receive a good education, maybe even to ultimately win admission to Oxford University, and so the Lawrences took the gamble. The price for this heightened exposure, however, was a family drawn even tighter into itself, the boys' lives circumscribed in comparison to those of their classmates, but for reasons those boys couldn't begin to fathom. All except Thomas Edward, that is. With the move to Oxford, the eight-year-old was now settling into the sixth home of his young life, and at some point during his first years at Polstead Road he partially unraveled the family secret. He kept the information to himself, however, never confronting his parents nor confiding in any of his brothers.

At the Oxford High School for Boys, Lawrence was known as an exceptionally bright but quiet student, one for whom team sports held no appeal and who, if not engaged in a solitary pursuit, preferred the company of his brothers or just a very small group of close friends. His bookish side—he had been a voracious reader even as a young child—was offset by a love of bicycle riding and a fondness for practical jokes. But there was something else as well. By early adolescence, "Ned," as he was known to family and friends, had developed the habit of constantly testing the limits of his endurance, whether in how far or fast he could bicycle or how long he could go without food or sleep or water. This wasn't the usual stuff of boyhood self-testing, but protracted ordeals that, through a kind of iron will, Ned could sustain to the point of collapse. So pronounced was this tendency that even his headmaster in the fourth form (equivalent to American eighth grade) took notice: "He was unlike the boys of his time," Henry Hall wrote in a remembrance of Lawrence, "for even in his schooldays he had a strong leaning toward the Stoics, an apparent indifference towards pleasure or pain."

Some of this may have stemmed from an increasingly severe home environment. As the Lawrence boys grew older, Sarah, the disciplinarian of the family, became both more religious and more given to physical punishment. These were not mere spankings, but rather protracted whippings with belts and switches, and in the remembrance of the Lawrence boys, Ned was by far her most frequent target. It established a disturbing pattern between mother and son. That Ned made a point of never crying or asking for leniency during these whippings—to the contrary, he seemed to derive satisfaction from his ability to display no emotion whatsoever—often had the effect of making the punishments worse, so much so that on several occasions the normally cowed Thomas Lawrence intervened to put a stop to them.

At around the age of fifteen, Ned abruptly stopped growing. With his brothers all eventually surpassing him in height, he became acutely aware of his shortness—variously pegged at between five foot three and five foot five—and this seemed to deepen an already pronounced shyness. About the same time, he developed a fascination with the tales of medieval knights, and with archaeology. He began taking long bicycle trips to churches in the English countryside, where he would conduct brass rubbings of memorial plaques. With his best friend of the time, he scoured the construction sites of new buildings going up in Oxford in search of old relics, and came upon a good number of them. These finds, mostly glass and pottery shards from the sixteenth and seventeenth centuries, soon led Ned to the Ashmolean Museum in central Oxford.

With the distinction of being the oldest public museum in Britain, and with an emphasis on charting the confluence of Eastern and Western cultures, the Ashmolean was to play a transformative role in Lawrence's life. Encouraged by its curators to whom he brought his construction site finds, the teenager soon became a familiar figure around the museum, dropping in after school, helping with odd chores on the weekends. For Lawrence, the Ashmolean became a window onto the world that lay beyond Oxford, its artifacts giving physicality to all the places and civilizations he constantly read about. Testament to his fascination with the past, as well as his already fierce streak of self-sufficiency, was that extended bicycle tour of the castles and cathedrals of Normandy in the summer of 1906.

Earning high marks at high school, in the autumn of 1907 Lawrence

was admitted to Jesus College of Oxford University, there to specialize in history. With an abiding interest in both military history and the
Middle Ages, he fashioned a thesis focusing on the architecture of medieval castles and fortifications. To that end, for the summer of 1908 recess,
he plotted a journey that dwarfed his earlier excursion to Normandy, an
elaborate twenty-four-hundred-mile bicycle trek that would take him to
nearly every significant such structure across the breadth of France. Staying in cheap pensions, or camping in the rough, he routinely pedaled more
than a hundred miles a day as he went from one ancient castle or battle-
ment to the next. At each, he took photographs, made sketches, and wrote
up exhaustive notes before getting back on his bicycle and pedaling on.

Initially, his letters back to Polstead Road assumed the same dry, even
tedious tone of those from his earlier travels. But then something changed.
It happened on August 2, 1908, when Lawrence reached the village of
Aigues-Mortes and he saw the Mediterranean Sea for the first time. In the
letter home describing that day, Lawrence displayed an exuberance and
sense of wonder that was quite out of character.

"I bathed today in the sea," he wrote, "the great sea, the greatest in the
world; you can imagine my feelings. . . . I felt that at last I had reached the
way to the South, and all the glorious East—Greece, Carthage, Egypt,
Tyre, Syria, Italy, Spain, Sicily, Crete—they were all there, and all within
reach of me. . . . Oh I must get down here—farther out—again! Really
this getting to the sea has almost overturned my mental balance; I would
accept a passage for Greece tomorrow."

It was almost as if he were describing a religious epiphany. In a way,
he was.

When Lawrence returned to Oxford and his studies that autumn, he
began to hatch a new—and infinitely more ambitious—journey, one that
would take him to the furthermost region of those he had contemplated
that day in Aigues-Mortes. Among the first to hear of this new scheme
was a man named David Hogarth.

A noted archaeologist who had worked and traveled extensively in the
Near East, Hogarth had only recently taken up the position of director,
or keeper, of the Ashmolean Museum. From the Ashmolean's assistant
curators he had undoubtedly heard mention of T. E. Lawrence—that the
shy Oxford student had been a fixture around the museum since his early
teens, that he showed a keen curiosity in archaeological work—but this
did not at all prepare Hogarth for the diminutive figure ushered into his
office one day in January 1909.

After his tour of the castles in France, Lawrence had now radically
expanded the idea for his senior thesis at Oxford. Put simply, there just

wasn't much new to be said or discovered by examining European medieval fortifications in isolation, whereas one of the enduring mysteries in the study of military architecture was the degree to which innovations in medieval battlements were of Western or Eastern origin: had the Christian Crusaders learned from their Muslim enemies while invading the Holy Land, or had the Muslims copied from the Crusaders? As Lawrence explained to Hogarth, what he proposed was a comprehensive survey of the Crusader castles of the Syrian Near East—and, in typical Lawrence fashion, not merely a visit to some of the more notable ones, but a tour of practically *all* of them. Lawrence planned to make this trek during the next Oxford summer recess, and alone.

Hogarth, already thrown by Lawrence's modest stature—he was now twenty but could easily pass for fifteen—was aghast at the plan. The expedition Lawrence proposed meant a journey of well over a thousand miles across deserts and rugged mountain ranges, where whatever roads and trails existed had only deteriorated since Roman times. What's more, summer was the absolute worst time to travel in Syria, a season when temperatures routinely reached 120 degrees in the interior. As Hogarth recounted the conversation to a Lawrence biographer, when he tried to diplomatically raise these issues, he was met with a steely resolve.

"I'm going," Lawrence said.

"Well, have you got the money?" Hogarth asked. "You'll want a guide and servants to carry your tent and baggage."

"I'm going to walk."

The scheme was becoming more preposterous all the time. "Europeans don't walk in Syria," Hogarth explained. "It isn't safe or pleasant."

"Well," Lawrence said, "I do."

Startled by the young man's brusque determination, Hogarth implored him to at least seek the counsel of a true expert. This was Charles Montagu Doughty, an explorer who had traversed much of the region Lawrence proposed to visit, and whose book *Travels in Arabia Deserta* was considered the definitive travelogue of the time. When contacted, Doughty was even more dismissive of the plan than Hogarth.

"In July and August the heat is very severe by day and night," he wrote Lawrence, "even at the altitude of Damascus (over 2,000 feet). It is a land of squalor, where a European can find little refreshment. Long daily marches on foot a prudent man who knows the country would, I think, consider out of the question. The populations only know their own wretched life and look upon any European wandering in their country with at best a veiled ill will."

In case he hadn't sufficiently made his point, Doughty continued,

"The distances to be traversed are very great. You would have nothing to draw upon but the slight margin of strength which you bring with you from Europe. Insufficient food, rest and sleep would soon begin to tell."

Such counsel might have dissuaded most people, but not Lawrence. For a young man already driven to test the very limits of his endurance, Doughty's letter read like a dare.

HE CERTAINLY LOOKED the part. With his bull shoulders, calloused hands, and Teddy Roosevelt handlebar mustache, William Yale, the new engineering level-man hired on to work the Culebra Cut in the summer of 1908, blended right in with the tens of thousands of other workers who had descended upon the jungles of Central America. They had come to take part in the most ambitious construction project in the history of mankind, the building of the Panama Canal.

Few of his coworkers might have guessed that in fact William Yale had no engineering background at all; instead, he had obtained the position of level-man, and the premium salary it garnered, through the efforts of a well-connected college friend. Surely even fewer might have guessed that the twenty-one-year-old—by all accounts a tireless and uncomplaining worker—was operating in an environment utterly alien to him, that as a scion of one of America's wealthiest and most illustrious families he had until very recently lived a life of privilege extraordinary even by the excessive standards of the day. To the American archetype of the self-made man, William Yale represented the dark and polar opposite, one born to tremendous advantage but who had lost it all in the blink of an eye.

Dating their arrival in America to the mid-1600s, the Yales of New England were a quintessential Yankee blueblood family, one that for 250 years had built an ever greater fortune through shipping, manufacturing, and exploiting all the riches the New World had to offer. True to their Presbyterian ethos, the Yales were also a family that believed in good works and education; in 1701, Elihu Yale, William's great-great-uncle, helped found the university in New Haven that still bears the family name.

Born in 1887, William certainly appeared destined to live in the familial tradition. The third son of William Henry Yale, an industrialist and Wall Street speculator, he grew up on a four-acre estate in Spuyten Duyvil, the bluff at the southwestern tip of the Bronx in New York City. With its commanding views of both Manhattan and the Hudson River, Spuyten Duyvil had long been favored by New York's moneyed class seeking to escape the noise and grime of the city, and the Yale estate was among the grandest. Through early childhood, William and his siblings, four brothers and two sisters, were educated by private tutors at the family mansion, took dance and social etiquette classes at Dodsworth's, Manhattan's preeminent dancing academy, and spent summers at the family's vast forested estate in the Black River valley of upstate New York. Like his two older brothers before him, for high school William was shipped off to the prestigious Lawrenceville School outside Princeton.

But even from an early age, the Yale boys probably had broader horizons than most other male offspring of the New York pampered set. This was due to their father. Beyond being an ardent political supporter of Teddy Roosevelt—the Yales fit squarely into the progressive Republican mold—William Henry Yale also subscribed to Roosevelt's notions of the ideal American man and of the dangers of "over-civilization," code for effeminacy. The true man, in this worldview, was a rugged individualist, physically fit as well as intellectually cultured, as equally at home leading men into battle or shooting big game on the prairie as chatting with the ladies in the salon. To this end, William Henry frequently took his sons on extended trips into the American wilderness and ensured that they were just as adept at hunting, fishing, and trapping as in displaying the proper manners at a Spuyten Duyvil garden party.

The "Roosevelt Man" paradigm seemed to take especially firm root in his namesake third son. During his summer break from Lawrenceville in 1902, fourteen-year-old William traveled with his father to Cuba to see the sights of the island, recently "liberated" from Spain, as well as to visit the family's newly acquired copper mines. Rather than immediately entering Yale University after high school—and there was never any question of which university all Yale boys would attend—William took a year off, and spent part of that time accompanying a wealthy friend and his family on a grand tour of the American West aboard their private railcar.

But much like T. E. Lawrence, when William Yale contemplated adulthood, he already regarded the conventional path so clearly delineated for him with an element of dread. "The routine life I had seen other young men take up seemed tasteless and meaningless," he would later write. "The thought of doing over and over again the same thing day after day, year after year was maddening to me. How others lived in the same town they grew up, married girls they had known all their lives, lived in the houses their families owned, went down, day in and day out, to their father's businesses, I could not understand."

Then the dilemma was settled for him. In October 1907, a panic on Wall Street sparked a nationwide run on banks and nearly halved the value of the New York Stock Exchange in a matter of days. Among the hardest hit by the panic was the heavily leveraged William Henry Yale, whose enormous fortune was virtually wiped out. When William came home that Christmas, having just started his freshman year at Yale, his father delivered almost unimaginable news: the nineteen-year-old student would now have to work to help cover his educational expenses; he was essentially on his own.

William's reaction to this news was mixed: shock, understandably, at the abrupt end to his privileged existence, but a shock leavened by a sense of liberation. Here was the chance to pursue the adventurous life he dreamed of. That summer, he took a leave from the university and shipped out to Panama.

That six-month sojourn in Central America proved a transformative experience. Instead of heirs and socialites, Yale's companions now were a motley and licentious crew of international adventurers and construction vagabonds, rough-cut men who taught the fallen aristocrat how to work and how to drink; by Yale's own account, it was only his mother's puritanical indoctrination that enabled him to withstand the determined appeals of the female professionals at the Navajo Bar in Panama City and escape with his chastity intact.

But if Panama opened a door, it was still a daunting one to step through. Upon returning to New Haven and completing his degree, William Yale found himself in a quandary. "The bottom had dropped out of my world. To ever get to where I could marry and live the life I was brought up to expect seemed utterly hopeless. I hadn't the foggiest idea how to make money. . . . What to do now? I was penniless, in debt, and knew nothing of the world, and at heart was intimidated by it."

He would eventually find an answer to that question. It would take the form of a notice soliciting applicants to the "foreign service school" of the Standard Oil Company of New York.

ANYONE WHO HAPPENED to be crossing the searingly hot plain west of Aleppo in northern Syria in early September 1909 would have encountered a perplexing sight: a young, painfully thin Englishman, a rucksack slung over his shoulders, tromping along while close on his heels trailed a squadron of Turkish cavalry.

A few days earlier, T. E. Lawrence had arrived in the remote foothill town of Sahyun, there to quietly survey yet another Crusader castle, and the local Ottoman provincial governor, or *kaimmakam*, had been so amazed at the sight of the young traveler that he insisted on treating Lawrence as a visiting dignitary. That meant staying in the governor's home and being lavishly waited upon, and it had also meant a personal bodyguard of cavalrymen when Lawrence set out for the five-day hike to Aleppo.

"It is rather amusing to contemplate a pedestrian guarded carefully by a troop of light horse [cavalry]," he wrote his family in describing the incident. "Of course everybody thinks I am mad to walk, and the escort offered me a mount on the average [of] once a half-hour; they couldn't understand my prejudice against anything with four legs."

Lawrence's walking tour of Syria that summer was comprised of two journeys. The first began in the coastal city of Beirut and consisted of a three-week jaunt south through the mountains of Lebanon to northern Palestine. After returning to Beirut and resting for a few days, he embarked on a far more elaborate and punishing trek north.

It was an adventure that changed his life. Everywhere the locals greeted him with both astonishment and overwhelming generosity. In village after village, residents would insist he eat with them, or stay the night as their guest, and despite their crushing poverty, very few would ever accept payment. "This is a glorious country for wandering in," he wrote his father in mid-August, "for hospitality is something more than a name."

His letters home conveyed a newfound happiness. In one letter to his mother at the end of August, he sounded like the modern college student who fancies that his travels have left him fundamentally transformed: "I will have such difficulty in becoming English again."

The difference in Lawrence's case was that this was to actually prove true.

Once back in Oxford for his senior year, Lawrence toiled on his thesis in the pleasant cottage his father had built for him in the garden of the Polstead Road home. The result carried the accurate if not exactly beckoning title *The Influence of the Crusades on European Military Architecture—to the End of the XIIth Century.*

The Oxford history department examiners were impressed enough by his original research—then, as now, most theses tended to be compendiums of others' work—that Lawrence was awarded first-class honors, the highest scholastic ranking and one of only ten such awards given by the history school that year. The distinction greatly enhanced his chances of pursuing an academic career, his newfound goal, and this was further helped along when the university arranged a stipend for him to conduct postgraduate work. Perhaps stemming from his teenaged archaeological finds in the Oxford construction sites, Lawrence had long had a special attraction to pottery, and it was to this he turned in his postgraduate research. To be sure, studying "Medieval Lead-Glazed Pottery from the 11th to the 16th Centuries" sounded a lot less exciting than tramping about Syria, but it was a first step toward the life he envisioned for himself.

But it was not to be. In the autumn of 1910, just days after arriving in France to begin his pottery research, Lawrence learned that David Hogarth was about to leave for northern Syria, there to oversee the inauguration of an archaeological dig for the British Museum at the ancient ruins of Carchemish. Abandoning France, Lawrence hurried back to Oxford to try to convince Hogarth to take him along.

HE WAS A small, sickly child born into a pitiless family. Even before reaching adolescence, Curt Prüfer, the only son of a Berlin schoolteacher, had suffered through a litany of ailments that included tuberculosis, kidney disease, and diphtheria. It was a failed treatment for this last affliction that left him with his soft, feathery voice.

The boy's frail health apparently did little to pull at the heartstrings of his parents, Carl and Agnes Prüfer. The father constantly criticized Curt for his purported laziness, while his mother rarely showed him affection or even attention. The emotional isolation didn't end there. According to Prüfer biographer Donald McKale, Curt had no childhood friends, and his sole bond of attachment throughout growing up was to his one sibling, a sister several years his senior. Tellingly, considering the schoolyard taunts he undoubtedly suffered due to his voice, the adult Curt Prüfer's favorite insult, one he would direct at entire nationalities and even his own married son, was the label of homosexual.

But in contrast to the spiritual poverty of his home life, Prüfer had been born into a fantastically exciting and tumultuous period in German history. In 1871, just ten years before his birth, Otto von Bismarck had capitalized on Prussia's crushing victory over France in the Franco-Prussian War to tear up the centuries-old patchwork of German principalities and duchies and forge the modern German nation.

Under a state-directed corporatist structure, Germany swiftly went from a primarily agrarian economy to being one of the most industrialized nations on earth, linked from one end to the other by a modern network of railroads, canals, and carriageways. A series of workers'-rights legislations, as well as the world's first national social welfare system, sent fractures through what had been one of the most rigidly class-stratified societies in Europe. Those fractures were widened further by the state's massive expansion of higher education. Once almost solely the province of the very elite, university was now accessible to the middle class, so much so that by the turn of the century they comprised half of all college graduates.

Equally dramatic was the new image and prowess of Germany abroad. From a dizzying mélange of squabbling fiefdoms—a mélange that Europe's established imperial powers had adroitly played off against one another for centuries—Germany was suddenly becoming an empire in its own right. Despite being a latecomer in the European "scramble for Africa," by the mid-1880s it had established colonies in western, southern, and eastern Africa; in a fit of grandiosity, it even planted its flag in the South Pacific island of Samoa, almost precisely the farthest spot from Germany on the planet.

But if Bismarck created the modern German state, it was another man who would truly catapult it onto the global stage, and fire the passions of young Germans like Curt Prüfer in the process. In 1888, Wilhelm II, the twenty-nine-year-old eldest grandchild of Queen Victoria of England, ascended to the German throne. With a fondness for military uniforms and bellicose language, as well as an undying resentment of the other European royal families, the young kaiser was determined to make his nation not just a regional power but a world one. This aggressiveness was of limited concern in other European capitals so long as the true levers of German authority lay in the steady hands of Chancellor Bismarck—within the incestuous orbit of European royalty, Wilhelm had long been pegged as an emotionally unstable but controllable hothead—but of considerably greater concern when Wilhelm forced Bismarck from office in 1890 and assumed autocratic powers. Absent the calming influence of the Iron Chancellor, and surrounding himself with palace sycophants and the Prussian military elite, Wilhelm nursed himself—and his subjects—on a particularly toxic nationalist mythology rooted in both a sense of victimization and superiority: that throughout history, Germany had been denied its rightful "place in the sun" through the treachery of others, that this colossal injustice was now to be remedied, through force of arms if necessary.

For a boy like Curt Prüfer coming of age at this juncture, it could almost be said that the new Germany created him. By the time he entered secondary school in 1896, a new national curriculum had been introduced, one that broke with the European classicist model in favor of one preaching nationalist pride and the primacy of the state and the emperor. It found a fervent disciple in the lonely, sickly boy from Berlin. Soundly rejecting his father's neosocialist liberalism, Curt also rebelled against his parents' narrow petit-bourgeois horizons, in particular their desire that he follow in Carl Prüfer's footsteps and become a schoolteacher. Instead, this German "New Man"—exceptionally bright and driven despite his father's harsh estimation—imagined a wholly different life for himself, and where he saw that life taking him was east.

Part of that attraction may have stemmed from the political currents of the day. Among all the jockeying European powers at the close of the nineteenth century, there was a growing tendency to regard diplomacy as a zero-sum game—any accord between one's competitors translated as a direct loss or threat to oneself—but nowhere was this tendency more pronounced than in Wilhelm's paranoia-tinged Germany. Throughout the 1890s, with growing signs of amity between France, Great Britain, and Russia, an amity spurred in no small part by alarm over Germany's rapid militarization, talk of "encirclement" increasingly came into vogue in Berlin. To escape this encirclement by its imperial rivals—France and Great Britain to one side, Russia to the other—a boxed-in Germany needed to look beyond for economic and political expansion, and the region holding the greatest promise was the Ottoman and Muslim East. This notion was greatly strengthened in 1898 when the kaiser made a triumphant tour of the Ottoman world and was royally feted wherever he went. For patriotic young Germans, the Near East was suddenly a beckoning frontier.

But for Curt Prüfer, probably the greater attraction derived from the exotic. At various times throughout the nineteenth century, archaeological discoveries in the Near East had spawned intense fascination among the European public, and probably nowhere had this been more true than in Germany. Dating back to Karl Lepsius's expeditions to the Egyptian pyramids in the 1840s and continuing through Heinrich Schliemann's excavations of Troy and Mycenae in the 1870s, German archaeologists had been at the forefront of exploration in the region, and responsible for many of the greatest finds. By the 1880s, with German scientists excavating burial tombs in the Luxor region of Upper Egypt, and Adolf Erman breaking the codes of pharaonic hieroglyphics at the University of Berlin, a new wave of popular interest had ushered in the so-called golden age of Egyptology. The craze captivated the young Prüfer much the way the dawning of the Space Age would enthrall a later generation. Even as a very young boy, he devoured the tales of adventure and discovery coming out of the Near East, and dreamed of the circumstances that might take him there.

That may have remained the stuff of childhood fantasy if not for Curt Prüfer's possession of a singular talent, a somewhat curious one in light of his speech difficulties. He was a prodigy when it came to mastering foreign languages, one of those rare people who could go from utter unfamiliarity to near fluency in a matter of months. He had thoroughly mastered French and English in secondary school, but as a young man he set his sights much further afield.

In partial acquiescence to his parents' conventional aspirations, in 1901 the twenty-year-old Prüfer enrolled in the University of Berlin to study law. At the same time, he took seminars in Oriental languages and quickly developed a proficiency in Turkish and Arabic, two of the more difficult languages on earth. Two years later, he dispensed with his legal studies altogether and, under the pretext that a drier climate might improve his frail health, moved to southern Italy to study Italian.

But Italy was not the East, and in that same summer of 1903, Prüfer set sail for Cairo. It was to be the first of three extended trips he would make over the next three years, partially supporting himself by writing travel articles for German cultural magazines as he worked toward a doctorate in Oriental studies.

Perhaps spurred by his own commoner background, the area of study Prüfer chose was a very unusual one for a European scholar of the time: an indigenous theatrical art form known as shadow plays that catered exclusively to the Egyptian working class. In his dissertation, he described visiting one of the coffeehouses where these plays were performed in the Was'a slum of Cairo.

"The galleries and benches on the main floor of this establishment are packed with people, mostly from the lowest strata of society. Here, donkey drivers, porters and pushcart vendors sit in a dense throng, peacefully smoking their hashish pipes. Members of the upper classes do not dare to enter the Was'a milieu for fear of damaging their good reputations."

The same held true for Cairo's expatriate community, of course, affording the young German scholar a glimpse into everyday Egyptian life virtually unique among Europeans. The time he spent in places like Was'a also enabled Prüfer to thoroughly master colloquial Arabic, a very different language from that spoken by the genteel class, and a skill that would stand him in very good stead in the years ahead.

By the beginning of 1906, Prüfer stood at a kind of crossroads. With his doctorate from the University of Erlangen in hand, he might easily have landed a teaching position in Germany—and, in what would have been a nice little turn of revenge, at a far more prestigious level than his primary schoolteacher father had attained—but he was anxious to return to the East. In rather quick succession, two strokes of luck were to make that possible.

That winter, he met Frances Ethel Pinkham, an American woman studying music in Berlin. A graduate of Wellesley College from a wealthy family in Lynn, Massachusetts, the thirty-eight-year-old Pinkham was, by the standards of the day, already well into spinsterhood when she met the solicitous and charming Oriental scholar thirteen years her junior. Following a brief romance, and over the fierce objections of Pinkham's parents, the couple married that April. Prüfer convinced his bride that they should move to Egypt so that he could further his studies and, hopefully, find suitable employment. While Pinkham's parents back in Lynn were no doubt aghast at the idea, in Cairo an opportunity for adventure and advancement soon presented itself to their new son-in-law.

During his previous stays in Cairo, Prüfer had frequently socialized with personnel from the German embassy, and these diplomats had been very impressed by his command of both classic and colloquial Arabic. In early 1907, with the embassy's current dragoman, or interpreter, slated for retirement, Prüfer was asked if he might be interested in the post. It's hard to imagine he pondered the offer for more than an instant. That February, Prüfer became the newest staff member of the German diplomatic legation to Egypt.

But something else awaited the unprepossessing twenty-six-year-old at the German embassy: a mentor, one of the most colorful—and in the eyes of the British, one of the most dangerous—personalities ever to stalk the Middle East.

THE RUINS OF Carchemish are situated on a rocky bluff over a bend of the Euphrates River, flush on the border between modern-day Turkey and Syria. Around it are rolling plains gradually giving over to grassy foothills. Overlooking an important ford of the Euphrates, the bluff has been inhabited for at least five thousand years, but achieved its greatest prominence at about 1100 BC during the Late Bronze Age. At that time, Carchemish was a principal city of the Hittite civilization, centered in the Anatolia region just to the north, and was well known to both the Egyptian pharaohs and the authors of the Old Testament; the Bible contains several references to the city, including a battle waged there between the Babylonian king Nebuchadnezzar and Pharaoh Necho II in the sixth century BC. This small corner of the Ottoman Empire was the place where T. E. Lawrence came to feel a deeper sense of belonging than anywhere else during his lifetime.

Having wheedled his way onto David Hogarth's archaeological expedition, Lawrence first reached Carchemish in February 1911. As the junior assistant on the excavation, his official duties were to photograph and sketch the dig as it progressed, as well as to keep a catalog of its various finds. His job quickly expanded far beyond this. As one of just two westerners permanently on-site to oversee a crew of some two hundred local workmen (Hogarth, although the overall administrator, would visit Carchemish only intermittently), Lawrence soon came to be something akin to a construction foreman. In this role he discovered, perhaps as much to his surprise as anyone else's, that he was a natural leader of men.

To be sure, this was partly due to his status as a European. Under a system dating back to the 1500s known as the Capitulations, the European powers had steadily wrung a series of ever more humiliating concessions from the sultans in Constantinople under the pretext of protecting the

Ottoman Empire's Christian minorities. By the beginning of the twentieth century, European citizens were effectively exempt from Ottoman law. "Really, this country, for the foreigner, is too glorious for words," Lawrence wrote to his family in the summer of 1912. "One is the baron of the feudal system."

But it was not merely this that made Lawrence a leader. He seemed to possess an instant affinity for the East, and in that affinity an almost instinctive appreciation for how its culture worked. By now quite fluent in Arabic, in Carchemish he labored ceaselessly to deepen that knowledge. He did so by quizzing the men in his work crews, by visiting them in their homes, by taking painstaking notes on all he learned. From their folkloric tales, to their views on politics, to charting out the complicated clan structure that determined regional allegiances, Lawrence gradually came to know this small corner of northern Syria and its people better than probably any other European of the time.

Of course, there is nothing more endearing than attention. To the extent that the workmen at Carchemish, drawn from the nearby town of Jerablus, had ever had prior dealings with a westerner, it had undoubtedly been of the most cursory and servile kind. They'd surely never met one who bothered to learn the names of their children and relatives and ancestors, who gladly accepted invitations into their modest homes, who showed genuine respect for their rituals and customs.

There was another aspect to Lawrence that impressed the locals as well. He seemed to have none of the softness or frailty they associated with Europeans; rather, he could work in the blazing heat for hours without pause, could walk or ride for days without complaint, soldiered through bouts of dysentery and malaria with the composed resignation of a local. To the Arabs of Jerablus, most everything about Lawrence spoke of a toughness, a stamina and an austerity, that made him seem less like a European and more like themselves. In Arab tradition, they rewarded that sense of kinship with a fierce and abiding loyalty. This cut both ways, for the longer he stayed in Syria and the more he was accepted by the locals, the less Lawrence came to think and act like a Briton.

More profoundly, his time in Syria caused him to fundamentally rethink his views on the "civilizing influence" of the West. This change found personification in the close relationship he developed with a young man from Jerablus named Dahoum. Starting out as a mere thirteen-year-old donkey boy at the Carchemish excavation site, the bright and extraordinarily handsome Dahoum was soon elevated by Lawrence to be a kind of personal assistant, and the two became inseparable, leading to whispered rumors that they might be lovers. Whatever the truth of those rumors, it was in the figure of Dahoum that Lawrence began to develop a new if rather romanticized notion of the essential nobility of the Arab race, admiring their asceticism as "the gospel of bareness," free from the taint of Western indulgence.

Writing his parents in 1911 from Jerablus, in a letter where he first introduced Dahoum as "an interesting character" whom he wished to help, he evinced views quite at odds with a British colonial sensibility: "Fortunately there is no foreign influence as yet in the district. If only you had seen the ruination caused by the French influence, and to a lesser degree by the American, you would never wish it extended. The perfectly hopeless vulgarity of the half-Europeanized Arab is appalling. Better a thousand times the Arab untouched. The foreigners come out here always to teach, whereas they had much better learn."

This wasn't a preoccupation one normally associated with an archaeologist. Even David Hogarth, despite his great affection for his protégé, was never convinced that Lawrence truly had the heart or temperament of a scholar. He had little of the meticulous doggedness of a man like Leonard Woolley, who in 1912 became the lead scientist at Carchemish. Instead, Lawrence's chief fascination seemed to be with the land and the people that surrounded him; it was there where his passion lay.

This passion also gave Lawrence a unique perspective on one of the more momentous developments of the early twentieth century: the protracted death throes of the Ottoman Empire. Most other Western eyewitnesses to that spectacle resided in the cities of the Middle East. Lawrence was one of the few who watched it play out in the countryside, where the great majority of Ottoman subjects still lived.

That death had been a very long time foretold. The Ottoman Empire had endured for nearly five centuries largely by allowing ethnic and religious minorities extraordinary freedom to govern themselves, so long as they paid their taxes and pledged ultimate allegiance to the sultans in Constantinople. This system had begun to crumble in the nineteenth century, buffeted by both the rise of nationalism and dramatic advances in communications and commerce. With astonishing speed, the world was becoming a smaller place, the industrializing nations of Europe were becoming exponentially more powerful, and an empire built on what essentially amounted to benign neglect of its component parts was an anachronism. By the 1850s, the Ottoman Empire was already "the sick man of Europe," its final collapse eagerly anticipated by the ascendant Western powers.

Through nimble alliance-making, the Ottomans had consistently managed to dodge that demise, even as their Western competitors nibbled at the empire's edges. In the 1870s, czarist Russia crushed an Ottoman army in the Balkans to win the independence of Romania, Serbia, and Montenegro. In 1881, France grabbed Tunisia. The following year, Great

Britain used the pretext of a nascent nationalist movement to snatch away Egypt.

Cruelly, the event that seemed to offer the Ottoman Empire its best hope for a renaissance merely accelerated the disintegration. In 1908, a reformist coup by a group of young military officers under the banner of the Committee of Union and Progress (CUP)—soon to become better known as the Young Turks—forced the despotic sultan to reinstate the parliamentary constitution he had abrogated thirty years earlier. Emboldened by their success, the Young Turks quickly launched a breathtakingly ambitious campaign designed to drag the empire into the twentieth century, including calls for the emancipation of women and the granting of full rights of citizenship to ethnic and religious minorities.

But if the CUP officers, most drawn from the European part of the empire and steeped in European liberalism, had expected the Western powers to embrace their cause, they were in for a rude surprise. Taking advantage of the political confusion in Constantinople, Austria-Hungary swiftly annexed Bosnia-Herzegovina. In other European capitals, including London, the Young Turks were regarded with the deepest suspicion, even derided as "crypto-Jews" bent on taking possession of the empire as part of some sinister plot by international Jewry. Within the Ottoman Empire, a virulent conservative backlash against the progressives quickly plunged the new parliamentary government into an era of political infighting and paralysis.

By 1911, the Young Turks had begun to solidify their hold on power, and had come up with three main rallying points in hopes of keeping their fractious empire together: modernization, the defense of Islam, and a call for a rejoining of the greater Turkic-speaking world, or Turanism. All of which sounded good, except that these three planks stood in direct opposition to one another.

The very progressivism of many of the Young Turks' social decrees may have played well with secularists and the empire's Jewish and Christian minorities, but they simultaneously enraged huge numbers of Muslim traditionalists. Similarly, while their increasingly jingoistic Turanist rhetoric surely excited the ethnic Turk populace, it just as surely alienated the non-Turkish populations—Arabs, Slavs, Armenians, Greeks—who now constituted a majority within the empire. As for wrapping themselves in the mantle of Islam's defenders, that might conceivably win over Turkish, Kurdish, and Arab Muslims, but it didn't do much for everyone else—including, for that matter, the sizable minority of Arabs who were Christians. In effect, by trying to find something to appeal to every segment of their polyglot society, the Young Turks were giving all of them something to hate and fear.

For Lawrence, a young man increasingly attuned to the political and social currents swirling around him, an inescapable conclusion began to form: little by little, the Ottoman Empire was coming apart at the seams. During his tenure at Jerablus, that process of disintegration accelerated, and what had been an intermittent nibbling at the Ottoman realm by the European powers was to become a feeding frenzy.

IN EARLY 1907, as Germany began to assert its assumed prerogatives as an imperial power, Curt Prüfer took up his post as embassy dragoman in Cairo.

On paper, the dragoman was merely the embassy interpreter, tasked to assist the ambassador at his diplomatic meetings, as well as to translate whatever documents the legation might address to the local government, or vice versa. In reality, an ambitious dragoman could become a virtual power unto himself. Then, as now, ambassadors were often a clueless and temporary bunch, products of a palace sinecure system and prone to be far more adept on the dance floor than at the negotiating table. Dragomen, on the other hand, represented continuity—many remained in their positions for decades—and through their translating work had intimate knowledge of most everything going on in every subsection of the embassy. Further, because they existed in a gray area between an embassy's diplomatic and consular branches, they could quietly pursue questionable activities, such as meeting with a regime's enemies, which might provoke an outcry if conducted by their superiors. This was crucial, for while nearly all the competing European imperial powers at the dawn of the twentieth century viewed their overseas legations as handy instruments for intelligence gathering, influence peddling, and general mischief making, the Germans were in a class by themselves. In keeping with Wilhelm II's pugnacious approach to foreign policy, German legations were forever being caught out in some ungentlemanly transgression—stealing government and industrial secrets, operating spy rings—that left their purportedly more high-minded British and French counterparts spluttering with indignation. At the center of many of these various scandals were the embassy dragomen.

In Egypt Prüfer had landed in one of the most important playgrounds for this muscular German approach to diplomacy, a place where Berlin saw the opportunity to both curry favor with the Ottoman leadership in Constantinople and chip away at the hegemony of their British rivals. That's because in 1882, under the pretext of defending the ruling clique from an independence-minded nationalist leader, Britain had invaded Egypt and effectively taken control of the country that had been under titular Ottoman rule for nearly four hundred years. The British hadn't stopped there. In May 1906, just nine months before Prüfer's arrival at the German embassy, they had exploited a minor diplomatic dispute in the Sinai, the vast peninsula standing to the east of the Suez Canal, to wrest that from the Ottomans as well. That episode had further fueled Egyptian discontent with British rule—as well as Constantinople's bitterness toward its former friend—and the Germans operating in Cairo saw nothing to lose and everything to gain by keeping that enmity at a low boil.

But perhaps the greatest asset Prüfer had to draw on in the Egyptian capital was his immediate supervisor at the embassy, a larger-than-life character named Count Max von Oppenheim.

Twenty-one years the dragoman's senior, Oppenheim was a gregarious, snappily attired bon vivant with a handlebar mustache and a fondness for both the ladies and the racetrack, and a member in good standing at Berlin's Union Club, the exclusive haunt of Germany's political and economic elite. Oppenheim joined the German diplomatic service in 1883. In short order, he had decamped for Syria, beginning a love affair with the Near East that would last for the next sixty years. An amateur archaeologist and ethnologist, he conducted archaeological expeditions in the countryside, enterprises that he personally financed from his banking family's fortune. In Oppenheim's case, the hobby eventually paid off; in 1899, he discovered one of the most important lost settlements of the Neolithic period, Tell Halaf, in northern Syria. (It is presumably on the strength of that discovery that Oppenheim bears the odd distinction of having a Montblanc pen named after him, joining such luminaries as Charlemagne, Copernicus, and Alexander the Great in the company's "patron of the arts" line.) The adventurer finally set up a semipermanent base of operations in Cairo in 1896, when he was given a vaguely defined attaché position in the consular section of the German embassy.

There were several controversial aspects to the count—no one was quite sure of the title's pedigree beyond its appearance on Oppenheim's business card—that set him apart from his diplomatic colleagues in the Egyptian capital. One was his propensity for "going native." This was most evident in his habit of gadding about clad in Arab robes, as well as his choosing to live in a "native" quarter of the city, but it also extended to his amorous arrangements. According to Sean McMeekin in *The Berlin-Baghdad Express*, "Every autumn, after his return from Berlin, Oppenheim's head servant Soliman would procure him a new slave girl (he called them his *Zeitfrauen*, or temporary concubines), who would become mistress of the harem until the following year, and who was herself served by two female attendants."

But the count was a man of catholic enthusiasms, and in addition to archaeology and horse racing and slave girls, there was one that Germany's imperial rivals in the Near East found particularly irksome: Max von Oppenheim wanted to rearrange the regional political chessboard through stoking the fires of Islamic jihad.

He had begun formulating the idea shortly after taking up his consular position in Cairo. In Oppenheim's estimation, the great Achilles' heels of Germany's principal European competitors—Great Britain, France, and Russia—were the Muslim populations to be found within their imperial borders, populations that deeply resented being under the thumb of Christian colonial powers. As the only major European power never to have attempted colonization in the Muslim world, Oppenheim propounded, Germany was uniquely positioned to turn this situation to its advantage—especially if it could forge an alliance with the Ottoman Empire. If it came to a Europe-wide war, Oppenheim posited in a flurry of reports to the German foreign ministry, and the Ottoman authorities in Constantinople could be persuaded to call for a holy war against the Christian occupiers of their former lands, what would happen in British-ruled Egypt, or French Tunisia, or the Russian Caucasus?

One person who was itching to find out was Kaiser Wilhelm II. Forwarded some of Oppenheim's "war by revolution" treatises, the German emperor quickly became a committed proponent of the jihad notion. Wilhem saw to it that Oppenheim, "my feared spy," was promoted at the Cairo embassy, assuming the somewhat ironic title of chief legal counsel.

Until the blessed day of pan-Islamic jihad came, there was plenty of work to be done in British Egypt. Through the early 1900s, Oppenheim spent much of his time—and not a little of his personal fortune—quietly wooing a broad cross section of the Egyptian elite opposed to British rule: tribal sheikhs, urban intellectuals, nationalists, and religious figures. While he had already won the kaiser to his jihadist ideas, in 1907 Oppenheim gained another adherent in the form of his new subordinate, Curt Prüfer. Enough with scholarly articles and Egyptian shadow plays; under the tutelage of his charismatic supervisor, Prüfer now saw the opportunity to spread gasoline over the region, put a match to it, and see what happened.

With his accent and command of Arabic far superior to Oppenheim's, the new dragoman became the key liaison between the embassy and the Egyptian capital's assorted malcontents. In particular, Prüfer carefully cultivated a friendship with the khedive (roughly equivalent to viceroy) of Egypt, Abbas Hilmi II, the local Ottoman head of state, whom the British had maintained on the throne even as they stripped him of all authority. Understandably, this arrangement had never sat well with the khedive, a resentment Prüfer did his best to nurture. The two German agents provocateurs didn't limit their ministrations to the Cairene mewling class. In early 1909, Prüfer and Oppenheim set out on a wide-ranging tour of the Egyptian and Syrian hinterlands, where, disguised in Bedouin garb, they endeavored to promote the twin causes of pan-Islam and anticolonialism among the tribesmen.

But one doesn't get Montblanc pens named after them by sticking to a routine, and in late 1910, Count von Oppenheim made a surprising announcement: he was leaving his legal counsel post at the embassy to return to his first true love of archaeology. Specifically, the count had decided it was high time to begin his excavations at Tell Halaf, the Neolithic ruins he had discovered in northern Syria, and which had now sat undisturbed for over a decade.

The understandable relief with which British authorities in Cairo greeted this news—they had been trying for years to find some pretext to have Oppenheim deported—was leavened by a healthy dose of skepticism, especially when a quick glance at a map revealed that Tell Halaf lay precisely alongside the proposed path of the Baghdad Railway. This was a massive public works project underwritten by the Ottoman government that was designed to link Constantinople to its easternmost—and reportedly, oil-rich—territory of Iraq (or Mesopotamia, as it was still commonly referred to in the West). Over the virulent objections of Britain and France, in 1905 the Ottomans had awarded the construction project, and the generous concessionary rights that went with it, to Germany.

But even if rid of "the kaiser's spy," the British in Egypt couldn't let their guard down. In his place, Count Max von Oppenheim had left behind in Cairo a very dedicated and resourceful protégé.

THE HEADQUARTERS FOR the Carchemish dig was a small compound about a half mile from the ruins, a former licorice company storehouse on the outskirts of the village of Jerablus. It was here that T. E. Lawrence and Leonard Woolley lived, as well as entertained the small groups of Western travelers who found their way to the excavation site with growing frequency. Over the course of their three years there, the two men continually added new rooms and storage sheds to the original structure, until the Jerablus "station" made for both a comfortable and expansive home. It was a place Lawrence came to regard as his sanctuary. As he wrote to his family in the summer of 1912, after having made a trip of just a few days to the Syrian coast, "I seem to have been months away from Jerablus, and am longing for its peace."

But in the Near East, the very notion of peace was rapidly becoming an anachronism as the crumbling of the Ottoman Empire gained momentum. In 1911, the Italians invaded Libya, setting off a bloody war that eventually led to an Ottoman defeat. Overlapping that conflict came the First Balkan War, in which the Ottomans lost most of their remaining European possessions, immediately followed by the Second Balkan War. The grim news had a cascading effect. By 1913, when the Young Turks staged a second coup to take over the reins of government outright, small-scale rebellions and separatist movements had sprung up across the breadth of what remained of the empire, with even local chieftains and clan leaders sensing that the moment had come to finally throw off the Ottoman yoke.

In this, the once-idyllic environs of northern Syria were in no way immune. Given the ethnic composition of the region—the population was overwhelmingly Arab or Kurd, with the presence of ethnic Turks largely limited to local representatives of the Ottoman power structure, its mayors and police and tax collectors—Lawrence had developed a rather simplistic moralist view of its inhabitants: love for the noble Arab; wary respect for the blustering Kurd; hatred for the cruel Turk. As a result, he was quite pleased when the local Kurdish tribes threatened an insurrection in 1912, and by the increasingly open defiance that he saw playing out in the streets of Jerablus by the once-cowed Arabs toward their Turkish overlords. The Ottoman thrall over the population—in Lawrence's view, a thrall based on fear and corruption and the sheer soul-grinding machinery of an inept bureaucracy—was rapidly slipping, and it was very hard to see how they might ever restore it. That estimation delighted him.

But it wasn't just the roiling within the Ottoman Empire that was being felt in northern Syria. There was also the spreading intrigue of the European imperial powers, all of them maneuvering everywhere in search of some advantage against their rivals. In particular, the arrival on the scene of the infamous Count Max von Oppenheim seemed a clear indication that the region was now part of the ever-expanding European chessboard. Having ostensibly returned to Syria to begin excavations at Tell Halaf, some one hundred miles to the east of Carchemish, Oppenheim dropped by the Jerablus station for a visit one afternoon in July 1912.

"He was such a horrible person," Lawrence wrote his youngest brother, "I hardly was polite—but was interesting instead [sic]. He said [the Carchemish ruins] were the most interesting and important discoveries he had ever seen barring his own."

Before long, Lawrence and Woolley began hearing rumors of the count's supposedly shoddy work at the Tell Halaf site, stories of great cartloads of treasures being illegally hauled away, bound for Berlin. They also couldn't help notice that after years of lackadaisical progress on the

Baghdad Railway—and in the Ottoman world, "lackadaisical" joined to "progress" tended to evoke geological comparisons—the pace of work suddenly accelerated once Oppenheim appeared. So accelerated, in fact, that by late 1912 the German engineers and their advance crews had set to work on one of the most technically complicated segments of the rail line, a trestle bridge over the fast-flowing Euphrates River. By remarkable coincidence, the site for that bridge was directly alongside the village of Jerablus.

Throughout 1913 and well into 1914, the two groups of Western workers who improbably found themselves in this same remote corner of northern Syria had an alternately amicable and contentious relationship. The German railwaymen in Jerablus assisted the British archaeologists by hauling away the discarded stone from their excavations for use in their railroad embankments. In turn, the Germans frequently sought out the Britons—and, with his fluent Arabic, especially Lawrence—to mediate in their perpetually tense relations with local workers. A chief source of that tension was the difficulty the Germans had in finding good help, their best workers routinely jumping ship for the higher wages and more respectful supervision of Lawrence and Woolley.

Very soon, these two groups would be on opposite sides of a world war, and a different railroad—the Hejaz line, running from Damascus seven hundred miles south to the city of Medina—would become the most vital transportation link in the Middle Eastern theater of that conflict. The knowledge Lawrence gained from watching the railway construction in Jerablus was undoubtedly of great assistance to him when, in a few years' time, he would make blowing up the Hejaz Railway a personal pastime.

AT MIDMORNING ON September 15, 1913, twenty-six-year-old William Yale was part of a three-man crew "pulling rods"—detaching and stacking drill sections, just about the most miserable job to be had in an oilfield—in the Kiefer field of northern Oklahoma when a courier on horseback approached. Minutes later, the Kiefer straw boss called Yale over to hand him a telegram. It was from the corporate headquarters of the Standard Oil Company of New York, and it was succinct: "Report to New York immediately."

After graduating from his eponymous university in 1910, Yale had struggled to find his calling until, in 1912, he came across a notice soliciting applicants for the "foreign service school" of the Standard Oil Company of New York. On a whim, he applied.

Operating out of Standard's corporate headquarters at 26 Broadway in New York, the "school" consisted of a four-month intensive lecture and seminar program, designed to educate its applicants in all aspects of the petroleum industry, as well as to instill in them the "Standard man" ideal. Just what that ideal might consist of was difficult to say, for by 1912 Standard Oil was the most infamous corporation in the history of international commerce, its name synonymous with capitalist greed run amok.

Through cutthroat tactics devised by its principal shareholder, John D. Rockefeller, Standard had so thoroughly dominated the U.S. petroleum industry over the previous four decades that by the early 1900s it controlled nearly 90 percent of the nation's oil production. For nearly as long, it had operated a complex web of front companies and shell corporations that had defeated the efforts of every "trust buster" lawman trying to break its stranglehold. Finally, in 1911, just the year before Yale's job application, the U.S. Supreme Court declared Standard to be an illegal monopoly and decreed it be broken up into thirty-four separate companies.

Whether this divestiture truly ended the Standard monopoly is still the subject of debate, but it did have the effect of forcing its component parts to specialize, either to focus on supplying regional domestic markets or on building international exports. Among the most aggressive in this latter sphere was the new Standard Oil Company of New York—often referred to by its acronym, Socony—the second largest of the thirty-four "baby Standards."

While other baby Standards turned inward, Socony looked at the great world beyond and saw a plethora of burgeoning markets thirsting for petroleum. It was to coordinate and standardize its marketing approaches in these far-flung spots that the company had launched its foreign service school. William Yale, an enthusiastic pupil, would call the program's teaching methods "far more effective and efficient" than anything he'd encountered at either prep school or university.

And the Socony administrators clearly liked what they saw in William Yale. At the conclusion of his coursework, he was selected to stay on and dispatched to take a firsthand look at oil production in the United States in preparation for future work abroad. Through the autumn of 1912, Yale shuttled to a variety of Standard oilfields in the Midwest, tasked only to write up weekly reports on what he observed and send them back to Socony headquarters.

But the endless tour of oilfields had soon become monotonous to the restless Yale. In early 1913, he wrote to his New York supervisors asking to be given a field job, arguing that if he was to learn any more about the oil business it would have to be by doing rather than observing. That letter undoubtedly further endeared him to 26 Broadway; the notion that a college man—an Ivy League graduate, no less—would request to toil as a laborer indicated just the sort of employee Standard was looking for. Yale was soon sent to the new Cushing field in western Oklahoma to work as a roustabout.

For a time, he reveled in the hard labor. Living in the middle of nowhere for weeks on end, Yale worked a succession of Oklahoma fields, where he cleared drill sites, laid piping, hauled machinery, and constructed derricks. He had been doing this for several months when the cable arrived from New York.

Just three days removed from the Kiefer field, Yale walked into the lobby of the Socony corporate headquarters at 26 Broadway in lower Manhattan. There, he was taken up to the thirteenth-floor office suite of Standard's vice president, William Bemis. Yale found two other men already waiting in the suite, hats in hand, and all three maintained a respectful silence as the officious Bemis fired off directives to his scurrying staff.

"My mind was in a dream world," Yale recounted, "as I listened to him dictating instructions to his secretary about shipments of kerosene oil to Shanghai, about contracts for asphalt to pave the streets of a city in India, and contracts with the Greek government for fuel oil to supply the Greek navy at Piraeus."

When finally Bemis turned his attention to the three waiting men, it was to inform them that they had been selected for a special overseas assignment, that in just two days' time they would board SS *Imperator* in New York harbor for its voyage to Calais, France. From there, they would travel overland across the length of Europe to Constantinople, where they would receive further instructions from the manager of Standard's branch office. Before dismissing them, Bemis stressed to the three men that they were embarking on a highly confidential mission. As such, they were to tell no one of their ultimate destination or of their affiliation with Standard Oil. Instead, they were to pass themselves off as wealthy "playboys" en route to a Grand Tour of the Holy Land, a charade lent credence by their deluxe travel accommodations: the *Imperator* was the newest and most luxurious passenger ship plying the Atlantic crossing, their rail passage to Constantinople was to be aboard the fabled Orient Express, and they would be traveling first-class the entire way.

But upholding the playboy ruse was easier said than done for Yale's two companions. J. C. Hill, the leader of the team, was a rough-around-the-edges crew boss from the steel mills of Pennsylvania. Rudolf McGovern was a dour and socially awkward geologist in his late twenties. Even if these two could manage to put on airs suggesting that they came from money—and that seemed doubtful—they hardly seemed prime candidates for a pilgrimage to biblical sites. Perhaps wisely, their answer to the playboy directive was to interact with the ship's other first-class passengers as little as possible.

William Yale had no such difficulties. To the contrary, the voyage was like a disorienting return to his former life. Among the *Imperator's* first-class passengers were a great many young people, the offspring of America's industrial magnates and landed aristocracy, setting off on their requisite Grand Tour of Europe, the sort of tame adventure that until a few years earlier would have been his lot.

Yale would recall one peculiar detail of that journey. The *Imperator* (German for emperor) was the new flagship of the Hamburg-America Line, and at every dinnertime its German officers rose to offer a toast to *"der Tag"* (the day). Unschooled in the nuances of German, Yale assumed that the gesture was in quaint celebration of the day just lived; it would be some time before he understood it was actually a kind of code, a toast in giddy anticipation of the coming world war, then less than a year away.

On September 15, 1913, the same day that William Yale received his cable at the Kiefer oilfield ordering him to New York, T. E. Lawrence was at the train station in Aleppo, sixty miles to the west of Carchemish, awaiting the arrival of his brother Will.

Of his four brothers, Lawrence had always been closest to Will, the middle child and just two years his junior. Upon learning that his brother was leaving England to take up a teaching position in India, he had implored Will to stop off in Syria en route.

Despite their closeness, the visit must have been the source of some anxiety for Lawrence, who had long since been consigned to the role of family bohemian; it was easy to imagine that his brother might be quite shocked by the primitiveness of his surroundings and to report back as much to Oxford. Lawrence needn't have worried. After the two spent some ten days together at Jerablus, Lawrence saw Will off at the local train station for the return to Aleppo, a moment Will recounted in a letter to their parents:

"You must not think of Ned as leading an uncivilized existence. When I saw him last as the train left the station, he was wearing white flannels, socks and red slippers, with a white Magdalen blazer, and was talking to the governor of Biredjik in lordly fashion."

That parting at Jerablus was to be the last time the brothers would ever see each other.

Chapter 3

Another and Another Nice Thing

Always my soul hungered for less than it had.

T. E. LAWRENCE, *SEVEN PILLARS OF WISDOM*

How do you put a collar on a leopard? Very carefully, according to the old joke, but in the autumn of 1913, T. E. Lawrence and Leonard Woolley were in need of a practical answer to that question. They had recently been given a young leopard as a gift by a government official in Aleppo, and had found that so long as he remained chained in the courtyard of the Jerablus compound, he made for a very effective watchdog. The problem, though, was that leopards grow very quickly, and it was now just a matter of time before he tore through the flimsy collar he had been delivered in.

The archaeologists' first idea was to throw a large slatted box over the cat, then reach through the slats to effect the collar exchange, but since the leopard was "not very sweet tempered" to begin with, according to Lawrence, this confinement only put him in a fouler mood. Their solution was a rather clever one. Slightly enlarging an opening in the box, they kept stuffing in burlap sacks until eventually the leopard was wedged so tightly that he couldn't move.

"Then we took the top off the box, collared him, and let him loose again," Lawrence wrote to his family. "He will make a most splendid carpet some day."

Along with learning how to recollar a leopard, it was in that autumn 1913 digging season at Carchemish, Lawrence's fifth, that he and Woolley would make a spectacular find—the site's main temple. It was an archaeologist's dream, the discovery of a lifetime, and it helped fuel in Lawrence a sense that he had found his true calling, and perhaps his true home. The spacious main living room of the Jerablus compound was now a cozy space adorned with artwork on the walls and carpets and animal hides on the floor, a library with books in seven languages, and an enormous fireplace constantly stoked with hot-burning olivewood. He revealed his feelings in a letter to a close friend from his Oxford days that autumn.

"I have got to like this place very much," he wrote, "and the people here—five or six of them—and the whole manner of living pleases me. . . . Carchemish will not be finished for another four or five years and I'm afraid that, after that, I'll probably go after another and another nice thing."

But heartbreakingly, funding from the British Museum—always extremely tight and always conditionally doled out from one season or year to the next—had been effectively exhausted. Unless an unforeseen new funding source suddenly appeared, the next digging season, spring 1914, was slated to be the last. This knowledge hung over Lawrence and Woolley, and it overshadowed their excitement over that season's discoveries with a deepening sense of despair. It was only when they began closing down the site in preparation for their off-season break that a new possibility presented itself.

Under the auspices of the Palestine Exploration Fund, a British Museum director explained, a group of Royal Engineers was about to embark on an archaeological survey of the so-called Wilderness of Zin of southernmost Palestine; might Lawrence and Woolley be interested in joining them during their upcoming break?

For Lawrence and Woolley, it presented a choice between spending two months of leisure in England, or trekking through one of the world's most inhospitable corners. But the lure of exploration really made this no choice at all; both men immediately signed on.

LATE ONE NIGHT in early October 1913, William Yale lay in his tent in the mountains of Anatolia, struck by a sense of wonder at how quickly a life could change. Just three weeks earlier he had been living in a two-room shanty and pulling rods in an Oklahoma oilfield, and now he was traveling through one of the most ruggedly beautiful landscapes on earth, a land only a handful of Americans had ever seen.

Adding to his sense of awe was that in all the time he'd spent in Oklahoma daydreaming about where Standard Oil might send him, he had scarcely considered the Near East. Instead, on that day he walked into the Socony headquarters in New York, he had assumed he was being dispatched as a sales representative to China.

Yale's misconception was understandable. In 1913, Socony was primarily an *exporter* of petroleum products, and China was by far its largest market. In comparison, the company's exports to the Ottoman Empire, primarily kerosene to fuel its embryonic industrial facilities, were minuscule. To put into perspective how minuscule, while Standard's kerosene represented the second biggest American export to the Ottoman Empire, the largest was Singer sewing machines.

But as the Standard vice president, William Bemis, had explained to the three men brought to his office that morning, they weren't being sent to the Near East to rustle up new purchasing clients, but rather to find and develop new sources of oil.

It was simple economics. By the end of 1913, the exponentially growing demand for oil and petroleum products around the globe meant that demand would soon outstrip supply. In the United States alone, the number of combustion-engine vehicles on the road had increased twentyfold in less than a decade, from some seventy-five thousand in 1905 to well over 1.5 million in 1913—and already a number of the oldest American oilfields were starting to run dry.

Oil was rapidly becoming a crucial military asset as well. In 1912, just a year before Yale's summoning to New York, the first lord of the admiralty of Great Britain, Winston Churchill, had made international headlines with his plan to convert the entire Royal Navy from coal to oil. As might be expected, this proposed modernization of the world's most powerful fleet was already causing the navies of other nations, including Germany, to scramble to follow suit.

As a consequence, both American and European oil companies were now rushing to find and exploit new fields wherever they might exist. One especially promising region was the Near East. In the 1870s, huge oil and gas deposits had been discovered around Baku on the Caspian Sea, and this had been followed by another large strike in the Persian Gulf in 1908. Those fields were quickly dominated by European consortiums, and the race was on to tap and lay claim to the next big find.

To that end, the Socony branch office in Constantinople had quietly obtained a six-month option from a consortium of three Jerusalem-based businessmen who held vast exploration concessionary rights in three different regions of the Ottoman Empire. It was to perform preliminary fieldwork in these concessionary zones that Yale, McGovern, and Hill had been dispatched from New York. As for the elaborate secrecy surrounding their mission, there were two reasons: to throw any potential competitors off the scent, naturally, but also to keep the Standard name in the background for as long as possible. Its recent breakup notwithstanding, the Standard brand was still regarded with such abiding distrust in the Near

East, as in many other parts of the world, that the easiest way to besmirch the reputation of a business rival was to accuse it of being a Standard Oil front.

But despite its stealth approach, there were indications that Standard Oil of New York was not quite the smoothly run, rapacious machine its progenitor had been. Indeed, one such indication was the composition of the team it had sent to explore the Ottoman concessions. J. C. Hill, the chief, was a Pittsburgh steel man with no experience in the oil industry. Rudolf McGovern was a college-trained geologist, but had never actually set foot in an oilfield. And while William Yale certainly knew his way around an oilfield, he had absolutely no knowledge of geology.

Certainly J. C. Hill had an unusual approach to exploration, one that might best be described as fatalistic. Arriving in Constantinople in early October, the team had set out for the first concessionary zone, a broad stretch of mountainous terrain in central Anatolia, just south of the Black Sea. Accompanied by a small team of local guides, the three Americans spent a couple of weeks roaming the high plateau on horseback, but each time McGovern pointed to a distant spot he deemed worthy of closer inspection, Hill thought better of it. A critical moment came when the group learned there was a boat heading back to Constantinople in thirty hours' time, and that there wouldn't be another for at least two weeks; they made the boat with just minutes to spare.

Their pace slowed considerably once they reached the second exploration zone, the Dead Sea valley in Palestine, in November 1913. Essentially a continuation of the Great Rift Valley of East Africa, from a geological standpoint the region held a good deal more promise than Anatolia. For several weeks, the team traveled the western shore of the Dead Sea, picking their way through shale screes and the surrounding limestone cliffs. Time and again, they found tantalizing clues to the presence of oil—lumps of pure asphalt floating in the sea, surface limestone so impregnated with petroleum that it gave off the odor of gasoline—but nothing to confirm that a commercially viable reservoir might lie beneath.

Then again, it was hard to say much with any definitiveness since Hill, employing the exploratory style he had honed in Anatolia, soon began to veto nearly every spot that McGovern recommended for closer investigation. At times it seemed to Yale that they weren't so much looking for oil as trying to hide from it.

Matters finally came to a head in early January when Hill announced that their work there was done and ordered the breaking of camp for the return journey to Jerusalem. Yale, fueled by three months of frustration, could hold his tongue no longer. He confronted Hill, and the two ended up in a heated argument.

Whether that argument had some effect or it was mere coincidence, on the very next day, as the group climbed into the Judean foothills for the return to Jerusalem, Hill suddenly drew up his horse to gaze at a mountainous outcrop some thirty miles to the south. It was a strange geological formation, an irregular massif rising from the surrounding desert plain. Examined through binoculars, there appeared to be pools of something collected at the mountain base, something shimmering and iridescent.

"There." J. C. Hill pointed off to the mountains of Kornub. "That is where we will find oil."

Events moved very quickly after that. Hurrying his bedraggled caravan back to Jerusalem, Hill immediately cabled Socony headquarters with news of his "find." By return telegram, he was ordered to gather up the two primary concession holders of the Palestine tracts, Jerusalem businessmen Ismail Hakki Bey and Suleiman Nassif, and personally deliver them to the Socony office in Cairo as soon as possible. In Hill's absence, Yale and Rudolf McGovern were to go on to Kornub and conduct tests to determine just how immense this new strike might be.

Hastily hiring guides and camp orderlies for the expedition, Yale and McGovern decamped from Jerusalem around January 6, only to meet T. E. Lawrence and his companions outside Beersheva a few days later. Following that humiliating encounter, the Socony party continued south until they at last reached the desolate peaks of Kornub. What they were to discover there would have momentous consequences.

ON MARCH 15, 1913, Aaron Aaronsohn was invited to a luncheon at an exclusive club in Washington, D.C. The guest of honor was former president Theodore Roosevelt.

Maybe it was out of respect that Aaronsohn's hosts, two prominent American Jewish leaders named Julian Mack and Felix Frankfurter, sat their guest beside the former president, or maybe it was born of a sense of mischief; both Aaronsohn and Roosevelt, still referred to as "the Colonel" by his intimates, had hard-earned reputations for being nonstop talkers, and their table companions may have thought it amusing to see who would win out. To the amazement of Mack and Frankfurter, it was President Roosevelt who barely got a word in; instead he listened to Aaronsohn with rapt attention. Aaronsohn clearly appreciated the uniqueness of his achievement; he wrote in his diary that night that "from now on, my reputation will be the man who made the Colonel shut up for 101 minutes."

Much like the former president, Aaron Aaronsohn came on like a force of nature. A towering man given to portliness, he was both brilliant and arrogant, passionate and combative, one of those people who seem to believe they are always the most interesting person in a room. In the case of the thirty-seven-year-old Aaronsohn, he was usually right.

By March 1913, he had also emerged as one of the most persuasive spokesmen for a cause that had recently gained currency in certain Jewish circles: Zionism. Calling for a return of the Jewish diaspora to their ancestral homeland of Eretz (Greater) Israel, the Zionist movement had gained some adherents among international Jewry over the previous two decades, but more frequently had been met with skepticism, even hostility. What made Aaronsohn so influential was that his Zionist arguments were not based on political or religious abstractions, but on the purely practical, almost the mundane: agriculture. Already recognized as one of the most accomplished agronomists in the Middle East, Aaronsohn had spent thirty-one of his thirty-seven years in Palestine, and he was now conducting a wide range of scientific experiments—on plants and trees and soils—that might restore the region to the verdant land it had been in ancient times. All high-minded Zionist principles aside, he frequently pointed out, the first prerequisite for the Jews' return to Israel was to have something to eat; Aaronsohn knew how to feed them.

He hadn't come to any of this easily. The eldest child of a Jewish grain merchant, Aaronsohn was born in 1876 in a small town in central Romania. He was just two when the Russo-Turkish War led to Romania's independence from the Ottoman Empire. For the nation's large Jewish population, what had been a tolerably bad existence under a Muslim autocracy quickly became an intolerably bad one under a Christian democracy. Effectively barred from obtaining citizenship, which also meant being barred from most schools and professions, the Jews began a mass exodus out of Romania. In 1882, when Aaron was six, his parents joined the flight. Rather than make for the émigrés' preferred destination of the United States, however, the Aaronsohns joined some 250 other Romanian Jews in sailing for the Palestine region of Ottoman Syria.

The group settled on a barren tract of rocky hillside near the port city of Haifa, an outpost they named Samarin. There they quickly discovered that the "land flowing with milk and honey" described in the Book of Exodus had changed a very great deal in the interim. The few Samarin settlers who knew how to farm—most had been small merchants back in Romania—were soon defeated by the arid landscape and poor soil. Within the year, the émigrés were so destitute they were forced to pawn their sacred Torah scrolls.

Salvation came in the form of the enormously wealthy French Jewish financier Baron Edmond de Rothschild. An early supporter and benefactor of Jewish immigration to Palestine, Rothschild had already established or bailed out a number of Jewish colonies in the region, and in 1884 he did the same with Samarin, renaming it Zichron Yaakov (Jacob's Memorial), in honor of his deceased father. As the community soon discovered, though, Rothschild's patronage came at a very steep price. In agreeing to lend financial support, his first condition had been "that he alone shall be the colony's sole lord and that all things in its domain be under his rule"—and he hadn't been kidding. The residents of Zichron Yaakov were told what crops they could grow, how they should dress, even who had earned the right to marry, and Rothschild's resident agents made sure the rules were enforced.

But for the young and extraordinarily bright Aaron Aaronsohn, this feudalistic system had its benefits. In 1893, at the age of sixteen, he was chosen by Rothschild's agents to be educated in France, all expenses paid, and for the next two years he studied agronomy and botany at the Grignon Institute outside Paris, one of the most prestigious agricultural academies in Europe. When he returned to Palestine, it was not to take up the life of a Rothschild serf in Zichron Yaakov but to serve as an agricultural "instructor" at another of the baron's settlements. The arrangement didn't last long. Within a year, Aaronsohn, just nineteen but already headstrong and impatient, broke with the baron and his agents and struck out on his own.

Finding work as an agricultural advisor to large absentee landowners, he also began meticulously studying and cataloging the flora and geology of Palestine. In this endeavor, his intense curiosity and indefatigable energy soon became legendary. By his midtwenties, already fluent in a half dozen languages, Aaronsohn began publishing articles in European agronomy journals. No one in the tightly knit and highly credentialed fraternity of European agronomists had ever heard of their colleague in Palestine, and the frequency and eclectic range of Aaronsohn's work—learned studies on everything from sesame oil extraction to silk production—led some to wonder whether the name was a pseudonym for a collective of scientists.

His true breakthrough came in 1906 with his discovery of wild emmer wheat, a progenitor of cultivated wheat long thought extinct, growing on the slopes of Mount Hermon. At a time when the world's population was still over 80 percent agrarian, the find made international headlines and won the young, virtually self-taught Jewish scientist the recognition of his peers around the globe. Three years later, he accepted an invitation from the U.S. Department of Agriculture to conduct a wide-ranging tour of the American West. There he was treated as something of a celebrity, offered college professorships, his highly anticipated lectures attended by overflowing audiences. But Aaronsohn's time in the United States—his stay extended to nearly eight months—also exposed him to the currents of modern Jewish political thought, and especially to some of the foremost leaders of the American Zionist movement.

While the notion of a return to Israel had been a cornerstone of Jewish faith for millennia—for nearly two thousand years, Jewish Yom Kippur and Passover services have ended with the recitation, "next year in Jerusalem"—it was a Hungarian writer, Theodor Herzl, who transformed it into a modern political idea. In the face of institutionalized anti-Semitism in even the most "enlightened" nations of Europe, and the periodic massacre of Jews in places like czarist Russia, Herzl had argued in his 1896 book *The Jewish State* that international Jewry could only ever be truly safe and free by establishing their own homeland in the ancient land of Israel. The following year, Herzl presided over the first meeting of the World Zionist Congress in Switzerland, an event that electrified Jewish audiences around the world.

It also provoked a furious backlash. In both Europe and the United States, many Jewish leaders—perhaps most—saw Zionism as a dangerous instrument that would isolate Jews from the nations of their birth, and provide fuel to the long-repeated accusation of Jews harboring a divided loyalty; some even suspected Zionism to be an anti-Semitic plot. For the anti-Zionists, the answer to the "Jewish Question" was not Israel but assimilation, full political and economic participation in the nations of their births, a goal finally coming within reach in much of Europe through the spread of democracy.

The "assimilationists" also appeared to have a powerful practical argument in their favor. Already by the early 1900s, some sixty thousand Jews lived in the Holy Land, and the great majority of them were either desperately poor or subsisting on subscriptions raised by their religious brethren abroad. Considering this, how could the wastelands of Palestine possibly sustain any significant percentage of the some ten million Jews then scattered about the globe?

It was in retort to this question that Aaron Aaronsohn—not just an agronomist, but an amateur archaeologist and an avid reader of history—could pose a compelling one of his own. What had sustained the Romans and the Babylonians and the Assyrians? From both archaeological excavations and old histories, it was clear that Palestine had once supported populations much greater than the estimated 700,000 inhabitants of the early 1900s, and it wasn't as if the water sources or soil beds that sustained those civilizations had simply vanished. Rather, they had been lost to time, and were waiting to be rediscovered, retapped. Aaronsohn also had a persuasive modern example to point to. During his travels in the American West, he had made a special study of California, a place with very similar climate and soil conditions to Palestine. With water diverted from the Sierra Nevada, California's Central Valley was already becoming the agricultural breadbasket of America and bringing in a flood of new settlers. The very same, Aaronsohn argued, could be achieved in Palestine, and with his unrivaled knowledge of the region, he was the man to do it.

In the face of such optimism, not to say arrogance, an expanding circle of wealthy American Jews warmed to Aaronsohn's vision of a restored Israel. Before he left the United States in the autumn of 1909, a consortium of these businessmen and philanthropists had raised some $20,000 toward the creation of the Jewish Agricultural Experiment Station in Palestine, a modern research center that Aaronsohn would oversee and that he vowed would become the preeminent such scientific facility in all the Middle East.

For his new venture, Aaronsohn set up operations on a bluff overlooking the Mediterranean some eight miles north of Zichron Yaakov, a place named Athlit. Over the next several years, he laid in fields of experimental seedbeds and orchards, built a complex of greenhouses and laboratories. He also saw to the construction of a large two-story building, housing for the facility's library and permanent workers, with a commanding view of the sea just one mile away. With a lack of sufficiently educated locals, Aaronsohn drew most of those permanent workers from among his own family—at various times all five of his siblings would be employed at Athlit—and it was they who oversaw its day-to-day operations, including supervising the field workers drawn from nearby Arab villages. "Before long," biographer Ronald Florence noted, "the experimental plots at the research center were producing more wheat, barley and oats per dunam [about one thousand square meters] than long-established farms on much better soils."

In light of his growing role as a recruiter for Zionism, it's somewhat curious that Aaronsohn appeared to have spent very little time thinking through its social or political ramifications. He could put more Jews on the ground in Palestine, of that he was certain, but what it meant or what form their governance might take was all rather vague.

But this same vagueness extended to the Zionist movement itself. Among "social" and religious Zionists, the goal was quite modest: increased Jewish immigration to Palestine for those who wished to go, with no upsetting of the existing local political framework. Indeed, many of the businessmen who had donated to Aaronsohn's research station considered themselves anti-Zionists, somehow imagining their involvement as apolitical, akin to helping rebuild a synagogue.

Even among those who embraced the idea of a "Jewish state," there was very little agreement on its definition. In 1901, Theodor Herzl had met with the Ottoman sultan in hopes of actually purchasing Palestine. When that overture went nowhere, most successive Zionist leaders had advocated an incremental approach, of Jewish financiers gradually buying up land in Palestine for settlement, while simultaneously negotiating with Constantinople—negotiations that might take the form of bribes or the paying off of a portion of the Ottomans' crushing foreign debt—to ensure Ottoman acceptance and protection of the new settlers. Whether such a scheme could ever lead to the kind of demographic shift allowing for Jewish majority rule was highly doubtful, however, given that Palestine's existing non-Jewish population outnumbered Jews by ten to one. By the time of Aaronsohn's luncheon with Teddy Roosevelt in 1913, however, a new, more promising prospect had presented itself. With the Ottoman Empire being torn at from all sides, its final collapse suddenly appeared imminent. If that fall did come and a European power took control of Palestine, the Zionists might be able to establish themselves under their protection. Both the most likely and most desirable such patron, in Aaronsohn's estimation, was Great Britain.

STEWART NEWCOMBE WAS a legendary figure in the Near East, although not in a uniformly positive way. At the age of thirty-five, the Boer War veteran had already surveyed and mapped vast tracts of Egypt and the Sudan for the British government, and had gained the reputation of being an indefatigable explorer, capable of the work of ten ordinary men. That was part of the problem. Due to his habit of driving others as hard as he drove himself, the Arabs who worked with him in the coming war would say of Captain Stewart Newcombe that "he was like fire, burning both his friends and enemies."

Not surprisingly then, Newcombe had been in a rather black mood as he left his camp in the Zin Desert on the morning of January 8 and made for Beersheva, a day's camel ride away. He was going there to meet up with the two eminent archaeologists, lately working on a dig in northern Syria, who had been assigned to his mission in southern Palestine. Although he fully appreciated the need for the archaeologists—they were the political cover that would allow his five military mapping teams to do their clandestine work—this operation was designed to be a fast-moving one over an unspeakably harsh landscape, and tending to the needs of two Oxford scholars was the last thing Newcombe needed. He had earlier sent ten camels to meet their boat in Gaza to transport their gear—archaeologists always had lots of gear—and he was coming out of the desert with more to handle the inevitable overflow.

A very pleasant surprise awaited him in Beersheva. "I expected to meet two somewhat elderly people; [instead] I found C. L. Woolley and T. E. Lawrence, who looked about twenty-four years of age and eighteen respectively.... My letters to them arranging for their reception had clearly been too polite. Undue deference ceased forthwith."

Far from needing a small camel caravan to haul their equipment, when Lawrence and Woolley had come off the boat in Gaza, accompanied by Lawrence's young assistant Dahoum, all their possessions had fit neatly onto the back of one small donkey. That had now been expanded somewhat by the purchase of camping and photographic supplies, but clearly the two young archaeologists appreciated the need for traveling light on the brutal terrain they were about to enter.

That evening, Newcombe spelled out to the men from Syria both what they were expected to do and the sub rosa purpose of the expedition. On this latter aspect, Lawrence had already pretty well figured things out. "We are obviously only meant as red herrings," he had written his parents en route to Palestine, "to give an archaeological colour to a political job."

That political job arose from a problem that Great Britain had largely brought upon itself. As the European power most dependent on control of the seas, Britain had been the driving force behind the construction of the Suez Canal in Egypt in the 1870s, seeing the linking of the Mediterranean to the Red Sea as a vital military and commercial shortcut in keeping its far-flung empire knitted together. So vital did it deem the canal that Britain had been willing to sacrifice its long-standing good relations with the Ottoman Empire in order to take possession of it outright, a feat accomplished by its 1882 invasion of Egypt under the pretext of quelling local unrest. That had delivered up the west bank of the Suez Canal, Egypt's de facto frontier, but it left the now hostile Ottomans still hovering on its east bank in the Sinai Peninsula. This problem was soon resolved; in 1906, Britain had capitalized on a minor diplomatic dispute to grab that territory also. The end result was something of a trade-off. The British now had their canal, along with the 120-mile-wide buffer zone of the Sinai Peninsula separating Egypt from the heavily settled Palestine region of southwest Syria. On the flip side, they had won the undying resentment of the Ottomans.

That was a small price to pay in 1882 and 1906, perhaps, but a rather different story by the beginning of 1914. With Europe stumbling ever closer toward a continent-wide war, the British were suddenly quite concerned by the sorry state of British-Ottoman relations, and by ominous signs that Constantinople was sliding into the orbit of Britain's avowed enemy, Germany. If the war everyone expected did come, the Suez Canal would be the crucial passageway for bringing British territorial troops from India and Australia to Europe; of course, if Turkey joined with Germany in that war, they would undoubtedly target the canal for this same reason. Britain's problems wouldn't end there. In the event that the enemy succeeded in crossing the canal and getting into Egypt itself, it was very likely to spark an anti-British insurrection by a population that thoroughly despised them, tying up British soldiers who would be needed for the fight in Europe.

In contemplating this scenario the British belatedly came to appreciate the downside to their Sinai buffer zone, one inherent to the very concept of buffer zones: how to know what lies on the other side? The British had a very good idea of what lay at the Sinai's northeastern tip—the populous and long-cultivated region of the Palestine coast—but they knew virtually nothing of the desert frontier that ran southeast from that coast to the Gulf of Aqaba, one hundred miles away. Were there roads there, water wells that might sustain an invasion force?

The person most preoccupied with finding out was Egypt's de facto ruler, the British agent and consul general, Horatio Herbert Kitchener. By 1914, Lord Kitchener was Britain's preeminent living war hero—he had crushed a native revolt in the Sudan during the Mahdi War in 1898, then led British forces to victory in the Boer War in 1902—but by one of those peculiar happenstances of history, as a young man Kitchener had been a geographical surveyor, and his crowning achievement was the mapping of Palestine. The one corner of Palestine that Kitchener and his cosurveyors had skipped over was the desolate wastelands of Zin—essentially the triangle-shaped lower half of modern-day Israel—the survey sponsors figuring there was simply no political or economic reason to include it. But it was precisely this unmapped triangle that now lay on the other side of the Sinai buffer zone.

Considering the enmity that had developed between the two empires, Kitchener had shown remarkable chutzpah in 1913 when "offering" the Ottomans the services of the British Royal Engineers to conduct a survey of Zin; unsurprisingly, Constantinople quickly turned the offer down. By happy coincidence, however, Zin also figured prominently in the biblical Book of Exodus, the region that Moses and the Israelites passed through at the end of their forty-year flight out of Egypt. This provided a handy theological and historical explanation for why a Christian nation might want to explore the region, and when the British tried this tack on Constantinople—repackaging their earlier offer so that it was now to be an archaeological survey of biblical sites under the auspices of the respected Palestine Exploration Fund—the ploy actually worked. It was this ruse that had brought Lawrence and Woolley to Beersheva, and that gave Newcombe the necessary cover for his military mapping teams.

Very quickly, whatever initial reservations Newcombe may have harbored at being saddled with the two archaeologists were erased. In Lawrence especially, he seemed to find a kindred spirit, a man so indifferent to creature comforts and possessed of such astounding endurance that it bordered on the masochistic.

He also detected a curious quirk in Lawrence's personality, a tendency to rise out of his core shyness in response to those who would obfuscate or stand in his way. An early example of this was his verbal torturing of the poor American oilmen in Beersheva. Most shy people tend to become more so when faced with a potentially confrontational situation, but with Lawrence and the Americans it had been precisely the opposite, the young archaeologist turning the encounter into a game of cat-and-mouse, with himself playing the cat. It indicated a streak of gamesmanship in Lawrence, a quality that would stand him in good stead as he faced off with the petty Ottoman officials who, Newcombe was sure, would try to obstruct their every move.

But in fact, far more than the Ottomans, it was the "Wilderness" of Zin itself that posed the greatest challenges to Lawrence and Woolley. Operating independently of the military survey teams, although frequently checked in on by Newcombe, they maintained a relentless pace over the bleak terrain, driving their camels and small team of camp orderlies to the point of ruin. At least these locals were accustomed to the region; coming from the more temperate climes of northern Syria, Lawrence and Woolley suffered terribly in the parched and sunbaked land.

These discomforts might have been partially offset if they'd found what they came to look for. They didn't. Instead, other than a few ruins dating from the Byzantine period or later, they found very few structures at all in the region—and certainly nothing suggesting an Exodus-era settlement.

But then there had always been something of a built-in fallacy to the Zin project, one the Ottomans might have deduced if they'd pondered matters a bit longer. In a landscape so inhospitable that even the hardy Bedouin nomads abandoned it in summer, why would Moses and the Israelites—forty years wandering in the desert and presumably eager to finally get somewhere nice—have lingered in this hellhole any longer than necessary? This was a point Lawrence touched on in a somewhat arch letter to his parents: "The Palestine Fund, of course, wants to find sites illustrating the Exodus, which is supposed to have passed this way. But of course a people 40 years out of Egypt could hardly leave much trace of themselves in their later camping grounds."

. . .

ON THE MORNING of November 12, 1913, Curt Prüfer made a most painful decision. For a brief time it had appeared that he might finally attain the respect and status he had always sought—as a scholar, as a sterling example of the new Germany—but then it had all turned to ash. Actually, it was worse than that, for in the bitter struggle waged over his candidacy to a prestigious position in the Egyptian power structure, Prüfer's British enemies had not only made sure he was denied the post, but professionally destroyed him in the process. On that morning, Prüfer sat at his desk in the German embassy and composed a terse letter of resignation from the foreign ministry, the institution that had been his home for the previous seven years. A few days later, the now former embassy official left for Jerusalem, there to await the arrival of his artist friend Richard von Below for their extended journey up the Nile.

In one of the more curious features of the European imperialist era, the dueling European powers often employed an intricate division-of-spoils system in their colonial realms with their imperial rivals, a way both to secure acceptance of their claims to hegemony and reduce those rivals' incentive for stirring local unrest.

From the standpoint of scholarly prestige, few foreigner-allotted positions in Cairo were more coveted than that of director of the khedival library. Since the signing of a bilateral accord in 1906, that post was reserved for a German. In late 1911, with the sitting German director slated for retirement, the German embassy put forward the name of Dr. Curt Prüfer as his replacement.

Its innocuous-sounding title notwithstanding, the post was a very sensitive one. In Ottoman times, the khedive had been the designated Egyptian head of state, and for the British to maintain the fiction that they had somehow been acting as a guarantor of Ottoman rule by their 1882 invasion, they had kept the khedive on as a figurehead. Since 1892, this had been Abbas Hilmi II. While Abbas was understandably never a big supporter of British rule to begin with, his dissatisfaction had dramatically deepened with Lord Kitchener's arrival on the scene in 1911. As the new British agent to Egypt, Kitchener had quickly grown so tired of Abbas—or as he preferred to call him, "this wicked little khedive"—that he'd begun stripping him of even his purely ceremonial duties. In response, Abbas had increasingly taken to using the offices of his "library" to stay in quiet contact with a host of Egyptian dissidents opposed to British rule.

Of course, what was bad for Britain was good for Germany, and by their control of the library directorship the Germans enjoyed the perfect cover to cultivate and maintain their own contacts with the anti-British Egyptian community. This was precisely what the outgoing German director had done, and in late 1911 the British had every expectation that Dr. Curt Prüfer, now promoted from dragoman to Oriental secretary at the German embassy, would uphold the tradition.

Certainly, Prüfer had done little to endear himself to the British authorities in Cairo, having continued with the pan-Islamic destabilizing efforts of his mentor, Max von Oppenheim. Most alarming to the Cairo authorities, Prüfer had long maintained a close relationship with a host of anti-British Egyptian figures, as well as with the disgruntled khedive himself. Indeed, on several occasions, Egyptian secret police had tracked the good doctor to clandestine meetings with some of British Egypt's most committed and dangerous enemies.

Consequently, placing such a man in the khedival library seemed a bit like putting an arsonist in a fireworks factory; shortly after Prüfer's name was put forward, the British diplomatically informed the Germans that his candidacy was "unsuitable." The Germans pressed their case, with the German ambassador in Cairo taking his spirited defense of Prüfer's nomination directly to Kitchener. At the end of October 1911 the German ambassador to Great Britain, Count Paul Metternich, took the matter all the way up to British foreign secretary Edward Grey.

But the more the Germans pushed on the Prüfer issue, the more suspicious the British became. In early 1912, Kitchener informed the German embassy that the issue had been referred to the Egyptian government's Ministry of Education, where Prüfer's candidacy had been rejected anew. It was an utterly transparent maneuver—the so-called Egyptian government would do exactly Britain's bidding—but it did finally bring an end to the matter. For Prüfer, it was a professionally devastating turn of events. Not only had he been publicly humiliated in losing the directorship, but with the intelligence reports of his intrigues now well known throughout the British government, he was effectively prevented from advancing further at the German embassy in Cairo.

But that was the least of it. However much the elitist structure of German society had been reformed in other spheres, those changes had not permeated into the diplomatic branch of the foreign ministry; in 1912, as in 1812, that branch was the province of the German aristocracy, its counts and princelings and noblemen. Indeed, no better example existed of the near impossibility of an outsider being admitted to this exclusive club than the long and futile struggle of Prüfer's mentor, Count von Oppenheim.

Although highly educated and clearly brilliant, Oppenheim possessed one fatal flaw in the eyes of the German diplomatic branch—he was of

Jewish ancestry—and that had been enough to defeat his many efforts over some two decades to win a transfer from the far less prestigious consular branch. He probably came closest in 1898, when his request was accompanied by a raft of supporting letters from gentile German aristocrats, friends of his from the Union Club in Berlin, except that Oppenheim had the misfortune of submitting his petition at the same time as another Jew. In the entire history of the German diplomatic service there had been only one Jewish member, a Rothschild, and the notion that there might suddenly be *two* more cast alarm.

"I am absolutely persuaded," a senior foreign ministry official wrote in response to the situation, "that what we have here is not a question of *one* Jew, but of his numerous coreligionists who will press through the breach which he makes. . . . If [even] one is let in, a cry of lamentation will ensue if others are refused." On such concerns, both applications were promptly denied.

On paper, the chances of Curt Prüfer—a lower-middle-class commoner with a doctorate from a middling university—passing into the foreign ministry's higher ranks looked nearly as bleak as Oppenheim's, but his Oriental secretary appointment had afforded a glimmer of hope; this was the one consular branch position where an elevation into the diplomatic branch occasionally occurred. Obviously, the odds of that happening would have been vastly improved had Prüfer assumed the library directorship. Conversely, having fought for that posting and lost, his odds now were exactly nil.

Through 1912 and most of 1913, Prüfer struggled on, but he found it impossible to escape the cloak of ignominy that had been cast over him. With the Egyptian secret police now watching his every move, even his adventurist activities as Oriental secretary were greatly curtailed. It was for this—and perhaps also a simple desire to try something completely new with his life—that he finally tendered his resignation and went off to join Richard von Below. What he went away with was an abiding hatred for the British, the "natural enemy" of Germany, now also the people who had destroyed his career.

On a broader level, though, the controversy that surrounded Prüfer over the library directorship neatly illustrated a particularly ominous feature of the early 1910s. While it already strained credulity that Lord Kitchener, the uncrowned sovereign of twelve million people in one of Britain's most important vassal states, had been compelled to personally engage in that controversy, how had it ever escalated to the point where the British foreign secretary and his closest advisors were enjoined? Did these men really have nothing better to do with their time than compose and debate lengthy memoranda over the job placement of a low-level German embassy official in Cairo?

In the answer to that question lies one of the keys to how World War I happened. By the early 1910s, with all the European powers perpetually jockeying for advantage, all of them constantly manufacturing crises in hopes of winning some small claim against their rivals, a unique kind of "fog of war" was setting in, one composed of a thousand petty slights and disputes and misunderstandings. It wasn't just the British foreign secretary whose time was taken up dealing with such things, but the foreign ministers—and in many cases, the prime ministers and presidents and kings—of all the powers, and often over struggles even less significant than that which entangled Curt Prüfer. Amid this din of complaint and trivial offense, how to know what really mattered, how to identify the true crisis when it came along?

THE GULF OF Aqaba is a narrow, hundred-mile-long inlet of the Red Sea that separates the craggy desert mountains of Arabia to one side from a similar set of mountains on the Sinai Peninsula to the other. At the northernmost end of the Aqaba inlet is the Jordanian town of the same name.

In 1914, Aqaba was nothing more than a tiny fishing village, its thousand or so inhabitants settled into a collection of crude huts sprinkled about the shoreline. Yet it was Aqaba, more than any other spot in the roughly four thousand square miles that he and his Royal Engineers were mapping, that obsessed Captain Stewart Newcombe.

In trying to anticipate the path an invasion force might take from Ottoman Palestine to reach the Suez Canal, certainly the most logical route was across the very top of the Sinai Peninsula, close to the Mediterranean. This was an established land crossing going back millennia, and its water sources, if meager, had been tapped and welled for just as long. Inland, the harsh Zin Desert seemed to afford few real possibilities, an assessment gradually being confirmed by Newcombe's men. By early February 1914, they had surveyed much of the border region's interior, and while finding a few Bedouin trails and wells, had uncovered nothing capable of sustaining an invasion force of any size.

But in all this, Aqaba, lying at the very southern end of the Sinai-Palestine demarcation line, represented a wild card. With its outlet on the Red Sea, troops could be ferried into the village and then marched west. For well over a decade, persistent rumors had the Turks secretly building a railroad spur linking Aqaba to the Arabian interior, complementing the mountain trail already in existence. Rumors aside, it was known that at least two "roads" originated somewhere in the Quweira mountains above Aqaba, trails long used by local Bedouin to launch raids into the Sinai. Taken all together, it meant the Turks might have the potential of launching an invasion force across the Sinai from the very southern end of the buffer zone, even while British attention was focused at the more obvious northern end.

Understandably, then, Stewart Newcombe viewed getting into Aqaba as the most crucial aspect of his entire mission to Zin. In mid-February 1914, he turned his attention to how he might do it and who should accompany him.

History is often the tale of small moments—chance encounters or casual decisions or sheer coincidence—that seem of little consequence at the time, but somehow fuse with other small moments to produce something momentous, the proverbial flapping of a butterfly's wings that triggers a hurricane. Such was the case with Captain Newcombe's choosing a companion for the journey to Aqaba.

Theoretically, he could have pulled any one of the Royal Engineers off his five surveying parties, but as much as their technical expertise might come in handy, he was expecting a cold reception in the village, and the sight of two British officers rolling in would be unlikely to improve it. He also could have chosen Leonard Woolley, whose somewhat fusty manner would lend credence to this being a foray of purely scientific interest. But instead he chose Lawrence. One reason was that he genuinely enjoyed his company, but another was Lawrence's peculiar skill at polite belligerence that Newcombe had observed in a variety of forms since the early days of the expedition, a skill likely to be called upon in Aqaba.

Joined by Dahoum, Newcombe and Lawrence showed up in Aqaba in mid-February, and, just as Newcombe had expected, their welcome was a decidedly icy one. The municipal governor, professing to have no knowledge of their project, immediately forbade them from doing any mapping or photographing or archaeological work in the region. But just as Newcombe had also expected, these strictures only spurred Lawrence to greater initiative. "I photographed what I could," Lawrence would recount in a letter to a friend, Edward Leeds, "I archaeologised everywhere."

Of special interest to Lawrence—and this interest may have mainly derived from the opportunity to flagrantly disregard the governor's orders—were the ruins of a fortress on a small island just a few hundred yards off the Aqaba shore. He secretly arranged for a boatman to take him to the island, only to have the man promptly arrested by the governor's police. Undeterred, Lawrence crafted a crude inflatable raft and, together with Dahoum, paddled out to the island.

It was an easy enough passage going out, but rather a different story on the return. With both the current and wind against them, it took Lawrence and Dahoum hours to make the shore, at which point the local police, long since alerted, took them into custody. The furious governor placed the pair under armed escort for their journey out of Aqaba. Unfortunately for the men detailed to this mission, the unwanted entourage simply provided Lawrence with an amusing new challenge.

"I learnt that their orders were not to let me out of their sight," he wrote his family a week later from a town fifty miles to the north, "and I took them two days afoot over such hills and wadis as did [them in]. I have been camped here for two days, and they are still struggling in from all over the compass."

As a bonus, during this forced march Lawrence had stumbled across the two "great cross-roads" that the Bedouin raiding parties used for their forays into the Sinai.

All of this would prove profoundly useful to Lawrence. In just a little over three years' time, he would use the knowledge gained from his escapades in Aqaba to conquer that strategic village in a manner that no one else could conceive of, a feat of arms still considered one of the most daring military exploits of modern times.

UPON PARTING WAYS with J. C. Hill in Jerusalem in early January, William Yale and Rudolf McGovern set out for the Kornub massif. Reaching it a few days after their humiliating encounter with Lawrence in Beersheva, they immediately had reason to recall a very basic law of chemical properties: namely, that it is not just oil mixed with water that gives off an iridescent sheen. In the right concentrations, a wide variety of minerals can, including iron, and it was precisely this—stagnant water rich in iron tailings—that Hill had observed through his binoculars from thirty miles away.

Crestfallen but determined to make the most of their arduous trip, Yale and McGovern spent several days collecting rock samples and drilling boreholes. From this, they determined there *was* oil in Kornub—McGovern was fairly certain of that—but whether it existed in anything near commercially viable quantities seemed unlikely. The two then returned to Jerusalem, there to relay the sobering news to Socony headquarters.

Curiously, and for reasons Yale and McGovern couldn't begin to fathom at the time, 26 Broadway didn't seem to share their sense of disappointment. The two were told to lie low in Jerusalem, which they did until mid-March, and were then dispatched for more fruitless exploration of the last of the three prospective concessionary zones, in the hill region of Thrace just to the west of Constantinople. Tucked away in the backwaters of the Ottoman Empire, Yale remained unaware that news of the Kornub "strike" had triggered a complex diplomatic tug-of-war, one that was playing out across four continents and involving ambassadors, ministers of state, and some half dozen international corporations.

When the British had pinpointed the location of Socony's interests in Palestine, courtesy of Lawrence's interrogation of Yale outside Beersheva, alarm had spread throughout the government. With access to oil now considered a matter of national security in light of the Royal Navy's ongoing oil-conversion program, taking control of any new fields was not merely an economic concern but a political one. There followed a complicated series of maneuvers in which the British authorities tried to sabotage the Kornub deal and arrange for a British oil company to obtain the concessions. In this cause they relied on information from one of the Palestinian concession holders, Suleiman Nassif, who deftly played each side against the other to his own benefit. It was at this juncture that McGovern's disheartening report on Kornub finally reached New York, but by then it was too late. Caught up in the spirit of competition, Socony not only disregarded McGovern's findings but ultimately paid a far higher price for the Kornub concessions than intended.

None of this was known to Yale and McGovern until they returned to Constantinople from Thrace in late April. There they were met by their old boss, J. C. Hill, who informed them that, having just secured the Kornub concessions for a period of twenty-five years, Socony was now gearing up for a massive exploration project in the region, one that would entail building roads, erecting worker camps in the desert, bringing in trucks and drilling equipment and heavy machinery. Furthermore, Socony was sending the three of them to Egypt, there to oversee the purchasing and to coordinate the delivery of all the matériel needed. That this was an area of expertise in which they had no knowledge was deemed unimportant; by the late spring of 2014, Yale, McGovern, and Hill were in Egypt contemplating a daunting stack of purchasing manuals in Socony's Alexandria office.

But in this new task, the three men could draw on a powerful guiding principle: they were Standard men, and above all else, William Yale was increasingly coming to realize, that meant taking charge, making decisions. Within a few days of sifting through those purchasing manuals, and without ever seeking the counsel of someone who might know what they were doing, they had ordered up some $250,000 worth of drilling equipment (about $30 million in today's equivalent) for the inauguration of Socony's new operation in the Kornub. That equipment, purchased from a variety of vendors throughout the United States, would take several months to arrive in Palestine—actual drilling was scheduled to begin on November 1—but in the meantime, an enormous amount of work was to be done.

The first step was to cut a road from Hebron down through the Judean foothills, and then across some twenty miles of virtually trackless desert to Kornub. This aspect of the project would prove immensely important in the near future. Yale was put in charge of this, and he contracted the best road builder in Palestine to do it. Even so, there were glitches. A near riot developed in Hebron when the road surveyors took to marking the walls of houses in their path with crosses in white paint, a symbol the devoutly Muslim residents interpreted as marking them for conversion to Christianity. On another occasion, Bedouin riflemen attacked one of the construction crews out in the foothills; the assault was finally repelled by Socony's own private militia.

But as Yale was well aware, the biggest hurdles awaited at either end of that road. All the drilling equipment being brought over from the United States would need to come in at the Mediterranean port of Jaffa—except there were no cranes in Jaffa capable of unloading such heavy machinery. Then there was the niggling little detail to be worked out at the other end of the line. One thing that makes a desert a desert is, of course, a lack of water, and while McGovern had managed to locate a few small wells in the Kornub area, the supply seemed barely sufficient for the twenty-man work crew that would be living there, let alone provide the huge amounts needed for the highly water-dependent drilling process. As with so many other parts of the project, however, this issue failed to set off alarm bells within Socony, and if a problem isn't acknowledged, does it really need a solution?

As work got under way, Yale was held by an ever-deepening sense of foreboding. "Secretly," he wrote, "I dreaded the mess, which seemed an inevitable outcome of the systemless way the Chief [J. C. Hill] handled matters."

UPON HIS RETURN to Syria from his Zin adventure in early March, Lawrence found a letter waiting for him from David Hogarth. It contained wonderful news. Impressed by word of the previous season's discoveries, the British philanthropist who was the primary sponsor of the Carchemish project had finally set aside enough funds to keep the excavations going for an extended period—two more years at least, and possibly for as long as it took for the site to be thoroughly explored. With this cheerful news, Lawrence planned to quickly finish the Wilderness of Zin report for the Palestine Exploration Fund during his upcoming break in England, and then hurry back to Carchemish for an early beginning to the next digging season.

For his return to England, Lawrence planned to first detour to Baghdad and then pass down the Tigris River to the Indian Ocean, figuring the much longer sea voyage this would entail would give him more time to work on the Zin report. Instead, just as that season's dig was closing down in early June, a letter from Stewart Newcombe changed his plan.

Newcombe, his work in southern Palestine finished, had visited Carchemish in May en route to England. But of course Carchemish was not really en route to anywhere, and Newcombe's true motive for the detour had been to continue overland to Constantinople in order to spy on the progress being made by the Turks and Germans on the Baghdad Railway—and in particular on their tunneling projects in the Taurus and Amanus Mountains. He had succeeded in making the journey, but had been so closely watched as to be unable to study the tunneling work in any detail. In his June letter, Newcombe asked if Lawrence and Woolley might follow the same path on their return to England and glean what they could. Rather taking to their new roles as military intelligence sleuths, the archaeologists readily agreed.

That journey proved to be another extraordinarily fortuitous happenstance, but one that would ultimately play out very differently from Lawrence's trip to Aqaba. In the Taurus and Amanus Mountains he would identify a crucial—and potentially devastating—Achilles' heel of the Ottoman Empire, one that, despite his most strenuous efforts during the coming war, would never be exploited.

BACK IN HIS garden cottage at 2 Polstead Road in Oxford, Lawrence sat down to write a long letter to a friend, James Elroy Flecker, on the last Monday of June 1914. The bulk of the letter was taken up with a picaresque description of a melee that had occurred between the German railway engineers and their workers in Jerablus in May. But what is most interesting about the letter is what it doesn't mention. On the day that Lawrence wrote it—Monday, June 29—the front page of almost every newspaper in Britain told of the previous day's assassination of the heir to the Austro-Hungarian throne, Archduke Franz Ferdinand, together with his wife, in the streets of Sarajevo by Serbian revolutionaries.

The news out of Sarajevo seemed to make just as little impression on Curt Prüfer and William Yale. His long Nile cruise with Richard von Below over, by the end of June 1914, Prüfer was living in Munich, eking out a modest living giving public lectures on Oriental languages; in his diary, he made no mention of the Balkan assassinations. As for William Yale, hard at work on the road project below Hebron, it appears he didn't even hear of them until some weeks later.

All of which was actually quite understandable; the public had become thoroughly inured to the endless saber-rattling of the European imperial powers, the "crises" that seemed to boil up and fall away every few months, and there was no reason to think this one would play out any differently. But Sarajevo was the crisis that counted, because those who wanted war made it count. A very slow-burning fuse had been lit, one that would take over a month to burn through, but when it did, in the first days of August 1914, it would trigger a continent-wide war that would ultimately carry everyone down into the abyss together.

In his letter to Flecker on June 29, Lawrence wrote that he expected to be in England for another two or three weeks, and "thereafter Eastward" to Carchemish. But Lawrence's days as an archaeologist were over.

Chapter 4

To the Last Million

Sir: I have the honor to report that conditions are going
from bad to worse here.

U.S. CONSUL GENERAL IN BEIRUT,
STANLEY HOLLIS, TO SECRETARY OF STATE, NOVEMBER 9, 1914

On the afternoon of August 7, 1914, Lord Horatio Herbert Kitchener, Britain's newly appointed secretary of state for war, was called to his first cabinet meeting with Prime Minister Herbert Asquith and other senior ministers.

Kitchener's selection for the War Office had come about almost by chance. On a brief visit back to England from his post as British agent to Egypt, he was just boarding a ship to leave when war was declared. Asquith, figuring that appointing Britain's most famous military hero to lead that effort might have a salutary effect on public morale, had skipped over a long line of prospective candidates in giving the position to Kitchener.

At the time, boosting public morale seemed among the least of the prime minister's concerns. In Britain, as elsewhere across Europe, war euphoria had gripped the populace, with great crowds gathering in public squares to cheer the news. Most predictions were that this war would be a very quick one, and in villages and cities across the continent, reserve soldiers, anxious to escape the drudgery of factory and farm, despaired at not being called up before this grand adventure passed them by. The situation was slightly different in Britain, one of the few European nations without mandatory conscription, but within days of the war declaration the British government was already contemplating a halt in recruitment, adjudging that it already had more volunteers signed up than it could ever possibly need.

But in that summer of 1914, most everyone was overlooking a crucial detail: that the weapons of war had changed so radically over the previous forty years as to render the established notions of its conduct obsolete. It was rather simple stuff, easy to miss—the machine gun; the long-range artillery shell; barbed wire—but because of this oversight, Europe was about to tumble into an altogether different conflict from what most imagined.

One reason Europe's imperial powers missed the warning signs was that these new instruments of war had previously been employed almost exclusively against those who didn't have them—specifically, those non-Europeans who attempted to resist their imperial reach. In such situations, the new weapons had allowed for a lopsided slaughter not seen since the Spanish conquest of the Americas, and more than any other single factor had accounted for the dramatic expansion of Europe's colonial empires into Asia and Africa in the latter part of the nineteenth century.

It is perversely appropriate, then, that among the few people who did appreciate this new face of war and the problems it would pose was the man who had officiated over more of these one-sided battlefield slaughters than probably anyone else alive: Lord Kitchener. At the battle of Omdurman in the Sudan in 1898, Kitchener had trained his Maxim machine guns on horsemen charging with spears; at a cost of forty-seven British army dead, he had killed ten thousand of the enemy in a single morning. But what would happen when the other side had Maxims too? Kitchener had a pretty good idea. At that cabinet meeting on August 7, where some other ministers imagined a conflict lasting months or even weeks, the newly appointed war secretary predicted years. "It will not end," he told his colleagues, "until we have plumbed our manpower to the last million."

Naturally, these were words few wanted to hear, let alone pay heed to. And so as if imagining that nothing had really changed since the last great bout of European wars in Napoleonic times, the Scottish Highlanders gathered up their bagpipes and kilts, the French cuirassiers and Austrian lancers donned their armor breastplates and plumed helmets and, to the accompaniment of buglers and drums, marched gaily off to battle, not realizing until too late that their Europe was now to become an abattoir, a slaughtering pen into which, over the next four years, some ten million soldiers, along with an estimated six million civilians, would be hurried forward to their deaths.

One would need to return to the Dark Ages or the depredations of Genghis Khan to find a war as devastating. By point of comparison, over the previous century, during which it had expanded its empire to five continents, the British Empire had been involved in some forty different conflicts around the globe—colonial insurrections mostly, but including the Crimean and Boer wars—and had lost some forty thousand soldiers in the process. Over the next four years, it would lose over twenty times that number. In the disastrous Franco-Prussian War of 1870–71, France had suffered an estimated 270,000 battlefield casualties; in the present war, it was to surpass that number in the first three weeks. In this conflict, Germany would see 13 percent of its military-age male population killed, Serbia 15 percent of its *total* population, while in just a two-year span, 1913 to 1915, the life expectancy of a French male would drop from fifty years to twenty-seven. So inured would the architects of the carnage become to such statistics that at the launch of his 1916 Somme offensive, British general Douglas Haig could look over the first day's casualty rolls—with fifty-eight thousand Allied soldiers dead or wounded, it remains the bloodiest single day in the history of the English-speaking world—and judge that the numbers "cannot be considered severe."

The effect of all this on the collective European psyche would be utterly profound. Initial euphoria would give way to shock, shock to horror, and then, as the killing dragged on with no end in sight, horror to a kind of benumbed despair.

In the process, though, the European public would come to question some of the most basic assumptions about their societies. Among the things they would realize was that, stripped of all its high-minded justifications and rhetoric, at its core this war had many of the trappings of an extended family feud, a chance for Europe's kings and emperors—many of them related by blood—to act out old grievances and personal slights atop the heaped bodies of their loyal subjects. In turn, Europe's imperial structure had fostered a culture of decrepit military elites—aristocrats and aging war heroes and palace sycophants—whose sheer incompetence on the battlefield, as well as callousness toward those dying for them, was matched only by that of their rivals. Indeed, in looking at the conduct of the war and the almost preternatural idiocy displayed by *all* the competing powers, perhaps its most remarkable feature is that anyone finally won at all.

In the end, the European public would look back on their war celebrations of August 1914 as if from a different age entirely, a death dance performed by gullible primitives. It would also give rise to an exquisite irony. In this titanic struggle waged for empire—protecting it, expanding it, chipping away at others'—four of the six great imperial powers of Europe would disappear completely, while the two survivors, Britain and France, would be so shattered as to never fully recover. Into the breach would come two dueling totalitarian ideologies—communism and fascism—as well as a new imperial power—the United States—that, given the bad name its predecessors had attached to the label, would forever protest its innocence of being one.

But in August 1914 all this was in the future. For now, Europe was gripped by a kind of giddy relief that the years of posturing were over, that *der Tag* had finally arrived.

In this, the Lawrence family of Oxford was in no way immune. Within days of the war's declaration, Frank Lawrence, the second youngest and most military-minded of the five Lawrence boys, was given his commission as a second lieutenant in the 3rd Gloucester Battalion. In India, Will Lawrence swiftly made plans to return to England in order to enlist, while Bob, the eldest, signed on with the Royal Army Medical Corps. By month's end, that left just fourteen-year-old Arnold and twenty-six-year-old "Ned" at home.

For T. E. Lawrence, this home stay was imposed by forces beyond his control. Although the Ottoman Empire had not joined in the August rush to war, expectations in London were that it soon might—and probably on the side of the Central Powers of Germany and Austria-Hungary. If that came to pass, the mapping expedition of southern Palestine that Lawrence and Leonard Woolley had recently participated in could be of great military importance. Under orders from Kitchener himself, the two young archaeologists were told to forgo any thought of enlisting until they had completed their report. So as others his age trooped off to boot camp that August, Lawrence shuttled between his Polstead Road cottage and the archives of the Ashmolean Museum, feverishly putting the final touches on *The Wilderness of Zin*.

If Lawrence was mindful of the report's significance, his comparative lassitude infected him with a growing sense of desperation. In early September, he and Woolley contacted Stewart Newcombe, their supervisor on the Palestine expedition and now a ranking officer in military intelligence, seeking his help in landing positions there. Newcombe advised patience. Should Turkey enter the war on Germany's side, he explained, their services as Near East experts would be urgently needed, and arranging their appointment would only be hampered if in the meantime they threw themselves into the maw of the military bureaucracy.

That advice didn't sit at all well with Lawrence. Surely adding to his gloom was that in those opening days the war did seem headed for the early conclusion that most predicted—except with the wrong side winning.

In provoking the conflict, German strategy had been predicated on an extremely bold, even reckless scheme. The plan was to only lightly defend its eastern frontier and cede ground against Russia's advancing armies, while launching a massive offensive against the French and British armies to the west in hopes of knocking those countries out of the war before they could fully mobilize. With that front thus closed down, the Germans could then turn their full attention to the Russians.

By the beginning of September, it appeared as if the Germans might succeed beyond their wildest dreams. On the Western Front, their armies had swept through neutral Belgium and then turned south, scattering the disorganized French and British forces before them. They now stood on the banks of the Marne River, just thirty miles from Paris. The surprise had come on the Eastern Front, where rather than simply employing defensive stalling tactics as planned, a vastly outnumbered German army had leapt to the attack; it had already annihilated one blundering Russian invasion force, and was about to destroy another. "Home by Christmas" suddenly seemed a conservative slogan, and for the soldiers of the Triple Entente—Great Britain, France, and Russia—a haunting one.

But then in the second week of September the tide abruptly turned. In the engagement that would become known as the "miracle of the Marne," the British and French checked the German advance and began slowly to push them back through the French countryside. This war was not going to be the "short, cleansing thunderstorm" the German chancellor had so confidently predicted; instead, after six weeks of combat, as many as half a million men were already dead, and stalemate was setting in.

For Lawrence, to be holed up in the leafy confines of Oxford at such a time, poring over a half-inch-to-the-mile map of an empty desert a thousand miles from the nearest battlefield, must have felt a terribly painful academic exercise. What's more, he surely reasoned, the reversal of fortunes in France meant his purgatory was likely to continue; if the Turks hadn't come into the war when it appeared Germany was running the table, why do so now when the Germans were retreating?

"I am writing a learned work on Moses and his wanderings," he acidly wrote to a friend in Lebanon on September 18. "I have a horrible fear that the Turks do not intend to go to war."

IF LAWRENCE HADN'T appreciated the warning signs in the run-up to war, William Yale, overseeing the construction of the Standard Oil road in southern Palestine, missed them completely. In fact, just as a telegram delivered to an Oklahoma oilfield had presaged his being dispatched to the Near East, so a second telegram to his remote construction camp in the Palestinian desert nearly a year later informed him of the war's outbreak.

With all work on the road project brought to an immediate stop, Yale hurried back to Jerusalem that August. He found a city in tumult. Among the sizable expatriate community of Europeans and Americans, most families were already packing up for the journey home. Leaving ahead of them in answer to their governments' general mobilization calls were the French and German men of fighting age (the British wouldn't initiate a draft until early 1916).

"We went down to the railroad station to see them off," Yale remembered. "Like young collegians on their way to a football game they shouted, cheered, and sang. As the train for Jaffa pulled out of the yards, the Germans in one car sang enthusiastically *Deutschland über alles*, while the Frenchmen in another car sang just as lustily, *La Marseillaise*. The friends of yesterday were off on their great adventure."

In contrast to the frenzied activity around him, the American oilman suddenly found he had little to do. With the United States staying out of the war, Socony headquarters ordered Yale to remain in Palestine, figuring he could at least watch over the company's soon-to-arrive oil drilling equipment until they decided on their next move. But even this caretaker task was soon mooted. Invoking a state-of-emergency decree, the Ottoman government requisitioned the incoming fleet of Standard Oil trucks as soon as they were unloaded at the Jaffa docks. Shortly afterward, the British navy stopped the freighter bringing most of Socony's piping and drilling machinery to Palestine and diverted all of it to an impoundment lot in Egypt.

With the community of foreigners in Jerusalem now reduced to a handful, Yale passed his time that late summer by playing tennis and canasta, and engaging in long, obsessive discussions with his fellow expatriates about what might come next in world events. A special focus of these discussions was trying to read the tea leaves of regional politics, sifting for clues as to whether or not the Young Turks in Constantinople would take their country into the fray. For a young man given to action, this imposed quietude was maddening, and Yale grew increasingly anxious for something to do.

But the old admonishment to be careful what you wish for soon found application when Yale was asked to play minder to a dozen unruly American oil workers. The men, most from Texas or Oklahoma, had been part of the intended work crew at the Kornub drilling site, and had been aboard the same freighter that the British diverted to Egypt. With time on their hands and money in their pockets, the oil workers proceeded to cut such a scandalous swath through the streets of Cairo—no mean feat in that libertine city—that the local Socony office had sent telegrams to headquarters urging that they be returned to the United States. Instead,

26 Broadway decided to forward the men to Yale, perhaps hoping that a stint in the Holy Land might serve to reacquaint them with their Christian virtues.

If so, that hope was misplaced. If anything, the opportunity to tread the land of Jesus seemed to spur the oilmen to even more outrageous public behavior. In observing this, as well as their office's rapidly dwindling cash reserves—the war in Europe had brought a temporary halt to international money transfers—Yale and his supervisor decided that a neat solution to both problems lay in withholding the men's pay and instead placing them on five-dollar-a-week allowances. Sensitive to the workers' disappointment with this arrangement, on allowance day Yale took to disbursing the money with one hand while holding a loaded six-shooter in the other.

But his troublesome charges also served a very useful function. In constant contact with Jerusalem's most unsavory residents, the oilmen were like the proverbial canaries in a coal mine, the first recipients of every dark rumor floating through the city—and with the spreading war in Europe, those rumors were turning exceedingly dark. It was precisely at tense times like these that the rich mosaic of the Ottoman world—a mosaic composed of a myriad of religious and tribal and ethnic groups—could quite easily become a grim counterimage of itself, a place where the various communities drew protectively inward, and where ancient feuds and suspicions and jealousies exploded into violence. Not surprisingly, this danger was greatest in the most "mixed" corners of the empire, and with its mélange of Arab and Turk and Armenian, of Muslim and Jew and Christian, all living cheek by jowl, there was no more cosmopolitan city in the Near East than Jerusalem.

By the end of August, stories were floating in from the countryside of Muslim vigilante armies forming, of Jews and Armenians being attacked, and while most of these tales proved false, they fed the ever-thickening air of tension. In the Old City, shopkeepers were raising prices and hoarding their wares, ever more convinced that Constantinople would soon enter the war. What was still not at all clear, though, was which side it might join, and another fault line formed between those hoping for the Triple Entente of Britain, France, and Russia and those desiring the Central Powers of Germany and Austria-Hungary.

On September 8, the sense of menace took more personal form for Yale and the other foreigners remaining in the city. Taking advantage of the chaos in Europe, the Young Turk government announced an end to the Capitulations, the humiliating concessions extracted by Western powers over the previous four centuries that largely exempted foreigners from Ottoman law. Yale noticed the effect immediately. Previously obsequious local officials became haughty, demanding. On Jerusalem's narrow sidewalks, residents no longer automatically stepped to the street at the approach of a Western "white man." On one occasion, when Yale and a couple of other foreign residents were visiting the Mount of Olives, a group of young boys pelted them with stones. To Yale, Jerusalem more and more felt like a pile of tinder in search of a match.

FOR OTHERS IN Palestine, the revoking of the Capitulations took on far more ominous import than a little stone-throwing. Left particularly vulnerable were the tens of thousands of Jewish émigrés who had come into the region over the previous thirty years.

Most had come in two successive waves. The first, of which the Aaronsohn family had been a part, had been an exodus out of central and southeastern Europe in the 1880s. This was followed by a second aliyah (literally "ascent" in Hebrew) in the early 1900s, mainly composed of Russian Jews escaping a new round of czarist political persecution and state-sanctioned pogroms. Although culturally these groups were very different—most of the first-wave émigrés tended to be religious and socially conservative, while many in the second were secular socialists— what they shared was that under the terms of the Capitulations many remained citizens of their birthplace.

That arrangement had historically worked to the benefit of both the émigrés and the Western powers. With it, the Jews had recourse to the protection of their former homelands, just as those foreign governments were given legal pretext to meddle in Ottoman affairs under the guise of tending to their transplanted citizens. While this bizarre system gave rise to a number of paradoxes, surely none was more grotesque than the spectacle of czarist Russia stoutly defending the rights and well-being of its Jewish citizens in Palestine, while systematically brutalizing that same religious minority inside Russia. With the revoking of the Capitulations, all this was coming to an end. Additionally, if Turkey did finally join the war, at least one portion of this Jewish community was likely headed for an unpleasant future; with thousands of the first-wave émigrés still holding Austro-Hungarian passports, and thousands from the second holding Russian ones, one group or the other was going to end up being classified as "belligerent nationals." As had already happened to countless innocent civilians across the breadth of Europe, the losers in this lottery could then be subject to deportation or internment.

In all this, most of the residents of Zichron Yaakov, including the Aaronsohn family, actually benefited from a different paradox. These Romanian Jews had come to Palestine after being effectively barred from citizenship in an independent Romania. By default, they thus remained citizens of Romania's preindependence master, namely the Ottoman Empire. Unlike other Jews in Palestine, then, Aaron Aaronsohn and other Zichron residents could look upon the revocation of the Capitulations with a measure of equanimity, perhaps even a touch of schadenfreude.

That sentiment was extremely short-lived, however, for the very next day, September 9, Constantinople announced a general mobilization of its armed forces. Under the curious rationale that this was necessary to "preserve Ottoman neutrality," the mobilization called for male citizens between the ages of eighteen and thirty-five to show up for military conscription. Worse, this edict extended to most *all* citizens—traditionally, Jews and a number of Christian sects had been exempt—and the regime was further rescinding the age-old system whereby the affluent could escape service by payment of a special *bedel*, or tax.

Aaron Aaronsohn was sufficiently acquainted with the Ottoman way of governance to know that this last clause meant nothing of the sort—it simply meant that obtaining an exemption now would entail paying more bribes to more officials—but the mobilization deeply worried the agronomist on a broader level. As recent events in Europe illustrated, an army called up almost always meant an army going to war; once the machinery and bureaucracy of war had been set in motion and popular hysteria properly ginned up, there was simply no easy way to shut it all down again. Ever since the outbreak of the European conflict, Aaronsohn had heard a rash of conflicting rumors from his friends in the Ottoman military and political hierarchy over what Constantinople might do, and this cloudiness was exacerbated by the vague picture to be gleaned of what was occurring in Europe. In the face of such uncertainty, Aaronsohn, like most of the Jewish residents of Palestine, simply clung to the hope that reason might yet prevail and the war be avoided.

Interestingly, it appears his apprehensions had less to do with which side Turkey might join than with the act of joining itself. Part of this may have stemmed from a common denominator in European wars going back to the Crusades—no matter who won or lost, the one fairly reliable constant was that Jews somewhere were going to suffer—but it was also born of a particular feature of Ottoman war-making. In the event of conflict, both military and civilian authorities would suddenly have license to embark on a wholesale requisitioning spree—"pillaging" might be a more apt term—as they grabbed up whatever they deemed necessary for the war effort. While this campaign was sure to affect Arab and Jewish villages alike, it would naturally be more zealous in those modern or prosperous places that had more to offer—places like Zichron Yaakov and Athlit, for example. Already by mid-September 1914, the Aaronsohn family and their neighbors in Zichron began hiding away whatever they had of value, braced for the ruinous arrival of the requisition officer.

ON THE AFTERNOON of September 4, 1914, Curt Prüfer was in a room of the Hotel Germania in Constantinople meeting with a burly, blond-haired German man in his thirties named Robert Mors. Until recently, Mors had been a policeman in the Egyptian coastal city of Alexandria, and their main topic of conversation that afternoon was how they might destroy the British administration in Egypt through a campaign of bombings, assassinations, and Islamic insurrection. The two men even bandied about ideas on how best to blow up the Suez Canal.

Their meeting was remarkable on both a personal and political level. Just a month earlier, Prüfer had been scratching out a modest living delivering lectures on Oriental languages in Munich; now he was a key operative in an intelligence mission so secretive that its existence was known to probably fewer than three dozen people in the world. That's because the ultimate purpose of this mission was to bring the still-neutral Ottoman Empire into the war, and among those with no inkling of Prüfer's activities in Constantinople could be included virtually the entire Young Turk political leadership. Credit for this peculiar set of circumstances belonged to Prüfer's old mentor, Max von Oppenheim, and to one of the stranger diplomatic accords ever put to paper.

As the war clouds had thickened over Europe during that long summer of 1914, a clear majority of the thirty or so senior members of the Committee of Union and Progress (CUP), the junta that controlled the empire, wanted to stay clear of the coming European firestorm. A small faction, however, had energetically sought to form an alliance with the Triple Entente, while another, led by thirty-two-year-old war minister Enver Pasha, tried to do the same with the Central Powers. Enver won out. In a case of exquisitely poor timing, he had signed a mutual defense treaty with Germany on the afternoon of August 2, just hours before Germany declared war on Russia and the conflict began.

Except, as it turned out, Enver Pasha had conducted these negotiations without ever consulting most of his CUP colleagues; indeed, at the time of the accord's signing, only three or four of Enver's closest confederates were aware of it. Even more astounding, Enver continued to withhold this information from the rest of the Turkish government throughout the first weeks of the war. As the young war minister told his impatient German allies, he needed more time to lay the groundwork before dropping this little surprise on his ministerial colleagues. To that end, a precipitating event, something that might turn both the nation and the rest of the Young Turk leadership away from the prevailing neutralist sentiment, could prove very handy.

Enver had come to the right people for, as neutral Belgium had recently learned, precipitating events was something of a German specialty. To help out his secret Turkish ally, Kaiser Wilhelm II could think of no better guide than Max von Oppenheim and his preachings on pan-Islamic revolt. If Islamic insurrection could be fostered in the various Muslim territories controlled by the British—and most especially in that land Britain had stolen from Constantinople, Egypt—surely it would be obvious to both the leadership and populace of the Ottoman Empire that they needed to come into the war.

But if the ultimate goal was to bring Turkey in, at least some in the German high command that autumn saw an upside to it remaining neutral just a bit longer. So long as it did, the Ottoman Empire could serve as the ideal launch pad for German destabilization efforts, a kind of Trojan horse from which to carry out attacks on the surrounding British colonies with very little risk of repercussion. That neutrality could also serve as a convenient shield while Germany laid the groundwork for the most important military operation to be conducted in the region, an assault on the Suez Canal. In mid-August, the kaiser signed a secret directive calling for the creation of the Nachrichtenstelle für den Orient (Intelligence Bureau for the East), to be based in Constantinople and to serve as the central clearinghouse for Germany's subversion campaigns in the Near East. The director of that bureau was to be Max von Oppenheim. Among Oppenheim's first acts upon assuming the post was to put out an offer of employment to his former protégé, Curt Prüfer.

Oppenheim's confidence in his apprentice was certainly deserved. No sooner had he checked into the Hotel Germania on the evening of September 3 than Prüfer set to work. Early the next morning, he met with one of Enver Pasha's chief lieutenants, a young Turkish staff officer named Omar Fawzi Bey, and together they worked up a whole list of prospective projects to strike at British Egypt: hiring Bedouin tribesmen to attack isolated British garrisons along the Suez Canal; sneaking so-called *komitadji* units of underground fighters into the country to foment Islamic insurrection; launching a terror campaign of targeted assassinations and indiscriminate bombings. Even if he remained dubious of some of the more novel schemes put forward by Fawzi Bey and his confederates—one involved scuttling a cement-laden freighter at the narrowest point of the Suez Canal—Prüfer appreciated the enthusiasm and creative thinking that went into them.

When not plotting with Fawzi Bey or Sheikh Shawish, an Egyptian firebrand hated and feared by the British, Prüfer was in regular conference with the four or five other Nachrichtenstelle operatives who had already arrived in the Turkish capital. At these meetings, often also attended by the three or four German embassy officials clued to Oppenheim's scheme, ambitious plans were laid for sabotage and subversion campaigns throughout the Muslim world: in Egypt, in Russian Central Asia, in Afghanistan, even as far away as India.

It was at the conclusion of one such meeting on the afternoon of September 7 that Prüfer was brought before the man who had made it all possible, Minister of War Enver Pasha. Small, extravagantly uniformed, and extraordinarily handsome—"the handsomest man in the Turkish army," the *New York Times* gushed—Enver had piercing dark eyes and a dramatic mustache, upturned and waxed in the Prussian style. That was not coincidence. As the military liaison to Germany in the early 1910s, he had quickly assumed the manner and style of its military elite, and now fancied himself more Prussian than the Prussians. Although Curt Prüfer was never much given to psychoanalysis, the few words he scribbled into his diary that night in describing the thirty-two-year-old Enver—by four months Prüfer's junior—offer one of the more incisive portraits of the man who was to practically single-handedly destroy the Ottoman Empire: "A man of stone. A face immovable, well-formed, beautiful in the feminine sense. Groomed to the point of foppishness. Along with a streak of shocking hardness. 'We can be more cruel than the British.' The man wants something, but the something does not come."

But of all the meetings he attended and the schemes he heard in those first few days in Constantinople, Prüfer was most intrigued by the unique situation facing Robert Mors, the cashiered Alexandria policeman. Mors had happened to be out of Egypt when the war began and, not surprisingly in light of his German citizenship, been summarily dismissed from his post by the British authorities. But in one of those quaint touches of "gentlemen's war" that still typified World War I in its early days, the British were granting Mors safe passage back to Alexandria in order to collect his stranded family. To Prüfer, this made Mors the ideal conduit for launching his subversion campaign. Given his status as a privileged European, Mors was also far more likely than a local to be able to secrete contraband articles among his personal possessions—and here Prüfer was thinking of bomb-making components—and smuggle them into the country. To impress the former policeman on the importance of his mission, Prüfer arranged an audience with Enver Pasha the day before Mors was to sail for Alexandria with bombing detonators hidden in his luggage. The Turkish war minister warmly thanked Mors for his service.

Even though the British quickly suspected some sort of pact had been struck between Enver and the German high command, they remained utterly in the dark as to the specifics. Their apprehensions grew, however, once Prüfer and Oppenheim's other intelligence bureau operatives began showing up in Constantinople. "Even without [Turkey joining the] war," British ambassador Louis Mallet cabled to London on September 15, "German machinations are so various here that I should not be surprised if they managed to engineer some scheme against the Canal, either by means of a so-called neutral ship from [the] Syrian coast, or by agents on land."

Against this were the constant assurances the British ambassador was given by Ottoman government officials. From the sultan and prime minister on down, Mallet heard the steady refrain that Turkey had no militarist intentions and only wished to stay out of the European conflict. While certainly some of these protesting senior officials were dissembling, others were not; incredibly, many still had no inkling of Enver's August 2 accord with Germany.

Mallet took his suspicions directly to Enver on October 5. Along with his other talents, however, Enver was a skilled liar. Not only did he deny any sinister intent behind the troop movements in Palestine but, according to Mallet, "laughed at [the] idea of individual Germans undertaking irresponsible enterprises against [the] Canal or elsewhere."

Except the Turkish war minister was about to get caught out. A few days prior to Mallet's meeting with Enver, Robert Mors had been arrested at Alexandria harbor with his bombing detonators. Facing possible execution under Egypt's martial law statutes, he soon told his interrogators all he knew of the German-Turkish plots against Egypt, as well as of his best-wishes audience with Enver Pasha on the eve of his voyage. Mors was especially expansive when it came to his relationship with Omar Fawzi Bey and Curt Prüfer. For Prüfer, the most damning part came when the foiled smuggler readily admitted that the detonators in his luggage had been intended for use with bombs being manufactured in Egypt. When asked how he knew that, Mors replied, "Because once I found Sheikh Shawish sitting with Dr. Prüfer in the latter's room at the Hotel Germania. They were copying in Arabic a recipe for making bombs. . . . [It] contained directions, a list of the component chemicals, and a sketch of a bomb in the right-hand bottom corner."

The British in Cairo showed considerable forbearance in the Mors incident, presumably in hopes that the more moderate elements in the Constantinople regime might yet rein in the adventurist Enver and keep Turkey out of the war. At his hastily held court-martial, Mors was sentenced to life in prison, while all mention of his meeting with the Turkish war minister was withheld from the public record. Cairo authorities were less forgiving of the man who had once lived in their midst. For his central role in the Mors affair, Curt Prüfer was to soon have a British bounty on his head.

THE OLD War Office Building at the corner of Horse Guards Avenue and Whitehall in central London is an imposing neo-baroque structure, a five-story monolith of white Portland stone with thirty-foot-high cupolas at each of its corners. Inside, it has the feel of a particularly elegant gentlemen's club, with marble staircases linking its floors, great crystal chandeliers, and mosaic-tiled hallways. In the more select of its nearly one thousand rooms, the walls are oak-paneled with niches cut out for marble fireplaces. In autumn 1914, this building was headquarters to Great Britain's Imperial General Staff, those seniormost officers tasked with overseeing their nation's war effort. It was also to this building that T. E. Lawrence, at last done with his *Wilderness of Zin* report, was dispatched in mid-October to take up his new position as a civilian cartographer in the General Staff's Geographical Section.

By then, "Section" was rapidly becoming a misnomer, for within a week of Lawrence's arrival, the last of the office's military cartographers was shipped off to the battlefront in France, leaving just him and his immediate supervisor behind. Thus Lawrence quickly found himself doing the work of a half dozen men: organizing the various war-theater maps, adding new details as reports came in from the front, briefing senior commanders on those maps' salient features.

One might imagine that for a young man—Lawrence had just turned twenty-six—to be suddenly thrust into the very nerve center of his nation's military command, to be in daily conference with generals and admirals, would be a heady experience. But one would imagine wrong. To the contrary, Lawrence seemed to take a decidedly jaundiced view of his new surroundings, its denizens fresh grist for his mordant wit.

Part of his disdain may have stemmed from how much military culture resembled that of the English public school system of which he was a product: the endless bowing and scraping to authority; the rigidly defined hierarchical structure as denoted by the special ties worn by upperclassmen and prefects in the schools, by the number of hash marks and pips on coatsleeves in the military; the special privileges bestowed or denied as a result. As Lawrence quipped to a friend shortly after arriving at the War Office, it appeared that the truly grand staircases of the building were reserved for the exclusive use of field marshals and "charwomen," or cleaning ladies.

His lack of awe probably also derived from the overall caliber of the building's occupants. With most active-service military officers now in France, the General Staff had been filled out with men brought up from the reserves or mustered out of retirement, and even to Lawrence's untrained eye it was clear many hadn't a clue of what they were supposed to be doing. As in any institution, this sense of inadequacy was often masked by an aura of extreme self-importance: at the War Office, freshly minted colonels and generals were forever striding briskly down hallways, memos in hand, or calling urgent staff meetings, or sending one of the Boy Scout messenger boys up to the Geographical Section for the latest map of Battlefield X, to be supplied ten minutes ago.

One by-product of this climate of puffery, however, was that it led directly to Lawrence's being inducted into the military, the circumstances of which provided him with one of his favorite later anecdotes.

Shortly after starting at the General Staff, he was ushered into the august presence of General Henry Rawlinson. Rawlinson was about to leave London to take up command of British forces in Belgium, and Lawrence had been summoned to brief him on the newly updated Belgian field maps. Except, according to Lawrence, Rawlinson went apoplectic at the sight of his civilian dress, and bellowed, "I want to talk to an officer!" Since the Geographical Section now consisted of just two men, Lawrence was immediately bundled off to the Army and Navy Store, there to get himself fitted out as a second lieutenant, while the paperwork for his "commission" was hastily drawn up. The uniform wouldn't truly solve the problem, however; in the years ahead, Lawrence's disregard for military protocol, manifested both in a usually unkempt appearance and a relaxed manner that bordered on the insolent, would drive his superior officers to distraction time and again.

But if he was now in the military, however haphazardly, Lawrence's work at the War Office was bringing him no closer to the arena of action. Since he fell below the minimum height standard of the British army, he needed a situation where his expertise might outweigh his physical shortcomings, and the only possible scenario meeting that criterion was, once again, if Turkey came into the war.

This seemed more unlikely than ever. With the war settling into paralysis—on the Western Front both sides were now frantically throwing up trenchworks—where was the incentive for anyone else to wade into the morass? "Turkey seems at last to have made up its mind to lie down and be at peace with all the world," Lawrence lamented to Winifred Fontana, the wife of the British consul in Aleppo, on October 19. "I'm sorry, because I wanted to root them out of Syria, and now their blight will be more enduring than ever."

But just two weeks later, his fears were put to rest. On November 2, with Enver Pasha's faction having finally won out, Turkey came into the war on the side of Germany and Austria-Hungary.

For Lawrence, more good news soon followed. In the wake of Turkey's declaration, Stewart Newcombe was recalled from the French theater to head up a new military intelligence unit in Cairo, the city slated as headquarters for Britain's war effort in the Near Eastern theater. It was to be a very small unit, just a handful of men with extensive knowledge of the region, and Newcombe immediately tapped both Lawrence and Leonard Woolley to join it.

"Now it's Cairo," Lawrence wrote Winifred Fontana again in early December, clearly in a much-improved mood. "All goes well except among the Turks."

IT WAS A land denuded. Although Aaron Aaronsohn had been prepared for the onslaught of the requisition squads following the Ottomans' entry into the war, their depredations went beyond even his worst imaginings. Across Syria, crops, farm vehicles, and draft animals were seized and hauled away in the name of wartime exigency, their hapless owners indemnified with hastily scribbled receipts that all knew would never be redeemed. And just as the agronomist had feared, the pillaging appeared particularly uninhibited in the Jewish colonies. At Zichron Yaakov, according to biographer Ronald Florence, "Aaron Aaronsohn watched Turkish soldiers systematically take clothing (including women's lingerie and baby clothes), carts, wagons, water buffaloes, agricultural implements, tools, firearms, medical instruments (including those for obstetrics), microscopes, and the fence posts and barbed wire needed to protect the fields." Eventually, most of Zichron's irrigation piping would go as well, leaving its fields and orchards to wilt from lack of water. Aaronsohn was only able to avoid a similar despoiling of the agricultural research station at Athlit through the determined intercession of local Ottoman officials and the posting of armed guards.

The agronomist might have resigned himself to the idea that these plunderings were part of the inevitable sacrifices to be made in wartime if they actually served the war effort; instead, they were gutting Syria from within, doing the enemy's work for them. In his travels over the coming months, he would see great stacks of confiscated wheat rotting in government storage yards, an uncovered mound of three thousand sacks of sugar in the city of Nablus left to dissolve in the winter rains, "to the delight of the street boys." To repair a bridge in Beersheva, Aaronsohn later reported, engineers had put in a request for twenty-four barrels of cement. Instead, the zealous requisition squads had gathered up four hundred barrels, all of which "were destroyed by rain before being used, with the result that the bridge remained without repairs."

While it could be argued that the Jewish colonies suffered disproportionately in these seizures simply because they had more and better matériel to take, the actions of the Constantinople regime certainly added to their misfortunes. Within days of Turkey joining Germany and Austria-Hungary in the conflict, the caliph, the supreme religious authority in the Sunni Muslim world, issued a fatwa that this was now a holy war, that in protection of the faith it was the sacred duty of every Muslim to join the jihad against Islam's foreign, Christian enemies. Although this call to jihad lost some of its luster among those who noticed that the Ottomans had just joined an alliance with two Christian and imperial powers, it did have the intended effect of inflaming the Muslim masses; in towns and cities across the empire, young Muslim men took to the streets and military induction centers to declare their willingness to fight and die for the cause. Of course, this fatwa had the simultaneous effect of alarming the empire's Christian and Jewish populations, compelling the governor of Syria to issue a hasty explanation that the jihad only applied to its foreign enemies.

If that clarification mollified many in the Christian community, which comprised nearly 30 percent of the empire's inhabitants, its calming effect was far more limited in the Jewish community. Part of their continuing fear surely derived from their small numbers—"small" having an unfortunate tendency to translate as "vulnerable" in wartime—but it also stemmed from the contentious position the Jewish colonists occupied in the social fabric of Palestine.

Some of those problems the colonists had brought on themselves. In Zichron Yaakov, as in most other "first-wave" Jewish settlements, the émigrés had gradually built their way to prosperity through adopting Palestine's long-established fellaheen system, employing landless or tenant Arab peasants to perform much of the manual labor. By contrast, many of the socialist-minded Russian émigrés of the second aliyah denounced this arrangement as exploitive and feudalistic; in pursuit of creating "the new Jewish man," they propounded, all work should be done by Jews themselves. For the unfortunate fellaheen, it wasn't hard to see the downside to both these approaches, one perpetuating the plantation system that had kept their families impoverished and disenfranchised for generations, the other denying them employment ostensibly for their own good—or, as Aaron Aaronsohn would caustically put it, "generously forbidding them to work at all."

Exacerbating the friction was that in the eyes of many of their Muslim Arab neighbors, the Jews were a *dhimmi*, or inferior people. Even for those Palestinians whose lives were unaffected by the Jewish influx, perhaps actually improved by it, the image of Jews living better than themselves—to say nothing of the further level of privilege many enjoyed courtesy of the Capitulations—added another layer of bitterness. Beginning with the first aliyah, there had been sporadic attacks on Jewish colonies by local villagers, and the occasional murder of a colonist caught out alone on the road.

But the colonists hadn't accepted this situation passively. In the early 1900s, several Jewish paramilitary forces, most notably the Gideonites and Bar Giora, were formed on settlements particularly hard hit by marauders, and they began contracting their protection services out to other colonies. It didn't take a clairvoyant to see where this would lead; before long, the Gideonites and Bar Giora were conducting punitive raids against Arab villages they deemed as hostile or responsible for prior attacks, ensuring new rounds of retaliatory attacks by the Arabs.

Taken together, then, by the autumn of 1914 the Jewish colonists in Palestine understandably felt nervous. Between the jihad fatwa and the requisition seizures and the revoking of the Capitulations, the most pressing question was just how much the local Ottoman officials—many not partial to the Jews at the best of times—would come to their aid if matters turned truly nasty.

In Zichron Yaakov, an answer to this question soon began to form, and it was not a comforting one. Aaron Aaronsohn's younger brother Alex had been caught up in the army's conscription sweeps of September, and when he finally managed to finagle a medical release and return home two months later it was with disturbing news: after the call to jihad, Alex and all the other Jews and Christians in his conscription unit had been stripped of their weapons and consigned to labor battalions. Then, in late November, came a new edict demanding that privately owned firearms be handed in to the authorities, resulting in another army requisition squad descending on Zichron Yaakov. When the residents professed to have no weapons—they had taken the precaution of burying them in a nearby field—the Turkish commander grabbed up four men, including the luckless Alex Aaronsohn, and hauled them off to Nablus to be beaten until they remembered otherwise. It wasn't until the same commander allegedly threatened to turn his attentions to the young women of Zichron that the weapons were finally surrendered, and Alex and the others released.

For many of the Jewish émigrés across Palestine, it was all beginning to feel like a prelude to the pogroms they thought they had left behind in Europe, especially when in early December the Young Turk who governed Palestine, Djemal Pasha, announced that the citizens of "belligerent nations" must either take Ottoman citizenship or face deportation. This naturally most directly affected the Russian Jewish minority, and within days, some eight hundred Russian Jews were rounded up in Jaffa for expulsion. The docks of that city were soon crowded with other Jews trying to get out on any ship that would take them, and to any safe haven that might accept them.

A number of Zichron Yaakov residents joined in this exodus, but the Aaronsohn family was not among them. Even though the family patriarch, sixty-six-year-old Ephraim, was still alive, it was really his eldest son who now decided important matters in the family, and for Aaron Aaronsohn there was no decision to be made. Palestine was their home. Moreover, it was the site of all his scientific work, and of the dream that sustained him. "I am always watched," he wrote one of his American benefactors in mid-January, "and well-intentioned friends are strongly advising me to leave the country as soon as I have the opportunity. But I have no intention to run away—yet." Still, Aaronsohn's faith in the state had been deeply shaken. "As a staunch supporter of the Turks from olden days, I feel sorry and ashamed for all I have heard and seen in these last weeks."

ON THE MORNING of December 15, 1914, a French steamer six days out of Marseilles approached the low, hazy horizon of northern Egypt. Among those on board was T. E. Lawrence, come to take up his new position with the military intelligence unit of the British Egyptian Expeditionary Force in Cairo. Accompanying him was the man who would be his immediate supervisor in that post, Captain Stewart Newcombe.

Cairo in 1914 was a city of less than one million, a place of wide boulevards and beautiful parks, of elegant riverfront promenades along the Nile. At that time, the Great Pyramids of Giza were some ten miles beyond the city's reach, their hard-stone crowns visible from the rooftop of most any tall building downtown.

But even more than its physical appearance, what made 1914 Cairo such a beguiling place was its status as one of the world's greatest crossroads, its layer upon layer of history going back over a millennium. The Old City remained a labyrinthine maze of alleyways and tiny shops, old palaces and mosques tucked into its back streets, and even if the occupying British had managed to erect a European veneer here and there in their thirty years of rule, the Egyptian capital remained a deeply exotic and mysterious place, unknowable in the way of all truly grand cities.

This was certainly part of what had entranced Lawrence upon his first visit to Cairo three years earlier. But if the city was physically little changed from 1911, in other ways 1914 Cairo was virtually unrecognizable. Since the outbreak of war in Europe, it had become a transit point for hundreds of thousands of territorial troops from India, Australia, and New Zealand passing through the Suez Canal on their way to the Western Front. As happens with R&R stops in most every war, these soldiers had quickly turned much of Cairo into a vast red-light district, places where most anything and anyone could be purchased for the right price.

That situation, scandalous to conservative Cairenes, had only grown worse in the days since Turkey joined the war. With a Turkish assault on the Suez Canal now all but certain—indeed, the governor of Syria, Djemal Pasha, had publicly vowed as much at the end of November—tens of thousands of British and territorial troops were now being held back in Egypt to meet the threat. This was rapidly turning Cairo into a military encampment in its own right, its downtown streets awash with strutting officers and columns of marching foot soldiers. If the Cairenes had never been thrilled about the presence of their British imperial overseers at the best of times—and they hadn't—they regarded them now with a seething and growing antipathy.

To provide office space and lodging for the officers tasked to manage this burgeoning military force, the British quickly took over most of the city's finer hotels. One of these was the Savoy, an eclectic blend of British Victorian and Indian Moghul architectures near the east bank of the Nile. Upon their arrival, the staff of Stewart Newcombe's new military intelligence unit set up shop in three large rooms on an upper floor of the Savoy, while taking bedrooms at the Grand Continental Hotel immediately adjacent.

Initially the unit consisted of just five men, and was more likely to be taken for some kind of Oxbridge peer-review panel than a group dedicated to the black arts of intelligence and counterespionage. Along with the two Oxford-educated archaeologists, Lawrence and Woolley, were two young aristocrats, George Lloyd and Aubrey Herbert, both sitting members of Parliament. Soon after arriving in Cairo, Lawrence wrote to his old friend Edward Leeds at the Ashmolean Museum to describe their various functions: "Woolley looks after personnel, is sweet to callers in many tongues, and keeps lists of persons useful or objectionable. One [George] Lloyd, who is an M.P. of sorts and otherwise not bad, looks after Mesopotamia, and Aubrey Herbert, who is a quaint person, looks after Turkish politics. Between them in their spare time they locate the Turkish army, which is a job calling for magnifiers." As for his own duties, Lawrence wrote, "I am bottle-washer and office boy pencil-sharpener and pen wiper."

In truth, Lawrence was far more than that. Because he had briefly worked in the Geographical Section of the London War Office, he was put in charge of the unit's mapping room. As all braced for the coming

Suez attack, this was an assignment that kept him working from early morning to late at night.

If he was finally a bit closer to the action, one thing that hadn't changed was Lawrence's gift for irritating his military superiors. Within weeks of his arrival a number of senior officers began grumbling about the slight young man in the Savoy mapping room, both his cheeky manner and unkempt appearance. But Lawrence's talent for annoying was not limited to his appearance and speech; he was also a very skilled writer. As the intelligence unit's acknowledged "Syria hand," in early 1915 he set to work on a long report describing the topography, culture, and ethnic divisions of that broad swath of the Ottoman Empire. Not for Lawrence the tentative, modifier-laden language that, then as now, tended to lard such background reports; instead, in "Syria: The Raw Material" he laid out his opinion of its various cities and peoples in refreshingly blunt—at times comically arrogant—prose. Typical was his withering appraisal of Jerusalem: "Jerusalem is a dirty town which all Semitic religions have made holy. . . . In it the united forces of the past are so strong that the city fails to have a present; its people, with the rarest exceptions, are characterless as hotel servants, living on the crowd of visitors passing through."

The remarkable utility of that first sentence—its ability in a mere twelve words to denigrate one of the world's most fabled cities, three major religions, and to offend the Christian sensibilities of every high-ranking British diplomat or general who might read it—was surely the source of considerable pride to Lawrence.

WILLIAM YALE INDULGED in portentous language as he described the mood aboard the refugee-packed freighter that carried him from Beirut to Alexandria in mid-November 1914. Having just escaped the dreadful wartime pall that had descended over Ottoman Palestine, he wrote that "to everyone on board ship, Egypt was a place of refuge where there was nothing to fear. It never occurred to me then that a different kind of terror would soon engulf the land of the Pharaohs."

Rather than pillaging soldiers or religion-crazed vigilantes, however, the terror to which Yale referred took the form of tens of thousands of transiting Australian soldiers who, having been released after weeks spent on board crammed transport ships from their homeland, were rapidly transforming ancient Cairo into a raucous whiskey-soaked bordello. Even his experience with the boisterous American roustabouts in Jerusalem couldn't prepare Yale, ever the puritanical Yankee at heart, for the scenes he saw constantly playing out in the city's streets: the fights, the pawings of passing women, the soldiers blacked out in gutters from drink. In his estimation, such outrageous carryings-on could only tarnish British prestige in the eyes of the locals, "for the Egyptians, like many others in the Near East, looked upon the British as a coldly superior race. These hot-blooded, lusty, undisciplined Australians of 1914 . . . were a revelation."

From his perch in Jerusalem, Yale had been eyewitness to the Ottoman Empire's long, slow tumble into the war. On November 3, as word of the Turkish war declaration spread, crowds of Muslim men had begun gathering in the Old City, their numbers constantly swelled by others pouring in from the outlying villages. That evening, Yale and other Western expatriates watched from an upper balcony of the Grand New Hotel as an unending stream of young men passed through the Old City's Jaffa Gate on their way to Al-Aqsa Mosque, Jerusalem's holiest Muslim shrine, beating their chests and chanting their readiness to die for the faith.

"[It] sent shivers up and down our spines," he would recall. "Consciously or unconsciously, we sensed in every fiber of our being, that these men were stirred with that same religious fervor with which, some 800 years before on this self-same street, their ancestors had matched forces with our Crusading forebears."

It had also helped convince Yale and his supervisor, A. G. Dana, that it was time to get out. Three days later they were at Jaffa harbor negotiating their way on board a refugee-laden freighter. By a circuitous route aboard other overladen ships, they finally reached Egypt, and the new terror of carousing Australian soldiers, on November 17.

Their arrival was noted by an alert British intelligence officer. On the Alexandria dock, Yale was escorted to an office to be debriefed on all he had seen or heard in Palestine in recent days. To his questioner's pleasant surprise, it seemed the American oilman had been very observant during his flight from Syria, and was able to provide estimates of Turkish troop strengths in a number of towns and cities in southern Palestine. He also confirmed that German officers were everywhere in the region and that along with truck convoys of war matériel and battalions of marching Turkish soldiers, the Germans appeared to be heading south.

In Cairo, Yale was forced to wait while his bosses back at 26 Broadway decided what to do with him and the other Socony employees scattered across the Middle East. From the standpoint of Standard's Kornub project, the Ottoman entry into the war only made a bad situation worse. With the British and French navies now imposing a blockade of their new enemy's coastline—and in the Ottoman era this meant the entire eastern Mediterranean shoreline, from Palestine to the southeastern corner of Europe—there certainly would be no early opportunity to develop that concession. The fundamental question facing Socony, then, was whether to retreat from the Middle East for the time being and bring their people home, or to keep them in place in hopes of some hard-to-foresee improvement in the near future.

Yale was still waiting for the answer when, one day in late December, there came a knock on the door of his room at the National Hotel. He didn't immediately recognize his visitor—the man was young and in a British army uniform, two characteristics that described much of Cairo just then—but there was something in the gaze of his piercing blue eyes that stirred a memory.

"Hello, Yale," the visitor said with an amused, lopsided grin. "You don't remember me, do you? I'm Lawrence of British Intelligence. We met at Beersheva last January."

Yale remembered then, and no doubt also remembered the delight with which the cocky young archaeologist had set out to demolish his "playboy" cover story.

As quickly became evident, this meeting, too, was to be an interrogation of sorts. Even before entering the war, Constantinople had been moving troops down into Palestine in obvious preparation for an attack on the Suez Canal, and that pace was now accelerating. Lawrence, having himself arrived in Egypt just days earlier, had thought to scan the registry logs of incoming foreigners and had come upon Yale's name. He now wanted to learn everything there was to know about the road that Standard Oil had been building below Hebron: its precise route, its composition and drainage, whether it could be used by the Turks to bring heavy weaponry south.

"When he secured all the information I had," Yale recalled, "he began talking about the situation in Palestine. I soon discovered that, although I had just arrived from there, this officer knew far more than I did. It was then that I began to learn of the efficiency of the British Intelligence Service and to understand something of the ability of young Lawrence."

That evening, Lawrence wrote up his findings for his superiors at military intelligence. It made for rather unpleasant reading. While the Hebron-Beersheva road was not finished, Socony had completed work on the most difficult stretch, the descent through the Judean hills to the edge of the desert. Perhaps drawing on his engineering experience at the Panama Canal, William Yale had made sure the road was cut with a gradual enough gradient to allow for heavy-truck traffic—one so gradual, in fact, that the roadbed could easily be converted to a railroad. Until then, British war planners had assumed that any significant Turkish-German advance toward the Suez from southern Palestine would be largely confined to the established narrow pathway close to the Mediterranean shoreline. With their Hebron road, Standard Oil and William Yale had inadvertently provided the Turks with the capability of expanding their field of operations by some thirty miles.

ON THE MORNING of November 21, 1914, less than three weeks after Turkey entered World War I, Ahmed Djemal Pasha, one of the "Three Pashas" triumvirate that now ruled the Ottoman Empire, left Constantinople to take up his new dual positions as commander of the Fourth Army and governor of Syria. His true authority was far greater than the titles suggested: supreme military and political ruler of all Ottoman lands south of Anatolia and west of Iraq, an area that comprised over half of the empire's remaining total landmass. As befitting that authority, his first order of business was to lead the Turkish army to the Suez Canal and strike at the heart of British Egypt.

Over the next three years, Djemal Pasha would come to thoroughly dominate life in Syria, his actions credited with causing much of what was to come. In his dual capacities as a military and political leader, he would also come into regular contact with—and at varying times employ the services of—three very different men: Aaron Aaronsohn, Curt Prüfer, and William Yale.

In some respects, the short, powerfully built Djemal seemed an unlikely choice for such a position. Born in 1872 to a low-level Ottoman officer, he had sought a career in the military as a matter of course, and risen unremarkably through the ranks before throwing his lot in with the reformist-minded conspirators of the Committee of Union and Progress in the early 1900s. A fairly obscure figure until the 1913 coup that enabled the CUP to rule by fiat, Ahmed Djemal was then appointed military governor of Constantinople. Less than a year later, with the emergence of the so-called Three Pashas triumvirate, the forty-two-year-old officer became one of the three public faces of the shadowy committee that controlled the empire.

Undoubtedly one reason for Djemal's elevation was his personal magnetism. As Henry Morgenthau, the American ambassador to Turkey, would recall, "Whenever he shook your hand, gripping you with a vise-like grasp and looking at you with those roving, penetrating eyes, the man's personal force became impressive." This does not imply that Morgenthau at all cared for Djemal, instead seeing in his charisma a malevolent force best rendered in overheated, racialist-tinged prose. "His eyes were black and piercing, their sharpness, the rapidity and keenness with which they darted from one object to another, taking in apparently everything with a few lightning-like glances, signalized cunning, remorselessness, and selfishness to an extreme degree. Even his laugh, which disclosed all his white teeth, was unpleasant and animal-like."

A more nuanced view was offered by another American who had extensive dealings with Djemal during the war. Howard Bliss, the president of the Syrian Protestant College in Beirut, would recall observing the governor at an afternoon tea party in wartime Beirut, a social event to which even the expatriate citizens of Turkey's foes had been invited. Djemal was "gay, debonair, interested, wandering about with his hands in his pockets, or lounging on the arm of a big chair, the other arm of which was occupied by a charming European lady." Noting the governor's love of children and overt displays of affection toward his wife—"unusual among Orientals"—Bliss saw in Djemal a man caught between an overwhelming vanity and a core kindness, "a character teeming with conflicting elements: cruelty and clemency, firmness and caprice, ideality [*sic*] and hedonism, self-seeking and patriotism."

These conflicting personality traits mirrored Djemal's political views. Indeed, he seemed to embody the internal contradictions that lay at the heart of the Young Turk movement, caught as it was between West and East, modernity and tradition, between awed admiration of the European powers and bitter resentment. A devout Muslim who embraced the jihadist credo of pan-Islam, Djemal had also been one of the most vocal Young Turk leaders in advocating that the empire's ethnic and religious minorities be given full civil rights. An aesthete who loved European music and literature, and who enjoyed nothing more than practicing his French in the expatriate salons of Constantinople, he also exhorted his countrymen to purge their nation of corrupting Western influence. Dreaming of a Turkish and Islamic renaissance that would return the Ottoman Empire to its ancient splendor, he was at heart a technocrat, intent on pulling his nation into modernity through the building of roads and railways and schools.

"He had the ambition of creating a Syria which he could exhibit with pride to an admiring Europe," Bliss wrote. "I think it would not be unfair to call him a personal patriot. He was inordinately vain. He wanted a reformed Turkey, but he wanted pre-eminently to be known as the Chief Reformer."

To try to achieve that, Djemal would rely on the skills he had honed in his fitful rise through the treacherous political currents of the CUP, the ability to turn in the blink of an eye from graciousness to ferocity, an adroitness with both the peace offering and the dagger. As those who lived in the lands encompassed by his new southern posting were soon to discover, Djemal Pasha could be wonderfully solicitous in trying to keep potential enemies on his side, but if flattery and sinecures and promises didn't appear to do the trick, he was perfectly willing to go with the old standbys of exile and execution.

As his train pulled out of Constantinople's Haidar Pasha station, the challenges of reforming Syria were soon to be put in stark relief—the initial hurdle Djemal faced was just getting there. The first part of that long journey went smoothly enough, a pleasant two-day train ride through central Anatolia, but the troubles started when they reached the depot town of Mustafa Bey, at the northern edge of the Gulf of Alexandretta. There, embarrassed officials informed Djemal that the onward track to the city of Alexandretta (modern-day Iskenderun) had recently washed out in a number of places. The pasha switched to an automobile, but only briefly; after mere yards on the main "highway" to Alexandretta, the car was mired up to its wheel wells in mud. A four-hour horseback ride finally brought Djemal to the seaside town of Dort Yol. There, a tiny two-man tramcar was found that, certain optimists believed, might be light enough to navigate the damaged coastal rail line and finally deliver the pasha and his chief of staff to Alexandretta, ten miles farther along.

"Never shall I forget this journey by trolley on the slippery track," Djemal wrote. "More than once we went in danger of our lives as in pouring rain we passed along the coast, which was watched by enemy ships.... We reached Alexandretta after a journey during which the trolley passed over rails which, in some places, hung suspended over a void for fifteen to twenty metres, and in others were under water."

But more bad news awaited the pasha. The road onward to Aleppo, the only link between Alexandretta and the interior of northern Syria, was now impassable—although "impassable" was perhaps an understatement. Repairs had been started on the road some time earlier, but had progressed no further than removing all its crowning stones. Those stones now lay in high stacks along either side, leaving the road to form, in Djemal's words, "a perfect canal." As he would exclaim in his memoir, "And here is the only road which keeps my army in touch with the home country!"

By the time Djemal finally reached his headquarters in Damascus on December 6, more than two weeks after his departure from Constantinople, he'd come to a fairly obvious conclusion: the Suez attack should be postponed until some of the very basic issues of supply lines and infrastructure were dealt with. He made the mistake, though, of sharing this thought with the young German intelligence officer who had been awaiting his arrival in Damascus and had been assigned to serve as Djemal's liaison to the German high command: Major Curt Prüfer.

To Prüfer, there could be no question of delaying the Suez offensive. As he wrote to Max Oppenheim after learning of Djemal's hesitation, support for the jihad among the Syrians was tepid to begin with, and in the event of a postponement, "undoubtedly the carefully manufactured enthusiasm would disappear and the old indifference, if not hostility, takes its place." What's more, such a delay would provoke "the total discouragement of the Egyptians, who are cowards anyway."

It was a rather curious stance for Prüfer to take, since most of his letter to Oppenheim consisted of reasons why an attack on the canal was almost sure to fail, his contention that "the means are not sufficient to the task." But Prüfer may have had a darker motive in urging it forward. In Constantinople, he had been eyewitness to the protracted struggle to bring Turkey into the war, and as he surely knew from intelligence reports reaching him in Damascus, there were still those in the CUP leadership maneuvering to back out of the German alliance and sue for peace with the Entente. An assault on the Suez would end all that. From that point on, Turkey would be joined at the hip to Germany, and it would win or die along with it.

Shortly afterward, Djemal received a terse cable from Constantinople: the Suez attack was to go forward without delay.

Chapter 5

A Despicable Mess

So far as Syria is concerned,
it is France and not Turkey that is the enemy.

T. E. LAWRENCE TO HIS FAMILY, FEBRUARY 1915

Soon after taking up his post at the Savoy Hotel, Lawrence comman-deered the largest wall in the office and covered it with a massive sectioned map of the Ottoman world. In his idle moments, he would stand against the opposite wall and gaze upon it for as long as time permitted, taking in all its vastness.

By January 1915, he was awaiting the Turkish attack on the Suez Canal with a certain impatience. One reason was that he had little doubt of its outcome. To reach the canal, the Turks first had to cross 120 miles of the inhospitable Sinai Peninsula. From his knowledge of that expanse, and especially of its limited water sources, Lawrence was convinced the attacking force would, by necessity, be quite small—surely not the 100,000 soldiers some alarmists in the British military hierarchy were suggesting—and thus easily repelled.

But the chief reason for his impatience was that he was already con-templating the next chapter in the Near East war, the one to come once the Turkish assault had been turned back. It would then be time for the British to go on the offensive, and gazing upon his maps at the Savoy, Lawrence was seeking out those places where an invading force might strike at the Ottoman Empire to most devastating effect.

One truly odd feature of that map had undoubtedly long since occurred to him: despite its enormous size and tenuous political cohesion, from the standpoint of geography that empire was astoundingly well protected.

The political and spiritual core of the Ottoman world was of course the ancient city of Constantinople, along with the mountainous region of Anatolia, the ancestral heartland of the Turks, that lay to its east. This concentration inevitably conjured a tantalizing prospect to British war planners, the chance to "decapitate" their enemy: if that city and that region could be seized, there was little doubt that all else would quickly collapse.

Except that any possible path to doing so presented enormous obstacles. With both of Turkey's European neighbors, Greece and Bulgaria, still neutral in the war, there was little maneuvering room to try an overland approach on Constantinople from the west. In theory, Britain's Russian allies could attempt an eastern advance from their position at the far end of Anatolia, but already being bled white by the Germans on the Eastern Front, the Russians were likely to exhaust their available manpower and matériel before getting very far in the mountainous terrain. As for a southern approach, that meant either a ground force trudging up through the Anatolian heartland where local resistance would be fierce—and, again, the mountains—or a naval flotilla running the gauntlet of Turkish forts lining the three-mile-wide Dardanelles strait. There was simply no easy way.

But the alternative, to start at some point on the Ottoman Empire's periphery, looked even worse. British Indian forces had seized the oilfields of southern Iraq in the first days of the war, but an overland march from there meant a seven-hundred-mile slog through river swamplands and desert before the Anatolian frontier was even reached. Likewise, an advance from Egypt meant first crossing the desolate Sinai Peninsula, then crashing up against Turkish forces massed in the narrow chokepoint of southern Palestine.

But amid this whole great expanse, there did exist one exquisitely vulnerable point in the Ottoman Empire's wall of natural defenses. It was the Gulf of Alexandretta, at that spot in northwest Syria where the long north-south coastline of the eastern Mediterranean shore bumps up against the far more rugged coastline of Anatolia. Not only was Alexandretta possessed of the best deep natural harbor in the eastern Mediterranean, a critical asset for amphibious operations, but the relatively flat landscape just to its east afforded ample room for ground troops to maneuver for a push farther inland.

But these were military considerations, ones that a number of senior British officers in Egypt had cottoned to even before Lawrence's arrival. What Lawrence uniquely saw, both from his familiarity with the region—Jerablus lay just one hundred miles east of Alexandretta—and his firsthand view of Ottoman society, was the political.

One of the great hidden dangers for any empire going to war is that within its borders are often large communities of people who want absolutely nothing to do with it. And the longer a war and its deprivations continue, the more resentful these communities become, and the more susceptible to the promises and propaganda of one's enemies. Most of the dueling empires of Europe were grappling with this internal danger as their war stretched on, but whatever problems the Europeans faced in this regard—and in some cases they were considerable—paled to insignificance next to those facing the Young Turks in Constantinople. Quite simply, given the extremely polyglot nature of their realm, most any course of action they might take that would win the support of one segment of the population was all but guaranteed to alienate another. This quandary had been illustrated by the mixed results of the call to jihad in November. While that call had momentarily excited the Muslim youth, it had terrified the empire's non-Muslim populations. At the same time, many conservative Muslim Arabs, already mistrustful of the Young Turks' perceived favoritism toward ethnic Turks, viewed it as a cynical attempt by an increasingly secular regime to play the religion card.

But if the Ottoman Empire was a mosaic, it was also one of distinct patterns, where various "colors" predominated or diminished across its expanse. And if one studied this mosaic from a slight remove, there was one spot on this great expanse where many of these patterns came to a confluence, creating a kind of ethnic and religious ground zero: Alexandretta.

Already, for reasons of distance and the relatively scant resources being allotted to it, Lawrence was convinced that a conventional war against Turkey wouldn't work. Instead, the British needed to pursue a so-called irregular strategy. That meant taking advantage of the internal fissures of their enemy's society, forging alliances with its malcontents. The Alexandretta Basin was the demarcation line between the Turkish world of Anatolia to the north and the great Arab world to the south—and as Lawrence well knew from his years at Jerablus, the Arabs of northern Syria had grown to deeply resent their Turkish overseers. Alexandretta also stood at the edge of the heartland of the Armenians, a people who had suffered periodic massacres at the hands of their Turkish neighbors; surely no people had more reason to rebel against Constantinople than they. In Lawrence's view, quite aside from its purely military advantages, a British landing at Alexandretta was almost certain to spark uprisings of both Syrians and Armenians against the Turks, uprisings that would naturally complement the British effort.

But Lawrence also had firsthand information that made the idea even more enticing. The principal highway linking Anatolia to the south passed through the Alexandretta Basin, and as Lawrence knew from his time in the region, that highway was in terrible condition. In addition, the Hejaz Railway that linked Constantinople to its Arab realms passed through the basin—or, to put it more accurately, partially linked, because what Lawrence also knew, courtesy of his journey through the region six months earlier at the behest of Stewart Newcombe, was that two crucial spans of that railway in the Taurus and Amanus Mountains north of Alexandretta were nowhere near completion. This meant that the Turks would have no way of responding quickly if an invasion force took control of the basin, and in the slowness of their response, all points to the south, cut off from resupply or reinforcement, might quickly fall. With just a comparative handful of soldiers in Alexandretta, then—Lawrence estimated a mere two or three thousand would be needed—the British had the potential of not only splitting the Ottoman Empire in two, but of taking one-third of its population and over half of its land area out of the war in one fell swoop.

Lawrence wasn't alone in identifying Alexandretta's extraordinary vulnerability; the Turks were keenly aware of it too—so keenly, in fact, that it had already caused them to submit to one of the more humiliating episodes of World War I.

On December 20, 1914, a lone British warship, HMS *Doris*, had appeared off Alexandretta and, in a brazen game of bluff, issued an ultimatum to the local Turkish commander: release all foreign prisoners in the town, as well as surrender all ammunition and railway rolling stock, or face bombardment. In desperation, for they had no guns to resist such an attack, the Turks had threatened to kill one British prisoner for every one of their citizens killed in the bombardment. That threat, in blatant violation of the Geneva and Hague war conventions, had sparked outrage within the diplomatic community and been quickly countermanded by the Young Turk leadership in Constantinople. Instead, a bizarre compromise was reached: in return for the British not shelling the town, the Turks agreed to destroy the two train engines that were sitting in Alexandretta station. Except, the embarrassed Turks were soon forced to admit, they had neither the explosives nor the expertise to uphold their end of the deal, so on the morning of December 22, a demolitions expert from the *Doris* was given safe passage to come ashore and blow the trains up. Understandably, the British government's attention to the *Doris* affair largely centered on the death-threat aspect, but to Lawrence the incident laid bare just how panicked the Turks were of what could be done to them in Alexandretta.

Although a mere second lieutenant relegated to collating maps, by virtue of his attachment to the military intelligence unit Lawrence was in the unique position of having his ideas disseminated to the highest levels of the British war-planning structure. It is surely no coincidence that while an Alexandretta landing had been discussed before, the scheme took on new urgency shortly after his arrival in Cairo. Judging by its tell-tale idiosyncratic approach to grammar, Lawrence was almost certainly the author of a crucial January 5, 1915, military intelligence memorandum on the subject: "We have been informed from two good sources that the Germans in command in Syria dread nothing so much as a landing by us in the north of Syria—they say themselves that this would be followed by a general defection of their Arab troops. There is no doubt that this fear is well founded, and that a general Arab revolt, directed by the Pan-Arab military league, would be the immediate result of our occupation of Alexandretta."

The lobbying had an effect. On January 15, 1915, just one month after his arrival in Cairo, Lawrence sent an update to his old mentor in Oxford, David Hogarth. Because the letter had to clear military censors, he adopted a deliberately vague tone: "Our particular job goes well. We all pulled together hard for a month to twist 'them' from what we thought was a wrong line they were taking—and we seem to have succeeded completely, so that we today have got all we want for the moment, and therefore feel absolutely bored."

The "them" he alluded to were senior British war planners in Cairo and London, while the "job" was an amphibious landing at Alexandretta. The only holdup now, it seemed to Lawrence, was for the long-awaited Turkish assault on the Suez Canal to be put safely in the past.

So GREAT WAS his men's morale that for a brief time even Djemal Pasha was stirred by the thought that it just might work out after all. "Everyone was absolutely convinced that certainly the Canal would be crossed," he recalled, "that we should dig ourselves in securely on the further bank, and that the Egyptian patriots would then rise and attack the English in the rear."

One source of this soaring optimism within the ranks of the Ottoman Fourth Army at the end of January 1915 was the extraordinary fortitude they had shown in crossing the Sinai, a shining example of what was possible when Turkish doggedness was joined to German organization. Making that 120-mile crossing had been months in the planning and involved almost superhuman logistical arrangements. Overseen by German officers, engineering units had fanned out across the desert beforehand, tapping wells for the oncoming troops, building rainwater reservoirs, and laying in depots of ammunition. Great teams of oxen had hauled the disassembled pontoon bridges needed to ford the Suez Canal, as well as the army's heavy artillery, while some twelve thousand camels had been gathered up from as far away as central Arabia to ferry supplies. In early January, the army of thirteen thousand men set out along three different paths through the desert, and despite the deprivations of that march—each man's daily food ration consisted of just a half pound of biscuits and a handful of olives—by the end of the month the attack force was encamped just a few miles east of the canal, ready to strike. Certainly the British in Egypt knew an attack was imminent—their spotter planes had photographed and occasionally shot at some of the Turkish formations—but they seemed to have no idea how large the force might be or where along the hundred-mile length of the canal it would come. It was this that had put Djemal's troops in such good spirits.

"I used to talk to the troops every night about the victory in store," he wrote, "and what a glorious victory it would be. I wanted to keep the sacred flame alive in the whole force. . . . If, by some unanticipated stroke of good fortune, this enterprise . . . had brought us success, we should naturally have regarded it as a good omen for the final liberation of Islam and the Ottoman Empire."

One man who little shared in these high hopes was Major Curt Prüfer. Along with a small contingent of other German junior officers, he had endured the hard rigors of that desert crossing, and attributed all its success to the meticulous planning of the chief German military advisor to Djemal, a lieutenant colonel with the colorful name of Friedrich Kress von Kressenstein. Still, planning had its limits, and even if Prüfer wasn't a professional soldier—just like T. E. Lawrence, he had received his officer's commission with no actual military training—he appreciated that the changed face of modern war almost surely meant problems for the coming offensive. In particular, in the age of aerial reconnaissance, then just in its infancy, the British undoubtedly had a far better idea of their enemy's strength and intentions than the Turks imagined.

This was confirmed to Prüfer by his own reconnaissance missions to the canal. The plan of attack called for the Turkish army's flanks to make diversionary feints at the north and south ends of the waterway, while the main force of some sixty-five hundred men stormed across near its midpoint, just above the Great Bitter Lake. When Prüfer joined a forward scouting party that crept close to the canal on the morning of January 25, he observed just two British dredgers and a handful of small lighter boats in the lake. Three days later, however, the British presence had grown to several transport ships and two cruisers, a number that expanded to some twenty ships by January 30. In the meantime, Prüfer had experienced a close call when a British warplane dropped two bombs on the main head-quarters encampment.

"I confess that the hammering of the bombs, the powerful explosions and the black billowing smoke, frightened me," he noted in his diary, "although I did my best to hide it. In the camp, everyone ran pell-mell."

To Prüfer, it all pointed to a coming disaster. "The enemy cruisers in the lake control the situation," he wrote upon returning from the January 30 scouting mission. "We will be destroyed before we have actually come into the vicinity of the channel." That night, he ate his "hangman's meal," asparagus and French toast.

The assault finally came in the early-morning hours of February 3, 1915. Taking advantage of a brief sandstorm that screened their actions from view, Turkish engineers hastily assembled their ten pontoon bridges at the water's edge as the foot soldiers massed behind, ready to charge across. At a crucial moment, however, a British searchlight picked up the activity; in a barrage of rifle and artillery fire, seven of the pontoon bridges were quickly destroyed. That may have been a blessing in disguise for the Fourth Army, for it limited the slaughter. As it was, the approximately six hundred Turkish soldiers who had managed to reach the far shore before their escape routes were cut off were all either soon killed or compelled to surrender.

Prüfer had been given the quixotic task of leading forward a long wagon train hauling sandbags; the plan called for the sandbags to be used both to block the canal and to create a bridge to the far shore. Instead, he spent most of the day scrambling from one point of chaos on the front lines to the next as British naval shells exploded all around.

By nightfall, Djemal and his senior German advisors concluded that the situation was hopeless, and a general retreat back across the Sinai des-ert began. To most everyone's surprise, the British made no attempt to pursue the fleeing army, enabling its withdrawal to be as orderly and dis-ciplined as had been its advance.

Despite his own bleak assessment on the eve of battle, the setback on the canal seemed to cast Curt Prüfer into despondency. Nursing a slight arm wound—he'd apparently been hit by shrapnel during the assault—he holed up in Hafir el Andscha, an oasis town at the eastern edge of the Sinai, to file dispatches to Max von Oppenheim and Hans von Wangen-heim, the German ambassador to Turkey. He was blunt, even derisive, over the campaign's failure to trigger an Egyptian uprising.

"Despite all our agitation," he wrote Oppenheim, "despite the thousands of [jihadist] pamphlets, we did not have any deserters. . . . The Egyptians are even cowardly in desperation, and lack any genuine love of fatherland."

But his disappointment clearly had deeper roots. Ever since teaming up with Max von Oppenheim, the former Oriental scholar had fervently embraced the notion of a pan-Islamic jihad against Germany's imperial enemies. Not just the battle but the entire Sinai campaign gave the lie to that. From the very outset, tensions were evident between the Turkish and Arab components of the assault force, and these had only worsened with time. Many of the Arab units fled as soon as the shooting began, or never deployed in the first place, while some went over to the enemy. Prüfer heaped particular scorn on the Bedouin nomad warriors, many of whom he had personally recruited to act as scouts and who similarly melted away on the decisive day. Indeed, just about the only unifying element detectable among this fractious lot was antipathy for their German advisors; even many Turkish officers had adopted a policy of "passive resistance" to any direction offered by the Germans throughout the campaign.

"The holy war," Prüfer informed his old mentor from Hafir el Andscha, "is a tragicomedy."

Djemal Pasha had a rather more upbeat assessment. While the assault obviously hadn't led to the Egyptian uprising he had hoped for, the action would cause the British to keep more troops in reserve in Egypt, making fewer available to fight elsewhere. Moreover, by his calling off the engagement when he did, his army was still largely intact. At the same time, as they made their respective ways back across the Sinai, Djemal and Prüfer undoubtedly shared a mounting sense of unease. Given the tit-for-tat nature of the war, a British retaliatory offensive would come soon. The only question was where, and from their own recent difficult journeys across Syria, both knew the likeliest spot: the Alexandretta Basin.

It wasn't just the broken railways and "canal" roads of that chokepoint that were cause for worry. In the nationwide scramble for reliable front-line troops, the Turks had been forced to leave the safeguarding of the Alexandretta region to two second-rate divisions composed almost exclusively of Syrian Arabs. Resentful of their Turkish overseers at the best of times—and these weren't the best of times in the Ottoman world—it was highly probable that these Arab units would quickly collapse at the first sign of an Allied landing, perhaps even switch sides.

In fact, Djemal Pasha's anxiety over Alexandretta had already led him to commit a singularly reckless act. Desperate to mask the city's abject vulnerability, it was he who had issued the threat to execute British prisoners back in December when HMS *Doris* stood offshore. Now, in the wake of Suez, the Syrian governor was sure the British would turn to Turkey's Achilles' heel once more, and this time there would be no negotiating, no way to stop them.

THROUGHOUT HISTORY, THERE have been occasions when a vastly superior military force has managed, against all odds, to snatch defeat from all but certain victory. The phenomenon usually has root in one of three causes: arrogance, such a blinding belief in one's own military or cultural superiority as to fail to take the enemy seriously; political interference; or tunnel vision, that curious tendency among war planners and generals to believe a flawed approach might be rectified simply by pouring more men and firepower into the fray. In early 1915, the British military would navigate its way to a fiasco of such colossal proportions as to require all three of these factors to work in concert.

With the brushing back of the Turkish assault on the Suez on February 3, Lawrence and other members of the intelligence unit in Cairo assumed that plans for a landing at Alexandretta would immediately get under way. Instead, the war strategists in London had already begun focusing on a different spot on the Ottoman coastline: the Dardanelles strait below Constantinople.

One of the earth's more peculiar natural formations, the Dardanelles is a narrow, fjordlike waterway flanked by the Turkish Asian mainland on its eastern bank and the mountainous Gallipoli peninsula on its western. After a twisting thirty-mile-long course between the mountains, the gorge opens up at its northern confluence to the inland Sea of Marmara, at the far end of which lies Constantinople, or modern-day Istanbul. For obvious reasons, the southern entrance to the Dardanelles, letting onto the Mediterranean, has always been regarded as the maritime gateway to that city, and since ancient times every civilization that has controlled the region has maintained fortifications there. The Ottoman forts that dotted the high slopes above the strait in early 1915 had been erected on the ruins of Byzantine forts, which in turn had been built on the ruins of Greek and Roman ones.

"Forcing the Narrows" had been an alluring notion for British war planners ever since Turkey came into the war, and for none more so than the first lord of the admiralty, Winston Churchill. As he repeatedly pointed out to the British cabinet—often to the point of tiresomeness, as was his style—with a defenseless Constantinople lying just to the north of that strait, here lay the chance to swiftly decapitate their Turkish adversaries and take them out of the war. Further arguing for a Dardanelles breakthrough was an appeal for aid from Russia, hard pressed by German and Austro-Hungarian forces in the north. With Russia's northern ports either iced in or patrolled by marauding German U-boats, the only possible maritime route for such aid, Churchill argued, was from the south.

As consensus for a Dardanelles naval operation grew in London, those in Cairo advocating an Alexandretta landing found themselves increasingly outmaneuvered; with the Royal Navy focused on the former, they were told, it would be spread too thin to support an operation in the latter. On its face, this contention was absurd. Even the most pessimistic War Office assessment had concluded that Alexandretta could be seized by about 20,000 troops—far more than the two to three thousand envisioned by Lawrence, but still a pittance compared with the numbers idly staring across no-man's-land on the Western Front. The real issue was institutional myopia. Since the Dardanelles had now become the first priority in the Near East, any action at Alexandretta fell under the classification of a diversion, and among senior British war planners, with their nineteenth-century notions of massing all available force at a single point, diversion was shorthand for distraction.

Joined to this was stone-cold arrogance. Turkey was a third-rate power, its soldiers ill-fed, ill-trained, poorly armed, and mutinous. In just the past five years, they had been beaten by the Italians, the Bulgarians, the Greeks, the Serbs, and the Montenegrins. Most recently, they had been swatted away from the Suez Canal and slaughtered by the Russians at the battle of Sarikamish in eastern Turkey. "Taking the Turkish Army as a whole," one British officer had reported to his superiors in November 1914, "I should say it was [a] militia only moderately trained, and composed as a rule of tough but slow-witted peasants as liable to panic before the unexpected as most uneducated men." Just what chance did this rabble have against the might of the British Empire? Ergo, why nip at their heels at Alexandretta when they could be beheaded at Constantinople?

But there was an altogether different issue at play as well, one that had nothing to do with military strategies or hubris and everything to do with politics. Since the start of the war, the French had laid claim to Syria, a spoils-of-war prize that it would take possession of once the conflict ended. Even though the Alexandretta enclave fell just outside the generally recognized borders of greater Syria, all the British talk of the Syrian uprising that was sure to follow an Alexandretta landing—talk, ironically enough, that Lawrence himself had done much to generate in his reports to London—made the French extremely edgy. Put simply, if there was to be an Allied move into the Syrian region, the French wanted to be in on it from the outset in order to take control of the situation. That was understandable as far as the argument went, perhaps, but then came the kicker: since France, hard pressed on the Western Front, had no troops to spare for such an enterprise, it meant that the entire region, including Alexandretta, should be militarily off-limits even to its allies.

Whether justified or not, in Lawrence's mind it was this French objection, far more than British War Office shortsightedness, that scuttled the Alexandretta plan. In mid-February, as word of the French position circulated among the stunned Savoy Hotel intelligence staff, he wrote a short letter to his parents in which he bitterly noted, "So far as Syria is concerned, it is France and not Turkey that is the enemy."

Initially, however, it appeared that Lawrence's indignation might be misplaced, and the Dardanelles gambit a success. On February 19, a joint British and French flotilla appeared off the southern entrance to the strait and with their long-range guns proceeded to shell the Turkish fortresses there at will. With the Turks able to muster only token return fire, most of their outer forts were soon pounded to rubble, leading the British fleet commander to confidently predict that by methodically working its way up the strait and destroying whatever Turkish fortifications remained, his armada might reach Constantinople within two weeks' time. That city's residents clearly agreed with him. As the Allied fleet sailed off to resupply for the big push, Constantinople's imminent fall seemed such a foregone conclusion that the nation's gold reserves were rushed to a safe haven in the Turkish interior, and many senior government officials quietly hatched personal contingency plans to flee.

One who didn't share this view was T. E. Lawrence. To the contrary, holding out hope that until the Dardanelles operation got under way in earnest there might still be a chance to overrule the French, he used the lull after the February 19 bombardments to continue pushing for an Alexandretta landing, but to little avail. With the senior British military command now deaf to his arguments, he finally reached out to the one person he knew who was well connected to the British political hierarchy, David Hogarth.

Although Lawrence had always assumed an informal, collegial tone with his mentor, his letter to Hogarth on March 18 was of a very different order: beseeching, even demanding. After outlining the crucial importance of taking Alexandretta—"the key of the whole place, as you know"—and warning of the danger should it fall into the hands of any other power, he all but gave Hogarth a set of marching orders to combat the various forces lined up against the plan: "Can you get someone to suggest to Winston [Churchill] that there is a petrol spring on the beach (very favourably advised on by many engineers, but concessions always refused by the Turks), huge iron deposits near Durt Yol 10 miles to the north and coal also. . . . Then go to the F.O. [Foreign Office] if possible. Point out that in [the] Baghdad Convention, France gave up Alexandretta to [the] Germans, and agreed that it formed no part of Syria. Swear that it doesn't form part of Syria—and you know it speaks Turkish.... By occupying Alexandretta with 10,000 men we are impregnable."

Whether or not Hogarth actually had the clout to execute such instructions, it was already too late. On the very day Lawrence sent his letter, March 18, the Allied fleet returned to the mouth of the Dardanelles to resume their bombardment campaign. This time, matters didn't go at all as planned.

For the first three hours, the Allied armada pounded away at the coastal forts with much the same ease as in February. The trouble started when the first line of ships was commanded to fall back to make room for the second. During the February bombardment, the Turks had taken note of an odd habit of the Allied fleet, that when reversing course they almost invariably turned their ships to starboard; on the chance that this tradition would continue, they had recently laid a single string of mines in an inlet the Allies would traverse on a starboard turn. Sure enough, at about 2 p.m. the retiring Allied first line steered directly into the minefield. In quick succession, three warships were sunk, and three more heavily damaged.

Although the term "mission creep," with all its negative connotations, didn't exist in 1915, it probably should have. In analyzing the March 18 minefield fiasco, British war planners came to the reasonable conclusion that the Dardanelles couldn't be cleared by sea power alone. What they failed to conclude was that the campaign should be abandoned in favor of something different. To the contrary, the Allies were now going to double down, with the naval effort at the strait to be augmented by a ground offensive.

It would be some time before anyone realized it, but that decision was to be one of the most fateful of World War I, ultimately extinguishing any hope that the conflict in the Middle East—and by extension, that in Europe—might be brought to an early end. In the interim, the regime in Constantinople, which just days earlier had been flirting with abandoning the capital, was given a new lease on life as the Allies again paused operations in order to cobble their ground force together.

IN THE MIDWINTER of 1915, the Standard Oil Company of New York finally decided what to do with William Yale. Releasing him from Cairo, that modern-day Sodom and Gomorrah so assaultive to his Yankee sensibilities, he was ordered to return to Constantinople.

With greater cunning than perhaps any other international corporation, Socony had looked upon the unfolding tragedy of World War I and been determined to play it to their advantage. In fact, in the very first days of the war it had come up with a plan whereby it might supply the petroleum needs of *both* warring European blocs by reflagging its tankers to the registry of neutral nations. While that scheme had been exposed, Yale discovered that Socony had now devised an ingenious new system to smuggle oil to Turkey through neutral Bulgaria. But this was minor compared with what Standard was planning next, and it was to achieve that greater plan that Yale had been brought back to Turkey.

What the bosses at 26 Broadway had come to realize was that so long as the Europe-wide war continued—and, just as crucially, so long as the United States kept out of it—they had the vast territories of the Ottoman Empire practically to themselves. With their British, French, and Russian competitors boxed out until the war ended, they now had a golden opportunity to grab up as many oil concessions in the Near East as they desired—and since they were the only major company still in operation in the region, they could do so at rock-bottom prices. The scheme traded on Turkey's desperate need for oil, a vital commodity if it was to have any hope of competing militarily. The oil coming through Socony's Bulgarian smuggling operation was a pittance compared with what was needed, and to meet this need Standard held out a possible solution: Palestine.

In various geological studies going back to the late 1800s, data suggested that central Palestine might well be the site of one of the world's great untapped oil reservoirs. The mapping team that William Yale had been a part of in 1913–14 had examined only a tiny portion of that area, some forty-five thousand acres, limited as it was by the boundaries of the concessionary zones. Standard wanted to massively increase its Palestine holdings, and it now saw a way to make that happen.

Just prior to Yale's return, Socony officials in Constantinople had told the Ottoman government that after careful consideration, they had regretfully concluded that the area covered by their seven concessions in Kornub was simply too small to be financially viable to exploit. If such a conclusion seemed odd coming so soon after Socony had embarked on a massive effort to develop those concessions, a naturally more pressing question for an oil-starved regime in the midst of a war was, just how many more acres did Standard feel they needed? The answer: a half million more, or, put in more tangible terms, pretty much the entire breadth of central Judea from the Dead Sea to the Mediterranean, an area covering about one-tenth of the current state of Israel.

Except there was a key detail in all this that Socony saw no reason to trouble the Turks with. It had no intention of actually drilling for oil, let alone refining it, until after the war was over. Its sole goal was to use the "golden hour" that the war afforded to lock up those 500,000 acres for the future, a future that, provided the right pressure was brought to bear on the right diplomats and politicians, wouldn't depend in any way on which side eventually won.

As the Socony employee with the most experience in Palestine, William Yale was to be the point man for getting control of that land. The first job at hand, though, was to change Turkey's mining laws; these were archaic and complex and an impediment to the kind of land grab Standard was hoping to achieve. To this end, the Constantinople Socony office set to work compiling a comprehensive set of new mining-law recommendations for the Turkish parliament—an undertaking eased by their having put the secretary of the Turkish senate on their payroll—and also placed Yale on the drafting committee. In just this way, the twenty-seven-year-old Yale, less than eighteen months removed from his roustabout duties in an Oklahoma oilfield, became instrumental in rewriting the commercial laws of a foreign empire.

THE GERMAN HOSPICE is a magnificent building of yellow stone and slate that sits on the ridgeline of the Mount of Olives in Jerusalem. Today its austere lines are softened by the cypress and pine trees that surround it, but when it was constructed in the early 1900s, under the orders and specifications of Kaiser Wilhelm II of Germany, its bare grounds and prominent position on the ridge gave it more than a passing resemblance to a Bavarian castle.

Built to accommodate German pilgrims and clergy visiting the Holy Land, the hospice has the feel of a particularly pleasant medieval monastery, rough-stone stairways connecting its different floors, open internal passageways giving onto views of its cloistered gardens. On the ground floor is a great chapel made of stone, its fusion of stained glass windows and Moorish-style archways reminiscent of the Great Cathedral in Córdoba. So grand is the hospice that Djemal Pasha chose to make it his Jerusalem headquarters during World War I, the city where he and his German liaison officer, Curt Prüfer, returned after their ill-fated Suez sojourn in February 1915.

In Jerusalem, the governor quickly became known for exhibiting a degree of irritability in the administration of his office. His new personal secretary, a twenty-one-year-old reserve officer named Falih Rifki, caught a glimpse of this on the first day he showed up for work at the hospice in the winter of 1915. Ushered into Djemal's inner sanctum, Rifki watched as the governor briskly signed his way through a high stack of papers placed before him and then taken away by three attending officers, oblivious to the twenty or so other men who stood in one corner of the room, pale and trembling with fear. When Djemal at last finished with his paperwork and turned to the clustered men, elders from the Palestinian town of Nablus, it was to ask if they understood the gravity of their unspecified crimes. The Nablus elders, apparently not appreciating that the question was meant to be rhetorical, began to protest their innocence and plead for mercy.

"Silence!" Djemal thundered. "Do you know what the punishment is for these crimes? Execution! Execution!" He let that news sink in for a bit, before continuing in a calmer tone, "But you may thank God for the sublime mercy of the Ottoman state. For the moment I shall content myself with exiling you and your families to Anatolia."

After the men had offered their profuse thanks and been hustled out, Djemal turned to Rifki with a shrug. "What can one do? That's how we get things done here."

The episode rather exemplified Djemal Pasha's managerial style, a man for whom the term "mercurial" might have been coined. Forever oscillating between raging severity and gentle magnanimity, often within the same conversation, he kept everyone around him permanently off balance, incapable of predicting his likely response to a situation. Howard Bliss, the president of the Syrian Protestant College in Beirut, recalled a meeting between Djemal and a favor-seeking Briton at which the governor bluntly refused every request made of him, until a sealed envelope was opportunely delivered by an aide. Reading the contents, Djemal broke into a broad smile.

"I now can grant all your requests," he announced. "I have just received a decoration from the Czar of Bulgaria, and at such times I always grant the first favors presented."

One effect of this style, of course, was that issues were never truly resolved; knowing that most any harsh edict might be countermanded or, conversely, a granted favor soon rescinded, petitioners learned to beseech Djemal for consideration when he was reported to be in a good mood—or, trusting in the law of averages, to simply beseech him repeatedly.

In his defense, though, it's not as if the Syrian governor didn't have a lot of things to be irritable about. Indeed, by the middle of March 1915 he was buffeted by such an array of crises as might cause the most cheerful person to feel a bit put-upon. Under the circumstances, the first of these crises, manifested on the morning of March 22, bordered on the perverse: locusts.

The Spanish consul in Jerusalem, a dapper young man named Antonio de la Cierva, Conde de Ballobar, happened to be working in his office that morning when he noticed the sky suddenly darken dramatically, as if there were occurring a solar eclipse. "Upon peeking out from the balcony I saw that an immense cloud had completely obscured the light of the sun." As Ballobar watched, the cloud descended, revealed itself to be millions upon millions of locusts. "The ground, the balconies, the roofs, the entire city and then the countryside, everything was covered by these wretched little animals."

Just as quickly as it had appeared, the horde moved on, headed east toward Jericho, but in subsequent days, reports of the locust plague started coming in from across the breadth of central Palestine. They told of entire orchards and fields stripped bare of every leaf and seedling within hours, of farm animals and briefly unattended infants being blinded, the insects feeding on the liquid in their eyes.

The Holy Land had experienced locust plagues in the past, but nothing in modern memory compared to this. Nor could it have come at a worse moment. Joined to the pressures of the war effort—tens of thousands of Syrian farmers had been drafted, the requisitioning of farm animals and machinery had been wanton—the pestilence was sure to make an already troubled spring planting season infinitely worse, and cause massive food shortages and price increases. Indeed, Consul Ballobar noted, within hours of the locust swarm touching down in Jerusalem, wheat prices in the city's bazaars had spiked.

True to his self-image as a reformer, Djemal Pasha didn't form a committee or appoint some toady to deal with the problem, the typical Ottoman response to a crisis. Instead, he immediately summoned Syria's most celebrated agricultural scientist, the thirty-nine-year-old Jewish émigré Aaron Aaronsohn.

The meeting between the two fiercely headstrong men took place on March 27 and, per Djemal's preference, was conducted in French. It got off to a rocky start. Along with outlining the modern techniques that could be used to combat the infestation, Aaronsohn took the opportunity to bluntly criticize the army's wholesale requisitions that had left the region on the brink of ruin even before the locusts appeared. According to the story Aaronsohn would later tell, the governor finally interrupted his tirade with a simple question: "What if I were to have you hanged?"

In a clever retort, alluding to both his considerable girth and to his network of influential friends abroad, the agronomist replied, "Your Excellency, the weight of my body would break the gallows with a noise loud enough to be heard in America."

Djemal apparently liked that answer. Before the ending of their meeting, he had appointed Aaronsohn inspector in chief of a new locust eradication program, and granted him near-dictatorial powers to carry it out. If any petty officials got in Aaronsohn's way, the governor let it be known, they would have to answer to him.

But if the locust plague could be delegated to an expert, that was not the case with Djemal's other concerns that March.

For some time he had been sitting on information that suggested the empire's "Arab problem" might be far more serious than anyone in Constantinople appreciated, that in Syria they might be sitting on something of a volcano.

Shortly after Turkey joined the war in November, a unit of Turkish counterintelligence officers had broken into the shuttered French consulate in Beirut, and there they had found a passel of documents in a concealed wall safe. Those papers laid bare a long-standing secret relationship between the French consul and a number of Arab leaders in Beirut and Damascus opposed to the Young Turk government. Not just opposed; many of the proposals these men had put to the French consul—for Syrian independence, for a French protectorate in Lebanon—were nothing short of traitorous.

But administering a corrective to the querulous Nablus elders had been one thing; moving against the Beirut and Damascus consulate plotters was a good deal trickier. Many were well known throughout the Arab world, and their execution or exile might provoke the very Arab rebellion Turkey sought to avoid. It might also raise alarm in the greater Arab Muslim world, including in the "captive" lands of Egypt and French North Africa, just when Constantinople was trying to stir these communities to the cause of pan-Islamic jihad. Consequently, Djemal had seen no choice but to adopt a wait-and-see approach. Tucking the Beirut dossier away in his Damascus office, he had endeavored to keep the malcontents close by feigning normalcy and reverting to the old Ottoman standby of handing out sinecures and honorary positions. That tactic might ultimately win the plotters to his side, or conversely reveal how extensive their conspiratorial circles actually were, but it was still worrisome to have these traitors at large at the very moment that an Allied invasion of Syria had suddenly grown more likely.

But in Syria, every problem had its counterproblem. Whereas the Beirut dissidents consisted almost exclusively of so-called progressives, Arab urban liberals infused with European ideas of nationalism and self-determination, in late March Djemal also faced a crisis with Arab conservatives, those spurred to outrage by the Young Turks' modernist—and, to their eyes, secularist—reforms. This conservative crisis was about to quite literally show up at the governor's door in the form of a soft-spoken thirty-one-year-old man named Sheikh Faisal ibn Hussein.

Faisal was the third of four sons of Emir Hussein, a tribal leader in the immense Hejaz region of western Arabia. Of much greater import, Faisal's father was the sherif, or religious leader, of the Muslim holy cities of Mecca and Medina, the most recent scion of the Hashemite clan that had served as the guardians of the Islamic holy land since the tenth century.

Relations between the Young Turks and Emir Hussein had been strained from the very outset, and time had done nothing to improve matters. Almost medieval in his conservatism, over the years Hussein had viewed the stream of liberalist edicts emanating from Constantinople with ever-deepening antipathy; his discontent ranged from the Young Turks' emancipation of women and promotion of minority rights, to its chipping away at the civic authority of religious leaders, even to its efforts to curb slavery, still a common practice in the Hejaz. Tellingly, the most tangible focus of Emir Hussein's rancor was the proposed extension of the Hejaz Railway from Medina to Mecca. Far from viewing the extension as a sign of progress, a way to ease the travel of Muslim pilgrims making the hajj to the holy city, Hussein saw it as a Trojan horse for Constantinople to exert greater control over the region, and specifically over him. The result had been an endless series of clashes between the Constantinople-appointed Hejaz civilian governors and the emir and his sons.

The tensions had only grown worse—and the consequences obviously far graver—since Turkey came into the war. Given that he was one of the most respected religious figures in the Muslim world, Hussein's noncommittal response to the call to jihad in November was quickly noted by all, and was viewed as a major reason for its tepid effect thus far. Similarly, appeals for national unity in the war effort had done nothing to bring about a rapprochement in the long-standing feud between Ali, Hussein's eldest son, and the current governor of Medina, a feud that at times had come close to open combat. Then there had been the emir's feeble response to Djemal's request for volunteers to join in the Suez assault. Instead of the thousands of tribal fighters the regime had counted on, Abdullah, Hussein's second son, had shown up in Syria with a mere handful.

Yet despite all this provocation, Hussein and his sons had to be handled with even greater delicacy than the Beirut malcontents. If from a narrow military standpoint the Hejaz lacked the strategic importance of Syria—it consisted of a few small cities surrounded by vast deserts at the farthest fringe of the empire—the Hashemite emir's singular ability to bestow or deny his religious blessing on Constantinople's actions gave him extraordinary power. Thus a kind of standoff ensued. Obviously, the Young Turks either wanted Hussein to fall in line or to be rid of him, but to move against him in too crude a fashion was to invite a ferocious conservative backlash. For his part, Hussein had to know that there was a limit to the Young Turks' patience, that pushing them too far was to invite in the soldiers.

That standoff had recently experienced a perilous rupture. In January, Hussein's eldest son, Ali, claimed to have uncovered a plot by the governor of Medina to overthrow Hussein and replace him with a more pliant religious figure. This was the reason for Faisal's impending arrival in Syria. Emir Hussein was sending him out of the deserts of Arabia to confront the Constantinople regime, both to express his outrage at the overthrow plot and to demand that the provincial governor be removed.

But here, at last, was something approximating good news for Djemal Pasha, for if there was anyone within the troublesome Hussein family who he felt might be the voice of reason, it was Faisal. Like his older brothers, Faisal had been raised and educated within the sultan's inner court in Constantinople, but it appeared this civilizing influence had taken special hold in Hussein's unassuming third son. In Faisal there was a caution, even a timidity, that might be exploited with gentle words and charm—and though the unlucky Nablus elders hauled into his office might have gone away with a differing opinion, charm was something of a Djemal specialty. When Faisal and his retinue rolled into town, the governor intended to greet him with all the pomp and fanfare of a visiting dignitary.

LESS THAN A mile away from the German Hospice, at the German military headquarters in downtown Jerusalem, Curt Prüfer also took a keen interest in the imminent arrival of Faisal ibn Hussein. He had a rather harder-edged view, however, of how to win the Hussein family to the Turco-German cause. Back in October 1914, even before Djemal Pasha's arrival in Syria, Prüfer had dispatched his own spies to the Hejaz to get a sense of where Emir Hussein's true loyalties lay. His conclusion, as he'd reported to Max von Oppenheim in early November, was that the emir in Mecca was essentially on the payroll of British Egypt and thus "English through and through."

Beyond his obvious political and religious differences with the Young Turks, the problem with Hussein extended to geography. One of the most isolated and impoverished regions of the Ottoman Empire, the Hejaz had an economy that was almost wholly dependent on the annual hajj, or pilgrimage, by the Muslim faithful to Mecca, the bulk of whom came from either India or Egypt. The arid Hejaz also relied on imported grain to feed its people, and much of that came across the Red Sea from Egypt or British Sudan in the form of government-subsidized religious offerings. With the British navy's undisputed control of the Red Sea, it would be a simple matter to cut off both the pilgrim traffic and food supplies to the Hejaz, an action that would quickly take the region to utter ruin. This was the sword that hung over his head, Hussein had intimated to Constantinople, and the underlying reason why he had to tread so carefully before the regime's demands.

But to Curt Prüfer it was all a rather outrageous bluff. Put simply, the British would never risk incurring the wrath of the Muslim world by starving out, let alone invading, the Islamic holy land; Germany should be so lucky. At the same time, Hussein, as the guardian of Mecca and Medina, wouldn't dare go over to the British, for that same Muslim wrath would then be directed at him. Instead, the wily old emir in Mecca was playing both sides, keeping the British at bay—and their food subsidies and pilgrim traffic intact—through advertising his differences with Constantinople, and keeping Constantinople at bay through touting the contrived British threat.

The problem was, the Turks would not challenge Hussein nor allow their allies to do so. Since arriving in the region, Prüfer and the other German intelligence agents had been explicitly forbidden from involving themselves in Hejazi affairs in any way. Even during Faisal's upcoming visit, Djemal intended to screen the young sheikh from his German advisors as much as possible. Instead, the Syrian governor would undoubtedly pursue the same course the Young Turks had adopted with the Hussein family for the past six years—solicitousness and flattery blended with veiled threats—and to the same negligible effect.

What made all this especially maddening to Prüfer was that Hussein was one of the linchpins in bringing the pan-Islamic jihad to full flower. Without the Hashemite leader's blessing, that fatwa remained a concoction of the Young Turk regime; with his blessing, fires might be ignited throughout the Middle East and beyond.

In his November report to Oppenheim, Prüfer had concluded that the emir was "luckily powerless and in our hands." The challenge now was to convince everyone else—Djemal, the Young Turks in Constantinople, Hussein himself—that this was true.

THERE IS LITTLE indication that Lawrence was following events in the Arabian Peninsula, or was even aware of them, during his first few months with the intelligence unit in Cairo—understandable given his almost obsessive focus on Syria. That changed when he made the acquaintance of Ronald Storrs, the British Oriental secretary to Egypt.

With his pencil-thin mustache and fondness for white linen suits, Storrs cut a dandyish figure among the predominantly uniformed British population of wartime Cairo, a Cambridge-educated aesthete with an encyclopedic knowledge of opera, Renaissance art, and classical literature. Shipping out to Egypt as a young man, he had passed through a

T. E. Lawrence (far left) and his four brothers (left
to right): Frank, Arnold, Robert, and Will. While T. E.
waged "paper-combat" in Cairo during 1915, both Frank
and Will would be killed on the Western Front.

Bodleian ref: MS. Photog. c. 122, fol. 3

Scholar, spy, and notorious ladies' man: Curt Prüfer in Cairo, 1906 © *Trina Prufer*

Fallen aristocrat William Yale was the only American intelligence agent in the Middle East during World War I— even while he secretly remained on the payroll of Standard Oil. © *Milne Special Collections, University of New Hampshire Library*

A towering figure: Aaron Aaronsohn, brilliant scientist, ardent Zionist, and mastermind of the most successful spy ring in the Middle East

Englishmen abroad: T. E. Lawrence (right) and Leonard Woolley at the archaeological ruins of Carchemish, 1912. Lawrence would recall his time at Carchemish as the happiest of his life.

Stewart Newcombe, Lawrence's supervisor on the mysterious Wilderness of Zin expedition and the man who brought him to wartime Cairo for intelligence work © *Marist Archives and Special Collections, Lowell Thomas Papers*

Dahoum, Lawrence's young assistant at Carchemish, to whom he dedicated *Seven Pillars of Wisdom*
© *The British Library Board, MS 50584, f.115–116*

After his vast family fortune evaporated, William Yale signed on with Standard Oil for a clandestine mission to the prewar Ottoman Empire in search of oil.
© Milne Special Collections, University of New Hampshire Library

Playboys in the Holy Land: To keep their mission secret, Yale and his Standard Oil partners (J. C. Hill, second from left, and Rudolf McGovern, second from right) were told to masquerade as wealthy "playboys" on a tour of biblical sights—to limited success. *© Milne Special Collections, University of New Hampshire Library*

Kaiser Wilhelm II, the Caesar of Germany. A generation of his subjects, including Curt Prüfer, was stirred by Wilhelm's bellicose demand that Germany assume its rightful "place in the sun."

(BELOW, LEFT) "The Kaiser's spy" and Curt Prüfer's mentor, Count Max von Oppenheim. While indulging his passion for archaeology, slave girls, and the racetrack, Oppenheim dreamed of setting the Middle East aflame through Islamic jihad.

(BELOW, RIGHT) Prüfer on the eve of the Turkish assault on the Suez Canal, February 1915. Despite predicting disaster in his private diary, he urged the attack forward.
© Trina Prufer

(LEFT) Lord Kitchener, appointed the British war secretary in August 1914. Where others foresaw a quick and painless war, Kitchener predicted one that would sap British manpower "to the last million."
© *UIG History / Science & Society Picture Library*

(ABOVE) Diplomatic gadfly and amateur extraordinaire Mark Sykes. "The imaginative advocate of unconvincing world movements," a disdainful Lawrence wrote of Sykes, "a bundle of prejudices, intuitions, half-sciences."

(LEFT) Reginald Wingate, the sirdar of the Egyptian army and British high commissioner to Egypt. He apparently never figured out T. E. Lawrence's double cross. *Photo by Hulton Archive/ Getty Images*

Ahmed Djemal Pasha (in white coat), the Ottoman governor-general of Syria. Over the course of the war, William Yale, Curt Prüfer, and Aaron Aaronsohn would all have close dealings with the mercurial Djemal.

"The handsomest man in the Turkish army," Ottoman minister of war Enver Pasha, who conspired with Curt Prüfer to destroy the Suez Canal © *DIZ Muenchen GmbH, Sueddeutsche Zeitung Photo/Alamy*

Mustafa Kemal "Ataturk," the hero of Gallipoli and the founder of the modern Turkish republic
Library of Congress

number of positions in the British administration there before winning appointment as Oriental secretary in 1909 at the age of twenty-eight.

It was a position he was born for. Along with being a decorous presence at the official receptions and galas of which the British community in Cairo was especially fond, Storrs acted as the right-hand man of the resident British consul general to Egypt, a behind-the-scenes monitor of the nation's myriad political intrigues. His star had risen considerably when Lord Kitchener assumed that post in 1911. Quickly coming to regard Storrs as his most trusted lieutenant—the Oriental secretary had been instrumental in torpedoing Curt Prüfer's appointment to the khedival library directorship, for example—Kitchener had maintained their relationship even after his appointment to war secretary in August 1914. Since he fully intended to return to his Egyptian post once the war was over, Kitchener had left his protégé behind in Cairo to serve as his eyes and ears.

But there was rather more to it than that. In Kitchener's service, Ronald Storrs was the crucial conduit in a game of political intrigue so sensitive it was known to only a handful of men in Cairo, London, and Mecca, the possessor of perhaps the most dangerous secret in the Middle East. By befriending T. E. Lawrence and bringing him in on that secret, Storrs would set the young intelligence officer on the course that was to bring him fame and glory.

At least initially, that friendship was based on the supremely ordinary, a mutual love of classical literature. As the rather fusty Storrs related of Lawrence in his memoir, "We had no literary differences, except that he preferred Homer to Dante and disliked my preference for Theocritus before Aristophanes."

At some point in the winter of 1915, their discussions turned to more current topics, specifically to the covert mission that Storrs was conducting for Lord Kitchener.

The story had begun a year earlier, in February 1914, when Abdullah ibn Hussein, the thirty-two-year-old second son of Emir Hussein of Mecca, came calling in Cairo. While the emir's disenchantment with the Constantinople regime was becoming fairly common knowledge by that point, Abdullah pushed matters into a whole new realm; granted a brief meeting with Kitchener, he attempted to sound out the consul general on what British reaction would be to an outright Arab revolt in the Hejaz.

Kitchener took pains to sidestep the query. After all, Britain and Turkey were still at peace then, and it simply wouldn't do for the former to encourage revolt in the latter. When Abdullah returned to Cairo two months later hoping for a second meeting, Kitchener foisted him off on his Oriental secretary.

Whatever limited subtlety Abdullah had managed with Kitchener, it was absent from his meeting with Storrs. "I found myself being asked categorically whether Britain would present the Grand Sharif [Hussein] with a dozen, or even a half dozen machine guns," Storrs recalled. "When I enquired what could possibly be their purpose, he replied (like all rearmers) for defence; and, pressed further, added that the defence would be against attack from the Turks. I needed no special instructions to inform him that we could never entertain the idea of supplying arms to be used against a friendly power."

But that second meeting with Abdullah had been in April 1914, and by the following September, matters had changed a great deal. As he waited to see if Turkey would come into the war, now–War Secretary Kitchener had reason to recall his earlier conversation with Hussein's son and to appreciate that he might have a unique opportunity awaiting him in Arabia. Rather than work through senior officials in the British military or civilian administrations in Egypt, Kitchener sent an encrypted cable to his old Cairo office: "Tell Storrs to send secret and carefully chosen messenger from me to the Sharif Abdullah to ascertain whether, should present German influence in Constantinople coerce [Turkey into] . . . war against Great Britain, he and his father and Arabs of the Hejaz would be with us or against us."

Hussein's reply, which arrived just as Turkey joined the war, was tantalizing. While stating that he would endeavor to stay neutral, Hussein hinted that with sufficient external support and concrete promises from Britain to stay out of internal Arabian affairs, he might lead his "immediate followers into revolt."

Seizing on that prospect, Kitchener swiftly sent another message that dramatically upped the ante. Should the Arabs join with Britain, rather than merely stay neutral, Kitchener wrote, "Great Britain will guarantee the independence, rights and privileges of the Sherifate against all external foreign aggression, in particular that of the Ottomans. Till now we have defended and befriended Islam in the person of the Turks [sic]; henceforward it shall be in that of the noble Arab."

But then Hussein seemed to equivocate somewhat. In his next letter, received by Storrs in December, the emir repeated his intention to "avoid any action detrimental to the British," but also indicated that any outright break with Turkey would have to wait until sometime in the indefinite future. And there the matter rested. In the months since Hussein had sent that last message, there had been no word out of Mecca.

To Lawrence, the details of this secret correspondence with Hussein came as something of a revelation. Since arriving in Cairo, he had devoted great energy to gauging the possibility of an Arab revolt in Syria, a revolt that, almost by definition, would be reliant on so-called progressives: businessmen and intellectuals disaffected by the corruption of the Constantinople regime, minorities yearning for equality, Arab officers and conscripts frustrated by the military's Turkish chauvinism. Of conservative Arabia he knew virtually nothing.

Yet from a political standpoint, Lawrence quickly appreciated the Hejazi potential. An alliance with Hussein would inoculate the British against the charge that it was fomenting rebellion as a means of taking over the Middle East; as guardian of the holy cities, it would be quite unthinkable to most Muslims that Emir Hussein had entered a partnership with land-grabbing infidels. To the contrary, a revolt starting in the Hejaz and under his leadership would carry the imprimatur of religious sanction, neatly nullifying the Islam-versus-Crusaders propaganda being promoted by the Turks and Max von Oppenheim.

But trying to assess where things stood in the absence of any new communication from Hussein was a perplexing process. On the one hand, he did appear to be living up to his promise of neutrality, as evidenced by his continuing noncommittal stance on the call to jihad. On the other hand, he had recently sent his third son, Faisal, to meet with Djemal Pasha in Syria, and to then proceed to Constantinople for more meetings with the Young Turk leadership. Since Faisal was generally considered to be the most moderate and sober-minded of Hussein's sons, the obvious conclusion was that Hussein was inching his way back toward a rapprochement with Constantinople and that the brief, tantalizing prospect of an Arab revolt in the Hejaz had slipped from British hands.

For his part, Lawrence soon had far more pressing concerns than trying to read the tea leaves of Hejazi politics. By early April 1915, all attention in British Egypt had turned to the upcoming naval and ground offensive against the Dardanelles.

DURING THE FIRST weeks of April, a vast flotilla of ships began to assemble along the northern coast of Egypt, while in the tent cities that dotted the shoreline, tens of thousands of soldiers were kept busy hauling supplies and practicing combat drills. They were members of the newly formed Mediterranean Expeditionary Force (Med-Ex for short) soon to be on their way to strike at the head and heart of the Turkish enemy. Despite the tedium of their wait, the mood of the troops was exuberant, keen.

With T. E. Lawrence, the sentiment was foreboding. The trepidation he had felt from the outset of the Dardanelles operation only deepened after he and other members of the Cairo intelligence unit were sent up to the staging area to brief its commanders on what they might expect at the other end. "The Med-Ex came out, beastly ill-prepared," Lawrence wrote David Hogarth on April 20, "with no knowledge of where it was going, or what it would meet, or what it was going to do." Most shocking of all to Lawrence, to plot their ground offensive, the Med-Ex senior staff had arrived in Egypt with exactly two copies of an obsolete quarter-inch-to-the-mile map of the Dardanelles region.

But when it came to committing folly, British war planners were just warming up. The principal landing zones for Med-Ex, it had been decided, would be on the Gallipoli peninsula, that thin ribbon of rugged mountains that forms the Dardanelles' western shore. Rarely more than six or seven miles across, the peninsula runs northward for some fifty miles before finally broadening out onto the European mainland. In selecting where to go ashore, the British could have chosen any number of spots along Gallipoli's length where a ground force, once gaining the ridgeline and climbing down to the opposite shore—a distance of less than three miles in places—would have split the Ottoman army in two and trapped any enemy forces positioned below that line. Of course, the best option might have been to sidestep the peninsula completely and put in at the Gulf of Saros at its northern end. An invasion force coming ashore in that broad bay would not only maroon all the Turkish troops garrisoned on Gallipoli, but would then have a virtually unimpeded path through easy countryside to Constantinople, just 100 miles away. This was certainly the greatest fear of General Liman von Sanders, the German commander recently appointed by the Turkish government to oversee the Dardanelles defense; in anticipation of a landing at Saros, he had placed his headquarters and fully a third of his army there.

The one possibility that Sanders tended to discount entirely was a landing at Gallipoli's southern tip, simply because the most basic rules of military logic—even mere common sense—argued against it. Not only would a landing force there be vulnerable to defenders dug in on the heights above them, but completely exposed to whatever long-range Turkish artillery remained operable in their nearby fortresses. And even if such a force managed to scale the heights and seize those forts, the Turkish defenders could then begin a slow withdrawal up the peninsula, throwing up new trenchlines as they went, neatly replicating the static trench warfare that had so paralyzed the armies on the Western Front. Indeed, one would be hard pressed to find a worse landing site most anywhere on the three-thousand-mile-long Mediterranean coast of the Ottoman Empire—yet it was precisely here that Med-Ex was going ashore.

Along with condescension for the enemy, always a perilous mind-set for an army, that decision was apparently born of sheer bureaucratic obduracy. Since the Dardanelles campaign had been conceived as a naval operation, the success or failure of the expanded mission would continue to be judged through the narrow lens of its original objective—clearing the straits—leaving its planners quite blind to the idea of trying a different approach that might ultimately achieve the same end. Incredibly, it seems the Gallipoli strategists had less rejected alternative landing sites than never seriously considered them.

In late April, the Med-Ex soldiers on the Egyptian coast began piling into the troopships that would take them across the eastern Mediterranean to Gallipoli. Lawrence, looking back over his failed efforts of the previous months, not just Alexandretta but a range of other schemes that he and the Cairo intelligence unit had concocted only to see shelved, could scarcely conceal his anger in another letter to Hogarth:

"Arabian affairs have gone all to pot. I've never seen a more despicable mess made of a show. It makes one howl with fury, for we had a ripping chance there." He ended on a somewhat forlorn note: "Push on A[lexandretta] therefore, if you can; it seems to me the only thing left for us."

When he wrote that letter, on April 26, Lawrence did not know how bad the mess was about to become. Just the day before, Med-Ex had gone ashore at Gallipoli.

AT ABOUT 6:15 on the morning of April 25, SS *River Clyde*, a converted collier out of Liverpool, closed on a small, gently arcing beach—code-named V Beach—at Cape Helles, the southern tip of the Gallipoli peninsula. Crammed belowdecks were some two thousand British soldiers. Coming in on the gentle seas alongside the *Clyde* were five or six launches, each towing several open cutters, likewise crammed to their gunwales with more soldiers. At about one hundred yards out, the cutter skippers cast off their towlines and distributed oars so that their crews might row the rest of the way to shore. From that shore came no sign of life at all. It appeared, just as hoped, that the landing at Cape Helles had caught the Turks completely off guard.

A damned good thing, too, for the slapdash preparations made for those going ashore at V Beach—and the notion of sending men onto an enemy beach in unarmored and motorless wooden boats wasn't the worst of it—suggested trouble if they met any resistance. In an Alexandria shipyard, workers had started in on a camouflage paint job of the *River Clyde* but had run out of time; as a result, as the collier approached V Beach that morning, its muted battleship gray was offset by enormous splotches of tan primer, making it stand out against the sea as if illuminated. Then there was the small matter of the *Clyde* being unable to actually reach the beach. The plan instead was to run her aground offshore and then to maneuver several fishing boats into the gap, lashing them together to create a makeshift bridge from ship to shore. At that point, the disembarking soldiers would emerge from four portals cut into the Clyde's bow, pass along two gangways to the fishing boats, then clamber over those until finally they reached the beach. It's hard to imagine that such blithe preparations would have attended a landing against Stone Age Pacific Islanders, let alone against a modern army, but such was the contempt with which British war planners held the Turks.

As the cutters neared the beach, the only sounds floating over the quiet bay were of boat engines and the dipping of oars, of men talking and laughing—perhaps a bit louder than normal out of relief at their uneventful landing. It was when the lead boats were just yards off the beach that the Turkish machine gunners, secreted in strategic vantage points along the shoreline, opened up.

The men in the open cutters never had a chance. One after another, these boats were shot to pieces or capsized, the gear-laden soldiers within them drowning in the surf or picked off after becoming entangled in the barbed wire that been strung below the water's surface. Most of the very few who made it onto the beach alive were soon cut down by raking machine-gun fire.

Those coming off the *Clyde* fared little better. Time and again, work crews emerged from the protected steel hull to try to lash the ersatz pontoon bridge together, only to be shot down almost immediately or to similarly drown in the surf. When finally a bridge of sorts was established, the soldiers emerging onto the gangways were easy targets; of the first company of two hundred men to go out the portals, only eleven reached shore. Many of the early casualties on the gangways actually died of suffocation, pinned beneath the growing heaps of dead and wounded of those coming behind. Whoever did manage to make the beach huddled for safety behind a six-foot-high sand escarpment at its landward edge, scant protection against machine-gun bullets. By late afternoon, there were so many dead men in the water that, as a British captain on the scene observed, "the sea near the shore was a red blood colour, which could be seen hundreds of yards away."

By the end of that first day, the advance landing forces at Gallipoli had already suffered nearly four thousand casualties, or considerably more than the total number of men Lawrence had projected would be needed to secure Alexandretta. So bewildered was General von Sanders by his enemy's idiocy that for the next day he remained convinced the southern landing was a mere feint and that the main invasion force was still coming elsewhere. This left it to a local Ottoman divisional commander, Lieutenant Colonel Mustafa Kemal, acting on his own accord, to repeatedly hurl his men against the invaders clinging to their tiny beachheads in an attempt to throw them back into the sea.

The first-day objective of those landing on Cape Helles had been to secure a small village some four miles inland, and then to advance on the Turkish forts just above. Over the next seven months, the British would never reach that village, but would suffer nearly a quarter of a million casualties trying. As for the Ottoman commander, Mustafa Kemal, the world would soon hear more about him; in 1922, he would emerge as the savior of the reconstituted Turkish republic and become better known by his honorific, Kemal Ataturk.

BUT IT WASN'T just the estimated half million soldiers killed or wounded on either side of the trenchline who would fall victim to the consequences of Gallipoli. On the very day the British came ashore, April 25, the Constantinople regime ordered the roundup of some two hundred Armenian intellectuals and business leaders whom it accused of being potential fifth columnists for the invaders. It was the beginning of a brutal "cleansing operation" against the Ottoman Empire's Christian minority—a genocide in the view of many—that would result in the deaths of as many as a million Armenians and Assyrians over the next year.

It would be some time before Lawrence and other British officers involved in the Middle Eastern theater came to appreciate that there had been yet another casualty at Gallipoli: the chance for a sweeping Arab revolt against the Turks, one that conceivably could have stretched from the Hejaz to northern Syria and clear over to Iraq. The details of this missed opportunity wouldn't be fully known for well over a year, not until Lawrence came face-to-face with Emir Hussein's soft-spoken third son, Faisal, and learned there had been a good deal more to his journey north in the spring of 1915 than met the eye.

In January 1915, at almost the same time that he learned of the Medina governor's plot to overthrow him, Emir Hussein had been visited in Mecca by a Syrian man named Fawzi al-Bakri. A long-standing and trusted member of the emir's retinue, on that visit al-Bakri had revealed that he was also a high-ranking member of al-Fatat, a secret society of Arab nationalists headquartered in his hometown of Damascus with cells throughout Syria and Iraq. Having learned of Hussein's secret correspondence with the British, the al-Fatat leadership had sent al-Bakri to Mecca with a proposal: a joint revolt against Constantinople by al-Fatat in Syria and the emir's forces in Hejaz, to be supported by the British and with Hussein serving as its spiritual leader.

Rather than give a definitive reply to this proposal, the cautious Hussein had instead sent Faisal north on a dual mission: to gauge the family's current standing in Constantinople, but also to assess the true prospects for an alliance with al-Fatat.

Arriving in Damascus in late March, Faisal politely declined Djemal Pasha's invitation to stay at the governor's mansion, explaining that he had already accepted the hospitality of a prominent Damascene family: the al-Bakris. In that home, shielded by high walls, Faisal held a long series of talks with the al-Fatat conspirators, and it was the delicate negotiations at those talks that largely explained why his stay in Damascus, originally intended to be brief, extended to some three weeks.

Journeying on to Constantinople, the young sheikh deftly worked the other side of the street. In meetings with the other two members of the Young Turk triumvirate, Enver and Talaat, as well as the newly arrived Max von Oppenheim, Faisal repeatedly expressed his family's fealty to the Ottoman cause, going so far as to sign an accord with Enver that appeared to finally put to rest many of the issues standing between Constantinople and his father. In mid-May, and to the accompaniment of an elaborate farewell ceremony organized by a grateful regime, he boarded a train at Haidar Pasha station for the return to Syria.

But that journey was into a world transformed. Just weeks after the landings in Gallipoli, already tens of thousands of Armenians were being banished from their homes and sent into internal exile, and the view out Faisal's train window was onto an unending horror show of starving women and children—and suspiciously few men—being herded along to God knows where at bayonet point. From the standpoint of the proposed Arab revolt, more grim news awaited him in Damascus. From his al-Fatat confederates, Faisal learned that many of the Arab-dominated military units in the region—units the conspirators had counted on for support when the revolt came—were already being dispatched to the Gallipoli killing fields, replaced by regime-loyal Turkish regiments.

Despite the radically changed atmosphere, perhaps because of it, the al-Fatat plotters had urged on Faisal a document to take to his father, and through him to the British in Egypt. Soon to become known as the Damascus Protocol, it consisted of a list of conditions whereby, with British assistance, al-Fatat might still be able to launch their revolt. As Faisal set out for his return to Mecca, the sole copy of the protocol was hidden in the boot of his most trusted bodyguard.

In preparing for Faisal's arrival in Syria back in March, Djemal Pasha had regarded the emir's third son as his last best hope to quell Hussein's restive heart. In fact, the Syrian governor was quite right in this estimation, if for all the wrong reasons. At a Hussein family conclave held at their summer palace in June, it would be Abdullah and Ali who would lobby their father for immediate rebellion against Constantinople, while Faisal, recent witness to all that Gallipoli had wrought—the Armenians dying en masse along the Anatolian roadways, the dispersal of the Arab units from northern Syria—would urge caution.

The knowledge of all this lay in the future for T. E. Lawrence. In the days and weeks after the Gallipoli landings, as he read through the cascade of grim battle reports coming over the wire at the Savoy Hotel in Cairo, it may have been just as well that he remained ignorant of the Damascus Protocol and of the would-be British allies waiting in Syria and the Hejaz. An absolute precondition for their revolt, the al-Fatat conspirators and Hussein would belatedly inform Cairo, a prerequisite upon which all their actions depended, was a British landing at Alexandretta.

Chapter 6

The Keepers of Secrets

You know, men do nearly all die laughing, because they know death is
very terrible, and a thing to be forgotten till after it has come.

T. E. LAWRENCE, IN A LETTER TO HIS MOTHER, 1916

F inding the demands of his mapping-room duties at the Savoy at least
temporarily eased by the departure of the Med-Ex army, in April
1915 Lawrence took over the task of editing an intelligence digest, a compendium of reports from around the region to be distributed to the upper
echelons of the British military command. He described the undertaking
with his trademark sarcasm to a friend in England:

"We edit a daily newspaper, absolutely uncensored, for the edification
of twenty-eight generals; the circulation increases automatically as they
invent new generals. This paper is my only joy. One can give the Turkish
point of view (in imaginary conversations with prisoners) of the proceedings of admirals and generals one dislikes, and I rub it in in my capacity
as editor-in-chief. There is also a weekly letter to 'Mother' [the London
War Office] in which one japes on a grander scale yet."

It was, of course, precisely this flippant attitude, one Lawrence seemed
determined to flaunt both in his correspondence and in person, that so
incensed his military superiors. But his defiance of soldierly protocol also
underscored a deeper truth: Lawrence was fundamentally not of them,
and was becoming less so all the time.

In just four months in the war theater, he had watched as Britain's best
hope for an early victory over the Turks was shelved for no better reason
than politics and institutional inertia; in its place, the "great thinkers" had

come up with Gallipoli. From what the Oxford scholar had seen, military culture was a world of hidebound careerists looking for a knighthood or their next medal, and of underlings loath to question the powerful, with countless thousands dying as a result.

What's more, by dint of his position in the Cairo military intelligence unit, Lawrence was uniquely positioned to know the truth behind the lies and propaganda on an ongoing basis. Every day he saw the raw battlefield reports coming into the Savoy Hotel from the various war theaters, and these told a tale of staggering incompetence and callousness: of soldiers ordered to stay in formation as they advanced over open ground toward enemy machine-gun nests; of hundreds dying to capture and lose and capture again a single village, a single hillock. Certainly a select group of other junior-ranked men had access to this information too—generals' aides and officers in similar military intelligence units in the various war theaters—but most of these were aspirants to the system, willing cogs in the vast, dumb meat-grinding machinery that none dared acknowledge as such.

THE GERMAN MILITARY mission in Jerusalem was housed in the Hospice for Russian Pilgrims, in the pleasant and orderly neighborhood just north of the Old City known as the Russian Compound. It was there that Curt Prüfer could often be found through the late winter of 1915, poring over intelligence cables and calculating his next move.

With a bit of distance from the event, the disillusionment he'd felt for the concept of holy war in the immediate aftermath of the Suez assault had eased somewhat. He recognized that with the Turkish forces getting no farther than the canal's banks, the idea remained an essentially untested one. He also recognized that despite that first setback, British Egypt could not be left alone, that so long as it existed, it posed the primary threat to the German-Turkish alliance in the Middle East. So a new assault was necessary, this time supported by far greater firepower, including German artillery and aircraft, as well as far better military intelligence, an apparatus that could provide details on what the British on the far side of the canal were planning, where their troops were deployed.

The problem was, Prüfer's own extensive intelligence network inside Egypt had also fallen victim to the Suez assault. In the first days of the war, he'd been able to use his Egyptian contacts to compile a comprehensive view of the enemy's preparations; in one memorable November 1914 report, he'd written of British defenseworks in the future tense—that is, of enemy installations still in the construction or planning stage. All that had been shut down in the run-up to Suez. As Prüfer reported to his superiors in late February, his own "bitter, practical experience" at the canal showed that most of the Bedouin and Egyptians he'd hastily recruited as replacement spies had been worthless, prone to "leaving honor and patriotism high and dry in the face of the temptations of the circling British agents who are not at all stingy with [gold] sovereigns." Germany might conceivably follow the British example and buy its way to a new informant network inside Egypt, Prüfer pointed out, but that would leave it dependent on whatever unverifiable intelligence these paid agents passed on, "functioning with these people" rather than actually managing them. In pondering this dilemma, the intelligence officer hit upon a rather shrewd idea: Jewish spies.

That idea's genesis may have stemmed from the company Prüfer was keeping at the time. Her name was Minna Weizmann, a dynamic and very pretty Jewish émigré in her mid-twenties from the town of Motal in White Russia (modern-day Belarus). From a prominent and highly educated family, Weizmann had embraced socialism from an early age, and had seized her chance to escape the hated czarist regime while at medical school in Berlin; in 1913, she'd immigrated to Palestine, becoming one of the few women physicians in Syria. It had been in Jerusalem in early 1914 that she and Curt Prüfer, recently resigned from the German embassy in Cairo, first met.

Although details of their relationship are sketchy, fragmentary evidence suggests the union was a special one for both. A rumor finding its way into German intelligence reports held that on the eve of Prüfer's departure for the Suez offensive in January, Weizmann had spent the night in his Jerusalem hotel room, behavior so scandalous for the time as to be ruinous for any woman not a prostitute. For his part, there are indications that Weizmann was a good deal more than just another amorous conquest for the ever-roving Prüfer; his wartime diaries contain several references to "my dear Fanny," Weizmann's nickname, signs of an affection rather absent in the few mentions of his American wife, Frances Pinkham, who is usually referred to merely as "Fr."

But if the bond with Minna Weizmann was true love, it was a love Curt Prüfer was willing to put to a higher purpose.

When Turkey came into the war, there were tens of thousands of Russian Jews scattered across Syrian Palestine who, like Minna Weizmann, still retained Russian citizenship. Constantinople had quickly given these now "belligerent nationals" a stark choice: become Ottoman citizens or face deportation or internal exile. In response, thousands of the émigrés had surrendered their Russian passports in favor of Ottoman ones, while thousands more had crowded into packed ships at Jaffa harbor in search of a new home. In March 1915, this exodus from Palestine was continuing—warships from the neutral United States were now complementing merchant vessels—and where most of these refugees were ending up was in British Egypt. As Prüfer pointed out in a proposal he sent to both Djemal Pasha and Max von Oppenheim, establishing a successful spy network in Egypt required "people who can be introduced into the country without suspicion, and have the necessary astuteness and sang-froid. We can find a number of such people amongst the Jewish population in this country."

Giving this spy ring its reliability, in Prüfer's estimation, would be the Russian Jews' abiding hatred of the anti-Semitic czarist regime. Operating on the premise that the friend of one's enemy is the enemy, he reasoned there might be many members of this community in Palestine who would jump at the chance to work against czarist Russian interests by striking at her ally in the region, British Egypt. Best of all, as Russian passport holders, these spies could simply join the ongoing refugee boatlift to Egypt without arousing suspicion.

But if it was already a feat to insert intelligence operatives into an enemy country in wartime, that still left the question of how to get them or their information out. Here Prüfer's scheme was truly clever. In March 1915, Italy remained a neutral nation (it would join the Triple Entente that May), and there was regular ship traffic between Italian ports and Egypt. Rather than try to communicate with or return to Turkey, Prüfer's spies would transit to Italy and pass their information on to the German embassy in Rome. At that point, they could either make for Turkey overland or, if their cover remained intact, return to Egypt for another round of intelligence gathering.

Warming to his topic, Prüfer further directed that the operatives should be divided into two cells, one composed of men, the other of women. Both cells "will try to steal relevant [British] documents or make copies of them. They will also try to get friendly with people who might be able to supply such information." Lest there be any confusion over what "friendly" meant, Prüfer spelled it out. "Above all, the women agents—who must be young and not without charms—should try to get into relationships with influential people who may, in a moment of weakness borne of intimacy, let escape information that could be useful to us."

His proposal received an enthusiastic response from Oppenheim, as well as from Ambassador von Wangenheim in Constantinople, and in early April Prüfer began his recruitment drive. In short order, he'd managed to procure the services of two Jewish émigrés, Isaac Cohn and Moses Rothschild, who were leaving Palestine for Egypt. While Rothschild made contact with a German spy nest at Shepheard's Hotel, the favored lodging and watering hole of the British high command in Cairo, Cohn undertook an extensive tour of the British coastal defenses in Alexandria and along the Suez Canal.

The spymaster clearly took his new enterprise very seriously and as a true patriot was ready to let whatever affections he felt for Minna Weizmann be trumped by those he held for the kaiser. In early May 1915, Weizmann made the crossing to Egypt as the newest member of Prüfer's spy ring. She probably needed little in the way of persuading; as both a Jew and a socialist, she might as well have been wearing a czarist bull's-eye on her back, and here was the chance for both adventure and revenge.

Initially, Weizmann did very well in her new vocation, her hospital work and the novelty of being a female physician giving her entrée to the upper echelons of British Cairo society. Her luck didn't hold, however. Under the cover of accompanying a badly wounded French soldier home, she managed to reach Italy, but there was observed meeting with the German ambassador in Rome. Unmasked, she was hauled back to Egypt, where she faced a decidedly grim future: internment in a British prisoner-of-war camp at the very least, and possibly execution. Instead, Weizmann's considerable charms combined with old-fashioned chivalry produced a far more pleasant outcome. As related by a Swiss woman who crossed paths with Minna that August and heard her story, "she was so beloved in Cairo and Alexandria, and held in such respect that people gave her unwavering denial [of being a spy] credence." Ironically, even the czar's consul in Cairo vouched for Minna's innocence and arranged for her safe passage back to Russia. It was while staying at a hotel in Romania, in transit to the homeland she had escaped from two years earlier, that Weizmann desperately reached out to the Swiss woman.

"She revealed everything to me," Hilla Steinbach-Schuh explained to a German official, "and fervently begged me to inform the German embassy in Constantinople of her deportation, especially that Herr Prüfer should be advised of this."

But the remarkably tender treatment shown Minna Weizmann—she would not only survive the war, but eventually return to Palestine to work for the medical service of the Zionist women's organization, Hadassah— may have also stemmed from her lineage. Her older brother was Chaim Weizmann, a renowned chemist who had immigrated to Great Britain in 1904 and who in 1915 was already working closely with the British munitions industry to improve their war-making capability; Chaim would go on to become the first president of the state of Israel, while Minna's nephew Ezer would serve as its seventh. That lineage may also explain why Minna has been largely excised from the history books, and even from the Weizmann family's memory (Chaim made not a single reference to his sister in his memoirs); for "the first family of Israel" to count among its members someone who not only spied for Germany but whose spymaster lover went on to become a senior Nazi diplomat is surely one of those awkward family stories best left untold.

Even before learning of Minna Weizmann's fate, however, Curt Prüfer had seen his fledgling Egyptian spy ring largely shut down, a result of Italy's joining the Triple Entente in May and the consequent severing of the German embassy "ratline." Still, Prüfer's bold initiative had greatly impressed his superiors in both the military and intelligence spheres. As Lieutenant Colonel Kress von Kressenstein, the commander of German forces in Palestine, informed Berlin, "Curt Prüfer is indispensable as the leader of the intelligence service."

ON MAY 9, 1915, T. E. Lawrence's younger brother, twenty-two-year-old Frank, stationed in the Arras sector of the Western Front, was doing repair work on a forward trench in preparation for an assault when he was struck by three shrapnel fragments from a German artillery shell. Whether it was true or not, for soldiers routinely dissemble about such things, Frank's commanding officer reported in his condolence letter to the Lawrence parents that their son had died instantly.

The news shattered Sarah Lawrence. By most accounts, Frank had been her favorite child, and since being shipped off to France in February he had written her long, discursive letters filled with descriptions of the foibles of military life and his everyday existence at the front.

T. E. Lawrence learned of Frank's death in a telegram from his parents in mid-May. For whatever reason, he waited to respond until he had received more information from his father through the mail. It wasn't until June 4 that he finally scribbled out a hasty note to his parents on a telegram form:

> I haven't written since I got your wire as I was waiting for details. Today I got Father's two letters. They are very comfortable reading, and I hope that when I die there will be nothing more to regret. The only thing I feel a little is that there was no need, surely, to go into mourning for him? I cannot see any cause at all. In any case, to die for one's country is a sort of privilege. Mother and you will find it more painful and harder to live for it than he did to die, but I think that at this time, it is one's duty to show no signs that would distress others, and to appear bereaved is surely under this condemnation.
>
> So please, keep a brave face to the world. We cannot all go fighting, but we can do that, which is in the same kind. N[ed].

Perhaps the note's most interesting aspect, beyond its startling cold-ness, was Lawrence's invocation of a kind of puerile patriotism that he had long derided. In any event, Sarah Lawrence was hardly in the mood to adhere to this stiff advice from her son. Shortly after, she wrote Ned another letter, in which she evidently (evidently because this letter has never been found) upbraided him for not expressing his love for her in her hour of grief. If Sarah Lawrence hoped this would stir a softening in her second son, she was to be disappointed:

> *Poor Dear Mother,*
> *I got your letter this morning, and it has grieved me very much. You* <u>*will*</u> *never never understand any of us after we are grown up a little.* <u>*Don't*</u> *you ever feel that we love you without our telling you so? I feel such a contemptible worm for having to write this way about things. If you only knew that if one thinks deeply about anything, one would rather die than say anything about it. You know, men do nearly all die laughing, because they know death is very terrible, and a thing to be forgotten till after it has come.*
> *There, put that aside, and bear a brave face to the world about Frank. In a time of such fearful stress in our country it is one's duty to watch very carefully lest one of the weaker ones be offended; and you know, we were always the stronger, and if they see you broken down they will all grow fearful about their ones at the front.*

Lawrence next wrote his parents about a week later; he made no reference to Frank—indeed, he rarely mentioned him by name in any subsequent correspondence—and instead spent the bulk of the brief note describing the weather just then in Cairo.

DJEMAL PASHA WAS in a much-improved mood by early June 1915. He had good reason to be. When the Allied forces had come ashore at Gal-lipoli on April 25, it largely mooted the possibility of a landing somewhere in Syria. Better yet, with both sides pouring more men and matériel into that narrow strip of battlefield, the Syrian governor had been provided with the means to be rid of the more troublesome military units in his zone. In response to Constantinople's urgent call for reinforcements, Dje-mal had immediately begun dispatching his Arab-dominated regiments in northern Syria to Gallipoli, replacing them with newly mustered Turk-ish formations from the Anatolian interior—utterly green soldiers, per-haps, but at least their loyalty could be relied upon. And of course, the removal of the potentially mutinous Arab troops meant that the schemes of the French consulate plotters, and whatever other separatist-minded Arab traitors might be skulking about, were now far less dangerous.

There had also been good news in regard to the troublesome Hussein family in the Hejaz. Building on the lavish treatment he had bestowed upon Faisal in Jerusalem and Damascus, Djemal had sent word to Constantinople that the charm offensive should continue once the young sheikh reached the Ottoman capital. That directive had been followed; in early May, the offending Medina civilian governor was transferred, allowing Faisal and Enver Pasha to fashion an accord that suggested a full rapprochement between the Young Turks and the irksome Hussein in Mecca. That was certainly the estimation of Max von Oppenheim, who had two long meetings with Faisal in Constantinople, and of Djemal himself when Faisal returned to Syria in late May. In an emotional address before Djemal's senior military staff at the German Hospice, Hussein's son had professed his undying loyalty to both the empire and the cause of pan-Islamic jihad.

There had even been some progress with the locust plague. Certainly the ravages of that infestation would be sorely felt in the autumn harvest, but through the energetic efforts of the Jewish scientist Aaron Aaronsohn and his modern trenching techniques, it appeared that full-scale catastrophe had been averted.

Yet amid this brighter outlook, a new crisis had engulfed the empire—or rather, an old one had erupted anew.

Within the Ottoman court, the Christian Armenians of Anatolia had long been regarded as potential fifth columnists for Christian invaders—and especially for its Russian archenemies—and for just as long the Armenians had suffered periodic massacres at the hands of their Turkish and Kurdish Muslim neighbors. The most recent bout of slaughter, in the 1890s, had led to the deaths of at least fifty thousand Armenians in a matter of days.

This historical animus had been rekindled by the regime's call to jihad against the "Christian enemies" in November 1914. The Armenians—ethnically and linguistically apart, as well as numerous enough to pose a plausible threat—were uniquely vulnerable to a spark that might set off a new wave of anti-Armenian fury. That spark had come with a Russian offensive into eastern Anatolia, when the Armenians became the perfect scapegoats for explaining away Turkish setbacks on the battlefield. Thus the stage was set: in the rhetoric of the Constantinople regime, and in the minds of many of its Turkish and Kurdish subjects, the some two million Armenians of Anatolia were now the enemy within.

On April 24, on the eve of the Allied landings at Gallipoli, Interior Minister Talaat had ordered the arrest of hundreds of Armenian civic leaders in Constantinople, and simultaneously instructed the governors of those provinces with a substantial Armenian population to immediately close down on all Armenian "revolutionary and political organizations" and arrest their leaders. This directive, carrying the suggestion that a credible Armenian secessionist movement actually existed, had terrible consequences; in the eyes of many government officials in the hinterlands, *all* Armenians were the enemy. Within days of Talaat's directive, tens of thousands of ordinary Armenian civilians were being pulled from their homes, to be force-marched to some unspecified "relocation zone" elsewhere, or in many cases simply butchered where they stood.

Given the porousness of Turkey's frontiers, as well as the presence of Western mission schools throughout the empire, reports had soon started coming into Constantinople telling of massacres of Armenians across the breadth of Anatolia, of corpses lining the routes of their forced marches into the countryside. As the horror stories multiplied, on May 24, the foreign ministers of the Triple Entente issued a proclamation vowing that the Young Turk leadership would be held responsible for "these new crimes of Turkey against humanity and civilization."

Constantinople's response was one of defiance; three days after the Entente proclamation, the Turkish cabinet approved the "Provisional Law of Relocation." Without specifically citing the Armenians, the law stated that the army was now "authorized and compelled to crush in the most severe way" any sign of resistance or aggression among the population. To do so, it had the power "to transfer and relocate the populations of villages and towns, either individually or collectively, in response to military needs, or in response to any signs of treachery or betrayal." As for where this potentially vast sea of internal deportees might be sent, Talaat and Enver had already selected a spot: gathered up from across Anatolia, most would be herded down to the barren reaches of northern Syria. The insanity inherent in this scheme, of uprooting a vast population and casting it into a land already devastated by the deprivations of war, would play out to obscene result: by best estimate, some 800,000 of the Armenian deportees were to perish—starved, shot, or beaten to death—en route.

The consensus among historians is that Djemal Pasha stood very much apart from his Young Turk coleaders in his response to the expulsions. In June, the first survivors of the death marches began to trickle into the north Syrian city of Aleppo, a way station toward their intended destination, the "relocation zone" of Deir al-Zour some one hundred miles to the east. Visiting Aleppo, Djemal Pasha was horrified by what he saw. Reiterating a March decree that commanded his army to protect the Armenians, he lobbied Constantinople to impose the order on military units where it really mattered, in Anatolia. That plea was ignored.

Getting no satisfaction from Constantinople, Djemal allowed thousands of Armenians to remain in Aleppo rather than continue their death march, and despite the deepening hunger and food shortages spreading through Syria, he ordered an increase of government food aid to the refugees. Testament to his love of order and regulations, he issued a rash of new edicts directing that the army regulate and maintain the food supply for the Armenians, that cars and horses be procured for their transportation, even that each refugee be given a financial allowance. But implicit in the stacks of documents that the Syrian governor signed in his office each day was the notion that his regime actually had the wherewithal to carry out these initiatives, never mind that all evidence—evidence that started just outside Djemal's office windows and stretched to the farthest corners of his realm—argued otherwise. It was as if he fancied himself the administrator of a canton of peacetime Switzerland, rather than of a poor and highly fractured region the size of Italy that was being ravaged by war, hunger, and disease. In the face of the Armenian crisis, as with so many other problems that came his way, Djemal responded with a mixture of bluster, threats, and pleas, and when none of that worked, he simply averted his gaze. By September, with the crisis worsening, he issued a new edict, making it a criminal offense to photograph the Armenians.

SOMETHING UNEXPECTED HAPPENED to Aaron Aaronsohn in the Palestinian village of Katra, when an elderly Arab man approached him with the words "zatna mamnounin"—"we are grateful to you." As the agronomist noted in his diary that evening, "the Arabs did not speak that way to Jews only twenty years ago. The job I undertake is a hard one indeed, but to compel the natives to declare, even if they are false in their hearts, zatna mamnounin to the Jews, for them to realize they are helpless in such calamities if we don't help them out, that is already worthwhile."

As the head of Djemal's locust eradication program, Aaronsohn traveled the length of the Syrian plague zone that spring of 1915, giving public lectures and holding field workshops on how best to combat the pestilence. At his urging, Djemal Pasha decreed that every man, woman, and child was to collect six rotels, about forty pounds, of locust eggs for destruction or face an exorbitant fine.

But even for a man of unflagging energy, there were times when the enormity of the task cast Aaronsohn into despair. Despite all the eradication efforts, the swarms continued to expand—at least one was credibly measured at one mile wide and seven miles long—as did the scope of their destruction. Ever more of lowland Judea, normally a verdant green at that time of year, became a study in brown: mile after mile of orchards stripped bare of both fruit and leaf, fields so devoid of vegetation they appeared set in winter fallow.

As crises everywhere have a tendency to do, the locust plague also laid bare the inequalities and deficiencies of Syrian society. Despite the extraordinary powers given him by Djemal, the response Aaronsohn typically encountered among local bureaucrats and military officers he tried to enlist to the eradication effort fell somewhere between uninterest and defiance. In Jaffa, he had been compelled to shame the *kaimmakam*, or local governor, into attending his public lecture, only to watch the man pointedly leave the auditorium halfway through. The old man in the village of Katra notwithstanding, the far more common response in Arab villages was resignation; to them, the locusts were *djesh Allah*, or "God's army," and it was futile, perhaps even sacrilegious, to resist it. Also laid bare was officialdom's resentment of the Jewish colonists, which was always simmering just beneath the surface. Ottoman tax officials were punctilious in handing out fines for insufficient egg collection in Jewish villages, while those same shortfalls—and in many cases complete inactivity—in Arab villages were ignored. In a particularly outrageous case, Aaronsohn reported, shortly after all the plowhorses in the Jewish settlement of Petah Tikvah had been taken away under the war requisitions statute, their owners were fined under the locust eradication statute for failing to plow their fields. Time and again, he threatened to resign from his inspector-general position in disgust, only to receive new assurances from Djemal that the problems and inequities would be addressed, that a new day of harmony and collective effort was just around the corner.

At least part of Aaronsohn's discontent, however, was rooted in the deeply personal, a change that had come over him during his travels through Palestine. For the first time, he had begun to question the Ottoman Empire's ability to survive—or, perhaps more accurately, the ability of the Jewish community to survive in her thrall. It went far beyond the petty harassments and corruption he had witnessed. At most every Jewish settlement he'd visited, he had been approached by frightened residents who told of growing tension with their Arab neighbors, of overt threats from local officials brandishing weapons.

The warning signs didn't attach solely to the Jews. In April, Aaronsohn had dispatched his brother Alex to Lebanon, both to see if the locusts had reached there and to check on their youngest sister, Rivka, who had been hustled off to Beirut during those tense days when the Turkish army was searching for Zichron's arms cache. Under the terms of the Capitulations, Christian-dominated Lebanon had always enjoyed a great measure of freedom from Constantinople, and had become a proud and prosperous Francophile enclave in Syria; as Alex reported back, even though Lebanon had escaped the locusts, it was now a sad and broken place, with Turkish soldiers everywhere and even the normally haughty Beirutis living in dread of what might come next. By early June came the most alarming reports yet, dark rumors about the massacre of Armenians in Anatolia. It was just around this time that Aaronsohn's brooding led him to two interlocking conclusions: the Jews in Palestine had to break with the Ottoman Empire. To achieve that break, they had to actively work for its downfall.

The agronomist was undoubtedly helped in reaching this conclusion by his assistant at Athlit, Absalom Feinberg, a twenty-six-year-old firebrand who was engaged to Aaronsohn's sister Rivka. In his home village of Hadera, a Jewish colony just ten miles south of Zichron, Feinberg had formed a local chapter of the Gideonites, the paramilitary organization that both protected Jewish settlements and launched reprisal raids against their perceived Arab enemies. It was an activity well suited to his political outlook, for to Feinberg the Arab-Jewish struggle in Palestine was a contest between "culture and savagery," and there was little doubt which role the Arabs fulfilled. "I have lived among them all my life," he would write, "and it would be difficult to sway me from my opinion that there is no more cowardly, hypocritical, and false race than this one."

But if there was one "race" Feinberg detested even more than the Arab, it was the Turk, and ever since arriving at Athlit he had preached to Aaron Aaronsohn the gospel of revolt, on the need for the Jews of Palestine to rise up and throw off the Turkish yoke.

Aaronsohn, fourteen years Feinberg's senior, may have laughed off his assistant's fiery oratory as the passion of youth, but a turning point of sorts had been reached that previous January when Feinberg and twelve other Hadera residents were arrested on the spurious charge of spying for the British. Managing to escape, Feinberg had made straight for Aaronsohn.

To win the release of the Hadera men, the agronomist contemplated taking the path he had trod so often before—working his network of contacts in the Ottoman bureaucracy, dispensing bribes where needed—but this time Feinberg would have none of it. "Our worst enemy is the Turk," he told Aaronsohn. "Now that the hour of his downfall has struck, can we stand by and do nothing? The Turks are right to suspect us. They know the ruin they are planning for us. Anyone without a rabbit's heart would be proud to spy against them if it would help to bring the English."

Certainly, Feinberg's views hadn't softened during the long days and weeks he had spent with Aaronsohn on the locust eradication campaign. Instead, by that June, it was the agronomist who had been converted.

As for how to work against the Turks—which by extension meant helping the British—the answer was fairly obvious. Over the course of the locust eradication effort, Aaronsohn and his various assistants had covered the length of Palestine, and the scientist now had a stack of reports on his desk detailing local conditions and resources for much of the region. The lists of available resources had quite naturally included the size and location of army camps, supply depots, and gasoline storage facilities, all vital information for a large-scale civic campaign but also for an enemy army. More specifically, these reports and Aaronsohn's own travels confirmed that the Turkish army was concentrated in just a few towns and cities in Palestine, that virtually the entire coastline had been left undefended save for a few motley crews of local gendarmes and rural militia. The British clearly didn't know this or they might have stormed ashore long ago, and this was the most crucial intelligence that Aaronsohn could provide them, a detailed, mile-by-mile report on the opposition to be faced—or more accurately, not to be faced—along the length of Palestine's coast.

As to the question of getting word to the British that a spy ring was waiting to be at their service in Palestine, the answer was even more obvious. In Beirut and Haifa, American warships were continuing to evacuate "neutrals" who wanted to leave the Ottoman Empire, and both port cities boasted thriving black markets in forged documents. While nothing in Syria was easy anymore, getting a messenger on board one of the Egypt-bound evacuation ships was little more than a matter of money and luck.

For Aaronsohn, it was also clear who this messenger should be. Twice in the opening days of the war, his brother Alex had run afoul of the Ottoman authorities, and he was now locked in a dangerous feud with a local functionary. Furthermore, Alex spoke flawless English, courtesy of a three-year residence in New York. So it was that in mid-July 1915 Alex Aaronsohn boarded USS *Des Moines* in Beirut's harbor. Joining him was his "wife," Rivka Aaronsohn. Once past the American warship's first port of call, the Greek island of Rhodes, the couple would continue on to Egypt, where Alex would make straight for the British military intelligence office in Cairo.

THE TRIP DOWN had been a delight: two weeks on a first-class train surrounded by beautiful scenery, broken here and there by stopovers in exquisitely picturesque Anatolian towns. Best of all, William Yale had fallen into the company of Abdul Rahman Pasha al-Yusuf, a member of the Turkish parliament and one of the wealthiest noblemen of Damascus, and been accorded lavish hospitality as the pasha's temporary "adopted son." In fact, just about the only disagreeable moments on the entire journey had been the bedbugs at the hotel in Eskisehir and the sight of the starving Armenian refugees massed along the rail siding in Tarsus. "It was a sad sight to see the poor people," Yale blandly recalled, "uprooted from their homes, going to an unknown destination, the shadow of a great tragedy looming over them." If the American oilman felt any moral uneasiness about his or his company's role in collaborating with the regime that was orchestrating this tragedy, he kept it to himself; William Yale had a delicate task to perform.

After just a few days in the Syrian capital, he took reluctant leave of the pasha to continue on to Jerusalem, where his first order of business was to arrange a meeting with Djemal Pasha. With a haste rather out of character for the Ottoman government, he soon received a summons to the German Hospice on the Mount of Olives.

As his horse-drawn carriage climbed the steep cobblestoned road up the mount on the appointed day, Yale found himself growing increasingly nervous. "I practiced the salaams and salutations I had learned on the trip from Constantinople," he wrote, "and wondered whether they were the proper ones to use for such a powerful person as Djemal."

Yale's anxiety was more than just a case of starstruck jitters. He had come to Jerusalem to secure concessionary rights to a half million acres of Palestine for Standard Oil, and as he well knew, the success or failure of that enterprise rested on his meeting with the Syrian governor. He wasn't at all sure how it might go.

Passing through the wrought-iron gates of the German Hospice, Yale's horse carriage drew to a stop before the main entrance of the magnificent building, where liveried sentries stepped forward to help him down. With his papers and maps, the American oilman was ushered into the ornate main hall, then down a long stone corridor to the anteroom of Djemal's inner sanctum.

As Yale waited there, he fell into conversation with one of the governor's young aides, a naval attaché who spoke English. Welcoming this distraction from his anxiety, Yale became so engrossed in their talk that he took little notice of those coming and going from the room, including the short uniformed man with the close-cropped black beard who eventually emerged from a side door. It wasn't until this man strode briskly up to the receptionist's desk, hopped up on one corner of it, and fixed him with an intent stare that Yale realized it was Djemal Pasha.

"Well, Mr. Yale," he said in elegant French, "get your maps and papers out and show me what you want."

Djemal's informality had the effect of instantly dissolving Yale's nervousness—but also of filling him with a sudden regret. At the last minute, he had decided that asking for the entire half million acres that Standard wanted in Palestine was simply too audacious a request to make at this first meeting with the governor, so Yale had brought only half his maps to the German Hospice. These he quickly spread upon the receptionist desk and pointed out a broad swath of central Judea. Djemal looked on, but judging by the impatient nodding of his head, he wasn't keen on hearing a lot of details. After just a few moments he straightened and gave another curt nod. "Tell me what you need and I'll issue the necessary orders at once."

It was only at that instant, Yale would later contend, that he grasped the gulf of understanding that stood between him and the Syrian governor. If there was oil in Palestine, Djemal Pasha naturally wanted it found and quickly tapped so that his transport trucks could move and his armies could fight their war. But Standard had no intention of doing that. Instead, Yale had come to Palestine merely to buy up concessions and put dibs on the region for Standard in the postwar era.

"As I look back on it now," Yale recounted some twenty years later, "I regret that I didn't tell him the truth."

But he didn't. Instead, with Djemal Pasha's support, Yale quickly obtained the necessary official papers and organized a field expedition. In short order, and with Turkish soldiers and local officials ensuring the full compliance of tribal sheikhs, he had nailed down the mineral concessionary rights to some quarter million acres of central Palestine. His Socony superiors back in Constantinople were understandably thrilled with the news, but apparently so was the Turkish leadership. First, Standard had helped them skirt the British naval blockade by smuggling oil in from Bulgaria, and now Standard was taking the further step—or so the Turks thought—of helping them develop their own oil resources. In late July, the regime resolved to show their gratitude to their friends in Socony's Constantinople office in the time-honored tradition of empires everywhere: the bestowing of medals.

For more fainthearted men, the idea of accepting medals from the Ottoman regime at that particular juncture might have given pause. The expatriate community in Constantinople was by then awash in reports of what was being done to the Armenians, fresh accounts almost daily of the inhabitants of yet another village being slaughtered, of hundreds or thousands more being starved or beaten to death during their marches into exile. But the men of Socony hadn't attained their positions by mixing morality with business, or by pandering to whatever humanitarian concern was currently in vogue. On July 28, the three senior officers of its Constantinople branch—William Bemis, Oscar Gunkel, and Lucien I. Thomas—were ushered into Dolmabahçe Palace for an audience with the sultan. At that ceremony, the Socony officials were awarded the Order of the Osmanieh, one of the highest civilian awards given by the Ottoman Empire, for their "numerous humanitarian services."

IN MID-JULY 1915, T. E. Lawrence sat down to answer a letter he had recently received from his closest sibling, his younger brother Will. At that time, Will was undergoing training at the Cambridge Barracks in Portsmouth to serve as an aerial observer for the Royal Flying Corps.

Given Lawrence's almost pathological reticence to express intimacy, it must have been especially difficult for him to turn to what had been the thrust of Will's letter to him: the death in May of their younger brother, Frank. "Frank's death was, as you say, a shock because it was so unexpected," he wrote. "I don't think one can regret it overmuch, because it is a very good way to take, after all. The hugeness of this war has made one change one's perspective, I think, and I for one can hardly see details at all."

In closing, though, Lawrence struck a softer, almost plaintive tone. "I wonder when it will all end and peace follow? All the relief I get [is] in *The Greek Anthology*, Heredia, Morris and a few others. Do you?"

In July 1915, the war was not yet even a quarter done; there were still more than three years of slaughter and ruin ahead. But the seeds for Lawrence's own dramatic role in that conflict were just then being sown. Those seeds were born of two seemingly disparate events: the arrival in Cairo of a strange letter secreted out of Mecca, and the crossing of an enigmatic twenty-four-year-old man over the torn and shell-pitted no-man's-land of Gallipoli.

BY THE MIDSUMMER of 1915 on Gallipoli, so many men were dying in such a confined space—in some spots, the opposing trenchlines were less than thirty yards apart—that informal truces began to be called in order to gather up the dead. The arrangements were usually worked out by local commanders, so that at a specified time grave-digging parties from both sides would step out into no-man's-land and begin their ghastly work.

This certainly appeared to be the intent of the Ottoman lieutenant who, on the morning of August 20, climbed from his army's forward trench and, under the cover of a white flag, started across no-man's-land. Instead, upon reaching the British line, the young officer announced to his startled hosts that he wished to surrender.

Following standard procedure, the man was bound and blindfolded and passed down through the Med-Ex trenchworks to regimental headquarters. If standard procedure had continued to be followed, he would have been interrogated there by an intelligence officer, then sent on to the central prisoner-of-war stockade before eventual transfer to a POW camp in Cyprus or Egypt. But there was nothing at all standard about this prisoner. His name was Mohammed al-Faroki, and despite his unassuming appearance—he was just twenty-four and very slight—the story he told was so remarkable that successive British officers felt their superiors needed to hear it.

He claimed to be a member of a secret military society called al-Ahd (the Awakening), comprised largely of Arab officers like himself, that had been waiting in vain for months for the right conditions to stage a revolt against their Turkish overseers. Rumors of shadowy fifth-column networks inside the Ottoman Empire had become rather commonplace by that summer, but what was different about Faroki was that he supplied a list of his alleged al-Ahd coconspirators, most of them high-ranking officers, complete with details on which units they commanded and where they were currently deployed.

Testament to the importance given the lieutenant's claims, on August 25, General Ian Hamilton, the overall commander of the Gallipoli campaign, fired off a report to War Secretary Kitchener himself. Deciding that the intelligence unit in Cairo was best equipped to judge the truthfulness of the lieutenant's story, London ordered Faroki put on board a warship bound for Egypt.

At least initially, neither Gilbert Clayton, the overall commander of the British military intelligence unit in Cairo, nor any of his subordinates knew quite what to make of the young man brought to their Savoy Hotel offices on September 10. Their attention was piqued, however, when Faroki suggested the British had squandered a profound military opportunity by not going ashore at Alexandretta in the spring of 1915.

According to Faroki, not only had Alexandretta been guarded primarily by Arab-conscript units at the time, with many of their commanders committed al-Ahd members, but these units had even carefully sabotaged the city's defensive fortifications in anticipation of an imminent British landing force. Those efforts had come to naught, obviously, when the British instead launched their disastrous Gallipoli campaign. That wasn't the worst of it, however. Once Gallipoli started, Djemal Pasha had swiftly sent the Arab units in Alexandretta to the battlefront; as a result, Faroki explained, many of the would-be conspirators of al-Ahd now lay dead on the Gallipoli hillsides, killed by the very "enemy" they had hoped to join.

Up to this point, much of Faroki's story was easy enough to verify. The founder of al-Ahd, a man named Abdul Aziz al-Masri, was living in exile in Cairo, and he was brought in to vouch for Faroki's bona fides.

As for his claim that Alexandretta had been guarded by troops anxious to mutiny, this was precisely what Lawrence had ascertained from his interviews with Ottoman prisoners and had stressed in his lobbying for a landing there. But Faroki had more to tell. A lot more.

For some time, he claimed, he had served as a kind of liaison between al-Ahd and another Arab secret society, al-Fatat, in Damascus. From this linking, al-Ahd had learned of the covert negotiations between al-Fatat and Emir Hussein in Mecca toward staging a joint uprising against the Turks. In the process, al-Ahd had also learned of the secret correspondence between Emir Hussein and the British in Cairo. The upshot of all this was that, if armed and supported by Britain, both Arab secret societies, the civilian al-Fatat and the military al-Ahd, were now prepared to join Emir Hussein in revolt against the Turks.

Such a partnership would come with a price, though: British recognition of an independent Arab nation encompassing virtually the entire Arab world, from Iraq in the east to Syria in the west and extending down to the tip of the Arabian Peninsula. The precise parameters of this Arab nation were open to some limited negotiation—the would-be rebels recognized Britain's colonial claim to Aden and its commercial interests in southern Iraq—but the one absolute precondition was that the French were not to have a controlling presence anywhere. If all that was agreed to, Faroki explained, then the British could have their revolution in the heart of the Ottoman world.

It was here that the young lieutenant's story began to strain credulity. Obviously, Faroki had learned of the secret correspondence between Emir Hussein and Ronald Storrs from somewhere, but apparently no one in the Cairo military intelligence unit had even heard of al-Fatat. As for Faroki's assertion that this cell spoke for a vast network of anti-Ottoman conspirators in Syria, Lawrence, given his long familiarity with the Syrian political scene, was probably in the best position to gauge that claim's veracity, but nothing he had gleaned either before or during the war suggested that such an extensive network existed. Even if it did, anyone with a rudimentary knowledge of Arab society was likely to find the notion of the progressive military and intellectual castes of Syria and Iraq joining in alliance with the archconservative Emir Hussein in Mecca a bit far-fetched.

Except for one thing. Just weeks before Faroki came across at Gallipoli, Hussein had ended an eight-month silence and finally sent a new message to Ronald Storrs. Absent from this letter was Hussein's earlier ambivalence, as well as his sense of proportion. Now he purported to speak for "the whole of the Arab nation," and his demands for cooperation with the British had ballooned beyond mere noninterference in the

Hejaz, to British recognition of independence for practically the entire Arab world.

So grandiose did Storrs find Hussein's demands—he acidly commented that they were "far more than he has the right, the hope, or the power to expect"—that he and Henry McMahon, the new British high commissioner for Egypt, decided that the best response was to simply ignore them altogether. This had been done in McMahon's reply to Hussein, sent shortly before Faroki's appearance.

Everything changed, though, when the specifics of Hussein's July letter were matched up against Faroki's September statements, for what was immediately apparent was that their stipulations and territorial demands almost precisely matched. Viewed in this light, Hussein's vague reference to "the whole of the Arab nation" took on a very different meaning, perhaps not delusions of grandeur by the Hejazi emir but rather an allusion to his secret partnership with the al-Fatat and al-Ahd conspirators. It suddenly occurred to British officials in Cairo that they might have seriously underestimated Hussein, that far more than potentially triggering an insurrection in a remote corner of the Ottoman Empire, the enigmatic old man in Mecca just might hold the key to the entire Middle Eastern theater of the war.

But there was still more. With his customary opaqueness, Hussein had introduced the specter of a ticking clock in his last missive, saying that Britain had thirty days from the receipt of his letter to accept or reject his terms, beyond which the Arabs "reserve to themselves complete freedom of action." Storrs and McMahon had paid little attention to this veiled threat at the time, but as Mohammed al-Faroki now informed them, this ultimatum was the result of a tantalizing offer recently made to Hussein by Djemal Pasha: full Arab independence in the postwar era, provided the Arabs lent wholehearted support to the Turkish-German war effort in the meantime.

The choice before the British, then, could not have appeared more stark: come to an agreement with Hussein and his coconspirators that might paralyze the Ottoman Empire from within, or, conversely, watch Hussein and the Arabs make their peace with Constantinople, a peace that would undoubtedly result in a reinvigorated call to jihad against the Allies, and just might be the spark to finally set the Muslim populations of their colonies aflame. With Prime Minister Asquith and his cabinet kept fully apprised, British diplomats in London and Cairo scrambled to send off a new and far more respectful message to the emir in Mecca. Thus began one of history's most controversial exchanges of secret messages, the so-called McMahon-Hussein Correspondence, the ramifications of which would soon embroil the British government—as well as its future agent in Arabia, T. E. Lawrence—in a complex web of misunderstandings, conflicting promises, and deceit.

In the short term, the revelations of Mohammed al-Faroki enabled Lawrence to return to the goal that had consumed him ever since arriving in Cairo nine months earlier: a British landing at Alexandretta.

FROM THE ATHLIT promontory on clear days, Aaron Aaronsohn and Absalom Feinberg could easily make out the British and French warships that trolled the Palestinian coastline, imposing their blockade. It would be off one of these warships, they'd assumed, that they would eventually receive a message from Alex in Cairo—perhaps delivered by Alex himself. As the days and weeks passed, however, their confidence in this wavered.

After nearly a month with no word, Aaronsohn and Feinberg settled on a risky backup plan. If the wait lasted much longer, Feinberg would take one of the small fishing boats that plied the coast, head straight out for one of the blockade ships, and try to talk his way on board. In mid-August, though, word came that the blockade was being tightened, the Allied warships now given license to destroy on sight any vessel they deemed suspicious; since this criterion surely attached to a strange vessel trying to make an approach, it rendered the backup plan less a risky venture than a suicidal one. Then came more bad news. In late August, it was announced (erroneously, it would turn out) that the refugee boatlift was coming to an end, that USS *Des Moines* would be making just one more call at Haifa harbor on August 30. When that American warship sailed over the horizon, the conspirators believed, so too would their last best chance to make contact with the British.

To Feinberg's urging that he go out on the ship, Aaronsohn stoutly refused. Instead, it was Feinberg, in disguise and carrying a forged Russian passport, who talked his way aboard the *Des Moines*. A week later, he found himself on the docks of Alexandria, Egypt.

Feinberg had just one contact in Egypt, but it turned out to be a good one: a young Christian Arab originally from Haifa who was now working as a courier for the British naval intelligence headquarters at Port Said. In Port Said, Feinberg tracked down his old friend, who quickly arranged a meeting with one of the unit's intelligence officers. That officer happened to be T. E. Lawrence's old partner at Carchemish as well as on the Zin expedition, Leonard Woolley.

What Feinberg didn't know—could not have known—was that Alex Aaronsohn had in fact made contact with British intelligence in Egypt. After a series of rebuffs, he'd finally gained an audience with a senior member of the military intelligence staff in Cairo on August 18. That officer had been T. E. Lawrence's other partner on the Zin expedition, Captain Stewart Newcombe. But that meeting had not gone at all well. Newcombe had taken a wary view of Alex Aaronsohn from the start, and that wariness only deepened when the earnest twenty-six-year-old began detailing the Jewish spy network supposedly standing by in Palestine to aid the British. It had been just two months since Minna Weizmann, Curt Prüfer's protégée, was unmasked as a spy, and British intelligence agents in Egypt were now alerted to the German scheme of employing Jewish refugees from Palestine as conduits. But perhaps what most aroused Newcombe's suspicion was that Alex Aaronsohn appeared to want nothing tangible in return for his services. As a senior intelligence officer, Newcombe was constantly besieged by self-proclaimed spies who, in return for their "valuable information," wanted money or weapons or help with legal problems; it simply didn't gibe that Alex Aaronsohn was offering up this purported treasure trove of information out of the goodness of his heart. As a result, and in what was surely one of the greatest miscalculations of his intelligence career, Newcombe had not only rebuffed Aaronsohn's offer, but ordered him from the country. Of course, Alex had no way of communicating any of this to his brother anxiously waiting back in Palestine; on September 3, just three days before Absalom Feinberg arrived in Alexandria, Alex and his sister Rivka had gone out of that same harbor on a ship bound for New York.

But Feinberg was to have much better luck with Leonard Woolley. Implicitly trusting the intense young man who had been brought before him, Woolley devised a system whereby a British spy ship might periodically troll past the research station in Athlit. Through a prearranged series of codes, the conspirators would signal out to the spy ship when there was information to be collected, and under the cover of darkness, either a small boat or a swimmer would be sent ashore to retrieve it.

There was only one way to both establish the coding system and test the efficacy of this plan: by sneaking Feinberg back into Palestine aboard one of the spy ships. After concluding his arrangements with Woolley, Feinberg waited for the right conditions—a calm sea, a moonless night—for his voyage home.

ONE PERSON WHO knew nothing of Newcombe's and Woolley's dealings with the would-be spies from Palestine that late summer was their former Zin expedition partner, T. E. Lawrence. This was partly due to the compartmentalization policy adhered to by British intelligence in Egypt, and partly to Lawrence's intense focus on one issue: a British landing at Alexandretta. By mid-October, the last pieces of that plan appeared to be falling into place, and the letter he penned to his parents strived for that delicate balance between excitement and sufficient obliqueness to get past the military censors:

"There is going to be a rather busy winter in the Levant," he wrote. "I am pleased on the whole with things. They have gone against us so far that our Government has become more reasonable, and the final settlement out here, though it will take long, will I think, be very satisfactory. We have to thank our [past] failures for that."

For Lawrence, the most excruciating aspect of Faroki's story was his description of the situation that had existed in Alexandretta in the winter of 1915, carrying as it did the suggestion that a British landing force might have practically strolled ashore there. Obviously, circumstances were much changed now, the al-Ahd-dominated military units long since moved elsewhere, but in the autumn of 1915, Lawrence and other advocates of an Alexandretta landing could point to several new factors that made their argument nearly as compelling.

Having sat out the first year of the war, Bulgaria had finally come in on the side of the Central Powers in late September. This meant the enemy now had an unbroken land route and rail line connecting Germany to Turkey, allowing for the quick and easy transfer of troops and weaponry. At the same time, British war planners, finally accepting Gallipoli for the fiasco it had been all along, were quietly drawing up plans for a withdrawal. Taken together, these two developments meant British Egypt was likely to be targeted anew, and by a much-better-equipped enemy. To hamper such an offensive, taking control of the Alexandretta Basin would not merely disrupt the enemy's main supply line, but sever it—and if that action did in fact spark a regional Arab uprising, the Turks would have a whole new set of problems to deal with.

Another new factor argued for Alexandretta, one for which the mercurial personality of Djemal Pasha could be thanked. In tacit opposition to his co-pashas in Constantinople, Djemal had given refuge to at least eighty thousand Armenian survivors of the Anatolian killing fields, and had organized many of the Armenian men into labor battalions. These refugees and labor battalions were concentrated in the Alexandretta region—some eight thousand had been put to work on the railroad tunnels being cut through the Amanus and Taurus Mountains—and even if they might be grateful to the pasha who had at least temporarily saved their lives, this Armenian population would most certainly regard arriving British soldiers as liberators and rush to their side. Attending that, of course, would be the public relations coup—an aspect of war Lawrence was always sensitive to—of Britain freeing untold thousands of Christian Armenians from servitude or death.

Through the strenuous lobbying of Lawrence and other members of the Cairo military intelligence staff, by late October the two most important British officials in Egypt—High Commissioner Henry McMahon and Major General John Maxwell, commander of the Egyptian Expeditionary Force—had been won over to the revived Alexandretta scheme. Better yet, these two men were about to hold a summit meeting with a visiting Lord Kitchener to decide the future course of the war in the eastern Mediterranean. The stars were finally aligning, so much so that Lawrence felt confident the seemingly impregnable walls of military idiocy were about to be breached.

"Things are boiling over this weekend," Lawrence wrote to a friend on November 4, on the eve of the Kitchener summit meeting, "and we have never been so busy before! This is a good omen, and a thing to make one very content."

The meeting between Kitchener, McMahon, and Maxwell took place on a ship off the Aegean island of Mudros on November 10 and 11. After an initial reluctance, the war secretary, too, came to embrace the Alexandretta plan, and fired off a cable to the prime minister urging its immediate approval.

But in London the idea had a more mixed reception. Amid the continuing carnage on the Western Front, the British high command was already struggling to find enough new men to throw into that meat grinder, and the notion of siphoning off matériel and soldiers—the revised Alexandretta plan now called for as many as 100,000 troops—was a difficult sell. Additionally, the misadventure at Gallipoli was hardly an advertisement for the wisdom of new amphibious landings on the Ottoman Front. In a flurry of cables passed between Kitchener's ship and various ministries in London, a debate ensued.

At this crucial moment, a French liaison officer attached to Kitchener's shipboard retinue decided the matter, firing off a cable to Paris alerting his government to the British deliberations.

Having been under the impression that they had killed off the Alexandretta scheme back in the winter of 1915, the French government now felt compelled to do so in more explicit form. On November 13, the French military attaché in London handed a letter to General William Robertson, the chief of the British Imperial General Staff and overall commander of the British army. After reasserting France's economic and political interests in Syria, the letter stated that "French public opinion could not be indifferent to anything that would be attempted in a country that they consider already as being intended to become a part of the future [French-controlled] Syria; and they would require of the French Government that not only could no military operation be undertaken in this particular country before it has been concerted between the Allies, but even that, should such an action be taken, the greater part of the task should be entrusted to the French troops and the Generals commanding them."

Its obtuse diplomatic language aside, the letter essentially repeated France's earlier objections to an Alexandretta landing: since France intended to take over Syria after the war, French forces needed to be in the vanguard of any military operation in the area, and since no French troops could currently be spared for such a mission, that precluded any mission being conducted at all. What was shocking this time around, though, was that the French would actually commit such a squalid argument to paper. British historian Basil Liddell Hart wrote of the French directive that "this must surely be one of the most astounding documents ever presented to an Ally when engaged in a life and death struggle. For it imposed what was really a veto on the best opportunity of cutting the common enemy's life-line and of protecting our own." By acquiescing to such an outrage, Liddell Hart contended, the British General Staff were essentially "accessories to the crime," that crime being that the British in Egypt had now been given no alternative but to await another assault on the Suez Canal, and to then launch their own attack against the very strongest point of the Turkish line—the narrow front of southern Palestine—an approach that was to ultimately cost them fifty thousand more casualties.

To the disbelief of Lawrence and others on the intelligence staff in Cairo, the Alexandretta plan was quashed anew, never to seriously be raised again.

Back in February 1915, when the plan had first been scuttled, Lawrence had bitterly suggested to his family that France was the true enemy in Syria. In the wake of the second scuttling in November 1915 was born an enmity that would cause him to view all future French actions in the region with utter distrust.

SOON AFTER THE death of her son Frank, Sarah Lawrence had chided her second son, "Ned," for something that clearly remained a sore point: his failure to visit Frank at his military boot camp in late 1914, prior to Ned's departure for Egypt. T. E. Lawrence had responded to his mother's criticism with a logic so matter-of-fact as to border on the perverse. "I didn't go say goodbye to Frank," he explained, "because he would rather I didn't, and I knew there was little chance of my seeing him again; in which case, we were better without a parting."

Lawrence had responded very differently in March 1915 when he learned that the ship transporting his brother Will back to England from India was passing through the Suez Canal. Not having seen Will since his visit to Carchemish in 1913, Lawrence had briefly put aside his work at the Savoy Hotel, mounted his Triumph motorcycle, and raced the eighty miles out to Port Suez to meet his brother's ship when it docked.

Just before he got there, however, a skirmish broke out somewhere along the canal, delaying Will's ship. Instead of a face-to-face meeting, all the brothers were able to arrange was a brief ship-to-shore telephone conversation. That same evening, Lawrence remounted his motorcycle and returned to his work in Cairo.

In volunteering to serve as an aerial spotter for the Royal Flying Corps, Will had chosen a position that came with one of the shortest life expectancies for any soldier in World War I. On October 23, 1915, Will was killed when his plane was shot down over France, his body never recovered. He was twenty-six years old, and had been at the front for less than a week.

The effect of losing two brothers in just five months seemed to draw Lawrence even deeper into his emotional shell. For the next several months, his letters home grew steadily more infrequent and terse. Indeed, while he had quickly dropped nearly all mention of Frank in writing to his parents, there is no record of his even acknowledging Will's death at the time, save for one oblique allusion. It was in a short note he sent home that December:

> I'm writing just a few words this morning, because it has surprised me by being Christmas day. I'm afraid that for you it will be no very happy day; however you have still Bob and Arnie left at home, which is far more than many people can have. Look forward all the time. Everything here is as usual, only we had a shower of rain yesterday, and it has been cool lately.

Chapter 7

Treachery

It seems to me that we are rather in the position of the hunters who
divided up the skin of the bear before they had killed it. I personally
cannot foresee the situation in which we may find ourselves
at the end of the war, and I therefore think that any discussion at the
present time of how we are going to cut up the Turkish Empire is chiefly
of academic interest.

BRITISH GENERAL GEORGE MACDONOGH,
DIRECTOR OF MILITARY INTELLIGENCE, JANUARY 7, 1916

On November 16, 1915, T. E. Lawrence penned a note to an old friend, Edward Leeds, one of the Ashmolean curators back in Oxford. It had been just three weeks since the death of his brother Will, and Lawrence was in a forlorn mood. After apologizing for his long silence, he told Leeds it was partly due to the demands of his job, "and partly because I'm rather low because first one and now another of my brothers has been killed. Of course, I've been away a lot from them, and so it doesn't come on one like a shock at all, but I rather dread Oxford and what it may be like if one comes back. Also they were both younger than I am, and it doesn't seem right, somehow, that I should go on living peacefully in Cairo."

If war is an inherently confounding experience, Lawrence could be forgiven that November for finding his particularly so. In the eleven months since he had arrived in Cairo, he had been largely confined to a suite of offices in the Savoy Hotel, a world away from the Western Front killing fields that had taken the lives of his brothers. Even more bewildering, he had expended his greatest energies not on battling the enemy, but engaged in "paper-combat" against the parochial interests of Britain's military bureaucracy and those of its closest ally, France.

The uselessness of those struggles was plain to see on the great map of the Ottoman Empire tacked to the wall of the Savoy offices. In November 1915, after a year of war in that theater and the deaths of hundreds of thousands, the map remained virtually unchanged.

In Gallipoli, the Mediterranean Expeditionary Force still clung to their blood-soaked beachheads, but even those tiny toeholds in Turkey were soon to disappear; in a cruel irony, the Allied withdrawal from Gallipoli, just then about to get under way, was to be the only well-executed phase of the entire campaign. In Anatolia, the suffering of the Armenians continued unabated, and was now being joined by that of the would-be Arab secessionists in Syria, their leadership decimated by Djemal Pasha's secret police. A landing in Alexandretta that might have aided both groups now seemed a dead issue, even if for reasons no one in Cairo could quite discern (it would still be some weeks before the London War Office got around to informing Egypt of the French government's formal spiking of the plan). In its stead, there was now growing talk of a conventional frontal assault against the entrenched Turkish forces at the far end of the Sinai in Palestine. Should that offensive be successful—and the example of Gallipoli offered scant reason to think it would—the British army would then be consigned to a long, slow grind north toward the Turkish heartland. Just about the only bright spot anywhere on that map was in Iraq. There, a British Indian army had steadily advanced up the Tigris River over the past seven months, and by mid-November stood at the gates of Baghdad. Even if that city at the Ottoman periphery were taken, however, it was hard to see its material effect on Constantinople, a thousand miles away.

Almost by default, then, Lawrence had increasingly looked to Arabia as the one place left that afforded a ray of hope, where the unconventional war he was convinced was needed to defeat the Turks might be waged. This hope had been given new vigor just days earlier. In the wake of Mohammed al-Faroki's revelations, the British high commissioner in Egypt, Henry McMahon, had rushed off a new letter to Emir Hussein acceding to nearly all his territorial demands for an independent Arab nation in payment for a British-allied Arab revolt. On November 5, an equally accommodating reply had come in to Cairo from Hussein. A few smaller points still needed to be worked out, but there was now a broad agreement in place for an Arab uprising against Turkey.

Not that Lawrence could possibly have imagined that this truly resolved matters. To the contrary, a perverse mind-set had settled in among the warring European powers by that autumn of 1915, one that suggested the situation in the Middle East was about to become far more complicated and contentious.

To understand this mind-set, one had to appreciate the paralysis that held over the larger map of the war. On the Western Front, the four-hundred-mile-long strip of no-man's-land separating the French and British armies from those of the Germans had barely moved in a year. While much less static, a different kind of stalemate had set in on the Eastern Front. There, after being mauled by German forces on its northwestern frontier in the first days of the war, Russia had taken revenge on the hapless Austro-Hungarian armies on its southwestern, only to be mauled anew when Germany came to Austria-Hungary's rescue. It established a deadly pattern—Russian success against Austria-Hungary negated by German success against Russia—that would continue into 1917. For sheer mindless futility, though, it was hard to compete with the newly opened Southern Front in northeastern Italy. Having belatedly joined the war on the side of the Entente, by November 1915 Italy had already flung its army four times against a vastly outnumbered Austro-Hungarian force commanding the heights of a rugged mountain valley, only to be slaughtered each time; before war's end, there would be twelve battles in the Isonzo valley, resulting in some 600,000 Italian casualties.

Of course, stasis is a two-way street, and if this broader map yielded no good news for the Entente, the same held true for the Central Powers.

Given this stunning lack of progress earned at such horrific cost, it might seem reasonable to imagine that the thoughts of the various warring nations would now turn toward peace, to trying to find some way out of the mess. Instead, precisely the opposite was happening.

It's a question that has faced peoples and nations at war since the beginning of time, and usually produced a terrible answer: in contemplating all the lives already lost, the treasure squandered, how to ever admit it was for nothing? Since such an admission is unthinkable, and the status quo untenable, the only option left is to escalate. Thus among the warring states in Europe at the end of 1915 it was no longer a matter of satisfying what had brought them into the conflict in the first place—and in many cases, those reasons had been shockingly trivial—but to expand beyond them, the acceptable terms for peace not lowered, but raised. This conflict was no longer about playing for small advantage against one's imperial rivals, but about hobbling them forever, ensuring that they might never again have the capability to wage such a devastating and pointless war.

But defeating one's enemies is only half the game; for a war to be truly justifiable one has to materially gain. In modern European custom, that need had been sated by the payment of war reparations into the victor's coffers, the grabbing of a disputed province here or there, but that seemed rather picayune in view of this conflict's cost. Instead, all the slaughter was to be justified by a new golden age of empire, the victors far richer, far grander than before. Naturally, this simply propelled the cycle to its logical, murderous conclusion. When contemplating all to be conferred upon the eventual winners, and all to be taken from the losers, how to possibly quit now? No, what was required was greater commitment—more soldiers, more money, more loss—to be redeemed when victory finally came with more territory, more wealth, more power.

While the Central Powers had their own imperial wish list in the event of victory, one that also grew more grandiose as time went on, for the Entente powers of Great Britain, France, and Russia there really was only one place that offered the prospect of redemption on the scale required: the fractured and varied lands of the Ottoman Empire. Indeed, by the autumn of 1915 that empire was now often referred to by cynics in the Entente capitals simply as "the Great Loot."

For all three powers, the war in the Middle East was now to become about satisfying the imperial cravings—desiderata, as it was politely known—they had long harbored. The czars of Russia had been angling to grab Constantinople for at least two hundred years. Similarly, France had enjoyed a special status as protector of the Ottoman Empire's Catholic population in Syria since the sixteenth century; if that empire was to be dismantled, then that region should rightly go to her. For its part, Britain had long been obsessed with protecting the land approaches to India, its "jewel in the crown," from encroachment by its imperial rivals—paradoxically, Russia and France foremost among them. Then there was the religion factor. All three of the principal Entente powers were devoutly Christian nations in 1915, and even after six hundred years it still grated many that the Christian Holy Land lay in Muslim hands. In carving up the Ottoman Empire there was finally the chance to replay the Crusades to a happier ending.

What probably most propelled these old desires into the realm of possibility were the secret negotiations between Britain and Emir Hussein. As those negotiations became less secret among the Allies, and the prospect of an Arab revolt more real, it produced not so much a piquing of imperial appetites as a mighty collective slavering.

By late November, France, tipped to Britain's dealings with Hussein and anxious to stake its claim, would hastily compile its own ambitious set of desiderata for the region. French demands would soon be joined by those of Russia. Confronted by the gluttonous wishes of its principal allies—allies today perhaps, but probably rivals again tomorrow—Britain would suddenly decide that it too was in an acquisitive mood, and never mind the promises it had so recently made to Hussein. Maneuvering for their own spot at the feeding trough would ultimately come Italy and even neutral Greece. All of this would quickly make military considerations in the Middle East subordinate to political ones, and move the decision-making process away from military officers in the field to diplomats and politicians huddled in staterooms. If the chief distinguishing characteristic of the former had been their ineptitude, at least their intent had been clear; with the rise of the statesmen, and with different power blocs jockeying for advantage, all was about to become shrouded in treachery and byzantine maneuver.

By coincidence, the man who was to play a singular role in generating that intrigue arrived in Cairo on November 17, 1915, just the day after Lawrence had complained to Edward Leeds of his peaceful life there. His name was Mark Sykes—or, more formally, Sir Tatton Benvenuto Mark Sykes, 6th Baronet of Sledmere.

Few people in history have so heedlessly caused so much tragedy. At the age of thirty-six, the handsome if slightly doughy Sykes epitomized that remarkable subclass of British aristocrats of the late imperial age known as the "Amateurs." Despite its somewhat derogatory modern connotation, the term derives from the Latin "for the love of," and in this context denoted a select group of wealthy and usually titled young men whose breeding, education, and freedom from careerist pressures—it was considered terribly déclassé for such men to hold down bona fide jobs—allowed them to dabble over a broad range of interests and find all doors flung open to them. Raised on a thirty-thousand-acre ancestral estate as the only child of a Yorkshire aristocrat, Sykes, like so many of his fellow Amateurs, seemed intent on living the lives of ten "ordinary" men. Educated at Cambridge, he had traveled extensively throughout the Ottoman Empire, authored four books, been a soldier in the Boer War, served as parliamentary secretary to the chief administrator of Ireland and honorary attaché to the British embassy in Constantinople—and those were just the highlights up to the age of twenty-five. In the succeeding eleven years before his arrival in Cairo that autumn, he had married and had sired five children—a sixth would soon be on the way—won a reputation as an accomplished caricaturist, invented an early version of the overhead projector and, since 1912, served as the Conservative member of Parliament for Hull Central.

Sykes's appearance in Cairo was a result of the most recent addition to his résumé. The previous spring, Lord Kitchener had appointed him as an advisor to the de Bunsen Committee, an interdepartmental government board designed to guide the British cabinet on Middle Eastern affairs. Unsurprisingly, Sykes had quickly emerged as the dominant member of that committee, and in July 1915 set out on an extended fact-finding mission to the region with the intention of imparting his firsthand impressions to the cabinet upon his return.

Lawrence and Sykes first met that August, during Sykes's stopover in Cairo on the outgoing leg of his fact-finding mission. Like most everyone else, Lawrence took a quick liking to the charming and personable MP. He and others in the Cairo intelligence staff were also gratified to finally find someone in the senior branches of the British government who appeared to appreciate their ideas for unconventional warfare. That estimate was initially fortified upon Sykes's return to Egypt in November; he had spent the previous two months meeting with officials in British India, a group vehemently opposed to the war-by-proxy plots emanating out of British Egypt, and the returned Sykes made no secret that his sympathies lay with the Egyptian approach.

Yet for all his astounding achievements, Mark Sykes exemplified another characteristic common among the British ruling class of the Edwardian age, a breezy arrogance that held that most of the world's messy problems were capable of neat solution, that the British had the answers to many of them, and that it was their special burden—no less tiresome for being God-given—to enlighten the rest of humanity to that fact. Sykes's special skill in this regard was a talent for bold and refreshingly concise writing, the ability to break down complex issues into neat bulleted-point formulas that provided the illusion of almost mathematical simplicity. He was a master of the PowerPoint presentation nearly a century before it existed.

One example—there were to be many more in the years just ahead—was an analysis he composed during his August stopover in Cairo that purported to chart the various intellectual elements at work in the Middle East. After first dividing those elements between the "Ancients" and the "Moderns," Sykes offered up subcategories. Thus, Class I of the Ancients were the orthodox ("hard, unyielding, bigoted and fanatical"), while Class I of the Moderns ("the highest type") denoted "a person of good family who has entirely absorbed a Western education," not to be confused with the Class II Moderns, who were "the poor, incompetent, or criminal who have received an inferior European education and whose minds by circumstances or temperament or both are driven into more sinister channels than the first class." Not content to end there, Sykes proceeded to apply his formula to various regions of the Middle East, offering his British readers an easy-to-follow guide to their nation's standing in each. It was not a pretty picture in a place like Egypt, frankly: from the Class I, II, and III Ancients, absolute hostility, benevolent apathy, and mild approval, respectively, joined to constitutional opposition and unforgiving enmity among the Class I and II Moderns.

It certainly wasn't the first time such silly racialist formulas had been put to paper, but it spoke volumes to the British leadership's own smugness—as well, no doubt, to their perpetually harried states in grappling with a conflict that spanned the globe—that such drivel, well organized and confidently stated, took on the flavor of wisdom. Upon Sykes's return to London and a bravura performance before the de Bunsen Committee, the British government would essentially hand off to the thirty-six-year-old Amateur one of the thorniest—and from a historical standpoint, most profoundly important—assignments of World War I: sorting out the competing territorial claims of Great Britain and her allies in the Middle East.

Only belatedly would British leaders recognize another aspect of Sykes's character, one that might have given them pause had they spotted it earlier. Perhaps to be expected given his frenetic pace and catholic range of interests, Mark Sykes had a very hard time keeping his facts, even his own beliefs, straight. Impressed by the last person he had spoken with, or the last idea that had popped into his fecund mind, he was forever contradicting positions or policies he had advocated earlier—often mere days earlier.

Lawrence began to get a glimmer of this in the time he spent around Sykes during that November stopover. There was something altogether disquieting about the cavalier way the young MP disregarded inconvenient evidence that didn't fit his currently held view, often only to seize on that same evidence when his opinion changed. As Lawrence would later write in *Seven Pillars*, Sykes was "the imaginative advocate of unconvincing world movements . . . a bundle of prejudices, intuitions, half-sciences. His ideas were of the outside, and he lacked patience to test his materials before choosing his style of building. He would take an aspect of the truth, detach it from its circumstances, inflate it, twist and model it."

But there was yet another side to Sykes's personality that boded ill for the crucial role he was about to assume. It seems the man was something of a sneak. Whether due to a need to prove he was always the cleverest person in the room, or a con man's desire to get one over simply for the sport of it, the young Amateur would make an art form out of bending the truth to suit his needs, of playing one side against another by withholding or manipulating crucial information. The result would be a most peculiar place in history for Mark Sykes: it's hard to think of any figure who, with no true malice intended and neither a nation nor an army at his disposal, was to wreak more havoc on the twentieth century than the personable and brilliant young aristocrat from Yorkshire, havoc that a small group of his countrymen, including T. E. Lawrence, would try very hard to set right.

Which isn't to suggest that Sykes uniquely possessed these traits. Indeed, when it came to duplicity, the Amateur had a lot of very accomplished competitors in the Middle East just then.

AT THE SAME time that Sykes was holding court in Cairo, an enigmatic robed figure was circulating through the bazaars and teahouses of a number of towns in western Syria. He was an exceedingly soft-spoken man in his midthirties, well-off and cultured, judging by the quality of his dress and classic Arabic diction. Because of his pale complexion and blue eyes, most who encountered him probably took the traveler for a Circassian, that ancient mountain people originally from the Black Sea region, many of whom have almost Nordic features. This was a misconception Curt Prüfer likely made no effort to correct. He was conducting this clandestine mission at the behest of Djemal Pasha. Its purpose was to find out where the real sympathies of the people of Syria lay.

By that autumn, the need for an unbiased assessment of Syrian public opinion was becoming acute both for the governor and his German advisors. With the Allied misadventure in Gallipoli showing signs of winding down, there was once again the threat of an enemy landing somewhere on the Syrian coast. If the Allies put ashore in Lebanon, how would the Lebanese Christians and the Druze religious minority respond? And what of the Jews, centered just below in Palestine? With the persecution of the Armenians in Anatolia continuing unabated, surely many in Syria's Jewish community were worried they might be next. Above all, what of the Arabs? Djemal Pasha had already begun to move against the Arab conspirators unmasked in the French consulate documents, and Emir Hussein in Mecca was a continuing source of concern, but what of the great masses of Arabs elsewhere?

For five weeks, and assuming a variety of personas and disguises, Prüfer wandered Syria. Along the way he talked with Jewish colonists, Arab shopkeepers, and Christian landowners, with westernized aristocrats and Bedouin sheikhs and fellaheen. By early December 1915, the German spy felt he'd sufficiently taken the nation's pulse to report his findings to Djemal and the German embassy in Constantinople.

In brief, he had found the greatest discontent among the Christians, nearly all of whom, he believed, secretly sympathized with the Entente powers. But Prüfer saw little real danger here, both because of the Syrian Christians' comparatively small numbers and because their "aptitude for treason" was surpassed by a "cowardice that prevents them from trying to realize their dreams."

Of somewhat greater concern, in his estimation, was the Jewish population, and specifically of that subgroup among them known as the Zionists. While "official Zionism says it only wants to create in Palestine a center for Jewish language and civilization, and is not at all interested in politics," Prüfer wrote, this was clearly not true. Rather, their ultimate aim was to create an autonomous Jewish state in Palestine, a goal far more likely to be achieved by an Entente victory than a Central Powers one. Still, and for much the same reasons as with the Christians, Prüfer saw little cause for alarm: "Being by nature cowardly and without initiative, the Jews will not dare to commit subversive acts unless an armed enemy force was already in the country."

Most heartening was what the German spy had discerned in the Arab Muslim community, by far the largest of the three. Partly due to the "fair and severe" measures Djemal had already conducted against those Arab leaders suspected of secessionist leanings, Prüfer found the Arab independence movement in a greatly weakened state. "Among the middle classes, reformism has barely any supporters," he wrote, "and among the small landowners, merchants and workers, who constitute the bulk of the population, the government and its cause seems to be popular." Even if an Arab uprising was somehow launched, Prüfer suggested in his usual trenchant way, it would receive little mass support "due to the frivolousness of the population."

This generally rosy assessment came with a major caveat, however; if the British did put ashore in Syria, latent sympathies would come to the fore. In that eventuality, the invaders could certainly find willing local collaborators. Prüfer provided Djemal with a long list of the names of "unreliables," mostly prominent Christian and Muslim Arab businessmen, as well as "all Zionist party chiefs," who should be immediately sent into internal exile in the case of an Allied landing.

This last suggestion triggered alarm within the German embassy. Just that August, Djemal had made use of the documents seized from the French consulate in Beirut to execute eleven prominent Arab leaders in one of the city's main squares. That event had stirred outrage in the Arab world, and Germany certainly didn't need one of its own intelligence officers providing the Syrian governor with more names for his hit list. In forwarding the report to the foreign ministry in Berlin, the German ambassador in Constantinople noted that he'd given Prüfer the following warning: "At the slightest indiscretion, the population could raise the charge that we are causing rigorous measures, like expulsions. In the future, please couch your suggestions to Djemal of this nature with cautious restraint."

That admonition may have come too late. With Prüfer's report already in hand, the Syrian governor seemed to conclude that his flexible approach to problem-solving—alternating between the rose and the dagger without readily discernible pattern—was the best way to outwit his growing list of enemies. On December 18, he had ordered a much larger roundup of those implicated in the French consulate files, a dragnet ultimately ensnaring some sixty members of the Arab intelligentsia of Beirut and Damascus.

Perhaps those arrests put Djemal in a happier mood, for he showed far greater magnanimity when another man of increasingly questionable loyalty, Aaron Aaronsohn, came calling at his Damascus office in January.

THE SPY SHIP never came.

On the moonless night of November 8, 1915, Absalom Feinberg had finally been slipped back ashore at Athlit from a British spy ship, and had immediately given an ecstatic Aaron Aaronsohn the good news: he'd made contact, the British eagerly awaited whatever intelligence they could pass on, and arrangements were now in place to make that happen.

With the spy ship scheduled to return in two weeks, the two men immediately set out on long-range reconnaissance missions to update their information, Aaronsohn heading north, Feinberg to the south. Under the guise of conducting scientific surveys for the agricultural research station, they surreptitiously noted the location of new Turkish army camps and supply depots and trenchworks, tracked the movements of trains and troop formations, meticulously jotted down in tiny script in their notebooks most anything they thought might be useful to the British.

But when they returned to Athlit and waited on the appointed night, the spy ship didn't come, nor on the next night, or the one after. As their wait dragged into early December, Aaronsohn and Feinberg grew increasingly puzzled, and then anxious; obviously, something somewhere had gone wrong, but the longer their wait extended, the more likely their nocturnal activities would come to the attention of the Turkish militia's night patrols. On the other hand, if they relaxed their vigil and missed the boat's appearance, the British might conclude that the conspirators had backed out or been caught and simply give up.

Despairing of the spy ship ever showing, by December 8, the impetuous Feinberg had come up with a new plan: he would reestablish contact by somehow maneuvering his way past the Turkish armies massed in southern Palestine, then cross over the Sinai no-man's-land to the British lines at the far end. If stopped by a Turkish patrol, he would claim to be doing fieldwork on locusts. That alibi had the benefit of credence. Just days earlier, a great new swarm of locusts had appeared over Judea, the first since the previous spring, and Aaronsohn had determined they were coming from Egypt over the Sinai land bridge. It still seemed a terribly risky venture, but, consumed by his own anxieties over reaching the British, Aaronsohn relented; Feinberg set out for the south that very night.

Soon after there came anxiety of a very different sort. In Constantinople, Aaronsohn's younger sister Sarah had for some time been looking for a way to escape her unhappy marriage and return to her family in Palestine. In mid-November, with her husband away on an extended business trip, she found her opening upon hearing that a Jewish relief official would soon be departing Constantinople for a tour of the Jewish colonies. Pleading to be taken along, on November 26, the twenty-five-year-old Sarah boarded a train at Haidar Pasha station and set off on the long journey home.

Dark rumors had abounded for months of what was happening to the Armenians in the Anatolian countryside, but the combination of poor communications and rigorous censorship had enabled the Ottoman regime to conceal the extent of the brutality from the general population to a fairly remarkable degree. This didn't apply, of course, to anyone whose travels took them through the killing fields. By the time Sarah Aaronsohn was reunited with her brother in Palestine on December 16, she was in a state of shock over what she had witnessed during her journey. The agronomist would later recount that "she saw the bodies of hundreds of Armenian men, women and children lying on both sides of the railway. Sometimes Turkish women were seen searching the corpses for anything that might be of value; at other times dogs were observed feeding on the bodies. There were hundreds of bleached skeletons." In the grisliest incident, Sarah claimed she had watched as her train was besieged by thousands of starving Armenians at one remote station; in the stampede, dozens fell beneath the wheels of the train, much to the delight of its conductor. Sarah fainted away at the spectacle, only to be remonstrated by two Turkish officers when she came to for her evident lack of patriotism.

Aaron Aaronsohn had long heard the Armenian horror stories on his own travels, but had tended to discount them as part of the eternal Syrian rumor mill. To have them confirmed by his sister—and to learn the slaughter was ongoing—made it all hideously real. It also led the agronomist inexorably to a grim question: who next? If the Young Turks could perpetrate this atrocity against the nation's two million Armenians, how much easier to do the same to its eighty thousand Jews?

Then came more bad news. In the Sinai, Absalom Feinberg had been stopped by a Turkish army patrol not at all impressed by his locust fieldwork cover story. Instead, they had hauled him back to Beersheva under suspicion of being a spy. In early January, he was transferred to the prison in Jerusalem to await possible trial; if found guilty of the worst potential charge against him, that of treason, Feinberg would undoubtedly have a quick appointment with the gibbet-gallows.

It was out of concern for his coconspirator's life that brought Aaron Aaronsohn to Djemal Pasha's Damascus office on the afternoon of January 12. Sensing that appeals for mercy or protestations of innocence may not work in this case, the agronomist turned to the same instrument that had failed Feinberg: locusts. To combat the new infestation, he told Djemal, he would return to his post as inspector general of the locust eradication program, the position he had finally left in disgust over government interference eight months before. The one precondition, however, was that Aaronsohn have the services of his most valuable and important assistant, a young man named Absalom Feinberg recently caught up in some misunderstanding in the Sinai.

On Djemal's order, Feinberg was swiftly released from his Jerusalem jail. Any euphoria the two would-be spies may have felt was undoubtedly tempered, however: their long and fruitless campaign to reach the British remained stalled.

No ONE GRASPED the whole picture. Given the chaos of war and the difficulty of communications, different branches of the British government negotiated with different wartime allies—or with parties they hoped to turn into allies—with no one realizing until too late that the agreements thus forged might conflict with one another. It was not a matter of duplicity, but rather a regrettable instance of the right hand not knowing what the left was doing.

This is one commonly held view of historians looking at the tangle of secret agreements that the British entered into regarding the Middle East in 1915 and 1916. A second, minority view holds that there was really no tangle at all, and entire books, enough to fill a great groaning bookshelf, have been devoted to teasing out the carefully chosen modifiers and conditionals placed within these various agreements to absolve their crafters of any charge of bad faith.

In truth, the first view is a fiction, and the second merely squalid, akin to arguing that a promise wasn't a promise because one's fingers were crossed. To the degree that the British right hand didn't know what the left was doing, it was because a select group of men at the highest reaches of its government went to great lengths to ensure it. To that end, they created a labyrinth of information firewalls—deceptions, in a less charitable assessment—to make sure that crucial knowledge was withheld from Britain's wartime allies and even from many of her own seniormost diplomats and military commanders.

Somewhat ironically, one of the first entities to come in for this treatment was the British Empire's own "jewel in the crown," British India.

By the beginning of the twentieth century, the British Empire had devolved into a unique kind of colonial solar system, a galaxy in which its principal satellites operated with increasing autonomy from the central "star" of Britain. Nowhere was this truer than in India, where the British administration in Simla (as the British government of India was commonly referred to, even though Simla was only its summer capital) pursued its own domestic agenda and, to a remarkable degree, even its own foreign policy.

But if British India maintained an aloof relationship with London, it had a downright frosty one with British Egypt, especially after it was informed of the negotiations between Cairo and Emir Hussein in 1915. Ever since the creation of the Indian Raj in 1858, the Arabian Peninsula had been recognized as falling within India's sphere of influence, and its administrators were loath to accept either the intrusions or opinions of Egypt, that Johnny-come-lately to the scene. More to the point, the largest Muslim population in the world, some eighty million souls, was to be found in India, a number that dwarfed the Muslim population of the Ottoman Empire by a factor of four. As Simla officials pointed out to London, it seemed a very dangerous game to encourage native revolt with promises of autonomy or independence in one part of the Muslim world while ruthlessly quashing any hint of Muslim rebellion born of those same desires in another—as British India had been doing for decades.

For that reason, when Cairo's negotiations with Emir Hussein reached a critical phase in the autumn of 1915, Simla had launched a fierce counterattack in London, denouncing the secret talks at every turn—so fierce, in fact, that by late October, when officials in London and Cairo were scrambling to fashion a suitable response to Hussein's extravagant demands, Lord Kitchener's solution was to simply cut India out of the conversation. It wasn't until a reply had already been sent acceding to most all of Hussein's demands that the viceroy of India was first told of the startling development and given the feeble excuse that, in the press of events, there just hadn't been time to consult him.

With India thus frozen out of the equation, Emir Hussein had cut a very good deal for himself—or so he thought. In his crucial October 24 letter, the British high commissioner to Egypt, Henry McMahon, declared that, subject to certain modifications, "Great Britain is prepared to recognize and support the independence of the Arabs in all the regions within the limits demanded by the Sherif of Mecca." While the two men continued to haggle over those proposed modifications in subsequent letters—the most contentious were British demands for "special administrative arrangements" in the oil-rich Iraqi districts of Baghdad and Basra, and for the exclusion of the northwestern corner of Syria—Emir Hussein had every reason to believe that a great independent Arab nation had been promised, one encompassing nearly the entire Arabian Peninsula and stretching east to the frontier with Persia, north to the Anatolian heartland of Turkey, and west to the Mediterranean Sea and the border of Egypt.

But Hussein might have wanted to pay closer attention to a conditional clause McMahon had unobtrusively inserted into his letter, the caveat that these pledges only applied "wherein Great Britain is free to act without detriment to the interest of her ally, France." In other words, if the French had a problem with some aspect of the deal, their resistance might override British acceptance.

That the French were likely to have such a problem, the British knew only too well. The previous summer, the French ambassador to Great Britain had spelled out to Foreign Secretary Grey precisely what territory his nation intended to grab in the Middle East. This included all of greater Syria, or the most valuable lands now promised to Hussein.

How to get around such a dilemma? By simply not telling the French of the deal struck with Hussein. Instead, in late November, French diplomats were invited to London to discuss their desiderata for the Near East. With remarkable disingenuousness, British officials expressed surprise when the French reiterated that they wanted pretty much the whole thing: Lebanon, Palestine, the Syrian interior, Iraq. Thus the stage was set for one of the strangest—and with the advantage of hindsight, most destructive—diplomatic accords ever penned: the Sykes-Picot Agreement.

In just a few days of meetings in early January 1916, two midlevel diplomats, Mark Sykes and François Georges-Picot—by coincidence, the same man who as French consul in Beirut had carried on a secret correspondence with Arab dissidents and had left those documents behind to be discovered by Djemal Pasha's secret police—cobbled together a future map of the Middle East that bore absolutely no relation to the one envisioned by Emir Hussein. Instead, French imperial avarice fueled British imperial competition, so that the truly independent Arab nation was now to be largely limited to the desert wastelands of Arabia, with the French taking direct control of greater Syria, and the British taking outright all of Iraq. In addition, two great swatches of the interior, essentially everything north and inland of Hussein's kingdom of the Hejaz, would be indirectly controlled, quasi-independent but with Britain and France holding "priority of right of enterprise." It was in these so-called Zone A and B enclaves where the negotiators' cynicism was most naked; since neither

Sykes nor Picot believed the Arabs were truly capable of governing themselves, they could pledge independence for these enclaves secure in the knowledge that they would end up as British and French vassal states. In their spare time, the two diplomats even came up with a new designation for Palestine. Rather than be part of the future Arab nation—its technical default status since McMahon had never mentioned Palestine in any of his proposed modifications with Hussein—it was now to fall under the joint administration of France, Great Britain, and Russia.

In Picot's defense, he couldn't have known how much his territorial demands conflicted with those of Emir Hussein. That's because his British counterpart never chose to tell him. As incredible as it might seem, during those crucial days of early January 1916 when much of the future map of the Middle East was being drawn, there was just one person in the world who knew the full details of both the McMahon-Hussein Correspondence and the emerging Sykes-Picot compact, and who might have grasped the extent to which Arab, French, and British goals in the region had now been set on a collision course: Mark Sykes.

But if Sykes did grasp this, he wasn't saying. To the contrary, his accord with Picot meant new firewalls now had to be erected, to keep in the dark not only Emir Hussein but also all those British officials in Egypt who were aware of the agreement with him and still ascribed to the old-fashioned notion that a nation should abide by its promises. Just as British India had been frozen out in the autumn of 1915, so now British Egypt would be frozen out in the spring of 1916 as the Sykes-Picot Agreement was debated in Entente capitals. To Cairo's repeated queries on the status of the Anglo-French negotiations, Sykes and other London officials only allowed that they were ongoing, and that certainly Egypt would be closely consulted before any final agreement was reached. Instead, it would be May 1916 before anyone in Cairo saw a copy of Sykes-Picot, and by then it was a fait accompli, a secret pact agreed to by the cabinets of Britain, France, and Russia. As T. E. Lawrence would recall, the reaction among the stunned Cairo military intelligence staff upon finally reading the agreement had been a collective urge to vomit.

But for Lawrence in the winter of 1916, all of this lay in the future. Behind his desk at the Savoy Hotel, he continued his "bottle-washing" and mapmaking and "paper-combat."

In this last sphere, his efforts had taken on a tinge of the absurd. At least in the past, his bureaucratic battles had been waged against the perfidious French; now they were being fought against the continuing intrigues of his own countrymen in British India. Apparently operating on the premise that until Emir Hussein actually launched his revolt the pact made with him might be scuttled, Simla was engaged in a relentless effort in London to that end, warning of both Hussein's unsuitability and of the disaster to come if a unified Arab nation was encouraged to form (a fear that obviously would have been eased had Simla known about Sykes-Picot, which they didn't). What made this ongoing campaign somewhat curious in Lawrence's view was that by the winter of 1916, India seemed to have rather enough problems in its own immediate sphere to worry about.

At least back in the autumn, Simla had been in a position to argue that it was they, and not British Egypt, who'd actually achieved something against the Ottoman Empire. Building on the ease with which they'd seized the petroleum fields of southern Iraq, in April 1915 the commander of the Indian Expeditionary Force (IEF) had sent a force of twenty thousand men up the Tigris River. Disdaining to form alliances with any of the local Arab tribes, let alone prattle on about autonomy or independence, General Charles Townshend had led his army to success after success in time-honored British military tradition—sallying forth to thrash whoever might stand in their way—so that by October his force stood at the gates of Baghdad. In light of this, Simla's straight-ahead approach to war-making appeared to have much to recommend it over the exotic and incendiary hearts-and-minds notions wafting out of Cairo.

But a great deal had changed in the interim. Rather than a triumphant entry into Baghdad, Townshend's army had been fought to a bloody stalemate on the city's outskirts in late November. Far advanced from his supply lines and with no prospect of quick reinforcement, Townshend had then made a strategic withdrawal one hundred miles down the Tigris to the riverfront town of Kut. By February 1916, the garrison in Kut was reportedly under a deepening siege—British India seemed in no hurry to provide a lot of details—even as a relief column battled its way up the Tigris to come to its aid.

Still, Simla's whisper campaign against Cairo and its embrace of Hussein had continued. In late January, Lawrence wrote a long report, "Politics of Mecca," designed to allay concerns back in London—concerns feverishly stoked by India—of what a unified Arab nation under Hussein's leadership might mean to Britain's long-term interests in the region. Perhaps tailoring his message to what the British leadership wanted to hear, Lawrence opined that the notion of such a monolith was far-fetched, that "if properly handled [the Arabs] would remain in a state of political mosaic, a tissue of small jealous principalities incapable of cohesion."

The following month, India appeared to try the opposite tack of belittling Hussein. They did so by inserting into the *Intelligence Bulletin for the Middle East*, a highly classified digest of information restricted to top-ranking military and civilian officials, an interview with a man named Abdul Aziz ibn-Saud. A tribal chieftain from the northeastern corner of Arabia, ibn-Saud called Hussein "essentially a trivial and unstable character," and made it clear that neither he nor most other Arabian tribal chieftains would ever accede to his leadership. Even if Hussein took the risky step of declaring himself caliph, the supreme religious-political figure in the Islamic world, ibn-Saud argued, it "would not make any difference to his status among other Chiefs and there would be no question of their accepting any control from him, any more than they do now."

To Lawrence, that interview represented a new, and potentially very dangerous, escalation in the competition between Cairo and Simla. That's because Abdul Aziz ibn-Saud was not just another tribal malcontent bent on retaining his autonomy, but Hussein's most formidable rival in all of Arabia. Having embraced an extremely austere form of fundamentalist Islam known as Wahhabism, over the previous fifteen years ibn-Saud had led his desert warriors into battle against one recalcitrant Arab tribe after another with a kind of evangelical zeal. The discipline of the Wahhabists was legendary; in that time, ibn-Saud's reach had expanded from a small string of oasis villages in the Riyadh region to cover a vast expanse of northeastern Arabia. Meanwhile, Ibn-Saud was also British India's man in Arabia, with a close relationship going back to before the war.

It was bad enough, in Lawrence's estimation, that Simla was using the *Intelligence Bulletin* to promote a man with views so antithetical to British values, but the gambit also underscored a situation almost laughably absurd had it not been so perilous: in their battle for primacy over Arabian policy, two different branches of the British crown were backing two sworn rivals. Surely that was less a recipe for a successful Arab revolt than for civil war—which of course may have been Simla's true goal all along.

In his riposte to the ibn-Saud interview, similarly disseminated to the upper reaches of the British government, Lawrence argued that despite posing as Islamic reformists "with all the narrow minded bigotry of the puritan," ibn-Saud and his Wahhabists were hardly representative of Islam. Instead, as he warned in "The Politics of Mecca," the Wahhabist sect was composed of marginal medievalists, "and if it prevailed, we would have in place of the tolerant, rather comfortable Islam of Mecca and Damascus, the fanaticism of Nejd . . . intensified and swollen by success."

As with many of Lawrence's other predictions, his warning about ibn-Saud and the Wahhabists was ultimately to prove true. In 1923, ibn-Saud would conquer much of the Arabian Peninsula and, to honor his clan, give it the name Saudi Arabia. For the next ninety years, the vast and profligate Saudi royal family would survive by essentially buying off the doctrinaire Wahhabists who had brought them to power, financially subsidizing their activities so long as their disciples directed their jihadist efforts abroad. The most famous product of this arrangement was to be a man named Osama bin Laden.

Far more immediately, however, Lawrence was to see his war-of-words campaign against British India sidelined by more pressing matters. That March, he was selected for a mission so clandestine, and so assaultive to British notions of honor, that its true nature would be largely expunged from the history books. In a nice touch of irony, it was a mission made necessary by a catastrophe of British India's creation, a series of events that reached an ugly denouement in the early morning hours of March 8, 1916.

AT ABOUT 6:30 on that morning, Lieutenant General Fenton Aylmer, the future 13th Baronet of Donadea, received some startling news. In his army's nighttime march on the town of Dujaila in central Iraq, the 36th Indian Infantry Brigade had become disoriented in the dark. Rather than stop at their preassigned forward position to wait out the dawn artillery bombardment of the enemy, segments of the brigade had continued on across the barren Dujaila plain and directly into the Turks' forward line. More specifically, they had stumbled squarely up the approaches to "the Citadel," a forty-foot-high earthen fortress that commanded the surrounding flatlands and formed the strongpoint of the Turkish defenseworks.

It sounded like a blueprint for slaughter, but it hadn't quite played out that way. The runner who appeared at Aylmer's headquarters that morning reported that, by all appearances, the fortress was either deserted or manned by a tiny skeleton guard; the 36th Indian Infantry Brigade was at the gates of the Citadel, and it was theirs for the taking.

It was the pivotal moment in Aylmer's long and bloody campaign to relieve General Townshend's army in Kut, now just eight miles farther up the Tigris River. With the astounding report out of the Citadel, here was not only the chance to win the battle of Dujaila before it had properly begun, but to begin to atone for the colossal missteps that had characterized Aylmer's advance over the previous two months.

By March 1916, the various armies of Europe had devised a simple rote method for attacking their entrenched foes: a sustained artillery bombardment of the enemy's forward defenses, one that might last a few hours or several days depending on the scale of the planned assault, followed by an infantry rush across no-man's-land. The problems with these tactics were manifest at every step. Most such bombardments caused relatively few casualties, since the defenders simply retreated to back trenches—or, in the more sophisticated trenchworks of the Western Front, into heavily protected underground bunkers—to await their conclusion. Naturally, these preliminary barrages also alerted the defenders both that an assault was coming and its precise location.

Once the shelling ceased, the attacking infantry units climbed out of their forward staging trenches to begin their advance across no-man's-land. Unfortunately for them, the end of the artillery barrage also cued the defenders that the ground assault was now under way, enabling them to quickly return to their own forward trenches and mow down the exposed attackers as they approached. In just this way, by early 1916, men had died by the hundreds of thousands in trenchworks across the breadth of Europe.

Despite the failure of these tactics across a wide spectrum of Europe's varied topography, Lieutenant General Aylmer had apparently seen no means to improve upon them on the flat and featureless landscape of central Iraq. It also seemed to escape him that it was these same ruinous tactics, employed by General Townshend in his effort to take Baghdad, that were necessitating his rescue mission in the first place. In the two months since he had set off for Kut with some twenty thousand British and Indian troops, Aylmer had three times hurled his men in frontal assaults over bare ground against the entrenched Turks. Each time, the British Indian army had eventually carried the field, if only through sheer numerical dominance—they outnumbered the Turks by at least two to one—and only at astounding cost; in the first two weeks, the relief force had suffered some ten thousand casualties, or half its strength.

This was no cause for undue alarm among senior commanders downstream, apparently, for they soon began shuttling some fifteen thousand more men up to Aylmer for a second push. By early March, this replenished force had advanced upriver until it came to the Turkish trenchline in Dujaila, the last obstacle standing between the rescuers and Kut just beyond. Having learned at least a little from his earlier battles, Aylmer had decided on a night march to the very edge of the Turks' artillery range in Dujaila, a quick sunrise bombardment, and then a dash for the Citadel that dominated the pancake-flat plain. It was shortly before dawn, while his guns were being silently unlimbered into place for the coming barrage, that he learned of the 36th Indian's remarkable news.

But Fenton Aylmer was clearly not a man who liked surprises, even good ones. After hastily conferring with his senior commanders, it was decided that the preemptive capture of the Turkish stronghold posed too great a departure from the battle plans already worked out to be adequately supported. The 36th Indian was ordered away from the Citadel and back to the main British line; from there, they could recross the plain and seize the fortress once the opening artillery bombardment had been completed.

When finally the British bombardment commenced—not at dawn as planned, but at 8 a.m.—all element of surprise had been lost, the Dujaila Citadel hurriedly manned by Turkish troops ferried over from across the river. It was another hour before the British frontal assault began. Very quickly, another four thousand imperial troops had fallen in no-man's-land, without a single one reaching the Citadel.

That engagement at Dujaila represented the last best chance the British had to save their besieged army in Kut. Over the previous two months, they had suffered fourteen thousand casualties trying to rescue an army of twelve thousand—and they weren't quite done yet. For his efforts, Fenton Aylmer was quietly relieved of command three days after Dujaila and shuffled off to a back-base job. Perhaps in recognition of his uneven achievements in Iraq, as well as his attempted cover-up of the Citadel fiasco—his official battle report would make no mention of the 36th Indian's report—his knighthood would be delayed until 1922.

In the wake of the Dujaila debacle, and in light of the dire situation facing Townshend's army at Kut—reports indicated the garrison would run out of food by mid-April—Lord Kitchener set to hatching a desperate scheme. In its pursuit, on the morning of March 22, 1916, the passenger ship *Royal George* slipped from its berth at Port Suez and turned south into the Red Sea, embarking on a fourteen-day journey around the Arabian Peninsula to southern Iraq. On board was T. E. Lawrence. He carried with him a letter of introduction from High Commissioner Henry McMahon to Sir Percy Cox, British India's chief political officer in Iraq.

"My dear Cox," the letter read, "I send these few lines to introduce Captain Lawrence who is starting today for Mesopotamia under orders from the W.O. [War Office] to give his services in regards to Arab matters. He is one of the best of our very able intelligence staff here and has a thorough knowledge of the Arab question in all its bearings. I feel sure that you will find him of great use. We are very sorry to lose so valuable a man from our staff here.

"I hope things are going well on your side. We are anxiously awaiting news of Townshend's relief but have heard nothing for ages."

The purpose of Lawrence's mission was actually twofold, one overt, the other very much veiled. In view of the ongoing crisis at Kut, Kitchener and his allies in the Egyptian intelligence staff hoped the British Indian commanders in Iraq might finally see the wisdom of trying to work with the indigenous Arab tribes that should have been their natural allies all along. The plan was to start sending out a group of Iraqi Arab officers who had defected from the Turks and were now working for the British in Egypt, so that they might forge alliances with local Iraqi tribal leaders, as well as peel away disgruntled Arab units of the Ottoman army.

It was hard to imagine how any of this could be done in time to save Townshend, however, and this gave rise to the second purpose of Lawrence's mission. Under orders from Kitchener himself, an attempt was to be made to bribe the Turkish commander of the Kut siege into letting Townshend's army go in return for one million English pounds' worth of gold.

If Lawrence resented being the bearer of this shameful instruction, almost without precedent in British military history, he never let on. Then again, he'd very recently been given two reminders of the puffery and hypocrisy of military culture.

A year and a half earlier, he had been magically elevated from civilian to second lieutenant because a general visiting the General Staff map room demanded to be briefed by an officer. Now Lawrence's superiors in Cairo had abruptly rushed through his temporary promotion to captain, effective his first day at sea, presumably to spare the very senior military commanders he would be meeting in Iraq from the indignity of conferring with a second lieutenant.

A rather more baffling episode had occurred just four days before he'd boarded the *Royal George*. On March 18, the small French military legation in Cairo had been temporarily recalled to France and, in long-standing military tradition among the European powers, the occasion was marked by the liberal disbursement of medals and honorifics. Quite inexplicably, considering his consistent efforts to thwart French ambitions in the region, the outgoing legation had selected Lawrence for the Légion d'Honneur, one of France's highest awards. Compounding their error, the following year they awarded him the Croix de Guerre avec palme.

Over the course of his wartime service, Lawrence was awarded a number of medals and ribbons, but with his profound disdain for such things, he either threw them away or never bothered to collect them. He made an exception in the case of the Croix de Guerre; after the war, according to his brother, he found amusement in placing the medal around the neck of a friend's dog and parading it through the streets of Oxford.

ON THE MORNING of April 5, the *Royal George* slipped into the bay of the dreary, low-slung port city of Basra, and a Royal Navy launch was sent out to collect its most important passenger, the newly minted Captain T. E. Lawrence.

As Lawrence soon discovered in Basra, the overt objective of his mission to Iraq, to coax British Indian commanders into launching a hearts-and-minds campaign among the local tribes, had already been mooted. In a series of cables to London while he had been in transit, the new commander in chief of the Indian Army Expeditionary Force in Iraq, General Percy Lake, had already dismissed the scheme as "undesirable and inconvenient."

But as Lawrence conferred with that leadership during his first days in Basra, it was clear that another, more insidious element had doomed his political mission, a toxic fusion of racism and British notions of military superiority. Despite the fresh example of the disaster at Gallipoli—maybe even because of it—many senior British commanders simply couldn't accept that they might lose to the "rabble" of the Ottoman army yet again. This attitude wasn't isolated to the narrow-minded generals of British India, but extended all the way to the supreme commander of British forces, General William Robertson, back in London. Upon hearing of the generous surrender terms offered to Townshend by Khalil Pasha, the Turkish commander at Kut, after the defeat of Aylmer's relief column, Robertson had responded, "My general information is to the effect that the difficulties of the Turks are serious. I regard Khalil Bey's overtures as a confirmation of this and as an indication that, given determined action on our part, success is assured."

In other words, in the upside-down worldview that this war against its military and cultural inferiors had induced in the British high command, an offer of honorable surrender was only evidence of the enemy's weakness, and that two relief efforts had ended in abject failure meant a third was sure to succeed.

By the time Lawrence was shuttled up the Tigris River to join the frontline headquarters staff on April 15, this third relief effort was well under way. After the fiasco at Dujaila, there had been a wholesale shakeup of that staff, with Aylmer replaced by a certain Major General George Gorringe. Unfortunately, the changes hadn't extended to the tactical playbook. Displaying the same fondness for frontal assaults against an entrenched enemy as his predecessor, Gorringe neatly replicated the record of Aylmer's first relief effort—ten thousand dead and wounded, no breakthrough—in almost precisely the same two-week span.

That final failure ended the uncomfortable existence Lawrence had endured ever since reaching the *Snakefly*, the British headquarters ship docked in the Tigris River below Kut. As word had spread among the officers on board of the clandestine purpose of his mission—to try to ransom out the Kut garrison—the young captain from Egypt had been pointedly shunned by most everyone. But now, having suffered some twenty-three thousand casualties across nine separate engagements without ever reaching Kut, and with that trapped garrison rapidly nearing starvation, the generals in charge belatedly accepted that Kitchener's scheme was the only option left.

But even at this eleventh hour, there would be time for an element of farce. Since neither General Townshend nor the commanders hoping to rescue him wished to have such an ignominious endeavor attached to their reputations, through the last days of April, Townshend and General Lake waged a duel of cablegrams, each arguing that the other should carry out the negotiations. Instead, it would ultimately fall on three junior officers—Colonel Edward Beach, Captain Aubrey Herbert, and Captain T. E. Lawrence—to make one last attempt to save the dying men of Kut.

IT HAD ALL the trappings of a Victorian parlor-room melodrama: the dashing and excessively handsome young nobleman, a requisite coterie of flirtatious but chaste women, the cold-blooded archvillain, even the innocent abroad, that out-of-his-depth character who, after various twists and turns, would provide the story with its moral conclusion. Where the small expatriate community of wartime Jerusalem differed from any theatrical counterparts was in the consequences to be paid for ending up on the wrong side of the narrative: imprisonment, exile, even execution. What was also different, of course, was the world that lay beyond those parlor-room windows, not the pleasant English countryside or a tony London street, but a city consumed by death, its streets and alleyways littered with those succumbed to starvation or typhus, its public squares frequently featuring men hanging from gibbet-gallows.

For William Yale, it was an exceedingly strange, fishbowl existence. With very little to do in the way of work, most every afternoon he met up to play bridge with an eclectic group of friends—a Greek doctor, an Armenian doctor, a retired Turkish colonel, and the Greek bishop of Jerusalem—that diversion giving over in the evenings to larger gatherings in the salons of various middle-aged expatriate women. At these soirees, dominated by dancing and the playing of parlor games, a peculiar sexual dynamic took place. Since there were few single expatriate women remaining in Jerusalem—and any attention paid to one could be quickly interpreted as an interest to marry—the single men flirted, openly and competitively, with the married women in attendance, often in plain view and with the acquiescence of their husbands. It was all quite harmless and innocent.

But there was nothing truly harmless in wartime Jerusalem, as Yale discovered when he became the favorite of Madame Alexis Frey, an attractive middle-aged French widow who enjoyed the status of grande dame of the city's salon scene. Yale's standing with Frey so rankled one of his competitors, a middle-aged Christian Arab who headed the Turkish Tobacco Régie, or monopoly, in Syria, that the man took Yale aside one day to make a proposal. "How about we divide the ladies of Jerusalem up between the two of us," the businessman said. "For myself, I will reserve Madame Frey, and you can have all the rest."

Yale initially dismissed the proposition as a joke, but thought differently when he next went to the Régie office to purchase his monthly ration of cigarettes, only to be told by the clerks they'd been instructed to not sell to him. That posed a problem since, true to its definition, the Régie was the only place tobacco could be obtained in wartime Jerusalem. Shortly afterward, Yale was informed by the Jerusalem chief of police that his challenger from the Régie was plotting intrigues against him.

"I began to realize that I was up against a jealous, unscrupulous person who would go to great lengths to rid himself of a rival," Yale recalled. "As my business demanded that my position should be such that I be on friendly terms with the Turkish officials and authorities, I saw I was playing a dangerous game. I decided to let Madame Frey settle the issue, so I told her to send Monsieur X packing or our affair was over."

When Madame Frey explained that that was quite impossible given the Régie man's prominence, the American oilman withdrew from the Frey salon in a huff. Yale's manservant, a grizzled old Kurd named Mustapha Kharpoutli, came up with an alternative solution. "Oh Master," he counseled Yale, "I know where 'the pig' goes every evening, so give the order and I will finish with him." As Kharpoutli explained, the Régie man left a particular woman's house every night at midnight. "It's on a lonely street. I will kill him tonight if you tell me to."

Yale declined that offer, and shortly after his friends engineered a brief rapprochement with Alexis Frey. It was a risky business, for the city's thicket of martial law edicts afforded almost endless possibilities for a rival to exact revenge; during Frey's next curfew-violating salon, her home was raided and half the attendees hauled off to jail, presumably after a tip-off from the jealous Régie man.

The episode served to remind Yale that his life now was like a game of musical chairs, one with extremely high stakes. The ultimate arbiter of that game, of course, was Djemal Pasha. On his word, most anyone could be cast into prison or summarily banished to some distant village in the Syrian wastelands—if often only to be just as swiftly released or restored according to Djemal's whim.

To stay in Djemal's good graces, or to soften the punishment when that failed, the foreign community in Jerusalem most often looked to two men. One was the dashing consul from neutral Spain, Antonio de la Cierva, Conde de Ballobar, who, having assumed the consular duties of most all the European "belligerent" nations, was extraordinarily well informed and influential. William Yale's relationship with the Conde de

Ballobar was a tricky one: a good ally to have if matters went awry, but also his most formidable competition when it came to fishing in Jerusalem's sparse pool of attractive and available women.

For day-to-day protection, Yale was much more likely to turn to another pillar of Jerusalem society, a charming middle-aged aristocrat named Ismail Hakki Bey al-Husseini, one of the three Jerusalem businessmen from whom Socony had obtained the original Kornub concessions back in the spring of 1914. Yale had developed a friendship with Ismail Bey during his extended stay in Palestine prior to the war's outbreak. That had quickly resumed upon Yale's return in 1915, and by the spring of 1916 the oilman considered Ismail Bey his closest friend in the Middle East. Of course, it probably didn't hurt that the Husseinis were one of the most powerful and well-respected families in all of southern Syria, Ismail Bey being a particularly prominent member.

But if the expatriate community had its protectors, it also had its predators. Of these, none was more dreaded than a young German officer who flitted in and out of the city with some regularity, Curt Prüfer. As Count de Ballobar noted of Prüfer, despite "his harmless appearance [he] is nothing less than a secret agent of the German government," and "in possession of an extraordinary talent." What made Prüfer such a figure of menace, quite beyond the creepiness factor of his whispery voice, was that he seemed to be the one German whom Djemal Pasha trusted implicitly. Run afoul of Curt Prüfer, and even the determined entreaties of Count de Ballobar or Ismail Hakki Bey might prove useless. Even the entreaties of Djemal Pasha, in fact. One afternoon, Yale happened to be visiting an expatriate couple he was friendly with when their front door was kicked in by Prüfer and two accompanying policemen. While the couple had claimed to be Swiss, it was an open secret within the foreign community—and to Djemal Pasha—that they were actually French, a detail Prüfer had apparently just uncovered. When he demanded the couple be cast into internal exile, an unhappy Djemal had no choice but to sign the expulsion order.

Prüfer's authority became especially worrisome to William Yale in the winter of 1916 when he discovered that he and the German intelligence agent were locked in a three-way competition—the third was the ubiquitous Ballobar—for the same woman, a beautiful Jewish-American girl living in Jerusalem. Concerned that her American suitor might soon be arrested, the girl finally confided to Yale that Prüfer frequently interrogated her about him and his activities. "Clearly I was under suspicion."

Surviving in wartime Syria required not only a finely honed selfishness, but a hardening of the heart. In this, Yale, the consummate survivor, was not at all immune. Every day for months on end, he had to step over the bodies of the dead and dying as he traversed Jerusalem. Every week he heard stories of those who had fallen from favor being disappeared, either figuratively in the form of banishment or quite literally in the form of the gibbet-gallows. To protect himself and his interests in such a place, he became increasingly cold-blooded, too, so much so that he would eventually turn on his closest friend. To his later embarrassment, this didn't stem from matters of personal safety; William Yale did it for oil.

Prior to his first meeting with Djemal Pasha in the spring of 1915, Yale had decided to divide Socony's petition for concessionary rights in Palestine into two separate requests, figuring that to ask for the entire half million acres desired at one fell swoop was to invite a backlash. The problem was that, having long since sewn up the concessionary rights to the first quarter million acres and done nothing with them, by the spring of 1916 the oilman had still not mustered the gall to ask after the second.

What he needed was some kind of opening to alter the playing field, but just what that might be was hard to imagine—especially since Djemal had clearly cottoned to Socony's game. At the beginning of 1916, the Constantinople office had labored mightily to obtain concessionary rights to several large tracts around Damascus, going so far as to make the American consul in that city, Samuel Edelman, their point man in the effort. In late March, however, after Edelman took the matter up with "the supreme factor in these regions"—an obvious reference to Djemal—he cabled back to Socony with some bad news. "[Djemal] says that while recently in Constantinople, the Minister of Mines said to him [that] Standard Oil was not working for the benefit or interest of Turkey, but to shut off competition. So long as this suspicion hangs over you, [it] will not be possible to obtain further concessions."

Shortly after that rebuff, however, an opening suddenly presented itself when Yale was once again summoned to Djemal's headquarters at the German Hospice. As the governor explained, he had recently received reports from military officers in the field of a large pool of oil collected at the base of a mountain in the southern desert. Since this oil was already on the surface, Djemal pointed out, it should be an easy matter to start collecting and refining it at once. As a personal favor, he wanted Yale to go and investigate the site, a small chain of mountains below Beersheva known as Kornub.

Yale instantly realized this "find" was the very same one that J. C. Hill had spotted from a Judean hillside two years earlier, and which he and Rudolf McGovern had ascertained to be iron tailings. But this seemed a detail not worth mentioning to Djemal Pasha. Instead, Yale said he would be happy to investigate the Kornub site, so long as the governor could see his way to approving a few more concessionary tracts. When he left the

German Hospice that day, the Standard representative had the pasha's consent to another quarter million acres of Palestine.

But while preparing for this next concession-procurement expedition Yale suddenly encountered a problem with his best friend, Ismail Hakki Bey. During the first great concession-buying expedition of the previous summer, Ismail Bey had succumbed to Yale's entreaties to accompany him on the vague assurance that Socony would compensate him for his services; even though the businessman had no proprietary interest in those concessions, he had relented. To be sure, that collaboration was rooted in more than mere friendship for both men. While Ismail Bey's cultured company was a welcome addition to the scrofulous assortment of soldiers and government functionaries who formed the rest of Yale's retinue, the American also looked to his well-connected friend to smooth out any difficulties that might arise with stubborn landowners or extortionate local officials. From Ismail Bey's perspective, with Socony clearly planning a massive exploration project in Palestine at some point in the future, it only made good business sense to attach to the undertaking however he could.

But when approached by Yale in the late spring of 1916 for his help with the next round of concession-buying, Ismail Bey balked. In the Arab way of doing business, one's word was inviolate. Ismail Bey had now seen enough of the American way to know that Yale's assurances of compensation were quite meaningless; what he needed was a written contract. Confronted by this request, Yale explained that as a mere purchasing agent for Socony, he hadn't the authority to pen such a guarantee, but that if Ismail Bey "wished to know my personal opinion, it was that he had better have confidence in the Company."

That wasn't good enough for Ismail Bey; he informed his friend that without such a written guarantee, he couldn't help him.

This placed Yale in a most difficult spot. Over the course of their two-and-a-half-year friendship, he'd come to know all of Ismail Bey's seven children, and had frequently dined in his Jerusalem home. As in any true friendship, the two had also shared confidences: on Yale's part, of the British nurse he had met in Jerusalem before the war and hoped one day to marry; on Ismail Bey's part, of his low opinion of the Ottoman government in general, and his resentment of Djemal Pasha in particular. Compounding Yale's difficulty was the very prominence of the Husseini name in Syria. Since Ismail Bey had relatives scattered in high government positions throughout the region, a rift between them might not be a matter of simply parting ways; if the businessman chose to stand in his way, the same doors that had previously been flung open for Socony could now be slammed shut.

As Yale recounted in his memoir, "I looked at him and said, 'Well, Ismail Bey, much as I will dislike doing it, if you do not agree to cooperate with me, I shall go at once to Djemal Pasha and tell him that you are blocking me, that you are pro-British and are tied up with British interests."

It marked a dramatic transformation in William Yale. In 1911, while working for a wealthy Bostonian industrialist, Yale had refused the pleas of his own bankrupted and desperate father for an introduction to his employer, feeling that trading on his position to arrange such a meeting would be improper. Just five years later, Yale was threatening his best friend with probable death—and not an easy death, but likely one that would only come after protracted torture and after his wives and children had been cast into a destitute exile—over a business deal.

But it worked. "I studied his face anxiously as I awaited his response," Yale would recall. "Rather abruptly he replied, 'I'll assist you; I'll trust the Company.' And he did work loyally with me as long as I represented the Company in Palestine."

KHALIL PASHA'S HEADQUARTERS encampment consisted of a single round tent set some four miles back from the front lines at Kut. It was midafternoon before the three British officers, having at last completed their grueling blindfolded journey from no-man's-land, were ushered inside.

Khalil was a trim man in his midthirties with piercing brown eyes and the handlebar mustache favored by Turkish officers—by all Turkish males, in fact—and despite the desolation of his surroundings, he still retained something of the dapper manner he had perfected in the salons of Constantinople. Aubrey Herbert, during his prewar days as an honorary consul in the Ottoman capital, had come to know Khalil quite well, and once he and his companions had settled in the tent he tried to break the ice with some opening pleasantries. "Where was it that I met Your Excellency last?" Herbert asked in French.

Khalil apparently had a good memory. "At a dance at the British embassy," he replied, also in French. From there, though, the conversation took a far more somber turn.

It was April 29, and the three British officers had set out for this meeting early that morning, climbing over the forward parapet of a British trenchline and into no-man's-land under the cover of a white flag. Before them stretched six hundred yards of waist-high meadow grass, at the far end of which rose the earthen berm of the Turks' trenchworks. Walking to a spot roughly equidistant between the two lines, they stopped and waited for several hours for some response from the Turkish side, buffeted both by the steadily rising heat and by the swarms of blowflies feeding on the rotting corpses that lay all about them. At last, the three men were taken over to the Turkish line, where they were blindfolded and put on horses to take them to Khalil's headquarters. Having badly hurt his knee in a fall a few days earlier, Lawrence quickly found that he couldn't ride; taken off his horse but still in blindfold, he was led by the hand by a Turkish soldier, stumbling and limping the four miles to Khalil's tent.

In stepping out into no-man's-land that morning, all three men were acutely aware of the humiliating nature of the task they'd been given. So dishonorable was this bribery attempt that Edward Beach would never publicly reveal the mission's true purpose, Lawrence would only write of it in the most euphemistic fashion, while Aubrey Herbert couldn't even bring himself to commit the words to the anonymity of his private diary; writing in his journal the previous evening, he noted that the only items they had to bargain with were "Townshend's guns, exchange of Turkish prisoners, and another thing." Even this ambiguity was ultimately too revealing; when Herbert's diary was published after the war, that clause was excised altogether.

But as the three officers soon learned in Khalil Pasha's tent, they actually had even less to bargain with than that. Unbeknownst to them when they'd set out, early that morning an increasingly unhinged Townshend had abruptly agreed to an unconditional surrender. Following military protocol, he then destroyed his remaining pieces of artillery. This act infuriated Khalil Pasha—he had desperately wanted to get his hands on those guns—and it left Beach, Herbert, and Lawrence with little to offer the Turkish commander beyond the gold ransom.

This the British officers couched in terms of a kind of humanitarian assistance package for the civilian residents of Kut. Surely, they suggested, those innocents had suffered just as badly as the trapped British soldiers through the five-month siege, and some form of financial recompense seemed in order. Khalil Pasha saw through the artifice at once and airily brushed the proposal away.

The negotiating party fared a bit better in asking for a transfer of wounded soldiers. With the Kut garrison now surrendered, the Turkish commander agreed to let British steamers come up with food supplies and take out the worst wounded. This concession encouraged Colonel Beach, the senior negotiator, to try his last card: an exchange of able-bodied prisoners, the survivors in Kut in return for the Ottoman prisoners the British had taken since first coming ashore in Iraq.

With an arch expression, Khalil offered an alternative arrangement, a one-for-one exchange of British soldiers for Turkish ones, a separate exchange for Indian soldiers and Arabs. The British officers weren't quite sure what to make of this offer, but when Herbert remarked that many Arab troops in the enemy army had fought valiantly and Khalil would be lucky to have them back, the Turkish commander's manner abruptly changed. Holding up a list of the POWs held by the British, Khalil pointed out the preponderance of Arab names. "Perhaps one of our [Turkish] men in ten is weak or cowardly," he said, "but it's only one in a hundred of the Arabs who are brave. . . . You can send them back to me if you like, but I have already condemned them to death. I shall like to have them to hang."

Realizing they were being toyed with, the British officers dropped the matter. A short time later, Khalil Pasha gave an affected yawn and announced that he was tired, that he still had many other matters to attend. So ended the last chance to rescue the garrison in Kut. From Khalil's headquarters, Lawrence, Herbert, and Beach were escorted back to the front line but, as darkness had now fallen, were invited to stay the night inside a Turkish encampment. As Lawrence pointedly wrote in his diary, "they gave us a most excellent dinner in Turkish style."

The following morning, the three officers were led down to the river-bank. In the daylight, they saw one body after another floating by on the Tigris's swift current. They were Ottoman soldiers, succumbed to cholera or typhus or battle wounds, and so indifferent were their commanders that their bodies had been tossed into the river rather than buried.

That same day, Townshend formally surrendered his forces at Kut. Both his army and the relief columns that were slaughtered trying to rescue it had been composed largely of Indian soldiers, and to whatever degree racism had contributed to their expendable treatment by their British commanders, those men were now to suffer even worse at the hands of the Turks. With most put to work essentially as slave labor on the Baghdad Railway, of the ten thousand Indian soldiers and camp-followers who went into captivity at Kut, as few as one-third would live to see the war's end.

A happier fate was in store for General Townshend. Taken to Constantinople, he spent the remainder of the war in a pleasant villa on an island in the Bosporus, where he was given use of a Turkish naval yacht and frequently attended diplomatic receptions at the Ottoman court. Joining him in Constantinople were his three prized Yorkshire terriers, pets that, despite the near-starvation conditions in Kut, had weathered the ordeal quite nicely. In a testament to the element of collegiality that persisted among the imperial ruling classes even in wartime, a number of Turkish government officials sent Townshend congratulatory notes on the occasion of his knighthood by King George V in October 1916.

.   .   .

ON A MORNING in early April, a courier on horseback appeared at the al-Bakri farmstead outside Damascus summoning Faisal Hussein to Djemal Pasha's offices in the city. This was hardly out of the ordinary. Faisal had returned to the Syrian capital at Djemal's request three months earlier and had frequent dealings with the governor. When Faisal arrived at Djemal's office that morning, however, he found him in a strangely cool, controlled mood.

After coffee had been served and pleasantries exchanged, Djemal slid a piece of paper across his desk. It was a telegram from Enver Pasha in Constantinople, and it concerned a letter the generalissimo had just received from Faisal's father in Mecca. It was less a letter than an ultimatum: if the Young Turks wished to retain his friendship, Hussein warned, they needed to recognize him as the hereditary ruler of the Hejaz, and to end the ongoing trial of the five dozen Arab nationalist leaders in Lebanon.

It placed Faisal in a very dangerous spot. Upon his return to Damascus in January, he had quickly discovered that the odds for a successful Arab revolt in Syria had radically diminished since his earlier visit. Many of the would-be political leaders of such a revolt had been banished or gone into hiding as a result of Djemal's purges, while the military component had been decimated at Gallipoli. While Faisal had alerted his father to this changed situation, judging by his petulant telegram, Hussein didn't grasp just how dire matters stood.

"Effendim," Djemal recounted Faisal as saying, "you've no idea what a grief this is to me. This telegram is certainly the result of some great misunderstanding. I can positively assure you that my father means nothing wrong."

Instead, Faisal attributed the "misunderstanding" to his father's difficulty with the Turkish language; obviously, some scribe had mistranslated his father's Arabic text and mangled it into something far different than intended. In Djemal's office that morning, Faisal offered to cable his father and, by explaining that his words had been misconstrued, undoubtedly obtain his immediate renunciation of the offending letter.

But as tiresome as Djemal Pasha was finding the machinations of Hussein and his sons, he also rather enjoyed watching Faisal squirm. Dismissing the young sheikh from his office, he instead composed his own letter to Emir Hussein. After explaining why he couldn't possibly release the Damascus defendants—"a government which pardoned traitors would be accused of weakness"—Djemal further suggested that with the nation in a war where its very survival was at stake, this perhaps wasn't the best time for Hussein to pursue the business of making his title hereditary. He then took the gloves off: "I should also draw your attention to the following aspect of the matter. Let us assume the Government complied with your demand solely because they wanted to keep you from being troublesome in the difficult times through which we are passing. If the war came to a victorious conclusion, who could prevent the Government from dealing with you with the greatest severity once it is over?"

However imperfect his knowledge of the Turkish language, Emir Hussein surely understood the threat in those words. And just in case there was still any uncertainty, Djemal soon turned his attention to the Lebanon show-trial defendants. On May 5, and despite Faisal's continued pleas for clemency, he signed execution orders for twenty-one of those found guilty. Early the next morning, the condemned were led into public squares in Damascus and Beirut and hanged.

In concert with another event, those executions finally brought the long, tortured dance between the Young Turks and the Hashemite ruler in Arabia to an end. Just weeks earlier, Djemal Pasha had dispatched a new force of some thirty-five hundred crack troops to Medina. He had assured Hussein that the unit was en route to Yemen, at the southwestern corner of the Arabian Peninsula, but Hussein wasn't convinced, suspecting they were really coming for him. In the wake of the May 6 executions, Hussein decided the time for dithering was over, and sent word to Faisal to get out of Damascus.

At about the same time that Faisal was preparing to do so, Djemal Pasha received another supplicant, Aaron Aaronsohn. In the four months since he had returned to his post as head of the locust eradication program, the agronomist had been a fairly frequent visitor to the governor's Damascus office during his travels through the region. He'd been happy to be able to report to Djemal that the second wave of locusts hadn't spawned, and so posed no threat in the future; even by late March, their numbers had begun to dwindle. What he hadn't shared with the Syrian governor, of course, was that he'd used the cover of his scientific fieldwork to establish an extensive network of prospective Jewish spies across Palestine.

Putting that network together had been exceedingly delicate work for Aaronsohn. Within the Jewish *yeshuv*, or community, was one faction that actively supported the Central Powers, another that secretly supported the Entente, while the vast majority simply wanted to stay out of the whole mess and hope for the best. What united almost everyone, however, was staunch opposition to any action that might bring more adverse Ottoman attention; even for those quietly praying for the British to come, they would lend their assistance once they were ashore, but to do anything beforehand was just too dangerous for everyone. Only by very gingerly sounding out their friends and acquaintances had Aaronsohn and

Feinberg managed to recruit some dozen like-minded members of the community willing to spy for Great Britain preemptively.

That remained a theoretical enterprise, however. Over the course of that winter, there had been several sightings of the British spy ships off the coast of Athlit, and the British had even sent messages ashore, but through an improbable string of bad luck, contact had never been made. For Aaron Aaronsohn, it was a maddening predicament. Three times they'd tried to connect with the British, and three times it had gone wrong, with the last try nearly resulting in Feinberg's death. Then, in the early spring of 1916, he came up with a new idea.

From his travels, Aaronsohn had learned that the Turkish army suffered from a massive shortage of lubricating oil; indeed, he could scarcely have not learned it since the earsplitting screech of oilless axles had become a kind of perpetual background music in Syria. Reading through a scientific journal one day, the agronomist came upon an article about a team of European scientists who had devised a method of converting sesame seed oil into lubricating oil. If there was one thing the Ottoman Empire had no shortage of it was sesame seeds, and it was with this proposal—to learn the extraction method from scientists in Germany and apply it to the Turkish war effort—that Aaronsohn came to Djemal's Damascus office one day in May.

Travel anywhere in the Ottoman Empire now required a *vesika*, or permit, and one of the few people who could approve the sort of journey Aaronsohn was proposing was Djemal Pasha himself. The governor was undoubtedly very suspicious. He didn't really trust Aaronsohn—or pretty much any Jew, for that matter—and there had recently been that strange business of his assistant caught wandering in the Sinai. To let such a man out of his clutches, even for a visit to an allied nation, was to take a great chance.

Against this, though, was Djemal's desperate need for lubricating oil for his army, a need the Standard Oil Company of New York seemed in no hurry to fulfill despite the staggering concessions he'd given them in Syria. In his usual brusque way, the governor quickly granted Aaronsohn's *vesika* for passage to Constantinople; once there, the scientist would need to clear more bureaucratic hurdles before continuing on to Berlin. But, of course, Aaronsohn had no intention of stopping at Berlin. Instead, he hoped to slip across the German frontier into a neutral country and there make contact with British intelligence; he just hadn't figured out that part of the plan yet.

.   .   .

LAWRENCE SET OUT for the return to Cairo from Iraq aboard a British troopship on May 11. In the past year, he had lost two brothers to this conflict that seemed to have no end, and if by mid-1916 the bankruptcy of the British war effort was everywhere evident, nowhere was it more so than here on its eastern flank. In just thirteen months, Britain had suffered some 350,000 casualties at the hands of "the sick man of Europe," had failed—and failed totally—where a ragtag collection of Balkan militias and armed peasants had repeatedly succeeded just three years earlier. As if that weren't enough, he was just then returning from an experience that, on both a personal and historical level, laid bare that bankruptcy like no other: a futile bid to save the lives of twelve thousand starving and defeated men, a shameful act of groveling in which he'd been forced to take part because the generals who had cast those men to their doom felt it beneath their dignity to do so.

Lawrence would come away from his Iraqi sojourn with two abiding thoughts. One was of the self-defeating arrogance with which the British Indian army had blundered into the country: "By brute force they marched into Basra. The enemy troops in Irak [*sic*] were nearly all Arabs in the unenviable predicament of having to fight on behalf of their [Turkish] secular oppressors against a [British] people long envisaged as liberators, but who obstinately refused to play the part." Their already keen sense of superiority swollen by Basra's easy capture, the British Indian commanders had been contemptuous of local support, even of the need for a defendable supply line, and had instead heedlessly marched their men up the Tigris to ruin. It may have been with the Iraq debacle in mind that Lawrence would later remark, "British generals often gave away in stupidity what they had gained in ignorance."

On a more philosophical level, what Lawrence took from Kut was a deepening antipathy for the imperialist cause. As he would write in *Seven Pillars*, "We pay for these things too much in honour and in innocent lives. I went up the Tigris with one hundred Devon Territorials, young, clean, delightful fellows, full of the power of happiness and of making women and children glad. By them one saw vividly how great it was to be their kin, and English. And we were casting them by the thousands into the fire to the worst of deaths, not to win the war but that the corn and rice and oil of Mesopotamia might be ours. . . . All our subject provinces to me were not worth one dead Englishman."

Still, Lawrence was determined that it should not have all been in vain. During his fourteen-day journey back to Egypt, he composed a long report on all he had been witness to in Iraq, a scathing critique of everything from the British Indian army's docking and warehousing systems, to the inadequacy of its seniormost generals, to the mindless stupidity of their battlefield strategies. But this, too, was to be an effort wasted. After reading Lawrence's incendiary report and learning it was to be passed on to General Archibald Murray, the overall commander of British forces in Egypt, senior officers in the Cairo military intelligence unit decided it was far too indelicate for the general's sensibilities; shortly before the report was to be sent to Murray, they carefully scissored out all of Lawrence's most inflammatory passages, thus ensuring that even now the grim lessons of Kut would stay unlearned. So thoroughly did the censors do their job that it is believed only one copy of Lawrence's original Iraq report survived intact.

FOR ANYONE SEEKING to justify the web of conflicting agreements that Great Britain had spun for itself in the Middle East by the spring of 1916, there were actually several strong arguments close at hand.

Perhaps the most obvious is succinctly conveyed in the old maxim that all is fair in love and war. By May 1916, the war had already killed millions of young men across Europe, and the future appeared to promise only more of the same; if double dealing and unsupportable promises might inch that conflict toward some kind of conclusion, who could reasonably argue against it?

There was also a matter of semantics, of how one defined "independence." While today the word's meaning seems obvious and universal, that was not at all the case in 1916. For many Europeans, steeped in the condescension of the late imperial age, independence didn't mean letting native peoples actually govern themselves, but something far more paternalistic: a new round of "the white man's burden," the tutoring—and, of course, the exploiting—of native peoples until they might sufficiently grasp the ways of modern civilization to stand on their own at some indeterminate point in the future. For those holding such a view—and this probably included not only a majority of the senior statesmen of Great Britain but of every other nation in Europe—the distance between "independence" on the one hand, and "mandates" or "zones of control" or "suzerainty" on the other, didn't appear to be the chasm of contradiction that others saw.

There was also a simple, cynical argument to be made: that the tangle of competing promises didn't much matter because it was probably all going to end up as an academic exercise anyway. Even the most starry-eyed imperialist had to recognize there was something faintly ludicrous about Britain and France sitting around and divvying up the postwar Middle East at a time when, if not outright losing that war, they certainly weren't winning it. As for Emir Hussein, he had been talking about an insurrection against Constantinople since even before the war, and there was still precious little sign of it happening. In the unlikely event that both the Arab revolt *did* come off, and the Entente *did* manage to win the war, the complications would be the best sort of problem to have, one that could be dealt with down the road.

By popular account, on the morning of June 5, 1916, Emir Hussein climbed to a tower of his palace in Mecca and fired an old musket in the direction of the city's Turkish fort. It was the signal to rebellion, and by the end of that day Hussein's followers had launched attacks against a number of Turkish strongpoints across the length of the Hejaz.

By an odd twist of fate, the westerner who had done more than any other to bring that revolt to fruition would never learn of it. Shortly before 5:00 p.m. on that same day, a Royal Navy battleship cruiser, HMS *Hampshire*, left its port in northern Scotland to transport War Secretary Horatio Kitchener to Russia. Less than three hours later, the *Hampshire* struck a German mine and quickly sank in high seas. Nearly every man on board perished, including Kitchener.

Just two weeks earlier, Lawrence had returned from his failed mission to Iraq to resume his desk job at the Savoy Hotel. His future looked much like his past: paper-shuffling, mapmaking, writing up strategies and reports that would never be acted on. Instead, with the news out of Mecca, he would soon have the war of his dreams, one that would catapult him into prominence, and then into legend.

Part Two

Chapter 8

The Battle Joined

The Hejaz war is one of dervishes against regular troops—and we are
on the side of the dervishes.

T. E. LAWRENCE, NOVEMBER 3, 1916

To break the tedium of the hot, slow voyage down the Red Sea, the
officers of HMS *Lama* organized an impromptu pistol-shooting competition on the afternoon of October 15, 1916, their second day out from
Port Suez. Taking advantage of a calm sea, they lined bottles along one
of the converted merchant steamer's rails, then gathered by the far rail to
take turns attempting to blast them to pieces.

The activity was not particularly pleasing to the *Lama*'s most important passenger, the Oriental secretary to Egypt, Ronald Storrs. He had
hoped for a nap in the torpor following lunch, but found it impossible
amid all the gunfire, especially once the ship officers advanced to experi-
menting with a captured Turkish black-powder rifle. "A detonation about
equal to that of an 18-pounder cannon," Storrs noted in his diary. "Conceived the idea, for my return, of holding up any northbound vessel and
boarding her."

One of the standouts in the shooting competition was Storrs's traveling companion, T. E. Lawrence, who had taken up target practice as a
hobby during his days at Carchemish and become an expert marksman.
Excepting Lawrence's fondness for gunplay, Storrs was quite pleased to
have his friend along on this trip. On his two earlier passages down the
Red Sea to Jeddah, the Oriental secretary had despaired at the lack of
interesting company. Already on this one, the "supercerebral" Lawrence

had given him a painstaking tutorial on the Playfair Cipher, an ingenious cryptographic system as simple to construct as it was hard to decode, and, as was their habit back in Cairo, the two had spent much of the rest of the time discussing classical literature and art.

As with Storrs's earlier trips to Jeddah, this October voyage was a result of the Arab Revolt, now a little more than four months old. Having served as a principal conduit between the British government and Emir Hussein in the laborious negotiations leading up to that event, the Oriental secretary had been a natural choice to continue in the role once the battle was joined. By October 1916, however, the Arab Revolt was fast reaching a crisis point, and it was an open question just how much longer it might remain a concern to Ronald Storrs or anyone else.

Testament to its tenuous slapdash nature was the manner in which the outside world had learned of it in the first place. That had coincided with Storrs's first voyage to Arabia in June.

From coded messages secreted out of Mecca, the launch date for the long-delayed uprising had finally been set for June 16, and so Storrs had gone across to Jeddah from the Sudan on June 1 to meet up with Abdullah, the emir's second son and—should it actually come off—the rebellion's chief field commander. Except Abdullah was nowhere to be found. After dispatching an envoy to Mecca with a request that Abdullah come to the coast as soon as possible, Storrs had spent the next four days trolling the Arabian shoreline aboard a British warship looking for some sign of either Turkish or Arab military activity. The dreary port towns had appeared even more soporific than usual.

On June 5, the envoy had finally returned from Mecca with a message from Abdullah. "To the most honoured and respected Mr. Storrs," the letter began. "I deeply regret I am unable to meet you personally, but an urgent need has called me and taken me, so my brother will come to you with all the news." That brother was twenty-year-old Zeid, the youngest of Hussein's four sons, and Storrs was directed to go to Samima, a tiny coastal village south of Jeddah, where Zeid would make his appearance the following morning. Whatever exasperation Storrs felt over these complications was tempered by a peculiar development: according to the envoy, the date for the revolt's launch had been moved up from June 16 to June 10. The Oriental secretary had long come to accept that timetables rarely held in the Arab world, but he could hardly recall an occasion when one had been moved *forward*.

Yet when finally he made contact with Zeid on the following morning, the revised launch date now a mere four days away, there was little hint of urgency. Instead, the cryptic young man had ushered Storrs into his field tent erected on the beach, where he engaged in extended pleasantries and chitchat while a retainer prepared coffee. Once the coffee was served, Zeid handed Storrs an "execrably written" letter from his father, detailing his plans for the coming revolt, as well as a request for £70,000 worth of gold to help bankroll the rebel forces. When Storrs pressed Hussein's son on precisely how they intended to defeat the enemy, it became evident that tactical considerations remained at the rudimentary stage. "We will summon the Turks to surrender," Zeid replied, "and shoot them if they refuse."

The Oriental secretary had barely been able to hide his impatience. The British had been funneling gold and rifles to Hussein for many months now, and Storrs had heard these grand plans—plans unblemished by any attempt at actual execution—for nearly as long; as he and other British agents had informed Hussein many times, no more funds would be released until the revolt began. It was when Storrs reiterated this message on the Samima beach that Zeid finally got around to dropping an interesting bit of news: "I am then happy to be able to announce to you that it began yesterday at Medina."

Hustling Zeid and his chief lieutenant back to the waiting warship, Storrs settled the two men at a hastily prepared breakfast table on the afterbridge, where he and the two military intelligence officers who had accompanied him from Cairo pumped the young sheikh for details. After alerting Cairo to the news, and quickly composing notes of congratulation to Hussein and Abdullah, Storrs gathered up whatever items were close at hand that might provide immediate encouragement to the rebel leaders: £10,000 worth of gold from the ship's safe; five cartons of cigarettes for Faisal and Abdullah, the two smokers in the family; the promise of a Maxim machine gun, to be delivered in one week's time. Lending all this momentous activity a homey touch was the wanderings of a small desert gazelle, bought in some Red Sea bazaar as a ship's mascot, that alternated between pronging the visitors with his horns in a bid for attention and feeding on whatever cigarettes were left lying about.

It had taken some time for clear battle lines to be drawn in the Hejaz. Capitalizing on the element of surprise of the first few days, Hussein's rebels quickly overpowered the tiny Turkish force in Mecca and, with the help of a British naval bombardment, the all-important port of Jeddah. In Taif, Hussein's "summer capital" in the mountains below Mecca, Abdullah's fighters took possession of the town while isolating the Turkish garrison of some three hundred troops in their well-defended fort. Matters didn't go nearly so well in Medina, the Hejaz's largest city. There, the rebels, emboldened by reports of the quick success in Mecca, had charged into the teeth of a vastly larger and entrenched Turkish garrison, some ten thousand soldiers, and been slaughtered by machine-gun and artillery fire. A month into the revolt, an uneasy stasis had set in, Hussein's forces firmly in control of Mecca and Jeddah and several of the smaller southern coastal towns, the Turks just as firmly in control of the railhead city of Medina, 150 miles to the north of Mecca, as well as the coastal towns on the Red Sea's upper reaches.

From a political standpoint, news of the Arab Revolt had been joyously received in Cairo and London. Coming on the heels of the fiascoes at Gallipoli and Kut, here at long last was some good news out of the Middle East. Most crucially, by virtue of his violent break with Constantinople, Hussein—both custodian of Islam's holiest shrines and one of the Arab world's most respected leaders—had fairly laid to rest any lingering fear that the Turks and Germans might finally galvanize their pan-Islamic jihad.

From a military standpoint, however, the British response was a good deal more equivocal. Obviously, if the Arab rebels succeeded in tying down large numbers of Turkish troops in the Arabian Peninsula, that would help protect the British army's right flank in an offensive into Palestine, an operation now in the planning stages in Cairo. On the other hand, by failing to spark a broader Arab uprising—in Syria and elsewhere, the Hejaz revolt had been met with a resounding silence—Hussein's forces were left extremely vulnerable to a Turkish counterattack and, given their spotty conduct thus far, unlikely to prosper in such a contest. In that case, troops and matériel from the British expeditionary army in Egypt might have to be siphoned off to aid the rebels at the very moment that the commander of that army, General Archibald Murray, was jealous to hold every available resource for his prospective push into Palestine.

And that scenario was to invite a much greater risk, one that might swiftly turn the Arab Revolt applauded by Britain's more politically minded war planners into the stuff of their worst nightmares. That's because it was not just the holy cities of Mecca and Medina that, by Koranic dictate, were off-limits to non-Islamic "infidels"; to only a slightly lesser degree this held true for the entire Hejaz. A hint of this had attended Ronald Storrs's first voyage to Arabia in June, when Zeid had refused to allow Storrs's two military intelligence colleagues to accompany him ashore; instead, the Oriental secretary had been compelled to come alone. In the following months, Hussein had concocted a bit of scriptural wiggle room to permit a very small group of British logistics officers to man a supply operation in the coastal town of Rabegh, but strictly restricted their presence to the shoreline. To allow them to venture farther inland, let alone to bring in whole units of rescuing British Christian soldiers in the event of a major rebel setback, would be to play directly into the hands of Turkish propagandists and risk the immolation of all concerned: Hussein no longer regarded as merely a traitor to the Ottoman Empire but to Islam as well; Britain's imperialist, Crusader intentions laid bare before an enraged Muslim world.

In the face of this dilemma, Britain had tried to work at the margins, bringing weaponry and gold to the Hejaz rebels through Rabegh, while ferrying over whatever Muslim troops could readily be spared—primarily Egyptians, along with a few Syrian and Iraqi defectors—to provide training and a small on-the-ground presence. That clearly wasn't enough, though, and as the summer of 1916 wore on, with the rebels' disorganization becoming more apparent and the signs of a Turkish counteroffensive more imminent, the debate in Cairo and London between those seeking a broader involvement and those urging continued caution took on a deepening urgency. Matters were not at all helped by Emir Hussein. Indeed, well into the autumn he had carried on a version of this debate all by himself depending on the latest news from the battlefront, alternately rejecting plans to bring in non-Muslim troops and pleading that any available troops be sent immediately, periodically shifting to the middle ground of asking Cairo to keep such troops on standby for possible intervention down the road.

By October, however, the time for such dithering had come to an end. The Turkish garrison in Medina was now stronger than at the revolt's outset, having been reinforced by rail, and had recently pummeled a rebel attack force led by Faisal, Hussein's third son. With Faisal's warriors now withdrawn into the mountains, there were clear signs that the Turks were preparing to march out of Medina with the goal of both splitting the rebel armies in two and wresting back control of Mecca. In response to the crisis, and to the increasingly anxious appeals of his sons from their various battlefronts, Hussein had finally acceded to the deployment of British troops to the Hejaz.

It was this development that was bringing Ronald Storrs to Jeddah for the third time. In answer to Hussein's request, and over the grumblings of General Murray in Cairo, the British War Committee in London had just agreed to send a brigade of British troops to the Hejaz—anywhere between three and five thousand soldiers—along with a fleet of airplanes. For the Oriental secretary, the opportunity to be the bearer of good news, together with the companionship of T. E. Lawrence, at least partially compensated for the growing distaste he felt for these tedious voyages and for the town of Jeddah itself.

Lawrence had been quite aware of the intense debate that the Arab Revolt had spawned in the upper reaches of the British war machine over the previous months. That awareness came both from his perch within the Cairo intelligence apparatus—the revolt had begun less than two weeks after his return from Iraq—and from his friendship with Storrs. Still, with his area of expertise centered squarely on Syria, he'd remained very much on the outside of these deliberations. In fact, by the time he joined Storrs on the *Lama* that October, his chief contribution to the Hejaz effort could hardly have been more prosaic: postage stamps.

In thinking of how to counteract Turkey's blanket silence on the Arab Revolt in its early days, Storrs had struck upon the idea of issuing "Republic of Hejaz" postage stamps, a cheap and effective way to prove to the outside world that a break had occurred. When he'd asked Emir Hussein for a suitably Islamic design, however, the resulting sketch bore an eerie resemblance to an English lighthouse. Storrs had then enlisted the help of his most learned Arabist friend, Lawrence, and the two spent a leisurely afternoon wandering the Arab Museum in Cairo selecting suitable motifs. Since, as Storrs related, "it was quickly apparent that Lawrence already possessed or had immediately assimilated a complete working technique of philatelic and three-colour reproduction," the Oriental secretary placed his friend in charge of getting the stamps made.

The postage stamp project coincided with a particularly trying time for Lawrence. Ever since coming to Cairo, he and the other eccentrics in Stewart Newcombe's tiny political intelligence unit at the Savoy had been officially attached to the resident Egyptian army, an arrangement Lawrence was quite happy with since the alternative was to fall under the umbrella of the ponderous and fiercely hierarchical structure of General Murray's Egyptian Expeditionary Force (EEF), the "regular" army tasked to take the war to the Turks. However, as part of a bureaucratic reorganization that summer—one of a half dozen wartime reorganizations of the British administration in Cairo that sowed chaos each time—Lawrence had been transferred into an intelligence unit wholly under EEF control. Worse, the reassignment placed Lawrence under the direction of a commanding officer he had little respect for, and required he leave Cairo for the sleepy Suez Canal port town of Ismailia. Lawrence had swiftly requested a transfer back to "the Intrusives" (the name the Savoy Hotel unit had chosen for itself in recognition of their repute within the military bureaucracy), but been just as swiftly denied. "I interpreted this," Lawrence wrote, "not without some friendly evidence, as a method of keeping me away from the Arab affair."

But Lawrence was nothing if not resourceful, and he had next thought to put one of his more pronounced personality traits to good use: the ability to annoy. With his new colleagues in Ismailia, he noted, "I took every opportunity to run into them their comparative ignorance and inefficiency in the department of intelligence (not difficult!) and irritated them yet further by literary airs, correcting Shavian split infinitives and tautologies in their reports."

The strategy worked. In late September 1916, upon learning of Ronald Storrs's upcoming voyage to Jeddah, Lawrence requested a ten-day leave from his new post, which his aggravated superiors were only too happy to grant. In just this way, and in no official capacity save entourage to Ronald Storrs, Lawrence set sail for Arabia for the first time.

Shortly after dawn on October 16, the *Lama* entered the wide bay of Jeddah harbor and made for the port on its sheltered far shore. In the early sun, Lawrence observed only light and shadow among the buildings of that town, while beyond it was "the dazzle of league after league of featureless sand." As the steamer approached its berth, he was to experience that phenomenon common to most who approach Arabia from the water, that moment when the sea-cooled air abruptly collides with that blowing off the land. As Lawrence would write, it was at that instant when "the heat of Arabia came out like a drawn sword and struck us speechless."

IT WAS AN awkward meeting papered over with British politeness. Coming off the *Lama* in midmorning, Storrs and Lawrence made the short walk through Jeddah's narrow streets to the handsome three-story building that housed the British consulate, there to be greeted by the resident British agent, Lieutenant Colonel Cyril Wilson. Wilson led his visitors into a cool and pleasingly shuttered reception room—it was not yet ten o'clock, but the whitewashed buildings of Jeddah already radiated a blinding glare—and ordered up refreshments.

Ronald Storrs had long acquaintance with the slender, mustachioed Wilson, a career army officer previously attached to the British administration in the Sudan, but time had done nothing to improve his opinion of the man. He found Wilson dull and irritable, with a hint of the hysteric—"totally unsuited for anything beyond provincial administration," he'd once written—and thus completely out of his depth in the important position he'd assumed in July, that of British representative to Emir Hussein's Hejaz "government." In fact, the chief reason Storrs hadn't raised his objections to Wilson more forcefully back in Cairo was out of mortal fear that should the man be sacked, Storrs himself might be sent to Jeddah as his replacement.

For his part, Wilson seemed to resent these visits by the Oriental secretary, the automatic deference shown him by Emir Hussein and his emissaries while he, the officer on the ground, saw to all the frustrating and thankless spadework of British policy.

There was also a bit of history between Wilson and Lawrence. Some months earlier in Cairo, the lieutenant colonel had spotted Lawrence wearing an Arab headdress while in uniform, and soundly rebuked him for the offense. There was little indication the intelligence officer had taken the criticisms of his appearance to heart in the interim, however, judging by the sweat-stained uniform with which Lawrence had arrived at the consulate door.

Still, all those in the reception room being British, none of this friction was voiced or even acknowledged. Instead, Storrs and Wilson feigned collegiality as they discussed the current situation in the Hejaz and that day's schedule. In adherence to Arab custom, the first order of business was for them to pay a courtesy call on Sheikh Abdullah, encamped some four miles out of town, as prelude to a more substantive meeting to be held that evening at the consulate. Leaving Lawrence to his own devices, the two senior men set out on horseback for Abdullah's camp in late morning.

When the trio reconvened at the mission building in early afternoon, however, it was to unpleasant news. A cable had arrived from Cairo announcing that, upon further reflection, the War Committee had chosen to recall both the brigade of British troops and the fleet of airplanes slated for imminent arrival in Rabegh. To add insult to injury, the £10,000 of gold that Storrs had brought with him on the *Lama* for disbursement to Abdullah was to be at least temporarily withheld. After their morning visit to Abdullah, during which Storrs and Wilson were the recipients of lavish Arab hospitality, they quite dreaded the sheikh's impending visit to the consulate.

Accompanied by his elaborately costumed court retainers and slaves, Abdullah arrived shortly after five o'clock. Lawrence's first impression was of a particularly jolly man—perhaps heightened just then by Abdullah's recent success in the city of Taif, where the long-resistant Turkish garrison had at last surrendered—with a touch of the voluptuary; though he was not yet thirty-five, the sheikh's face was already taking on the rounded form of one who enjoyed his pleasures and indulged his appetites. His jollity didn't last long. Dispensing with the elaborate pleasantries that normally accompanied such meetings, no sooner had Abdullah and his chief lieutenants settled in the consulate reception room than Wilson began reading aloud from the Cairo cable as Storrs translated into Arabic. Abdullah listened with a hard-to-read stoicism.

Once the reading was finished, Abdullah began to plead his case to Storrs, a turn in the conversation the Oriental secretary tried to forestall by explaining he had absolutely no authority in military matters. It was more than a little disingenuous coming from the man who had penned the secret overture to Hussein back in 1914, and for the first time, the Britons in the room were witness to a flash of Abdullah's temper. "Pardon me," he interrupted, "it was your letter and your messages that began this thing with us, and you know it from the beginning, and from before the beginning."

Duly chastened, Storrs and his two countrymen mutely listened as their visitor delivered a long soliloquy on the current grim state of affairs in the Hejaz and the signal role Great Britain had played in bringing it about. "He gave a fairly accurate historical summary of the negotiations," Storrs ruefully noted in his diary, "quoting several times [His Majesty's Government's] promise that we would do everything possible to help the Arabs."

The conversation lasted for a couple of hours, Abdullah outlining all his current difficulties, Storrs and Wilson promising to do all in their limited power to get this latest decision reversed. Toward the meeting's conclusion, the sheikh turned to the task he clearly wished to avoid: calling his father to break the news. The consulate telephone was brought out and a call put through to Emir Hussein's private line, Mecca 1.

To Storrs's surprise, the emir seemed to take the disappointment rather in stride, stating once again his full confidence in his British partners and his faith that all would work out in the end. When at last Abdullah departed from the mission building that evening, with plans made for his return the next morning, he left his British hosts, as Storrs would relate, "in a state of admiration for him and disgust with ourselves."

One person who had spoken very little through that long, tense meeting—indeed, he may not have spoken at all—was T. E. Lawrence. Part of the reason was obvious: he had no official capacity in being there, and for him to offer an unsolicited opinion at such a delicate encounter would have been a shocking breach of protocol. At the same time, this remove allowed Lawrence to spend the time closely studying Abdullah—or as he himself described it, "playing for effect, watching, criticizing him."

If Emir Hussein was the undisputed spiritual leader of the Arab Revolt, Abdullah was its undisputed field marshal; so manifest was this point that among the British military officers and diplomats involved in the Hejaz affair, it had barely even come up for discussion. Abdullah was his father's most trusted son, the emissary he had sent to Cairo in 1914 to sound out the British over his secessionist plans, the military commander who had seen to the capture of Taif, the family representative who sat down and negotiated with their British advisors.

Yet even at this first meeting, Lawrence had his doubts. Despite the somberness of the conversation at the consulate, he suspected in Abdullah "a constant cheerfulness," the mien of an astute politician but not necessarily a sincere one, a man of overwhelming ambition. But there was more to it than that. In poring over the intelligence reports coming out of the Hejaz over the previous four months, Lawrence had tried to analyze why the revolt had settled into dismal stasis after such a promising start. He had concluded that, at its core, what the rebellion lacked was true leadership, "not intellect, nor judgment, nor political wisdom, but the flame of enthusiasm that would set the desert on fire." What it needed was a prophet, and as that meeting at the consulate had extended, "I became more and more sure that Abdullah was too balanced, too cool, too humourous to be a prophet—especially the armed prophet who, if history be true, succeeded in revolutions."

All of which, had Lawrence voiced these thoughts to his senior colleagues, might have drawn an obvious response: who cares what you think? But Lawrence didn't voice them. Instead, it seems clear that already by the evening of October 16, not yet in Arabia a half day, he had taken it upon himself to calculate a new course for the Arab Revolt, one that would cast him in a central role. That role, as he described it in a moment of profound self-certainty—or breath-catching arrogance, depending on one's perspective—was "to find the yet unknown master-spirit of the affair, and measure his capacity to carry the revolt to the goal I had conceived for it." For any of that to happen, though, would require stealth on Lawrence's part, an ability to keep his own counsel and to quietly look for those openings that might allow him to pursue his agenda. Over the course of that meeting with Abdullah, Lawrence had found his first opening, one he would try to exploit as early as the following morning.

But that long day of October 16, 1916, was not yet over. Before it was, Lawrence was to encounter another personality whose presence loomed large over the Hejaz, one who, by negative example, would soon further clarify the mission Lawrence was creating for himself.

TOWARD THE END of the dinner at the French mission house in Jeddah, Colonel Édouard Brémond raised his champagne glass in toast to his British guests. "I have just heard," he announced, "that my only male relation up till now not killed or wounded in the war has been seriously injured. It is thus my duty and my pride to drink to the Alliance, and to say how much pleasure it gives me to be associated with Englishmen."

That poignant moment on the night of October 16 left a deep impression on Ronald Storrs. "The un-French absence of *panache* in his delivery was very striking. I drank to his cousin's recovery and the success of the French Mission."

Now settled into a somewhat portly middle age, the forty-seven-year-old Brémond was the exemplar of the French imperial soldier, guided by an unwavering belief in both his nation's greatness and the righteousness of its *mission civilisatrice*, or "civilizing mission," to spread Gallic enlightenment and culture to the world's disadvantaged. For most of his military career, he had served in France's North African possessions, Algeria and then Morocco, and from his experiences battling rebellious tribes had gained the reputation of being an expert in irregular warfare. Promotion came steadily if unspectacularly: supervisor of the Moroccan ports police, deputy head of the French military mission to Morocco, administrator of the city of Rabat.

In the run-up to World War I, Brémond had been recalled to France and rushed to the front. As with so many of the French officer class in that horrific first month of the war, Brémond's tenure there was pitifully brief, ending when he was shot through the chest while leading his men into battle on the Belgian frontier. After recuperating from his wounds, he was given command of an infantry regiment, the 64th, where for the next two years he watched his military comrades, as well as his male relatives, fall one by one to the Western Front slaughter. A release of sorts presented itself in the summer of 1916 with the outbreak of the Arab Revolt. In deciding to send a small military mission to the region, the French Defense Ministry had looked to Brémond—"a practicing light in native warfare, a success in French Africa"—and seen the perfect man to lead it.

In fact, the colonel was the ideal candidate for reasons that went beyond his long experience in the Muslim world. As with so many of its actions in the Middle Eastern theater of the war, there was a hidden agenda to the French mission to the Hejaz, one that required both cunning and deviousness to execute. By good luck, these traits were very well honed in Édouard Brémond.

Encouraging the Arabs to revolt had of course been a British operation from the outset, and one that had made the French leadership, with their imperial designs on Syria and Lebanon, very nervous when they'd caught wind of it. Their concerns had been eased by the signing of the secret Sykes-Picot agreement, codifying their Middle Eastern claims, but had come rushing back when the Arab Revolt became a reality. All talk of the Entente Cordiale aside, the French simply didn't trust their British allies to stand by their promises in the region, and with the revolt in the Hejaz, they had now unleashed a revolutionary force that might not be containable even if the British so desired. French anxiety had only deepened when their proposal to send a token military force to the region, a way to protect their future claim and monitor events on the ground, was politely but firmly rebuffed by the British; the situation in the Hejaz was so fluid and delicate, London had argued, that the introduction of another foreign military presence just then could only complicate matters.

So the French pursued a Trojan horse approach instead. The two-hundred-man military unit that sailed out of Marseilles harbor under Colonel Brémond's command in August 1916 was officially titled the French military mission to Egypt. The British couldn't very well bar such a mission from its closest ally, even if it begged the question of just what the French soldiers intended to do in Egypt. To this, Colonel Brémond had a ready answer: to facilitate the passage of Muslim pilgrims from French territories, primarily Morocco and Algeria, seeking to make the hajj to Mecca. The British couldn't very well object to this either, since their army and navy were already providing escort for thousands of Egyptians and Indian Muslims making their own pilgrimage to Mecca.

It had been the last step in this little scheme that even the British had to grudgingly admire for its audacity. Accompanying a group of Moroccan pilgrims to Jeddah in mid-September, Brémond had disembarked, seen to the rental of a suitably impressive building, and announced the arrival of the French military mission to the Hejaz. In short order, he fired off a cable to the French Ministry of Foreign Affairs, urging the establishment of a permanent diplomatic mission to Hussein's administration. When that request was approved, the French military and diplomatic presence in Arabia was technically equal to that of the British, a fait accompli that London found quite impossible to counteract; after all, Paris could argue, here was the opportunity for the two great allies to jointly plan for the region's future on a basis of equality, a course sure to only broaden their eternal bonds of friendship. This was the situation facing Storrs and Lawrence when they arrived in Jeddah in mid-October.

But Brémond's cunning was not limited to the shell game he had executed in establishing his Hejaz mission; it extended to the goal of the mission itself. As he expounded during that dinner at the French consulate on October 16, his overt role in the Hejaz was to show French support for the Arab Revolt, and to ascertain how France might be able to assist it. His covert role, however, was to try to limit the scope of that revolt, to keep it and its aspirations for an Arab nation well away from those Arab lands that France coveted in the postwar era. As for how that might be done, Brémond had a neat, if supremely cynical, plan.

Above all else, he explained to his British guests that night, the Arabs must not be allowed to take Medina. So long as the Turkish garrison there held out, and so long as the Arabs concentrated their blood and treasure on seizing it, the rebellion would remain safely bottled up in the Hejaz. Should Medina fall, he warned, then the Arabs would naturally turn their attention to the north, to liberating from the Turkish yoke their Arab brethren in Palestine and Syria and Iraq, a campaign that would inevitably conflict with British and French imperial designs in the region.

It was cold-blooded perhaps, but a strategy quite brilliant in its simplicity: while trying to help a foreign rebellion succeed was always an iffy proposition, arranging for it to *not* succeed was infinitely easier.

Yet at that dinner at the French consulate, Colonel Brémond was laboring under at least two great misconceptions. The first was that this element of connivance—of lending support to the Arab Revolt as a means to hobble it—was actually necessary. If Brémond had known of the Sykes-Picot Agreement, with its promise of a French Syria and Lebanon, he might have been far more sanguine over the future course of the Arab Revolt. But Sykes-Picot was known to only a very small handful of French government officials, and this group did not include those midlevel military and foreign ministry bureaucrats tasked to defend France's claims in the Middle East. Incredibly, this information had also been withheld from the man sent to Arabia to serve as the frontline guardian of those claims.

Brémond's second misconception was in assuming that, as he held forth to his British guests that evening, he was among friends—or at least, like-minded imperialists. He was not, and he most especially was not of the young British captain who sat at the dining table and barely spoke. As Brémond was soon to discover, in T. E. Lawrence he had a very formidable opponent. What's more, advantage had just passed to Lawrence. At the French consulate, Brémond had laid his hand bare; Lawrence had revealed nothing.

PRECEDED BY A phalanx of slaves, Abdullah rode on a white mare into the courtyard of the British consulate at about ten o'clock the following morning. He was more somber than the day before, and once settled into the consulate reception room, he explained why. He had just received a cable from his brother Faisal at his mountain encampment north of Rabegh reporting that two Turkish warplanes had bombed his camp the previous afternoon; while inflicting little damage, they had sown terror among the tribesmen, most of whom had never seen such machines before. The news was especially pointed, considering the attack came on the same day the British had canceled plans to send their own fleet of airplanes to Arabia.

This drew a response from Lawrence, who suggested that this Turkish show of force shouldn't be cause for much alarm. "Very few Turkish airplanes last more than four or five days," he breezily explained.

It was probably with this comment that Abdullah truly took notice of Lawrence—a mere background presence the previous day—for the first time. He soon had reason to take even greater notice when the conversation turned to a discussion on the location of various Turkish forces around the Middle East. "As Syrian, Circassian, Anatolian, Mesopotamian names came up," Ronald Storrs recalled, "Lawrence at once stated exactly which [Turkish] unit was in each position, until Abdullah turned to me in amazement: 'Is this man God, to know everything?' "

In his memoirs, Storrs attributed his friend's remarkable performance that morning to happy coincidence stemming from Lawrence's labors in the Cairo mapmaking room. Perhaps, or perhaps Lawrence was merely bluffing. Either way, the effect was the same, and it provided Lawrence with the platform to roll out his scheme.

The chief difficulty the British faced in assisting the Arab Revolt, he explained to Abdullah, was a lack of reliable information on what was actually taking place on the ground. What was needed was an objective observer, one who could gain the ear of senior British war planners, to provide a comprehensive report on the situation, both on the problems that seemed to be plaguing the supply pipeline in the port town of Rabegh and on the logistical needs of Faisal's forces in the mountains to the north. Since time was clearly of the essence, Lawrence put himself forth as the man who might carry out this mission.

It was an innocuous enough proposal, and one Abdullah immediately agreed to, suggesting that once Lawrence was in Rabegh, he would arrange for Faisal to come down from the mountains to meet with him. To this, Lawrence politely demurred. He needed to appraise the situation inland for himself, which meant he needed to go to Faisal, not the other way around. Given the stricture against non-Muslims traveling to the interior, it was a bold request. Even Cyril Wilson, who had met Faisal twice and whom Emir Hussein greatly respected, had only been permitted to step down at port towns and wait for Faisal's appearance.

With Storrs joining in the lobbying effort, Abdullah was gradually won over to the idea—no doubt the current tenuousness of the Arab position had a loosening effect—but the ultimate decision rested with the more formidable Hussein. As Abdullah expected, his father was extremely ambivalent to the plan when he was called on the Mecca trunk line, spurring Storrs to take command of the telephone receiver.

"Storrs in full blast was a delight to listen to in the mere matter of Arabic speech," Lawrence would recall, "and also a lesson to every Englishman alive of how to deal with suspicious or unwilling Orientals. It was nearly impossible to resist him for more than a few minutes, and in this case [he] also had his way."

But it was a qualified victory. The most Hussein would allow was for Lawrence to put in at Rabegh, and there to meet with his eldest son, Ali; if Ali "thought fit," he would then arrange Lawrence's onward journey to meet Faisal. It was not at all hard to see how this was going to end up. Ali had a reputation for caution, and for the cautious, the default answer is always no. Storrs and Lawrence resolved to push the matter when Abdullah returned to the British consulate for dinner that evening.

At that dinner, Storrs and Lawrence urged Abdullah to write formal letters of introduction to Ali and Faisal, figuring this would greatly enhance the odds of Lawrence being given permission to travel inland. This Abdullah was initially very reluctant to do, but, gaining his father's approval over the telephone line, Lawrence recounted, Abdullah finally penned "direct written instructions to Ali to mount me as well and as quickly as possible, and convey me, by sure hand, to Faisal's camp."

Early on the morning of October 19, HMS *Lama* put into Rabegh harbor. For the rest of his life, an image would stick in Ronald Storrs's mind of Lawrence standing on the pier and waving goodbye as Storrs's ship turned and made for Egypt. Lawrence's Arabian adventure had begun.

LAWRENCE'S HUNCH ABOUT Ali proved absolutely correct; the eldest Hussein son was staggered when he was handed the letter from Abdullah dictating their father's permission for the young British army captain to travel inland. However, with the fealty with which all the Hussein sons showed their father, Ali saw no choice but to acquiesce, and he set about arranging Lawrence's journey.

Situated at the edge of a broad desert plain, the nondescript little port of Rabegh seemed an unlikely spot to hold anyone's attention for very long, let alone to be the strategic linchpin in the war for control of the Arabian Peninsula. Yet, situated midway between Mecca and Medina, Rabegh was a crucial way station on the "pilgrims' road"—little more than a camel track marked by stone cairns—that linked those two holy cities, which meant it stood squarely in the path of any Turkish army moving south to retake Mecca. Rabegh was also the chief transshipment point for British supplies and weaponry coming down from Egypt to be distributed to the rebels fighting inland—or *not* distributed, merely vanishing somewhere en route, as more often seemed to be the case.

If Rabegh was not the most appealing place, the two and a half days Lawrence spent there did provide him with the chance to meet two more of Emir Hussein's sons, and to submit them to the same sort of character study he had performed on Abdullah in Jeddah.

By coincidence, Zeid, the youngest, had recently arrived to help Ali sort out the supply-line problems. A half brother to Hussein's other three sons, Zeid was a handsome youth of twenty, who had inherited the pale complexion and softer features of his Turkish mother. Although he was clearly quite intelligent, both his youth and non-Arab appearance would have made him an unlikely rebel commander even if he possessed leadership traits, which he did not. "Is fond of riding about and playing tricks," Lawrence noted. "Humorous in outlook, and perhaps a little better balanced, because less intense, than his brothers. Shy."

Despite the strained circumstances of their first meeting, Lawrence took a quick liking to Ali. "His manner was dignified and admirable, but direct," he wrote, "and he struck me as a pleasant gentleman, conscientious." But there was a forlorn, tired air to Hussein's eldest son, his skin sallow, his mouth "sad and drooping," that made him seem far older than his thirty-seven years. Without apparent ambition for himself, Lawrence observed, Ali also seemed to fall under the sway of whatever more dynamic personality happened to be nearby, hardly the hallmark of a natural leader. Still, Lawrence much preferred Ali to Abdullah, noting that "if Faisal should turn out to be no prophet, the revolt would make shift well enough with Ali for its head." Perhaps, but it was a make-do assessment that considerably raised the stakes for Lawrence's meeting with Faisal.

He set out for that meeting on the night of October 21. Indicative of Ali's abiding concern over the journey—part of the hundred-mile trek would be through areas controlled by tribes hostile to the revolt—were the elaborate precautions he'd taken, keeping news of Lawrence's departure and destination secret from even his closest household slaves. To serve as Lawrence's guides, he had chosen two of his most trusted lieutenants, a father and son who, by the unwritten law of the Arabian tribes, were expected to lay down their lives to protect their charge. Ali further directed the three men to avoid all settlements along the route and to travel at night as much as possible, even that Lawrence wear a headdress over his army uniform so as to cast a sufficiently Arab-looking silhouette in the moonlight.

The potential for danger notwithstanding, very soon after setting out Lawrence's preoccupation turned to the more mundane, the grinding physical discomfort of riding a camel again after two years sitting behind a desk at the Savoy Hotel. Since its pronounced and narrow spine lies just below the skin, riding a camel is a wholly different experience from riding a horse, more akin to sitting atop a swaying metal rod. Even the best Bedouin saddle—little more than a wood-and-leather frame covered in blankets—can only slightly dull the pain for the green rider. Most such riders can rarely withstand the suffering for more than two or three hours without a break, but Lawrence was to have no such luxury on this journey; instead, what lay before him was an ordeal of some thirty hours in the saddle broken only by two short breaks. He spurred himself on by summoning the extraordinary endurance he had shown in the past—on his bicycle tours of France, on his twelve-hundred-mile hike through Syria—and by holding the thought that at the other end awaited the last of the Hussein brothers, the man who might prove to be his "prophet" of war.

Despite his discomfort—or maybe as a way to distract from it—Lawrence made a careful study of the terrain they were crossing, jotting down notes in his small army-issue notebook as he rode. He was traversing a land only a handful of outsiders had ever glimpsed, one steeped in a desert culture little changed in millennia, but with just enough similarities to the Syria he knew so well as to be thoroughly disorienting. In Syria he had made a hobby of sorting out the complicated clan and tribal structures, the complex rules that governed their interaction, but in Arabia all those rules were far more layered, far more rigidly upheld.

"Each hill and valley in it had a man who was its acknowledged owner," he wrote, "and [who] would quickly assert the right of his family or clan to it against aggression. Even the wells and trees had their masters, who allowed men to make firewood of the one and drink of the other freely, as much as was required for their need, but who would instantly check anyone trying to turn the property to account. . . . The desert was held in a crazed communism by which Nature and the elements were for the free use of every known friendly person for his own purposes and no more."

In Syria, the price for transgression was most often ostracism, perhaps the handing over of a sheep in fine; in the sere and harsh landscape of Arabia, it was death.

But if still the amateur anthropologist, Lawrence was also taking note of the topography of the Hejaz through the eyes of a military man: where sources of water might be found, the trails an army might navigate to best advantage. In this way, he happened upon a glaring hole in his own army's contingency plans.

In preparing for the defense of Rabegh—which by definition also meant the defense of Mecca—British officers advising the rebels had mapped out the Turks' most likely approaches, ones predicated on the existence of trails and the supply of water, and overseen the building of outlying guardposts accordingly. Yet on his journey to Faisal's camp, Lawrence came upon two seasonal watercourses that didn't appear on any British maps, and that would allow an attacking army to either fall on Rabegh from an unforeseen direction or to sidestep the port town completely on its way to Mecca. How had the British advisors, who had now been in Rabegh for three months, remained ignorant of these watercourses, and why had the local Arabs, who surely knew of them, not raised the alarm? Quite simply, because quarantined as they were on the shoreline, the British hadn't been aware enough of their surroundings to formulate the question, and without the question, the Arabs hadn't been aware enough of British concerns to offer the information. To Lawrence, it underscored both the difficulty in trying to marry two such very different cultures for the purpose of making war, and the potential for disaster in Hussein's stricture against nonbelievers traveling inland; no matter how many British troops were brought over, so long as they were isolated on the coast, in their ability to gauge danger they might as well be in blindfolds.

In the early afternoon of October 23, Lawrence's party rounded a wall of high stone cliffs to suddenly find themselves in the verdant valley of Wadi Safra, the refuge for Faisal's rebel army that had so recently been humbled outside Medina. As they ascended toward the headwaters, Lawrence began to see small encampments of armed men scattered among the hillside villages, camps that steadily grew in size and proliferation until they seemed to fill most every level stretch of land.

At last the party entered Hamra, a village of about one hundred homes, and drew up before a long, low house where a sword-wielding slave stood guard. Dismounting from his camel, Lawrence was admitted into the inner courtyard to see the profile of a man standing in the far doorway. "[He] looked very tall and pillar-like," he wrote, "very slender, in his long white silk robes and his brown headcloth bound with a brilliant scarlet and gold cord. His eyelids were drooped, and his black beard and colorless face were like a mask against the strange, still watchfulness of his body."

It was Faisal ibn Hussein. As Lawrence would later write in *Seven Pillars of Wisdom*, "I felt at first glance that this was the man I had come to Arabia to seek, the leader who would bring the Arab Revolt to full glory."

MAYBE, BUT IN actual fact, their initial meeting did not go well. Ushered into the home, Lawrence joined Faisal and a dozen or so other men, chieftains of various tribes that had joined the revolt, in a dimly lit room covered with carpets. As did his brothers, Faisal possessed a courtly graciousness, and he thanked Lawrence for making the long and difficult journey to visit him. This preamble soon gave way, though, to a more somber discussion of his recent string of military setbacks at the hands of the Turks.

Of Hussein's sons, Faisal and his followers had borne the greatest amount of fighting since the start of the revolt, and had done so while receiving the least in the way of supplies and funds. Most recently, he explained to his visitor, his men had been on the verge of a great victory at Bir Abbas, on Medina's outskirts. Instead, for lack of artillery to counteract that brought to bear by the Turks, his army had foundered and then been scattered. The remnants of that army—many had peeled away and returned to their homes—were now encamped there with him in the mountain safeness of Hamra, awaiting the Turks' next move. That was how things stood. Properly supplied and armed, Faisal contended, his men were capable of anything, but if the current situation persisted, where they had to beg the British for every ounce of matériel—most of which never reached the front lines anyway—then the future course of the uprising was already written. When the Turks came out of their stronghold in Medina and marched for the coast, a march that now seemed imminent, it would leave Faisal with the choice of either being stranded in the mountains or beating a retreat back toward Mecca. The first option would mean slow annihilation, the second rapid disintegration, for just as had occurred after Bir Abbas, many of his followers would refuse to flee so far away from their tribal areas—they would just go home.

Even as he listened, Lawrence intently studied Faisal, looking for clues to both his personality and the nature of the hold he had over the other men crowded into the room. "He was a man of moods," he noted, "flickering between glory and despair, and just now dead tired. He looked years older than thirty-one, and his dark, appealing eyes, set a little sloping in his face, were bloodshot, and his hollow cheeks deeply lined and puckered with reflection.... In appearance he was tall, graceful and vigorous, with the most beautiful gait, and a royal dignity of head and shoulders. Of course he knew it, and a great part of his public expression was by sign and gesture."

Maybe it was also Faisal's exhaustion that caused him to speak far more bluntly than his brothers had of the element of distrust that lay at the core of the Arabs' relationship with Britain, a distrust reflected in everything from Hussein's tortuous two-year negotiation with Storrs and McMahon to the restricting of British advisors to the coast. Since history clearly showed the British didn't help others out of the goodness of their heart, Faisal asked, just what was it they wanted of the Hejaz?

As many other British officers had done with other members of Hussein's Hashemite clan, in the dimly lit home in Hamra, Lawrence patiently reassured Faisal that the British had absolutely no territorial interests in the Hejaz. That assurance lost some of its luster, Faisal pointed out, when it was recalled that the British had said precisely the same thing about the Sudan before grabbing it.

Their somewhat prickly conversation extended through dinner, then started up again at 6:30 the next morning when Faisal showed up at Lawrence's tent. In these talks, Lawrence found Hussein's third son to be "most unreasonable," and yet there was something about the passion with which he spoke, the hard determination behind it, that Lawrence found profoundly compelling. It was a passion he'd found lacking in both Abdullah or Ali, and it fueled his conviction that in Faisal he had found his leader.

That conviction was strengthened when Lawrence spent several hours that day wandering among the rebel encampments, falling into conversation with whoever crossed his path. One of the first things that struck him was the range of tribes they represented. In the ever-fractious world of Arabia, rare was the man who could unite even the various tribes and clans in his immediate area, but here in Wadi Safra were thousands of men representing nearly every tribal group across the breadth of the western Hejaz, some a full two weeks' journey away from their homelands. Even more remarkable, this was an army that had been put to flight by the Turks just a week earlier, and yet their morale and confidence in ultimate victory seemed utterly unshaken. The man who had molded that unity and spurred that confidence was Faisal.

That evening, having been in Wadi Safra for only slightly more than twenty-four hours, Lawrence stopped by Faisal's headquarters to say goodbye. Their parting conversation was more relaxed than those of earlier, with Faisal thanking Lawrence for coming and Lawrence holding out the vague hope that perhaps his trip would prove of some benefit. With that, he mounted a new camel and, with a squad of fourteen warriors as bodyguards, made for the nearest rebel-held Red Sea port, the town of Yenbo, where a British ship might collect him for his return to Egypt. He was anxious to get there, for he was now firmly convinced that in Faisal ibn Hussein the revolt had found its prophet. "It was all and more than we had hoped for," he wrote, "much more than our halting course deserved. The aim of my trip was fulfilled."

Chapter 9

The Man Who Would Be Kingmaker

[Faisal] is hot tempered, proud and impatient, sometimes unreasonable
and runs off easily at tangents. Possesses far more personal magnetism
and life than his brothers, but less prudence. Obviously very clever,
perhaps not over scrupulous . . . Had he been brought up the wrong way
might have become a barrack yard officer. A popular idol, and ambitious;
full of dreams, and the capacity to realize them.

T. E. LAWRENCE ON FAISAL IBN HUSSEIN, OCTOBER 30, 1916

Doggedness and good luck had made Lawrence's visit to the Hejaz
an extraordinarily successful one. In a mere ten days, he had met
all four of Emir Hussein's sons, as well as the principal Allied envoys in
Jeddah. He had also seen firsthand the British efforts at establishing a
supply line for the rebels at Rabegh, and been the first outsider to journey
inland for a look at the actual battlefront. Now, as he rode into Yenbo on
the morning of October 26, 1916, he was anxious to get back to Cairo to
report on his findings.

In that dusty little port town, however, his fortunes suddenly flagged.
A British warship had been scheduled to make a Yenbo port of call, but
the appointed day came and went with no sign of it. With no choice but
to wait—for a total of five days, it would turn out—Lawrence took up
quarters in a modest three-story house overlooking the tiny waterfront,
the home of Faisal's local liaison officer, and there set to work writing up
the impressions of his journey. In his usual crabbed hand, and with only a
blue fountain pen and some scrap paper by way of supplies, over the next
five days he would put some seventeen thousand words to paper.

It was also in that house in Yenbo where the dueling legends of T. E. Lawrence were to be born. To his lionizers, Lawrence's acute grasp of the situation on the ground in Arabia, combined with his brilliance at conveying that understanding into words, was about to make him a man born to the hour, a prime example of the phenomenon in which a particular kind of genius is finally joined to the circumstances he has spent his entire life working toward. To his detractors, what was about to happen could be largely, even wholly, attributed to random chance, that the myriad small events which were to transpire over the next three weeks and so improbably turn to Lawrence's advantage—the strange coincidences, the timing and mistiming of messages, the byzantine maneuverings by generals and statesmen—were beyond any prediction. If all these factors were tossed into some giant cosmic hopper, so this narrative goes, it never would have played out in quite the same sequence again.

The specifics of Lawrence's résumé that October would actually appear to provide fodder for the latter version of the legend. At Yenbo, he was a twenty-eight-year-old army captain without a single day of military training; at that time, policy in Arabia was being debated at the highest levels of the British military and political leadership. True, he was the first British officer to glimpse the rebel fighters in the field, but that glimpse had lasted all of twenty-six hours and essentially consisted of watching them lounge about a valley encampment, hardly the basis for an authoritative analysis. Nor were most of his observations truly unique; among the handful of British military officers who had preceded him to the Hejaz, nearly all had noted the completely ad hoc nature of the Arab "army," its lack of anything approaching conventional military discipline, even its abject terror of enemy artillery and airplanes.

But of course, Lawrence hadn't merely his brief sojourn to Faisal's camp to draw on, but the years he had spent immersing himself in Arab culture in Carchemish. From this he'd gained a profound appreciation for how clan and tribal alliances worked, how that structure might play out on the battlefield, and how unusual it was to find a leader capable of forging a coalition of tribes for anything more than a very short-term goal. In addition, starting as a young boy and continuing through his years at Oxford, Lawrence had obsessively focused on one very particular field of scholarship—medieval military history—and warfare in early-twentieth-century Arabia bore striking similarities to that in fourteenth-century Europe. These similarities extended from how a fighting force was recruited, to its leadership structure—trade out sheikhs and emirs for lords and thanes and princes—to how that fighting force maneuvered in the field. In 1916 Hejaz, much like 1356 France, an army on the move was wholly dependent on satisfying its most elemental needs—

water, the availability of draft animals, forage—and this dictated where it went, whom it fought, and when. Lawrence, with a knowledge of medieval military strategies surpassed by but a small handful of people alive, found many of the features of the Arabian battlefield instantly recognizable, and certainly far more familiar than to a professionally trained officer steeped in Napoleonic or even current Western Front precepts.

With this cultural and scholarly grounding, Lawrence immediately saw the utter futility of trying to transform the Arab rebel fighting force into something it was not, and never would be—namely, a conventional European-style army. The only way forward, he argued in the reports he penned in Yenbo, was for the British to accept the Arab way of war, and to adapt their strategies and expectations accordingly.

But even this was not terribly controversial or original as far as it went—after all, even the most hidebound military officer recognizes the need to adjust to the men and matériel at his disposal—but from his brief time in the Hejaz, Lawrence had come to two specific conclusions that were much more so.

In light of the woeful lack of military success since the early days of the Arab Revolt, there was a growing consensus in both London and Cairo that a sizable British force would have to be dispatched to the Hejaz to bolster the rebel forces; the most common figure bandied about was a brigade, or at least three thousand soldiers. In October, Emir Hussein continued to vacillate about this idea, worried that such an "infidel" presence in the Muslim holy land would undermine his standing with the tribes currently joined to him. From his own travels, and especially from the wariness he had encountered in Faisal's camp, Lawrence concluded that Hussein's apprehensions were absolutely valid; while a small group of European advisors and trainers setting up shop on the coastline would be "joyously welcomed," he wrote, any larger force was likely to be resented and play into Turkish propaganda about Christian Crusaders. By arguing for this minimal presence, Lawrence was placing himself against the majority opinion of the British military command staff, including that held by the two British officers who'd spent the most time in the Hejaz, Lt. Colonel Cyril Wilson and his deputy, Alfred Parker.

Even more potentially contentious was Lawrence's notion that the true "prophet" of the revolt was the soft-spoken and austere Faisal. Going back to even before the war, British officials had regarded the gregarious and dynamic Abdullah as their chief ally in the Hejaz, the son in closest counsel to the mercurial Hussein, and nothing since the revolt's outbreak had changed that view. To the contrary, it was to Abdullah that those officials continued to turn in hopes of divining what the old man might be thinking, and in charting the next stage in the fighting. By contrast, prior to Lawrence, the only British officials to have met Faisal were Wilson and Parker, and then to rather thin conclusion; if liking Faisal on a personal level, Wilson had sensed in the emir's third son "a man who can't stand the racket" of combat—essentially, a coward—an estimation he had conveyed to the British leadership. When it came to promoting Faisal as the revolt's real leader, Lawrence constituted a minority of precisely one.

And so, against the very long odds on both these points, just how did Lawrence eventually win out? A case of genius not to be denied, or sheer dumb luck?

What the purveyors of both dueling legends tend to overlook is that, already at Yenbo, Lawrence had a formidable, if rather unglamorous, weapon in his arsenal. From his position at the inner circle of the military intelligence apparatus in Cairo, he possessed an intimate grasp of the British military and political power structure deciding policy in Arabia. But "structure" is far too charitable a word. In fact, it was a bureaucratic quagmire, a maze of overlapping ministries and competing agendas and feuding personalities. From his reading at the Savoy Hotel—and virtually nothing was so classified as to be beyond his purview—Lawrence knew who all the principal players were in this morass, the opinions they held, and, perhaps most important, who their rivals were. Along with writing up his reports, the five-day wait in Yenbo gave him time to contemplate the mind-numbingly complex political chessboard that lay before him, and to devise a strategy whereby he might play off the competing factions and see his ideas win out.

He would be assisted in this by something else often overlooked: the nature of communications at the time. In some spheres, this was fantastically advanced from just decades earlier, in others still quite primitive. In 1916, the mimeograph machine could make hundreds, even thousands of copies of an important document; for most everything else, there was the century-old technology of carbon paper. Via the wireless telegraph, a message could be sent from London to Buenos Aires in a matter of minutes, while delivering that same message to someone just ten miles away in a place like Arabia required the dispatch of a courier on foot or horseback. Lawrence would prove very adept at using both the advances and deficiencies in communications to his advantage, repeatedly breaching protocol to get messages to his allies quickly, conveniently failing to receive undesired orders—"garbled transmission" was a favorite excuse—until it was too late and the matter decided. Joined to a certain ruthless streak, it all enabled T. E. Lawrence to emerge as a kind of exemplar of the bureaucratic infighter, with a prowess that even the most devious palace intriguer or tenure-track college professor might envy.

Over the next three weeks, Lawrence would be employed as point man—hatchet man might be a more apt term—by a variety of British officials seeking to promote their agendas over those of their rivals. In that role, the twenty-eight-year-old captain would adroitly work all sides of the street, allowing him to administer a brutal blow to French designs in the region, undermine an immensely powerful British official, and help catalyze a fundamental shift in British policy in Arabia. In the process, he would also alter the course of the Arab Revolt, and his own role within it.

It was an ascendancy that got off to a shaky start, however. On October 31, HMS *Suva*, under the command of a career naval officer named William "Ginger" Boyle, so nicknamed for his red hair, put in to Yenbo to finally free Lawrence from his enforced Arabian interlude.

"I had heard of a Captain Lawrence being on the coast," Boyle would recall in his memoirs. "I had assumed he was one of the military officers sent over and was a little astonished when a small, untidily dressed and most unmilitary figure strolled up to me on board . . . hands in pockets and so without a salute." Noticing that Lawrence had three captain stars on one shoulder strap but inexplicably none on the other, the no-nonsense Boyle refused even to acknowledge his passenger and instead pointed him over to his first lieutenant; the ship captain was gratified when the lieutenant roundly upbraided Lawrence for his lack of manners.

In his own recollection of that meeting, Lawrence conceded his failure to make a good first impression on Ginger Boyle but was more inclined to attribute the problem to genetics. "Red-haired men," he pointed out, "are seldom patient."

BY ALL ACCOUNTS, Édouard Brémond had taken little notice of the quiet British army captain who attended his dinner at the French mission on October 16. There was little reason he should have. The French colonel's principal guests that evening had been his British counterpart in Jeddah, Cyril Wilson, and the visiting Oriental secretary for Egypt, Ronald Storrs, a gregarious and witty table companion. By contrast, Captain Lawrence had been so slight in stature and so youthful in face that, in his ill-fitting uniform, he might easily have been mistaken for an adolescent playing at soldier. Brémond had ample reason to revisit that assessment when Lawrence returned to the French mission dining hall at the beginning of November. At that dinner, the unassuming young officer of three weeks before was loquacious, even commandeering of the conversation, and Brémond was aghast at what he was saying.

When HMS *Suva* had turned into Yenbo bay on October 31, Lawrence had assumed he would soon be on his way back to Cairo. Instead, Cyril Wilson's deputy in the Hejaz, Colonel Alfred Parker, had come up on the *Suva* to hear firsthand what Lawrence had found at Faisal's camp. Impressed by his insights, Parker had suggested that Lawrence first make for Khartoum in order to confer with Reginald Wingate, the governor-general of the Sudan and one of the most important British officials involved in Arabian affairs. As a result, the *Suva* had carried Lawrence two hundred miles back down the coast to Jeddah, where a second ship was readied to take him on the short hop across the Red Sea to the Sudan. Testament to the sudden interest in his mission, this second ship, HMS *Euryalus*, was the flagship of the Red Sea fleet and under the personal direction of the fleet commander, Admiral Rosslyn Wemyss.

Hearing of all this, Colonel Brémond was also keen to learn what the young army captain had observed in Faisal's camp and, perhaps even more, just what he intended to tell Reginald Wingate. This had prompted his invitation to Lawrence and Wemyss to be his dinner guests in Jeddah. At that gathering, it soon became clear that most every opinion Captain Lawrence had formed ran directly counter to what the French colonel was trying to achieve in Arabia.

Since setting up shop in Jeddah in early September, Brémond had lobbied for a greatly expanded Allied military presence in the Hejaz. Certainly part of his argument had root in his very low opinion of the fighting capability of Hussein's rebels. Time and again, he had proposed that the two hundred French technical advisors who were under his command and currently sitting idle in Egypt be brought down to Rabegh, where they might start transforming the Arabs into a credible fighting force. Of course, such a small force would be completely vulnerable in the event of a Turkish attack on that port town, Brémond argued, so he further proposed that a sizable contingent of British soldiers—at least a brigade, perhaps two—be brought from Egypt to secure the area and provide protection. If the French colonel had his way, the Western military presence in the Hejaz would be expanded from a tiny handful of men—himself, Wilson, and Parker, the few British logistics officers scattered along the shoreline—to anywhere between three thousand and ten thousand.

Left unspoken in this proposition was how it neatly dovetailed with France's—or at least Colonel Brémond's—hidden agenda. With a large force of Allied troops on the ground, it would be that much easier to monitor and control events, and to prevent the Arab Revolt from spreading north into Syria. Even better, with an absolutely minimal French investment, its two hundred soldiers alongside Britain's thousands, France would achieve a physical military presence in the Middle East, and further stake its claim to being a joint and equal partner with Britain in the region.

Even without grasping Brémond's ulterior motives, the commander of the Egyptian Expeditionary Force in Cairo, General Archibald Murray, had given the idea a frosty reception. Tasked to launch an offensive into southern Palestine on the far side of the Sinai Peninsula, and with his army already being periodically poached by Western Front commanders looking for fresh bodies to fling against the Germans in France, Murray was adamantly opposed to parting with any more of his men for the "side-show" in Arabia.

Brémond had enjoyed much better luck in his approach to Reginald Wingate. Indeed, the Sudan governor-general was a perfect British foil for the Frenchman, a fervent believer in the importance of the Arab rebellion, but just as fervently convinced that the rebels could never carry the day on their own. Along with Brémond's counsel, Wingate's conviction on this point was constantly reinforced by the two political officers he had sent to Arabia, Wilson and Parker, both of whom believed the revolt would soon collapse if foreign troops didn't come in. Of course, it was easy enough for Wingate to lobby for such a move, since he didn't have the soldiers to send; instead, they would have to be taken off Murray in Egypt. The way Brémond figured it, with Wingate as an ally it was simply a mat-ter of waiting for the next Arab setback, at which point they could join forces and, sidestepping Murray, appeal directly to London for a military deployment.

Brémond didn't have to wait long. In fact, an opportunity had pre-sented itself in those same few days that Lawrence was stranded in Yenbo. In late October, news had come in of a large Turkish force closing on Rabegh. The report had sown panic among the Arab forces in the foothills above that vital port town, triggering a stampede toward the coast. Seeing their opening, Wingate and Brémond had moved quickly. Wingate fired off a cable to London urging that an Anglo-French force be readied to land at Rabegh. Following Wingate's lead, Brémond had a note passed to the British Foreign Office announcing that while he was fully prepared to speed his idled soldiers and artillery guns to Rabegh's relief, it would be "highly imprudent" to do so "unless they could be protected by a suf-ficient escort to secure their not falling into enemy hands." As for just what size "escort" the French colonel was looking for, Wingate provided his government with the specifics: a minimum of six battalions, or some six thousand British soldiers.

Faced with such an urgent appeal, the British War Committee came close to approving the proposal, and probably would have if not for the strenuous objections of General Murray, the man on the hook for supply-ing those six thousand troops. On November 2, the War Committee had declined to order any deployments out of Egypt, but instead suggested that Brémond and Wingate rustle up whatever soldiers they could under their commands and rush them to Rabegh—a suggestion that obviously led the coescalationists right back to square one.

If disappointed by London's decision, Brémond was surely heartened by a new bit of information that came in that same day. As Alfred Parker in Rabegh reported, there was no Turkish force closing on that town, and there never had been; rather, the entire crisis had been sparked by an erroneous rumor. The embarrassing episode, Parker acidly noted, "proves that Rabegh force could not stand for a moment if threatened. . . . I consider best solution would be British Govt. [War Committee] to reconsider their decision and land brigade at Rabegh."

That was music to Brémond's ears, and he could be confident that a new chance to lobby the War Committee would soon present itself; after all, if the rebels had been put to flight by a rumor, what was going to happen when the Turks launched a bona fide attack?

It was at this precise juncture, however, that T. E. Lawrence reappeared in Jeddah.

As Lawrence expounded over dinner at the French mission, from the time he had spent with Ali in Rabegh and Faisal in Hamra, he was now convinced that any Allied military presence in Arabia should be an absolutely minimal one; Hussein's rebels would gladly receive weapons and military training from Christian "infidel" advisors, whether they were French or British, but anything more expansive was sure to fuel fears of a European takeover and cause the revolt's destruction from within.

This was an analysis upon which reasonable men could disagree—and Brémond did disagree, strenuously—but what truly stunned him was Lawrence's further contention that, quite aside from the religious issue, such a force was altogether unnecessary. In his view, the strength of the Arab fighters was as a defensive force, and commanding as they did the narrow gorges and defiles that stood between Medina and the coast, their position was all but impregnable to any conceivable approach a Turkish army might make. So long as the Arabs held those heights—and it was hard to see how they might ever be dislodged given that the terrain was completely unsuited to the Turks' advantage in artillery and airplanes—Rabegh was perfectly safe.

Brémond was too polite a host to point out that this assertion was being made by a man who had observed the rebels in the field for all of one day, but he surely asked how this view squared with the recent rebel stampede above Rabegh; apparently the Arabs didn't share in the belief of their positions' impregnability if they were willing to abandon them on a rumor. It was perhaps in reply to this line of questioning that Lawrence made a further assertion: it had been Ali's men who had panicked at Rabegh, not Faisal's, and it was Faisal who was the true leader of the revolt.

Even more than Lawrence's other opinions, it was this declaration that flabbergasted Brémond. The colonel had yet to meet Faisal, but nothing he'd heard suggested Hussein's third son as either a natural or decisive leader; instead, as Brémond would shortly report to Paris, "[Faisal] talks a lot but says nothing. He acts little and does nothing."

But from a French perspective, the thought of promoting Faisal's leadership was also alarming. By all accounts, he was far more distrusting of the European allies than his older brothers. There was also the matter of his long dalliance with the pro-independence Arab conspirators in Syria. Even if Djemal Pasha had hunted down many of those conspirators, no doubt parts of the network still existed, and for a France eager to keep the Arab Revolt well away from Syria, there could be no prospect more worrisome than the ascent of Faisal.

Brémond might have been tempted to write Lawrence off as a particularly irksome dinner guest, his bold assertions those of a naïf infused with a sense of self-importance, save for a couple of details. One was his manner. He stated his views with utter and unshakable confidence, a confidence bordering on the impertinent when it came to military protocol; no matter the seniority or rank of those who disagreed with him, the army captain with the icy blue eyes refused to back down. Another was the effect he'd had on Admiral Wemyss. Whatever the admiral's views on a deployment to Arabia had been previously, it was clear he was much impressed by Lawrence, and now held very similar opinions; in fact, Wemyss was planning to accompany Lawrence to Khartoum so that they might make their case to Wingate jointly. Not surprisingly, it made Édouard Brémond extremely apprehensive of what might happen once these two came into contact with the man who up until then had been his closest British ally.

After that dinner in Jeddah, Colonel Brémond disparagingly remarked that Lawrence had become a "vassal" of Faisal. As he got to know Lawrence better in the months ahead, however, Brémond would conclude he'd had it the wrong way around, that the unassuming little British captain had a selfish, even sinister, motive in promoting Faisal. If a British brigade was put ashore in Arabia, a proper military command structure would be established, one that would leave no role for an inexperienced desk officer like Captain Lawrence. Absent that intervention, it would be up to Hussein's sons to carry the day, and in the soft and hesitant figure of Faisal, Brémond deduced, Lawrence had found a man he might bend to his will, allowing him to become the unseen kingmaker of Arabia.

. . .

ON THE SAME day that Lawrence set out for Faisal's camp in the mountains, October 22, a most curious drama had unfolded in northern Scotland. It began when a Scandinavian-American Line passenger ship, the *Oskar II*, put in at the coal refueling station in the Orkney Islands town of Kirkwall.

Although the *Oskar II* was transiting between two neutral countries—she was out of Denmark and bound for New York City—the Orkneys were an extremely sensitive area for the British military, the site of their main wartime naval base in the harbor known as Scapa Flow. Always on the lookout for spies or saboteurs, a team of British police inspectors boarded the Swedish-registered ship for a routine check of the passports and luggage of its passengers. On that day, they found someone of great interest. He was a stout forty-one-year-old Ottoman citizen who had recently crossed into neutral Denmark from Germany.

Detaining the man on deck in plain view of other passengers, the inspectors made a thorough search of his cabin; as they subsequently informed the *Oskar II* captain in the presence of gawking passengers, they found it "full of German stuff." Taken off the ship in a police launch, the man was held that night under guard at a Kirkwall hotel, then transferred the next day to the Scottish mainland. Brought to London, by the morning of October 25 he was undergoing questioning by Basil Thomson, the head of Scotland Yard's Criminal Investigation Department, and the official in charge of tracking subversives and spies in wartime Britain.

It wasn't until the *Oskar II* reached New York City that the British detention of Aaron Aaronsohn became publicly known. It immediately caused a stir in certain circles, especially within the American Zionist community and among those agricultural scientists who had come to know Aaronsohn during his extended prewar visits to the United States. For members of both these groups, it seemed utterly inconceivable that the Jewish agronomist might be an agent for the Central Powers, the accusation implicit in his detention at Kirkwall. On the other hand, there was the disquieting fact that he had chosen to remain in Ottoman-ruled Palestine at the war's outbreak, even as many other Jewish émigrés had fled to neutral nations or British-ruled Egypt. Then there was the highly suspicious nature of his journey across war-torn central Europe to reach Denmark. Certainly that trip could not have been made without the approval of high officials in both the Turkish and German governments.

At least one of Aaronsohn's fellow passengers on the *Oskar II* fervently believed in his innocence. A German Jewish socialite named Olga Bernhardt, she had become very friendly with the agronomist during the voyage from Copenhagen, and she sought to publicize his plight once she reached America. That effort badly backfired when, apparently alerted by Bernhardt, the *New York Evening Post* instead characterized Aaronsohn's detention as that of a dangerous Turkish spy. With that, any campaign within the American scientific or Jewish communities to win his release quickly fizzled.

Which actually suited Aaron Aaronsohn just fine. That's because his "arrest" at Kirkwall had been an elaborate charade. He was a spy, or at least he very much wanted to be, but for the other side in the conflict, and his removal from the *Oskar II* with its theatric touches—placing him under guard in public view, the semipublic announcement of what had been found in his luggage—was tailored to throw German and Turkish counterintelligence agents off the scent and protect his spy ring back in Palestine. This couldn't have been achieved by Aaronsohn simply falling from view. Instead, he needed the Germans and Turks to "know" that his intention had been to go to America, that the British had grabbed their "dangerous Turkish spy" off the decks of the *Oskar II* quite by chance. To this end, the portrait rendered of him by the *Evening Post* was just a bonus. As Aaronsohn noted in his diary that night in his Kirkwall hotel room, "The game is in play."

It was very much a marathon game. It had been well over three months since Aaronsohn had left Palestine with Djemal Pasha's *vesika*, or travel permit, in hand. First, there had been a monthlong delay in Constantinople as he negotiated the bureaucratic maze to obtain the documentation needed for his further passage to Vienna. From the Austrian capital, it had been a simple matter to continue on to Berlin, but then came another monthlong delay as he tried to figure out the crossing into neutral Denmark. The scientist had finally achieved that in mid-September, but then more hurdles: first, making contact with British counterintelligence agents, then convincing them his incredible story was true.

The British spy handlers in Denmark may not have been thoroughly assured on this last point, but after some hesitation, they decided it would be Scotland Yard's problem to sort out. In mid-October, they arranged to put Aaronsohn on board the *Oskar II*, sailing from Copenhagen harbor on the nineteenth, while further arranging his detention in Kirkwall in three days' time. Thus the British were finally about to "bring in from the cold" a would-be spy who had spent over a year desperately trying to get their attention.

As he waited for the *Oskar II* to sail, Aaronsohn was acutely aware that he was about to cross a point of no return, that whatever happened next, his former life as a simple scientist in Palestine was gone forever. In Copenhagen, he wrote several coded letters that, through intermediaries, he hoped would reach his coconspirators back in Athlit; in them, he wrote with happy anticipation about his imminent departure for New York—for the benefit of German and Turkish counterintelligence agents—but used certain words and phrases to indicate that his real destination was Britain.

He also wrote a very long letter to Judge Julian Mack, one of the American benefactors of the Athlit research station, in which he laid bare his reasons for the dangerous path he was now taking. In what was part confession—indeed, this was how Aaronsohn would later describe it—and part manifesto, he wrote out an anguished narrative of what had occurred in Palestine over the previous two years, how it had inexorably brought him to the point where he was prepared to betray the nation that had given his family refuge. "Would I have left the country and openly taken service on the English side," he wrote, "it would already have been bad enough. My character, my standing would be impaired. But I did worse. I stood where I was, I organized a whole movement, I became connected with the Intelligence Office, as people who are afraid of words call it. I do not like mincing words. Put it clearly, and I became a Spy."

Aaronsohn intended the letter to be shown to other American Jewish benefactors of the research station, many of whom did not consider themselves Zionists and were sure to be shocked by its contents. This may have been the reason for its oratorical, even somewhat histrionic tone as the scientist explained what he and his confederates felt they were fighting for: "Nobody can say we were doing it for the sake of vile money. . . . We are not doing it for honours either. . . . We do not do it for vengeance; we do it because we hope we are serving our Jewish cause. . . . We considered it our duty to do our share, and we are still foolish enough to believe in right and justice and recognition of the Cause we are serving."

That was all well and good, but a loftiness unlikely to fully satisfy Basil Thomson. As the head of Scotland Yard's Criminal Investigation Department, Thomson had interviewed hundreds of would-be spies by the close of 1916, and interrogated many more who had proven to be German moles. Certainly neither the résumé nor the recent travels of the man brought into his office on October 25 were the stuff to inspire confidence.

Yet the longer Aaron Aaronsohn talked, the more Thomson was persuaded that here was the genuine article, a man anxious to help the British war effort—albeit for his own motives—and possessed of the skills and acumen to do so. It was not just Aaronsohn's meticulously observed details of the Turkish war machine—a bit out of date now, perhaps, but Aaronsohn claimed to have a network in place to constantly update them—but his seemingly encyclopedic knowledge of most every aspect of the region. For the detective, the decisive moment came when the topic turned to the British army's current slow-motion advance across the Sinai Peninsula in prelude to their offensive into Palestine.

One key reason for that army's glacial pace over the arid wasteland was the need to haul water all the way from Egypt. That had meant laying a pipeline, which had also necessitated the building of a railroad. According to Aaronsohn, Thomson recounted in his memoir, it all could have been avoided. "There is water right there in the desert, three hundred feet down," he said. "All you have to do is drill for it."

"How do you know that?" Thomson would recall asking.

Aaronsohn shrugged. "The rocks indicate it. And [first-century Jewish-Roman chronicler] Flavius Josephus corroborates it. He wrote that he could walk for a whole day south from Caesarea and never leave flourishing gardens.... Where there were gardens, there must have been water. Where is that water now?"

"And what can you do?" Thomson asked.

"If I were with the British army, I could show the engineers where to drill. I guarantee that they would find enough water for the army without having to bring a single drop from Cairo."

Impressed, Thomson decided to pass Aaronsohn on to the central headquarters of the British military, the Imperial General Staff on Whitehall Street. There, a young major, Walter Gribbon, was detailed to further debrief the agronomist, a first step toward determining just what should be done with him. On October 28, three days after arriving in London, Aaronsohn wrote his brother Alexander and sister Rivka in New York. Along with great relief at finally reaching England—"for the past few nights I have slept in peace, untroubled by nightmares"—he admitted to a pang of regret:

"Here, I had the good fortune to meet eager ears and open minds. I have reason to believe that had our [British] friends been better informed sooner, they would have acted in consequence. Had I come earlier I should have probably served our cause better, spared our country some suffering, and rendered more efficient service to our friends."

When he wrote those words, Aaronsohn didn't know the half of it. On the previous day, as he was again being debriefed by Walter Gribbon, a friendly, slightly chubby man in his midthirties had come into the office to briefly sit in on the proceedings. During a break in Gribbon's questioning, the visitor inquired after Aaronsohn's views on Zionism, of where exactly he placed himself amid the galaxy of Jewish political thought. The visitor had listened intently and, before leaving, handed Aaronsohn a calling card, asking if he might be so good as to drop by the indicated address at

9:30 a.m. in three days' time. Aaronsohn readily agreed. The address on the calling card was 30 Broadway Gate, the London residence of the MP from Hull Central, Sir Mark Sykes.

BY NOVEMBER 15, 1916, Brigadier General Gilbert Clayton faced a conundrum as old as the superior-subordinate relationship: how to sabotage the plans of his boss without revealing his own hand in the endeavor. Adding to Clayton's difficulties on that day was that to come up with a feasible scheme, he urgently needed to speak with one of his own subordinates, Captain T. E. Lawrence. Unfortunately, Lawrence was quite unreachable, in transit somewhere along the thousand-mile stretch of desert and Nile River towns that lay between Khartoum and Cairo.

The problem was that, once again, Reginald Wingate was lobbying London for a large-scale military intervention in Arabia, and this time suggesting that both Lawrence and Sheikh Faisal were in favor of it. Until Lawrence resurfaced, there was no way of knowing what he might have said to Wingate, and thus no easy way to thwart the plan.

In whatever course he chose, however, Gilbert Clayton did have a distinct built-in advantage. That's because within the maze of overlapping bureaucracies the British had created in wartime Egypt, no one was precisely sure where Clayton's job duties began and where they ended. That uncertainty had stood the unassuming spymaster with the pencil-thin mustache in very good stead in past crises, and it was about to do so again.

At the war's outset, Clayton had been the chief British intelligence officer in Cairo, a post that made him the overall supervisor of Lawrence and the other Intrusives who set up shop at the Savoy Hotel in late 1914. In turn, Clayton had answered to the chief British civil authority in Egypt, High Commissioner Henry McMahon. Keeping matters simple, all ultimately answered to the Foreign Office in London.

That neat chain of command had turned both murky and contentious when Egypt became the chief staging ground for British military operations against the Ottoman Empire, operations that fell under the aegis of the War Office. In the inevitable turf war between the resident administration and the incoming generals of the Egyptian Expeditionary Force, those military intelligence units answerable to the War Office—Cairo was suddenly awash in them—saw little reason to tolerate a competing one answerable to the Foreign Office. Tensions had only grown worse when Clayton's Intrusives were given a clearer mandate in early 1916 and institutionalized as the Arab Bureau. For months afterward, General Archibald Murray, the commander of the Egyptian Expeditionary

Force—or EEF—tried unsuccessfully to wrest control of Clayton's outfit from McMahon, before finally settling for a quasi-supervisory role.

But the battle for primacy in Cairo was actually a three-way fight, and just to keep things lively, this third contender was a thousand miles away in Khartoum. Reginald Wingate, the governor-general of the Sudan, was also the sirdar, or commander in chief, of the Egyptian army, a wholly different military force than Murray's EEF. As might be predicted, none of these three men—McMahon, Murray, Wingate—liked each other very much, and joined to their intrigues against one another were the competing bureaucracies of London and British India, each with its own set of interests and allies and adversaries in the Egyptian capital. On top of this was the official indigenous Egyptian government that, though it was quite toothless, various British officials periodically felt the need to pretend to consult in order to maintain the appearance that the wishes of the actual inhabitants of Egypt somehow mattered.

Amid this impenetrable tangle, though, one name had a way of popping up with surprising regularity: Gilbert Clayton. By the autumn of 1916, the spymaster was simultaneously the head of the Arab Bureau (answerable to McMahon), the "Cairo Agent of the Sirdar" (Wingate), and the chief liaison officer between EEF (Murray) and the British Egyptian civilian administration (McMahon). In his spare time, he also directed an internal spying network that kept watch on both local dissident leaders and representatives of the indigenous Egyptian government, a task simplified by the fact that the two were often one and the same. As Lawrence would later write of Clayton, "It was not easy to descry his influence. He was like water, or permeating oil, creeping silently and insistently through everything. It was not possible to say where Clayton was and was not, and how much really belonged to him."

Paradoxically, considering the sabotage mission he was contemplating that November, of the various competitors, Gilbert Clayton was personally closest to Wingate. A trim man in his midfifties with a fine white mustache, Wingate was a legend in East Africa, having fought alongside Kitchener in the Mahdi War of the late 1890s, and then staying on to rule over British Sudan for the next seventeen years. For five of those years, Clayton had served as Wingate's personal secretary in Khartoum, and he'd been deeply impressed by the man's political acumen. The sirdar had also been one of the first British leaders in the region to appreciate the importance of the Arab Revolt in the summer of 1916, and had been tireless in promoting their cause to London.

The recurrent sticking point, however, was that nearly all of Wingate's information on Arabia came either from the two Sudan hands he had sent

there, Cyril Wilson and Alfred Parker, or from Colonel Édouard Brémond. From these three, the sirdar had heard a steady litany of the rebels'
incompetence, an unending drumbeat on the need for a large Allied force.
This was a course that virtually everyone in the Arab Bureau strongly
opposed, and it had been partly in hopes of bringing a new perspective
to the matter that Clayton had arranged to send T. E. Lawrence on his
fact-finding mission to the Hejaz in October. As Clayton had expected,
the visit had convinced Lawrence that escalation would be folly—which
was also why he had approved Lawrence's detour to Khartoum in order to
brief Wingate directly.

At first, that stratagem appeared to pay off. Lawrence had arrived in
Khartoum on November 7, just days after Wingate's first intervention
request had been vetoed by the War Committee, and whatever Lawrence
said to the sirdar seemed to greatly mollify him. Obviously impressed
by Lawrence's knowledge of the Arab world, and by his account of the
defensive capabilities of Faisal's troops, Wingate cabled Clayton that same
day outlining a radically scaled-back plan: to urge Brémond to send his
technical advisors on to the Hejaz but without the thousands of British
troops as protection, and to give Faisal's men the "moral and material
support (aeroplanes, guns and machine guns) necessary to enable them to
continue their defensive [*sic*] in hills."

But if Clayton thought that settled the matter, he was soon set right.
The next day, November 8, the French government had pressed the War
Committee to reconsider its decision, stressing that while Brémond was
anxious to send his advisors to Rabegh, "they cannot provide the kind of
field force that British infantry would form. Sending these French units
to Rabegh on their own would mean unnecessarily risking their sacrifice,
thereby handing to the Turks the guns and machine guns intended for the
Sherif's army."

In his own cable shortly afterward, Wingate had thrown his support
to the Brémond/French argument anew, even if tempered somewhat by
Lawrence's influence. Since it was possible that Faisal might on his own
block a Turkish advance toward Rabegh, as Lawrence maintained, Wingate suggested that a British brigade be readied for deployment but only
sent ashore "at the last moment." The sirdar further intimated that this
was a course of action approved by the one British officer who had actually been to the war front, Captain Lawrence.

To Clayton, reading this cable in Cairo, it made little sense. Lawrence had surely been around the military long enough to know that a
force readied for deployment *would* be deployed, bringing about the very
situation—the implosion of the Arab Revolt—that he had warned against.
How had Lawrence possibly acquiesced to this? It was a question with no

immediate answer. Lawrence had left Khartoum on November 11, and would be incommunicado until he reached Cairo. In the meantime, the War Committee, under intense French pressure, was pondering its next move.

No record exists of what was said when Clayton finally sat Lawrence down in the Arab Bureau offices on November 16, and neither man was to detail that meeting in their later writing. From anecdotal evidence, it appears Lawrence either maintained that Wingate had somehow misunderstood him, or, if admitting to having agreed to Wingate's plan, claimed he thought he was responding to a purely hypothetical scenario.

But if Lawrence did equivocate about his meetings with Wingate, there is another possible explanation. On November 6, the day before he had arrived in Khartoum, it was announced that Henry McMahon was being dismissed as Egyptian high commissioner, to be replaced by Reginald Wingate. That news put Lawrence in a nasty squeeze in Khartoum; he was not only sitting across from the biggest proescalationist in the British power structure, but the man about to become his overall boss. With this in mind, the most likely scenario is that Lawrence agreed with Wingate's proposal to his face in Khartoum, in hopes that he could help in its scuttling once he got back to the more amenable climes of Cairo.

Certainly that was what he now set out to do. At the end of his meeting with Clayton on November 16, Lawrence returned to his office and quickly wrote up a new memorandum on the situation in the Hejaz, one so blunt and shorn of niceties that it left no room for misinterpretation. In terms of length, there is probably no document that more profoundly influenced the British war effort in Arabia than the four-page memorandum he handed to Gilbert Clayton the next day.

In that memo, Lawrence held up and then knocked down virtually every possible argument for a large Allied military presence in Arabia—and he did so by turning the escalationists' own arguments against them. While it was true that the Arabs couldn't defend Rabegh if the Turks broke through Faisal's mountain defenses, he pointed out, neither could an Allied force held somewhere in reserve as Wingate proposed. That's because, once through the mountains, the Turks would reach the port town in a mere four days, hardly time for even a fully readied force standing by in Egypt to be brought down and deployed.

This, then, left the argument of deploying now, while Faisal's men still held the mountains, but the issue there was deep-rooted Arab distrust. "They are our very good friends while we respect their independence," Lawrence wrote. "They are deeply grateful for the help we have given them, but they fear lest we may make it a claim upon them afterwards. We have appropriated too many Moslem countries for them to have any real trust in our disinterestedness and they are terribly afraid of an English occupation of Hejaz. If the British with or without the Sherif's approval landed at Rabegh an armed force strong enough to . . . organize a position there, they would, I am convinced, say 'we are betrayed' and scatter to their tents."

This was, of course, the same basic argument other antiescalationists had been making all along, but Lawrence was able to give it a wholly new twist by virtue of his firsthand look at the region. As he'd discovered in his trek to Faisal's camp, there were other water sources in the mountains above Rabegh that, until then, no one had known about. If Arab resistance in those mountains collapsed—a collapse that, again, was sure to accompany an Allied escalation—the Turks could draw on those water sources to sidestep Rabegh altogether and continue on toward Mecca unimpeded. In this scenario, the port town would be transformed from vitally strategic to utterly superfluous.

But Lawrence wasn't done yet. Recognizing that Colonel Brémond and his French superiors were the prime movers behind the escalation push—and were likely to continue that push no matter what the War Committee decided during this latest go-around—he set out to demolish their rationale for needing a British protection force for their technical unit in Rabegh. If the Turks did break through the mountains to advance on Rabegh, he pointed out, the Allies would still have four days' notice before they got there. In that scenario, the Royal Navy would have more than enough time to evacuate two hundred French military advisors, but probably not enough time to also evacuate thousands of British troops and all their valuable war matériel. Remarkably, this rather glaring hole in the French argument doesn't seem to have been noticed by anyone previously.

Except, Lawrence maintained, the French plan had never been about defending Rabegh anyway. Rather, it was about safeguarding their imperialist designs in the Middle East by seeking to destroy the Arab Revolt from within: "They say, 'Above all things the Arabs must not take Medina. This can be assured if an allied force landed at Rabegh. The tribal contingents will go home, and we will be the sole bulwark of the Sherif in Mecca. At the end of the war we give him Medina as his reward.' This is of course a definite policy, agreeable to their larger schemes," but the result, Lawrence contended, would be to leave, "the Franco-British force a disconsolate monument on the dusty beach at Rabegh."

It was an astounding accusation to make against Britain's closest ally, built as it was on an extrapolation—and a rather sweeping mischaracterization—of what Colonel Brémond had told Lawrence in Jeddah. But perhaps it was not so astounding to a British military leadership grown increasingly resentful and suspicious of their French allies.

On the Western Front, the British were now doing a majority of the fighting—and dying—as a shattered and depleted French army tried to rebuild itself. Over the past five months, in a campaign meant to relieve pressure on the battered French garrison in Verdun, British general Douglas Haig had repeatedly and futilely hurled his army against the German trenchworks along the river Somme; the 400,000 British dead and wounded at the Somme were double that suffered by the French. On the more local front, surely any British commander privy to the manner in which the French had repeatedly blocked the Alexandretta plan, as well as their continuing ambivalence over the coming British offensive in Palestine—an ambivalence born of fears that success would take the British into regions the French were claiming for themselves in the postwar world—were prepared to accept most any charge of Gallic perfidy at face value. Of course, Lawrence's accusation was also guaranteed to play well to the imperialist segment of the British government, eager to somehow keep France out of the Middle East altogether.

The effect of Lawrence's memo, then, was to transform the question of an Allied troop deployment to Arabia from its military context and propel it into the political. To wit, those in the British power structure favoring escalation might actually be unwitting dupes of a cleverly constructed French trap, one designed to both sabotage the Arab Revolt and, by the diversion of British troops to Arabia, hobble the offensive in Palestine. By the autumn of 1916, it was hard to conceive of any accusation more injurious to a British officer's reputation than that of useful fool to the French, but however obliquely, this was essentially the charge Lawrence was laying before Reginald Wingate.

But what to do with such an incendiary document? This was the new dilemma facing Gilbert Clayton on the morning of November 17. As Lawrence was attached to the Arab Bureau, standard procedure called for Clayton to first forward the memo to the bureau's overseer, Henry McMahon. That, however, would have been preaching to the choir, and as McMahon was already on his way out as high commissioner, anything he might do with the document could have only muted effect. Conversely, Clayton had the option of sending it to Reginald Wingate in hopes that the sirdar might finally see the error of his escalationist ways and change course—except Lawrence had been so derisive of the standby-force plan that the man who had authored it was bound to get his back up.

When it comes to political infighting, though, sometimes one's bitterest enemy can be turned into a temporary ally. Ever since arriving in Cairo, General Archibald Murray had set out to control or neuter Gilbert Clayton and his Arab Bureau in any way he could. In a fit of pique after failing to have the bureau put under his command, Murray had gone so far as to order his own intelligence units not to cooperate with Clayton's out-fit. Of more immediate interest to Clayton on November 17, however, was Murray's implacable opposition to sending troops to Arabia. He'd made his feelings on the topic clear at an interagency conference in September.

"There is no good telling me that you only want this and that," he'd railed at Wingate's deputy, Cyril Wilson. "From the experience of war, and experience of recent campaigns, it is absolutely clear that you start and you grow. You start with a brigade, that brigade wants some artil-lery, then aeroplanes and camels. Then comes a request that the force be moved to another point about ten miles [away], which it is absolutely essential to hold. So the campaign grows."

With all this in mind, it apparently occurred to Clayton that Archibald Murray might be just the man who'd know what to do with Lawrence's memo.

For the EEF commander, that four-page report must have arrived like a rare gift. Here was not only a précis that dismantled the intervention argument on its merits, but, as an added windfall, hinted darkly that it was all a French plot. He ordered that its author be immediately brought to his office.

Archibald Murray was a famously nervous man. During a pivotal moment in the opening days of the war, he had fainted away from the unrelenting tension, an episode that spurred shocked whispers through-out the British high command and probably contributed to Murray's demotion from army chief of staff, the number two position in the mili-tary hierarchy, in 1915. His transfer to Egypt hadn't seemed to improve matters, as Lawrence discovered when, answering Murray's summons to headquarters that day, he was intercepted by Murray's deputy, Gen-eral Lynden-Bell. As Lawrence recounted, "I was astonished when, as I came in, [Bell] jumped to his feet, leaped forward, and gripped me by the shoulder, hissing, 'Now you're not to frighten him; don't you forget what I say!'" The task before Lawrence, Bell instructed, was to give Murray "a reassuring picture of affairs, and yet not a rosy picture, since they could not afford excursions either way."

Lawrence seems to have managed this delicate balancing act when finally set before Murray. And despite Murray's reputation for jumpiness, it soon became clear that when it came to bureaucratic knifework, he had a pretty steady hand himself. Shortly after Lawrence left his office, he fired off a cable to Wingate: "I have just seen Lawrence on his return from visiting Faisal, and his opinion, in which I understand you and Faisal concur, is so strongly against the dispatch of white troops to Arabia that I venture to suggest for your consideration that the CIGS [Chief of Impe-rial General Staff William Robertson] should at once be informed."

Perhaps this request for Wingate's "consideration" was intended as rhetorical flourish, for Murray had actually sent Lawrence's memo to Robertson fifteen minutes earlier. As for Wingate concurring with Lawrence's views, that would be a hard matter for Wingate to judge since Murray didn't bother sending him a copy of the memo.

In London, Lawrence's report played to great effect, and was quickly circulated through the upper reaches of both the Foreign and War Offices. As usually happens in such cases, those who agreed with the report burnished the résumé of its author to lend authority to his assertions. On November 19, General Robertson, himself no fan of intervention in Arabia, forwarded the memo to the cabinet while describing its author as a man "said to have an intimate knowledge of the Turks and the Arabs."

To those in the cabinet unfamiliar with the intricacies of Arabian policy, perhaps the memorandum's most persuasive aspect was its anti-French tilt. Interestingly, one official who tried to counter that effect was Mark Sykes. "Captain Lawrence's statement in regard to the French attitude to the Arabs," he complained to the Foreign Office, "and his reference to their larger schemes of policy, must be the result of some misunderstanding, either by Captain Lawrence of the French, or by the French officers of their own Government's intentions, as it seems in no way to fit in with anything said or thought here or in Paris."

His was a lonely voice, however, and little match for the antiescalation/anti-French officials who now had their own "expert" in the field to tout. Henry McMahon joined his efforts to that campaign in a cable to Charles Hardinge, the permanent under secretary at the Foreign Office. Noting that he'd always feared that an Allied intervention in Arabia would corrode Arab morale, McMahon wrote that Lawrence, "whom I knew to be a very shrewd observer, has confirmed my opinion on this point. He has moreover told me, as doubtless you will hear from the Sirdar [Wingate], that the French hold the same view, and it is with this very object that they are magnifying the dangers of the present situation and advocating action at Rabegh. Colonel Brémond even went so far in a moment of confidence as to tell Lawrence that the French object was to thus disintegrate Arab effort. . . . It is as well to remember this in any proposals that the French may now or hereafter make in regard to our joint assistance to the Sherif."

Amid the tumult, Lawrence even saw his stock rise among those regular army staff officers in Cairo who had previously held both him and the Arab Bureau in contempt. "They began to be polite to me," he wrote, "and to say that I was observant, with a pungent style, and character."

In the face of such an onslaught, the War Committee quietly shelved the Rabegh proposal anew, but not before a rather humorous last act. It wasn't until November 21, four days after Lawrence's memo reached London, that Reginald Wingate finally saw the analysis with which he supposedly fully concurred. After his angry cable demanding to know why he'd been kept out of the loop, the War Committee mildly rebuked Murray for failing to first solicit Wingate's opinion, suggesting that "there is apparently lack of co-ordination in [this] matter."

Murray begged to differ. "I have always taken special care to keep Sirdar fully informed of all I am doing," he cabled London back, "and as far as I know we are working in the closest touch. You may rely on me in this matter. As regards Lawrence's report. As Lawrence had just come to me after spending several days with the Sirdar I naturally understood he was fully in possession of Lawrence's news. In fact Lawrence informed me to this effect."

A PERSONALITY TIC of Aaron Aaronsohn's was to keep constant track of the exercise he got in a day—the time spent bicycling, or the miles walked—and to note it in his diary. It may have been born of his long and only intermittently successful campaign to keep his weight down, but the long walks he took during his stay in London served an additional purpose: a way to distract himself from the maddening inertia of the British government. As he noted in his diary for November 11, 1916, a day in which he had covered some twelve miles, "If I brooded continually over the situation, it would be enough to drive me mad. What slowness in decisions! It will soon be two months since I have left Berlin, and after all nothing of consequence has been done to discover [sic] the Athlit people."

Certainly the scientist had done his part. In the nearly three weeks he'd been in London, he had compiled two long reports for his British hosts, one chronicling the plight of the Armenians in Syria, the other on conditions inside Palestine. This second report, running to forty-six pages, provided the British with probably their most comprehensive look inside any corner of the Ottoman Empire since the war had begun. Along with a thorough rundown of the political and economic situation of the region, Aaronsohn detailed the health and medical crises facing it, the condition of its roads and railways, and meticulously listed the location and size of most every Turkish garrison guarding the Syrian coast. He even noted how many gendarmes currently policed Beirut, and what weapons they carried.

Nevertheless, Aaronsohn continued to be shuttled from office to office, ministry to ministry, repeatedly asked to tell his whole story over from the beginning. From no quarter, it seemed, was any effort being made toward returning him to the war theater, let alone trying to establish contact with his spy network back in Palestine.

Part of the issue was surely simple bureaucratic ineptitude, but perhaps joined to this was a kind of collective disbelief on British officials' part at what they'd been handed. Then as now, intelligence agents were accustomed to getting small slivers of information from a wide variety of sources and trying to fit those slivers together to form a portrait; it was very unusual, even suspicious, to be handed all of it in one fell swoop. Contributing to this was an element of blithe anti-Semitism that permeated the British government at the time—as it did most European governments—which provided as a starting point that a Jew wasn't to be completely trusted until he proved himself worthy. In the arena of espionage, that created a paradox hard to rise out of. In an eleven-page analysis of Aaronsohn's Palestine report, an intelligence officer with the War Trade Intelligence Department conceded that the information was "very correct" wherever it could be verified, but also noted the informant was a Zionist and "of the Romanian type of Jew." That description apparently validated the agent's conclusion: "Of course we do not know the object of his visit to this country, but he might be just as observant of things here as he has been in Turkey and a purveyor of information of the conditions in England if he should get back to Turkey."

Naturally, all this was quite invisible to Aaronsohn. Instead, as the interminable delay in London dragged on, the scientist increasingly fretted that perhaps the problem stemmed from the conversation he'd had at 30 Broadway Gate on October 30.

Answering that invitation to call on Mark Sykes, Aaronsohn had appeared at the London townhouse promptly at 9:30. Repairing to the exquisitely furnished study, the two men had soon been joined by a third. This was Gerald FitzMaurice, the former dragoman to the British embassy in Constantinople and now one of Sykes's key allies in the British power structure. While Aaronsohn provided few details of what the three discussed during their ninety-minute conversation—"we talk of Zionism," he noted in his diary—he'd initially thought it had gone very well. Weeks later, though, with his London stay reaching the one-month mark, he fell to second-guessing. "I was probably too open with them," he wrote on November 24, "and they took it as a ruse. Or they are distracted or turning a blind eye. Or maybe they saw it as naivete on my part."

In fact, Aaronsohn's apprehensions couldn't have been more misplaced. Even if he kept it fairly discreet, Mark Sykes could be counted among a small but influential group of British statesmen who had begun turning their thoughts to the creation of a Jewish enclave in Palestine. What's more, in Aaron Aaronsohn he saw a man who might play a signal role in bringing that idea to fruition.

Part of Sykes's motive was rooted in religiosity. A devout Catholic, he regarded a return of the ancient tribe of Israel to the Holy Land as a way to correct a nearly two-thousand-year-old wrong. That view had taken on new passion and urgency with the massacres of the Armenians. To Sykes, in that ongoing atrocity, the Ottoman Empire had proven it could never again be trusted to protect its religious minority populations. At war's end, the Christian and Jewish Holy Land of Palestine would be taken from it, and the failure of the Crusades made right.

But it was not just religiosity; Sykes also saw a potentially huge political advantage in this. The Jews were an influential but deeply factionalized presence throughout the Western world, with most either staying neutral or siding with the Central Powers so far in the war. A chief cause was the inclusion of the notoriously anti-Semitic czarist Russia in the Entente; even many British Jews could barely bring themselves to support an alliance that included the despised regime in Petrograd. By the Entente's coming out in strong support of a Jewish homeland in Palestine, Sykes believed, it would inevitably turn the opinion of international Jewry toward its side. In turn, the advocacy of American Jews—a small but powerful constituency—might finally provide the spur for bringing the United States into the war.

This idea had already been promoted by a British statesman far more powerful than Mark Sykes. In March 1915, the home secretary, Herbert Samuel, had put to the cabinet that Palestine be made a British protectorate at war's end, and Jewish emigration actively encouraged toward the eventual creation of a majority-Jewish enclave. That resolution had been quickly and quietly shot down by the cabinet—the potential ramifications of such a momentous course of action were too far-reaching to countenance—but the notion had lingered on. When put in charge of hashing out an agreement with Georges-Picot on a framework for the postwar Middle East, Mark Sykes had taken it up again.

Immediately a potential obstacle presented itself. In his correspondence with Emir Hussein, Henry McMahon had specifically listed all those territories to be excluded from Arab sovereignty or subject to later negotiation, but nowhere had he mentioned—let alone made a claim for—Palestine. A strict reading of that correspondence, therefore, could only lead to the conclusion that Palestine was to be part of the independent Arab nation. That was not such a big obstacle as far as Mark Sykes was concerned; since he and Georges-Picot were ignoring most other promises made to Hussein as they carved the Middle East into imperial spheres, what was the harm in adding Palestine to the mix? In the draft version of the Sykes-Picot Agreement, that Syrian province had been penciled in to fall under the "international administration" of Britain, France, and Russia.

But even this arrangement wouldn't bring about the British-protected Jewish state that Sykes envisioned, nor could it possibly be a harmonious one. As he conceded in a March 1916 cable to George Buchanan, the British ambassador to Russia, "Arab Christians and Moslems alike would fight in the matter to the last man against Jewish Dominion in Palestine." At the same time, the Jews were stoutly opposed to an international administration there, while the French and Russians would most certainly oppose a solely British one. To break the logjam, Sykes informed Buchanan, he'd bandied about a new idea with Georges-Picot.

A peculiar signature of Sykes's "solutions" was a kind of quasi-scientific notion that fantastic intricacy might lead to ultimate simplicity, as if the world were a motor vehicle in which, once its myriad moving parts were properly aligned, all would hum along nicely. So it was with his new idea for Palestine. Invoking Herbert Samuel's cabinet resolution of a year before, he proposed that Palestine be put under a British protectorate; that Emir Hussein appoint one of his sons as the sultan of an independent Palestine; that Britain and France jointly act as the sultanate's guarantor; while simultaneously a "privileged chartered company" be established for the purpose of buying up land for Jewish colonization. "I regret complicated problem requires complex settlement," Sykes concluded to Buchanan, "but under above France gets a position in Palestine, Russian demands are satisfied, Arabs have a Prince, Zionists get constitutional position and have British protection, which I understand they desire."

But lest the champagne be uncorked too soon, Sykes's neat formula elided some inconvenient realities. First, Samuel's proposal of the previous year had been rejected out of hand by the cabinet. Second, Sykes had floated his plan without clearing it with any of his superiors—and floated it to the chief French negotiator deciding the future composition of the Middle East, no less. The day after Sykes's cable to Buchanan had reached his desk, Foreign Secretary Edward Grey wrote a withering rebuke, ordering Sykes to "obliterate from his memory that the Samuel's Cabinet memorandum made any mention of a British Protectorate. . . . I told Mr. Samuel at the time that a British Protectorate was quite out of the question and Sir M. Sykes should never mention the subject without making this clear."

That slapdown may have led to greater discretion on Sykes's part, but it certainly didn't cool his ardor for thinking creatively when it came to Palestine. Through the spring and summer of 1916, he held a series of private discussions with Moses Gaster, a leader of the British Zionist movement, to keep the ideas percolating. It was when he met Aaron Aaronsohn, however, that his passions returned to full flourish. According to Sykes's biographer, Roger Adelson, "If Rabbi Gaster a few months before had provided Sykes with the grace-note of Zionism in Europe, here was Aaronsohn who had actually played the trumpet in Palestine. Sykes liked the sound of it."

Zionist historian Isaiah Friedman was more specific: "How deeply Sir Mark Sykes was impressed by Aaronsohn can be gathered from the confident and close relations which later developed between them." Citing other British wartime officials who would soon be heavily influenced by Aaronsohn's views, Friedman argued that "it would be reasonable to suppose that it was he who was the decisive influence in Sykes's conversion to Zionism."

Indeed, even if he second-guessed it as his days in London dragged on, Aaronsohn's diary entry on the Broadway Gate meeting alluded to the alliance that was already taking form. "FitzMaurice is in favour of the 'fait accompli' in Palestine," he jotted, meaning a Jewish homeland, "[but] the Allies are not yet in agreement. . . . [Sykes] hopes we will succeed in altering the English viewpoint, 'but it requires work.'"

Where Aaronsohn would contribute to that work was in Cairo. On November 24, the same day that he worried in his diary over the impression he might have made on Sykes, the scientist began packing for the ship that would take him to Egypt. There he would join forces with British military intelligence and try to reactivate his long-dormant spy ring. In Egypt Aaronsohn would also eventually reunite with Mark Sykes. Together, they would concoct a scheme that was to help dramatically reshape the British government's view on the creation of a British-protected Jewish homeland in Palestine.

DESPITE THE FUROR his November 17 memo had spawned, with Lawrence's brief sojourn to the Hejaz at an end, there were no plans to send him back. To the contrary, Gilbert Clayton intended to put his literary skills and fluency in Arabic to use in a new desk job in Cairo, heading up the Arab Bureau's fledgling propaganda department. That Lawrence was to escape this mundane fate was due to the intercession of a most unlikely patron: Reginald Wingate.

Shortly after learning he would be taking over from McMahon in Cairo, and thus in direct charge of the Hejaz operation, Wingate had petitioned for an expanded roster of advisors and intelligence officers to serve in Arabia; of most pressing concern was to attach a liaison officer to Faisal in the mountains above Rabegh. The logical choice to head up this British military mission, all agreed, was Lawrence's titular supervisor at the Arab Bureau, Stewart Newcombe. But with Newcombe on assignment in Europe until sometime in December, Wingate urged that someone else be sent as his temporary stand-in, and he quite naturally thought of the impressive young captain who had just visited him in Khartoum. On November 12, the day after Lawrence left the Sudanese capital, Wingate cabled Clayton in Cairo suggesting that Lawrence be sent back to Yenbo to manage things until Newcombe arrived. Clayton, thinking of the propaganda department he wanted Lawrence to head, tried to deflect the request, but Wingate wouldn't take no for an answer.

"Pending Newcombe's arrival," he reiterated on November 14, "I wish Lawrence to proceed to Yenbo by first possible opportunity. It is vitally important to have an officer of his exceptional knowledge of Arabs in close touch with Faisal [at this] critical juncture." He then reassured Clayton this was to be only a temporary measure, and that Lawrence would be returned to Cairo once Newcombe came on the scene. Under such pressure, Clayton had no choice but to relent.

Of course, all this occurred before Lawrence wrote his incendiary memorandum taking direct aim at Wingate's plans in Arabia. By the time Wingate saw that memo, his lavish praise of Lawrence was already a matter of record, as was his insistence that Lawrence return to Yenbo. Even if Wingate wished to punish the young captain for his temerity, there was now no graceful way to do it.

But excelling at bureaucratic infighting is not simply about coming out on top. True mastery comes with the ability to so cover one's tracks as to appear utterly blameless, and this was a game Clayton and Lawrence played with consummate skill. Before the month of November was over, Colonel Brémond would receive a stern telegram from the commander in chief of the French armed forces, Marshal Joseph Joffre. After obliquely referring to an "agreement" worked out with the British—the Sykes-Picot pact—Joffre rebuked Brémond for ever suggesting that France wished to prevent an Arab capture of Medina. "The already known state of mind of the British and the Sherif could lead to the belief that we are trying to renege on the arrangements made and could have serious consequences for the development of our plans in the Levant. It is important, therefore, that your attitude does not lend itself to such an interpretation."

The sandbagging of Reginald Wingate was even more impressive, however. On November 23, as the tempest over Lawrence's memorandum continued to rage, Clayton sent a "private" cable to Wingate in Khartoum suggesting that all blame for the controversy rested with Murray. Perhaps calculating that the bad blood between the sirdar and the EEF commander meant the particulars would never get sorted out, Clayton went so far as to suggest that it was Murray who had compelled Lawrence to write the offending report.

Evidently, Wingate had a pronounced naïve streak: "I have no doubt that Lawrence has done all this in perfectly good faith," he wrote Cyril Wilson on the same day he received Clayton's cable, "but he appears to me to be a visionary and his amateur soldiering has evidently given him an exaggerated idea of the soundness of his views on purely military matters." Clearly alluding to Murray, he went on, "I am principally annoyed in all this matter, not so much on account of the apparent want of straightness on the part of certain people who should be above that sort of thing, but on account of the huge loss of time when I am working at very high pressure."

Either Wingate never did figure out the extent to which he had been played by Clayton and Lawrence, or he was an unusually forgiving man; in just eight months, he would spearhead the effort to award Lawrence the Victoria Cross, Britain's highest military honor, for valor in the field.

But not everyone was so quick to ascribe the best of intentions to the upstart army captain. One who took a far more jaundiced view was Cyril Wilson, the British official who had most closely observed Lawrence in Arabia, and would serve as Lawrence's direct superior officer upon his return. Wilson argued strongly against that return on even a temporary basis, and when presented with a fait accompli let Gilbert Clayton know his feelings. "Lawrence wants kicking," he wrote the Arab Bureau head, "and kicking *hard* at that; then he would improve. At present I look upon him as a bumptious young ass who spoils his undoubted knowledge of Syrian Arabs etc. by making himself out to be the only authority on war, engineering, running [His Majesty's] ships and everything else. He put every single person's back up I've met, from the Admiral down to the most junior fellow on the Red Sea."

Of all the deceptions put to paper about the events of that November, however, surely the most brazen was one Lawrence penned about himself. It concerned that day toward the end of the month when he was summoned to Clayton's office and told he was being sent back to Arabia as a temporary liaison officer to Faisal ibn Hussein. According to Lawrence's account in *Seven Pillars*, "I urged my complete unfitness for the job."

Chapter 10

Neatly in the Void

The situation is so interesting that I think I will fail to come back.

T. E. LAWRENCE, IN ARABIA, TO
CAIRO HEADQUARTERS, DECEMBER 27, 1916

From the crest of the hill, the night-wrapped valley of Nakhl Mubarak yielded a startling sight. As Lawrence would recount, glimpsed through the fronds of the date-palm plantations was "the flame-lit smoke of many fires," while the valley echoed with the braying of thousands of excited camels, gunshots, and the calls of men lost in the darkness.

Accompanied by four tribal escorts, Lawrence had set out from the port of Yenbo earlier that evening, December 2, 1916. Their destination was Faisal's camp in the mountainous enclave of Kheif Hussein, some forty-five miles inland. With good camels beneath them and riding steadily, the group had anticipated making the camp just around daybreak. Instead, a mere five hours into their ride and just twenty-five miles from the coast, they came upon this puzzling scene in Nakhl Mubarak; no one in Lawrence's party had any idea who these masses of armed men in the valley below might be.

Dismounting, the group quietly descended from the ridgeline until they came to a deserted home at the valley's edge. After corralling the camels and secreting his British charge within the home, the lead escort slipped a cartridge into his carbine and set out alone on foot to investigate. He shortly returned with shocking news: the men were Faisal's army. Remounting their camels, the group proceeded into the heart of the valley, the scene more bewildering to Lawrence by the minute. "There were hundreds of fires of thorn-wood, and round them were Arabs making coffee or eating, or sleeping muffled like dead men in their cloaks, packed together closely in the confusion of camels."

They found Faisal at the center of the encampment, sitting before his tent with several aides and a scribe. With illumination provided by slaves holding lanterns, he was alternately dictating orders and listening to battlefield reports being read aloud to him, the picture of placidity. It was some time before he dismissed his retinue so that he might explain the situation to his British guest. That situation wasn't good; it was little short of disastrous, in fact.

During Lawrence's first visit in October, Faisal had outlined an elaborate plan to take his war campaign north, a way to reduce the Turkish threat to Rabegh and Mecca by giving the enemy something new to worry about. That scheme depended on Faisal working in close concert with the fighting units of his three brothers. While Abdullah harassed the Turkish forces around Medina, Faisal would move the bulk of his army northwest through the mountains to Kheif Hussein before closing on the Turkish-held port of Wejh, some two hundred miles above Yenbo. Simultaneously, Zeid would come up to protect the approaches to Yenbo, while Ali brought his army out of Rabegh to guard a crucial intersection on the pilgrims' road to Mecca.

Lawrence had thought the plan too complicated by half, reliant as it was on a level of coordination among the four brothers nearly impossible to achieve across the great expanse of western Arabia. He'd conveyed his doubts to Gilbert Clayton in his reports at the time, but apparently had been less persuasive with Faisal; in mid-November, Faisal had put the scheme into effect.

For a short while all had gone accordingly, with Faisal taking most of his forces north to Kheif Hussein. At his back, however, twenty-year-old Zeid inexplicably left one of the mountain paths leading to Yenbo completely unguarded, and it was this path that a Turkish mounted patrol found. Suddenly finding the Turks between them and their escape route to the coast, Zeid's charges had promptly scattered in disarray. That had only been stage one of the fiasco, however. When they learned of Zeid's collapse, and fearful that they too might soon be stranded in the mountains, Faisal's followers had succumbed to a similar panicked stampede from Kheif Hussein. Faisal and his lieutenants had finally halted the flight there in Nakhl Mubarak, but even this, he confided to Lawrence that night, probably wouldn't hold; with the advancing Turks now to the east and south, it seemed just a matter of time before his entire force—what was left of it—fell all the way back to Yenbo port itself.

Operating on practically no sleep, Lawrence spent the next forty-eight hours alternately conferring with Faisal and circulating among the fighters in Nakhl Mubarak , trying to better gauge the magnitude of the crisis. He then raced back to Yenbo to raise the alarm. When he sat down to send an urgent message to Clayton on the morning of December 5, he was in a state of both exhaustion and despondency. "I had better preface by saying that I rode all Saturday night, had alarms and excursions all Sunday night, and rode again all last night, so my total of sleep is only three hours in the last three nights and I feel rather pessimistic. All the same, things are bad."

As Lawrence well knew, the Arab rout in the mountains was much more than just a military setback. Uniting the northern tribes to his leadership had required months of painstaking and delicate work on Faisal's part, and that was now rapidly coming apart. In his report to Clayton, Lawrence enumerated those tribes that had already abandoned Faisal—or appeared ready to—and warned how those defections not only threatened to leave the road open to a Turkish capture of Mecca, but to a collapse of the Arab Revolt itself. The crucial point, Lawrence wrote, was that Faisal was now "a tribal leader, not a leader of tribes," and it would take a long time to repair the damage. In this, too, there was a parallel to the Crusader armies of the Middle Ages that Lawrence had studied; the extreme fragility of alliances between disparate and largely autonomous groups meant unity was always one small setback away from unraveling.

But it was also a personal fiasco for Lawrence. In his October reports, he had readily conceded the difficulty of ever organizing the Arab fighters into a conventional fighting force—he'd figured that a single company of Turkish soldiers, properly entrenched in open country, could defeat them—but had been both eloquent and persuasive in emphasizing their potency as a defensive force. "Their real sphere is guerrilla warfare. . . . Their initiative, great knowledge of the country, and mobility, make them formidable in the hills." Not just formidable; in Lawrence's estimation, in such a role they would be all but impregnable. "From what I have seen of the hills between Bir Abbas and Bir Ibn Hassani," he had written, "I do not see how, short of treachery on the part of the hill tribe[s], the Turks can risk forcing their way through." To the contrary, with the hills "a very paradise for snipers," he was confident that a mere one or two hundred men could successfully hold any possible line of Turkish approach toward the coast.

This conviction was one of the cornerstones of Lawrence's argument against sending Allied troops into Arabia, and he had maintained it even after troubling evidence to the contrary. At the beginning of November, after rumors of a Turkish advance had sent Ali's men fleeing from the hills above Rabegh, Lawrence had intimated to Édouard Brémond that matters would have turned out differently if Faisal had been in charge. As events now made clear, in this estimation he had been absolutely one hundred percent wrong.

Perhaps it was embarrassment over how badly he had misjudged the situation, or perhaps even in his exhaustion Lawrence remained the ever-vigilant bureaucratic strategist, but before sending off his pessimistic cable to Clayton, he thought to scribble a postscript. If reprinted in the *Arab Bulletin*, his cable would soon be read by all those in the British leadership who had been won to his nonintervention argument, so he jotted, "don't use any of above in Bulletin or elsewhere; it is not just—because I am done up."

In response to the deepening crisis, British naval ships began massing off Yenbo; if the worst did come to pass and Faisal's men were put to siege in that town, the ships might at least lay down artillery fire on the surrounding open plain to slow the Turkish advance. True to Faisal's prediction, on the morning of December 9, the vanguard of his spent force began drifting into the port with the news that they'd been flushed from Nakhl Mubarak by another Turkish push; by the time the last stragglers came in, the some five thousand warriors Lawrence had seen under Faisal's banner just one week earlier had been reduced to fewer than two thousand. While a handful of the missing three thousand had fallen in battle, the vast majority had simply abandoned the fight and gone home to their villages.

So dispiriting was the atmosphere that even Lawrence now had second thoughts about his most stoutly held belief. Writing to Clayton again on December 11, he announced that "Faisal has now swung around to the belief in a British force [being deployed] at Rabegh. I have wired this to you, and I see myself that his arguments have force. If Zeid had not been so slack, this would never have got to this pass." He added a bitter afterthought: "The Arabs, outside their hills, are worthless."

On that same day, Lawrence painted an even more dire picture to Cyril Wilson. Without British troops in Rabegh, he wrote, Faisal was now of the opinion that the whole revolution might collapse within three weeks' time.

To THE PUZZLEMENT of many residents, on the morning of May 31, 1916, a German warplane had appeared in the skies over Jerusalem and proceeded to execute a series of tight circles just to the west of the walled Old City. Finally, a small weighted object was thrown from the plane that landed in the street directly in front of the Hotel Fast, the favored watering hole of German officers in Jerusalem. Upon closer inspection, the packet was found to be a bundled German flag with a note inside from Curt Prüfer. He was returning to the city that evening, the note explained, and he wanted his cook to prepare a "good dinner" for him. It was the sort of flamboyant act that Prüfer probably never would have performed in his prior incarnation as a spy chief, but it was very much in keeping with the colorful antics of his new comrades in arms, the spotters and machine gunners and flying "aces" of the German Fliegertruppen, or Flying Corps.

In preparation for a renewed Turco-German offensive against the Suez Canal, in the early spring of 1916 a new German air squadron had been brought down and based in Beersheva, at the eastern end of the Sinai Peninsula. Tiring of his propaganda and surveillance duties in Syria and eager to play an active role in the coming attack, Prüfer had petitioned to be made an aerial spotter for Field Aviation Detachment 300.

The request was a somewhat puzzling one, given that Prüfer had remained dubious about the wisdom of a second attempt on the Suez since having participated in the first. As far back as August 1915, in a detailed report to the German ambassador in Constantinople, he'd argued that for such an offensive to have even a minimal chance of success, it could not at all resemble Djemal's haphazard "reconnaissance in force" of the previous February, but would require a massive investment of manpower and resources: road- and railway-building crews, crack Turkish troops, German aircraft and officers and artillery. Of course, he pointed out, the very scale of that investment meant a multiplying of the logistical hurdles in keeping such a force supplied and fed and watered across the Sinai sands. Simultaneously, it rendered the notion of somehow catching the British by surprise "unthinkable." "With all their war machines," he wrote, "you'd have to conduct a siege and bash their defenses with artillery before you could march into Egypt, after which you would need to maintain a line of supply from Palestine and Syria."

But even if all this could be accomplished, Prüfer had pointed out, capturing the canal just might not ultimately be very significant. After all, with the British navy in complete command of the seas, it wasn't as if the Suez would suddenly become useful to the Germans or Turks. As for the argument that cinching off this maritime shortcut would disrupt the flow of British territorial troops to Europe by forcing them to take the long way around Africa's Cape of Good Hope, this was certainly true, but the two- to three-week delay that would cause hardly rose above the level of inconvenience. To the German intelligence agent, the plans for a second Suez operation had seemed to underscore the old maxim that war can kill all things except bad ideas.

Against this, though, a powerful, personal lure had worked on him:

Detachment 300, the "glamour" of air war. In contrast to the hideous reality of life and death in the trenches, an aura of romance had instantly attached to this newest form of warfare, with the pilot aces of all sides transformed into newsreel heroes and matinee idols. Prüfer, never much of a man's man, clearly reveled in being in the company of such *Übermenschen* at Beersheva, and the months he spent with Detachment 300 were undoubtedly among the happiest of his life, a carefree time of late-night drinking sessions, or flying off to Jerusalem or Jaffa at a moment's notice to attend diplomatic receptions or social dances. There seemed to be an almost starstruck quality to it; in contrast to the scant details Prüfer normally jotted in his wartime diary—when he bothered to keep it at all—he made careful note of the names of most all the Detachment 300 pilots for posterity. In the dropping of his note in front of the Hotel Fast to order up a meal, the soft-spoken former scholar was emulating the pranks of his new, larger-than-life comrades—and undoubtedly deriving considerable pride over his excellent aim.

Very shortly after that lark, however, had come news of the Arab Revolt in the Hejaz. Apparently forgetting his own oft-repeated assertion that the Arabs were too cowardly to ever rebel, Prüfer's first response had been a certain smugness, remarking in his diary, "I rightly warned them about the Sherif [Hussein]." As the revolt spread, however, and one Turkish garrison after another in Arabia came under siege, he remembered his old mentor, Max von Oppenheim, and the tremendous efforts the propaganda chief had made to forestall this day from coming. "The situation in Arabia goes badly for the Turks," he noted in early July. "Poor Oppenheim!"

But Prüfer had soon turned his attention back to more immediate concerns, as preparations got under way for the new Suez offensive. As an aerial spotter, he quite literally had a bird's-eye view when the Turkish vanguard launched its attack against the British railhead at Romani, some twenty-five miles east of the canal, on the morning of August 4, 1916. While that vantage point afforded him the opportunity to hurl a few bombs down on the enemy—bombs that in those early days of air combat were little more than large hand grenades—it also allowed him to grasp the full magnitude of the Turco-German defeat as it unfolded over the next two days.

Hoping to catch the British in a flanking move, the attacking force was instead caught out in the open and enveloped. By the afternoon of August 5, the Turkish army was in headlong retreat, having suffered some six thousand casualties, about one-third its total strength, and a toll that undoubtedly would have been higher if the British hadn't slowed their pursuit out of sheer exhaustion in the 120-degree heat.

The rout at Romani ended forever the Turco-German dream of "liberating" Egypt. It also ended Prüfer's four-month idyll with Detachment 300, for it forced him to finally acknowledge something he'd tried very hard to ignore: he was desperately ill. There had been terse little clues to it in his diary for some time—"I am unwell," he had noted back in mid-May—but now, his face sunken and his weight down to little more than a hundred pounds, even his handwriting betrayed him; gone was his emphatic, jerky script, replaced by a trembling, barely legible scrawl. Diagnosed as suffering from both cholera and tuberculosis, he was placed on medical leave and shuttled back to Germany in early October. After several weeks' recuperation in a Berlin hospital, he began helping out in the mapping division of the Reserve General Staff on Wilhelmstrasse.

In that capacity, the arc of Curt Prüfer's wartime experience completed a curious reverse symmetry with that of one of his adversaries in the field, British army captain T. E. Lawrence. During the first two years of the war, Lawrence had spent most of his time deskbound in the mapping room of the Arab Bureau in Cairo, while Curt Prüfer seemed to be everywhere: launching sabotage and spying missions against British Egypt, participating in two major offensives, unmasking potential enemies of the Ottoman and German cause throughout Syria. By the end of 1916, it was now Lawrence who was in the field as Prüfer whiled away his days in a mapping room in Berlin.

And a most prosaic existence it was. By January 1917, with his medical leave in Germany extended, Prüfer found himself battling with the local food rationing office in Berlin over his bread allotment. As he complained in cables to both his former colleagues in Constantinople and senior officials at the foreign ministry, without written confirmation of his leave extension, the Bread Commission was refusing to issue him the required ration card, and he beseeched their help in sorting out the problem as soon as possible. It was a very long way from dropping dinner orders out of airplanes.

Furthermore, there was the strong likelihood that it was with such mundane concerns that Curt Prüfer's wartime career would end. With his congenitally frail health, the Orientalist had only been inducted into the German military back in 1914 through the intercession of Max von Oppenheim, and his health was obviously far more ravaged now. Once again, though, the self-proclaimed baron from Cologne would come to his protégé's aid, offering Prüfer an escape route from his semi-invalid duties in Berlin.

Having thus far failed to ignite a pan-Islamic jihad in the Middle East that would play to Germany's political and military benefit, Oppenheim, according to Prüfer biographer Donald McKale, was now expanding his ambitions into the economic sphere. What he envisioned, in the wake of the coming Central Powers victory, was a vast German economic consortium that might dominate commerce and resource development throughout the region for decades to come. In the count's scheme, the vehicle for this domination was to be a unique partnership between the German government and the nation's private industrial conglomerates, the two working hand in glove for both personal and national interest. A man with a deep, perhaps exaggerated appreciation for the power of the printed word, Oppenheim worked up an alluring packet of brochures and prospectuses to dazzle German businessmen with visions of the wealth that could soon be theirs in the far-off lands of the Ottoman Empire.

As Oppenheim explained to would-be investors, nothing more exemplified the symbiotic relationship between public and private that he envisioned for the East than the role soon to be assumed by his young protégé, Curt Prüfer, in Constantinople. As the new head of the German intelligence bureau there, Prüfer would also serve as the primary conduit for investors trying to navigate Turkey's bureaucratic shoals. German industrialists could hardly ask for a better friend; here was a man who not only knew the region and Young Turk power structure intimately, but had a proven record of getting things done by whatever creative means necessary.

Just as with his notion of anticolonial Islamic jihad, Max von Oppenheim's economic scheme would prove a bit ahead of its time, presaging as it did the so-called national corporatism model first successfully harnessed by Italian fascist leader Benito Mussolini in the 1920s, and then to even more spectacular effect a decade later by Mussolini's protégé, Adolf Hitler. For Curt Prüfer in 1917, however, it simply meant a return to the field. In late February, he bid goodbye to his mapping-room colleagues in Berlin and set out for the Middle East once more.

FOR COLONEL ÉDOUARD BRÉMOND, watching Captain T. E. Lawrence come off the deck of HMS *Suva* in Jeddah harbor on December 12 must have been a particularly gladdening sight, something very much like revenge. Even if he'd yet to put together that Lawrence was the prime mover behind the rebuke he had received from the French War Ministry weeks earlier, Brémond most certainly now recognized him as a troublemaker, the man who more than any other British field officer had poisoned the well for sending Allied troops to Arabia. But now a rather different figure stood before the French colonel, one shorn of his arrogance and supreme self-assurance. Lawrence was just coming in from Yenbo, where he had witnessed firsthand the pell-mell retreat of Faisal's forces before

King Hussein of the Hejaz
© *Marist Archives and Special Collections,*
Lowell Thomas Papers

Ronald Storrs, the liaison in
the secret negotiations between
Hussein and the British, and the
man who brought T. E. Lawrence
into the Arab Revolt
© *Marist Archives and Special Collections,*
Lowell Thomas Papers

"The armed prophet," Faisal ibn Hussein, King Hussein's third son and T. E. Lawrence's chief ally during the Arab Revolt

Interminable talks and languorous meals: a tribal council at Faisal's roving war headquarters, 1917. Unique among his military officer colleagues, Lawrence understood that the British had to adapt to the Arab way of war.
© *Marist Archives and Special Collections, Lowell Thomas Papers*

With a keen insight into how tribal politics worked, Lawrence was the only British officer in Arabia to be truly accepted into Faisal's inner circle. Faisal (third from right) and his tribal lieutenants, with Lawrence at lower right.
© *Marist Archives and Special Collections, Lowell Thomas Papers*

War at its most primal. Lawrence's decisions on when and where to attack the Turks were largely dictated by the availability of water and forage.

© *www.rogersstudy.co.uk. March 1917. Photo by Captain Thomas Henderson*

Gilbert Clayton, Britain's chief spymaster in Egypt and T. E. Lawrence's supervisor. By autumn 1917, Clayton was so concerned at the risks Lawrence was taking that he planned to remove him from the battlefield, "but the time is not yet, as he is wanted just now."

(BELOW) A detachment of the Ottoman Camel Corps in southern Palestine, 1916.
Until the guerrilla tactics advocated by Lawrence and others were finally adopted, British forces were repeatedly humiliated by the antiquated and outnumbered Turkish army.

Lawrence's powers of endurance, exemplified by his marathon camel treks, astounded even his hardiest Bedouin companions. © *Imperial War Museum (Q 60212)*

A spectacle out of the Middle Ages:
Faisal (center in white robe), leading
his tribal army for the assault on Wejh

© *Imperial War Museum (Q 58863)*

The entrance to Aaronsohn's Jewish Agricultural Experiment Station at Athlit, the headquarters of his NILI spy ring

(BELOW, LEFT) Aaronsohn's younger sister, twenty-seven-year-old Sarah, masterfully operated the NILI spy ring inside Palestine despite ever-mounting peril.

(BELOW, RIGHT) As Germany's spymaster, Curt Prüfer was one of the most feared figures in the Middle East during World War I, but he never suspected there was a Jewish spy ring operating out of Athlit.

the advancing Turks, and the experience seemed to have stripped the irksome little captain of his romantic notions of the brave Arab warrior.

Perhaps it was the belief that they were finally on the same page, or perhaps Brémond couldn't resist the temptation to stick the knife in a little, but on the Jeddah dock he informed Lawrence that he was just then on his way to meet with Reginald Wingate in Khartoum. In light of the unfolding crisis on the Arabian coast, he intended to once again press for the dispatch of an Anglo-French force to Rabegh.

Lawrence had no doubt Brémond would find a receptive audience. Sure enough, on December 14, and with Colonel Brémond at his side, Wingate fired off another secret cable to the Foreign Office and General Murray in Cairo urging that a brigade be sent as soon as possible. "I can see no alternative or practical means of assisting Arabs, and of saving Sherif's movement from collapse," Wingate wrote. "Sherif has cancelled his original application to us to dispatch European troops, but is [now] genuinely alarmed at situation and, in Colonel Brémond's opinion, with a little pressure would again ask for them." The immediate question before them, Wingate argued, "is whether we shall make a last attempt to save Sherif and his Arabs in spite of themselves."

Except, unbeknownst to most everyone at that moment, the immediate crisis in western Arabia had actually already passed. On the night of December 11, just hours after Lawrence left Yenbo on the *Suva*, a large Turkish force had approached the town, only to hesitate upon seeing the British ships in the harbor, their searchlights illuminating the surrounding countryside as if in daylight. Apparently the Arabs' mortal fear of artillery was shared by the Turks, for this force soon turned back from Yenbo; within days, aerial reconnaissance showed it had retreated into the mountains, perhaps was even on its way back to Medina. While this development didn't necessarily mean an end of the Turkish threat to the coastal towns, it did create breathing space—and breathing space wasn't at all helpful to the two escalationists in Khartoum. In coming weeks, Wingate and Brémond would find several more occasions to press for intervention, but they had lost their last best chance with the Turkish withdrawal outside Yenbo.

Within several days of that threat passing, a somewhat chastened Lawrence was back in Yenbo, trying to figure out with Faisal what might come next. They were aided in their planning by a rather momentous development in London. Just weeks earlier, the coalition government of Herbert Asquith had fallen, and been replaced by a new coalition government led by David Lloyd George. The new prime minister was determined to break with the "Westerner" mind-set that had prevailed in London since the beginning of the war, which held that ultimate victory could only be achieved on the Western Front. That mind-set had led to the deaths of some 400,000 British soldiers by the end of 1916, with no end or breakthrough in sight. Instead, Lloyd George wanted to pursue an "Easterner" policy, to try to "knock out the props" of the enemy war machine by striking at its weakest spots. At least by comparison to the seemingly impregnable wall of the Western Front, that meant the Balkans and the Ottoman Empire.

Shortly after Lawrence's return to Yenbo, this new focus became evident in an increased British presence on the Hejazi coast—not the thousands of regulars hoped for by Wingate and Brémond, but rather an assortment of instructors and advisors tasked to transform the undisciplined Arab rebel bands into a credible fighting force. The most interesting of these expanded operations took place in Yenbo, the northernmost rebel-held port and now deemed relatively safe from Turkish attack. With the Hejaz Railway, the Turks' lifeline to their garrison in Medina, situated a mere ninety miles inland, the British envisioned using Yenbo as the staging ground for a committed campaign of sabotage attacks on the railroad, and to this end they brought in a colorful figure named Herbert Garland. A tall, rangy Scotsman, Garland had been a chemist before the war and by tinkering in the training grounds in Cairo had become a self-taught expert in blowing things up. In the few forays the Arabs had conducted against the Hejaz Railway prior to his arrival, they had simply torn up the tracks with picks and shovels, a very simple business to mend, and Garland now set about teaching them the fine art of placing an explosive charge beneath a rail in such a way as to mangle it beyond repair. In the doldrum rebuilding days at Yenbo of early January 1917, one of Major Garland's most attentive students was T. E. Lawrence.

But despite his dealings with Garland and the several other British advisors now setting up shop in the port town, there was something that set Lawrence quite apart from his countrymen. Part of it was obvious: his dress.

During Lawrence's visit to the Arab encampment in Nakhl Mubarak in early December, Faisal had suggested he dispense with his British army uniform in favor of Arab dress; that way, the British liaison officer could circulate through the camp and call upon Faisal at his leisure without drawing undue attention. Lawrence had taken to this suggestion with alacrity, donning the white robes and gold sashing normally reserved for a senior sheikh. He had changed out of those robes during his brief run down the coast to Jeddah, but had immediately put them on again upon his return to Yenbo.

Yet he stood apart for far more than just his attire. Taking his temporary posting as Faisal's liaison very much to heart, Lawrence largely eschewed the British tent settlement at the water's edge to spend most of his time at the sprawling Arab encampment several miles inland. There, and with far more tolerance than most other British officers might reasonably muster, he set about adapting to the peculiar lassitude with which Faisal ran his "army."

The typical day started with a dawn wake-up call by an imam, then a leisurely breakfast where Faisal conferred with his senior aides and various tribal leaders. This was followed by a long morning stretch during which any man in the encampment could come to petition Faisal over some concern or grievance; as Lawrence quickly noted, few of these audiences had any direct connection to the war effort. This open-house session only ended with the serving of lunch, often a two-hour affair attended by more aides and tribal leaders, after which Faisal might spend a couple of hours dictating messages to his scribes. That work done, it was more chitchat until an evening meal consumed at an even more languorous pace than the previous one. After that, more dictations by Faisal, more conversations with elders, the reading of reports from various scouting parties, an unhurried, undirected process that might stretch well past midnight—even right up to the imam's dawn call that signaled it was all about to start over again.

For a famously impatient and ascetic man like T. E. Lawrence, it must have been a kind of agony. In normal times, he was so indifferent to food and meals that his preference was to eat standing up and to finish in less than five minutes. Probably even more trying for a man who abhorred physical contact—he avoided even the shaking of hands if he could do so without offense—was the easy affection on constant display in the Arab camp, the endless embraces and kissing of cheeks, the casual holding of hands.

But Lawrence also recognized that this was the Arab way of war and peace. Faisal was not just a wartime leader, but a Hejazi chieftain, and the long, seemingly purposeless conversations were the glue that kept his fractious coalition together. In this culture, Faisal was not a general who issued orders—at least not to men not of his tribe—but a consensus builder compelled to cajole, counsel, and listen. Certainly, none of this was going to change to accommodate the Arabs' British advisors. To the contrary, Lawrence understood, it was he and his countrymen who had to adapt if they hoped to be accepted and effective. It was a pretty simple truism, but one that many of his colleagues, steeped in British notions of both military and cultural hierarchy, had a very hard time with.

Animating Lawrence's determination to adapt was the figure of Faisal ibn Hussein himself. Even in the darkest days of the revolt, when he had visited the Arabs' temporary refuge at Nakhl Mubarak, Lawrence had been struck by Faisal's unshaken ambition, a quality that had tempered his own pessimism over the situation. As he had reported to Gilbert Clayton on December 5, "I heard [Faisal] address the head of one battalion last night before sending them out to an advanced position over the Turkish camp at Bir Said. He did not say much, no noise about it, but it was all exactly right and the people rushed over one another with joy to kiss his headrope when he finished. He has had a nasty knock in Zeid's retreat, and he realized perfectly well that it was the ruin of all his six months' work up here in the hills tying tribe to tribe and fixing each in its proper area. Yet he took it all in public as a joke, chaffing people on the way they had run away, jeering at them like children, but without in the least hurting their feelings, and making the others feel that nothing much had happened that could not be put right. He is magnificent, for to me privately he was most horribly cut up."

Faisal had displayed that same spirit in Yenbo. On December 20, when it was clear the Turks were falling back toward Medina, he had beseeched his brother Ali to come north out of Rabegh with his army of some seven thousand, while Faisal took his own forces back up into the mountains; the hope was to catch the withdrawing Turks in a pincer movement. Alas, Ali proved no better a warrior leader than brother Zeid. Within days, his army had panicked and turned back for Rabegh on yet another erroneous rumor of a Turkish force ahead, and a disappointed Faisal saw no option but to return with his own men to Yenbo.

To most other British officers who observed the incident, it was another example of the ineptitude of the Arab forces, that at least twice now they had fled the field on the mere rumor of a Turkish presence. Lawrence saw things quite differently. Fresh from their recent rout in the mountains, the prudent course would have been for Faisal to keep his men under the protection of the British naval guns at Yenbo while they regrouped; instead, he had tried to leap to the offensive the moment an opportunity presented itself. It spoke of a determination in Faisal sorely lacking in his brothers.

In a similar vein, with both Rabegh and Yenbo now looking at least temporarily secure, Faisal returned to the idea of taking his campaign north and seizing the port town of Wejh. With Wejh in rebel hands, not only would the British supply line from Egypt be brought two hundred miles closer, but the easier terrain would allow for more frequent raids inland against the Hejaz Railway. Over long discussions with Lawrence, the two came up with a stripped-down version of Faisal's earlier plan, one that relied far less heavily on support from his now proven unreliable brothers.

But planning that advance must have been a bittersweet exercise for

Lawrence. As he well knew, his time in Arabia was rapidly drawing to a close. Despite a series of delays in Europe, Stewart Newcombe would soon be on his way to take up his permanent position with Faisal, and Lawrence bundled back to his desk job at the Arab Bureau.

It was a fate he had tried to forestall through a campaign of quiet subversion ever since returning to the Hejaz. A chief target of that campaign had been his temporary field supervisor, Lieutenant Colonel Cyril Wilson. Quite aware of Wilson's fierce opposition to even his temporary posting in Arabia, Lawrence had sought to sidestep the resident agent in Jeddah by playing directly to the higher powers in Cairo. That scheme had started with his very first cable back to Gilbert Clayton on December 5. "One of the things not fixed when I came down here," Lawrence wrote, "was my [supervisory] chief, and my manner of reporting. It is probably through Colonel Wilson, but as there is a post going to Egypt tonight I am sending this direct."

In fact, it had been made perfectly clear to Lawrence that Wilson was his chief in the field, so his confusion on this point was more than a little disingenuous. It established a precedent, however, one that Lawrence soon reemployed when Wilson tried to clip his wings by appointing him to the lowly post of supply officer in Yenbo. In protesting this assignment to Clayton—"I regard myself as primarily an Intelligence Officer, or liaison with Faisal"—Lawrence also thought to explain that he was sending his latest reports to Cairo, rather than routing them through Wilson, because "if they are to be any good at all they should reach you within a reasonable period of dispatch—and to send them to Jeddah is only [the] waste of a week or ten days." That rationale would have lost some of its persuasiveness had it been known that Lawrence was actually on a ship en route to Jeddah when he wrote it.

As December wore on, his campaign became only more overt. Not for Lawrence any beseeching pleas for reconsideration; instead, he assumed the posture that his continuing on in Arabia was a foregone conclusion. "If I am to stay here," he wrote Clayton's deputy at the end of the month, once again sidestepping Wilson, "I will need all sorts of things. Have you any news of Newcombe? The situation is so interesting that I think I will fail to come back. I want to rub off my British habits and go off with Faisal for a bit." As if that desire was somehow already a part of his government's planning, Lawrence then laid out his intentions. "When I have someone to take over here from me, I'll go off. Wadi Ais is the unknown area of N. Hejaz, and I want to drop up and see it, [and] anything behind Rudhwa will be worth while."

.　.　.

IT WAS LESS a failed regime, perhaps, than a fantastically deluded one. Across the breadth of Syria by the close of 1916, an estimated half-million people had already died of starvation or disease, and conditions appeared slated to only grow worse in the new year. On the military front, Turkish forces had been thrown back from the Suez Canal anew, the garrison in Medina was one of the last holdouts against the Arab rebels in the Hejaz, and the British were once again marching up the Tigris toward Baghdad. Yet in his governor's mansions in Jerusalem and Damascus, Djemal Pasha continued to pore over blueprints for new canalworks and roadways, continued to attend ribbon-cutting ceremonies for the inauguration of schools and hospitals. It was as if he clung more tenaciously to his self-image as a progressive reformer *because* of the cascade of ruin all around him rather than in spite of it.

Perhaps one reason was that the Syrian governor was becoming ever more divorced from the power elites in Constantinople. In the Ottoman capital, the criticisms of Djemal had reached new heights with the outbreak of the Arab Revolt, but in what was now an established pattern, those criticisms ran the gamut from his having been too harsh—a common view, one embraced by most historians, was that his executions of the Arab nationalist leaders had provoked the rebellion—to his being far too lenient. To this latter charge, Djemal's penchant for glibness didn't help his cause; when Julius Loytved-Hardegg, the German consul in Damascus, asked whatever had possessed him to allow Faisal ibn Hussein to leave for Arabia on the eve of the revolt, Djemal replied that he'd done it to test Faisal's true colors. As Loytved-Hardegg acerbically noted in his report of the meeting, "the present time doesn't seem especially appropriate" for such a test.

Also irritating to Constantinople was Djemal's curious streak of courtliness toward Europeans in general, and the French in particular, as evidenced by his continuing to allow many of these "belligerent nationals" to stay on in Syria without restriction. A notable exception to his Europhilia was the European nation to which his government was militarily allied; Djemal loathed most everything about Germany and its culture, and could be quite expansive in enumerating its deficiencies to anyone within earshot.

As the war ground on, however, and Frenchmen became a rarer commodity in Syria—thanks in no small part to the ferreting-out skills of German agents like Curt Prüfer—the governor seemed to transfer his affections to a different expatriate community, the Americans. To the cloistered faithful of the American Colony, a conservative religious sect that had established itself in Jerusalem in the 1890s, Djemal was a frequent and welcome guest; surviving photographs show Colony children crawling over Djemal's lap, much to his evident delight. Similarly, Howard

Bliss, the president of the Syrian Protestant College (later the American University of Beirut), was so grateful for Djemal's support of the institution, ensuring that it received subsidized food shipments in the midst of the Lebanon famine, that in late January 1917 he invited the governor to be the university's commencement speaker.

At that time, the U.S. consul in Damascus, Samuel Edelman, was having his own rather odd experience with Djemal, one that began with his answering a summons to the governor's Damascus office on January 20. For some months, Edelman had been trying to arrange the safe passage from Syria of some five hundred American citizens eager to escape the worsening conditions, but his efforts had been stymied by Ottoman authorities. Certainly not helping matters was the recent reelection of Woodrow Wilson as president. Despite the campaign slogan that had helped carry him to reelection—"He kept us out of the war"—there were growing signs that Wilson intended to bring the United States in on the side of the Allies, and Constantinople was understandably loath to release hundreds of foreigners with firsthand knowledge of the situation in Syria, and whose government might soon join the enemy camp. In his meeting with Edelman on January 20, Djemal offered a novel solution. As the nonplussed consul cabled to his embassy in Constantinople, Djemal would now agree to let the five hundred Americans leave so long as they gave their word of honor "not to discuss Ottoman affairs until the end of war." Not surprisingly, American diplomats swiftly agreed to these patently unenforceable terms and set about arranging the departure of their citizens from Syria.

But it wasn't as if Djemal was compliant to the entreaties of all Americans. One who didn't get his way in one particular incident was the Standard Oil representative in Syria, William Yale.

Despite the steadily worsening conditions in Jerusalem, the American oilman had proven himself supremely adaptable to his surroundings. With the Turkish currency collapsed in value and speculators subject to hanging, Yale had embarked on a complicated black-market scheme that involved the buying and reselling of gold and paper scrip in different towns across Palestine that, after expenses, netted him a tidy 10 percent profit. On one occasion, when the governor of Jerusalem had balked at renewing Socony's concessionary permits, Yale had blackmailed the man by threatening to denounce him to the Young Turk leadership in Constantinople, as well as to inform the governor's wife of his illicit love affair.

Yale's special appeal to Djemal Pasha came in the autumn of 1916, and it arose when a trusted—or perhaps bribed—censor at the telegraph office in Jerusalem came to Yale and his business partner, Ismail Hakki Bey, with disturbing news. According to the censor, Djemal had just received an anonymous letter accusing Ismail Bey of belonging to a revolutionary group with ties to the Arab Revolt leader, Faisal Hussein. Further, the letter stated that "a young American was financing the group," a clear reference to Yale.

Since such an accusation, if believed, was tantamount to a death sentence, the two men rushed to Djemal's office at the German Hospice and demanded to see the letter. To their profound shock, they recognized the handwriting as that of Selim Ayoub, one of the other two Jerusalem businessmen involved in the Kornub oil concessions. "Ismail Bey and I were so angry at the man's underhanded, unscrupulous action," Yale recalled, "we demanded that he and his whole family be exiled."

In his memoir, Yale professed to have been on "intimate, friendly terms" with Ayoub and his family, and he surely knew what such a banishment would mean to the man's wife and children: utter destitution in the best of circumstances, slow death from disease or starvation in the worst. Yale also seemed to have rather forgotten that he'd threatened Ismail Bey with a very similar charge the year before. In any event, Djemal refused to give the aggrieved oilmen full satisfaction; while agreeing to send Selim Ayoub into exile, he decreed that the rest of the Ayoub family could remain in Jerusalem. With twenty years' distance on the event, Yale would note in his memoirs, "I am glad that Djemal acted less cruelly than the rest of us."

THE MARCH ON Wejh began at an oasis village northeast of Yenbo, and in wondrously exotic fashion. To Lawrence, the scene was both splendid and barbaric, as if the medieval histories he had devoured as a child had suddenly come to life. "Faisal in front, in white," he wrote. "[Chieftain] Sharraf on his right, in red headcloth and henna-dyed tunic and cloak, myself on his left in white and red. Behind us 3 banners of purple silk with gold spikes, behind them 3 drummers playing a march, and behind them a wild bouncing mass of 1,200 camels of the bodyguard, all packed as closely as they could move, the men in every variety of colored clothes and the camels nearly as brilliant in their trappings—and the whole crowd singing at the tops of their voices a war song in honor of Faisal and his family! It looked like a river of camels, for we filled up the wadi to the tops of its banks, and poured along in a quarter-of-a-mile long stream."

For Lawrence, this entrancing spectacle was to be very short-lived. Despite all his maneuverings of the past month, earlier that morning a cable had arrived in Yenbo announcing that Stewart Newcombe was finally on his way from Egypt; Lawrence was instructed to wait in Yenbo for his replacement's arrival, at which point his posting in Arabia would come to an end. As a result, after accompanying the grand cavalcade north for a mere hour or so, Lawrence had no choice but to bid Faisal farewell and return to the coast.

But there was to be no handover of authority in Yenbo. Instead, with Newcombe encountering another last-minute delay in Cairo, it was decided the two officers would meet up in the small rebel-held port of Um Lejj, halfway along the coast to Wejh, where they could intercept Faisal's army as it moved north. Accordingly, on January 14, Lawrence hopped on HMS *Suva* and made the short run up to Um Lejj and a reunion with Faisal. With the rebel force pausing there to reprovision, it was a fleeting reminder to Lawrence of both the adventure he'd had over the previous six weeks and of all he was about to miss. "I wish I had not to go back to Egypt," he wistfully wrote his family from Um Lejj on January 16. "Anyway, I have had a change."

Except there was still no word of Newcombe. By the seventeenth, and with the rebel march scheduled to resume the next morning, Lawrence quietly entertained the hope that perhaps his superior still might not make it in time, in which case he would have "no choice" but to accompany Faisal on to Wejh. By that evening, and with still no sign of Newcombe, Lawrence's hopes seemed realized; leaving a note for Newcombe in Um Lejj—"So I miss you by a day!"—he raced out to the desert to rejoin Faisal.

In fact, it was by considerably less than a day. No sooner had the Arab army broken camp that morning, Lawrence happily ensconced alongside Faisal, than two horsemen appeared coming from Um Lejj at a full gallop. One of them was Newcombe, finally arrived to take up his position as head of the British military mission to the Hejaz.

By instruction, Lawrence was to now return to Um Lejj and board the next ship for Cairo. On the spur of the moment, however, Stewart Newcombe decided on a different plan. This handover was far too rushed, and while he'd no doubt stumble his way to a familiarity with Faisal and his chief lieutenants during the continuing trek to Wejh, that process might be greatly eased if his stand-in of the past six weeks remained on hand to make the introductions. When Newcombe suggested this alternative to Lawrence, he encountered no resistance.

DURING HIS LONG and dreary days of waiting in London, Aaron Aaronsohn had fixed his gaze on Cairo, the place where he imagined British inertia might finally be overcome. It wasn't quite working out that way. "A hundred times daily I curse the moment when we decided to work with them," he raged in his diary on January 5, 1917. "Better for us to stagnate with the Turks and keep our illusions about the Allies than to approach them and see this hopeless incompetency. If the Boches [Germans] are finally beaten by these *kakers* they will have reason to doubt God and Justice."

Aaronsohn had arrived in Port Said in mid-December with the intention of immediately proceeding to Cairo to present his letters of introduction to Gilbert Clayton at the Arab Bureau. Instead, the British authorities meeting his ship had been more impressed by his dubious legal status—he was still a citizen of the Ottoman Empire—and had quarantined him in Alexandria. Shortly afterward, a young captain from the Eastern Mediterranean Special Intelligence Bureau (EMSIB), William Edmonds, showed up with the news that he was to serve as Aaronsohn's liaison.

The agronomist's initial high opinion of Edmonds—"not only very intelligent but very shrewd as well"—rapidly diminished when it became clear the intelligence agent's function was more to mollify Aaronsohn with the appearance of progress than to actually liaise him to anyone of substance. An indication of where Aaronsohn stood in the larger scheme of things was revealed when he inquired into the possibility of being reimbursed for some of the expenses he'd incurred in reaching London and then coming on to Egypt, a cost he estimated at about £1,500. Edmonds blanched at the figure; with the miserliness with which British officialdom was already infamous, he pointed out that no expenses could be reimbursed without proper receipts, and instead proposed placing Aaronsohn on a stipend of £1 a day, a sum that didn't even cover his Alexandria hotel bill. The proud scientist immediately refused.

"Until now," he vented in his diary that night, "I have encountered nothing but distrust and reticence, smallness and pettiness. I must try and control my nerves so that I can establish another connection with Absa," he wrote, referring to Absalom Feinberg, the deputy he had left behind in Athlit. "Then, he can continue the work if he wants to. So far as I am concerned, I have had enough of it. I am not going to continue working under such conditions."

Driving Aaronsohn's pique was that he'd heard nothing of what might be happening in Palestine for the past eight months. His whole purpose in coming to Egypt had been to finally link the British with his spy network in Athlit, and instead he was wasting his time quibbling about receipts and meeting with low-level functionaries.

What the scientist didn't appreciate was that he still wasn't fully trusted. Just as with the intelligence analyst back in London who'd concluded that Aaronsohn's information was so accurate it might indicate he was really a Turkish spy, so that analyst's counterparts in Cairo were grappling with the conundrum that this suspicion posed: how to link up with Aaronsohn's spy network, should it actually exist, while simultaneously blocking him from making contact with his Turkish counterintelligence handlers, if that was his true game? Aaronsohn may have unwittingly added to these doubts by repeatedly asking to talk with the intelligence officer that Absalom Feinberg had made contact with in 1915, Leonard Woolley. His British handlers were very slow to inform Aaronsohn that Woolley was now a Turkish captive, his ship having been torpedoed in the Gulf of Alexandretta over the summer, and Aaronsohn's constant invoking of Woolley's name in the absence of that information surely raised more eyebrows.

Shortly before Christmas, the British thought they'd come up with a clever way around their dilemma. Edmonds informed Aaronsohn that, at long last, a spy ship was being dispatched to make contact with Athlit; might Aaronsohn care to send along a personal message? The agronomist saw through the ploy at once and flew into one of his trademark tempers. Unless he went on the boat personally, he told Edmonds, he'd simply end all relations then and there; far better that than allowing the British to send in "some blunderer" who might get all his people killed.

In the face of this ultimatum, a compromise was reached: Aaronsohn could go along on the boat, but would not be allowed ashore. In his stead, couriers would be sent in on a launch under the cover of darkness carrying instructions from him, as well as some of his small personal items that his confederates might recognize, thus convincing them the instructions were genuine. Allowing sufficient time for contact to be made, the launch would then go back in to retrieve the couriers off the beach. Time would be short, however, since the spy ship obviously needed to be well over the horizon and gone from sight before sunrise.

As at most every other stage of this star-crossed venture, now entering its seventeenth month, there was to be a snag. With Aaronsohn on board, the spy ship, a small converted trawler named the *Goeland*, slipped out of Port Said on Christmas Eve, and reached the coast off Athlit by the following afternoon. Aaronsohn made out someone waving a black cloth from the second-floor balcony of the research station, an identification that might have been more definitive had anyone on the ship's crew thought to bring along a decent pair of binoculars. Waiting for the cover of nightfall to make contact, the *Goeland* then headed out to the open sea, only to sail directly into a strong squall, a typical occurrence in the eastern Mediterranean at that time of year. Consequently, it was nearly 2 a.m. before the seas had calmed enough to allow it to return to Athlit and release the launch with the two couriers on board, one carrying Aaronsohn's instructions to his conspirators, the other his monogrammed penknife and special magnifying glass. No sooner had the launch disappeared into the darkness than the storm kicked back up.

Within the hour, the launch returned with troubling news. With the surf too rough to make a beach landing, the couriers had been instructed to swim the last little distance to shore. And with dawn fast approaching—already they could see a bivouac fire to the north, presumably that of a Turkish shore patrol—there was now no time to go back in to collect them; the couriers would have to fend for themselves. Throttling up its engines, the *Goeland* headed out to open waters once more. For Aaronsohn, it was one more maddening experience to join all the others; he had at last glimpsed Athlit again, but had no way of knowing for certain if successful contact had been made.

His mood improved when in early January he was finally permitted to leave Alexandria for Cairo. Taking a room at the Continental Hotel, he made the rounds of the different officials in the Arab Bureau, and at last began finding a receptive audience. Chief among these was another aristocratic Amateur and member of Parliament, a thirty-one-year-old Oxford graduate recently arrived in Cairo named William Ormsby-Gore. If not quite up to Mark Sykes's overachiever status, Ormsby-Gore was also a great dabbler over an eclectic array of interests, including the notion of establishing a Jewish homeland in Palestine—a cause with special resonance since he had recently converted to Judaism. In the months ahead, he and Sykes would emerge as two of the most important figures in the British power structure pushing for the creation of such a Jewish homeland, and one of their primary vehicles in furthering that cause would be Aaron Aaronsohn.

In the meantime, though, Ormsby-Gore sought to bolster the agronomist's flagging spirits however he could. Under his urging, another spy ship was sent to make contact with Athlit in mid-January; alas, this mission, too, ran into bad weather, and was aborted even before the Palestine coast had been reached. Ormsby-Gore also passed Aaronsohn along to two other members of the Arab Bureau, Philip Graves and Major Windham Deedes, who shared the MP's belief in the enormous benefits that might be derived by activating the scientist's intelligence network. These sympathizers managed to insert a portion of an Aaronsohn report on the Jewish colonies in Palestine into the *Arab Bulletin*, including the pointed comment that the Zionists' greatest desire was "for autonomy through the benevolence of a friendly protecting power," marking one of the very few times a non-British correspondent gained a hearing in the intelligence compendium. Still, it reflected how far the agronomist remained from the inner circle of power in Cairo that he could imagine Windham Deedes as being "in charge of the Intelligence Service," as he noted in his diary, rather than cued to his true status as a mere midlevel analyst.

Slowly but surely, then, Aaronsohn finally began making some headway, but as he well knew, "slowly" was his enemy. That became manifestly clear on January 25. As he was returning to his room at the Continental Hotel that afternoon, he spotted his erstwhile liaison, Captain Edmonds, lounging near the staircase; he noted that the young officer seemed "mysterious in attitude."

"You are the very man I am looking for," Edmonds said. "You must go immediately to Port Said. One of your men came across the desert." It was shocking news to Aaronsohn, but, true to form, Edmonds refused to provide any details other than the man's name: Joseph Lishansky.

"Is he wounded I wonder?" Aaronsohn wrote in his diary before rushing off to Port Said. "Why do they send me to him instead of sending him here? These gentlemen are so uselessly and so unfortunately mysterious!"

As he discovered in Port Said, his apprehensions were exactly right—Lishansky was wounded—but the story got much worse from there. Having despaired of ever hearing from Aaronsohn, and with the situation in Palestine growing ever more bleak, in mid-December Lishansky and Absalom Feinberg had decided to make another attempt to reach Egypt overland; in a cruel twist of fate, they had set off from Athlit just days before the *Goeland* couriers had come ashore with Aaronsohn's instructions. After a harrowing journey across the Sinai no-man's-land, the two men had been nearly to the British lines when they were spotted by a band of Bedouin raiders. In the ensuing gunfight, Lishansky escaped with relatively minor wounds, but Feinberg had been shot in the back and was presumably dead.

The news shattered Aaronsohn; Feinberg was not only his deputy at Athlit, but his closest friend. "So Absa, the brave, was shot by vile, rapacious Bedouins," he lamented in his diary; "he fell dying into the hands of those whom he despised most."

There was little time for grieving, however, for Aaronsohn instantly appreciated the new problem Feinberg's apparent death raised: if the Turks found and identified his body, they would surely set to tearing Athlit apart and rounding up his associates. Rushing back to Cairo, Aaronsohn went in frantic search of his newfound friends in the Arab Bureau, and found Windham Deedes.

The frustrations of nearly two years came out in a torrent. Amid tears, he blamed Feinberg's death on the incompetence and cynicism of the British war machine, and warned that his death was a mere harbinger of the many to come if the Turks uncovered his spy ring—as now seemed highly likely. "I spoke with fire and sorrow," Aaronsohn noted in his diary. "[Deedes] listened to me kindly. . . . He assured me that in future there would be no more humiliation and distrust and that everything would go well."

True to Deedes's word, a spy ship was immediately readied to make another run to Athlit. This time, Aaronsohn distinctly saw signals from the research station's balcony, and a launch was cast off to take his messages ashore. In an eerie reprise of the earlier voyage, however, another storm descended at just that moment, compelling the launch to stay offshore and a lone courier to swim the last stretch to the beach. After a tense hour's wait, the swimmer reappeared on the shore with two men from Athlit, but by now the storm was raging; unable to swim out to the launch, this courier, too, was left behind.

More bad news soon followed. Guided by Lishansky's description of the attack, a Bedouin tracker was sent out into the Sinai in search of Absalom Feinberg. He found nothing. "So our brave Knight is dead!" Aaronsohn wrote in his diary. "Without even confessing it to myself, I had entertained a wild hope that he had survived. But now, we can do nothing except to complete the work for which he gave his life."

But this, too, was hardly a consoling thought to Aaron Aaronsohn. With Absalom Feinberg now dead and his brother Alex in America, the full burden and peril of operating the spy ring would fall squarely on the only person left in Palestine whom the scientist implicitly trusted: his twenty-seven-year-old sister Sarah.

IN *SEVEN PILLARS OF WISDOM*, Lawrence described the Arab army that left Um Lejj for the march on Wejh on January 18 in exalted terms. Coming just a little over a month since the debacle above Yenbo, Faisal now stood at the head of a force of some ten thousand warriors drawn from a half-dozen different tribes and many more clans. Lawrence underscored the importance of that moment by invoking the words of a young sheikh of the Beidawi tribe, Abd el Karim, as he gazed over the sea of tent encampments:

"He called me out to look, and swept his arm round, saying half-sadly, 'We are no longer Arabs but a People.' He was half-proud too, for the advance on Wejh was their biggest effort, the first time in memory that the manhood of a tribe, with transport, arms and food for [covering] two hundred miles, had left its district and marched into another's territory without the hope of plunder or the stimulus of blood feud."

Perhaps, but born of such high purpose, it must have been rather anticlimactic when Faisal's forces cleared the dunes south of Wejh a week later to find the port town already a shattered, smoking ruin. It was an embarrassing sight for Faisal ibn Hussein, and only slightly less so for that British member of his entourage who had become his greatest supporter.

By the timetable worked out with senior British officers at Um Lejj,

Faisal's men were supposed to have reached Wejh fully two days earlier. At that point, a coordinated land-and-sea operation was to be launched, with Faisal's forces closing from the landward side while the British naval flotilla waiting offshore would ferry ashore the some 550 Arab fighters they had transported up from Yenbo.

But as the British armada maneuvered into position leading up to H-Hour on January 23, Faisal's army had been nowhere to be seen. That night, the commander of the British fleet, Admiral Rosslyn Wemyss, decided that, for "sanitary reasons" alone, he simply had to put the Arab warriors on his ships ashore. Following a brief bombardment on the morning of January 24, the shipborne Arab fighters had been ferried into Wejh under the command of two British officers.

The ensuing battle was a chaotic and fitful affair, one that lasted most of that day and left some twenty of the Arab fighters dead. No doubt contributing to its slow pace—the Turkish garrison of two hundred was outnumbered nearly three to one and demoralized—was the Arab habit of breaking off their attacks to loot and ransack whatever new buildings they occupied. One of the British officers in charge of the ground operation, Captain Norman Bray, was shocked by the rebels' behavior, noting in his battle report that the result of their freebooting ways was a town "ransacked from roof to floor." This was the scene that Faisal and Lawrence rode into the following day.

For his part, Lawrence struggled mightily to put the very best gloss on matters, offering in his own report a number of unconvincing explanations to account for their delay in reaching Wejh. Lawrence's reflexively contrarian response to criticisms of the Arabs by his British comrades was nothing new. Back on the night of December 11, when Turkish forces had approached the outskirts of Yenbo, a British pilot had unsparingly described the panic that gripped Faisal's forces within the town. His account stood in marked contrast to Lawrence's own version of events. "The garrison was called out about 10 PM by means of criers sent round the streets," he reported. "The men all turned out without visible excitement, and proceeded to their posts round the town wall without making a noise, or firing a shot."

The easiest explanation for this divergence of accounts was that the pilot had actually been in Yenbo at the time, whereas Lawrence had not; earlier that same day, he had left Yenbo by ship, a detail left obscure in his report.

This variance in viewpoints also extended to the figure of Faisal ibn Hussein. In his December report, that same British pilot had reported that Faisal "is easily frightened and lives in constant dread of a Turkish advance, though he seems to conceal that fear from his army." Another

British officer, Major Charles Vickery, caustically commented after observing Faisal's force in Wejh that "it is not known how far other She-rifial leaders interest themselves in the training of their troops, but certainly Sherif Faisal ignores it." Most appalling to British officers had been Faisal's decision to take up quarters on a British warship in Yenbo harbor during those dark December days when a Turkish attack seemed imminent, leaving his men onshore to fend for themselves.

All of this, of course, stood at great odds to Lawrence's own analysis; as he'd said of Faisal even during the grim interlude in Nakhl Mubarak, "he is magnificent." It also revealed something quite remarkable: after just three months in the field, Lawrence was not only the chief booster of Faisal and the Arabs, but their most determined apologist.

Among those who noticed this was Faisal himself. Knowing that Lawrence was now scheduled to return to Cairo—and probably having seen enough of the hard-nosed Newcombe during the march up from Um Lejj to realize theirs would be a less congenial relationship—Faisal sent off a secret cable to Cyril Wilson in Jeddah on the same day that he reached Wejh. As Wilson relayed to Gilbert Clayton in Cairo, Faisal "is most anxious that Lawrence should not return to Cairo, as he has given such very great assistance."

Confronted by this direct request from Faisal, Clayton found it quite impossible to find a way to refuse. Within days, the paperwork was readied to make Lawrence's posting to the Hejaz permanent. At last, Lawrence was to be free: free of his desk at the Savoy Hotel, free, ultimately, to remake the war in Arabia to his own image.

Chapter 11

A Mist of Deceits

A man might clearly destroy himself, but it was repugnant that the
innocence and the ideals of the Arabs should enlist in my sordid service
for me to destroy. We needed to win the war, and their inspiration
had proved the best tool out here. The effort should have been its own
reward—might yet be for the deceived—but we, the masters,
had promised them results in our false contract,
and that was bargaining with life.

T. E. LAWRENCE, *SEVEN PILLARS OF WISDOM*

With the taking of Wejh, the setbacks and embarrassments that had plagued the Arab rebel cause in recent months were being consigned to history. Lawrence made every effort to hasten the process of forgetfulness along.

After that town's capture in late January 1917, he was briefly brought back to Cairo in preparation for his return to Arabia on a permanent basis. In the Egyptian capital, he kept up a wearying pace. Along with catching up on his long-neglected reports and making additions to *The Handbook of the Hejaz*, a primer the Arab Bureau was compiling to help familiarize British officers being dispatched there, Lawrence shuttled between the offices of the British military leadership to provide them with firsthand accounts of what was occurring across the Red Sea. With all, he presented a very optimistic view of where matters stood—he even managed to concoct plausible-sounding excuses for Faisal's late arrival to Wejh—and insisted there was a newfound fortitude and enthusiasm for battle among the western Arabian tribes. His assessment stood in marked contrast to those of other British officers present at Wejh, but success has a way of choosing winners in such disagreements.

"The circle of Arab well-wishers was now strangely increased," Lawrence archly recalled. "In the army, our shares rose as we showed profits. [General] Lynden-Bell stood firmly our friend and swore that method was coming out of the Arab madness. Sir Archibald Murray realized with a sudden shock that more Turkish troops were fighting the Arabs than were fighting him, and began to remember how he had always favored the Arab revolt."

Perhaps none were so pleased as Lawrence's superior, General Gilbert Clayton. To be sure, Faisal's insistence that Lawrence stay on as his permanent liaison necessitated a bit of bureaucratic reconfiguring—Clayton needed to ensure that neither Cyril Wilson in Jeddah nor Stewart Newcombe, the recently arrived head of the British military mission, felt infringed upon—but these were trivial matters when set against the achievement: after all the distrust that had marked Arab-British relations over the previous two years, suspicions that had remained despite the ministrations of generals and senior diplomats, the chief Arab field commander now regarded a lowly British officer as his most indispensable advisor.

So hectic was Lawrence's pace in Cairo that he apparently took little notice of a visitor to the Arab Bureau offices on the morning of February 1, 1917. It had been just a few days since Aaron Aaronsohn learned of the death of his chief spying partner, Absalom Feinberg, in the Sinai desert, and he was now being treated with a kind of contrite respect within the British military intelligence apparatus; he'd come to the Savoy Hotel that morning to lend his advice to a British officer compiling a dossier on the Palestine political situation. While Lawrence made no record of their brief conversation, Aaronsohn was sufficiently struck by it to make note in his diary that night. "At the Arab Bureau there was a young 2nd lieutenant (Laurens)," he wrote, "an archaeologist—very well informed on Palestine questions—but rather conceited."

Perhaps one reason Lawrence forgot about his first encounter with Aaronsohn—they would meet again, and to far greater consequence—was that just two days later a chain of events began that would fundamentally transform his mission in the Middle East. It started on the morning of February 3, with a visit to the Savoy Hotel by his nemesis, Colonel Édouard Brémond.

CUNNING AND RESOURCEFULNESS are characteristics that generally well serve a military officer. If judged by those traits alone, Édouard Brémond should not have been a mere colonel in the French armed forces, but a field marshal.

As he'd shown repeatedly during his time in Arabia, if Brémond found one approach to a desired goal blocked, he immediately set out in search of another. And if that first goal was made unattainable or redundant, he simply recalibrated his sights to something else. What made this agility even more impressive was that, as both political and military point man for French policy in Arabia, Édouard Brémond was juggling two largely contradictory agendas at once: to ensure that France enjoyed equal standing with her ally, Great Britain, in all matters related to the war effort there, but also to try to limit that war effort from within.

His long and ultimately fruitless campaign to put an Allied force ashore in Rabegh had been only the most overt of these efforts. During the same period, he had been urging on Hussein the establishment of a French-Ottoman bank in Jeddah, an institution that might lend financial credits to the Hejaz government at very attractive rates. British officers examining Brémond's bank proposal had quickly judged it to be an economic trap—with no means to pay back the loans, the Hussein regime would soon become beholden to its French creditors—and scuttled the plan. Then there was the colonel's perennial lobbying to have French officers attached as advisors to the various Arab rebel formations; while he achieved some success with Abdullah and Ali—a half dozen French specialists had been dispatched to their camps in December—he'd had little with Faisal, who remained deeply wary of Gallic intentions.

With the advance on Wejh, Brémond had seen a new opportunity. Once that Red Sea port was captured from the Turks, the entire focus of the Arabian conflict would shift north some two hundred miles. That would render the Turkish threat to Jeddah and Mecca essentially moot—and with it any argument for an Allied force in Rabegh—but it would offer up an even more enticing target: the Turks' last principal outpost on the Red Sea, the small port of Aqaba.

Observed on a map, Aqaba's extraordinary strategic importance was plain to anyone. Situated at the end of a hundred-mile long ribbon of water that forms the southeastern boundary of the Sinai Peninsula, the port was ideally situated to serve both as a staging ground for attacks into the population centers of southern Palestine, a mere hundred miles to the north, and for launching raids on the Hejaz Railway, the lifeline of the Turkish garrison in Medina, just sixty miles to the east. In fact, Brémond had broached the idea of an assault on Aqaba with his British military counterparts shortly after his arrival in Cairo in the summer of 1916. The notion had found considerable favor among the British, but with the Arab

Revolt still struggling very far to the south at that time, had been deemed premature.

By late January 1917, it was premature no more. Not only did the Arabs now control the Red Sea coast as far north as Wejh, but General Murray's ponderous advance across the Sinai Peninsula in prelude to his Palestine offensive was nearly complete. Lying in the gap between these two forces was Aqaba. Its control by the Allies would secure Murray's right flank, ensuring that no Turkish counteroffensive could be launched from that direction, and it would bring the Arab rebels much closer to their British army suppliers in Egypt.

Of course, the plan might also finally bring about the fulfillment of Brémond's not-so-secret agenda: keeping the Arab Revolt bottled up in the Hejaz. Far away from the Islamic holy cities of Mecca and Medina, King Hussein (he had declared himself such in late October) could hardly object to a sizable British and French presence in Aqaba. And with that presence, the principal Allies could dictate to their Arab junior partners just where they might go and what they might do; any Arab dissent on that point and the pipeline of Allied weapons and gold upon which they depended could simply be cut off. Better yet, all of this could be accomplished under the guise of helping the rebel cause by moving their forward base to a place where they could more easily carry out their railway attacks.

In mid-January, even before Wejh had been taken, Brémond began discussing this idea with his superiors in Paris, and found enthusiastic support. While Paris would pursue the matter at the departmental level in London, the French liaison in Cairo and Brémond in Jeddah were commanded to lobby for the Aqaba scheme among the regional British leadership. Brémond knew just where to turn. In addition to touting the plan to British officers in the Hejaz, he put it before his most reliable ally in the Cairo power structure, Reginald Wingate, newly ensconced as British high commissioner to Egypt. Wingate liked the idea so much that he immediately took it to General Archibald Murray.

By the usual standards of British politeness and understatement, Murray's response was withering. "In reply to your letter referring to Brémond's proposal," he wrote Wingate on January 22, "my opinion, from the purely military point of view, is that the [previous] objections to landing a force at Rabegh apply with equal if not greater force to a landing at Aqaba." Therein followed Murray's usual litany of fears about mission creep, before he turned to demolishing Wingate's contention that control of Aqaba would enable the Allies to strike inland at the Hejaz Railway. "The country in the neighborhood of Aqaba is extremely rough and rocky," the general explained, and any push inland would be over a terrain only certain rare breeds of camels could traverse. "To sum up, therefore," Murray wrote, "the French proposal to land troops at Aqaba offers, from a military point of view, so few advantages and such serious disadvantages, that I can only suppose that it has been put forward without due consideration and I do not propose to entertain it."

Along with testiness, another feature of Archibald Murray's leadership style was a tendency to needlessly compartmentalize information. As he well knew when writing to Wingate, the chief impediment to an eastern advance from Aqaba was not simply "rough and rocky" terrain but that terrain's near impassability. A few months earlier he had detailed a junior officer in the Arab Bureau office to analyze a series of aerial reconnaissance photos taken of the Aqaba region. In his report, that officer had pointed out that the port was nestled in the very shadows of a massive range of rugged mountains that rose steadily for thirty miles inland before descending over an equally inhospitable landscape to the interior desert where the Hejaz Railway lay. The only way through that wall of rock was a narrow gorge known as the Wadi Itm, along which the Turks had built a network of fortified blockhouses and trenchworks, leaving any military force foolhardy enough to attempt a crossing exposed to constant ambush and sniper fire. The issue, then, was not *taking* Aqaba—that was the easy part—but in ever being able to move off its beach. A heedless move here was to invite a miniature replay of the Gallipoli debacle—or a full-scale reprise, depending on how determined military commanders became to compound their initial error.

Inexplicably, however, Murray chose not to share this salient information with Wingate, nor evidently with the growing chorus of other British officers advocating an Aqaba landing. In the absence of that information, Murray's scornful reply to the proposal appeared to be just another manifestation of his timidity and bad temper. That was certainly the view Colonel Brémond came away with upon hearing the news through the diplomatic filter of Reginald Wingate.

"You can confidentially inform Brémond," Wingate cabled his underlings in Jeddah on January 24, "that we have already given fullest consideration here to [the] proposal to land troops at Aqaba, but in view of our present military commitments in Sinai and elsewhere it must be discarded. We fully recognize the advantages of this scheme, but the troops and transport necessary to undertake a successful expedition against the railway [from Aqaba] are not available."

To Édouard Brémond, a man who'd previously been able to play Wingate to great effect, all this apparently sounded less like an emphatic "no" than a coquettish "maybe." Days later, the French colonel boarded a naval frigate in Jeddah harbor for the run up the coast to Wejh to put his proposal directly to the one man whose desires just might override Murray's: Faisal ibn Hussein.

The two men met on the afternoon of January 30, with the more fluent Arabic-speaking Stewart Newcombe acting as interpreter. Brémond informed Faisal that he was on his way to Egypt to inspect his men at Port Suez, before continuing on to Cairo. There, he intended to lobby the British high command to send a brigade to seize Aqaba, a force to be complemented by two French-Senegalese battalions that were sitting idle in the French port of Djibouti, at the southern mouth of the Red Sea.

Although Faisal had also set his sights on Aqaba, he refused to endorse Brémond's plan; as Newcombe would report, "Faisal afterwards told me that he would like British troops to help him, but did not want any help from the French or to have anything to do with them." On the heels of that meeting in Wejh, Brémond immediately proceeded to Port Suez and then to Cairo, where he sought out a most unlikely listener. "[Brémond] called to felicitate me on the capture of Wejh," Lawrence recounted in *Seven Pillars*, "saying that it confirmed his belief in my military talent and encouraged him to expect my help in an extension of our success." That "extension," of course, was the colonel's scheme for an Allied landing at Aqaba.

Whatever possessed Brémond to tip his hand to Lawrence? The simplest explanation—that he saw the Aqaba plan as so beneficial to all concerned that even the obstreperous Lawrence might embrace it—is also the least likely. By now, Brémond was fully aware of Lawrence's abiding distrust both of him and of French intentions in the Middle East, a distrust so deep that he was likely to oppose any French proposal on the basis of its origin alone. Indeed, by Lawrence's own account, he instantly heard in Brémond's Aqaba plan an echo of his hidden motive in the Rabegh scheme, a way for the Allies to assume de facto control over the Arab Revolt and keep it out of Syria.

But what Brémond surely didn't appreciate was that the man sitting across from him that morning at the Savoy probably knew the Aqaba region as well as any European alive. Not only had Lawrence negotiated that landscape during his 1914 Wilderness of Zin expedition, but it was he who had studied the Aqaba aerial maps at the behest of General Murray, to deeply pessimistic results. Brémond may have envisioned Aqaba being a grand cul-de-sac for the Arabs, but in Lawrence's estimation, it would be for any British and French troops sent there, too.

When Lawrence tried to explain this to Brémond, however, the Frenchman remained utterly sanguine. In fact, he let drop that once his lobbying efforts in Cairo were done, he intended to return to Wejh to prod Faisal further on the matter.

There may have rested the colonel's true motive in seeking Lawrence out that morning. The little Oxford upstart had been the most eloquent—and, as bad luck would have it, influential—of Brémond's British opponents during the Rabegh episode, and the Frenchman surely didn't want Lawrence on hand in Cairo to pour water on any pro-Aqaba fires he might light among the British high command. By further letting slip that he would soon return to Wejh for another meeting with Faisal, Brémond may have been hoping that Lawrence would immediately make haste for Arabia, thereby removing himself from the arena where decisions were actually made.

If this was Brémond's goal, it worked perfectly. "Now I had not warned Faisal that Brémond was a crook," Lawrence recounted. "Newcombe was there [in Wejh], with his friendly desire to get moves on. . . . It seemed best for me to hurry down and put my side on their guard against the [Aqaba] notion."

Within hours of his meeting with Brémond, Lawrence left Cairo for Port Suez, there to board the first ship for Wejh.

IT WAS A small but telling sign of the changes that war had brought. In June 1915, when William Yale had taken his first carriage ride to the Mount of Olives to meet Djemal Pasha, the horses had trotted up the steep cobblestoned road with ease. Now, in February 1917, that same journey was torturously slow, the emaciated horses in their harnesses so weakened from two years of food shortages that it appeared they might die in the effort. "It seemed we would never reach the German Hospice," Yale recalled. The oilman persevered, though, for it was absolutely vital that he reach the Syrian governor.

By that winter of 1917, Yale could feel the walls closing in on him in Jerusalem. Part of it had to do with his nationality. Over the past two and a half years of war, the grudging respect with which the United States had initially been regarded by nearly all the combatants, its annoying stance of neutrality offset by its efforts at peacemaking, had steadily eroded to something approaching disgust. In Britain and France, it took the form of a despair that the American government might ever recognize how its own welfare dictated that it side with the "democracies" against the "dictatorships." In the Central Power nations, it took the form of a growing bitterness at an American foreign policy that, for all Woodrow Wilson's pious talk of being a neutral arbitrator, clearly favored the Entente. And for all concerned was a deepening anger that under the cloak of defending the sacred tenet of "free trade," the United States continued to finance and do business with both sides in the conflict, growing ever richer while Europe bled.

By early 1917, however, with Woodrow Wilson's reelection campaign safely behind him, there were growing signs that the status quo might soon end, with the United States entering the war on the side of the Entente. Should that happen, those Americans still residing in Central Power nations could expect to come in for some unpleasant treatment, and probably none more so than William Yale. With his bare-knuckled approach to commerce—bribery, threats, and blackmail had been his stock-in-trade—the oilman had made a lot of enemies during his time in Palestine, business rivals and aggrieved local government officials who might quite enjoy seeing the long-protected American "neutral" reclassified as a "belligerent" and hauled off to an internment camp.

Yet as the menacing signs had built that winter, a personal sense of duty had prevented Yale from asking the Standard Oil office in Constantinople for permission to leave Jerusalem. Instead, he and his trusty bodyguard, Mustapha Kharpoutli, made contingency plans to try a dash for British Egypt should the Americans come into the war, even as both knew the odds of success in such an enterprise were virtually nil.

Then, on February 1, Germany had announced a resumption of its unrestricted U-boat campaign against all merchant vessels supplying its European enemies, a move that would inevitably target American ships and seemed almost designed to provoke an American war declaration. That didn't immediately materialize, but just days later, after Wilson took the interim step of breaking off diplomatic relations with Germany, Yale received the cable he'd been desperately awaiting: the Standard office in Constantinople ordered him to leave Palestine and make his way to the Ottoman capital. In great relief, the American swiftly packed up his office papers and personal belongings, eleven suitcases and footlockers in all, in preparation for the long train ride north.

It was then that Yale discovered he was caught in something of a riddle. As with everyone else in wartime Syria, he needed a travel permit, or *vesika*, in order to leave Jerusalem. Since he was a foreigner, however, his permit had to be personally authorized by Djemal Pasha, and Djemal now rarely left Damascus. For agonizing days, Yale tried to think of some way out of this conundrum, until finally he received a tip that Djemal was coming to Jerusalem on a brief fact-finding mission. It was this that spurred his anxious trip up the Mount of Olives that February morning.

But even as he waited in the main hallway of the German Hospice for the chance to buttonhole the Syrian governor, William Yale found his trademark self-confidence deserting him. "America was on the verge of war with Germany," he recalled, "and there was nothing I could do to be of use to Djemal Pasha. To make matters worse, I had [earlier] been accused of being a member of a revolutionary Arab group. Certainly I could not expect Djemal Pasha to feel kindly towards me."

Perhaps another factor weighing on Yale was the singularly unproductive role he had performed at the behest of his employers while in Jerusalem. Despite being given concession over a vast swath of Judea by Djemal Pasha, Standard Oil had failed to produce a single drop of Palestinian oil for the Turkish military machine.

As Yale waited in the hospice foyer, Djemal at last emerged from a far doorway and, surrounded by a coterie of high-ranking German and Turkish military officers, strode briskly down the corridor toward him. But the oilman froze, didn't even try to get the governor's attention as he swept past. Appalled by his own timidity, Yale simply stared after the receding entourage until someone called to him, "Mr. Yale, what on earth are you doing here?"

Turning, Yale saw that his questioner was a man named Zaki Bey, the former military governor of Jerusalem. A courtly and cultured figure, in the early days of the war, Zaki Bey had endeavored to shield Jerusalem's foreign community from the harsher edicts of both the Constantinople regime—he had reportedly warned the Greek Orthodox patriarch to hide his church's valuables ahead of a government seizure warrant—and the resident German intelligence corps. For his conciliatory actions, Zaki Bey had ultimately been forced from office by the Germans, but had somehow remained a member in good standing of Djemal Pasha's inner circle. Just as important, given the circumstances of the moment, Zaki Bey was a member in good standing of William Yale's biweekly bridge club. After hearing of the American's predicament, the former governor tore off the last page of a government document, hastily scribbled out a travel authorization on the back, and sped down the corridor in pursuit of Djemal. Shortly afterward, he returned, the signed *vesika* in hand.

"As the horses jogged wearily down the Mount of Olives," Yale wrote, "I hummed with joy. After two long years of exile during which time I had seen the increasing misery of war entangle those about me, I now held in my hand a paper which would start me on my way home."

Of course, what the future held once he reached that home was an open question. If the Americans did finally enter the war, Standard Oil's operation in the Middle East would be shut down for a long time to come. Thus idled, Yale would probably be let go or shunted back to the lowly work he'd performed in the American oilfields. In contemplating this uncertainty, the oilman apparently decided that whatever debt of gratitude he might owe to Djemal Pasha for allowing his escape from Palestine, it was a debt best kept to acceptable limits. During the long train ride back to Constantinople, a grinding, stop-and-start ordeal of nearly three weeks, Yale took very careful note of all that he observed out its windows: German and Turkish troop movements, the status of railway construction projects, the location of military encampments and ammunition storehouses. Depending on what the future brought, that information might be of great use to someone—and it might also be very useful to William Yale.

LAWRENCE'S WORST FEARS had been misplaced, as he discovered when he reached Wejh on February 6 and rushed into hurried conference with Faisal. It was certainly true that the Arab leader was keen to move on Aqaba, but he was just as keen that the French play no role in it; if anything, his meeting with Colonel Brémond a week earlier had served to only deepen Faisal's distrust of the Frenchman.

At the same time, Lawrence was perhaps secretly grateful to Brémond for having raised the Aqaba issue, for it had alerted him to the great struggle inevitably to come over that town's fate. In fact, that struggle was already under way, and the French colonel's gambit was but one small part of it.

Wejh was now the forward base camp of the Arab Revolt, and almost every day new tribal delegations were coming in to meet with Faisal and sign on to the revolutionary cause. Most of these tribes were from the desert and mountain expanses to the east and north, the revolutionary frontier opened by Wejh's capture, and these new recruits naturally wanted to take action in their own backyard. That meant rolling up the Red Sea coast toward Aqaba. Simultaneously, Faisal was coming under intense pressure from his Arab military advisors—primarily Syrian officers who had been captured or had deserted the Ottoman cause—to carry the fight farther north into their homeland. Both the shortest and easiest path to do so lay through Aqaba.

To these clamorings could be added those of the British officers now operating in the Hejaz, beginning with the head of the military mission, Stewart Newcombe. For the British field officers, Aqaba's seizure would mean a much shorter communication and supply line to Egypt, as well as control of the entire northern Arabian coastline. Even Gilbert Clayton back in Cairo urged in a January memo that the brigade once slated for Rabegh be put ashore at Aqaba. In the face of this chorus, Lawrence surely realized that his protestations on the town's physical obstacles would ultimately be drowned out. Indeed, if the examples of Kut and Gallipoli and a score of battlefields on the Western Front were any guide, the very impracticality of an Aqaba landing would draw British war planners to it like moths to the flame.

Lawrence's contrarian view was unlikely to be much better received by the Arabs. As with all revolutionary movements, the animating force behind the Arab Revolt was passion, and that was a sentiment fueled by daring and boldness, quite antithetical to pleadings for caution or restraint. Besides, if Aqaba were excluded, the Arabs' only other viable path into Syria was the inland route along the Hejaz Railway, a perilous option so long as the Turkish garrison in Medina stood at their backs. That option also meant relying on a very long and tenuous supply line to the coast, a line that would become more tenuous the farther north the Arabs pushed—although this concern possibly lay more in the theoretical realm than the practical; given the Arabs' current rate of progress in the inland theater of operations, it might not be the current generation of fighters that reached Damascus, but their grandchildren.

For all these reasons, Lawrence could strenuously counsel Faisal against going to Aqaba, could even expound on the trap he believed Édouard Brémond was setting for him there, but it was unlikely to serve as anything more than a temporary brake. But due to his unique position in the British intelligence apparatus—privy to the innermost strategic and political planning being done in Cairo, but also operating in the field where those plans were to be implemented—Lawrence perceived something else as well.

In 1917, the European powers still held to the imperial mind-set that one's claim to primacy in a place was directly linked to the expenditure of blood and treasure in taking it, that legitimacy was established by quite literally planting one's flag in the soil. This ultimately was why the French, with precious few troops to spare for operations in the Middle East, had scuttled the British plans to go ashore in the Gulf of Alexandretta in 1915, why they remained so uneasy about Murray's upcoming offensive into Palestine, and why, conversely, they wanted every available French soldier in the region to partake in any storming of Aqaba. It was only their physical presence, so they believed, that ensured their imperial claims would be honored.

This was not a peculiarly Gallic outlook, but one that very much infected the British as well. In all the talk of taking Aqaba, what most everyone envisioned, including Faisal, was basically a replay of the Wejh operation: an amphibious landing of Arab troops aboard British vessels, an advance against the Turkish garrison heavily supported by British naval guns, a new influx of British supplies and matériel once the town had fallen. Except Aqaba, in contrast to Wejh, was a town of enormous strategic importance to the British, and one that lay far outside the Islamic "holy land" zone that had caused them to tread so gingerly in the environs of Mecca. Having expended British blood and treasure to seize it, the British military planners' temptation to claim Aqaba as their own—and simultaneously to relegate the Arabs to a subservient role—would prove all but irresistible. When that happened, the Arabs would be caught by the throat. For the first time, the two principal Entente allies, Britain and France, would have a sizable joint military force in the Middle East, and if forced to choose between French and Arab wishes, there could be little question which side British leaders in Cairo—or if not Cairo, London—would come down on. The most likely result would be the marooning of the Arabs in Aqaba, either explicitly or tacitly blocked from continuing north.

In short, then, Édouard Brémond was the least of Faisal's problems. As the Rabegh episode had shown, Lawrence could handily outmaneuver Brémond by playing the anti-French card when Gallic interests clashed with those of the British, but it would be a very different game in a situation where British and French interests dovetailed. In essence, Faisal was well primed to spot French perfidy, but what about British perfidy?

As for why Lawrence might perceive all of this while others didn't, and why he was so ready to doubt the fidelity of his own government, the answer was simple: the Sykes-Picot Agreement. So long as that pact stood, British betrayal of the Arab cause in deference to its French ally was virtually preordained, most all the pledges contained in the McMahon-Hussein Correspondence to be nullified. Indeed, because of that pact, the British government might have their own strong motive for putting the Arabs in a box at Aqaba; by denying them the opportunity to actively participate in the liberation of Syria and other Arab lands, the British could then renege on their promises to the Arabs with a much clearer conscience.

But in trying to explain all this to Faisal—to impress upon him the need to turn away from the trap in Aqaba and make for Syria by the inland route; to not trust in the French, but not in the British either—Lawrence had only one potential instrument at his disposal: once again, Sykes-Picot.

In the British army of 1917—as indeed, in any wartime army at any point in history—the divulging of a secret treaty to a third party was considered a consummate act of treason, one sure to win the offender a long prison sentence if not an appointment with a firing squad. Yet at some point during those early days of February in Wejh, Lawrence took Faisal aside and did precisely that, revealing to him both the existence and the salient details of Sykes-Picot.

That Lawrence appreciated the enormity of what he had done is clear from the subsequent efforts he made to cover his tracks. In his own writings, as well as in queries put to him by various biographers, he remained resolutely vague about when he first learned of Sykes-Picot and how much he knew of its specifics, implying that he hadn't been in a position to actually tell Faisal very much. In fact, Sykes-Picot is not at all a complex document—it runs a mere three pages—and Lawrence almost certainly had a complete familiarity with it no later than June 1916, when it was circulated through the intelligence offices in Cairo. Similarly, in *Seven Pillars* he fashioned a false chronology whereby his hasty return to Wejh after meeting with Brémond in Cairo was born of the need to warn Faisal of the Frenchman's plan—"[Brémond] ended his talk ominously by saying that, anyhow, he was going down to put the [Aqaba] scheme to Faisal in Wejh"—an assertion that only worked by failing to mention that Brémond had already put the scheme to Faisal four days earlier. Lawrence's purpose for this omission, presumably, was to establish the idea, if it ever did come to light that he had divulged Sykes-Picot to Faisal at this juncture, that he had only done so to sabotage the conniving French. For British readers and officials alike in postwar Britain, this anti-French twist would make for a far more pleasing explanation than the alternative, his action less a treasonous offense than a perfectly understandable, even admirable, one.

It was all a construct that Lawrence's biographers—at least those in the lionizing camp—have been more than willing to accept. Yet in doing so they have glided past one of the most important and fascinating riddles of T. E. Lawrence's life. How was it that a man less than four months in Arabia had come to so identify with the Arab cause that he was willing to betray the secrets of his own nation to assist it, to in effect transfer his allegiance from his homeland to a people he still barely knew?

Surely part of it was rooted in a peculiarly British sense of honor. To probably a greater degree than in any of the other warring nations in Europe, the British ruling class in 1917 still fiercely held to the notion that their word was their bond. Among the handful of British diplomats and military men aware of their government's secret policy in the Middle East—that the Arabs were being encouraged to fight and die on the strength of promises that had already been traded away—were many who regarded that policy as utterly shameful, an affront to British dignity. Lawrence may have felt this more viscerally by virtue of being where the fighting and dying was taking place, but he was hardly alone in his disgust.

Another part of it may have stemmed from the rekindling of boy-hood fantasies. As Lawrence would write, "I had dreamed, at the City School in Oxford, of hustling into form, while I lived, the new Asia which time was inexorably bringing upon us." Here in Arabia was suddenly the chance to be the knight-errant of his childhood readings, the liberator of an enslaved and broken people, and with this came a sense of purpose far stronger than any appeal to petty nationalism or to an empire that every day was further proving its unworthiness and obsolescence.

Whatever the combination of motives—and Lawrence may not have fully grasped them himself—the effect of his revelation to Faisal was both immediate and dramatic. The Arab leader now understood that despite their promises, the British were not going to simply cede Syria; if the Arabs wanted it, they would have to fight for it. Within days of Lawrence's return to Wejh, other British officers were noting with puzzlement how Faisal had suddenly cooled on the idea of an Aqaba operation; instead, his sole focus was on carrying his rebellion to points farther north, into the Syrian heartland itself.

It was the same news Édouard Brémond heard on his next visit to Wejh on February 18. With Lawrence sitting in, Faisal informed the French colonel that he was now firmly opposed to an Aqaba landing, and instead intended to redouble his efforts inland. He once again turned down Brémond's offer of French advisors, explaining that he had no need for them, and even offered an arch apology for the ever-broadening scale of his military plans; he would happily concentrate his efforts on Medina, he told Brémond, if only he had the same French artillery "to reply to the guns which the French had supplied to the Turks." Outflanked once again, Lawrence gleefully noted, Brémond had little choice but "to retire from the battle in good order."

In subsequent weeks, the various British officers stationed in Wejh continually tried to rein in Faisal's suddenly lofty plans, to get him to focus on the immediate matters at hand. To little avail. As one of those officers, Major Pierce Joyce, would write on April 1, "I am still of the opinion that Sherif Faisal's whole attention is directed towards the North. . . . I have endeavored to confine Faisal to local ambitions and military operations, but from somewhere he has developed very wide ideas."

As for where Faisal might have developed those ideas, senior British officers remained baffled. Certainly, they didn't suspect Captain Lawrence. In an early March report to Cairo, Cyril Wilson's deputy in Jeddah singled Lawrence out for praise, calling him of "inestimable value."

FOR DJEMAL PASHA, the options were narrowing. Since the beginning of the year, the signs that the British would soon launch their long-awaited offensive in southern Palestine had grown increasingly obvious. By February, Turkish units had steadily ceded ground all the way to the outskirts of the town of Gaza, and still the British were closing; German aerial spotters reported a veritable sea of tent encampments and supply depots strung along the new, British-laid railway clear back to El Arish, forty miles away. While estimates of the British attack force varied, the one certainty was that it vastly outnumbered the some twenty thousand Turkish defenders standing to meet it.

It was a disparity that Djemal despaired of closing, for everywhere across the empire, the Ottoman army was stretched to the breaking point: actively engaged on two fronts in Europe, squared off against the Russians in eastern Anatolia, and now falling back before a second British Indian invasion force in Iraq. Even if any troops could be spared from these other fronts—and the reality was, they couldn't—it seemed all but impossible that they might reach Palestine in time to meet the British attack. With no other choice, then, Djemal had reluctantly turned his gaze to the ten thousand troops still holding Medina.

Any thought of abandoning that Arabian city was an extraordinarily painful one, which is probably why the governor had put it off until the eleventh hour. Not only did Medina anchor the southern terminus of the Hejaz Railway, but Turkish control was absolute, never seriously threatened by the disorganized and outgunned Arab rebels who sporadically sniped about its edges; as such, it stood as a bulwark against the schemes of Emir Hussein to spread his revolt north. To give up Medina, Islam's second holiest city, would also be to hand the rebels and their British paymasters a tremendous psychological victory, the mantle of religious primacy in the eyes of the greater Muslim world.

On the other hand, the Turkish troops in Medina were some of the finest to be found in the Ottoman Empire, and led by one of its ablest generals, Fakhri Pasha; their presence on the Palestine front could make the difference between victory and defeat. And so, under the urging of Enver Pasha and the German military high command in Constantinople, in late February Djemal sent down word that Medina was to be given up, its garrison to begin the long trek back up the Hejaz Railway to Syria and hurried into the trenchlines in Gaza.

That order drew an immediate and ferocious response from a man named Ali Haidar. In the wake of Hussein's revolt the previous summer, Constantinople had handpicked Haidar as the new "legitimate" mufti of Mecca and bundled him south to assume his position of supreme religious authority. Haidar had ventured no farther than Medina, of course, but there he had established a kind of "puppet papacy" in rivalry to Hussein's regime in Mecca. If rejected by most Hejazi Arabs, Haidar's claim to being the true guardian of Islam's holiest shrines had given sufficient pause to the international Muslim community to blunt Hussein's appeal. All that would be lost if Medina was abandoned. "The news horrified me," Haidar wrote in his memoir. "Hastily I sent a strongly-worded telegram to Djemal in which I said the very idea of deserting the Holy Tomb was utterly shameful, and that it should be protected to the last man, if necessary."

The mufti clearly knew his audience, for just days after issuing his Medina withdrawal order, Djemal abruptly rescinded it; the city would stay in Turkish hands, and the outnumbered troops bracing for the British attack in Palestine would have to manage as best they could on their own.

But in one of those odd little wrinkles of history, the brief and quickly resolved Turkish debate over the future of Medina was about to have far-reaching consequences. That's because British military cryptographers intercepted and decoded Djemal Pasha's cable ordering the garrison's withdrawal, but failed to intercept his subsequent cancellation order. As a result, the Arab rebels and their British advisors would devote their energies of the next several months responding to an event that wasn't going to happen. It was also in these circumstances that T. E. Lawrence would eventually have his greatest epiphany about the Arab Revolt and how it should be fought.

AS INSTRUCTED, LAWRENCE was waiting at the dock when the *Nur el Bahr*, an Egyptian patrol boat, put into Wejh on the morning of March 8. There he took delivery from a British army courier of two rather extraordinary documents.

The first was a transcript of Djemal Pasha's cable ordering the abandonment of Medina. As soon as could be organized, Djemal had instructed, the Turkish garrison was to begin moving up the Hejaz Railway, taking all artillery and other war matériel with them, and to form a new defensive line in the Syrian city of Maan, five hundred miles to the north. From there, whatever troops could be spared were to be rushed to the redoubt of Gaza in southern Palestine.

The second was a directive from Gilbert Clayton in Cairo. With General Murray's Palestine offensive now just weeks away, it was vital that no reinforcements reach the Turkish defenders in Gaza, which meant every effort should be made to halt the Medina garrison's departure. With the technical support of their British advisors, the Arab rebels were to dramatically expand their attacks on the Hejaz Railway, rendering as much damage to it as possible, and to make a blocking stand against the withdrawing Turkish units if necessary. With his usual propensity for discretion, Clayton suggested that neither Faisal nor the other Arab commanders need be informed of the reason for this escalation.

That directive placed Lawrence in another difficult spot. On the one hand, focusing on the railway played very much into his personal effort to get Faisal to concentrate on inland operations and to turn away from the attractive trap of Aqaba. On the other, taking Medina had been a primary objective of the Arab Revolt from the outset, and an Ottoman withdrawal from that city would be nearly as great a psychological victory to the rebels as an Ottoman surrender. Now the Arabs were being asked not only to forgo the prize they had fought so long for but to commit men to battle to prevent its delivery.

This, of course, was the motive behind Clayton's call for secrecy, but it raised at least two morally troublesome issues. If the Arabs were persuaded to occupy a stretch of the railway between Medina and Maan as a blocking force without being told why, then they also wouldn't know that they stood squarely in the path of the redeploying Medina garrison—and there could be few illusions about the outcome of the lightly armed Arab tribesmen crashing up against one of Turkey's best-equipped armies in the open desert. There was also the point that the Arabs were now being asked to fight—and, inevitably, to take casualties—in the Hejaz so as to lighten the burden and death toll of British troops in Gaza. Certainly, that came with the territory of membership in a military alliance, but just as certainly, in Lawrence's estimation, the British owed it to their Arab allies to tell them why.

Since he had technically committed treason just weeks earlier with his divulging of the Sykes-Picot Agreement, this edict was much easier for Lawrence to disobey. "In spite of General Clayton's orders," he wrote Cyril Wilson that evening, "I told [Faisal] something of the situation. It would have been impossible for me to have done anything myself on the necessary scale." As he would later recount in *Seven Pillars*, Faisal "rose, as ever, to a proposition of honour, and agreed instantly to do his best."

The immediate task was to get word of the new directive to Abdullah—with his followers massed near the Hejaz Railway at Wadi Ais, it would be they who would carry or lose the day—but given the past lassitude of Hussein's second son, Lawrence was convinced that both delivering that critical message and seeing it carried out had to be done by a British officer. With Stewart Newcombe and the handful of other British officers who knew the Hejaz interior already out on scouting or demolition missions, that left him. In the same hurried note he scribbled out for Cyril Wilson that evening, Lawrence explained that his plans were quite ad hoc given how little time he had to prepare:

"I think the weak point of the Turk [evacuation] plans lies in the trains of water and food. If we can cut the line on such a scale that they cannot repair it, or smash their locomotives, the force will come to a standstill. . . . If only we can hold them up for ten days. I'm afraid it will be touch and go.

I am taking some Garland mines with me, if I can find instantaneous fuse, and if there is time, I will set them as near Medina as possible: it is partly for this reason that I am going up myself."

Under the cover of darkness on the night of March 10, Lawrence set out with an escort of just fourteen fighters for the grinding five-day trek to Abdullah's camp.

It was a brutal journey from the outset. Lawrence was already in the grip of a severe bout of dysentery, and by noon of the following day was also afflicted with boils that covered his back. It was all he could do to stay in his camel's saddle as the small party plodded through one of the more desolate landscapes to be found in western Arabia. By the next day, March 12, his condition had worsened still, the dysentery twice causing him to faint "when the more difficult parts of the climb had asked too much of my strength."

Preoccupied by his own torments, Lawrence apparently failed to notice the growing friction among his small entourage, which was drawn from a fragile assortment of previously feuding tribes. What had been good-natured ribbing between them at the journey's outset had steadily escalated to the exchange of insults and veiled threats, a simmering stew of tension. Matters came to a head that same evening.

Taking shelter for the night in a mountain close known as Wadi Kitan, Lawrence fell into exhausted rest among the rocks. That ended with the report of a gunshot echoing through the canyon. Roused by one of his escorts, Lawrence was led over the rocks to view the body of a member of the traveling party, an Ageyl tribesman named Salem, dead with a bullet through the temple. With the skin around the entry wound burnt, it was clear the killing had been done at close range, which meant by another member of the group. Very quickly, the finger of suspicion fell upon a Moroccan named Hamed. During an ad hoc trial, Hamed ultimately confessed, and Salem's Ageyl brethren demanded blood for blood.

Over the preceding months, Lawrence had watched in fascinated admiration as Faisal had acted as peacemaker in scores of tribal feuds, disputes running the gamut of questions over foraging rights to decades-old—even centuries-old—blood vendettas. It was a role Faisal would continue to fulfill throughout the war. "An account of profit and loss would be struck between the parties," Lawrence later recalled, "with Faisal modulating and interceding between them, and often paying the balance, or contributing towards it from his own funds, to hurry on the pact. During two years Faisal so labored daily, putting together and arranging in their natural order the innumerable tiny pieces which made up Arabian society [that] there was no blood feud left active in any of the districts through which he had passed."

What made the system work was a collective faith in the mediator's impartiality, but it was an arrangement that came with a harsh side: when necessary, the peacemaker also had to act as the dispenser of justice.

The horror of what lay before him in Wadi Kitan seemed to slowly dawn on Lawrence. If the Ageyl insisted on Hamed's death, then it had to be so; this was the law of the desert. But while his execution by Salem's Ageyl kinsmen might ensure short-term peace on the journey to Abdullah's camp, once word of it reached the larger rebel community it was sure to spark a blood vendetta between the Ageyl, a very important and numerous tribe, and the many Moroccans who had joined the revolt. The only real solution, then, was for an impartial third party to carry out Hamed's execution, and in Wadi Kitan that night there was only one person who was "a stranger and kinless." As Lawrence would recall in *Seven Pillars*, "I made [Hamed] enter a narrow gully of the spur, a dank twilight place overgrown with weeds. Its sandy bed had been pitted by trickles of water down the cliffs in the late rain. . . . I stood in the entrance and gave him a few moments' delay, which he spent crying on the ground. Then I made him rise and shot him through the chest."

But the first bullet failed to kill the man. Instead, Hamed fell to the ground shrieking and thrashing, the blood spreading over his clothes in spurts. Lawrence fired again, but was so shaky he only struck Hamed's wrist. "He went on calling out, less loudly, now lying with his feet towards me, and I leant forward and shot him for the last time in the thick of his neck under the jaw. His body shivered a little."

It was the first man Lawrence had ever killed. Stumbling his way back up to his perch among the rocks, he immediately lay down and fell into exhausted sleep. By dawn, he was so ill that the others had to hoist him into his saddle to continue the journey.

AARON AARONSOHN HAD arrived—or at least he was sufficiently susceptible to kind words and respectful audiences to imagine so.

By the middle of March 1917, the man who had so long wandered the bureaucratic wilderness of Cairo was finally being recognized by the British intelligence community as one of their most important assets, the conduit for a fount of information beginning to come in from enemy-held Palestine. With tremendous satisfaction, the agronomist could note the steadily expanding number of British officers who had once given him short shrift, whether due to his temperament or his outsider status or his Jewishness—perhaps in some cases a combination of all three—but now sought his counsel, extending invitations for him to join their dinner table.

This breakthrough had begun in earnest in mid-February, when he had gone on board the spy ship *Managem* for yet another attempt to reach Athlit. This time, the weather had cooperated, and they had picked up one of Aaronsohn's confederates, a man named Liova Schneersohn. Best of all, the spy ring had been alerted to the British effort to make contact by the couriers left ashore on previous runs, and Schneersohn brought on board with him a trove of recent intelligence reports in a waterproof satchel.

"We left at once," the agronomist noted in his diary of February 20, "happy."

With that run, the link to the Athlit spy ring was finally firmly established, and in the weeks and months ahead, couriers on board the British coastal runners would collect a steady supply of reports on conditions inside Palestine. The British could only be amazed at the wealth of intelligence they received—as well as rueful at not having availed themselves of the opportunity first presented a year and a half earlier. With the Jewish spy ring gradually expanded to some two dozen operatives throughout Palestine, and many of them holding prominent positions in the local government, the Athlit ring detailed everything from the location of Turkish military supply depots, to the precise number of railway troop cars passing through the crucial junction town of Afuleh; in this last effort, they were helped by an enterprising agent who thought to open a refreshment stand alongside the train station. For their part, the Jewish conspirators finally gave their ring a code name, NILI, the Hebrew acronym for a passage from the Book of Samuel, *Nezah Israel Lo Ieshaker,* or "the Eternal One of Israel does not lie or relent." That was all a bit too exotic for the British, who continued to officially refer to Aaronsohn's spy ring simply as "Organization A."

Given the fast-approaching timetable for Murray's offensive in Palestine, just as welcomed was the detailed analysis of the region that Aaronsohn provided the British. A nineteen-page paper on the Palestinian economy authored by William Ormsby-Gore in February drew heavily on the agronomist's earlier reports; Reginald Wingate was so impressed, he sent a copy on to the new foreign secretary in London, Arthur Balfour. Aaronsohn was also enlisted to make additions and corrections to *The Military Handbook for South Syria,* a primer British officers would carry with them as they advanced beyond Gaza. When that primer began circulating in mid-March, its breadth of information was quickly noted, as well as its source. As Aaronsohn wrote in his diary on March 20, a military acquaintance had "congratulated me on my contribution to the Handbook, saying that everybody was talking about it at headquarters. It must be so, as [his official liaison, William Edmonds] told me today they were receiving reports from everywhere saying how delighted everybody was with my work."

Naturally, Aaronsohn was also pursuing his own agenda in all this. Part of that agenda was very overt—certainly, he'd never hidden the fact that his overriding motive for joining with the British was out of concern for the future of the Jewish settlers in Palestine—but some of it was a good deal subtler. In *The Military Handbook for South Syria*, for example, Aaronsohn included a detailed description of most all the Jewish settlements in Palestine, along with their adjacent Arab villages. In the quick character sketches he provided of the leaders in these communities was an element of score-settling, his allies invariably described as "intelligent" and "trustworthy," his enemies as just the opposite. Thus Aaronsohn's chief Arab nemesis in Athlit was marked down as an "extortionate parasite" and "fanatical Moslem," while a Jewish banker in Tiberias with whom he'd crossed swords was skewered for his "Oriental standard of honesty." The effect was to both preemptively steer the British toward his Zionist allies and to lend the Jewish settlers in Palestine a prominence far beyond the tiny fraction of the population they actually composed. Perhaps most crucially, Aaronsohn painted a very rosy picture of the reception General Murray was likely to receive once he'd broken through at Gaza and advanced into the Palestine heartland. "The attitude of the Jews all the world over towards the British regime is easy to be guessed," he wrote in late February. "Palestine under the British flag will draw steadily Jewish idealism, Jewish intelligence, Jewish capital and Jewish masses."

The agronomist surely knew that very little of this assertion was necessarily true. Among international Jewry, Zionism remained a deeply divisive issue, and within Palestine the vast majority of Jews continued to be either loyal to the Ottoman regime or resolutely apolitical. That didn't matter; Aaronsohn's audience was British military and political leaders, and extremely rare is the war-planning staff that can resist a tale which has its own soldiers being greeted as liberating heroes.

So greatly had Aaronsohn's star risen that on March 26 he was granted a prize that had eluded him since arriving in Egypt: an audience with General Gilbert Clayton. This meeting went so well it was followed by a far lengthier one a week later. In the interim, General Murray had at last launched his Palestine offensive, and first reports told of a smashing success—"a great victory over the Turks," Aaronsohn noted in his diary on March 29. On April 3, Clayton called the agronomist back to his office to hear his thoughts on how the British might drive home their advantage in the next stage of battle.

Aaron Aaronsohn was rarely bashful about sharing his opinions, and he wasn't that day with Gilbert Clayton. After asserting that at no time in history had Jerusalem been captured from the south or west, he advocated that the British army continue a northern sweep along the coastal plain, and then hook back to fall upon the city from the north. In contrast to other armchair generals, of course, Aaronsohn could draw upon his encyclopedic knowledge of the land—its trails and terrain and water sources—to lend weight to his advocacy. As he noted in his diary that night, "General Clayton listened to me with much interest. I left him dreaming over the map after an invitation to come back and see him every time I had such good suggestions to make." In the same entry, the scientist allowed himself a moment of exultation. "I have succeeded in making the right party understand that it is useless to beat around the bush. Palestine is a ripe fruit. A good shaking-up and it will fall in our hands."

Left unclear was just who this "our" might consist of: the Allies, the British, or the Zionists alone.

AT SUNSET ON March 28, Lawrence and his vanguard of rebel fighters climbed to the top of a rocky crag to peer over its edge. In the flat valley below, perhaps three miles away, lay Aba el Naam, a principal station and watering depot for the Hejaz Railway. In the failing light, Lawrence watched the Turkish army garrison—some four hundred soldiers, by best estimate—go through their evening drills.

It was reported that the Turks made frequent nighttime patrols around the perimeters of their railway garrisons to compensate for their sense of isolation. This was unpleasant news to Lawrence; his vanguard consisted of a mere thirty men, and they needed to rest after their three-day journey from Wadi Ais. A solution came to him. At nightfall, several men were dispatched to sneak close to the station and fire a few random shots in its direction. As Lawrence recounted, "The enemy, thinking it a prelude to attack, stood-to in their trenches all night, while we were comfortably sleeping."

It was a sleep Lawrence probably required more than his companions, for he was still recovering from the dysentery and fever that had held him in its grip for weeks. He also needed to have both his wits and strength about him for the assault he was planning on Aba el Naam.

After the ghastly events in Wadi Kitan, he had forced himself on, increasingly ill, until finally they made Abdullah's camp at Wadi Ais on the morning of March 15. There, after a brief conference with Abdullah in which he explained the need to immediately move against the railway, Lawrence excused himself to take a brief rest. Instead, he lay in his tent, racked with malaria, for the next ten days.

Adding to Lawrence's torment during those long days had been his knowledge of what was happening—or rather, not happening—during his incapacitation. Given Abdullah's reputation for indolence, Lawrence had figured all along that if any determined action were to be taken against the railroad, he would need to lead it himself—and this calculation proved prescient. In the infrequent moments when he was able to rally enough to venture outside his tent, Lawrence observed that Abdullah's camp had retained its climate of frivolity and relaxation just as before, that nothing like a military mobilization was taking place.

What's more, it became clear that Lawrence wasn't particularly welcome in Wadi Ais. Among Abdullah's inner coterie was a barely concealed distrust, even an animosity, toward the visiting British officer that their chief did little to dispel. For his part, Lawrence's once rather favorable opinion of Abdullah, tepid though it had been, steadily hardened into a contemptuous dislike: "His casual attractive fits of arbitrariness now seemed feeble tyranny disguised as whims," he wrote, "his friendliness became caprice, his good humor [a] love of pleasure.... Even his simplicity appeared false upon experience, and inherited religious prejudice was allowed rule over the keenness of his mind because it was less trouble to him than uncharted thought."

On March 25, at last sufficiently recovered from his illness to function, Lawrence strode into Abdullah's tent to announce he would lead an attack against the railway himself. That announcement was warmly received, for Abdullah "graciously permitted anything not calling directly upon his own energies." By approaching some of the sheikhs in Wadi Ais whom Lawrence perceived as actual warriors, he quickly won commitments for a tribally mixed assault party of some eight hundred men to fall upon the isolated train depot at Aba el Naam. The next morning, he set off ahead with his small vanguard to assess the site and work up a battle plan.

All during the day of March 29, Lawrence and his advance team moved into attack positions in the hills around the station, while closely watching the Turkish soldiers go about their routine: forming up for roll call, falling out for meals, performing desultory drills, still oblivious to the trap being set for them. Best yet, from Lawrence's perspective, was the train that chugged into view that morning and came to a halt at Aba el Naam; destroying a Turkish train would be a great bonus to the operation, and he fervently hoped it did not push off again before the main assault party arrived.

That force began to drift in that evening, but to Lawrence's dismay, it was not the eight hundred fighters he had been promised, but more on the order of three hundred. It forced him to quickly recalibrate what might be accomplished in the morning.

Throughout that night, Lawrence made his preparations. Small groups of fighters were dispatched to secrete themselves in the heights surrounding the station; once the assault got under way, the Turks would find themselves caught in an amphitheater of gunfire. One demolition team was sent to place a mine on the railway north of Aba el Naam, while he personally placed the one to the south, the first time he would put Herbert Garland's mine-laying tutorials to the personal test. It was also here where he set his sole machine gun, in a concealed gully a mere four hundred yards from the track. With Medina forty miles to the south, Lawrence figured this would be the direction the Turkish garrison would take in retreat—or conversely, the direction from which any reinforcements might come—and the machine gun with its three-man crew would turn the open ground into a slaughter yard. So exhaustive and time-consuming were his preparations that when finally the attack was launched shortly before dawn, Lawrence had to be shaken out of a fitful slumber to observe it.

It started very well. The Arabs' two mountain guns, or pack howitzers, had been tucked into hillside crevices with commanding views of the depot, and they opened up with devastating effect. Within moments, two of the station's stone buildings had taken direct hits, the depot's water tank had been punctured, and a train wagon parked on a siding set aflame. Simultaneously, the Turks scrambling for their trenches were discovering there was little protection to be found; with bullets coming in from three sides, they were just as likely to be shot in the back as in the front.

Amid the chaos, the train that had come into Aba el Naam the day before began to move off, attempting an escape south. As Lawrence watched in satisfaction, it tripped the mine he'd set, producing a puff of sand and scattered steel—but then, nothing. For what must have seemed an eternity, he waited for the machine-gun team hidden in the gully to open up, but all remained silent. Instead, the Turkish train engineers were able to dismount in perfect safety, slowly joist the engine's damaged front wheels back on the track, then gather steam for a limping journey on to Medina.

Shortly after, Lawrence called off the assault. Turkish reinforcements would surely soon be on their way, and those soldiers below who had survived the initial melee were now protected by the cloak of thick black smoke that enveloped the station from the burning wagon. The only alternative to withdrawal, Lawrence reasoned, was a frontal assault against the Turkish trenches, an option likely to be as murderously futile at Aba el Naam as it had been on a thousand other battlefields.

Measured in terms of casualties—the way military men usually gauge such things—the engagement had been a great success. At the cost of a single fighter wounded, the Arabs had killed or wounded some seventy Turkish soldiers, taken another thirty prisoner, and undoubtedly disrupted traffic on the Hejaz Railway for some days to come. For Lawrence, though, it was a hollow victory, diminished by the knowledge of what might have been. If the machine-gun crew in the gulley had acted as planned, the hobbled train would have been shot to pieces rather than allowed to escape; as Lawrence soon learned, the crew had simply abandoned their position once the fighting around the depot started, either because they wanted to witness it or because they felt exposed being so far removed from the main rebel force. Similarly, if he'd had the eight hundred fighters promised back in Wadi Ais rather than the three hundred who had shown up, the outnumbered garrison in Aba el Naam could have been annihilated. Denied the unqualified victory he'd hoped for, Lawrence would only say about the battle that "we did not wholly fail."

Surely deepening his disappointment was what the experience said of the Arab Revolt going forward. In urging Faisal to make for Syria by concentrating his attacks inland, Lawrence had vaguely talked of overrunning the isolated Turkish garrisons along the railway as they went. But what were the real prospects of that happening given the example of Aba el Naam? If the Arabs couldn't sufficiently organize to defeat four hundred backline guardpost soldiers in a skirmish where they had commanded the heights and enjoyed complete surprise, what would happen when they were confronted by the several-thousand-man garrisons that awaited in the larger rail towns in southern Syria—let alone the ten thousand frontline troops who stood at their backs in Medina?

Yet, in a different way, the engagement at Aba el Naam proved something of a seminal event for Lawrence, as it lent proof to an idea—perhaps more accurately, a constellation of ideas—he had begun to formulate. By his own account, that process had started during those long days of illness spent lying in his tent at Wadi Ais.

At its core was the question of what the Arab rebels were truly capable of in the face of the Turkish army. Virtually to a man, the British advisors sent to the Hejaz since the beginning of the revolt were derisive of the Arabs' fighting abilities. Indeed, Lawrence had shared something of that opinion with his observation that a single company of entrenched Turkish soldiers could put the entire rebel army to flight.

The problem with this view, Lawrence was coming to realize, was not just that it held the Arabs to European standards of warfare—standards totally unsuited to the Arabian terrain—but that it rather blinded those advisors to see the tremendous advantage that terrain might offer. In a word, space. Some j257,000 square miles of open space.

"And how would the Turks defend all that?" Lawrence asked. "No doubt by a trenchline across the bottom if we came like an army with banners, but suppose we were (as we might be) an influence, an idea, a thing intangible, invulnerable, without front or back, drifting about like a gas? ... Most wars were wars of contact, both forces striving into touch to avoid tactical surprise. Ours should be a war of detachment. We were to contain the enemy by the silent threat of a vast unknown desert, not disclosing ourselves till we attacked."

If alien to many in the hidebound British military structure of the day, none of this was truly revolutionary, but rather the classic strategy-by-default of weaker military forces throughout history. After all, if one is outmanned or outgunned, charging straight at the enemy only ensures getting to the cemetery or surrender table that much quicker. What was unique was how Lawrence saw its application to the Arabian war.

Ever since his arrival, the overriding goal of both the Arab rebels and their British advisors had been capturing Medina, the event that would rid Arabia of four centuries of Turkish rule and allow the theater of operations to move north. The current campaign to prevent the Turks' withdrawal from Medina had thrown a new complication into the mix, but the end goal hadn't changed; for Briton and Arab alike, seeing the Ottoman flag come down from Islam's second holiest city was the prize that would open the road to others. What Lawrence now saw was that Medina should not be taken, either by force or by surrender: "The Turk was harmless there. In prison in Egypt he would cost us food and guards. We wanted him to stay at Medina, and every other distant place, in the largest numbers."

The proper strategy going forward, in Lawrence's new estimation, was to keep the Turks settled into Medina almost indefinitely. To do that, it didn't mean shutting down the Hejaz Railway altogether, as the British were hoping to do, but rather allowing that supply line to operate at just enough capacity to keep the Turkish garrison on life support. Sustained enough to survive, but too weak to withdraw or go on the offensive, that garrison would then essentially become prisoners—even better than prisoners because the burden of sustaining them would continue to fall on the enemy.

This concept didn't apply only to Medina. Once that garrison was rendered impotent, Lawrence foresaw, the Arabs could take their rebellion into Syria and pursue the same strategy there: ceding the larger garrison towns to the Turks while they roamed the countryside striking at soft spots of their choosing, constantly disrupting the enemy supply lines until the Turkish presence was limited to an atoll of armed islands amid an Arab-liberated sea.

Once this idea of the Arab force "drifting about like a gas" came to him, it was probably inevitable that Lawrence's thoughts turned to that place on the map that had been a gnawing concern for over two months: Aqaba.

The tricky thing about Aqaba from the Arab perspective was that while it presented a trap should they go into it as junior partners of the British and French, the port was still vital for them if they hoped to push into Syria. If somehow the mountain range that lay between Aqaba and the Hejaz Railway could be wrested from the Turks, the Arabs would then enjoy a mere sixty-mile-long supply line for their operations in southern Syria, rather than the three-hundred-mile line from Wejh. But how to clear those mountains, and how to do it without being beholden to the British and French?

In pondering this dilemma earlier, Lawrence had settled on a rather obvious and conventional solution, pointing out that as the Arab forces moved north along the rail line, clearing the towns of Turks as they went, the Turkish garrison in the side spur of Aqaba would eventually be cut off; an Arab side force could then be sent over the mountains from the inland side to capture it. Now, however, with the "drifting like gas" concept to mind, he began formulating a far more audacious scheme. Taking Aqaba didn't have to wait until the Turks' inland garrison towns were taken, nor did it have to wait until the Arabs advanced north en masse. Instead, Lawrence believed that a very small and mobile force of Arab fighters might pass undetected all the way to the vicinity of Maan, the inland terminus of the road to Aqaba, and there conduct a series of seemingly random diversionary raids. With the Turks put on high alert by these attacks—which meant standing to in their defensive positions—and unsure where they might come next, the Arab force could then cross the mountains and fall on Aqaba from the landward side before anyone in the Turkish military leadership had time to react.

It was with these ideas in mind—still embryonic, certainly the staggering logistical issues involved not yet worked out—that Lawrence returned to Abdullah's camp from his railway raiding forays in early April. There he found a plaintive note from Faisal awaiting him.

"I was very sorry to hear that you were ill," Faisal wrote in awkward French. "I hope that you are already better and that you would like to come back to us in a short time, as soon as possible. Your presence with me is very indispensable, in view of urgency of questions and the pace of affairs." He closed in a somewhat whiny tone. "It was not at all your promise to stay there so long. So I hope that you will return here as soon as you receive this letter."

As quickly as he could manage, Lawrence set out for Wejh.

Chapter 12

An Audacious Scheme

So far as all ranks of the troops engaged were concerned, it was a
brilliant victory, and had the early part of the day been normal, victory
would have been secured.

LIEUTENANT GENERAL CHARLES DOBELL,
ON THE BRITISH DEFEAT AT GAZA, MARCH 28, 1917

With the ramshackle outskirts of Wejh just coming into view in the
predawn light, Lawrence ordered his small camel train to a halt.
He hadn't bathed since leaving Abdullah's camp four days earlier, and out
of a sense of propriety he wished to change out of his filthy, dust-caked
robes before presenting himself to Faisal.

It was April 14, 1917. Lawrence had been gone from Wejh for just a
little over a month, but he was returning to a world transformed. Indeed,
the changes that had occurred in that thirty-five-day span, both on the
global and Middle Eastern stages, were of such a magnitude he probably
had difficulty absorbing them all at once.

In mid-March, just days after he had set off for Abdullah's camp, the
three-hundred-year Romanov dynasty in Russia had come to an abrupt
end. Faced with paralyzing industrial strikes by workers demanding an
end to the war, and a semimutinous army that refused to move against
those workers, Czar Nicholas II had been forced to abdicate. The provisional government that had replaced the czar vowed to keep Russia in
the Entente, but with the chaos worsening, there was growing doubt in
other European capitals about just how long Petrograd might stand to that
commitment. In fact, though no one yet realized it, the seed of the new

Russian government's destruction had already been sown through one of the most successful subversion operations in world history. On April 1, the German secret police had quietly gathered up a group of leftist Russian exiles, men just as opposed to the new moderate regime as they had been to the czar, and arranged their passage home. Among the returning malcontents was a Marxist named Vladimir Ilyich Ulyanov, soon to become better known by his *nom de cadre*, Lenin.

But as unsettling as developments in Russia were to the British and French leadership, they proved a boon in another sphere. President Woodrow Wilson's loathing of the retrograde czarist regime had played a key role in his refusal to bring the United States into the war on the side of the Entente. With the new moderate government in Petrograd, Russia was suddenly "a fit partner for a League of Honor" in the American president's view. In concert with Germany's renewed U-boat war in the Atlantic, and the exposure of an outrageous German scheme to lure Mexico into attacking the United States, it had provided Wilson with the political cover to finally declare war on Germany at the beginning of April. Given the staggering logistics involved in building the tiny American peacetime army into a major fighting force, and then transporting it across the Atlantic, it would be a long time before the American "doughboys" might significantly contribute to the Western Front battlefields—most war planners estimated at least a year—but the news came as a tremendous relief in France and Great Britain, both sliding ever closer to financial collapse as the war ground on.

There had also been a momentous event in the Middle East. On March 26, the same day that Lawrence set out to attack the railway garrison at Aba el Naam, General Archibald Murray had at last thrown his army against the Turkish trenchworks at Gaza. In a confused and fitful battle that had continued into the following day, the British had repeatedly appeared on the verge of a decisive victory, only to find new ways to fritter away their advantage, finally calling off their assault as Turkish reinforcements drew near. The result was quite different from the "great success" that Aaron Aaronsohn had noted in his diary, or the "brilliant victory" that Murray's on-the-ground commander reported in his initial communiqué. Instead, and despite outnumbering the Turkish garrison by at least three to one, the attacking British had suffered over four thousand casualties while inflicting less than half that number on their enemy and leaving them in control of the battlefield. The outcome amply justified the taunting Turkish leaflet dropped on British lines in the aftermath: "You beat us at communiqués, but we beat you at Gaza." By the time of Lawrence's return to Wejh on April 14, General Murray was gearing up his forces in southern Palestine for another try.

In Lawrence's telling, though, that day was most memorable for yet another event: his first encounter with Auda Abu Tayi.

Since his first visit to the Hejaz, Lawrence had heard of the legendary exploits of Auda Abu Tayi, a leader of the fierce Howeitat tribe of northwestern Arabia. For even longer, Faisal had been waging a charm offensive to bring the chieftain in on the side of the rebel cause, sending emissaries with notes and presents and promises, entertaining a parade of Auda's tribal lieutenants. Now, with the capture of Wejh placing the rebels at the outer proximity of Howeitat territory, Auda had finally come down to the coast to meet Faisal in person. At some point during Faisal's and Lawrence's reunion meeting that day, Auda was invited to join them.

Whether wholly accurate or not, Lawrence was given to penning very incisive and closely observed first impressions of people—and few made a bigger first impression on him than Auda Abu Tayi. "He must be nearly fifty now (he admits forty)," Lawrence noted in a wartime dispatch, "and his black beard is tinged with white, but he is still tall and straight, loosely built, spare and powerful, and as active as a much younger man. His lined and haggard face is pure Bedouin: broad low forehead, high sharp hooked nose, brown-green eyes, slanting outward, large mouth."

Beyond Auda's arresting physical appearance lay his charisma and peerless reputation as a desert warrior. "He has married twenty-eight times, has been wounded thirteen times, and in his battles has seen all his tribesmen hurt and most of his relations killed. He has only reported his 'kill' since 1900, and they now stand at seventy-five Arabs; Turks are not counted by Auda when they are dead. Under his handling, the [Howeitat] have become the finest fighting force in Western Arabia. . . . He sees life as a saga and all events in it are significant and all personages heroic. His mind is packed (and generally overflows) with stories of old raids and epic poems of fights."

Although left unsaid, it would seem one reason Lawrence was so taken with Auda Abu Tayi was the stark contrast he drew to Faisal ibn Hussein. While Lawrence still had a profound appreciation for Faisal as the political guide of the Arab Revolt, the man who could gain and keep the fractious clans and tribes to the banner of the greater cause, it had become increasingly clear that King Hussein's third son was not a natural warrior. To the contrary, and in opposition to the image Lawrence had first presented to his army superiors, Faisal appeared to quite abhor violence and to go out of his way to avoid participating in it personally, "a man who can't stand the racket," as Cyril Wilson once drily observed.

This had been evident most recently amid the intensified campaign against the Hejaz Railway. To spur the Arab fighters to action, Lawrence had joined other British officers in urging Faisal to decamp from Wejh and make for the main rebel staging ground at Wadi Ais. Faisal had brushed aside these entreaties, alternately pleading a shortage of camels and the need to remain on the coast to personally meet with the various tribal delegations coming in to join the revolt, stances that led some British officers to quietly conclude the man was a bit of a coward. That assessment was neither fair nor true—certainly it had taken enormous courage to pull off the tightrope act that Faisal had performed for so many months between Djemal Pasha and the Arab nationalists in Damascus—but it was a very different type of courage than the unalloyed thirst for battle of a man like Auda Abu Tayi.

Further diminishing Faisal in Lawrence's eyes was a propensity for vacillation. Perhaps it came with being a conciliator and patient listener, but the emir—Faisal and his brothers had advanced to that title upon their father declaring himself king in October—had the disconcerting habit of falling away from seemingly firmly held positions under the urgings and opinions of whoever next caught his ear; as Lawrence would later remark, "Faisal always listened to his momentary adviser, despite his own better judgment."

As a recent example, back in February Lawrence had divulged to Faisal precisely why signing on to an Allied-managed attack on Aqaba posed a potential trap for the Arabs—and had put himself at great risk in doing so. Thus educated, Faisal had scotched all talk of a precipitous move on the port. After a brief absence from Wejh in early March, however, Lawrence had returned to discover Faisal once again fallen under the sway of his tribal allies, and back to advocating an immediate assault. It required another round of persuasion on Lawrence's part to talk Faisal down.

In fact, it seemed that yet another about-face had spurred Faisal's plaintive note to Lawrence in Wadi Ais pleading for his immediate return. In late March, rumors had reached Wejh that the French were about to launch an amphibious landing on the Syrian coast—some rumors held they were already ashore—raising the specter of Syria being stolen away in a French fait accompli. Faisal's apprehensions had been further stoked by a visit from Édouard Brémond on April 1, and a new press by the colonel to attach French "liaison" officers to the Arab forces in Wejh. Faisal had again rebuffed Brémond, but his visit had fueled the Arab leader's anxiety to make for Syria via Aqaba as soon as possible. As a result, one of Lawrence's first tasks upon reaching Wejh on April 14 was to ascertain that the French rumors were untrue, and to calm Faisal down once more. Along with being tiresome, this suggestibility in the emir was dangerous; Lawrence might refocus him now, but what would happen the next time an Aqaba-urging chieftain or the mischievous Colonel Brémond came calling?

There was an obvious answer, of course: to immediately make for

Aqaba—and with control of that port, for points farther north—by implementing the daring inland-approach scheme Lawrence had begun to map out in his mind. Moreover, among the Arab chieftains gathered in Wejh that day was just the sort of fearless, single-minded fighter who might bring that scheme to fruition: Auda Abu Tayi.

Except a new complication now presented itself, one directly tied to Faisal's changeability. Back at the beginning of March, amid Faisal's renewed anxiety to move on Aqaba, a British officer in Wejh had thought to apprise Gilbert Clayton of the news. Clayton had sent a top-secret directive in reply, one addressed to Lawrence and only two other British officers in Arabia. That directive hadn't reached Wejh by the time Lawrence had left for Abdullah's camp, but it was among the correspondence awaiting his return on April 14.

"The move to Aqaba on the part of Faisal," Clayton had written, "is not at present desirable." While claiming his main concern was that Faisal not be distracted from operations against the Hejaz Railway, Clayton hinted at the true reason in the letter's close. "It is questionable whether, in the present circumstances, the presence of an Arab force at Aqaba would be desirable, as it would unsettle tribes which are better left quiet until the time is more ripe."

Both from his own relationship with Gilbert Clayton, the consummate strategist, and from what he had gleaned in the corridors of the intelligence bureau in Cairo, Lawrence quickly grasped the subtext of the general's words. He'd been exactly right in his warnings to Faisal in February—the British wanted Aqaba for themselves—but to accomplish that, they didn't wish to merely put the Arabs in a box; they now didn't want the Arabs there at all. (In fact, Clayton would soon make this point explicit in a note to Reginald Wingate: "The occupation of Aqaba by Arab troops might well result in the Arabs claiming that place hereafter, and it is by no means improbable that after the war Aqaba may be of considerable importance to the future defence scheme of Egypt. It is thus essential that Aqaba should remain in British hands after the war.")

On April 14, Lawrence could try to deny the thrust of Clayton's March 8 directive any way he wished—that with the passage of five weeks, it was now out of date; that merely stating what was or was not "desirable" didn't rise to the level of an explicit order—but he surely understood the peculiarly oblique nature of British military-speak well enough to know that going ahead with his Aqaba plan now would be seen as a clear contravention of his superior's wishes. Then again, this was a man who just two months earlier had revealed to Faisal the details of a diplomatic pact so secret that only a handful of people in the upper reaches of the British government knew of its existence.

At some point during that remarkable day of April 14—and most likely when the three of them were alone in Faisal's tent—Lawrence put his Aqaba proposal to Faisal and Auda. In Auda's quick and hearty agreement to the proposal was confirmation of what Lawrence had sensed in the chieftain from the outset. "After a moment I knew," he wrote, "from the force and directness of the man, that we would attain our end. He had come down to us like a knight-errant, chafing at our delay in Wejh, anxious only to be acquiring merit for Arab freedom in his own lands. If his performance was one-half his desire, we should be prosperous and fortunate."

ON APRIL 18, 1917, just four days after Lawrence's return to Wejh, a French destroyer slipped from an Italian port and headed southeast into the Mediterranean. On board were the two midlevel government functionaries who, a year previously, had secretly carved the future Middle East into British and French spheres of control and lent their names to the process: Mark Sykes and François Georges-Picot. Their destination was Alexandria, Egypt, and their mission was to bring political order to the region's rapidly changing military situation.

Or at least so the situation had appeared when the idea of their journey had first been broached several months earlier. Despite a record of dismal stalemate on virtually every battlefront since the start of the war, neither the British or French government had broken itself of the habit of squabbling over the spoils of victory long before victory had been achieved. In early 1917, with General Archibald Murray gearing up for his march into Palestine, their wrangling had inevitably turned to the Middle East.

Intent on defending their imperial claim to Syria, France had launched a two-pronged initiative. The first had been to scrounge up its scant military units in the region for the purpose of attaching them to Murray's army. When this overture, couched as an act of Entente solidarity, was initially turned down by the British on the pretext that operational planning was too far advanced to allow for their integration, it had triggered furious French charges of betrayal. British commanders on the ground were forced to relent, but not at all happily. "Of course it is impossible to decline to have these French troops," Murray's deputy, General Lynden-Bell, confided to a member of the Arab Bureau in mid-March, "but you can imagine what a terrible nuisance they will be to us."

On the diplomatic front, Paris had also insisted that a French political officer accompany Murray's army as it advanced into Palestine, a further nuisance, of course, but one that London found just as difficult to refuse. When in January France had announced that this political officer was to be Georges-Picot, Britain suddenly found the need to have a political officer of its own to accompany him—and who better than Picot's old negotiating partner, Mark Sykes?

But this new mission put the MP for Hull in a somewhat tricky spot. During his discussions with Picot over where to draw their lines of Middle Eastern control, Sykes had never felt the need to inform the Frenchman—or any other Frenchman, for that matter—as to how those lines might conflict with commitments already made to King Hussein. Nowhere was this conflict more glaring than in Syria, a land the British had now essentially "sold twice," recognizing its independence in the McMahon-Hussein Correspondence, recognizing its domination by France in the Sykes-Picot Agreement.

This was not an immediate problem so long as Picot remained in France, Hussein's rebel armies remained in the Hejaz, and the Turks still ruled Syria, but now, with Archibald Murray's imminent march into Palestine and both Sykes and Picot slated to be in his train, those delicate walls of separation were about to crumble. As he anticipated his trip to Egypt, Mark Sykes could only have foreseen unpleasantness ahead.

But then a rather ingenious solution had come to him. What if, instead of to King Hussein, he brought Georges-Picot before a group of Syrian exiles with no knowledge of the promises made to the Arabs? In their ignorance, these Syrians might be grateful to accept whatever crumbs of limited self-rule the British and French were willing to throw their way, and that gratitude might in turn lead the French to soften their imperialist demands. On February 22, Sykes had written to Reginald Wingate, the British high commissioner to Egypt, asking for his help in organizing just such a delegation of Syrian exiles in Cairo, men with whom he and Picot could discuss the future status of their homeland. Should it be necessary to include a delegate from the Hejaz on the committee, Sykes suggested it be "a venerable and amenable person who will not want to ride or take much exercise." In a remarkable act of brio, Sykes also thought to enclose with this letter a series of quick sketches he had worked up toward the design of a new rebel flag. (Curiously, it may have been in flag design where Mark Sykes's true talents lay. King Hussein would eventually adopt one of Sykes's designs as his own.)

Startled by Sykes's cynical request, Wingate sent a cable to the Foreign Office pointing out that since it was to King Hussein that Britain had made its commitments, surely it should be Hussein who chose the delegation to meet with Sykes and Picot. Sykes quickly shot down that idea, suggesting to Wingate that "it does not appear necessary to give King Hussein the impression that the future of Syria is to be considered *de novo* [anew]." In any event, Sykes hinted, the high commissioner was making more of all this than need be. "What we really want are a few men of good standing, representatives of the Arab National Party, to represent the Syrian Moslem point of view, sign manifestos and approve any local arrangements that may be made."

As a result of these building pressures, it must have come as something of a guilty relief to Mark Sykes when, just as final preparations were being made for his and Picot's trip to Egypt, news came of Murray's March 26 setback at Gaza. Surely Murray's next push would succeed—it was hard to imagine Turkey's absurd streak of good luck lasting much longer against British might—but in the meantime, the delay would give Sykes time to navigate the complex minefield awaiting him in Cairo.

This minefield was not limited to the Syrian question. Over the past few months, Mark Sykes had been quietly working on another scheme that, if all worked out, would neatly outmaneuver his traveling partner, François Georges-Picot.

Under the original terms of Sykes-Picot, Palestine was to be separated from the rest of Syria and placed under the "international administration" of the three principal Entente powers, Britain, France, and Russia. Within months of coauthoring that arrangement, however, Sykes had seen the opportunity to go a good deal better. By playing to the various Palestinian constituencies—and most especially to Jewish Zionists, with their deep distrust of France and utter hatred for czarist Russia—it might be possible for Britain to scuttle the joint administration idea as unworkable, and to place Palestine under a solely British protectorate. Sykes had been harshly rebuked when he'd floated this idea past the Foreign Office leadership in the spring of 1916—Secretary Grey had instructed him to "obliterate" the thought from his memory—but now, a year later, the notion had flowered anew in Sykes's fertile mind.

One reason was that Secretary Grey was now a thing of the past, forced out of office with the rest of the Asquith government in December 1916. With its "Western" focus, the Asquith regime had always been wary of diplomatic schemes that might inflame relations with the ever-sensitive French, but that was a lesser concern with the new "Eastern"-tilting administration of David Lloyd George and his foreign minister, Arthur Balfour. Anxious for a breakthrough in the war somewhere—anywhere—they had brought a new emphasis to Eastern operations, and if success there meant stepping on French toes, it was a small price to pay.

Sykes had benefited from another important change in the new government. A chief complaint against the Asquith administration had been its lack of clear and constant direction in the war, and in response Lloyd George had created a so-called War Cabinet, a cabal of just five senior statesmen with sweeping powers to oversee most all aspects of the British military effort. Surely a sign of the new administration's appetite for creative solutions had been the promotion of Mark Sykes to the position of assistant secretary to the War Cabinet, placed in charge of Middle Eastern affairs.

Just as crucial had been Sykes's discussions with Aaron Aaronsohn in October and November. Following those conversations, and reanimated to the potential of using Zionism as a pro-British vehicle in Palestine, Sykes had quietly held a series of meetings with British Zionist leaders through the early winter of 1917. These discussions had culminated in an extraordinary conference with a group of leading British "Jewish gentlemen" at a London townhouse on the morning of February 7, 1917; what made this gathering extraordinary was Sykes's opening announcement that he was there without the knowledge of either the Foreign Office or the War Cabinet, and therefore their discussions had to remain secret. Among the eight men in attendance were Lord Walter Rothschild, former home secretary Herbert Samuel, and a man soon to figure very prominently in Sykes's Palestine schemes, the incoming president of the English Zionist Federation, Chaim Weizmann.

A forty-three-year-old émigré from czarist Russia, the dynamic, goateed Weizmann was an erstwhile chemistry lecturer at the University of Manchester who over the previous decade had emerged as one of the most articulate and persuasive voices of British Zionism. A prominent figure at international Zionist conferences, he was also intent on converting rhetoric to action; in 1908, he had helped create the Palestine Land Development Company, chartered to buy up agricultural land in Palestine for Jewish settlement. What had most brought Weizmann to the attention of British officials, however, was his work in chemistry. Shortly before his meeting with Sykes, he had developed a revolutionary process to create synthetic acetone, a key component in explosives, and in making his discovery available to the British munitions industry he had won the government's undying gratitude. (This surely negated any taint that might have attached to his also being the older brother of Minna Weizmann, the erstwhile lover of Curt Prüfer, who had been arrested as a German spy in Egypt in 1915.) Serendipitously, during his tenure at Manchester, Weizmann had also won the sympathies of his local member of Parliament to the Zionist cause; that MP was Arthur Balfour, the new British foreign secretary.

At that February 7 gathering, the British Jewish leaders had emphatically stated precisely what Mark Sykes hoped to hear: that there was simply no way the international Zionist movement in general, nor the Zionist settlers in Palestine in particular, would accept a joint Entente administration in Palestine. To the contrary, all demanded sole British control of the region, or, as one of the attendees put it, "a Jewish State in Palestine under the British Crown." In response, Sykes announced his readiness to present the Zionist viewpoint to the War Cabinet. He also suggested that the assembled dignitaries begin lobbying their religious brethren elsewhere to that goal, even "offering to make War Office telegraph facilities available to them so they could communicate secretly with leading Zionists in Paris, Petrograd, Rome and Washington D.C."

At the same time, the politician from Hull couldn't quite part with his penchants for blithe optimism and the dissembling statement. As far as Arab sensibilities were concerned, Sykes opined at the February 7 meeting, he could see no objection on their part to increased Jewish settlement in Palestine—an interesting assertion considering that, even at this late date, no Arab was aware the Entente powers had any designs on Palestine at all. (He obviously could not have known Lawrence was just then telling Faisal about the Sykes-Picot accord.) His suspicions undoubtedly aroused by Sykes's queries on the desirability of a joint administration, Lord Rothschild had then bluntly asked what promises had been made to the French in the region. To this, Sykes made the astonishing reply that "the French have no particular position in Palestine and are not entitled to anything there." These were just two more faulty assertions—the first perhaps an exercise in wishful thinking, the second an outright lie—to join all the others Mark Sykes had promulgated in recent months, an ever-growing corpus of half-truths and conflicting schemes that even he would soon begin having difficulty keeping straight.

In the meantime, he was clever enough to realize that all was very fluid, that a precipitating event or a changed set of circumstances on the ground might upend everything once again, rendering some of his entanglements moot and giving rise to new opportunities to achieve his goals—as variable as those goals might be. What's more, as he sailed to Egypt that April, Sykes was about to be reunited with a man who understood the need for bold action: Aaron Aaronsohn.

The agronomist from Athlit was a very different type of Zionist from those Sykes had quietly plotted with in London. Those men were sober-minded and cautious, their approach gentlemanly, whereas Aaronsohn was brash and impatient, a man hardened by his having actually lived the Zionist "dream" in Palestine. In comparison with some of those London confreres, he also had a much grander vision of what should happen in Palestine: not just an expanded Jewish presence under British protection, but an eventual outright Jewish state, one that would extend from the shores of the Mediterranean to east of the Jordan River and nearly to the gates of Damascus. Aaron Aaronsohn was a radical, but as Mark Sykes well knew, it was often the radical who catalyzed change.

What he couldn't have guessed just then was that he and Aaronsohn were about to be handed a bountiful gift from someone on the opposite side of the battlefield, Djemal Pasha.

TO THE ANNOYANCE of defense-minded military commanders throughout history, civilians have a tendency to stay put in their homes until an enemy invading force is just over the horizon. Then, once the arrows or bullets or missiles begin to fly, these civilians bundle up their families and as many possessions as time allows and take to the roads in whatever conveyance is available to them. Predictably, the most common result of this rushed exodus is severe traffic congestion—and often complete paralysis—on all paths leading away from the battlefront, making it extremely difficult for the defending force to bring reinforcements to the scene. To guard against this, armies have routinely forced civilians out of a likely battle zone well ahead of time—and at bayonet point if required. Due to the stasis of the battle lines, such forced evacuations had rarely been necessary on the Western Front through the first two and a half years of World War I, but they had been a common feature in the east, and most especially on the Ottoman Front.

It was a policy that came quite easily to the Ottomans, and for reasons that went beyond simple military expediency. Many times over the centuries, the sultans in Constantinople, mindful of both their comparative military weakness and the polyglot nature of their empire, had adopted a kind of scorched-earth policy in the face of external threat, uprooting entire populations that might tacitly or overtly collaborate with invaders. Time permitting, also removed from an invader's path were livestock, farm equipment, and food stores, most anything that might provide the enemy sustenance, and that which couldn't be taken away was burned, smashed, or poisoned.

For all their reformist ideas in other spheres, the Young Turks had seen little reason to revisit this tradition when they came to power in 1908; more likely, they'd simply been overwhelmed by the pace of events. During the Balkan Wars of 1912–13, entire civilian populations were forcibly ejected by most all the combatant armies, less for reasons of military convenience than in pursuit of a policy that a century later would become known as ethnic cleansing. That massive if largely forgotten human tragedy—hundreds of thousands of Turks, Bulgars, Macedonians, and Greeks were permanently expelled from their ancestral homes—set the precedent for the far more brutal and deadly expulsion of Anatolia's Armenian population beginning in the spring of 1915. Despite that ghastly recent example and his own efforts to ameliorate it, when Djemal Pasha found his own Syrian realm under threat in early 1917, it was to the policy of expulsion that he turned.

At first there was nothing controversial about it. In late February, with the British invaders massing below Gaza and clearly about to strike, he had ordered the evacuation of that town's population, perhaps twenty thousand civilians in all. It was a move the Syrian governor had every reason to congratulate himself on; when the British attack came in late March, the cleared roads to the north and east of Gaza had allowed the Turks to rush in reinforcements and carry the day.

In that battle's aftermath, Djemal and his German commanders studied the map of the larger southern Palestine region; surely the British were going to try again, and just as surely they would be more artful than to attack over the same ground twice. In trying to anticipate where that next strike might come, Djemal's concerns centered on the coastal town of Jaffa, some forty miles to the north.

Throughout March, rumors reaching Djemal's headquarters had held that the British might bypass the Turkish trenches in Gaza by making an amphibious landing to the north. Not only did the smooth beaches and gentle surf of Jaffa provide a nearly ideal site for such a landing, but so did the town's mixed population; among its forty thousand residents were some ten thousand Jews and perhaps four thousand Christians, minorities that were becoming increasingly disenchanted under Ottoman rule. While those initial concerns had been mooted by the failed British frontal assault at Gaza on March 26, they came rushing back in its aftermath, so much so that on March 28, Djemal ordered Jaffa's evacuation. After initially giving residents less than a week to organize their departures, Djemal relented to protests by Jewish leaders—Passover, one of the most sacred of Jewish holidays, was about to begin—and extended the deadline another eight days.

Despite the Ottoman government's proclivity for sunny proclamations at such times—there was usually much talk of extra trains being laid on to transport the uprooted to safety, of the pleasant temporary quarters being readied to ensure the refugees' continuing comfort—these evacuations were invariably messy, wretched affairs. For the criminally minded, they provided an opportunity to loot the homes of their departed neighbors, or to waylay exhausted and overburdened travelers on the road. Given the corruption endemic to all levels of Ottoman government, they also tended to be highly selective; those blessed with the right connections or the funds to bribe the right officials might be allowed to stay behind or only move to a town's outskirts, while others were being herded days or even weeks away. Perhaps inevitably, these abuses were likely to be most prevalent in a "mixed" town like Jaffa, a chance for the ethnic and religious animosities that always lurked below the surface of Ottoman society to be given full play.

Nevertheless, there was initially nothing about the evacuation of Jaffa to suggest it would be anything more than one of those little forgotten footnotes of war, another point of misery for a civilian population long grown accustomed to it. But in issuing his edict, Djemal Pasha unwittingly set in motion one of the most consequential disinformation campaigns of World War I. The first link in that chain of events occurred on the night of April 17, when a twenty-seven-year-old woman was helped aboard a British spy ship trolling off the coast of Palestine.

IT WAS A poignant reunion. Aaron Aaronsohn hadn't seen his younger sister Sarah in nearly a year, but there she was in Port Said, pale and weak but alive, having just come off the *Managem* from Athlit. Rushing her to his rooms at the Continental Hotel in central Cairo, Aaronsohn summoned a doctor, who diagnosed anemia and proffered iron tablets. Despite her exhausted state, Aaronsohn then began pumping his sister for news from Palestine.

To say that Sarah Aaronsohn was an independent spirit would have been a gross understatement. As a young woman growing up in Zichron Yaakov, she had fairly scandalized its more conservative residents with her insistence on riding horseback and participating in hunts in the surrounding foothills with the men. Like her male siblings, she was extremely well educated, had traveled—in her case, throughout central Europe—and possessed of a worldly sophistication quite out of keeping with a woman coming of age in the hardscrabble Jewish colonies in Palestine. Even if she had bowed to tradition by quickly marrying after the engagement of her younger sister, Rivka, to Absalom Feinberg—it was considered close to scandalous for an older sister not to marry first—she'd been modern enough to walk out on her unhappy marriage in Constantinople and not look back.

Perhaps most shocking for a woman in the early 1900s, Sarah Aaronsohn had made no attempt to hide either her intelligence or her natural leadership skills. While these qualities spurred resentment in some, others were totally enamored, and over the years the attractive Aaronsohn sister had gathered about her an ardent coterie of male suitors. She was not shy about trading on that attraction for her own higher purposes. Upon the death of Absalom Feinberg in the Sinai desert in January 1917, Sarah had assumed leadership of the NILI spy ring in Palestine, and among the operatives scattered across the region, a network she had helped expand to nearly two dozen, were several men clearly in love with her.

That element aside, Sarah Aaronsohn seemed uniquely suited to the perilous role into which she'd been thrust and, judging by the results, performed it more ably than either of NILI's original leaders—her temperamental brother; the impetuous Feinberg—might have done. As a woman, she was largely immune from the suspicions that attached to Palestine's westernized Jews in the eyes of Ottoman officials, and she had used that immunity to make extended reconnaissance trips through the countryside, just an innocent "lady's outing" should she ever be stopped. Once contact with the British had been established, she turned Athlit into her command post, sorting the bits of intelligence coming in from all over Palestine and ensuring it was organized in time for the next scheduled delivery to the spy ship offshore. One measure of her steeliness was her ability to keep the death of Absalom Feinberg, the man with whom she had shared a chaste love, a secret from the rest of the NILI ring. So as to maintain organizational morale, she held to the fiction concocted by her brother in Cairo that Feinberg had gone off to Europe to train as an Entente pilot.

Now, in mid-April 1917, Sarah Aaronsohn had come to Egypt with a disturbing story to tell. Three weeks earlier, she told her brother, Djemal Pasha had ordered Jaffa's evacuation. While this edict applied to the entire population of the town, it was hardly a surprise that the burden had fallen especially heavy on its Jewish residents; with transport scarce, they were forced to leave most of their possessions behind, while simultaneously suffering abuse and depredations by their long-resentful Muslim neighbors. According to Sarah, at least two Jewish men had been lynched on the Jaffa outskirts.

For Aaron Aaronsohn, the news was deeply alarming. Mindful as he was of the fate of the Armenians, the Jaffa expulsions suggested that something similar might now befall the Jews. He immediately set out to alert his associates in British intelligence of the potential humanitarian crisis looming in southern Palestine.

His timing couldn't have been worse. On the very day of Sarah Aaronsohn's arrival in Cairo, April 19, Archibald Murray had thrown his army against the Turkish trenches at Gaza a second time. Proving Djemal Pasha wrong, Murray chose to attack over precisely the same ground as in the first assault, although opting for an even more artless, human-wave approach. Just about the only British refinements since the First Battle of Gaza were the use of tanks and poison gas against the enemy, but even these couldn't alter the outcome; in the six thousand casualties the British suffered at the hands of the vastly outnumbered but victorious Turks was a debacle so sweeping as to be apparent to all.

Few could have been more dumbfounded than Aaron Aaronsohn. Back on March 12, prior to Murray's first attack, British planners had sought out his counsel based on his intimate knowledge of the topography of southern Palestine. The agronomist had been aghast that the British proposed to make their main thrust through an area south of the town known as Wadi Ghazzal, a stretch of flat ground broken by meandering streams, which then rose up to a gridwork of nearly impenetrable cactus-fenced animal pens. "I said I considered the ground very much to our disadvantage," Aaronsohn had written at the time, "and would give a great chance to the Turkish snipers. Wadis there are numerous and difficult to cross." Despite this admonition, in both Gaza assaults the British had made for the streams and cactus fences of Wadi Ghazzal like homing pigeons.

Of more immediate concern to Aaronsohn, with the latest Gaza disaster dominating the concerns of British Cairo, it was impossible to get anyone to pay attention to what might be happening to the Jewish population of Jaffa. Over the course of that next week, the scientist desperately approached most any British official he could think of, but got nowhere. Then his luck suddenly changed. It did so on April 27, when he was finally able to obtain an audience with Mark Sykes.

Since their arrival in Cairo five days earlier, most of Sykes's and Picot's time had been taken up in conferences with the "delegation" of Syrian exiles that Sykes had preselected to represent Arab interests in the region. Much of the urgency of these talks had dissipated with the grim news out of Gaza, but after several days of negotiations, Sykes felt confident that he'd managed to bridge the vast gulf between France's imperial designs in Syria and Britain's pledge to Syrian independence. A great aid in this bridging process was the fact that the three Syrian delegates were totally unaware a gulf existed.

"Main difficulty," Sykes explained in a cable to the director of military intelligence back in London, "was to manoeuvre the delegates, without showing them a map or letting them know that there was an actual geographical or detailed agreement [already in place], into asking for what we are ready to give them."

With the "Syrian Question" thus nicely resolving itself, at least temporarily, Sykes was able to carve out time for other things. High on that list was meeting with Aaron Aaronsohn, who had been beseeching Sykes's retinue for an appointment for days. Their reunion took place in a conference room of the Savoy Hotel on the morning of April 27.

"At last!" Aaronsohn wrote in his diary. "We immediately broached intimate subjects. He told me that since he was talking with a Jewish patriot, he would entrust me with very secret matters—some of which were not even known to the Foreign Office."

Sykes filled him in on his clandestine meeting with the British Zionist leaders at the London townhouse on February 7, as well as expounded on a new formula for Middle East peace he'd recently devised, a scheme that called for a grand alliance of the Jews, the Arabs, and the remnants of the Armenians. With such an alliance, Sykes confidently explained, the Arabs could be made compliant—they had to know that without Jewish and British support, their independence bid would fail—but would also gain the clout to defy the French. At the same time, such a pact would freeze out the grasping Italians, marginalize the Russians, create a pro-British buffer state in protection of Egypt and India, all while paying lip service to the anticolonial demands of Britain's newest ally, the United States. How the Arabophobic Aaronsohn responded to this dizzying graph-paper concoction—its complexity only surpassed by its absurdity—isn't known. Most likely, he simply listened in respectful silence; after all, he had pressing matters of his own to take up with Mark Sykes.

If other British officials had been too distracted to pay attention to the predicament of Jaffa's Jewish population, not so the War Cabinet's new assistant secretary. Instead, it appears Sykes instantly grasped the potential propaganda bonanza Aaronsohn's news provided, a way to propel those still noncommittal elements of international Jewry toward the Zionist-British cause. He quickly dispatched Aaronsohn to work up a memo on the Jaffa situation, and to meet with him again the next morning.

In writing on the plight of the Armenians five months earlier, Aaronsohn had paid grudging respect to Djemal Pasha, pointing out that despite his personality flaws and failures as an administrator, the Syrian governor had been resolute in trying to stop the Armenian massacres and in alleviating the suffering of the survivors. The agronomist had also at times benefited from Djemal's changeable and oddly courteous nature, his personal appeals to him winning the release of Absalom Feinberg after his arrest as a potential spy, as well as the modification of an array of edicts injurious to Jewish settlers. As he sat down to write his account for Mark Sykes on the afternoon of April 27, however, Aaronsohn appreciated that here was a golden opportunity to advance the Zionist cause, and to fully capitalize on that opportunity meant creative license would have to be taken. The primary victim of that creativity was to be Djemal Pasha.

Reconvening with Mark Sykes at 9:15 the next morning, Aaronsohn handed over his memorandum on Jaffa. In quick order, Sykes fired off a top-secret cable to the Foreign Office asking them to get hold of Chaim Weizmann at the English Zionist Federation and deliver the following message: "Aaron Aaronsohn asks me to inform you that Televiv [the Jewish enclave of Jaffa] has been sacked. 10,000 Palestinian Jews are now without home or food. Whole yeshuv [settlement] is threatened with destruction. Jemal [Pasha] has publicly stated that Armenian policy will now be applied to Jews. Pray inform [Jewish] centers without naming Aaron Aaronsohn or source of information."

The first to heed the call was the *Jewish Chronicle*, Britain's preeminent Zionist newspaper. On May 4, under subheadlines entitled "Grave Reports—Terrible Outrages—Threats of Wholesale Massacre," readers were informed, "It is with profound sorrow and concern that the *Jewish Chronicle* learns, from an absolutely reliable source, the very gravest news of the Jews in Palestine.... Tel Aviv, the beautiful Garden City suburb of Jaffa, has been sacked and lies a mere heap of ruins, while similar wanton destruction has in all probability taken place in other specifically Jewish parts of Palestine."

Taking up the fiction about statements made by the Syrian governor, the *Chronicle* continued, "But even worse is threatened. For the Turkish Governor, Djemal Pasha, has proclaimed his intention of the authorities [*sic*] to wipe out mercilessly the Jewish population of Palestine, his public statement being that the Armenian policy of massacre is to be applied to the Jews. If this dire and dastardly threat is carried into effect, it will mean not alone that thousands of Jews... will be put to the sword in cold blood, but that in addition the whole of the work of Palestinian re-settlement will be utterly destroyed."

Over the next few days, the grim news out of Palestine reverberated through Jewish communities in Britain, the United States, and continental Europe, and drew anguished appeals to their governments that some kind of action be taken. In the case of the British Foreign Office leadership, however, just what could be done was not at all clear. "I regret," one senior diplomat commented on the same day the *Chronicle* story appeared, "that no action by us seems in any way feasible."

But at least one British official saw in the Jaffa story the chance to take matters to an entirely new level, not just to sway international Jewish opinion but to bring pressure to bear on his own government. This was William Ormsby-Gore, the Conservative member of Parliament who had been so impressed by Aaron Aaronsohn during his time in Cairo at the Arab Bureau; in May 1917, Ormsby-Gore was back in London and working with Mark Sykes on the War Cabinet's Middle Eastern affairs desk. While Sykes had left Cairo for a brief trip to Arabia on April 30, thus falling out of easy communication, he found Ormsby-Gore's cable awaiting his return to Egypt on May 9.

"I think we ought to use pogroms in Palestine as propaganda,"

Ormsby-Gore wrote. "Any spicy tales of atrocity would be eagerly welcomed by the propaganda people here, and Aaron Aaronsohn could send some lurid stories to the Jewish papers."

Sykes received no argument from Aaronsohn. The two had another long meeting on May 11, at which, the scientist reported, they "discussed the question of American Jews and of the propaganda we could do there [*sic*] now in recruiting for the Palestine front. Sir Mark offered to forward any telegrams or letters which I might care to send."

Perhaps mindful of his own growing reputation for exaggeration, Sykes had the foresight to send Aaronsohn's new and expanded missive out under the signature of High Commissioner Reginald Wingate. "During Passover," Wingate's cable to London that same day read, "the entire Jewish population of Jaffa expelled towards north. Homes, property ransacked, population in flight robbed with connivance of Turkish Authorities. Jews resisting [were] pillaged, hanged. Thousands wandering helplessly on roads, starving." And now there was a frightening new development in the telling, an extending of the evacuations to the much larger Jewish population in Jerusalem. "Masses of young Jerusalem Jews deported, northward, destination unknown. Forcible evacuation of [Jerusalem Jewish] colony imminent."

Under Wingate's signature, circulation of this cable wasn't limited to the Foreign Office leadership; instead, it landed on the desks of the king, the prime minister, and the entire War Cabinet. At the same time, Aaronsohn gave Sykes a list of some fifty Zionist leaders throughout the world to be immediately notified. Now the Jaffa story went the 1917 version of viral. "Cruelties to Jews Deported in Jaffa," screamed a headline in the *New York Times*, "Djemal Pasha Blamed," while the American government, so recently enlisted to the war effort, joined an international chorus in denouncing this latest outrage by the Constantinople regime. Nowhere was that chorus louder than in Great Britain.

The Turks and their German allies might be forgiven for being slow to respond to this onslaught of condemnation; after all, the Jaffa evacuation had occurred in early April, and it was now mid-May. After initially refusing to dignify the charges with a response, Djemal Pasha finally flatly denied the accusations, pointing out that the entire population of Jaffa had been evacuated, not just its Jews, and that the process—unpleasant though it undoubtedly was for those affected—had been completed in an orderly and peaceful fashion; in fact, the governor had granted Jaffa's Jewish population special considerations during the operation denied others. As for the claims of Jews being "deported" from Jerusalem, the Syrian governor countered, there had been no evacuations there at all. These assertions were seconded by the regimes in Constantinople and Berlin, and even by a collection of Jewish leaders in Palestine, including Jerusalem's chief rabbi.

But it was too little too late. In the minds of much of the international public, the "pogrom" in Jaffa was already an established fact, the latest Central Powers atrocity to join the "rape of Belgium" and the massacres of the Armenians. It also alerted the Zionists and their British government allies to the tremendous tool they'd been handed. Coming so closely after the fall of the hated czar and the admission of the United States into the war, the Jaffa story helped accelerate a tectonic shift taking place among international Jewry, the growing conviction that their future lay with the Entente.

Of more immediate impact, it played to the argument of the more radical Zionists that any accommodation or compromise with Turkey was no longer possible. In early June, with the Jaffa story still raging, Aaron Aaronsohn penned cables to some of the most prominent leaders in the American Jewish community, men who continued to be cautious about wholeheartedly embracing the Zionist cause and who in some cases still imagined the future of Jewish settlement in Palestine as best served by Ottoman rule. To lend further authority to Aaronsohn's message—among its recipients was a sitting Supreme Court justice, Louis Brandeis, as well as a future one, Felix Frankfurter—Mark Sykes arranged for the cables to be routed through the British embassy in Washington for delivery. Typical was the cable received by Judge Mayer Sulzberger in Philadelphia:

"Turkish atrocities on Jewish populations in Palestine reported on reliable information," Aaronsohn wrote. "It is high time to abandon our previous forgiving attitude towards Turks. . . . Now that Turks have committed those crimes, Jewish attitude and American public opinion must undergo complete change. Only efficient way to quick release of Jewish populations from Turkish clutches is to attack latter thoroughly in the field and everywhere. . . . We must present a united front, and concentrate Jewish influence on wresting Palestine from Turkish hands."

In that same month of June, a rather different version of the Jaffa story began to emerge. In response to Entente appeals, Spain, Sweden, and the Vatican, all neutral entities in the conflict, sent envoys to investigate what had happened there. Both the Spanish and Vatican envoys quickly concluded that the reports of Jewish massacres and persecutions were without foundation, while their Swedish counterpart went even further. "In many ways," he wrote, "the Jewish community of Jaffa had fared far better—and certainly no worse—than the resident Moslem population in the evacuation." Shortly afterward, the U.S. consulate in Jerusalem also reported that the accounts of violence against the Jaffa Jews were "grossly exaggerated." Even Aaron Aaronsohn was ultimately forced to concede that the two Jewish men allegedly "lynched" in Jaffa had actually been arrested on charges of looting, and evidently not hung after all.

It didn't matter, of course. In war, truth is whatever people can be led to believe, and Djemal Pasha had just handed his enemies a "truth" that would change Middle Eastern history. The fiction of what happened in Jaffa in 1917—a fiction repeated as fact by most historians writing on the period since—would now become the ur-myth for the contention that the Jewish community in Palestine could never be safe under Muslim rule, that to survive it needed a state of its own.

ON APRIL 21, a British navy patrol boat put in to Wejh harbor with a cargo of intense interest to Captain T. E. Lawrence: eleven Turkish prisoners of war. Until the previous morning, the men had been part of the Turkish garrison defending Aqaba.

Acting on rumors that a German minelaying operation was under way in the vicinity of Aqaba, three British patrol boats had closed on the port just before dawn on April 20 and put ashore a landing party, catching the tiny garrison off guard. The brief ensuing gun battle left two Turkish soldiers dead, eleven captured, and the rest—some fifty or sixty by best estimate—taken to the hills. Since six of the prisoners were Syrian draftees and expressed a desire to join with the rebel forces of Faisal ibn Hussein, one of the British patrol boats had brought them down to Wejh for questioning.

Over the course of that day, Lawrence interrogated each of the Syrians in turn. From them he learned that while the Aqaba garrison fluctuated in size, it rarely consisted of more than one hundred soldiers. Of even greater import considering the scheme he was hatching, the total number of Turkish soldiers billeted in the blockhouses along the sixty-mile Wadi Itm trail between Aqaba and Maan was at most just two hundred more. It meant that Lawrence's plan just might work; if he could raise an Arab force at the eastern terminus of that trail and launch a lightning advance over the mountains, he could sweep the isolated Turkish garrisons before him and fall on Aqaba practically unopposed.

But just because Lawrence saw the opportunity before him, it didn't necessarily follow that anyone else in the British military would. Still in effect was Gilbert Clayton's March 8 directive that the Arabs not move on Aqaba. Instead, all attention was to remain focused on attacking the Hejaz Railway to block the Turkish garrison's withdrawal from Medina (it would still be some weeks before the British realized the Turks had no intention of leaving Medina), an imperative that allowed for no side adventures.

Of course, the best way to avoid having one's ideas shot down is to never explicitly voice them. Rather than take his proposal up with Clayton directly, Lawrence chose to engage the two other British officers then based in Wejh in a generalized discourse about the insights into guerrilla warfare he had gained during his convalescence in Wadi Ais. In particular, he would later claim, he expounded on the foolishness of trying to take Medina from the Turks, and the unfeasibility of trying to organize the Arabs into a blocking force on the Hejaz Railway. Instead, he suggested, they needed to spread the Turks thin by expanding the war front as much as possible. Among other things, that meant going north with "a highly mobile, highly equipped striking force of the smallest size, and use it successively at distributed points of the Turkish line."

To Lawrence's listeners in Wejh, both career military men, it may have all sounded intriguing, but also like little more than a distraction to the mission at hand. This was a reaction that Lawrence was rather counting on. "Everyone was too busy with his own work to give me specific authority to launch out on mine," he would recount. "All I gained was a hearing, and a qualified admission that my counter-offensive [idea] might be a useful diversion."

It's hard to imagine how his fellow officers might have lent Lawrence "specific authority" for his scheme, since it's clear from their own field reports that he never indicated that this diversionary force might make for Aqaba. Lawrence adopted an even more oblique manner in his approach to Cyril Wilson in Jeddah, informing his superior that Auda Abu Tayi would soon be taking a raiding party toward Maan, and that Lawrence was considering accompanying the party to ensure their actions complemented Britain's current military objectives. Wilson concurred, reporting to Clayton on May 1 that "Auda is to travel north, probably accompanied by Lawrence, with their first aim to disrupt the railway around Maan." Omitted was any mention of what their second aim might be.

In *Seven Pillars*, a book rife with self-justifications, Lawrence would offer a truly breathtaking one to explain his decision to strike out on his own: "The element I would withdraw from the railway scheme was only my single self and, in the circumstances, this amount was negligible, since I felt so strongly against it that my help there would have been half-hearted. So I decided to go my own way, with or without orders."

In other words, as Lawrence no longer saw the point in trying to shut down the railway, it was really best for all concerned that he go find something else to do. Small wonder why so many of his military superiors found the Oxford scholar infuriating.

Underlying this, though, was an even grander psychological rationalization for the action Lawrence was contemplating. In his mind, upholding the promises made to the Arabs truly would serve Great Britain's long-term interests, not just as a point of honor but as a way to minimize the influence of other European powers—allies today, perhaps, but surely competitors again tomorrow—throughout the region. A vital first step in this campaign was to allow the Arabs to take their revolution into Syria, and thus steal that land away from France. The core problem, in Lawrence's estimation, was that Great Britain had yet to grasp what was best for her, and he simply didn't have time to explain.

BEFORE SETTING OUT for Aqaba, Lawrence was to have one more fateful meeting in Wejh. It came on the morning of May 7, when a British destroyer briefly put into the harbor. On board was Mark Sykes.

The two had first met during Sykes's fact-finding mission to Egypt in 1915, and despite their vast differences in personality—Sykes gregarious and charming, Lawrence taciturn and painfully shy—had reportedly gotten along quite well. That didn't last long. As with most everyone else in the Cairo military intelligence office, Lawrence's opinion of the diplomat had rapidly soured once details of the Sykes-Picot Agreement became known to them in the spring of 1916. Certainly, Sykes's continuing fondness for firing off fatuous memos proposing neat solutions to the region's problems—proposals often in direct opposition to those he had advocated weeks or even days earlier—had done nothing to rehabilitate his image in Lawrence's eyes in the year since. In his view, Sykes fairly epitomized that vexing feature of Edwardian England, the aristocratic gadfly, a man who could gain a hearing for his reckless ideas by virtue of his pedigree and the breezy confidence with which he voiced them.

In their meeting on May 7, however, Lawrence was to discover something else about the man; for want of a more decorous term, Mark Sykes was also a liar.

Indeed, that the two were meeting in Wejh at all that day was a by-product of Sykes having been caught out in his latest round of trickery. The diplomat was just returning from an audience with King Hussein, an encounter Sykes had wished to avoid but which had been forced on him by the resident agent in Jeddah, Colonel Cyril Wilson.

For all his stiff-necked priggishness, the swagger-stick-toting Wilson had gradually emerged as the voice of conscience for British policy in the Middle East. In the long debate of late 1916 over whether a British brigade should be deployed in the Hejaz, Wilson had initially been among its fiercest advocates, and had been tasked by his superior, Reginald Wingate, to compel King Hussein to that view. Over the course of numerous meetings with Hussein, however, it had gradually occurred to the resident agent that perhaps the old man in Mecca knew his subjects and the politics of western Arabia better than the Allied advisors newly arrived to the scene. Ultimately, when Wingate had once again ordered his underling to lean on Hussein over the matter, Wilson, heretofore regarded as something of a Wingate yes-man, had essentially refused to do so and been instrumental in seeing the proposal finally shelved.

Wilson had had a far more visceral reaction upon learning of Sykes's scheme to avoid Hussein in favor of his sham negotiations with the Syrian "delegates" in Cairo. In late March he had sent a long and anguished letter to Clayton enumerating both the problems inevitably to come from this act of deception and the benefits to be derived by being honest with Hussein. "We now have a chance, which is not likely to occur again, of winning the gratitude of millions of Moslems of the [British] Empire," he wrote. "For Heaven's sake, let us be straight with the old man; I am convinced it will pay us in the end."

While that appeal had been in vain, it seemed the good colonel in Jeddah was quite capable of backroom maneuvers of his own. At his next meeting with Hussein, he urged the king to formally request a meeting with Mark Sykes. When Wilson forwarded that request to Reginald Wingate, another man who, despite his interventionist impulses, held to the British tradition of fair play, it quickly became an invitation Sykes couldn't refuse. On April 30, with his and Picot's conferences with the Syrian "delegates" in Cairo concluded, Sykes had boarded the British destroyer in Port Suez and set off for Jeddah.

Even for a supremely self-confident man, it must have been a stressful voyage. It was one thing to bamboozle a few preselected functionaries in Cairo with no knowledge of the McMahon-Hussein Correspondence; it would surely be quite another to fool one of its actual authors. But then, Sykes had other cards to play. Chief among them was his ability to control the flow of information. Just as he had arranged to have a first meeting with the Syrians in Cairo without Picot present, so now he would be meeting alone with Hussein. As a result, should any future dispute arise over what had or had not been discussed, it would be the word of a highly respected British envoy against that of a mercurial desert chieftain long known for forgetfulness and willful misinterpretation.

It might have all worked out just fine—at least for the time being, which was all Mark Sykes could reasonably hope for—if he hadn't decided to stop off in Wejh en route to confer with Faisal. By chance, Lawrence was away on a brief reconnaissance trip when Sykes called on May 2, but he got a full report from Faisal on what had transpired upon his return to Wejh two days later. By then, Sykes was already on his way to Jeddah and his meeting with King Hussein.

Judging by the report he sent to Reginald Wingate on the evening of May 5, Sykes's foray into shuttle diplomacy could scarcely have gone better: "On 2nd May, I saw Sherif Faisal at Wejh and explained to him the principle of the Anglo-French agreement in regard to an Arab confederation; after much argument he accepted the principle and seemed satisfied." That success had presaged one even more remarkable, for that very afternoon Sykes had met with King Hussein. "In accordance with my instructions, I explained the principle of the [Anglo-French] agreement as regards an Arab confederation or State. . . . I impressed upon the King the importance of Franco-Arab friendship and I at least got him to admit that it was essential to Arab development in Syria, but this after a very lengthy argument."

A close reader of that May 5 report might have been disquieted by the peculiar symmetry of these two meetings—forthrightness by Sykes in outlining French-British designs in the region, followed by Arab argument, followed ultimately by Arab acceptance—while the truly cynical might have concluded that, with his emphasis on the quarreling involved, Sykes was already laying in his defense should there be future disagreement with Faisal and Hussein over what had been said or agreed to. In the interim, though, the trip was a triumph of diplomacy, a crucial first step toward resolving the nettlesome issues that stood between Britain and France and their Arab allies.

"Please tell Monsieur Picot," Sykes ended his May 5 cable to Wingate, "that I am satisfied with my interview with Faisal and the King, as they both now stand at the same point as was reached at our last joint meeting with the 3 Syrian delegates in Cairo."

What Mark Sykes didn't know, of course, was that in Faisal ibn Hussein he had been speaking with a man quite aware of the Sykes-Picot Agreement—courtesy of T. E. Lawrence—and in no way did Sykes's vague and generalized discussion of that pact on May 2 match up with what the Arab leader already knew. Nevertheless, whether hewing to the Arab negotiating tradition of not tipping one's hand until absolutely necessary, or worried that Lawrence would be exposed as his source, Faisal had not confronted the diplomat over his obfuscations at the time.

Not that he was in any better position to do so when Sykes stopped back by on May 7. Faisal's knowledge of the true framework of Sykes-Picot, as opposed to the bastardized version Sykes had chosen to tell him, was the great and dangerous secret that he and Lawrence shared, and to reveal it now could only invite disaster: for Faisal, estrangement and perhaps abandonment by his British benefactors; for Lawrence, immediate transfer and probable court-martial.

On the other hand, Lawrence *did* have sanctioned knowledge of

Sykes-Picot, which meant he on his own could confront Sykes over the sanitized version told to Faisal—and, presumably, to Hussein. All indications are that Lawrence provoked just such a confrontation. Neither man was to make record of their meeting in Wejh, but it appears to have been a highly contentious one. From that day on, Lawrence's attitude toward Sykes would be hostile. For his part, Sykes would miss few chances to try to denigrate or marginalize Lawrence in any way he could.

On a more personal level, it seems that encounter with Sykes in Wejh came to simultaneously haunt Lawrence and to provide a certain kind of relief. He stood vindicated in not trusting in the honor of his government, and in imparting to Faisal its secret plan to betray the Arab cause. To whatever degree his conscience had been bothered by that decision, in the slippery schemes of Mark Sykes it was now cleansed.

At the same time, he appreciated that in his countryman was a particularly formidable rival. By comparison, Édouard Brémond was easy, his various schemes made predictable by his singular pursuit of French hegemony. Mark Sykes, by contrast, was a man ruled by whim, who didn't feel bound by—perhaps at times didn't even remember—the myriad promises that tripped so easily from his lips. He was able to stay ahead of it all by a talent for deceit, but since he was in a position of power, pulling the levers from Jeddah to London and all points in between, at the end of the day there would probably be no final appeal to British ideals of honor or justice, all would be sacrificed to convenience. The only recourse for the Arabs, then, was to try to change the facts on the ground, to strike a blow that might upend the plans of the dealmakers.

It was with such thoughts that, two days later, Lawrence set out on the long and dangerous trek toward Aqaba. For what would soon become one of the most audacious and celebrated military exploits of World War I, his accompanying "army" consisted of fewer than forty-five Arab warriors.

Chapter 13

Aqaba

Never doubt Great Britain's word.
She is wise and trustworthy; have no fear.
KING HUSSEIN TO HIS SON FAISAL, MAY 1917

His Sherifial Majesty [King Hussein] evidently suffers from the defects
of character and ignorance of system common to Oriental potentates. . . .
The task of guiding an Oriental ruler or government in the way
they should go is no light one—as I know to my cost—and you have my
fullest sympathy. It must be heartbreaking work at times.
REGINALD WINGATE TO CYRIL WILSON, JULY 20, 1917

It was a moment when the awful burden of leadership fell upon Law-rence as if a great weight, reminiscent of what had occurred in Wadi Kitan two months earlier. Then, the mantle of authority had required him to execute a man. Now it required him to try to save one, but quite possibly to lose his own life in the effort.

It was midmorning on May 24, his party's fifth day in El Houl. Arabic for "the Terror," El Houl is a vast trackless and waterless expanse in northern Arabia empty of even the smallest signs of life, and Lawrence had dreaded that leg of their journey to Syria ever since leaving Wejh. Reality had been worse than the imagining. Within hours of entering El Houl, the forty-five-man caravan had been buffeted by a ferocious headwind, "a half-gale," in Lawrence's estimation, "so dry that our shriveled lips cracked open, and the skin of our faces chapped." The wind, and the burning, blinding sand it kicked up, continued almost without pause for the next four days.

To endure in such situations, humans tend to retreat into a kind of closed-off mental state, their entire focus honed to simply trying to reach the end. Such was the case with Lawrence and Auda's party in El Houl, so much so that on the morning of May 24, no one seemed to take note of the riderless camel padding alongside the others. Perhaps they assumed she was one of the baggage camels that traditionally lagged behind, or that her rider had switched to another camel and was to be found elsewhere along their extended line. Most likely, in their semihibernative states they simply couldn't be roused to care. When finally Lawrence investigated the mysterious camel, he discovered it was the mount of Gasim.

"A fanged and yellow-faced outlaw," Gasim was a native of the Syrian city of Maan, and Lawrence had brought him along on the trek in hopes that he might make contact with other Arab nationalists in his hometown. Of course, this also made Gasim an outsider among the traveling Howeitat and Ageyl tribesmen and, in the harsh code of the desert, just as friendless in a crisis as the condemned Hamed had been at Wadi Kitan. As Lawrence recounted, Gasim's status now "shifted the difficulty to my shoulders."

Perhaps indicative of the stress El Houl had put on his own reasoning skills, Lawrence made a most foolhardy decision, not only to go back alone in search of Gasim, but not even to tell the others he was doing so. Within a very short distance, he discovered, all trace of their path had vanished, the camels' tracks in the sand swept away by the scouring wind, and then the caravan itself receded until it was lost in the murk. To somehow find Gasim and then return to the caravan, Lawrence could only rely on the compass readings he'd periodically noted in his diary and trust he hadn't erred.

It was fifteen days since they had set out. In Bedouin tradition, a number of tribal chiefs, including Faisal, had accompanied them the first few miles out of Wejh by way of farewell, and then the forty-five or so travelers had headed off into the northeastern darkness, the last anyone in the Hejaz would hear of them for over two months.

They traveled light. Along with a few rifles and 20,000 gold sovereigns—to be disbursed among Syrian tribal leaders they hoped to win to the rebel cause—each man carried in his saddlebags some forty-five pounds of flour. That and water would be their staples until they reached their initial staging ground, the Wadi Sirhan depression on the Syrian frontier, in an estimated three weeks' time.

Despite being struck by a new round of fever and boils, Lawrence would recall the first days of that journey in almost idyllic terms, the beginning of a great adventure. It was also during this time that there occurred one of the more intriguing side stories to his time in Arabia, the account of how he came to obtain his two camel orderlies, given the names Daud and Farraj in *Seven Pillars* (their actual names were Ali and Othman).

It occurred during a day of idleness when, as Lawrence rested his weary boil-covered body in the shadow of a rock escarpment, a young boy rushed up beseeching his help. Having fled from a nearby Ageyl encampment, Daud offered that his best friend, Farraj, was about to be severely beaten by the camp commander for accidentally burning down a tent; a word from Lawrence, the boy suggested, might stay the punishment. That theory was discredited when Lawrence took the matter up with the passing Ageyl camp commander, Saad, a few moments later. Explaining that the two boys were constantly getting into trouble and that an example had to be made, Saad instead offered a Solomon-like solution in deference to Lawrence's appeal: Daud could halve his friend's punishment by submitting to the other half himself. "Daud leaped at the chance," Lawrence wrote, "kissed my hand and Saad's and ran off up the valley."

In *Seven Pillars*, Lawrence would strongly suggest that the Farraj-Daud relationship was a sexual one, describing it as "an instance of the eastern boy-and-boy affection which the segregation of women made inevitable." In the process, Lawrence was to add to speculations—still a point of heated debate in some circles nearly a century later—about his own sexuality. Much of that speculation stems from his description of the "two bent figures, with pain in their eyes, but crooked smiles upon their lips," who showed up at his camp the next morning and begged to be taken on as his servants:

"These were Daud the hasty and his love-fellow, Farraj, a beautiful, soft-framed, girlish creature, with innocent smooth face and swimming eyes." After first trying to turn the boys away, explaining he had no need of servants, Lawrence finally relented, "mainly because they looked so young and clean." From that day on, the mischievous antics of Daud and Farraj would provide lighthearted relief to Lawrence's travels.

But already in these early days of the journey, the party faced a worrisome problem. Virtually all their camels, both the baggage and mounted ones, suffered from the virulent mange endemic to Wejh, and without even the rudimentary unguents to control it—butter was a traditional desert remedy—many were quickly going lame or mad from it. The epidemic may have contributed to the deaths of two of the baggage camels that, during a climb through a particularly narrow defile, lost their footing and plunged to the rocks below. None of this bode well as they came to the edge of El Houl.

"In all Faisal's stud of riding-camels," Lawrence noted, "there was not one healthy. In our little expedition every camel was weakening daily. [Auda's chief lieutenant] Nasir was full of anxiety lest many break down in the forced march before us and leave their riders stranded in the desert."

The torturous nature of the passage across El Houl was reflected in the small pocket diary Lawrence carried. Instead of the voluminous notes he normally kept on his travels, the few short fragments he managed there grew steadily more disjointed, almost nonsensical. And then, on the fifth day, Gasim disappeared.

In deciding to turn back for the lost man, Lawrence surely knew that Gasim was probably already dead; for anyone caught out in El Houl without shelter or water at that time of year, life expectancy could be measured in terms of hours. He surely also knew that if he'd made the slightest miscalculation in his compass readings, he too would soon expire. Still, he persevered—and finally, he was lucky. After an hour and a half of riding, he spotted a small black object in the far distance, an object that, as he approached, took the form of a staggering and delirious Gasim. Hoisting the man onto the back of his own camel, Lawrence turned and raced to find the others.

In David Lean's epic film, the rescue of Gasim would be immortalized in a ten-minute scene, culminating in Lawrence finally rejoining his comrades to their relieved and raucous cheers, his noble act cementing his image as a true "son of the desert." The reality was quite different. By the code of this brutal landscape, Gasim had brought his death upon himself by having failed to secure his camel when he stopped to relieve himself, and, rather than praised, Lawrence was berated by some of his comrades for having risked his life for one clearly so worthless. Furthermore, the caravan commander now administered another beating to Daud and Farraj for letting Lawrence go back alone.

ON MAY 26, 1917, two days after Lawrence's rescue of Gasim, King George V and his War Cabinet received some gladdening news. It came in the form of a top-secret cable from Reginald Wingate in Cairo, a report on Mark Sykes's latest triumphant visit to Arabia.

Following on Sykes's earlier solo visit, he and his French diplomatic counterpart, François Georges-Picot, had recently met with King Hussein in Jeddah in hopes of thrashing out a settlement between the Arabs and the French over the future status of Syria. Since their desires were almost diametrically opposed—Hussein still insisting that postwar Syria be part of a greater independent Arab nation, the French just as insistent that it come under French control—there had been little expectation of success. The first day's session confirmed this prognosis. After a tense three-hour confrontation on May 19, Picot and Hussein had parted ways even more intransigent than before.

It came as a shock, therefore, when the following morning Hussein had his interpreter read aloud to the European envoys a bold proposal: the king was now ready to accept the same future French role in the "Moslem-Syrian littoral"—presumably meaning the coastal, Lebanon portion of Syria—as the British were to assume in the Iraqi province of Baghdad. Since a victorious British army had recently placed Baghdad under military occupation, and the terms of the Sykes-Picot Agreement called for keeping the province under direct British control indefinitely, this Baghdad-Lebanon equation of Hussein's had the effect of suddenly ceding to the French most everything they were asking for in Lebanon. As Sykes reported to Wingate with what could only have been gross understatement, "Monsieur Picot received this very well and relations became cordial."

It was a remarkable achievement. Against all odds, Sykes had managed to make a crucial first cut through the great Gordian knot created by Britain's conflicting pacts and promises in the Middle East.

Yet for those familiar with Sykes's modus operandi there was something about this breakthrough that should have given pause. In contrast to his usual prolixity on all manner of topics, his full report on the Jeddah meetings, the most important diplomatic discussions between the Allies and King Hussein to date, ran a mere four pages, with Hussein's startling Lebanon concession dealt with in a single sentence. Additionally, neither Sykes nor Picot had pressed Hussein to commit his offer to paper, nor had they managed to obtain a copy of the pledge the king's interpreter had read aloud. Even those senior officials in the French Ministry of Foreign Affairs who had been fervently wishing for just such a resolution quickly began to suspect there was something altogether too neat about the deal struck in Jeddah.

Those concerns took tangible form when Stewart Newcombe arrived in Cairo on May 27 and walked into Gilbert Clayton's office. Both he and Cyril Wilson had been present for at least some of the proceedings in Jeddah, and had written up their own accounts of what had taken place. Newcombe also brought the written account of Fuad al-Kutab, Hussein's interpreter and the man who had actually presented the proposal. While they differed in specifics, all three indicated it had actually been Mark Sykes, not Hussein, who had first come up with the Lebanon-Baghdad formula. More troubling, the king appeared to have come away with a radically different idea from the Allied envoys of what that formula meant.

The most exercised over the matter was Cyril Wilson. "Although Sykes and Picot were very pleased at this happy result," he wrote, "and the Sherif had made the [Lebanon-Baghdad] proposition himself, I did not feel happy in my own my mind, and it struck me as possible that the Sherif, one of the most courteous of men, absolutely loyal to me and with complete faith in Great Britain, was verbally agreeing to a thing which he never would agree to if he knew our interpretation of what the Iraq situation is to be."

In his distressed—and rather repetitive—twelve-page letter to Clayton, Wilson detailed how he had repeatedly pressed Sykes to clarify exactly what Hussein intended by the offer, only to have his concerns brushed aside. Instead, Wilson reported, the entire affair had been marked by a breezy refusal on Sykes's part to get into particulars.

If less emotional, Newcombe's protest was in many ways more striking. His time in the Hejaz had been a difficult one, he had little faith in the Arab rebels as a viable fighting force, and yet the episode in Jeddah had left him perturbed. Central to his apprehensions was a conversation he'd had with Hussein's son Faisal, who had also been in Jeddah during the envoys' visit. In making his startling offer, Newcombe reported, "[Hussein] stated to Faisal very vehemently that he was perfectly willing to do this because Sir Mark Sykes, representing the British government, had told him to, and that as Sir Mark Sykes had advised him to leave everything in [his] hands, he felt glad to do so, having absolute trust in the British government."

From Newcombe's vantage point as a British officer, this assurance by Sykes, conjoined to Hussein's obviously limited awareness of what he was agreeing to, meant the British government now had a moral obligation to see the Arab Revolt through to the end. "Otherwise we are hoodwinking the Sherif and his people, and playing a very false game in which [British] officers attached to the Sherif's army are inevitably committed, and which I know causes anxiety in several officers' minds in case we let them down."

For all their unease, however, Wilson and Newcombe were either too diplomatic to call Sykes out directly, or too credulous to piece the whole scheme together. In actual fact, what had occurred in Jeddah was not a potential misunderstanding, but an intricate and very cleverly executed deception on Mark Sykes's part.

The cornerstone for that deception had been laid three weeks earlier, during Sykes's first visit to Arabia. In his similarly spare report of that trip, Sykes asserted that he had fully explained the Sykes-Picot Agreement to Hussein and Faisal, and won their grudging acceptance. While that wasn't at all Faisal's assessment of their meeting, the British envoy could be confident that British officialdom would surely take his word—a sitting member of Parliament and a baronet no less—over that of an erratic Arab tribal chieftain and his warrior son. Of course, there *was* at least one other person who knew that Sykes had lied about his candor during that first trip, and whom British officialdom just might listen to. This was T. E. Lawrence, but to Sykes's good fortune, Lawrence had now fallen from view, embarked on his northern trek, and he remained totally incommunicado during Sykes's crucial return visit to Jeddah with Picot.

It seems Sykes was inspired to his master deception by pondering the very issue that had made such a mess of the initial Picot-Hussein meeting on May 19: Picot's insistence that France enjoy the same role in coastal Syria as the British were to assume in Baghdad. At the time, Sykes had been deeply irritated by this linkage—he wanted to keep French and British desiderata in the Middle East quite separate—and he had left the discussions in a dispirited mood. However, once back on HMS *Northbrook*, the British warship that had brought the envoys to Jeddah and upon which they were staying, an obvious solution to his dilemma apparently occurred to Sykes.

The reason Hussein was resisting the Lebanon-Baghdad linkage was simply because he didn't want any French presence anywhere, not because he somehow knew Baghdad was slated to fall under permanent British control. The only way Hussein *could* have known that was if Sykes had told him of that clause in Sykes-Picot, and Sykes most certainly had not.

Instead, the last word Hussein had on British intentions in Baghdad was the vague accord he had reached with High Commissioner Henry McMahon back in late 1915. In their back-and-forth correspondence, McMahon had argued that, in light of Britain's economic interests in Iraq, the provinces of Basra and Baghdad would require "special administrative arrangements" within the future Arab nation, implying some measure of British control. In response, Hussein had offered to leave those provinces under British administration "for a short time," provided that "a suitable sum [was] paid as compensation to the Arab kingdom for the period of occupation." From all this, Sykes surmised, Hussein still held to the belief that any British presence in Iraq was to be along the lines of a short-term leasing arrangement, but that those provinces' ultimate inclusion in the greater independent Arab nation was secure. Indeed, on several recent occasions, Hussein had enigmatically assured his closest confidants, including both Faisal and Fuad al-Kutab, that he had an iron-clad British promise about Iraq's future "in his pocket," even as he refused to show them the actual letters from McMahon.

To Sykes, it opened up a tantalizing prospect. Between Hussein's ignorance of Sykes-Picot, and Picot's ignorance of the McMahon-Hussein Correspondence, it might be possible to forge an agreement in which both sides thought they were gaining the upper hand. The ultimate beauty there was that with both sides believing they'd essentially tricked the other, neither would want to risk scuttling the deal by getting into specifics. On that same afternoon of May 19, Sykes sent an urgent message ashore from the *Northbrook* asking that Fuad al-Kutab visit him.

At that meeting, Sykes impressed on Fuad the need to limit Hussein's overtures on the following day to just two points. The first, little more than a goodwill gesture, was for Hussein to announce that he would withhold support from a group of Syrian exiles who were soon to embark on an international lobbying campaign for Arab independence. The second, and obviously vastly more important, was for Hussein to cede to the Lebanon-Baghdad formula. To the nonplussed al-Kutab, Sykes was reassuring, repeatedly telling the advisor to leave the matter in his hands and he would see to everything.

Even so, Hussein was wary of agreeing to the plan. He finally relented, al-Kutab related, because "he knows that Sir Mark Sykes can fight for the Arabs better than he himself in political matters, and knows that Sir Mark Sykes speaks with the authority of the British government and will therefore be able to carry out his promises." Besides, Hussein reminded al-Kutab once more, he had "a letter from Sir Henry McMahon which promises all I wish. This I know is alright, as the British government will fulfill her word."

The following morning, Fuad delivered Hussein's proclamation as directed. That afternoon, as the *Northbrook* sailed out of Jeddah harbor, Georges-Picot could believe France had just been handed Lebanon, while King Hussein could believe he had just maneuvered France into accepting the future independence of all of Syria.

Even if not grasping the fraud that had been perpetrated, Wilson and Newcombe were sufficiently appalled by Sykes's cavalier approach to demand a full accounting in their letters to Clayton. Wilson urged that Sykes be compelled to put in writing what he believed had been agreed to in Jeddah, and that Hussein be told precisely what British intentions truly were. "If we are not going to see the Sherif through," Wilson wrote, "and we let him down badly after all his trust in us, the very 'enviable' post of Pilgrimage Officer at Jeddah will be vacant, because I certainly could not remain."

But when it came to political gamesmanship, the Arabs were not necessarily rubes themselves. With his secret knowledge of the Sykes-Picot Agreement, courtesy of Lawrence, Faisal was understandably aghast at what his father had agreed to, and quickly sought to turn the tables. On May 28, he issued a public proclamation to the Syrian people calling them to arms in the cause of Arab independence, while heaping praise on Great Britain for her aid in that mission. "Doubtless in doing so," Faisal wrote, "her sole object is to see in the world an independent Arab government, established and administered by the Arabs, without any modification of the boundaries of its country." The French came in for similar treatment. After thanking France for her past contributions in Syria, Faisal noted that "we are deeply grateful to her for having joined her Ally in recognizing our independence."

Far from an accord, then, the real result of Sykes's charade in Jeddah was a deepening of the gulf between Arab and Allied aspirations in the Middle East, a schism that was soon to have very ugly and lasting repercussions. In the interim, British policymakers reverted to the strategy they knew best: do nothing, see what comes next, and hope that it all works out in the end. When asked about Faisal's proclamation, so at odds with the agreement ostensibly reached days earlier, Sykes shrugged it off as a propaganda ploy meant for domestic Arab consumption. When Clayton finally got around to taking Wilson's and Newcombe's complaints to Sykes, it was with an escape clause built in. "I do not attach very great importance to this," he wrote of Hussein's apparent confusion, "as I think that events will be too strong for him and that, in the end, he will have to fall in line, or fall out."

One man who wouldn't let things drop was the dogged Cyril Wilson. In late June 1917, fully a month after he'd first sent his complaints to Cairo and received no satisfaction, he wrote to Reginald Wingate's deputy, Lieutenant Colonel Stewart Symes, urging that Sykes be made to write out a "short statement of fact" on exactly what had been agreed to at Jeddah. As Wilson pointedly noted, "there cannot be any harm in writing a fact [sic] which Sir Mark Sykes, I understand, states he clearly explained to the Sherif."

But paper trails had already caused enough problems in the Middle East, and Symes saw no reason to add to them. "The whole question is at present in a state of flux," he answered Wilson, "and depends entirely on various developments in the war. It is therefore quite impossible to lay down anything in the least definite, and all we can do is to keep the various factions in play so far as possible until the situation becomes more clear. It is a difficult position, I know, but there it is."

On a pathetic note, perhaps the stoutest defender of British honor in the wake of the Jeddah meetings was the man most victimized by them, King Hussein. Upon learning of the overture made on the decks of the *Northbrook*, Faisal got into a heated argument with his father, until Hussein finally cut him off with a rebuke: "These words are from a father to his son. Never doubt Great Britain's word. She is wise and trustworthy; have no fear."

. . .

IT WAS SUPPOSED to be a refuge, but Lawrence saw it very differently: a place of torment and pestilence, a nightmarish landscape to be escaped as soon as possible.

Running in a northwest-to-southeast diagonal through the borderlands of Arabia and Syria (modern-day Jordan), the two-hundred-mile-long Wadi Sirhan is more properly a geological depression, a hundred-million-year-old narrow drainage valley for when this desolate corner of the world had abundant water. In 1917, the wadi was where Auda Abu Tayi arranged to have his Howeitat kinsmen assemble to meet the tiny force he and Lawrence were bringing up from Wejh.

As Lawrence noted in *Seven Pillars*, with its ample water wells and relative lushness, Wadi Sirhan should have seemed a veritable paradise after their crossing of El Houl. Instead, at least two aspects made the place barely tolerable. The first was its poisonous snakes. There were horned vipers and puff adders and cobras, and they seemed to be everywhere— tucked beneath rocks, draped on bushes, coiled at water's edge—and as a man with an almost phobic fear of snakes, Lawrence never found a moment of true peace. Not that his fears were all that irrational; within days of arriving in Wadi Sirhan, three of the men who had made the passage from Wejh were dead from snakebites, and four others nearly so. Neither did the local "remedy" inspire much confidence, consisting as it did of binding a victim's wound with snakeskin plaster and then reciting Koranic verses over him until he died.

Then there were the banquets. Wadi Sirhan constituted the lower reaches of the domain of Nuri Shalaan, one of the most powerful tribal chieftains of southern Syria, and Auda had immediately set off to meet with Shalaan and gain his permission for the rebels' presence there. This left Lawrence to stand as one of the chief guests of honor at the nightly feasts of rice and mutton put on by the gathered Howeitat clans. As any westerner who has been their guest might attest, Bedouin hospitality can be so overwhelming as to border on the oppressive, and so it quickly became for Lawrence. Each night, different impoverished families competed to play host to the travelers from Wejh, and in Lawrence's lavish description of these banquets, what starts out as colorfully folkloric gradually veers toward the grotesque, especially when he lingers on the image of swollen-bellied children gathered at the periphery of the feasts, anxiously awaiting their chance to swoop in and snatch up any leavings from the communal tray.

"The landscape was of a hopelessness and sadness deeper than all the open deserts we had crossed," Lawrence wrote. "Sand or flint or a desert of bare rocks was exciting sometimes, and in certain lights had the monstrous beauty of sterile desolation; but there was something sinister, something actively evil in this snake-devoted Sirhan."

But Lawrence's torments went beyond reptiles and too much mutton. In those quiet days of waiting, with more and more tribes coming in to negotiate their alliance with the rebel emissaries, he became acutely aware of the cloak of deception he wore.

It was a deception that operated on multiple levels. On the day they had set out from Wejh, most of Lawrence's companions knew only the official reason for their journey: to rally the Syrian tribes and prepare for Faisal's advance north. Knowledge of the concrete objective, the capture of Aqaba, was held by only a very small handful of men. Indeed, it's possible the full plan was known only to Lawrence, that even Auda and Faisal hadn't the complete picture.

His romantic reputation aside, Auda was essentially a desert raider and, as such, primarily interested in plunder. Since there would be precious little by way of loot in Aqaba, Lawrence may well have kept matters vague at the outset, operating on the premise that at some point during the expedition he could convince Auda that Aqaba's capture would serve his long-term interests better than whatever more obvious spoils lay close to hand. As for Faisal, in the wake of Lawrence's departure from Wejh, he once again lobbied his British advisors for an early advance on Aqaba. Perhaps this was a ruse on Faisal's part, a way to further mask Lawrence's true destination from his colleagues, but it seems equally likely that the Arab leader did so because he hadn't been apprised of precisely what that destination was. Of course, these were mere tactical deceptions, made necessary by the exigencies of war, but it meant the ultimate onus of leadership—not to mention of possible failure and the catastrophe this would unleash on those around him—rested on Lawrence's shoulders alone.

What made all this infinitely more burdensome was the greater deception that lay beyond: the planned betrayal of the Arabs at the Allies' hands. It seems Lawrence had only grasped the full scope of this double cross at his meeting with Mark Sykes just before his departure from Wejh, and it clearly weighed heavily on him on the journey north. Of this, Lawrence obviously could confide even less in his traveling companions, and his sense of guilt became overwhelming in the face of the endless stream of tribal delegations coming into Wadi Sirhan to join the fight for Arab independence.

"They saw in me a free agent of the British Government," he wrote, "and demanded from me an endorsement of its written promises. So I had to join the conspiracy and, for what my word was worth, assured the men of their reward." It was a role that left Lawrence "continually and bitterly ashamed," for "it was evident from the beginning that if we won the war, these promises would be dead paper, and had I been an honest advisor of the Arabs, I would have advised them to go home and not risk their lives fighting for such stuff."

But of course Lawrence could do no such thing. As an alternative, he chose to remove himself from the scene. "Can't stand another day here," he jotted in his journal on June 5. "Will ride N[orth] and chuck it."

The choice of phrase, "chuck it," was an interesting one, for what Lawrence now proposed was a trek into the heart of Turkish-held Syria, a journey so hazardous as to be practically suicidal. In *Seven Pillars*, he would attempt to rationalize this decision by explaining that he wished to venture into the north to "sound its opinions and learn enough to lay definite plans. My general knowledge of Syria was fairly good, and some parts I knew exactly, but I felt that one more sight of it would put straight the ideas of strategic geography given me by the Crusades."

Implicit in this quest was the hope, slender though it might be, that if the Arab Revolt could be raised in the Syrian heartland, the imperialist designs of France might yet be subverted. Pressing up against this hope, though, was the far likelier outcome: that in revolt, the Syrians would fight and die for a cause already lost.

Lawrence's anguish at the situation was evident in the scribbled message he wrote Gilbert Clayton in the margin of his notebook. "Clayton. I've decided to go off alone to Damascus, hoping to get killed on the way. For all sakes try and clear this show up before it goes any further. We are calling them to fight for us on a lie, and I can't stand it." Figuring the notebook would eventually find its way into British hands should he die on his mission, Lawrence left the notebook in Wadi Sirhan and set off for the north in the company of just two guides.

It was to be perhaps his most audacious exploit of the entire war, a circuitous four-hundred-mile tour through enemy territory that carried him to the border of Lebanon and to the very outskirts of Damascus. The feat would win him a nomination for the Victoria Cross, Britain's highest military decoration, yet also endure as one of the most mysterious and least-documented episodes in Lawrence's life. This was very deliberately so. The sole report he would eventually submit to his superiors in Cairo recounting the odyssey would run to just four pages. In *Seven Pillars*, a 650-page book studded with exhaustive disquisitions on the flora and geological features of obscure desert basins, Lawrence's northern expedition is dispensed with in a few paragraphs and derided "as barren of consequence as it was unworthy of motive."

What is known about that journey is that, time and again, Lawrence secretly met with prospective allies in the Arab Revolt—tribal leaders and urban nationalists—only to be greeted with profound hesitation. It was the classic conundrum of guerrilla warfare: Faisal's rebels needed local support to pave their way into Syria, but the locals couldn't reasonably be asked to rise up without the aid and armed support of the rebels. In that riddle, and in how terribly wrong events could go if the right balance wasn't achieved, Lawrence felt the weight of his and Britain's deceit more keenly than ever.

From both a political and personally defining standpoint, Lawrence's most consequential encounter came toward the end of his journey, when he stopped in Azraq, a desert oasis in southeastern Syria, to meet with Emir Nuri Shalaan. Testament to Shalaan's preeminence in the region, it was to him that Auda Abu Tayi had sped weeks earlier seeking permission to use Wadi Sirhan as a gathering point for his Howeitat tribesmen. Since even before the Arab Revolt began, King Hussein had sent emissaries to Shalaan in an attempt to win him and his vast Rualla tribe to the cause, and for just as long the emir had nimbly danced along the knife's edge, hinting he might soon be ready to join the rebellion, only to then nudge back toward the Ottoman side. It wasn't just his authority that made Shalaan an imposing figure, however; in Lawrence's hand, the chieftain appeared almost the spectral personification of death itself:

"Very old, livid, and worn, with a gray sorrow and remorse upon him, and a bitter smile the only mobility of his face. Upon his coarse eyelashes the eyelids sagged down in tired folds, through which from the overhead sun, a red light glittered into his eye sockets and made them look like fiery pits in which the man was slowly burning."

But perhaps this somewhat overwrought description stemmed from something else about Nuri Shalaan. Despite his isolation in the desert, it seemed the Rualla chieftain was well informed on the various promises the British had made to Hussein and other Arab leaders in the Hejaz over the previous two years. By way of taking Lawrence's measure, Shalaan brought out copies of these conflicting documents, laid them before his visitor, and asked which ones he should believe. "I saw that with my answer I would gain or lose him," Lawrence recounted, "and in him the outcome of the Arab movement."

Lawrence counseled that Shalaan should trust in the most recent of the British promises. It seemed to assuage the desert chieftain, but of course simply brought a new measure of guilt to Lawrence's burdened conscience.

After that meeting with Shalaan, Lawrence returned to his companions waiting in Wadi Sirhan with an iron resolve to compel Britain to uphold her pledges to the Arabs. He would do so by personally leading the Arabs onto an expanded Syrian battlefield, a campaign that would enable them to lay claim to the lands they conquered and thus cheat the French of their imperial designs. "In other words," Lawrence wrote, "I presumed (seeing no other leader with the will and power) that I would survive the campaigns, and be able to defeat not merely the Turks on the battlefield, but my own country and its allies in the council-chamber."

This was, he admitted, "an immodest presumption."

LAWRENCE WASN'T THE only Western intelligence agent afoot in Syria that June. In fact, at one point during his impetuous reconnaissance trek to the north, he came within three miles of crossing paths with his old nemesis, Curt Prüfer.

Since returning from Germany in March, Prüfer had rarely left the comparative comfort of his desk job at the intelligence bureau headquarters in Constantinople. The grand partnership of German government and industry envisioned by Max von Oppenheim had largely withered on the vine, with German businessmen understandably loath to invest in a region grown more destitute and fractured by the day. Prüfer had instead spent much of his time trying to arrange for the publication of a new series of pro-German propaganda pamphlets, only to be beset with niggling queries from Berlin over printing costs and bureaucratic obstacles thrown up by obdurate Ottoman censors.

In mid-May, he decided to break from this tedious routine by conducting an extended inspection tour of the German propaganda centers and libraries that Oppenheim had established across Syria the year before. These field trips were also what made Prüfer a good intelligence agent, providing him with a firsthand view that often conflicted with the sugar-coated communiqués and cables that crossed his desk. Even so, on this outing he was in for a shock.

As often happens in war, by the spring of 1917 the outside world was gaining a rather clearer picture of what was happening inside the Ottoman Empire than the empire's own inhabitants. Much of that insight was coming from American consular officials who had begun vacating their posts following the break in U.S.-Ottoman diplomatic relations in April. In debriefings in Switzerland and Washington and London, these officials told of a land where hundreds of thousands of civilians had succumbed to disease or starvation, where vast territories were in a state of near-open rebellion, and where army units suffered desertion rates of 25, 30, even 40 percent. The more perceptive of these recent evacuees also reported on the growing friction between Turkish and German military units, a mutual antipathy that had occasionally led to violence, and of the general population's utter apathy, their most fervent desire simply for the war to end and life to become tolerable again.

Certainly, Prüfer had received glimmers of all this while in Constantinople. Even if downplayed, reports from the field told of food shortages and epidemics, of flagging morale among both the Turkish citizenry and soldiers. But none of that truly prepared Prüfer for the ravages awaiting him when he boarded an interior-bound train at Haidar Pasha station on May 21. Most telling from Prüfer's standpoint were the deprivations he personally had to endure on this journey. Gone were the special train cars put on for his comfort and the official banquets held in his honor. Instead, and despite being one of the most important German officials in the Middle East, his travel now was aboard packed and dilapidated trains that frequently broke down or were shunted to sidings for hours, even days, for no apparent reason, the only accommodation to be found in filthy and flea-infested hostels. The spare diary he kept of that two-month odyssey, brief entries made in a penciled scrawl, consisted of an almost unbroken litany of complaint.

Adding to Prüfer's misery, and rather epitomizing the ruin about him, was an intermittent toothache that steadily worsened until his entire jaw was inflamed. A dentist tentatively diagnosed scurvy, a disease now rampant in Syria and caused by a simple vitamin C deficiency. Until two years earlier Syria had been one of the great citrus-growing regions of the world, but in the face of a chronic coal shortage most of its fruit trees had been cut down to provide fuel for train engines.

Yet despite seeing all this with his own eyes, Curt Prüfer seemed determined to miss its import. As he reported to senior diplomats in Berlin, the reason his and Max Oppenheim's shared dream of pan-Islamic jihad had thus far failed to galvanize the Muslim masses was mostly just a matter of poor communication. "Hysterical propaganda that focuses on enemy atrocities are a waste of time," he wrote. "The peoples of the Turkish empire aren't stupid, they know what is going on around them."

Even with his criticisms, however, Prüfer failed to detect the fissures already cracked open all about him. He had frequently written that the Syrian Arabs were too cowardly to rise up against the Turks, and nothing he saw on this journey caused him to reassess that view. On June 3, while Prüfer was in Damascus, T. E. Lawrence was in a village a mere three miles away, plotting with an Arab nationalist leader on how to bring the Arab Revolt into the Syrian capital. Prüfer had been even more dismissive of the Jewish settlers in Palestine, calling them docile and obedient. June 12 saw the German intelligence chief staying at a crude little hotel in the Palestinian village of Zammarin, just one mile from the Jewish settlement of Zichron Yaakov that was the hub of the NILI spy network.

. . .

SARAH AARONSOHN'S VISIT to Cairo in mid-April had been planned as a very brief one, a chance to meet with her brother and for the two of them to coordinate NILI's activities for the coming months. On the next sailing of the *Managem*, Sarah and her chief NILI deputy, Joseph Lishansky, were to be slipped back ashore at Athlit and the spying campaign resumed. Instead, there had ensued such a string of bad luck—two abortive sailings, a bout of malaria that landed Sarah in a hospital for two weeks—that it seemed an open question whether she and Lishansky would ever get home at all. By the end of May, the pair were right back at their Egyptian starting point.

If Aaron Aaronsohn was understandably frustrated by these delays—he had never intended Joseph Lishansky to leave Athlit in the first place, and the spy network was surely foundering in both his and Sarah's absence—he was also experiencing a bit of a change of heart. A loner at the best of times, he nevertheless enjoyed his sister's companionship in Cairo and was coming to rely on her levelheaded advice in his battles with the British bureaucracy. He now decided it would be cruel to return her to Athlit after all. "I do not see the necessity of it," he confided in his diary on May 31, "now that the most precious time is past."

Convincing the iron-willed Sarah Aaronsohn of this, however, was an altogether different matter. When her brother broached the idea, her response was immediate and adamant: she was going back to Palestine no matter what. The agronomist tried a different tack. During her stay in Cairo, Sarah had become a familiar figure to many of the British officers her brother associated with, an object of admiration for the very dangerous work she was conducting. At the same time, some of these officers, imbued with an old-fashioned code of chivalry, had hinted to Aaron Aaronsohn that it was a tad unseemly for a woman to continue to face such "manly" perils. This view was most persistently put forward by Aaronsohn's erstwhile handler, William Edmonds, and Aaronsohn arranged for the EMSIB captain to raise it anew one evening while he and Sarah sat in the lounge of the Continental Hotel.

"Madam," Edmonds stiffly addressed Sarah, "the High Command has authorized me to thank you very much for all that you have done for us. They urge you not to return to Palestine. Egypt is open to you. You can stay here as long as you wish. What you have done up to now is valuable, and it is enough."

While thanking the captain for the offer, Sarah Aaronsohn instantly saw through the charade. Turning to her brother, she said, "If you know me, give me the means to return. If you don't provide them for me, I'll find my way back myself."

On June 15, the spy ship *Managem* sailed once more. This time it managed to reach Athlit, and both Sarah Aaronsohn and Joseph Lishansky went ashore. When Aaron Aaronsohn got the word, it provoked a complicated reaction, relief and regret intermixed. As events would prove, this latter sentiment was quite justified; he would never see either his sister or Lishansky again.

ON THEIR FAST racing camels, Auda and Lawrence set off ahead of the others to inspect the water wells of Bair. Following behind was the fighting force that had been painstakingly assembled in Wadi Sirhan over the previous three weeks: some five hundred tribal fighters, mostly Howeitat, ready to strike a blow against their Turkish overlords. All had left Wadi Sirhan two days before, June 18, in the highest of spirits.

As a consequence, what Auda and Lawrence discovered at Bair was deeply dispiriting. All three of the oasis's principal wells had recently been dynamited by the Turks, reduced to heaps of broken stones and still-smoldering timbers. By good luck, the charge they had placed on a fourth well a short distance away had failed to detonate, affording the rebel force just enough water to sustain themselves and their camels, but the larger message was a grim one: the Turks were onto them.

While it might seem counterintuitive, the desert is one of the more difficult places to keep one's presence a secret. Travelers are wedded to moving between available sources of water, and on a landscape where others are also constantly on the move, crossing a desert is rather akin to traveling a highway possessed of very few side roads. Among the tribes of southeastern Syria, a great many had heard of the rebel force being mustered in Wadi Sirhan by that third week in June, and inevitably, so had the Turks. By blowing the wells at Bair, the first principal water source west of Wadi Sirhan, the Turks hoped to block their enemy's advance before it even got under way.

While that mission had failed just enough to allow the rebels and their animals to stay alive in Bair, it cast grave doubt over the next proposed leg of their march. Seventy miles to the southwest of Bair stood the crossroads town of Maan, astride the Hejaz Railway and the strategic hub of the entire region. Lawrence's plan was to skirt below the heavily garrisoned town and continue toward Aqaba, but this scheme was dependent on finding water at Jefer, another series of desert wells just twenty-five miles to the northeast of Maan. The problem was that once the Turks in Maan figured out the rebels were heading for Aqaba—and at this point even "the most civilian owl could not fail to see that"—they could send a demolition team out to destroy the Jefer wells long before the rebels got there.

The key, then, was to devise a screen, to confuse the Turks both as to where the rebels currently were and where they might be headed. From Bair, emissaries were sent to area tribes with word that the rebel force was still organizing itself back in Wadi Sirhan; surely at least one of these tribes would pass this "intelligence" on to the Turks to curry favor. Simultaneously, small units of fighters were dispatched to conduct pinprick attacks throughout the region.

Lawrence had laid some of the groundwork for this screen during his earlier trip north. In early June, he had led a handful of local recruits and blown up a small bridge of the Hejaz Railway north of Damascus; that attack, occurring hundreds of miles from any previous action by the rebels, had so alarmed Turkish authorities that they'd briefly been convinced a local insurrection was about to get under way. For the expanded screening operation out of Bair, Lawrence chose to lead the most ambitious effort himself. On June 21, he and some one hundred fighters struck out from the oasis and made for the railhead town of Amman, 150 miles to the north.

It was to be a peculiar kind of exercise, and one that constantly put Lawrence's skills of persuasion to the test. Time and again, he had to stay his Arab companions from the pitched battles they desperately craved, reminding them this was meant to be a show of force, a game of bluff in which a destroyed railway culvert sent just as powerful a message to the enemy as a blown-up train. This wasn't at all the way the Arab tribesmen thought battle should be joined, but as they were scant in number and dependent on mobility, Lawrence was determined that they avoid protracted firefights or anything else that might delay their quick return to Bair. This imperative of speed, however, also had a nasty side effect; simply put, this was a force with neither the time nor the capacity to deal with prisoners.

While preparing the ambush on the Turkish garrison at Aba el Naam three months earlier, Lawrence and his companions had been inadvertently discovered by a wandering shepherd boy. Fearing the boy would alert the Turks to their presence if released, but with the shepherd increasingly distraught at being separated from his flock, the ambush party had finally resorted to a somewhat comical solution: they tied the boy to a tree for the duration of the battle, then cut him free as they fled. In their hit-and-run operations around Amman, the raiders hadn't the luxury of such consideration.

On one occasion, they encountered a traveling Circassian merchant. Unable to take him along as a prisoner but reluctant to let him go—

most Circassians were Turkish sympathizers—many in the raiding party argued for his quick execution. By way of compromise, they instead stripped the man naked and sliced the soles of his feet open with a dagger. "Odd as was the performance," Lawrence noted mildly, "it seemed effective and more merciful than death. The cuts would make him travel to the railway on hands and knees, a journey of an hour, and his nakedness would keep him in the shadow of the rocks till the sun was low." While the Circassian's ultimate fate is unknown, the merciful aspects of leaving a naked and crippled man out in the Syrian desert in June might reasonably be debated.

By the time the raiding party returned to Bair, Lawrence had every reason to feel confident. In response to their disinformation effort, the Turks had just dispatched a four-hundred-man cavalry unit to hunt down the phantom rebel force in Wadi Sirhan. Over the previous week, the Arabs had carried out a series of hit-and-run strikes across the length of southern Syria with no discernible pattern. By now, the Turks surely thought the next attack could come most anywhere, and were distracted from the still-distant target of Aqaba. With such confidence, the rebel force moved on the water wells of Jefer.

Sure enough, the Turks had destroyed the Jefer wells too, but with only slightly more efficiency than they'd shown at Bair. One of the wells was only partially collapsed, and a daylong repair effort restored it to use. While that project was under way, Lawrence received the most remarkable news of all.

A few days earlier, a flying column had been sent to rally the tribes residing in the foothills to the southwest of Maan and in the direction of Aqaba. Together, they had attacked the Turkish blockhouse at Fuweila, occupying a high point astride the Maan-Aqaba road. Initially that attack had accomplished little, the tribesmen easily driven off by the entrenched soldiers, but then the Turks in Fuweila had launched a reprisal raid. Falling on a nearby Howeitat settlement, they had cut the throats of everyone they found: one old man and a dozen women and children. Blind with rage, the Arab warriors had renewed their assault on the Fuweila blockhouse, overrun it, and slaughtered every soldier within. As a result, one of the chief Turkish strongpoints on the Aqaba road was suddenly gone, the path over the mountains virtually clear. Scrambling to action, the rebel force in Jefer raced for Fuweila.

Their excitement was to be short-lived. As they skirted below Maan on the afternoon of July 1, word came that a relief force of some 550 Turkish soldiers had left Maan en route to Fuweila that morning. That force was now somewhere on the road ahead of them.

It placed Lawrence in a deep quandary. With their greater mobility, the Arabs might be able to get ahead of the relief column and continue on toward Aqaba, but that would mean leaving a sizable Turkish force, already on the march, close behind them on the Wadi Itm trail—in effect, almost the precise scenario that Lawrence had persistently warned would be the result of an amphibious landing. There really was only one choice: to find the Turkish relief column and destroy it.

IT HAD BEEN nearly four years since William Yale sailed from New York harbor aboard SS *Imperator*, a "playboy" embarked on a tour of the Holy Land should any of his fellow passengers ask. Now, in mid-June 1917, he was returning to a city in the grips of a patriotic frenzy. Across Manhattan, buildings were festooned with enormous American flags, windows were framed with red-white-and-blue bunting, and a fevered excitement still carried on the air two months after President Wilson had brought the country into the war.

One reason for the sustained excitement may have been that it was still a long way off before war's more disagreeable aspects—specifically, dead and maimed soldiers—would begin to intrude on the festivities. Since 1914, Wilson had deliberately kept the American army near its paltry peacetime size as a roundabout way to defeat the interventionists; after all, with a standing army of just over 120,000 soldiers, about one-twentieth the size of any of the major European powers, what could the United States possibly contribute to the war effort? Most estimates were that it would be up to a year before an American army—now slated to grow to well over one million—might contribute to the European battlefield in any significant way.

Further slowing matters was evidence that, beyond the flag-waving, the American public was showing a marked hesitancy in signing on for the fighting and dying. Wilson had been under the impression that his high-blown rhetoric alone would serve to bring a flood of volunteers to the army recruitment centers, but it seems most of his countrymen got lost somewhere between his old boast that the United States was "too proud to fight" and his new exhortation that "the world must be made safe for democracy." By mid-May 1917, fewer than 100,000 young men had enlisted for this crusade, leading to the enactment of a draft law for the first time since the American Civil War. Consequently, when Yale stepped off his ship in New York harbor that June, one of his first errands was to register with the local Selective Service board.

The oilman could have harbored few illusions about what lay in store for him—as a twenty-nine-year-old single man with no dependents, draftees didn't come any more Class I than William Yale—and it was a prospect that filled him with dread. Part of it was that, as opposed to most of his countrymen, he had already seen the hideous face of modern war—not the slaughter in the trenches in France, but the equally grotesque spectacle of civilians dying en masse from starvation and disease in Syria. He'd observed subtler facets of it during his long slow journey across southern Europe to get home: the bread lines that had stretched for blocks in Vienna, the looks of crushing resignation among a company of French soldiers waiting on a train platform for transport to the front. He also undoubtedly saw exactly where military induction would take him. Perched as he was at the upper end of conscription age (thirty in May 1917, raised to forty-five just three months later), in combination with his college education and aristocratic pedigree, he would almost surely be shunted into an officer-training academy. Once there, given his business background and technical expertise, he would just as surely be further shunted along to the supply-and-logistics orbit of the quartermaster's office. And since the United States had only declared war on Germany, meaning practically everyone was to be sent to the Western Front, Yale would most likely spend his war "career" ticking off checklists at some supply depot well behind the lines in rural France.

This was not at all the future that the ambitious oilman saw for himself, and he was brash enough to believe that the four years he'd just spent in the Ottoman Empire might make him an attractive candidate for a more meaningful position somewhere in the governmental or military hierarchy. After spending a mere weekend at the Yale family's upstate New York retreat, reuniting with the parents and siblings he hadn't seen since 1913, William Yale returned to New York City and hit the hustings.

The result was demoralizing. Despite his calling on every business and college acquaintance he could think of, few had any suggestions for where an "Eastern hand" might fit into the larger scheme of things in a nation at war. He called on Socony headquarters at 26 Broadway, figuring that though their Middle Eastern operations were likely to remain suspended for the conflict's duration, they might find something else overseas for an employee who had served them so loyally and in such difficult circumstances. That plan fell through when, meeting with one of the Socony directors, the pugnacious Yale lambasted the company's recent decision to stop paying the salaries of their native employees in the Middle East, pointing out that this pittance for a corporation like Socony was life-sustaining for those trapped in the war zone. Alas, Yale discovered after being ordered from the office, his listener had been the author of that directive.

Despairing of finding anything in New York, he went to Washington, D.C., sustained by the thought that in the locus of power, surely someone would appreciate what he had to offer. As his calling card, Yale wrote up a detailed report on all he had seen and heard in Syria. "Three years of war," he wrote, "have reduced Palestine to a deplorable condition, the villages depleted by military drafts, devastated by cholera, typhus and recurrent fever, and typhoid has resulted in reducing the population [by] probably over 25%." The situation was even worse in Lebanon, he reported, where, according to one of his Turkish military informants, at least 30,000 civilians had already starved to death, and unconfirmed rumors put the figure at over 100,000.

Of possibly greater interest to his prospective readers was the oilman's attention to military matters. Yale had clearly put his long rail journey from Jerusalem to Constantinople to good use, listing a number of critical bridges and embankments along the line that, if bombed, would all but cripple the Turks' ability to bring supplies or reinforcements from Anatolia to Syria or Iraq. He also pinpointed the location of an array of critical German military installations along the route, including a wireless relay station in the Amanus Mountains made conspicuous by the Swiss chalet-style German barracks alongside it. "I saw also German aeroplanes and hospital units going south. One German aeroplane division of twenty-three aeroplanes, I was informed by the German captain in charge, was on its way to Beersheva." He was even able to report that between 150 and 200 German transport trucks were now carrying supplies to Turkish forces in southern Palestine "over a new military road which connects Jerusalem, Hebron and Beersheba," while tactfully omitting that this was the same road on which he had overseen construction for Standard Oil in 1914.

In recent weeks, Allied officials had started to glean something of conditions inside the Ottoman Empire from debriefings of the evacuated American consular officers, but these were nothing compared to William Yale's report. Even if three months out of date, it represented one of the most detailed and reliable analyses of the situation in Syria to emerge since the beginning of the war. On June 27, Yale strode into the State, War and Navy Building (now the Old Executive Office Building) next to the White House and dropped his report off at the offices of the secretary of state himself, Robert Lansing. He followed up with a personal letter to Lansing three days later.

After noting that "the disposition of Palestine will probably be one of the big questions to be decided" in any postwar peace conference, Yale suggested to the secretary that "if the United States of America is to play her part in the solution of a problem so intricate and important, her statesmen must have at their disposition reports of unbiased men who had a first-hand knowledge of the country and its people. It is for such service, whether it be in diplomatic or secret service work, or relief work in Palestine, that I am prepared to resign my present position with the Standard Oil Company of New York, and offer my services to the Government of the United States."

Perhaps his four years abroad left Yale blind to the complexity—to some minds, the hypocrisy—of the new Wilson doctrine. Yes, the American president fully intended to impose his notion of "a lasting peace" on the warring world—that had been his price for entering the conflict—but, reflective of his nation's isolationist core, this was to be done while involving the United States in as few long-term foreign entanglements as possible. As a consequence, the very item Yale imagined to be his ace in the hole, his expertise in enabling the United States to "play her part" in the Middle East, was exactly the sort of thing the Wilson administration hoped to avoid. Little surprise, then, that his overture to Lansing was met with a resounding silence. The baffled oilman then drew on an old Yale University contact to funnel his report to the head of the U.S. Army's Intelligence Department, only to meet the same response.

Out of desperation, Yale played what must have seemed his very last card. During his journey across Europe that spring, he had met with the British military attaché to Switzerland and asked about the possibility of joining on with British military intelligence. The attaché had not been at all encouraging but, impressed by Yale's breadth of knowledge on the Middle East, suggested that if no other options presented themselves once he returned home, Yale might call on the British ambassador to Washington, Cecil Spring-Rice. With the military attaché's note of introduction in hand, Yale did so on the morning of July 9.

Serendipity had an odd way of intervening at crucial moments in William Yale's life, but never in quite so unlikely a way as on July 9. In calling at the British embassy, Yale fully expected to be told the ambassador was away or in a meeting, the same brush-off he'd received from many other men far less busy or powerful over the previous month. Instead, he was immediately ushered into Spring-Rice's office.

"Where did you get your name?" the astonished ambassador asked by way of greeting. "My first wife was a Yale, one of the last members of the family in Wales!"

IT WAS LESS a battle than a massacre. As dawn of July 2 broke, the Arab warriors circled through the hills surrounding the pass at Fuweila in cautious search of the Turkish relief battalion. They found them in a mountain close just below Fuweila known as Aba el Lissan, encamped and still asleep along the banks of a stream. Incredibly, the Turkish commander hadn't taken the precaution of putting scouts on the surrounding ridgelines, enabling the Arabs to quietly spread out among the overhanging rocks and encircle their slumbering enemy. Once in position, they began to snipe at the men trapped below.

It became a ferociously hot day, the hottest Lawrence could ever remember in Arabia, and this greatly contributed to the desultory nature of the fight. Despite the overwhelming advantage afforded by their command of the heights, the Arab attackers found they could only lie upon the rocks to shoot down at the enemy for a few moments at a time; to linger any longer was to be burned through their thin robes, even to have skin peeled from their bodies in swatches. Into the afternoon, the erratic contest continued, the Turks below huddling in clefts along the stream for protection, the Arabs above them hopping from one overlook to the next in search of a clean shot.

By Lawrence's account, it was a flippant comment on his part that finally changed the battle's tenor. Overcome by the heat, he had sought refuge in the shade of a narrow gulley that also offered up a thin rivulet of water. He was found there by Auda Abu Tayi.

"Well, how is it with the Howeitat?" Auda teased, recalling Lawrence's past gibes at his tribesmen. "All talk and no work?"

Lawrence teased back, remarking that the Howeitat "shoot a lot and hit a little."

The remark seemed to enrage the chieftain. Flinging his headgear to the ground, he charged back up the hill shouting for his men to disengage and to take to their horses waiting below. Fearing his comment had so offended Auda that the Howeitat were now leaving the fight, Lawrence clambered up the slope to make amends. He found Auda standing alone and glowering down at the enemy. "Get your camel if you want to see the old man's work," Auda said.

Hurrying down to the protected hollow where the main camel-mounted Arab force had waited all day to make their charge into Aba el Lissan, Lawrence mounted his prized camel, Naama, and climbed to a nearby ridge. He was just in time to see Auda and his fifty Howeitat horsemen charge into the valley from an adjacent ridge at full gallop.

"As we watched," Lawrence recalled in *Seven Pillars*, "two or three [Howeitat] went down, but the rest thundered forward at marvelous speed, and the Turkish infantry, huddled together under the cliff ready to cut their desperate way out towards Maan in the first dusk, began to sway in and out, and finally broke before the rush."

The 350 camel troops were swiftly ordered forward as well. Among the Turkish infantrymen, trapped and exhausted and now being charged by a mounted enemy from two sides, any semblance of defense swiftly collapsed. Suddenly, it was every man for himself, and in Aba el Lissan that day, this simply meant death came quicker.

By his account, Lawrence missed much of it. Due both to Naama's speed and to his position at the fore of the camel charge, he had found himself well out in front of his attacking comrades; Lawrence had managed to get off just a few rounds with his pistol before Naama was shot dead beneath him, sending him plummeting to a rough landing among the rocks. When finally he gathered his wits about him, the battle was already winding down. To his chagrin, he also discovered that Naama hadn't actually been killed by the Turks; judging by her fatal wound, a point-blank shot to the back of the head, Lawrence had accidentally shot her himself.

The carnage in Aba el Lissan was as vicious as it was one-sided. Just two Arab fighters were killed in the attack, and a handful wounded. By contrast, of the 550 Turkish soldiers trapped in the valley, perhaps 100 managed to make their escape in the direction of Maan, leaving some 160 captive and another 300 dead or dying. As Lawrence would allude in *Seven Pillars,* some of these deaths were not the result of battle, but of the Arabs' thirst for vengeance for the killing of the Howeitat civilians several days before.

There now came another test of Lawrence's leadership. From his interrogation of one of the prisoners, he learned that Maan itself was very lightly garrisoned—and considerably more so now given the fate of the Aba el Lissan relief column. As word of this spread among the Arab fighters, a clamor went up for the force to double back and fall upon the railhead town; Maan offered up a golden opportunity for plunder, while the sad little port town of Aqaba offered nothing.

It was an absolutely pivotal moment, and Lawrence could feel the objective that had borne him these past two months slipping away. Even if the Arab fighters managed to take Maan, it would be a purely temporary victory; the Turks would counterattack in force, and that would see the path to Aqaba, now virtually clear, shut down forever. What's more, it would effectively mean the end of the fighting force he and Auda and the other tribal chieftains had so patiently cobbled together. By July 2, they had "no guns, no base nearer than Wejh, no communications, no money even, for our gold was exhausted, and we were issuing our own notes, promises to pay 'when Aqaba is taken' for daily expenses." Aqaba now had to be taken as a matter of survival.

With Auda's help, Lawrence at last managed to turn the warriors away from the easy promise of Maan. Both to put more distance between their men and that temptation and out of fear of attack by Turks or marauding rival tribes, they resolved to set out for Aqaba that same night. But this decision raised another, troubling issue: what to do with the enemy wounded? It was agreed that those able to walk would join their fellow prisoners and, watched over by a rearguard detail, be herded along in the direction of Aqaba. As for the twenty or so Turks too badly wounded to travel, they were to be left behind, placed beside the stream so that at least their imminent deaths might not come from thirst.

While the Arab warriors began breaking camp for the onward night march, Lawrence set off alone down the valley to where the day's slaughter had taken place. He hoped to gather enough coats or blankets off the Turkish corpses to make those being left by the streambank a bit more comfortable in their last hours, but he found that scavenging parties had already discovered the dead and stripped them naked. The scene, and Lawrence's reaction to it, was to lead to one of the eeriest passages in his autobiography:

> *The dead men looked wonderfully beautiful. The night was shining gently down, softening them into new ivory. Turks were white-skinned on their clothed parts, much whiter than the Arabs, and these soldiers had been very young. Close round them lapped the dark wormwood, now heavy with dew, in which the ends of the moonbeams sparkled like sea-spray. The corpses seemed flung so pitifully on the ground, huddled anyhow in low heaps. Surely if straightened they would be comfortable at last. So I put them all in order, one by one, very wearied myself, and longing to be of these quiet ones, not of the restless, noisy, aching mob up the valley, quarrelling over their plunder, boasting of their speed and strength to endure God knew how many toils and pains of this sort.*

At last turning away from the dead, Lawrence rejoined the warriors for the march on to Aqaba, now just forty miles away over the mountains.

IN LAWRENCE'S TWO-MONTH absence, the Anglo-Arab military campaign in the Hejaz continued in its usual fitful rhythm. Through May and June, British demolition parties, usually accompanied by bands of Arab warriors, made their periodic forays inland to do damage to the Hejaz Railway. Their reports noted the occasional success—a blown bridge here, a wrecked train there—but even more frequently complained of the unreliability and lack of discipline among their Arab confederates. Higher up the chain of command, British commanders remained exercised about galvanizing the rebels to finally carry out their blocking operation in the El Ula region northwest of Medina, but the sense of imperative for the scheme was gradually withering under the evidence that the Turks had no intention of leaving Medina. Faisal, now enjoying the title of Commander of Arab Forces, had instead set his sights on his march into Syria. Among those British officers privy to Faisal's fantastically ambitious blueprint for that advance—this from a man who had barely budged from Wejh in four months—enthusiasm tended to be restrained. "It is somewhat difficult to examine in any detail Sherif Faisal's plan," one such officer reported at the end of May, "which is characterized throughout by a remarkable freedom from conventional restrictions in regard to time, space, arrangements for supply, or the disposition and possible action of the enemy."

Looking over the reports from the field, Gilbert Clayton in Cairo filed a weekly status report on the Hejaz situation to the director of military intelligence in London. Throughout May and June, these memoranda were usually prefaced by the comment that very little had changed since the previous one. But if all remained static in the Hejaz—"satisfactory" was the word Clayton preferred—by late June, his spies inside Syria were reporting a rather dramatic uptick in rebel activity. By the time Clayton penned his report of July 5, these reports were coming in from all across southern Syria: "active hostility" by the Howeitat tribe near Maan; an attack on the Turkish garrison at Fuweila; a raid on a Turkish camel-grazing party near Shobek; a sabotage operation on the rail line outside Bir el Shedia.

"It is not known what are the present whereabouts of Captain Lawrence, who left for the Maan area or Jebel Druze area some time ago," Clayton noted in that same report, "but lately an Arab rumor came into Wejh to the effect that he and the small party with him had blown up a large iron bridge south of Maan. These activities in the Maan area are probably the outcome of Captain Lawrence's arrival in that neighborhood."

Gilbert Clayton had it only partly right. What he couldn't have known was that Lawrence and his Arab confederates were actually responsible for nearly all the actions in southern Syria he reported on that day, just as they had been for most of the other attacks across the breadth of Syria, some of them over three hundred miles behind enemy lines, that had taken place over the previous month. He also couldn't have known that on July 5, Lawrence was not in the neighborhood of Maan, but rather sixty miles to the southwest, negotiating the surrender of the Turkish garrison in Aqaba.

After the massacre at Aba el Lissan, Lawrence and the Arab warriors had raced toward the sea. As they crested the mountains and descended the Wadi Itm toward Aqaba, the fighters passed one empty Turkish blockhouse and trenchline after another, final proof of the brilliance of Lawrence's contrarian scheme. "The enemy had never imagined attack from the interior," he noted, "and of all their great works, not one trench or post faced inland."

In contrast to its dramatic rendering in David Lean's movie, the fall of Aqaba was somewhat anticlimactic. After a tense two-day standoff, with both sides running desperately short of food, the Turkish commander finally accepted that his situation was hopeless and surrendered the port on July 6 with barely a shot fired. With the white flag raised, the rebels raced into Aqaba on their camels and splashed into the sea in celebration of their audacious victory.

But for Lawrence, the long ordeal was not quite over or the triumph secure. There were now nearly twelve hundred men crowded into Aqaba, some six hundred Arab fighters and an equal number of Turkish prisoners, but desperately little food. He also knew that it would only be a matter of time—and likely a short time—before the Turks in the Syrian interior mustered a sufficient force to march over the mountains to retake Aqaba. Such an advance might be slowed by manning the mountain guardhouses with rebel units, but as Lawrence knew from past bad experience, relying on Arab tribesmen to hold defensive positions, even formidable ones, was never a safe bet. Just as vital as Aqaba's fall, then, was to now get word of it to the British so that supplies and reinforcements could be rushed in.

The next day, and accompanied by just eight warriors, Lawrence set out in the direction of Egypt, hoping to cross the 150 miles of desert that lay between Aqaba and the British lines at the Suez before it was too late.

July 6, 1917: In one of the most daring military exploits of World War I, Arab rebels under Lawrence's leadership captured the strategically vital port of Aqaba. © *Imperial War Museum (Q 59193)*

Auda Abu Tayi, a legendary warrior and Lawrence's chief ally in seizing Aqaba. © *Marist Archives and Special Collections, Lowell Thomas Papers*

The British and French hoped to deny their Arab allies control of Aqaba. Without their knowledge, Lawrence devised the audacious scheme for the Arabs to get there first. © *Marist Archives and Special Collections, Lowell Thomas Papers*

"We turned our Hotchkiss on the prisoners and made an end of them." As the war dragged on, Lawrence became an ever more pitiless battlefield commander. © *Marist Archives and Special Collections, Lowell Thomas Papers*

A primary target of the British and Arab rebels was the Hejaz Railway, the lifeline of the Turkish army. By his count, Lawrence personally destroyed seventy-nine bridges during the war.

The chessboard changes. The Turks had no answer when the British introduced Rolls-Royce armored cars to the desert campaign.

Faisal ibn Hussein (in the front passenger seat) and other Arab rebel leaders being transported across the desert, 1918

THREE PHOTOS: © *Marist Archives and Special Collections, Lowell Thomas Papers*

British Zionist leader Chaim Weizmann (left) and Faisal
ibn Hussein, June 4, 1918. The following year, with
Lawrence as intermediary, the two joined forces at the
Paris Peace Conference to call for a combined Arab-Jewish
state in Palestine. This effort was ultimately sabotaged by
British and French imperial machinations.

The "Big Four" at the Paris Peace Conference. Left to
right, David Lloyd George (Great Britain), Vittorio
Orlando (Italy), Georges Clemenceau (France), and
Woodrow Wilson (United States). Lloyd George and
Clemenceau made a secret pact to divide up the Middle
East before Wilson reached Paris. *Library of Congress*

The betrayal revealed. Lawrence on the balcony of the Victoria Hotel in Damascus, October 3, 1918, after the fateful meeting between Allenby and Faisal. The next day Lawrence would leave Syria, never to return. © *Imperial War Museum (Q 114044)*

"I imagine leaves must feel like this after they have fallen
from their tree," Lawrence wrote a friend one week before
the motorcycle accident that killed him. This is one of the
last formal portraits taken of Lawrence, in December 1934.
Bodleian MS. Photogr. c. 126, fol. 75r

Part Three

Chapter 14

Hubris

Do not try to do too much with your own hands. Better the Arabs
do it tolerably than that you do it perfectly. It is their war, and you are to
help them, not to win it for them. Actually also, under the very
odd conditions of Arabia, your practical work will not be as good
as perhaps you think it is.

T. E. LAWRENCE, ADVICE TO BRITISH OFFICERS,
IN *TWENTY-SEVEN ARTICLES*, AUGUST 1917

O n the morning of July 10, 1917, Gilbert Clayton was seeing to one of
his drearier tasks, composing the weekly status report on the Arabian war theater for the military intelligence director in London. As he
had done many times in recent months with only the slightest variation,
he prefaced the memo with the comment that "nothing has occurred of
great importance in the Hejaz since I last wrote," before providing a quick
rundown of battle plans yet to be acted upon, small successes that should
have been greater, opportunities squandered.

Shortly after the report went out the door to the telegraph office, a
tiny figure in a dirty Arab robe wandered into Clayton's office. Taking his
visitor for a local favor seeker, or perhaps an enterprising beggar boy, the
distracted general was in the process of shooing him out the door when
he noticed the familiar lopsided grin, the piercing light blue eyes. It was
T. E. Lawrence.

Sitting his emaciated subordinate down, Clayton urgently pressed
for details on all that had transpired in the two months since Lawrence
had set off into the Arabian interior and vanished from view. The general

then dashed off an excited postscript to his weekly status report: "Since writing the above and just as I send it to the mail, Captain Lawrence has arrived after a journey through enemy country which is little short of marvelous." There followed a brief synopsis of the capture of Aqaba, as well as of Lawrence's intelligence-gathering mission across Syria. "I have not yet been able to discuss his journey with Lawrence as he has only just arrived and is somewhat exhausted by 1,300 miles on a camel in the last 30 days. . . . I think, however, that you would be interested in the above brief sketch of a very remarkable performance, calling for a display of courage, resource and endurance which is conspicuous even in these days when gallant deeds are of daily occurrence."

Ironically, some of Lawrence's greatest travails in reaching Cairo had come in trying to navigate the British lines. The previous afternoon, he and his small band of escorts had reached the eastern bank of the Suez Canal, having made the 150-mile trek from Aqaba in an astounding forty-nine hours, only to find the British guardposts there abandoned (due to a cholera outbreak, Lawrence would later learn). Finding an operable field telephone, he repeatedly called over to the army's ferry transport office on the opposite shore to request a boat, only to be just as repeatedly hung up on. At last he reached a logistics officer who knew him from Wejh, and a launch was sent.

In that first moment of safety, two months to the day since he had set out from Wejh, Lawrence's strength finally gave out, and it was all he could do to drag himself to the Port Suez officers' billet at the Sinai Hotel. "After conquering its first hostile impression of me and my dress," he wrote, "[the hotel] produced the hot baths and the cold drinks (six of them) and the dinner and bed of my dreams."

His ordeal continued into the next day. Barefoot and still clad in his ragged Arab robes, Lawrence was repeatedly stopped and questioned by military police during his train journey to Cairo. His luck turned on the train platform at Ismailia when he caught the notice of a senior British naval officer who recognized him from his Red Sea crossings. It was a fortunate meeting; the military high command in Cairo was quickly alerted to what had happened in Aqaba, and by that afternoon the first supplies and reinforcements were being rushed to the rebel-held port.

On the Ismailia platform, Lawrence also learned of a major development that had occurred in his absence. Following his defeat at the Second Battle of Gaza, Archibald Murray had been removed from command of the Egyptian Expeditionary Force. His replacement, a cavalry general named Edmund Allenby, had arrived in Cairo less than two weeks earlier. Initially, Lawrence greeted this news with dismay. It had taken months of painstaking ministrations by himself and Clayton and everyone else at the Arab Bureau to even partially win over the prickly Murray to the idea of supporting the Arab Revolt. Now they would have to start over from scratch, and Lawrence envisioned many more months lost in the education of Edmund Allenby.

But upon reaching Cairo, Lawrence was to discover something else. Already, word of his exploits was spreading through the British military command, and to electrifying effect. Coming on the heels of the defeat at Gaza, the stasis in the Hejaz, and the ceaselessly grim news from Europe—another Allied offensive on the Western Front had failed, the French army was mutinying, the Russian government was collapsing— here was some genuinely cheering news, a sterling example of British daring and pluck. Even beyond the fantastic manner in which it had been achieved, Aqaba's capture meant the Arab war effort had abruptly leapfrogged 250 miles to the north and made the task of carrying that effort into Syria dramatically simpler.

Curiously, though, it was Lawrence's subsidiary feat, his long and perilous journey through the Syrian heartland, that seemed to most capture the imagination and accolades of his countrymen. Part of it was surely the romantic image it conjured, one with many antecedents in British military lore: the lone adventurer (never mind that Lawrence had actually been accompanied by two scouts) sneaking behind enemy lines in disguise and with a bounty on his head, his clandestine meetings with would-be conspirators, the threat of betrayal and tortured death stalking his every turn. Certainly it was this aspect that most inspired Reginald Wingate in recommending Lawrence be awarded the Victoria Cross, Britain's highest military decoration. As Wingate pointed out, what "considerably enhanced the gallantry" of Lawrence's exploit was that it had been conducted amid "a highly venal population" even with a £5,000 Turkish reward on his head.

Lawrence, as noted, minimized the importance of that trek. Indeed, the few details he ever provided on it were in an obliquely worded four-page report he wrote immediately upon his arrival in Cairo. Ever the strategist, however, he evidently realized that in the official reaction to his Syrian adventure, he had been handed a powerful instrument to further his goals. He deftly wielded that instrument when brought before the new EEF commander, General Edmund Allenby.

Given the elaborate decorum that existed within the British military of 1917, it's hard to imagine a more incongruous meeting than the one that took place at the Cairo General Headquarters on the afternoon of July 12. Nicknamed "Bloody Bull" for his explosive temper, Edmund Allenby was a towering man with the physique of a boxer gone slightly to seed, an intimidating presence even when not clad in his general's dress uniform.

On the opposite side of his desk sat the wraithlike Captain T. E. Lawrence, perhaps 135 pounds when healthy but now reduced to less than a hundred by the rigors of his desert exploits, dressed in a white Arab robe and turban and, by his own account (though it seems improbable), shoeless; Lawrence's uniform had been destroyed by moths during his long absence from Cairo, so he would claim, and he had yet to find time to replace it.

Lawrence surely knew something of Allenby's war record, including that it was a somewhat checkered one. During the British withdrawal at the battle of Mons in August 1914, Allenby had ordered his cavalry regiment to stand their ground before a much larger advancing German force, thereby enabling the rest of the beleaguered army to make an orderly retreat. Coincidentally, it was during that same battle that Archibald Murray, then the chief of the Imperial General Staff and monitoring the British retreat from a central command post, had fainted away from the tension. Much more recently, however, Allenby's star had been eclipsed at the battle of Arras, where he was criticized for being slow to take advantage of breaches in the German line to drive his men forward—a relative point, perhaps, in an engagement that saw the British advance less than two miles at the cost of 150,000 casualties.

As with Murray, then, Allenby's transfer to Egypt was meant as a demotion, but where this had induced a kind of crippling caution in Murray, Lawrence sensed it might spur something very different in Allenby. In the general's office that afternoon, he proceeded to paint a wondrously ambitious portrait of what the Arab rebels now stood poised to achieve. So long as Aqaba was quickly bolstered as the chief staging point, he explained, the Arabs could at last take their fight into the Syrian heartland. And not in any small way; in Lawrence's telling, there was now the opportunity to set the whole region aflame.

To complement the threadbare report on his Syrian spying mission, Lawrence had made a little hand-drawn map to illustrate his plan to the general. It depicted no fewer than seven prospective Arab forces attacking the Turks across the length of Syria, as far west as the Lebanon coast and as far north as the cities of Homs and Hama, one hundred miles above Damascus. While he cautioned in his cover note that "there is little hope of things working out just as planned," if even some aspects of Lawrence's blueprint came to fruition, the bulk of Turkish forces deployed across northern and eastern Syria would find themselves stranded, unable to advance or even to easily retreat.

There was a catch, though. For this grand Arab uprising to succeed, Lawrence told Allenby, it required a simultaneous British army breakthrough in southern Palestine. Once that had been achieved, the two forces could move north in lethal tandem, the Arab irregulars shutting down the Hejaz Railway and marooning the Turks in their garrison towns in eastern Syria, while the British army, their inland flank protected by the Arabs' actions, advanced up the western coastal shelf. In Lawrence's plotting, even the quick capture of Damascus and Jerusalem were within the realm of possibility.

But there was another small catch. The fighters who would serve as the crucial linchpin to this Arab strike force, the Bedouin of eastern Syria, traditionally trekked farther east in autumn in search of better forage for their camels, effectively leaving the war theater. To make use of these essential warriors, Lawrence explained, action would have to commence no later than mid-September, or in about two months' time.

It's not altogether clear how much of this extravagant vision Lawrence himself actually believed. Even if flushed by his recent triumph at Aqaba, he was surely still too much the pragmatist to imagine that all the inertia and tribal squabbling that forever shadowed the Arab Revolt would somehow now melt away. He'd also undoubtedly had enough experience with the British military to know that haste was not its strong suit. Most likely, in putting forward his grandiose scheme he saw the chance to win over the new British commander in chief—unschooled in the sluggish pace with which events moved in the region, eager to redeem his soldier's reputation in the wake of Arras—to his own vision of a joint Arab-British liberation of Syria. It was a vision Allenby would have to embrace or reject quickly, of course, since Lawrence had also set a ticking clock.

But if there was an element of bluff in all this, who could possibly catch him out? T. E. Lawrence was now a celebrity in Cairo, the magical manager of Arab tribes, as well as the only British officer to have personally taken the pulse of their potential fifth columnists inside Syria. Even if he knew those prospective collaborators were nowhere near ready to rise up in two months, it's not as if anyone else knew. Instead, so long as the almost inevitable delay tripped up the British timetable, his secret knowledge of Arab unpreparedness would remain safe, and in the meantime he would have forged an alliance—and a mutual dependency—that couldn't be broken.

In *Seven Pillars*, Lawrence all but admitted to this game: "Allenby could not make out how much [of me] was genuine performer and how much charlatan. The problem was working behind his eyes, and I left him unhelped to solve it."

And it was a performance that succeeded brilliantly. At the end of their meeting, the general raised his chin and announced, "Well, I will do for you what I can."

If he kept it low-key with Lawrence, Allenby let his enthusiasm be known to his superiors, including General William Robertson, chief of the Imperial General Staff and the overall coordinator of the British war effort. "The advantages offered by Arab co-operation on lines proposed by Captain Lawrence," he cabled Robertson on July 19, "are, in my opinion, of such importance that no effort should be spared to reap full benefit therefrom.... If successfully carried out, such a movement, in conjunction with [British] offensive operations in Palestine, may cause a collapse of the Turkish campaigns in the Hejaz and in Syria and produce far-reaching results, both political as well as military." So vital did Allenby view the scheme that he passed on Lawrence's concern of losing the eastern Bedouin to their autumn grazing grounds should there be a delay. "I therefore ought to be prepared to undertake such operations as may be possible with the force at my disposal by the middle of September."

Even Robertson, a committed "Westerner" loath to entertain ambitious plans in the East, was quickly sold on the idea; at the culmination of a flurry of cables between Cairo and London that July, he promised to immediately send Allenby as many as fifty thousand more troops for his upcoming Palestine offensive. It all marked an astounding turnaround in fortunes for the Arab Revolt. Just two months earlier, the rebels had been regarded as little more than a sideshow nuisance by Archibald Murray; now they were setting the timetable for the next British offensive in Palestine.

But the newly strengthened Arab-British alliance also signaled a change on the political front, one that General Allenby may not have appreciated or cared about, but that T. E. Lawrence most certainly did. Until recently, British planners had been pondering strategies to minimize the Arab rebels' role in Syria out of deference to their French allies. Now, by signing on to Allenby's plan—which really meant Lawrence's plan—the British military was setting on a course that completely ignored French concerns, and would eventually cast the whole framework of Sykes-Picot in doubt.

That was all a bit in the future, however, and in the interim, praise for Lawrence's exploits continued to come in from all quarters. Though he was found to be ineligible to receive the Victoria Cross (one of its stipulations is that the heroic deed must be observed by a fellow Briton), he was soon promoted to major, as well as named a Companion of the Order of the Bath, one of the highest levels in the British chivalric system available to junior military officers.

Amid his newfound celebrity, in early August Lawrence was asked to jot down his insights on working with Arabs for those British officers being sent for duty in the Hejaz, to share his secrets of success in a realm where so many others had come to crushing despair. The result was a short treatise he entitled *Twenty-Seven Articles*. Some of his recommendations were commonsense, while others must have seemed rather exotic to his pupils. "A slave brought up in the Hejaz is the best servant," he advised, "but there are rules against British subjects owning them, so they will have to be lent to you. In any case, take with you an Ageyli [tribesman] or two when you go up country. They are the most efficient couriers in Arabia, and understand camels."

Above all, Lawrence counseled his readers to shuck their English ways, to so totally immerse themselves in the local environment as to know its "families, clans and tribes, friends and enemies, wells, hills and roads."

Within the parochial British military culture of 1917, *Twenty-Seven Articles* had the force of revelation—and indeed, the tract continues to have profound influence today. Amid the American military "surge" in Iraq in 2006, the U.S. commander in chief, General David Petraeus, ordered his senior officers to read *Twenty-Seven Articles* so that they might gain clues on winning the hearts and minds of the Iraqi people. Presumably skipped over was Lawrence's opening admonition that his advice applied strictly to Bedouin—about 2 percent of the Iraqi population—and that interacting with Arab townspeople "require[s] totally different treatment."

AARON AARONSOHN AND Captain Ian Smith had never been close. From their first meeting, Smith, the EMSIB (Eastern Mediterranean Special Intelligence Bureau) liaison to the spy ships operating out of Port Said, had made little attempt to hide his low regard for the Jewish spy ring in Palestine. From that inauspicious beginning, Smith—"always an idiot" in the agronomist's estimation—had seemed to go out of his way to slight Aaronsohn and his confederates in ways large and small, as if it were the British who were doing a great favor to the Jewish spies rather than the reverse.

No amount of past insults, however, quite prepared Aaronsohn for those of July 1. Evidently irritated that Aaronsohn had complained of his shabby treatment to an officer in the Arab Bureau, Smith acidly told the NILI ringleader that his spies in Palestine "are no good. The work can be done much better by others."

Making the episode especially galling was that it came at a time when the British were piling on NILI's workload at every turn—and in ways that went far beyond intelligence gathering. In the wake of the sacking-of-Jaffa story in May, an international relief effort had gone up to raise funds for its Jewish victims. To the obvious question of how such funds might reach the needy within Palestine, someone in the British hierarchy hit on the just as obvious answer: the NILI network. And so long as the NILI opera-tives were distributing relief funds across Palestine, why not propaganda materials as well? And how about in their spare time, they also carry out sabotage attacks? At the beginning of June, plans had been drawn up to smuggle explosives ashore at Athlit so that a NILI team might blow up a crucial railroad bridge in the Jordan valley; toward that goal, Aaronsohn's chief lieutenant in Egypt, Liova Schneersohn, was now undergoing demo-lition training at a British army testing ground on the Cairo outskirts.

Aaronsohn had reluctantly agreed to each of these new demands put on his organization, seeing it as the price to be paid for British favor, but it made the insult from Ian Smith simply too much to bear. As he informed his allies in the Arab Bureau the day after that confrontation, since EMSIB apparently now had other and better operatives in Palestine, "I no longer had the right to endanger my people in continuing the work." Therefore, he was shutting down NILI.

Because it wasn't as if Aaronsohn lacked other reasons to feel grossly underappreciated that summer. At the core was the continuing mystery of just what his status was in Cairo, of where he and his organization fit into the larger scheme of things. In his meetings with Mark Sykes in April and May, Aaronsohn had learned that the British politician was working closely with two leaders of the English Zionist Federation, Chaim Weiz-mann and Nahum Sokolow, in London. In fact, during his time in Cairo, Sykes had urged Weizmann to come out to Egypt to spearhead the Zionist effort there but, in lieu of that, to appoint Aaronsohn as his local "repre-sentative." Aaronsohn had gone along with the plan out of deference to Sykes, even though he was quite at odds with the milder brand of Zionism of Weizmann and Sokolow—but then he had received absolutely no com-munication from either man since. So vague had his status remained, and so futile his own efforts to receive guidance from the Zionist Federation that, just days before his run-in with Smith, he had asked Gilbert Clayton to take the matter up with Mark Sykes. Even this, though, had yielded nothing.

Thus out of the loop, Aaronsohn also remained quite unaware that his cherished Zionist cause was actually making great strides in London—and largely through the efforts of the tireless if uncommunicative Chaim Weizmann.

The campaign to prod the British government into a public decla-ration in support of a Jewish homeland had recently undergone a major overhaul. At one time, Weizmann had stressed the effect that such a dec-laration would have on American Zionists, causing them to add their influential voice to those calling for an end to American neutrality and intervention on the side of the Entente; obviously, that argument had lost much of its luster with the United States' entry into the war. Also headed toward oblivion that summer was the parallel contention that such a declaration would spur Russian Jews to rally to the prowar government of Alexander Kerensky; with the chaos in Russia deepening by the day, Kerensky's problems were now far beyond the point where Jewish support might make much difference. In early June, though, Weizmann had found a potent new argument courtesy of the Central Powers.

As Weizmann explained in a June 12 meeting with Robert Cecil, the British assistant secretary of state for foreign affairs, for many months he had been hearing rumors that the German government was trying to enlist leaders of the German Jewish community to act as intermediaries for a prospective peace deal. Weizmann had long dismissed these rumors, but recently they had gained great credence; in fact, he told Cecil, he had heard that German Jewish leaders were now actively considering such a role, provided the kaiser's regime met their demand for a Jewish state in Palestine. This the German government was evidently contemplating, judging by the recent and unprecedented spate of articles in the German press in support of a Jewish homeland.

To the degree that any of this was substantially true, the message was plain—that if the British didn't play the Jewish-homeland card soon, the Germans surely would—and Robert Cecil was a quick pupil. The day after his meeting with Weizmann, he sent a confidential memorandum to his superior, Lord Charles Hardinge. "There can be no doubt that a complete change of front on the part of the German Government has taken place," Cecil wrote, "and that orders have been given to treat Zionism as an important political factor in the policy of the Central Empires." The purpose of that change, in his estimation, was to influence the opinion of international Jewry "and to utilize it in the interests of German propaganda against the Entente."

In hopes of averting this potentially calamitous outcome, Cecil explained, his recent visitor had put forward a helpful suggestion. "Dr. Weizmann concluded by urging very strongly that it was desirable from every point of view that His Majesty's Government should give an open expression of their sympathy with, and support of, Zionist aims, and should publicly recognize the justice of Jewish claims on Palestine."

With alarm bells over a possible German-sponsored Jewish state reverberating through the British Foreign Office that June, this was a suggestion that an increasing number of senior British officials were ready to heed.

If all this remained unknown to Aaron Aaronsohn, it was also unknown to those Arab Bureau officials who scrambled to put out the fire sparked by Captain Smith's comments of July 1. Instead, they were just trying to save Britain's most important spy network in Palestine from shutting down.

As part of a renewed effort to show Aaronsohn respect, Smith was forced to apologize for his comments, and the agronomist was soon given an audience with the new EEF commander in chief, Edmund Allenby. Their meeting took place on the morning of July 17, just five days after Allenby's discussions with T. E. Lawrence. In a leisurely conversation, Aaronsohn filled in the general on a variety of topics regarding Palestine, everything from its agricultural conditions to the fighting abilities of its Turkish garrison, and even provided character sketches of Djemal Pasha—"very much inclined to plot, and clever at it"—and the German commander in Syria. "The [commander in chief] listened with interest," Aaronsohn noted, "and questioned me intelligently, 'to the point.' He made an excellent impression on me."

In the afterglow of that meeting with Allenby, Aaronsohn may have felt he had at long last "arrived" with the British in Cairo. Then again, he'd felt that at various other times over the preceding seven months. The problem was, with the British forever striving to keep all options open, reluctant to ever give anyone either a positive or negative straight answer, there really was no such thing as having "arrived," the hearty embrace avoided for the cautious pat on the back. This was compounded in Aaronsohn's case by the new machinations in London over a possible declaration of support for a Jewish homeland, a generalized anxiety within much of the British government over where that might lead. As a result, the goal was to keep Aaronsohn happy but in limbo, to maintain that fine balance between encouraging his efforts and remaining circumspect as to their ultimate reward.

Fortunately, the British could rely on a man with considerable skill at such things, Reginald Wingate. "I gather," Wingate wrote a senior Foreign Office diplomat on July 23 upon learning of the government's latest tentative overture to the British Zionists, "that the matter is by no means decided, and that you wish me to keep Aaronsohn satisfied without telling him anything very definite. This has been done."

ON JULY 16, the captain of the British troopship HMS *Dufferin* was told to stand by at Port Suez in order to transport an important official down the Red Sea coast to Jeddah. The next morning, the ship's crew caught first sight of their distinguished guest when twenty-eight-year-old T. E. Lawrence sauntered up the gangway. It was a long way from the day, eight months earlier, when Lawrence had walked up another naval ship's gangway in Yenbo harbor only to be soundly rebuked for his unkempt uniform and insolent manner.

One measure of how greatly his stock had risen in the wake of Aqaba was the mission he was undertaking to Jeddah. In his discussions with Generals Allenby and Clayton, Lawrence had emphatically—and perhaps quite exaggeratedly—told of the abiding esteem with which the Syrians held Faisal ibn Hussein; they saw him as the Arabs' overall military commander, he had explained, and it was under his banner that they would rise in revolt. As with most everything else Lawrence stated in Cairo that July, his superiors had little way of either confirming or refuting this assertion, it simply becoming part of the narrative of what lay in store once the battle for Syria was joined.

From this, Lawrence saw the opening to go one better: to fully coordinate the joint Arab-British offensive in Syria—and, not coincidentally, to permanently weld the fortunes of the Arab cause to those of the British army—why not place Faisal and his forces directly under Allenby's military command? Lawrence had gained quick approval of this idea in Cairo, but there remained a huge potential roadblock: King Hussein. With his reputation for irascibility, along with his jealous efforts to control the rebel movement, it seemed highly likely the Hejazi king would reject the suggestion out of hand. Then again, he might just listen to Faisal's most trusted British advisor and the "hero of Aqaba." In short order, Lawrence found himself aboard the *Dufferin* bound for a meeting with Hussein.

But the mission to Jeddah was only the most visible sign of the young captain's new and profound influence over British policy in the region. Behind the scenes, Lawrence had already laid the groundwork for a dramatic restructuring of the British military presence in Arabia, one tailored to his specifications. As he rather immodestly explained in *Seven Pillars*, he had put the argument to Gilbert Clayton thus: "Aqaba had been taken on my plan by my effort. There was much more I felt inclined to do—and capable of doing—if he thought I had earned the right to be my own master."

During their week together in Cairo, Clayton had agreed to most of his subordinate's suggestions. With the war in the Hejaz essentially over—though the Turks still controlled Medina, they had now lost all offensive capability—the long and futile campaign to block the Hejaz Railway at El Ula could be brought to a merciful end. For the same reason, the main rebel base at Wejh was now to be virtually shuttered, with both its Arab forces and British logistics officers brought up to Aqaba. Assuming the role of de facto general, Lawrence plotted out the future deployments of those Arab armies to remain in the Hejaz, and worked up a list of the British army personnel to be retained, reassigned, or let go. Clayton had drawn the line, however, on Lawrence's bold proposal that he be given overall command at Aqaba, pointing out that having a junior officer order about his superiors just wasn't the British way. Instead, they jointly settled on one of Cyril Wilson's deputies, Major Pierce Joyce, for the Aqaba post, an easygoing and unambitious officer unlikely to get in Lawrence's way.

Nothing, however, more exemplified Lawrence's changed status than his reunion with Colonel Wilson in Jeddah. After Lawrence's first visit to Arabia eight months earlier, Wilson had angrily commented to Clayton that the arrogant junior officer "wants kicking, and kicking *hard*," and had tried to prevent his return to Arabia on even a temporary basis. By July 1917, however, the colonel had come to see Lawrence, now in the process of being promoted to major, as both an ally and probably the most important British field officer operating in the Hejaz.

Just prior to Lawrence's arrival in Jeddah, Wilson had received a memorandum from Clayton outlining the sweeping personnel changes being contemplated for the region, pointedly noting that he had come to these ideas in consultation with Captain Lawrence. This detail made one feature of the memorandum all the more striking: pushed aside was Stewart Newcombe, still the officially designated head of the British military mission to the Hejaz.

Far more than to anyone else, it was to Stewart Newcombe that Lawrence owed his position in the Middle East. But in Lawrence's cold-eyed view, war was war, and whatever sense of gratitude he felt for his mentor couldn't stand in the way of its conduct. Newcombe had endured a contentious tenure in the Hejaz, never quite adjusting to the Arabs' mysterious approach to war-making, and in myriad reports had complained bitterly of their lack of discipline and reliability. As Lawrence explained to Cyril Wilson upon his arrival in Jeddah, it had been decided that Newcombe would now be taken off the front and relegated to a rearguard role, effectively demoted. A surprised Wilson quickly acquiesced.

That same evening, Lawrence and Wilson met with King Hussein. It was Lawrence's first audience with the king, and he found him both charming and personable. That assessment may have been helped by Hussein's quick acceptance of the proposal to place Faisal and his army under Allenby's direct command.

A very different matter arose the following morning when Hussein summoned Lawrence to his Jeddah palace for a private meeting. With uncharacteristic bluntness, the king brought the conversation to a topic that had become something of a personal obsession: his meetings back in May with Mark Sykes and François Georges-Picot.

While the controversy over what had or had not been agreed to at those meetings continued to find small echo in certain branches of the British government, its import had been diminished by the pace and urgency of other events. Surely adding to its waning effect was the polite tone adopted by dissident eyewitnesses like Cyril Wilson, with his couched language alluding to "possible misunderstandings." It was not at all the tone Lawrence would adopt, and what had taken Wilson many discursive pages to relate, he did in less than one: "The main points," he cabled Clayton after his second meeting with Hussein, "are that he had altogether refused to permit any French annexation of Beirut and the Lebanon. . . . He is extremely pleased to have trapped M. Picot into the admission that France will be satisfied in Syria with the [same] position Great Britain desires in Iraq. . . . In conclusion the Sherif remarked on the shortness and informality of conversations, the absence of written documents and the fact that the only change in the situation caused by the meeting was the French renunciation of the ideas of annexation, permanent occupation, or suzerainty of any part of Syria."

Whether due to its brevity or the new celebrity of its author, within days that report was finding its way onto the desks of the seniormost officials of the British government. It had the effect of instantly resurrecting the debate over Britain's web of conflicting promises in the Middle East—as well as Mark Sykes's singular role in spinning that web.

But Lawrence's mission to Arabia was not quite done. While he was still in Jeddah, word came from Cairo that according to a reliable informant, Lawrence's chief partner in the Aqaba campaign, Auda Abu Tayi, was now secretly negotiating with the Turks to switch sides. Lawrence's immediate reaction was defensive—he suggested that perhaps it was actually a ruse on Auda's part to lull the Turks into inaction—but he evidently had less confidence in that theory than he let on. Within hours, he was on board a ship bound for Aqaba and a face-to-face confrontation with Auda.

Trekking inland on a fast camel, Lawrence found the Howeitat chieftain along with his two chief lieutenants, both also named by the informant as prospective traitors, in a tent outside the village of Guweira. For many hours they passed as reunited friends, until Lawrence invited Auda and one of the other conspirators to join him for a walk. Once they were alone, he challenged the two men with what he had been told. "They were anxious to know how I had learnt of their secret dealings," Lawrence recounted, "and how much more I knew. We were on a slippery ledge."

Indeed, a ledge that conceivably could have been fatal for Lawrence. Instead, drawing on his extraordinary skill in knowing how to converse with Arabs in even these minefield circumstances, he put on an elaborate performance—sympathy, flattery, and ridicule all fused into one—to first disarm and then win the men back to the rebel side. Once returned to Aqaba, Lawrence cabled Cairo that the business with Auda amounted to little more than a misunderstanding, that all was now "absolutely satisfactory."

As Lawrence later admitted, he frequently shaved the facts in what he passed on to Cairo about the Arab Revolt and its leaders, but suggested it was really to everyone's benefit. "Since [British] Egypt kept us alive by stinting herself, we must reduce impolitic truth to keep her confident and ourselves a legend. The crowd wanted book-heroes."

And like any good performer, Lawrence gave the crowd what they wanted.

ONCE THE MATTER of his Welsh ancestry got sorted out, William Yale and the British ambassador to the United States settled down to business.

In all likelihood, Yale had rather low expectations of what Cecil Spring-Rice might be able to provide him by way of job prospects. After all, the British already had an extensive intelligence apparatus devoted to the Middle East. But William Yale was canny enough to realize he had something to offer that very few others did: an oil connection. Over the previous four years, he had canvassed vast stretches of Palestine looking for potential oil deposits for Standard Oil of New York. Through office memoranda, he also knew where else across the Ottoman Empire his company had sought or obtained concessions. In the postwar world, who was to know if the occupying power in these regions would recognize the Socony concessions? Certainly if that occupying power had already publicly stated that future oil exploration and extraction was to be regarded as a matter of national security—a power like Great Britain, for instance—it seemed entirely possible it might toss out Socony's claims in favor of development by one of its own national syndicates. If so, having someone on board who had seen the preexisting maps and geological surveys could save a lot of time and trouble.

Whatever the motive, Ambassador Spring-Rice was sufficiently intrigued by his young visitor to ask that Yale drop off at the embassy a copy of his report on conditions in Syria. This Yale did the very next day, along with a two-page addendum noting the location of all principal German military installations in Jerusalem, with those locations further pinpointed on a map.

If Yale's Syria report had failed to interest American officials, the British reaction was quite different. The ambassador thought enough of it to rush a copy directly to Foreign Secretary Balfour, which drew an equally swift response from London; provided William Yale could obtain a draft waiver from the U.S. War Department, the secret cable instructed, Spring-Rice was to offer the twenty-nine-year-old oilman a lieutenant's commission in the British army, "with view to subsequent employment as intelligence officer to Egypt. His information is sure to be of value. Please take necessary action and wire result."

The required War Department waiver should have been little more than a formality now that the United States and Great Britain were war-time allies. But it was not, it turned out, such a formality in William Yale's case. That's because after languishing apparently unread at the State Department for over a month, his Syria report had finally landed on the desk of someone intrigued by its contents. That person was a man named Leland Harrison, the special assistant to the secretary of state, but that title didn't begin to convey the actual power he wielded.

The thirty-four-year-old Harrison enjoyed a similar Yankee blue-blood background to Yale's. After being educated at Eton and Harvard, he'd joined the U.S. diplomatic corps and held a succession of posts at some of the most important American overseas missions. His swift rise had been cemented when Secretary of State Robert Lansing brought him to Washington in 1915, where Harrison quickly gained a reputation as Lansing's most trusted lieutenant.

Both fierce Anglophiles, Lansing and Harrison had shared a deepening disenchantment with Woodrow Wilson's commitment to American neutrality in the war. Another source of Lansing's favor for Harrison was undoubtedly his subordinate's profound sense of discretion. One State Department staffer would say of Leland Harrison that "he was positively the most mysterious and secret man I have ever known. . . . He was almost a human sphinx, and when he did talk, his voice was so low that I had to strain my ears to catch the words."

Where this became significant was that prior to American entry in the war, Lansing had acted as the leader of a virtual shadow government within the Wilson administration, a secretive cabal that quietly maneuvered for intervention on the side of the Entente. Just how secretive was indicated by Lansing's creation of something called the Bureau of Secret Intelligence in 1916. In hopes of uncovering evidence of German treachery that would make the argument for intervention irresistible, the bureau's special agents spied on diplomats and businessmen from the Central Powers residing in the United States, an activity that obviously undercut Wilson's public vow of impartiality and would have infuriated other branches of government had they been told. But they weren't told. Instead, Lansing had used State Department discretionary funds to create the bureau, enabling it to operate without the approval or even the knowledge of Congress or most of the rest of Wilson's cabinet. Pulling Leland Harrison from the Latin American division, Lansing had placed his young protégé in charge of this "extra-legal" new office, tasked to overseeing "the collection and examination of all information of a secret nature."

While this element of conspiracy within the State Department had been somewhat mooted by American entry into the war, it provided Harrison with a precedent when, upon reading William Yale's Syria report, it occurred to him that it might be very useful for the United States to have its own source of intelligence in the Middle East. The snag was that such an enterprise fell out of the purview of the existing domestic intelligence agencies and, with the United States not at war with Turkey, beyond the scope of the army intelligence division as well. The solution was to bring Yale in under the umbrella of the Bureau of Secret Intelligence; to that end, he was summoned to the State Department in early August.

At that meeting, Harrison put forward a remarkable proposition: Yale would return to the Middle East as a "special agent" for the State Department. At a salary of $2,000 a year plus expenses, his mission would be to monitor and report on whatever was happening that might be of interest to the American government—or, perhaps more accurately, of interest to Leland Harrison. From his base in Cairo, Yale would send weekly dispatches through the American embassy's diplomatic pouch to Washington, where they would be routed exclusively to Harrison's attention. Unsurprisingly, Yale quickly accepted the offer. On August 14, and under Secretary Lansing's signature, he was named the State Department's special agent for the Middle East.

After a brief trip home to see his family in Alder Creek, on August 29 Yale boarded USS *New York* in New York harbor for another transatlantic crossing. En route to Cairo, he was to stop off in London and Paris to take a sounding of those British and French officials most directly involved with Middle Eastern affairs. As Harrison cabled to the American ambassador in London, "[Yale] is to keep us informed of the Near Eastern situation and, should the occasion arise, may be sent on trips for special investigation work. He is favorably known to the British authorities, who offered him a commission. Please do what you can to put him in touch with the right authorities."

In the second decade of the twenty-first century, it is difficult to fully grasp the utter provincialism of the United States as it entered World War I in 1917. Not only was its standing army one-twentieth the size of Germany's, but it was dwarfed in size by even some of Europe's smallest actors, including Romania, Bulgaria, and Portugal. In 1917, the entire Washington headquarters staff of the State Department fit into one wing of a six-story building adjacent to the White House, a structure it shared with the command staff of both the Departments of Navy and Army.

Those examples notwithstanding, perhaps more remarkable is this: for most of the remainder of the war, the American intelligence mission in the Middle East—a mission that would include the analysis of battlefield strategies and regional political currents, the interviewing of future heads of state, and the gathering of secrets against governments both friendly and hostile—would be conducted by a single twenty-nine-year-old man with no military, diplomatic, or intelligence training. To these deficiencies, William Yale could actually think of a few more: "I lacked a historical knowledge of the background of the problems I was studying. I had no philosophy of history, no method of interpretation, and very little understanding of the fundamental nature and function of the [regional] economic and social system."

Not that any of this caused him undue anxiety. An exemplar of the American can-do spirit, William Yale also held to the belief, quite common among his countrymen, that ignorance and lack of experience could actually bestow an advantage, might serve as the wellspring for "originality and boldness." If so, he promised to be a formidable force in the Middle East.

AARON AARONSOHN AND T. E. Lawrence had first crossed paths on February 1, 1917. That encounter made little impression on either man, save a quick note in Aaronsohn's diary that he'd found Captain "Laurens" knowledgeable but conceited. Their next meeting, on August 12 of that year, was one both would remember for a long time. In the interim, each had become a personality to reckon with in Cairo, Lawrence for his exploits in Arabia, Aaronsohn for his contribution to the British war effort through his NILI spy ring. Of course, both had also gained reputations for being outspoken in their views on the future of the Middle East. Their talk at the Arab Bureau offices quickly degenerated into mutual hostility.

Lawrence may have been alerted to the tone their conversation would take by an incendiary paper Aaronsohn had penned a few weeks earlier. By August 1917, with the specter of official British support for a Jewish homeland in Palestine inching closer to reality, even the more radical leaders of international Zionism had adopted the soothing language of conciliation: whatever the future political framework in Palestine, they stressed, the Jews would live in peaceful coexistence with their Arab and Christian neighbors, the fight against Turkish oppression a cause they all shared.

No such placating words were forthcoming from Aaron Aaronsohn. In his position paper, soon to be excerpted in the *Arab Bulletin*, the agronomist inveighed against the "squalid, superstitious, ignorant" Palestinian serfs known as the fellaheen, freely acknowledged that at times they had been forcibly removed from the land by Jewish settlers—and would be again if he had his way. As to the accusation that Jews kept themselves apart from their Arab neighbors, Aaronsohn not only confirmed the charge, but wrote, "We are glad of it. From national, cultural, educational, technical and mere hygienic points of view, this policy has had to be strictly adhered to; otherwise the whole Jewish Renaissance movement would fail." As a cautionary tale, he pointed to the alleged educational shortcomings in the assimilationist Jewish settlement of Rosh Pinah, which he attributed to the "unavoidably degrading effect that continued contact with the uneducated fellaheen had on the Jewish youth."

Surely most upsetting to the mainstream Zionist leaders and their British supporters, however, were his comments on the Arab Revolt. In paving the way for official support for a Jewish homeland, and in anticipation of Arab resistance to the idea, British officials from Mark Sykes on down had been energetically coaxing the Zionists to voice their solidarity with the Arab cause. Chaim Weizmann had led this chorus from London, but in Cairo, no one had given Aaronsohn the playsheet.

"[The Palestinian Jews] have no interest, and still less confidence, in the Arab Revolt," he wrote. "They are not in a position to take up arms against the Turk, and they would hesitate to join the Arabs, even if they were in a position to do it. So far as we know the Arabs, the man among them who will withstand a bribe is still to be born. . . . In order to help to defeat the Turk, [the Jews] will readily join the British forces, but it is doubtful whether they will ever trust the Arabs."

Hardly words to delight T. E. Lawrence, the self-appointed defender of that revolt in the West, but at their meeting, Aaronsohn seemed almost to go out of his way to provoke Lawrence further. The ultimate future of Palestine, he explained, was not a British protectorate in which a Jewish minority would be protected, but a de facto Jewish nation. This would be achieved both politically and economically, with Zionists simply buying up all the land between Gaza and Haifa and forcing the fellaheen from the land. Lawrence's response was equally blunt. The Jews in Palestine had two choices, he told the agronomist: either coexist with the Arab majority or see their throats cut.

"It was an interview without any evidence of friendliness," Aaronsohn noted in his diary with considerable understatement. "Lawrence had too much success at too early an age. He has a very high estimation of himself. He is lecturing me on our colonies, on the spirit of the people, on the feelings of the Arabs, and we would do well in being assimilated by them, etc. While listening to him I could almost imagine that I was attending the lecture of a Prussian scientific anti-Semite expressing himself in English. . . . He is openly against us. He must be of missionary stock."

But Lawrence was only the latest addition to the roster of people irritating Aaron Aaronsohn just then. Despite the peacemaking efforts of various British officers, a three-month-old feud with the anti-Zionist Jewish Committee in Alexandria raged unabated, and the agronomist was still being virtually ignored by Chaim Weizmann's Zionist Federation in London. So infuriated was Aaronsohn at the lack of respect being shown him from London that just days after his encounter with Lawrence, he wrote two long letters to Weizmann complaining of his treatment and, once again, threatening to disband NILI. When he repeated this threat to Reginald Wingate, it sparked another worried cable to the Foreign Office.

"It might help matters if Mr. Aaronsohn were to receive without delay the support for which he has asked," Wingate wrote Secretary Balfour on August 20. "An additional reason for not alienating him, and one which may perhaps appeal to you, is that the military authorities attach importance to retaining the use of the organization which he has created in Palestine. He is in a position to destroy this organization, and there is little doubt that, in his present frame of mind, he will be tempted to do so unless some concession is made to his views. How far his difference with the Zionists in England is due to questions of principle and how far to wounded susceptibilities I am unable to tell."

Shortly afterward, while riding his bicycle through the streets of Cairo one evening, Aaronsohn came up with a new idea: if the British Zionists wouldn't clarify matters with him, then he would go to Britain and force them to. When he put this plan to his British handlers, they readily concurred, no doubt relieved at the prospect of placing some distance between the NILI network and its potentially destructive creator. On September 13, Aaronsohn left Egypt bound for Marseilles.

But consumed by his myriad squabbles, as well as his need for recognition, it seems to have only fitfully occurred to the scientist that he was engaging in extremely risky behavior for someone who headed a clandestine spy ring. He also appeared to have quite forgotten the cover story designed to keep his family and coconspirators in Palestine safe, that as far as Ottoman authorities knew, he'd been lifted off a boat en route to the United States and was presumably cooling his heels in a British internment camp. Instead, Aaronsohn's name had now appeared in an array of official reports circulating between Cairo, London, and Paris. Worse, through both his dealings with British officials in Cairo and his continuing spat with the Jewish Committee in Alexandria, an ever-growing circle of people in Egypt were aware of NILI's existence. Even if none of these would deliberately harm the spy ring, how much longer before word of it finally reached Berlin or Constantinople?

Certainly, Aaron Aaronsohn's own family hadn't helped matters.

During his New York exile, his younger brother Alex had written of his escape from Turkey in an article for the *Atlantic Monthly* magazine; by August 1917, that article had been converted into a book, *With the Turks in Palestine*, which was now available in Cairo bookstores. Among Jewish settlements in Palestine, it was now an open secret that some sort of intelligence network was operating out of Athlit—and Sarah Aaronsohn's very conspicuous travels in the region gave many a good idea of exactly who was involved. Indeed, in July a delegation of Palestinian Jewish leaders had called on Sarah to demand she immediately stop her "activities," an ultimatum she had angrily spurned.

But if only because they were supposed to be professionals at such things, by far the greatest blame for the situation attached to those British officials tasked to manage the spy ring. Their cavalier manner bordered on the criminal. It was they who had come up with the idea of using the NILI network to distribute both British propaganda materials and relief funds for Jewish refugees, and while Aaronsohn had ultimately vetoed the first proposal, he had relented on the latter. As a result, when the first installment of aid went ashore at Athlit in mid-July in the form of gold sovereign coins, NILI operatives were no longer just exporters of intelligence but now importers of contraband gold, doubling their risk of detection. Most astounding of all, the British had repeatedly violated the most basic rule of running spies, which is to make sure one cell has no contact with another. By August 1917, the once-small fleet of spy ships operating out of Port Said had been steadily whittled down to the point where a single vessel, the *Managem*, was now conducting all missions. Out of necessity, this meant the *Managem* was transporting operatives of Britain's different intelligence networks in Palestine on the same voyages, neatly ensuring that if one spy was caught or defected, he or she was in a position to unmask everyone else.

Ultimately, it all spoke to the same personality flaw that had plagued the British in their war against the Turks from the outset, one shared in this instance by the Aaronsohns: hubris, contempt for one's enemy. And just as had occurred so many times since 1914, they would all soon have reason to regret it. On September 13, the same day Aaronsohn set sail for Europe, Turkish authorities in Palestine caught their first NILI spy.

It was the sort of store-clerk work Lawrence enjoyed the least. By late August, the process of converting Aqaba from a sleepy fishing port into the forward staging ground for the Arab Revolt was well under way, with a daily stream of British ships disgorging mountains of supplies. Those ships also brought in thousands of fighters—Muslim recruits from

Egypt, Arab warriors from Faisal's old base at Wejh—where they were joined by a surge of new tribal recruits coming in from the surrounding mountains. Since his return from Cairo on August 17, Lawrence's days in Aqaba had been spent dealing with the inevitable logistical foul-ups, and in trying to help bring some degree of order to the place. But perhaps such mundane duties helped distract from the larger problems at hand, for already the heady optimism and accelerated plans sparked by Aqaba's capture six weeks earlier had become a thing of the past.

As might have been foreseen, General Allenby's ambitious goal of launching his Palestine offensive by mid-September had been pushed back due to a host of delays in getting his army fully reequipped; planners in Cairo were now talking of a launch date no earlier than late October. Which maybe was just as well from Lawrence's perspective, since the Arabs were woefully unprepared too.

At the same time, Lawrence was living the old proverb of success having a thousand fathers. Exacerbated by its proximity to Cairo, Aqaba was now plagued by that most noxious of bureaucratic envoys, the advisor, each determined to prove his worth by coming up with his own list of dubious recommendations. In late August, a newly arrived intelligence officer, taken aback by the lack of professionalism among the Arab troops, urged on Cairo the immediate dispatch of the Imperial Camel Corps, an elite British camel cavalry force. Lawrence was forced to take time from his other duties to undermine the plan. "One squabble between a [Camel Corps] trooper and an Arab," he wrote Clayton on August 27, "or an incident with Bedouin women, would bring on general hostilities." Politic enough to concede some of the intelligence officer's other points, he closed on a dismissive note. "I don't think that any [report] of the Arab situation will be of much use to you unless its author can see for himself the difference between a national rising and a [military] campaign."

Coincidentally, when Clayton received that note, he was already considering doing a little field research of his own. On September 1, he arrived in Aqaba from Cairo, marking his first visit to the war front that had consumed his energies for over a year.

As always, it seemed the general had something of a hidden agenda to his visit. Over a month earlier, he'd received a curious letter from Mark Sykes in London. Clayton had seen no reason to share its contents with Lawrence during his subordinate's recent stay in Cairo—the two had been in daily contact at the Arab Bureau throughout the second week of August—but for reasons known only to him, he had brought the letter to Aqaba for that purpose.

When Sykes had returned to London from his Middle East sojourn that summer, it had been to a radically altered political landscape. As

Entente leaders were learning to their shock and dismay, President Woodrow Wilson's talk about making "the world safe for democracy" had been more than just sanctimonious rhetoric; the price for American intervention in the war was to be self-determination for oppressed peoples, and the annulment of the maze of secret pacts between governments—in effect, the beginning of the end of the imperial era. It was a measure of just how desperate Great Britain and France had become—between them, they had suffered some five million casualties in three years of war—that formerly voraciously acquisitive politicians in both capitals were now scrambling to learn the strange vocabulary of "non-annexation" and "autonomy."

Few were more adroit at executing this about-face than Mark Sykes. With astonishing speed, the politician had refashioned himself an enlightened postimperial statesman, a champion of self-determination. The best course in the Middle East, Sykes now argued, was for both Britain and France to renounce any imperialist claims whatsoever, since it was clear, as he informed Gilbert Clayton in his letter of July 22, that "colonialism is madness." In its place, what he envisioned was a kind of political finishing school administered by the Western powers, a period in which the benighted races of the Middle East might be instructed in Western values and systems and then sent on their merry way. Lest anyone find all this jarring coming from the coauthor of the most infamous imperial pact in modern history, Sykes had a handy solution; as he advised the War Cabinet in mid-July, henceforth all references to the Sykes-Picot Agreement should be discarded in favor of "the Anglo-French-Arab Agreement."

Not everyone was impressed by Sykes's new incarnation. Over time, a growing consensus in the Foreign Office leadership held that Britain had cut a very bad deal in Sykes-Picot, and blame had naturally affixed to its poorly supervised coauthor; as War Cabinet member George Curzon commented, "[Sykes] appears to think that the way to get rid of suspicion is always to recognize what the other party claims and to give up, when asked, our claims." Confidence in Sykes was further eroded by the continuing controversy over his and Picot's purported accord with King Hussein in May, and by his leadership role in promulgating the sacking-of-Jaffa story, now viewed by many as a backdoor scheme to prod the government into fully supporting the Zionist camp. Matters came to a head in early July when Arthur Nicolson, the under secretary of state for foreign affairs, had sought to unravel for the War Cabinet precisely what other commitments the government had made in the Middle East over the previous two years, and how those might square with its promises to King Hussein. All but calling Sykes a liar—"it is a little difficult to be sure that the papers in the Department represent the whole of what actually passed"—Nicolson urged that "the opinion of Sir Mark Sykes should be invited before the matter is pursued further, as he alone will be able to state with authority how far any evasion or modification of our engagements to [Hussein] are likely to be resented by Arab opinion."

In the face of such criticism, Sykes assumed a petulant, defensive crouch. Curiously, he also focused on a particular junior British army officer as a source of his troubles: Captain T. E. Lawrence. In a self-pitying note to Secretary Balfour's secretary on July 20, Sykes presented his two years of toil on Middle Eastern affairs as an exercise in thankless self-sacrifice. "Hitherto the work has been fairly successful, but I have had to contend, as you know, with many difficulties: the prejudices of the past both British and French, the mutual suspicions and susceptibilities of out-of-date minds, the anti-British policy of Brémond, the anti-French attitude of Lawrence."

But perhaps this focus wasn't so curious after all. Only a handful of people grasped the full tapestry of contradictions and half-truths Sykes had woven in the Middle East, but most of these—men like Gilbert Clayton and Reginald Wingate—were too much servants of the system to ever fully confront him; if things did blow up, they would keep their grumbling to a minimum and look for ways to muddle through. But then there was Lawrence, the non–club member who wouldn't hesitate in shaming Sykes if given the platform—and in the wake of his triumph at Aqaba, he increasingly had that platform.

In addition, Lawrence now had the ability to seriously damage the diplomatic framework Sykes had spent two years building. Imperfect though it was, it protected British interests in the region while giving a little bit of something to most everyone else. Now, with Lawrence's de facto military alliance with Allenby joined to his long-standing determination to wrest Syria from France, and quite suddenly the little captain was elevated from nuisance to formidable threat. It was apparently in hopes of neutralizing that threat, through both flattery and thinly veiled condescension, that Sykes devoted a portion of his July 22 letter to Clayton. It was that same letter Clayton brought with him to Aqaba to show Lawrence.

"Lawrence's move is splendid and I want him knighted," Sykes had written in reference to Aqaba's capture. "Tell him [that] now that he is a great man he must behave as such and be broad in his views. Ten years' tutelage under the Entente and the Arabs will be a nation. Complete independence [now] means Persia, poverty and chaos. Let him consider this, as he hopes for the people he is fighting for."

Combined with all he knew of Sykes's past machinations, and coming so close on the heels of his confrontation with Aaronsohn in Cairo, Lawrence could not stomach the letter's patronizing tone. Perhaps also it touched a chord of ego; if not a "great man," Lawrence was now most certainly his own, and he wasn't about to be dictated to by Mark Sykes. In a scathing seven-page letter to the politician, couched as an earnest request for guidance, he methodically held up each of Sykes's schemes to scrutiny before exposing their gaping holes: "What have you promised the Zionists, and what is their programme? I saw Aaronsohn in Cairo, and he said at once the Jews intended to acquire the land-rights of all Palestine from Gaza to Haifa, and have practical autonomy within. Is this acquisition to be by fair purchase or by forced sale and expropriation? . . . Do the Jews propose the complete expulsion of the Arab peasantry, or their reduction to a day-labourer class?"

He then turned to the matter of French "help" to the Arabs in developing Syria, the canard that Sykes had tried to foist on Hussein at Jeddah. "The Arabs can put their revolt through without French help, and therefore are disinclined to pay a price only to be made known to them in the future. . . . The Sherif will succeed, given time and a continuance of our help, [and] he will take by his own efforts (don't assume virtue for the mules and cartridges we supply him; the hands and heads are his) the sphere we allotted to our foreign-advised 'independent Syria,' and will expect to keep it without imposed foreign advisors. As he takes this sphere of his, he will also take parts of the other spheres not properly allotted to an Arab state [under Sykes-Picot]. His title to them will be a fairly strong one—that of conquest by means of the local inhabitants—and what are the two Powers going to do about it?"

At the letter's close, Lawrence assumed a slightly more conciliatory tone, recognizing the realpolitik reality that "we may have to sell our small friends in pay for our big friends," but pointed out that, contrary to Sykes's perpetually sunny pronouncements, "we are in rather a hole. Please tell me what, in your opinion, are the actual measures by which we will find a way out?"

The letter was perhaps the most searing indictment ever penned of Sykes's actions in the Middle East, but it was one the politician would never see. On September 7, with Clayton having returned to Cairo from his Aqaba visit, Lawrence routed the letter through his office for onward transmission to London; upon reading its contents, however, Clayton thought better of it. As he explained in a note to Lawrence, he didn't wish to provide Sykes with anything that "may raise him to activity," especially now that the increasingly discredited Sykes-Picot Agreement seemed headed for oblivion. "It is in fact dead," Clayton wrote, "and if we wait quietly, this fact will soon be realized. It was never a very workable instrument and it is now almost a lifeless monument."

In this appraisal, Gilbert Clayton couldn't have been more wrong, but Lawrence wasn't in a position to argue the point. In what was becoming something of a pattern between them, by the time Clayton sent his note, Lawrence had already set off for the interior and a new strike against the Turks.

WILLIAM YALE FIRST sensed something amiss when, checking into London's Savoy Hotel on September 7, he noticed the abundance of "painted ladies" circulating through its lobby. As he sadly noted in his diary the following day, it appeared the once-grand old hotel had become "to all intents and purposes a house of assignation."

The puritanical Yale had little time to dwell on the squalidness of his surroundings, however, for he was to stay very busy in London. Through Leland Harrison's helpful cable to the American ambassador, the new special agent gained quick entrée to many of the top British officials involved in Middle Eastern affairs. Amid these meetings, Yale was flattered to discover that his Syria report had been hailed as one of the most incisive documents to emerge from that vital corner of enemy territory, circulated and studied at some of the highest levels of the British political and military leadership; he was happy to meet with debriefers from various intelligence units, and to provide them with whatever further details he could.

Rather soon, though, Yale's attention turned away from trying to gain a broad view of the Middle Eastern situation—from his own experience in the region, he knew that any truly useful insights were likely to be found in Cairo—and toward a particular aspect of it: the British government's growing flirtation with the Jewish Zionist community.

His curiosity was piqued by a peculiar story circulating in British newspapers that told of an unnamed Jewish chemist who had supposedly given the government "certain secrets" pertaining to the manufacture of explosives. "This Jewish chemist," Yale wrote in his diary on September 12, "who, when asked what reward he desired, replied that personally he wished nothing, but that he was a Jew and that he wished that in a Peace Conference the Allies would give special consideration to the question of the Jews in Palestine." According to the newspaper accounts, the British government had secretly promised the scientist to do so.

Even if Yale didn't yet have the name of the chemist—it was Chaim Weizmann, of course—what he found intriguing was that the government had made no public attempt to deny or diminish the account, which strongly suggested it was true. Over his next week in London, the new American intelligence operative sounded out an array of officials on just what British policy might be in regard to the Jews in Palestine, only to receive an array of conflicting responses.

Perhaps one reason for this, Yale concluded, was that there seemed little agreement among British Jews over just what arrangement they hoped for. Some of those in the Zionist community argued for nothing less than a Jewish nation in Palestine, others merely for a guarantee of increased immigration, while some anti-Zionist leaders fiercely denounced the movement as a dangerous new tool for Jewish marginalization, a handy weapon for anti-Semites to question the loyalty of Jews to the nations of their birth. In trying to sort through the controversy, it seemed plain to Yale that the British government was contemplating some sort of overture in connection with the Jews and Palestine, but that precisely what that would be had not yet been decided.

After two weeks, Yale felt he had gleaned all he could in London, and was anxious to get on to Cairo. First, though, there was someone he very much wanted to talk with in Paris, a Zionist leader whose name had come up often in recent days, and who had just arrived in France from Egypt: Aaron Aaronsohn.

IT IS AN enduring myth about the battle for Arabia: the fantasy of the "clean war," of Arab warriors, stirred after centuries of crushing subjugation, rallying to the cry of freedom; of those same warriors bravely charging down sand dunes to fall upon their hapless and cruel oppressors.

Contrary to the charge of his detractors, T. E. Lawrence actually played a minimal role in creating this myth. Far more it stemmed from the need of a shattered postwar public to find even a trace of grandeur in a war so utterly grotesque. There was not a lot of material to work with from the Western Front, where countless thousands had simply vanished in puffs, atomized by artillery, or been entombed forever beneath its mud. By contrast, Arabia was all berobed warriors and charging camels and flapping banners, a touch of medieval pageantry amid the inglorious slaughter. That image and the need for it dimmed under the weight of a second, even more horrific world war, but then David Lean's 1962 film resurrected it for a new generation.

Lawrence's greatest contribution to the literature of war was that, despite his open advocacy for the Arab cause, fidelity to the truth compelled him to try to convey what it was really like. As he made clear in *Seven Pillars*, while many Arabs joined the fight out of a sincere desire to be rid of the Turks, sincerity was helped along by British gold and the prospect of bountiful loot. On the battlefield, the rebels' enemies were not just Turks but fellow Arabs, warriors from tribes that had missed out on the British gold or taken that of the Turks, clans with whom they had blood feuds or who were freelancers out scouting for loot themselves.

Nor did that battlefield bear much resemblance to the scenery of popular imagination. Instead of the picturesque expanses of sand dunes often associated with the region, much of the Arabian and Syrian deserts consist of dreary gravel plains and barren stone mountains, similar in many respects to the less picturesque corners of Utah or Arizona. In traversing this terrain, Lawrence and his Arab allies survived on a diet of mutton, camel meat, and bread in good times, raw flour in the less good. These meals were chased down with water often drawn from brackish springs or algae-covered ponds, or from wells contaminated by the Turks with rotting animal corpses. Seeking out shade to escape the withering heat of midday often meant encountering that strange and cruel phenomenon common to deserts the world over, great swarms of biting black flies.

But of all the components to the myth, perhaps the most erroneous is the notion of a "clean war." On this most severe of landscapes, the badly wounded on both sides were often left behind to die, the lucky ones dispatched with a bullet to the head. Subsisting on whatever was left over once their captors had their fill, prisoners died in droves from hunger and thirst—when the victors bothered to take prisoners at all. And in contrast to the clearly delineated death zones of the Western Front, this was a battlefield on which combatants and civilians were intermingled, where the completely innocent could suddenly find themselves caught amid the bullets and knives.

It was early on the afternoon of September 19 when the ten-car train rounded the bend from the south. Lawrence waited until the train's second engine had started over the short bridge, and then he detonated his fifty-pound gelignite mine. Instantly, a plume of black smoke shot a hundred feet into the air and billowed out to either side at least as far. Once the report of the explosion and the screech of ripping metal died away, there came a brief, eerie silence. Then the killing began in earnest.

To complement the Arab warriors he intended to recruit along the way, Lawrence had brought along from Aqaba two fellow Western officers—a Briton he nicknamed "Stokes" for the Stokes trench mortar he carried, an Australian nicknamed "Lewis" for the two Lewis machine guns in his care—and they had pre-positioned themselves and their weapons on a rocky ledge just three hundred yards from the bridge. As the smoke cleared, it was revealed that only the train's engines and lead carriage had fallen into the culvert below the collapsed bridge, the remaining seven carriages sitting upright and immobile on the tracks. Rows of Turkish soldiers sat on the roofs of these carriages, and they were now mowed down by the Lewis machine guns, "swept off the top like bales of cotton."

Starting to recover from their shock, a number of Turks scrambled for the relative shelter of the culvert under the bridge. The first mortar that Stokes fired at them went a little wide. After he adjusted the weapon's elevating screw, his second shell dropped directly in their midst. The sudden carnage there, Lawrence noted in his official report, caused the survivors to panic and race "towards some rough country 200 yards N.E. of the line. On their way there the Lewis gun[s] killed all but about twenty of them."

With Turkish resistance rapidly collapsing, the Arab fighters—just over one hundred men—dashed forward to begin their looting. Anxious to check on the damage to the engines, Lawrence scrambled down from his perch to join them.

Reaching the train, he discovered it had been carrying a mixed cargo, that along with the soldiers, several of its carriages were filled with civilians. Some of these were the families of Turkish officers returning to Damascus, others simple refugees. "To one side stood thirty or forty hysterical women," Lawrence recounted in *Seven Pillars*, "unveiled, tearing their clothes and hair, shrieking themselves distracted. The Arabs, without regard to them, went on wrecking [their] household goods, looting their absolute fill." Spotting Lawrence, the women fell on him to beg for mercy. They were soon joined by their husbands, who "seized my feet in a very agony of terror of instant death. A Turk so broken down was a nasty spectacle; I kicked them off as well as I could with bare feet, and finally broke free."

On his way to the train engines, Lawrence checked on the one carriage that had tumbled into the ravine. He found it had been a medical car, the wounded and ill laid out on stretchers for the journey, but all were now bunched in a bloody tangled heap at the bottom of the upended wagon. "One of those yet alive deliriously cried out the word 'typhus.' So I wedged shut the door and left them there, alone."

He was only slightly more helpful to a group of Austrian military advisors who had been on the train, and "who appealed to me quietly in Turkish for quarter." Intent on finishing up his demolition work, Lawrence left them under an Arab guard; moments later, the Austrians were killed, "all but two or three," as the result of some dispute.

In his official report on the engagement below Mudowarra, Lawrence estimated the number of Turkish dead at about seventy, at a cost of one Arab fighter. He lamented that amid the pandemonium, he'd had to rush his vandalism to the first train engine, and feared it was still capable of repair. "The conditions were not helpful to good work." He made no mention of dead civilians in the report, although considering the fusillade of bullets fired into the unarmored train in the first few minutes of the battle, their number must have been considerable. Similarly, he offered no explanation for the discrepancy between the ninety Turkish soldiers taken prisoner and the sixty-eight ultimately delivered to Aqaba.

For most who experience it, combat triggers a contradictory duel of emotions: horror at its gruesomeness, exhilaration at its unmitigated thrill. Reconciling these dueling reactions is probably more difficult for the soldier than for the civilian given the element of braggadocio that exists within his fraternity, and he is likely to be more candid about the complexity of his feelings—to the degree that candor is even possible—with a nonsoldier.

Upon his return to Aqaba from Mudowarra, Lawrence wrote to a military colleague, Walter Stirling. In the letter, he recounted the train attack in gleeful detail, noting the "beautiful shots" of the Stokes gun that had killed twelve Turks on the spot, and how his own share of the loot was "a superfine red Baluch prayer-rug." He continued, "I hope this sounds the fun it is. The only pity is the sweat to work [the Arabs] up, and the wild scramble while it lasts. It's the most amateurish, Buffalo-Billy sort of performance, and the only people who do it well are the Bedouin."

The day before, September 24, a seemingly very different Lawrence had written to his old friend Edward Leeds at the Ashmolean Museum in Oxford: "I hope when the nightmare ends that I will wake up and become alive again. This killing and killing of Turks is horrible. When you charge in at the finish and find them all over the place in bits, and still alive many of them, and you know that you have done hundreds in the same way before, and must do hundreds more if you can."

If Lawrence was already having difficulty reconciling this psychic divide, it was about to get worse.

Chapter 15

To the Flame

I only hope and trust TEL will get back safe. He is out and up against
it at this moment. If he comes through, it is a V[ictoria] C[Cross]—if
not—well, I don't care to think about it!

DAVID HOGARTH TO HIS WIFE, NOVEMBER 11, 1917

They had met several times before in Palestine. Back then, Aaron
Aaronsohn had been an eminent scientist, a pioneer in the field of
agronomy, and William Yale the regional representative of the Standard
Oil Company of New York. Now, in late September 1917, both had added
considerably to their résumés, Aaronsohn a leader in the international
Zionist movement, Yale a special agent for the U.S. State Department. But
what Yale didn't know about Aaron Aaronsohn—at least not yet—was
that he was also the mastermind of one of the most extensive spy rings in
the Middle East. And what Aaronsohn didn't know about William Yale
was that, his vague job title aside, he too was essentially a spy. As might
be expected, all this lent their meeting in Paris on September 25 a certain
circumspect quality.

Since arriving in the French capital four days earlier, Aaronsohn
had been trying to get a sense of where matters stood with the Zionist
cause before moving on to London. To that end, he'd first sought out his
old benefactor, Baron Edmond de Rothschild, who he knew was playing
a key behind-the-scenes role in the ongoing discussions with the French
and British governments. He'd come away disappointed.

"He listened very interestedly all the time I spoke to him," Aaronsohn would inform his brother Alex in a letter, "and asked me questions which I answered, but he would not let me touch on certain subjects, did not wish to speak about them, so that it was impossible for me to learn from him what I wished to know. . . . He feels, as we all do, that if Great Britain would only rule over our land, we could obtain great things, but as nothing certain is known [yet], he cannot allow himself to speak."

He'd had far better luck when Mark Sykes showed up in town. The two had a long meeting on September 23, followed by another the next morning. "He told me everything," Aaronsohn told his brother, "and showed me what a lot of enemies we have. Most of the opponents [are] from among our own people, and that is dangerous to our organization."

Evidently, one reason Sykes had sought out Aaronsohn in Paris was to play peacemaker. The British War Cabinet was once again taking up the debate over supporting a Jewish homeland in Palestine, and it was vital that the leading Zionists speak with one voice. That meant ending the ongoing friction between Aaronsohn and Chaim Weizmann's English Zionist Federation; as Sykes explained, Aaronsohn's angry letters to Weizmann of mid-September had been "like a thorn in the latter's eye."

Which frankly suited Aaronsohn just fine. As he haughtily told his brother, "Mark Sykes begs me to make peace with them and wants me to promise not to quarrel. He says that I should listen to Weizmann and to Sokolow. I told him that I was not going to London to quarrel, only to tell them their mistakes and to show them the way to do things properly. If they accept, well and good; if not I will go my own way."

William Yale may have gleaned something of this rift within the Zionist camp from his own interviews in London, but it likely was mere background noise to the more overt struggle between the British Zionists and anti-Zionists, and between the competing camps within the British government. If in seeking out Aaronsohn in Paris, Yale hoped for edification on all this, he didn't get it. As he noted in his diary that night—and would eventually report back to Leland Harrison in Washington—Aaronsohn "does not wish to see Jewish autonomy or a Jewish state at this time, saying that nothing would be more harm [sic] to the Zionists than that. [Rather,] he wishes to see either English, American or International government control of Palestine." What's more, Yale could report, after seeing to his business in London, Aaronsohn intended to continue on to the United States to call on his influential American Jewish contacts to press the point. What made this rather baffling was that while in London, Yale had met with one of Aaronsohn's closest allies, a businessman named Jack Mosseri. Even while extolling Aaronsohn's clear-eyed insights on the matter, Mosseri was advocating the establishment of an outright Jewish government in

Palestine, and the adoption of Hebrew as its official language. Following his meetings in Paris, Yale left for Cairo undoubtedly even more confused about where things stood on the Zionist question than before.

But he also left with something else. Either oblivious to Yale's job responsibilities or just a peculiarly credulous sort, Aaronsohn had entrusted his American visitor with a letter to be delivered to his brother Alex, now back in Cairo. Other than the rudimentary safeguard of being written in Hebrew, the letter was not encrypted in any way, and it was in this highly indiscreet dispatch that Aaronsohn detailed his meetings with Edmond de Rothschild and Mark Sykes and outlined all he knew of the current status of British-Zionist negotiations in London.

The spy chief hadn't ended there, though. Along with listing by name "our friends" in the British military hierarchy in Cairo who should be kept abreast of developments, Aaronsohn instructed his younger brother to put Georges-Picot, the French political agent who was on his way to Egypt, under surveillance. "Pascal," he wrote, referring to his chief assistant in Cairo, "will tell you how we can watch his movements." Aaronsohn had even imparted some advice to his brother about William Yale: "Get as pally as you can with him and watch him, for you will be able to get information from him which you need, especially about happenings in Egypt."

All of this might have been of tremendous interest both to Yale and to the agency he now represented. While the American government had been apprised of Britain's deliberations on the Jewish homeland question, no one from President Wilson on down was aware of the contentiousness it had spawned there—and they certainly didn't know of the behind-the-scenes role being played by Mark Sykes. But if Aaron Aaronsohn was shockingly careless in handing such a document to William Yale, he was also lucky. In his role as an intelligence agent, Yale fully intended to open and translate the letter before passing it on to Alex Aaronsohn, but, new to the spy game, he apparently didn't appreciate that these matters tended to be time-sensitive. By the time he got around to having Aaronsohn's letter translated and sent on to the State Department, it would be mid-December. By then, most of the explosive information he'd had in his possession for nearly three months would be rendered moot.

WITH THE AIRPLANE still a rarity in the Middle East in 1917, the one sent to collect Major Lawrence from Aqaba on the morning of October 12 was a clue to the importance being placed on his mission. Another was the identity of those waiting for him at the military field headquarters outside El Arish: Generals Allenby and Clayton, as well as Lawrence's old mentor from Oxford, David Hogarth, now the titular head of the Arab Bureau.

Lawrence had barely alit from the ninety-minute flight—in 1917, a plane's cruising speed was barely over one hundred miles per hour—before learning why he'd been summoned.

At very long last, a date had been set for Allenby's offensive against the Turkish line: October 28, or just a little more than two weeks away. It would take very different form from Archibald Murray's two failed attempts. In hopes of convincing the Turks that was not the case, the British would conduct a preliminary three-day bombardment of Gaza—the classic World War I prelude to a frontal assault—but then strike at the far more lightly defended town of Beersheva, thirty miles to the east. Once in possession of Beersheva and its vital water wells, the British would then push north and west, severing Gaza's supply lines to the Palestine interior. If all went accordingly, the Turkish army entrenched at Gaza would either be surrounded or forced to withdraw to avoid being trapped. The question for Lawrence was how the Arab rebels might assist in this great effort.

That was a question with no easy answer, because the very cleverness of the Beersheva scheme derived from its modesty. In a corner of the world where access to water was a general's first tactical consideration, one of the chief reasons for Murray's unimaginative frontal assaults at Gaza had been the need to quickly get his army to the water sources that lay behind the Turkish lines. Of course, this imperative had also made Murray's efforts all-or-nothing propositions—no lolling about on a desert battlefield in hopes of incremental gains—that he had lost. By contrast, once in control of Beersheva's water wells, Allenby's army had the luxury of closing on Gaza at a methodical pace; operational plans called for an offensive stretched out over at least a week. The downside—and this was where the modesty aspect played out—was that the deliberateness of the British advance would also give the Turks time to regroup. Allenby obviously hoped for more, but in all probability a successful offensive meant gaining a toehold in southwestern Palestine and little else; no race up the coastline, no dash for Jerusalem.

Consequently, it was very difficult to see what role the Arabs might play. If their contribution was to be in shutting down the Turkish supply line into Palestine, the logical place for them to strike was the rail junction town of Deraa in central Syria; from there, a railroad spur ran west off the Hejaz Railway and served as the Turks' principal lifeline in and out of the battle zone. Furthermore, from his June intelligence foray across Syria, Lawrence knew there were thousands of tribesmen in the Deraa region ready to join the revolt. On the other hand, any large-scale operation at Deraa would be to invite the tribesmen's slaughter if the British army advanced no farther than their Palestinian toehold 120 miles to the southwest.

Nor was there much the Arab rebels massed in Aqaba could do. Frankly—even though Lawrence was probably less than frank with his questioners at El Arish on this score—the situation there was a mess. For well over two months, the forces gathered there had been awaiting word on when the British army would finally strike at southern Palestine, the cue for their own foray into the Syrian heartland, and this wait had led to a spiraling logistical nightmare. With thousands of prospective warriors idling away in the port, an ever-greater amount of supplies had needed to be shipped in from Egypt to equip and feed them—as well as ever more British gold to keep them paid—which in turn had drawn in even more recruits. The situation had grown so bad that by early October, transport ships were being devoted to hauling in Egyptian forage just to feed the camels and horses, the hills around Aqaba having been stripped bare. As if matters weren't grim enough, a recent cholera outbreak had now brought the entire supply system to a virtual standstill as quarantining procedures were introduced.

But probably even more deleterious was the effect this holding-pattern existence was having on morale in Aqaba, for a sense of gloom had now begun to permeate the rebel ranks. With no one was this more evident than in Faisal himself. As the delay in pushing north extended, he had sunk into a deepening depression, convinced that the chance to wrest Syria for the Arab cause was slipping away. In his more bitter moments, he even accused the British of imposing this inaction deliberately, a maneuver to hand Syria to the French, and while the harried Major Joyce bore the brunt of Faisal's complaints, Lawrence had frequently been compelled to lend his soothing influence in meetings with the emir. To maintain the notion that *some* progress was being made, and perhaps also to at least temporarily escape the unhappy town, Lawrence had continued his raiding forays over the mountains—he'd just returned from another train attack when the summons to El Arish came—but it was all very pale stuff when set against the grand vision he had laid out in Cairo three months earlier.

Yet for political reasons—and maybe personal ones too—Lawrence felt it was vital that the Arabs contribute in some way to the upcoming offensive. And so in El Arish he came up a new plan.

If not by an attack on Deraa itself, there was another place where the railroad spur into Palestine could potentially be severed. It lay fifteen miles to the west of Deraa, where the line passed over a number of high bridges as it navigated the rugged Yarmuk gorge; if just one of those bridges could be destroyed, the effect would be the same. The further advantage to such an operation was that it could be conducted very much along the lines of the "traditional" train attack, a hit-and-run mission by a small and highly mobile Arab force.

There the similarities ended, however. The Yarmuk gorge was over two hundred miles from Aqaba, and in a comparatively densely populated region. On such a mission, any force coming from Aqaba would be negotiating an alien landscape, constant prey to Turkish army patrols and Turkish-allied local tribes. Those dangers would only multiply if they actually succeeded in the mission. As they tried to make their escape, the one certainty was that the raiders would be completely on their own, far beyond the reach of either the British or fellow rebels to come to their aid.

To these concerns, Lawrence offered a refinement: he would do it himself. Just as he'd done in taking Aqaba, he would set out with a small, handpicked force, one hopefully resourceful and unobtrusive enough to avoid detection, and he would recruit whomever else he needed along the way. After the operation, the local recruits could melt back into their villages as those in Lawrence's party scattered in search of safe haven.

To most who heard it in El Arish, Lawrence's idea seemed less a battle plan than a suicide mission. Moreover, these were men to whom Lawrence was not some faceless soldier, but a friend, a protégé, a young man they admired. Weighing against this, though, were the exigencies of war.

By mid-October 1917, the Entente war effort lay everywhere in tatters. Over the previous summer, the French army had been riven by mutinies, with entire regiments refusing to march into their trenchwork slaughter pens; while that crisis had now abated, the army of France remained a shaken, traumatized force. On the Eastern Front, the Germans had smashed yet another Russian offensive, a last desperate gamble by the dying Kerensky regime; before the end of that month of October, the Bolsheviks would seize power and sue for peace with Germany. On the Southern Front, the Italians had recently failed in their tenth and eleventh offensives against the Austrians in the Isonzo valley, and were about to experience a colossal collapse in the battle of Caporetto. Since July 31, the British commander on the Western Front, Douglas Haig, had been building on his reputation for callous butchery by persisting with an offensive even more futile than his previous outing at the Somme. By the time the battle of Passchendaele was finally called off in early November, the seventy thousand British soldiers who had perished in its mud fields would equate to one dead man for every two inches of ground gained.

Amid all this, just how much value could be put on the life of one more man—even of an "almost indispensable" one, as Gilbert Clayton had described Lawrence a year earlier—if he might in some small way advance the war effort? If Lawrence was brave or foolish or deluded enough to chance Yarmuk, certainly no one at headquarters was going to try to talk him out of it. Upon being briefed on the plan, General Allenby instructed that it be carried out on the night of November 5, 6, or 7.

. . .

ACCORDING TO POPULAR folklore, the agent of their destruction was a pigeon.

Since the early days of the war, the British had employed carrier pigeons to relay messages on the Western Front, and in the summer of 1917 someone in Cairo hit on the same idea as a way to maintain contact with the NILI operatives in Palestine. On paper, the notion had a lot going for it. It would help eliminate the need for the perilous and trouble-prone spy-ship runs from Egypt—with almost eerie regularity, these voyages had a way of coinciding with bad storms—as well as the risk to operational security inherent in face-to-face contact between spies and spy handlers. Carrier pigeons might also mean that crucial intelligence would reach British lines much faster. Between the difficulty in getting informants' reports to Athlit, and then the wait for the ship, the information Cairo received from NILI was often five or six weeks out of date.

The pigeons had proved something of a dud, though. On a test run in July, only one of the six birds released made it the one hundred miles to the British headquarters in the Sinai. Nevertheless, on August 30, Sarah Aaronsohn had turned to the method out of desperation. By then, the *Managem* hadn't put in at Athlit for nearly a month (little did Sarah Aaronsohn know that, apparently, the main reason for this inactivity was a British refusal to increase the pay of the man who made the swim from ship to shore to £30 a month); anxious to reestablish contact, she inserted her coded messages into tiny metal capsules, attached these to the legs of several pigeons, and set the birds loose. For insurance, she sent off two more pigeons four days later.

Sarah had always been leery of the system, and when she went down to the sea for a swim on the morning of September 4, her doubts were confirmed; perched atop a nearby water tank was one of the birds she'd released the day before, the telltale capsule still attached to its leg. Sure enough, rumors soon began circulating that a Turkish commander in Jaffa had intercepted a message-carrying pigeon, and even though Turkish authorities apparently couldn't break the code or pinpoint the bird's origin, they were now convinced that a spy ring was operating somewhere along the Palestine coast.

Then, in mid-September, came news of the arrest of Naaman Belkind in the Sinai. NILI's chief operative in southern Palestine, Belkind had been caught trying to cross over to the British lines. Suspected of being a spy, he was first tortured for information in Beersheva, then transferred to Damascus to undergo more elaborate interrogation. With Belkind's capture, Sarah Aaronsohn and other NILI agents feared it was only a matter of time before their network was exposed and the Turks came for them. So did those other residents of Zichron Yaakov who'd long been suspicious of the goings-on in town and in nearby Athlit. On September 18, the settlement's governing committee summoned Sarah Aaronsohn to a meeting where she was confronted over her *traife*, or "unclean," work.

"Today we don't want to hear any more explanations from you," they reportedly told her. "Only one word, the right answer: your promise to stop this work, which has gone beyond all bounds. . . . If you want to work at espionage, leave the territory and the lands of the Jews and go and work in some distant land."

It was amid this tightening peril that the *Managem* finally returned on September 22. Apprised of the situation on land, British authorities swiftly arranged for a British merchant ship docked in Cyprus, one large enough to evacuate as many residents of Zichron Yaakov as wished to leave, to make for Palestine. That ship appeared off the coast of the Jewish colony on the night of September 25.

In the interim, however, Sarah Aaronsohn and her confederates appeared to recover their resolve. Part of it may have stemmed from a belief that Belkind wouldn't break—after all, it had been nearly two weeks since his capture and the Turks still hadn't come for them—but even more was concern of what would happen to the far-flung NILI agents if those at its headquarters suddenly disappeared. As it was, only two people, a mother and her young son, went out on the rescue ship. To the suggestions of her lieutenants that she go out as well, Aaronsohn was adamant: "I want to be the last, not the first, to leave." Instead, Sarah would wait for the next visit of the *Managem*, arranged for October 12, during which she would gauge the state of things.

But it seems the NILI operatives hadn't considered another possible explanation for the lassitude of Turkish authorities, a rather ironic one under the circumstances. Both the Turks and their German allies remained stung by the tremendous propaganda victory the Allies had achieved with their talk of the Jewish "purge" in Jaffa back in May. The Germans were also well aware that the British government was considering calling for a Jewish homeland in Palestine as a way to win the international Zionist community to its side; indeed, the Germans were now rather desperately trying to come up with a counterformula to appeal to the Zionists. As a result, and even as reports of a Jewish spy ring in Palestine circulated in Constantinople and Berlin—because, in fact, Naaman Belkind *had* talked—the Germans were sternly warning their Turkish allies to be absolutely certain they had their culprits before making a move. All well and good to round up a crowd of Arabs or Turks and put them to the bastinado, but in the autumn of 1917, the Germans counseled, the Jews in Palestine needed to be treated with a little more finesse.

Then, at the end of September, the Turks were apparently handed the last piece of the puzzle—and responsibility for this didn't fall to an errant pigeon or Naaman Belkind, but to the British spy runners themselves. According to the postwar account of a Turkish intelligence chief in Syria, it came when two Arab spies were caught on the Palestinian coast. Under torture, the men offered that they had been put ashore from a British spy ship, and that they'd traveled on that ship in the company of Jewish spies. Those spies had been dropped off first, in the vicinity of the agricultural research station at Athlit.

For greater protection, Sarah Aaronsohn and her chief lieutenant, Joseph Lishansky, had recently moved into Zichron Yaakov, eight miles down the road from Athlit. They were there when, late on the night of October 2, the settlement was surrounded by Turkish soldiers. The roundup began the following morning, the soldiers and secret police, having already ransacked Athlit, working off a list of dozens of names. Among the first to be detained was Sarah Aaronsohn, along with her father, Ephraim, and brother Zvi. Managing a quick escape was the "ringleader" the Turks most hoped to catch, Joseph Lishansky; with their 1917 chauvinism, it apparently never occurred to them that the true ringleader might be a woman.

The paradox of having to take special care with members of the Jewish community lest German wrath be incurred was to now take perverse form and would turn the Turkish operation in Zichron Yaakov into a kind of slow-motion horror show. On that first day of "questioning," Sarah Aaronsohn's father and brother were severely beaten in front of her, the soldiers demanding to be told Lishansky's whereabouts, but she herself wasn't touched. Matters turned a good deal uglier the next morning. Ephraim and Zvi Aaronsohn, along with a number of other detained men, were led to the central square, where they were tied up and repeatedly whipped in an attempt to get those still in hiding to surrender. Struck by her icy defiance of the previous day, the Turks targeted Sarah for especially brutal treatment. Tied to the gatepost of her family's home on Zichron's main street, she was whipped and beaten with flexible batons, or bastinados. Still, she would reveal nothing, reportedly even taunting her torturers until she fell into unconsciousness.

One by one, those on the Turks' wanted list who were hiding began turning themselves in, tormented by the cries of their relatives. Or they were betrayed by others, for as the terror extended, a kind of group psychosis seized Zichron Yaakov. "For those who had long opposed NILI's activities," wrote one historian, "it was a time to prove their loyalty to the Turks and to settle old debts. As the Turks rounded up more men for the bastinado, four hysterical viragos ran through the streets, loudly rejoicing as each new victim was put under the Turkish whips, even falling upon the arrested men with blows and shouted abuse."

With still no sign of Lishansky, the authorities raised the stakes even higher. Summoning the settlement's governing committee, the Turkish commander threatened to lay waste to the village unless Lishansky was handed over. To reinforce the point, he announced that the following morning all those detained—some seventy in all—were to be transported to the main police station in Nazareth for further "questioning." Joining them would be seventeen Zichron elders chosen at random, to be released if Lishansky was surrendered, to share in the general unpleasantries if not. By that afternoon, Zichron residents were taking the settlement apart in search of Lishansky, while the governing committee posted a reward for his capture.

The ordeal reached its grim denouement the next day, Friday, October 5. As the captives were being loaded for transport to Nazareth, a bloodied and battered Sarah Aaronsohn asked permission to change into clean clothes for the journey. Led to her family home, she was allowed to step into a bathroom unattended, where she hastily wrote out a last note of instructions to those NILI operatives who remained. Then she withdrew a revolver she had secreted in a cubbyhole in anticipation of just such a situation and shot herself in the mouth.

Even this did not end the torment of Sarah Aaronsohn. While the bullet destroyed her mouth and severed her spinal cord, it missed her brain. For four days, she lingered in agony, attended to by German Catholic nuns, before finally expiring on the morning of October 9. By Jewish tradition, she was buried that same day in the Zichron cemetery, her death shroud a swatch of mosquito netting taken from her family home. She was twenty-seven years old.

On the night of October 12, three days after Sarah's death, the *Managem* reappeared off the coast of Athlit as scheduled. On board was Alex Aaronsohn, who was overseeing the Cairo office while Aaron was in Europe. He carried a message that had been forwarded by his brother.

On October 1, Aaron Aaronsohn had arrived in London from Paris. There, he had finally met Chaim Weizmann and quickly forged at least a temporary rapprochement with the Zionist Federation leader. Central to that rapprochement was Weizmann's recognition of the vital role NILI was playing in the Zionist cause, an appreciation he had expressed in a telegram to be disseminated to the NILI operatives: "We are doing our best to make sure that Palestine [will be] Jewish under British protection.

Your heroic stand encourages our strenuous efforts. Our hopes are great. Be strong and of good courage until the redemption of Israel."

It was this message that Alex Aaronsohn carried ashore with him that night at Athlit, but no one was there.

A CHANGE HAD come over Lawrence, a kind of quiet despondency. David Hogarth, his old mentor, had noticed it at the El Arish headquarters in mid-October. "He is not well," Hogarth wrote an Arab Bureau colleague afterward, "and talks rather hopelessly about the Arab future he once believed in."

Others had detected the change even earlier, including Lawrence himself. "I'm not going to last out this game much longer," he had confided to his friend Edward Leeds after the train attack at Mudowarra in September. "Nerves going and temper wearing thin, and one wants an unlimited account of both."

This new element of emotional fragility seemed to accelerate in the days after his meetings in El Arish. One who would bear unique eyewitness to it was a man named George Lloyd. Another of the aristocratic "Amateurs" who had found themselves in the Middle East during the war, Lloyd was a handsome, Cambridge-educated baronet and Conservative member of Parliament who had been recruited to Stewart Newcombe's military intelligence unit in Cairo in late 1914. Lloyd had soon chafed under Newcombe's austere leadership and arranged a transfer, but not before forming a friendship with a coworker nine years his junior in the small office, T. E. Lawrence.

As with so many other British aristocrats during the war, Lloyd had floated between job titles and assignments with rather dizzying regularity—stints with military command staffs in the field interspersed with the deskbound duties of parliamentary committees—but at least some of those assignments periodically returned him to the Middle East. With a background in banking, in the autumn of 1916, he had been brought down to study the financial status of King Hussein's regime in the wake of the Arab Revolt. His comprehensive report on the Hejaz economy—it essentially didn't have one—had included a damning analysis of Édouard Brémond's scheme to create the Ottoman French bank, and been instrumental in its scuttling.

By the autumn of 1917, however, Lloyd was marooned at a back-base office shuffling paper and anxious to return to the field. At the end of September he had written to Gilbert Clayton, listing those areas where he thought he might be of some service. In particular, he remembered his old colleague in the Cairo military intelligence office, who was now something of a legend. "I think I could be still more useful in a personal way to Lawrence," Lloyd wrote. "He is overworked and must be overstrained. If he is to remain in the field at his most responsible job, I do think he must have true companionship and relief of some other white man congenial to him. I could never in any way attempt to take the lead in that job. I am not even remotely qualified. But in his curious way, [Lawrence] has rather an addiction to me, and if he liked to have me with him to accompany him on his 'stunts,' I believe my presence might help to keep him going."

Its racialist note aside, the request was a rather extraordinary one, an aristocrat and sitting member of Parliament effectively asking to play Sancho Panza to Lawrence's Don Quixote. Clayton seized on the offer, and arranged Lloyd's immediate recall. He was waiting in Aqaba when Lawrence returned from El Arish on October 15.

For several days, the two friends caught up with each other as Lawrence laid plans for his imminent trek to Yarmuk. As Lloyd observed, those plans had a decidedly ad hoc nature. Along with just a very tiny cadre of Arab warriors, Lawrence would leave Aqaba with an Indian army machine-gun unit and one British officer, a demolitions expert named Lieutenant Wood, who was on semi-invalid status after having been shot in the head on the Western Front. Avoiding populated areas on the long trip north, Lawrence would then recruit his local operatives from among the clans of eastern Syria, and join them to followers of Abd el Kader, an Algerian exile who had been with the Arab Revolt since its inception and whose kinsmen lived in the Yarmuk area. After the attack, the local recruits would melt away, while those from Aqaba would scatter before their inevitable Turkish pursuers. It was further arranged that Lloyd would accompany Lawrence for at least the first few, safer days of the journey.

On October 20, Lloyd sent Clayton a cable outlining these plans, as well as his own first impressions of the situation in Aqaba. His breezy tone abruptly shifted in a postscript he marked "Private": "Lawrence is quite fit, but much oppressed by the risk and magnitude of the job before him. He opened his heart to me last night and told me that he felt there was so much for him still to do in this world, places to dig, peoples to help, that it seemed horrible to have it all cut off, as he feels it will be, for he feels that, while he may do the [Yarmuk] job, he has little or no chance of getting away himself. I tried to cheer him up, but of course it is true."

It was an unusually heartfelt message to be exchanged between two men for the times, let alone included in a military cable, and it may have been that George Lloyd hoped it would cause Clayton to cancel the operation. If so, he was soon set right. Allowing that he too was "very anxious" about his subordinate, Clayton replied that Lawrence's burdened mood was rather to be expected considering the mission before him. "He has a lion's heart, but even so, this strain must be very great," Clayton acknowledged. "Well, he is doing a great work and, as soon as may be, we must pull him out and not risk him further—but the time is not yet, as he is wanted just now."

TO AS MUCH pomp and ceremony as a war-ravaged nation could manage, the Young Turk regime put on a decorous reception for Abbas Hilmi II, the erstwhile khedive of Egypt. Along with bunting and a ceremonial guard, a host of dignitaries were on hand to greet the titular Ottoman sovereign of Egypt as his train pulled into Constantinople's Sirkeci station one afternoon in late October. Among those in attendance was an old friend and coconspirator of Abbas's, Dr. Curt Prüfer. Picking up where they had left off, the lives of the German spymaster and the pretender to the Egyptian throne were about to become entwined in intrigue once again.

When the Turks came into the war on the side of the Central Powers, the British had deposed Abbas—the "wicked little khedive," in Kitchener's memorable phrase—and cast him into a wandering exile, one that had eventually landed him in Switzerland. But Abbas was a born schemer, and in Switzerland he had a lot of time on his hands. Over the next three years, he had tirelessly negotiated with both sides in the conflict in hopes of regaining his throne in the postwar era, and it was a measure of his catholic approach to plotting that each side was very much aware of his dealings with the other. The Young Turk leadership in Constantinople had never had much use for Abbas at the best of times, and his artless carryings-on in Switzerland did little to endear them to his cause; indeed, they had spurned his every advance.

By 1916, however, the Germans had taken a rather different view of Abbas Hilmi. Whether born of a desire to stand by an old friend or—rather more likely—operating under the delusion that Abbas actually represented some constituency other than himself, the Germans had steadily come to regard the deposed khedive as their future power broker in Egypt once victory was achieved. After persistently encouraging Abbas and the Constantinople regime to reconcile, their efforts had finally come to fruition with Abbas's arrival in the Ottoman capital that October.

Over the next few months, Prüfer and the ex-khedive saw a great deal of each other, and together they formulated plans for the future of Egypt, one in which Abbas would be restored to his former splendor with the aid of his German friend. So close were the two men, and so important did Berlin consider their future Egyptian stakeholder, that Prüfer would soon virtually become Abbas's personal handler. It was an alliance that over the next year would take on the tinge of the bizarre, the spectacle of two men constructing a castle-in-the-sky fantasy even as the real world burned down around them.

THEY SET OUT on the evening of October 24, and very quickly George Lloyd appreciated what so enthralled Lawrence with these journeys into the desert interior, the sensation of passing into an otherworldly place where time stood still. "The view up the pass was magnificent," Lloyd wrote in his diary from that night, "400 feet of jagged towering basalt and granite rock on either side of us, and the moon shining in our faces." The Arab sheikh accompanying them, he noted, "rode ahead of us with two or three Biasha slaves and looked like some modern Saladin out to meet a crusade."

For the first few days, the journey north was easy, and as they wended their way through the spectacular landscape of the Wadi Rumm mountains, the two friends talked Middle Eastern strategies and concocted fanciful plans for a grand tour of Arabia after the war. "We would defy Victorian sentiment and have a retinue of slaves," Lloyd recounted, "and would have one camel to carry books only, and we would go to Jauf and Boreida and talk desert politics all day." Lawrence felt so at ease that he even talked a bit about his family and upbringing in Oxford, the happy days he had spent in Carchemish. For Lloyd, long accustomed to his friend's taciturn nature, the fact that Lawrence "talks very well" came as something of a surprise.

Already, though, disquieting elements were beginning to attach to the trip. One took the form of Abd el Kader, the Algerian exile who promised to lead Lawrence to his kinsmen in the Yarmuk region, but who frequently clashed with other members of the traveling party. Another was the personality of the British demolitions expert, Lieutenant Wood. After getting lost in the darkness on his first night out, the lieutenant had remained unhappy and aloof, rarely engaging with his countrymen except to complain about the rigors of the journey. It increased Lloyd's apprehensions because, due to yet another foul-up in the supply pipeline from Egypt, Lawrence would have to perform some extremely risky improvisations at the target site, and would need to rely on Wood to step in should anything go wrong.

Back at El Arish, Lawrence had asked Clayton for a thousand yards of a newly developed lightweight two-strand electric cable, to be used in connecting the gelignite mine he would attach to the Yarmuk bridge to its electric detonator; such a length would allow the demolition team to be well away from the bridge when they blew it up, as well as provide a reserve for any secondary acts of mayhem that might present themselves. Instead, just five hundred yards of the old single-strand cable had been delivered to Aqaba. Since this line needed to be doubled over, it placed Lawrence a maximum of 250 yards away from the blast. Further, there was a good chance he'd be trying to set his charge while being shot at. Although Lawrence hoped he could go about attaching the explosives to the under-girders of the bridge unnoticed by the Turkish guards above, the standby plan was for others in the raiding party to distract the Turks in a firefight from the surrounding hills. Should Lawrence become a casualty in the process—a not unlikely prospect—Wood was expected to take over the operation.

But all this supposed a sufficient raiding party could even be raised, because what Lawrence was already discovering was a pronounced reluctance among prospective recruits to sign on. Lloyd later wrote to Clayton that "anyone who can hold up a train and enable the Arabs to sack it commands temporarily their allegiance," and this was one of the keys to his friend's success. "To them he is Lawrence, the arch looter, the super-raider, the real leader of the right and only kind of *ghazzu* [warfare], and he never forgets that this is a large part of his claim to sovereignty over them." With those Lawrence approached to join the Yarmuk mission, however, interest very quickly died off once he explained that his target was not a train but a bridge.

There was another matter, too. Among his fellow British officers, Lawrence had gained the reputation of being a veritable "Indian scout," possessed of an uncanny ability to navigate his way through the desert. As George Lloyd was discovering, this wasn't exactly true. On two separate occasions, they had become lost during night treks, and Lawrence's insistence during the second incident that they merely needed to follow Orion to recover their way had instead led them directly toward a Turkish encampment. All these factors considered, Lloyd wrote Clayton, "I hope his chances are really much better than would appear at first sight."

Actually, they were potentially far worse than even Lloyd imagined. Shortly before leaving Aqaba, Lawrence had been warned that Abd el Kader was a traitor and now in the pay of the Turks. Lawrence hadn't thought to share that warning with Lloyd. Perhaps this was because the source was Lawrence's old antagonist in the Hejaz, Édouard Brémond.

In fact, the French colonel had undergone a profound transformation in recent months, especially in his view of the Arab Revolt. This may have stemmed from his finally being informed of the Sykes-Picot pact that ensured French control of Syria, or from a recognition that what he couldn't thwart he needed to embrace. Whatever the cause, by the autumn of 1917, the imperialist Brémond had curbed his obstructionist approach to British initiatives in the region and become energetic in trying to get French weaponry and financial subsidies to the Arabs. Lawrence was surely aware of this transformation in his old adversary, but, whether still held by an abiding belief in French treachery or determined to press on no matter the ever-mounting signs of peril, he had chosen to ignore Brémond's warning about Abd el Kader. If Brémond was wrong about anything, however, it may have only been the vintage of the Algerian's betrayal; as far back as November 1914, Curt Prüfer had met Abd el Kader and reported on his fidelity to the German-Turkish cause.

To ignore such a litany of bad omens suggested a kind of fatalistic resignation on Lawrence's part, as if he now saw himself on a mission where his own life simply didn't much matter. Lloyd saw indications of this during their journey north. At some point, Lawrence expounded that since the Arabs had never been privy to Sykes-Picot, they could hardly be bound to it; instead, by seizing Syria, they might create their own destiny. It was for this cause, Lawrence confided, that he was now risking his life—or, as Lloyd jotted in his handwritten notes of that remarkable conversation, "L not working for HMG [His Majesty's Government] but for Sherif [Hussein]."

On the evening of October 28, four days after leaving Aqaba, the two friends sat down to discuss what came next. They were rapidly approaching the true danger zone, the point of no return, and Lloyd's apprehensions over Lawrence's "stunt" had only deepened. As he'd done several times previously, Lloyd offered to stay on. Lawrence thanked him, but explained that "he felt that any additional individual who was not an expert at the actual demolition only added to his own risk." He then offered a more poignant reason for sending Lloyd back, a wish rooted in the recognition that he might soon die: "He would like me to go home to England," Lloyd noted in his diary, "for he felt that there was a risk that all his work would be ruined politically in Whitehall and he thought I could save this."

The next afternoon the two friends parted, Lloyd turning back toward Aqaba, Lawrence continuing on for Yarmuk.

UPON FINALLY REACHING Cairo in late October 1917, William Yale checked in with the American diplomat who was to act as his liaison. This turned out to be a rather feckless young fellow named Charles Knabenshue, who held the ambiguous title of chargé to the United States' Diplomatic Agency. Given the all-pervasive British intelligence network in Cairo, the two quickly concluded that Yale should present himself to the

British authorities more or less overtly; "otherwise," Knabenshue informed the State Department, "his independent activities would certainly become known to them through their agents and thus excite unfavorable suspicion." Consequently, the two Americans asked for an audience with the British high commissioner to Egypt, Reginald Wingate, at his earliest convenience. Most convenient, it turned out, was the very next day. Donning their best summer suits, Yale and Knabenshue set out for the white stone mansion on the banks of the Nile that served as the British Residency.

For Reginald Wingate, having another State Department official wandering about Cairo presented something of a mixed prospect. On the one hand, with the United States now joined to the Allied war effort, British officials had an obligation to build the bonds of trust and solidarity even in those arenas, like the Middle East, where the Americans did not intend to militarily engage. Additionally, the high commissioner had his own ulterior motive for playing nice with the Americans. As he contemplated the deepening political morass into which Great Britain was sliding in the region, its secret deals with the French and the Arabs now about to be complemented by a pledge to the Zionists, Wingate increasingly saw the United States as a potential rescuer from the muddle. Indeed, just days before Yale's arrival in Cairo, Wingate had posited to a rather startled Knabenshue that perhaps the Palestine deck of cards should be shuffled once again, that instead of Arab or French or international or Zionist or even British control in the postwar world, maybe the Americans would like to step in there and have a go at things. Wingate could rely on Knabenshue to relay such feelers to the State Department in a positive light—the diplomat was married to an Englishwoman and was an ardent Anglophile—but maybe Yale could serve as a useful seconding voice.

On the other hand, if forced to deal with another State Department official, Wingate and every other Briton in Cairo aware of the man's background undoubtedly wished that it *not* be William Yale. Part of it stemmed from the antipathy with which British officials at all levels regarded Yale's former employer, Standard Oil of New York. Time and again in the early days of the war, Socony tankers had been caught trying to elude the British naval blockade to supply oil to the Germans, a practice finally curtailed less through diplomatic appeals than by the British seizure of Socony ships. But only curtailed; just that summer, with the United States now officially at war with Germany, the Socony representative in Brazil had been caught red-handed selling oil to German front companies. In defending his actions, the man had blandly explained that business was business, and that if he didn't sell to the enemy, his competitors surely would. That William Yale came out of such a cold-blooded corporate culture did little to inspire British confidence.

Nor, of course, did Yale's specific service to that corporation. As the British in Cairo were well aware, the former Socony representative had just spent over two years living as a protected neutral in the heart of enemy territory, and even if London might be grateful for the intelligence Yale had passed on based on his tenure there, that gratitude was far more muted at the actual war front. In particular, British war planners in Cairo couldn't quite forget that much of the best highway in enemy-held Palestine, the Jerusalem-to-Beersheva road that served as the Turks' crucial supply lifeline to the Gaza front where British forces had twice foundered, had actually been built by Standard Oil back in 1914, nor that William Yale had been a supervisor on that project.

All this taken together, Wingate found himself in a bit of a quandary when, shortly after their first amicable meeting, Yale came back to him with a bold request. From somewhere, the State Department agent had learned of the existence of the *Arab Bulletin*, the weekly compendium of raw and top-secret intelligence gathered by the Arab Bureau from across the Middle East. So sensitive was the *Bulletin* that its distribution was limited to fewer than thirty of the seniormost political and military officials of the British Empire, along with just three representatives of Allied governments. William Yale now wanted access to it as well.

After careful consideration, Wingate acceded to the request, but only after imposing a typically British precondition. Yale could peruse the *Bulletin* for his own edification, but, on his word of honor, he was to never directly quote from it in any of his dispatches to the State Department.

No doubt such a gentlemanly arrangement worked just fine among the refined diplomatic classes of Europe, but in hindsight, the high commissioner might have wanted to more fully entertain his prejudices about William Yale's background; he had just given access to Britain's most time-sensitive secrets in the Middle East to a former employee of one of the most predatory corporations in human history, and William Yale didn't so much intend to quote from the *Bulletin* as to mine from it wholesale.

In his memoir, Yale justified that intent by a nice turn of circular logic: "The information the British gave me was not given to me personally, for I was but an agent of the United States government, and if I performed the function I was employed for by the government, I must transmit to the State Department what news I acquired.... The officials of other governments must understand such to be the case, hence any condition imposed by them has no validity. In consequence, I had no hesitancy in quoting these statements in the *Arab Bulletin* which I judged to be necessary."

While conceding the possibility of a gap in such logic—after all, for foreign officials to "understand" his situation, it rather depended on their being informed of it—Yale had a handy excuse for this, too; if his finely calibrated American moral compass had somehow been sent askew, it was surely due to the fact that "I had been living and dealing with European and Oriental officials for four years."

But there was something else about the young American special agent that Reginald Wingate didn't apprehend. William Yale wasn't actually a *former* employee of Socony at all. Rather, he was officially "on leave" from that corporation, a status that allowed him to continue to draw half his prewar salary. And even if British officials in Cairo were to ever grow suspicious of such a link, they were unlikely to uncover it, since Yale had arranged for his Socony checks to be issued to his mother and deposited in New York. In the months ahead, as he read through the *Arab Bulletin* and whatever other classified British intelligence came his way, Yale kept a careful lookout for any references to oil.

ON THE AFTERNOON of October 31, 1917, Aaron Aaronsohn and Chaim Weizmann waited in an antechamber of the British cabinet's conference room in Whitehall. They had been invited there by Mark Sykes for the honor of being the first to learn the result of the British leadership's latest deliberations on "the Zionist question."

At long last, the doors to the inner sanctum swung open, and a beaming Mark Sykes emerged. "Dr. Weizmann," he announced, "it's a boy."

The two Zionist leaders were then brought into the cabinet conference room to meet Prime Minister David Lloyd George, Foreign Secretary Arthur Balfour, and the other members of the government who had just then approved the wording of a statement on the future status of Jewish settlement in Palestine six months in the making. Testament to both that tortuous process and to the deep reservations many senior British officials still harbored on the issue was the curious manner in which the statement would now be delivered: a scribbled, seemingly off-the-cuff note of a mere three sentences from Secretary Balfour to British financier Walter Rothschild.

"His Majesty's Government view with favour," the salient clause read, "the establishment in Palestine of a national home for the Jewish people, and will use their best endeavors to facilitate the achievement of this object."

That handwritten note would soon become known as the Balfour Declaration, and from it would grow a controversy that continues to haunt the world to this day. For Aaron Aaronsohn, however, it was a first step toward his dream of a reconstituted Israel, the cause for which he and so many of his compatriots in Palestine had sacrificed so much. Aaronsohn was yet to know the full extent of those sacrifices, however. On that day of celebration at Whitehall, neither he nor anyone else outside Palestine had learned of the ugly events that had occurred at Zichron Yaakov three weeks earlier.

FOR GILBERT CLAYTON and David Hogarth and a handful of other British officers in Egypt that early November, a nagging concern began to intrude on their ebullient moods: where was Lawrence?

General Allenby's offensive had gone off like clockwork. Catching the Turkish forces around Beersheva off guard, the British cavalry had stormed into that desert town on the morning of October 31 and then pressed on. By November 7, the Turkish garrison at Gaza, their lines of reinforcement cut and in imminent danger of being encircled, had abandoned their trenchworks and begun a hasty withdrawal twenty miles up the coast. Bad weather prevented the British from pressing their advantage, but they had now finally pierced the first and strongest defensive wall of Palestine.

Yet as the days passed and the afterglow of that victory began to fade, those at El Arish who had been involved in the strategic planning with Lawrence grew increasingly troubled by the enduring silence from Yarmuk. As Gilbert Clayton confided to George Lloyd, now back in Aqaba, on November 12, "I am very anxious for news of Lawrence."

On that day, Lawrence and his raiding party were actually some eighty miles to the east of Yarmuk, hoping to salvage at least some small accomplishment from a mission where everything had gone wrong.

Reaching the desert fortress village of Azraq a few days after parting with Lloyd, Lawrence had found the Serahin tribesmen he hoped to enlist for Yarmuk reluctant to join; a chief reason was their deep mistrust of Abd el Kader, whom they too suspected of being a traitor. Swayed by an impassioned speech by Lawrence, the tribesmen finally joined on to the mission, but then Abd el Kader had abruptly disappeared en route to Yarmuk, last seen heading for a Turkish-held town. Still, Lawrence refused to turn back.

Despite it all, he very nearly succeeded. Reaching the railroad bridge at Tell al Shehab on the night of November 7, Lawrence and his demolition team had been hauling the gelignite down into the gorge under the very nose of a Turkish sentry when someone dropped a rifle against the rocks. Alerted by the sound, the half dozen Turkish guards rolled out of their guardhouse to begin firing wildly in all directions. Possessed of the unpleasant knowledge that gelignite explodes if hit by a bullet, Lawrence's porters summarily tossed their loads into the ravine and scrambled for safety. With little alternative, Lawrence joined them.

Men in war are among the most superstitious of people, but even one welded to pure rationality might have decided it was now time for the Yarmuk raiding party to call things off, to count its blessings at having survived for this long and make for safety. Instead, Lawrence seemed gripped by an almost demonic determination to wring at least some small shard of success from his mission. He decided to launch another train attack.

To do so, though, meant raising the danger stakes yet again. With his entourage running desperately short of food, he ordered some of its members away. This included the Indian machine-gun crews, which meant that even if the train attack came off, the raiders would have no heavy weaponry to protect them. What's more, due to the amount of electric cable lost at the Yarmuk bridge, whoever triggered the detonation would be positioned a mere fifty yards from the blast site. That person would be Lawrence.

The site he chose was an isolated stretch of track outside the village of Minifir on the main trunk line of the Hejaz Railway below Amman. Crouched behind a small bush to conceal his detonator but in plain view of the track, Lawrence first tried to blow up a long troop transport train. To the great good fortune of himself and the sixty men in his retinue hiding in nearby gulleys, the electric connection failed—they surely would have been massacred by the overwhelming Turkish force—and for agonizing minutes, Lawrence endured the puzzled stares of the Turkish soldiers on the slowly passing train, occasionally waving to them in forced friendliness.

Not that the odds of survival were much better with the somewhat smaller troop train Lawrence succeeded in striking the next day. Positioned so close to the explosion site, he was sent flying by the blast's concussion—a very lucky thing since a large chunk of the destroyed train engine landed directly atop the detonator mechanism that moments before had been between his knees. Dazed, Lawrence staggered to his feet to see that his shirt was torn to shreds and blood dripped from his left arm. As the dust and smoke cleared, he also saw just before him "the scalded and smoking upper half of a man," ripped in two by the blast; that portion of his body had flown fifty yards through the air.

"I duly felt that it was time to get away," Lawrence recounted in *Seven Pillars*, "but when I moved, I learnt that there was a great pain in my right foot, because of which I could only limp along, with my head swinging from the shock. Movement began to clear away this confusion, as I hobbled toward the upper valley, whence the Arabs were now shooting fast into the crowded coaches."

As Lawrence stumbled toward safety, the Turkish soldiers on the train took aim at him—albeit not very good aim; by his account, he was grazed by at least five of their bullets, "some of them uncomfortably deep." As he went, still in a state of shock, he willed himself on by chanting an odd refrain: "Oh, I wish this hadn't happened."

In the capture of Wejh ten months earlier, Lawrence had excoriated a British officer who had led an assault party ashore, an action that resulted in some twenty Arabs being killed, rather than simply waiting for the stranded Turkish garrison to surrender. "To me," he wrote of that engagement, "an unnecessary action, or shot, or casualty, was not only waste but sin. . . . Our rebels were not materials, like soldiers, but friends of ours, trusting our leadership. We were not in command nationally, but by invitation, and our men were volunteers—individuals, local men, relatives—so that a death was a personal sorrow to many in the army."

At Minifir, Lawrence had picked a fight with a Turkish force of some four hundred soldiers with a mere sixty followers; incredibly, some of these didn't even have weapons, and were reduced to throwing rocks at the hobbled train. About twenty were quickly shot down, including at least seven from among the group sent down to the tracks to rescue Lawrence. Of the contradiction between his response to the British officer's actions at Wejh and his own at Minifir, Lawrence seemed to remain quite oblivious—or perhaps, in the passage of those brutal ten months, he simply no longer cared.

"Next day," he wrote of Minifir's aftermath, "we moved into Azrak, having a great welcome and boasting—God forgive us—that we were victors."

Chapter 16

A Gathering Fury

With reference to the recent publication of your Excellency's
declaration to Lord Rothschild regarding Jews in Palestine, we
respectfully take the liberty to invite your Excellency's attention to
the fact that Palestine forms a vital part of Syria—as the heart is to the
body—admitting of no separation politically or sociologically.

THE SYRIAN COMMITTEE OF EGYPT TO BRITISH
FOREIGN SECRETARY BALFOUR, NOVEMBER 14, 1917

The British Authorities have replied to the Syrian Committee . . . that
the telegram to Mr. Balfour could not be transmitted at this time, but
that the British Authorities were pleased the Syrians in Egypt had made
known their sentiments in regard to the Zionist Question.

WILLIAM YALE TO STATE DEPARTMENT, DECEMBER 17, 1917

For the traveler venturing east from the Jordanian capital of Amman, there is little to relieve the eye. Within a few miles, the hilly contours of Amman are left behind and the land settles into an undulating plain of gravel and coarse sand. As a consequence, one's first thought upon coming to the high stone walls of the citadel of Azraq, some fifty miles across that dreary desert, is apt to be wonderment at its improbability. On this vast and empty landscape, how to account for such a massive fortress, its thirty-foot walls crowned by even higher watchtowers at its corners, ever having been built?

The answer is water, of course, an oasis that in ancient times provided the only source of sustenance over a surrounding area of nearly five thousand square miles. It was the Romans who first appreciated Azraq's strategic importance, erecting a small fort beside the oasis in the second century AD, but it was Saladin's Ayyubid empire a thousand years later that created the impressive monolith that still stands. Even today, the citadel dominates the town that shares its name, but in November 1917, when Lawrence and his small band of raiders fled to Azraq after their train attack at Minifir, that settlement consisted of a few stone huts, and the fortress must have risen up from the plain before them like an apparition.

Azraq was where Lawrence had met Nuri Shalaan, the emir of the Rualla tribe, the previous June, and he had noted at the time that it made for a perfect hideout. Along with water and shelter, the fortress provided a commanding view of the desert in all directions. Consequently, Lawrence had sent the Indian machine-gun crews there just prior to the Minifir attack, so that by the time he and the rest of the raiding party arrived on November 12, those guns were already mounted in the citadel's watchtowers, making the place all but invincible. So ideal was the oasis, in fact, that Lawrence quickly decided to make it the forward base for bringing the Arab Revolt to the Syrian heartland; within a day of arriving, he sent a courier on the two-hundred-mile journey to Aqaba with instructions for Faisal to begin bringing the vanguard of his army north.

Setting up shop in Azraq served a more cunning purpose, too. The settlement marked the northwestern boundary of Nuri Shalaan's dominion. Despite the repeated entreaties of Faisal, and Lawrence himself back in June, Shalaan continued to straddle the centerline of the war, quietly lending support to the Arab rebels one day, openly trading with the Turks the next. In Azraq, the rebels would be placing themselves squarely between the Rualla heartland and the Turkish-controlled Syrian market towns. "He hesitated to declare himself only because of his wealth in Syria," Lawrence wrote of Shalaan, "and the possible hurt to his tribesmen if they were deprived of their natural market. We, by living in one of his main manors, would keep him ashamed to go in to the enemy."

In Azraq, Lawrence's small retinue quickly became less a band of warriors than a pickup construction crew as they set to work making the citadel habitable for the much larger force soon to be on its way. They repaired its tumbled stone walls and fallen roofs, even refurbished the small mosque in its courtyard that had most recently been used as a sheep pen. As word of the rebels' presence spread through the district, their labors were interrupted by visits from tribal delegations, visits that invariably led to feasts and an atmosphere of general merriment. Lawrence found a pleasant respite from it all by taking up residence in the repaired watchroom of the southern tower.

Even for a book saturated with detail—some might say drowned by it—there is something quite remarkable about Lawrence's account of Azraq in *Seven Pillars*. For five pages, and in some of the most heart-felt writing of the entire memoir, he lingered over the idyll of his time there, the happy camaraderie that existed between his group of follow-ers and their visitors, lyrically described the mysterious wolves or jackals that howled outside the citadel's walls at night but were never seen. Even when the winter rains started, turning the fortress into a leaking, clammy prison where the only recourse was to huddle for warmth beneath sheep-skins, misery took on a distinctly heraldic quality. "It was icy cold as we hid there, motionless, from murky daylight until dark, our minds seemed suspended within these massive walls, through whose every shot-window the piercing mist streamed like a white pennant. Past and future flowed over us like an uneddying river. We dreamed ourselves into the spirit of the place; sieges and feasting, raids, murders, love-singing in the night."

Making all this rather more remarkable is that, at most, Lawrence stayed just six days in Azraq on this November visit, and possibly as few as three.

Perhaps the place took on its idyllic trappings in his mind because of what he had just endured. For the preceding month, ever since coming up with the plan to attack the Yarmuk bridge, Lawrence had lived in the constant shadow of the knowledge that he might soon die. In Azraq, that shadow had abruptly lifted.

Or perhaps it was due to what lay immediately ahead. Just days after reaching Azraq, Lawrence set off into the desert again in the company of three men. Their destination was the crucial rail junction town of Deraa, seventy miles to the northwest. There, Lawrence would endure the most horrific—and among his various biographers of the past half century, most fiercely debated—ordeal of his entire wartime experience.

THE DOUBLE CROSS, for this was certainly how Aaron Aaronsohn viewed it, was revealed on the afternoon of November 16, on the very eve of his departure from London. It was then that he finally received Chaim Weizmann's letter of instruction concerning his mission to the United States. The two had discussed that mission at such exhaustive length in recent days that Aaronsohn almost didn't bother to read the letter—but he did.

Weizmann's note instructed him, essentially, to shut up. "The carry-ing out of these complicated duties," he wrote, "makes it desirable for you to avoid making public speeches and journalistic interviews, and in order to prevent your being pressed to undertake such work we, in accordance with your desire, formally request you to confine yourself to the duties already specified." In case the point could be missed, Weizmann further ordered Aaronsohn to refrain from all "direct action, either by speech or letter, except through the medium of Mr. Brandeis," the leader of American Zionists.

Aaronsohn was made furious by the letter, not least by Weizmann's contention that he himself had asked for such a muzzle. "The old man is not a fool," he angrily noted in his diary that night, "but I am not so naïve either. . . . Verily, every day brings me another proof of Weizmann's hypocrisy."

Since arriving in London six weeks earlier, Aaronsohn had spent a good deal of time with the British Zionist leader. Their relationship was a complicated one, rooted in both mutual respect and mutual distrust, and they had developed a habit of getting along famously one day, falling to bickering the next. Just prior to Weizmann's demeaning letter of instruction, there had been much more of the former, and for a simple reason: in a matter of days, there had unfolded before their eyes the most dramatic and consequential events in the history of Zionism.

Chief among these was the Balfour Declaration, of course, but neatly coinciding with that had been news of the British army's rapid advance in Palestine. After breaking through at Beersheva, Allenby's forces had continued to push north, scattering the disorganized Turks before them. Although Aaronsohn didn't know it yet, on that very day of November 16, a British vanguard was marching unopposed into the coastal city of Jaffa, fifty miles from their starting point, even as other units closed on the foothills below Jerusalem. With astounding speed, what had seemed a distant, even theoretical, dream for nineteen hundred years—the return of the Jewish diaspora to their ancient homeland—was hurtling toward reality.

Understandably, the combination of these events was having an electrifying effect on the international Zionist community. From Jewish enclaves around the world, messages of gratitude for the Balfour Declaration had flooded into the British Foreign Office. That outpouring seemed to instantly affirm the argument that Chaim Weizmann and his allies in the British government had been pressing for months, that by declaring support for a Jewish homeland and working to make it happen, the Allies would find the world's Zionist community rushing to its side.

This reaction wasn't universal, however, and the fervency of support elsewhere made the muted reaction among American Zionists all the more striking. By mid-November, few American newspapers had seen fit to even mention the declaration—the *New York Times* dispensed with it in three very short paragraphs—while many noted American Jewish leaders had yet to publicly comment on it. Most conspicuous was the silence emanating from the Wilson administration, a situation Weizmann and the British government found particularly galling since the declaration had been rewritten—and substantially delayed—specifically to gain the American president's approval.

As Woodrow Wilson's closest advisor, Colonel Edward House, had informed the British back in September when the proposal was first explicitly put to the Americans, the president was prepared to go no further than a vague statement of "sympathy" for the Anglo-Zionist plan, and only this "provided it can be made without conveying any real commitment" on his part. By subsequently watering down the declaration's original proposed language, the British had managed to bring Wilson fully on board, but with a major caveat still attached; as House told London in mid-October, the president "asks that no mention of his approval shall be made when His Majesty's Government makes [the] formula public, as he has arranged that American Jews shall then ask him for his approval, which he will give publicly here."

Except that Wilson's silence had contributed to the hesitation of American Zionists on the matter, which in turn had enabled the president to maintain his silence. It was in hopes of countering this standoff that Aaron Aaronsohn, a familiar figure to many of those Zionists, was being dispatched to the United States.

The goals of his mission had been worked out at a high-level meeting at the British Foreign Office a few days earlier, one attended by both Weizmann and Mark Sykes. It was a highly ambitious agenda. As the officially designated liaison between the English Zionist Federation and its American counterpart, Aaronsohn was to "help our United States Organization to appreciate the actual significance of various political and military developments" in the Middle East, as well as to promote the "the rousing of Zionist enthusiasm, the stimulating of pro-Entente propaganda," and, in furtherance of Sykes's fanciful notion of a Jewish-Arab-Armenian consortium in the Middle East, "the consolidation and alliance of the Zionist forces with those of the Arabs and Armenians." In addition, Aaronsohn was to act as the official channel of communication between Weizmann and the leader of the American Zionist community, U.S. Supreme Court justice Louis Brandeis.

As daunting as this agenda was, Aaronsohn had accepted the assignment wholeheartedly, and he'd let his Zionist contacts in the United States know he was on his way. That simply added another layer of humiliation to Weizmann's letter of instruction on November 16.

But many people had tried to silence Aaron Aaronsohn over the years, and to precious little success. Quickly coming to regard Weizmann's strictures as something of a dare, the next morning the agronomist boarded a train at London's Euston station for the run up to Liverpool and the ship, SS *St. Paul*, that would take him to New York.

In Weizmann's defense, it wasn't merely a controlling nature that led him to try to muzzle Aaronsohn. While appreciative of the scientist's extensive contacts in the American Zionist community, Weizmann had spent enough time around Aaronsohn over the previous six weeks to grow apprehensive of his hotheaded personality. That was especially worrisome considering that there was actually something of a hidden agenda to his mission to the United States.

In anticipation of full British control of Palestine in the near future, as well as to allay the fears already being expressed by the Muslim and Christian communities of Palestine over the Balfour Declaration, Sykes and Weizmann had decided that a Zionist committee should be dispatched to the region as soon as possible to take stock of the situation. Sykes in particular was anxious that this committee include an American delegation, figuring that its presence would be viewed as tacit acceptance by President Wilson of both the Balfour Declaration and future British control of Palestine. But a rather daunting obstacle stood in the way. The United States had only declared war on Germany, and Wilson had made it clear he had no intention of becoming entangled in any affairs regarding the Ottoman Empire; thus it was highly doubtful that his administration would sanction an American delegation. This gave rise to Aaronsohn's sub rosa mission to the United States: to get American Zionist leaders to bring pressure on the Wilson government, not only to openly endorse the Balfour Declaration, but to reverse course and declare war on Turkey.

But when Aaronsohn arrived in the United States he received some crushing news. At the Zionist Federation office in New York on December 1, he was handed a cable from his youngest brother, Sam, newly arrived in Cairo. Nearly two full months after the event, Aaronsohn finally learned of the destruction of his NILI spy ring by the Turks. His brother's cable also told of the death of their sister Sarah, their father, Ephraim, and of the execution of Naaman Belkind.

"The sacrifice is accomplished," Aaronsohn wrote in his diary that night. "I knew that we still had to face the greatest misfortune, but it is one thing to fear it, and another to know that all hope is lost. Poor father, poor Sarati.... Her loss is the most cruel."

The news surely added a new layer of resentment in his feelings for Weizmann and the other Zionist leaders in Europe who sought to curb his influence. For two years, Aaronsohn and those closest to him had risked their lives for the Zionist cause—and many had now paid the ultimate price—while those in London and Paris went about their meetings and pamphleteering. That contrast was exquisitely underscored on December 2. Just a day after Aaronsohn received the sad news from Athlit, members of the English Zionist Federation gathered at London's Albert Hall for a gala celebration marking the one-month anniversary of the Balfour Declaration.

IT'S UNLIKELY THAT any writer ever recounted his or her own torture in more exacting, even loving, detail.

By Lawrence's account, it began on the morning of November 20. Several days earlier, he had left Azraq with his three escorts to survey the countryside around the vital railway town of Deraa. He now wanted a firsthand look at Deraa's rail complex itself. The only way to do that was brazenly, so that morning Lawrence and one of his escorts had ridden to an isolated stretch of railway several miles north of town and dismounted from their camels; on foot and in Arab dress, they had then begun simply walking the rails into Deraa.

All was going well until, passing a Turkish army encampment, the pair drew the notice of a suspicious sergeant. The officer collared Lawrence, announcing that "the Bey [chief] wants you," but for some reason allowed his companion to continue on.

For the rest of that day, Lawrence was held in a guardroom awaiting his audience with the bey and parrying suspicions that he was a Turkish army deserter. He did so by claiming to be a Circassian, a mountain people of the northern Caucasus who were exempt from conscription and known for their fair complexions and light-colored eyes. In the evening, guards came to take him to the bey's rooms, a man Lawrence would identify as "Nahi" in *Seven Pillars*, but whose actual name was Hajim Muhittin, the Deraa district governor.

It became clear this meeting was intended to be of a sexual nature when Hajim dismissed the guard detail and wrestled Lawrence onto his bed. When he managed to wriggle free, the governor summoned the guards, who pinioned Lawrence to the bed and began tearing away his clothes. Hajim's pawing began anew, until Lawrence kneed him in the groin.

With his naked victim again pinned to the bed by the guards, a furious Hajim now fell on Lawrence in a frenzy of both ardor and rage, kissing and spitting on him, biting into his neck until it drew blood, finally lifting up a fold of skin on his chest to skewer him with a bayonet. As Lawrence would recount, the bey then ordered the guards "to take me out and teach me everything."

What followed was an ordeal of horrific torture. Dragged into a nearby room, Lawrence was stretched over a bench where two of the guards "knelt on my ankles, bearing down on the back of my knees, while two more twisted my wrists till they cracked, and then crushed them and my neck against the wood." A short whip was then retrieved, and the four guards took turns lashing Lawrence on the back and buttocks scores, if not hundreds, of times. "At last when I was completely broken they seemed satisfied," he recalled in *Seven Pillars*. "Somehow I found myself off the bench, lying on my back on the dirty floor, where I snuggled down, dazed, panting for breath, but vaguely comfortable."

But his torment was not quite done and, in the telling, now took on a hallucinatory quality. Viciously kicked in the ribs by the officer in charge and ordered to stand, Lawrence instead smiled idly up at the man. At this effrontery, the officer "flung up his arm and hacked the full length of his whip into my groin. This doubled me half-over screaming, or rather, trying impotently to scream, only shuddering through my open mouth. One [of the guards] giggled with amusement. A voice cried, 'Shame, you've killed him.' Another slash followed. A roaring, and my eyes went black."

Perhaps not surprisingly, when Lawrence was finally dragged back to Hajim's quarters, "he now rejected me in haste, as a thing too torn and bloody for his bed." His ordeal at last over, Lawrence was hauled out to the courtyard and dumped in a shed where an Armenian "dresser," or male nurse, was summoned to wash and bandage him. Then his torturers simply walked away.

That they would do so was only the first in a remarkable—some would say highly improbable—sequence of events that would ultimately deliver Lawrence from his greatest tribulation. By his account, as dawn approached, he summoned the strength to get to his feet and explore his dreary surroundings. In the empty adjacent room, he found a "suit of shoddy clothes" hanging from a door. Managing to dress himself, he then climbed out a window to drop to the empty street outside. On unsteady feet, he proceeded to walk through the just-wakening town until at last he'd left it behind. Wheedling a ride from a passing camel-borne merchant, he finally came to the outlying village where he'd arranged to rendezvous with his Azraq companions. He found them there, their previous anxiety over his capture replaced by amazement at his escape.

"I told them a merry tale of bribery and trickery," Lawrence recounted, "which they promised to keep to themselves, laughing aloud at the simplicity of the Turks." That same afternoon, the group set out on horseback for the seventy-mile return to Azraq.

So, in brief, was Lawrence's account of that awful day—in brief, because the story of his brutalization at Deraa would extend over five lurid and excruciating-to-read pages in *Seven Pillars*. Yet there is something in the sheer accumulation of such ghastly detail that serves to cloud the narrative, to make vague what really happened. In describing his wrists being twisted until they "cracked," did Lawrence mean they were broken? And was he actually raped? There are several euphemistic clues to suggest so, but just as many to suggest the opposite. Even more puzzling are those lingering descriptions of his torture that take on a vaguely lascivious, voyeuristic quality. When he was lanced with the bayonet, for example, Lawrence noted that "the blood wavered down my side, and dripped to the front of my thigh. [Hajim] looked pleased and dabbled it over my stomach with his finger-tips." Later, while being kicked in the ribs after his flogging, he would recall that "a delicious warmth, probably sexual, was swelling through me."

Under the weight of such precise and overwhelming detail, many Lawrence biographers—most, in fact—have concluded that the incident at Deraa simply could not have happened as he described, even that it didn't occur at all. Put plainly, how could anyone subjected to the cruelties Lawrence claimed to have endured at Deraa been capable of escape? Even allowing for the fantastic string of good luck that brought him to that point, how did a man whose wrists had been "cracked" shortly before manage to climb out a window? Flogging so disrupts the central nervous system that many victims have difficulty even standing for several hours after receiving as few as thirty lashes; lashed exponentially more, how was Lawrence able to walk several miles through an enemy town unnoticed, then immediately set out on a seventy-mile horseback ride?

The implausibilities grow in light of Lawrence's subsequent actions. Just two days after returning to Azraq, he embarked on an arduous four-day camel ride to Aqaba. Once there, he made no mention of his Deraa ordeal to his British comrades. Questioned years later, several would recall that Lawrence had seemed preoccupied upon his return, one going so far as to say he was "pale and obviously distraught," but none reported seeing any cuts or bruises on their colleague, or that he displayed any obvious signs of physical discomfort. Indeed, upon seeing his protégé less than three weeks after the Deraa incident, David Hogarth would write to his wife that Lawrence looked "fitter and better than when I last saw him."

Casting further doubt on the Deraa story as rendered in *Seven Pillars* is the radically different first version that Lawrence provided nineteen months after the event. It was contained in a June 1919 letter to his army friend, Colonel Walter Stirling, and Lawrence backed into the account by way of listing the various betrayals of the Algerian turncoat, Abd el Kader. Not only had the Algerian sabotaged his Yarmuk bridge operation, Lawrence explained to Stirling, but he had been recognized by Hajim Muhittin, the Deraa governor, "by virtue of Abd el Kader's description of me. (I learnt all about his treachery from Hajim's conversation, and from my guards.) Hajim was an ardent pederast and took a fancy to me. So he kept me under guard till night, and then tried to have me. I was unwilling, and prevailed after some difficulty. Hajim sent me to the hospital and I escaped before dawn, being not as hurt as he thought. He was so ashamed of the muddle he had made that he hushed the whole thing up, and never reported my capture and escape. I got back to Azrak very annoyed with Abd el Kader."

When measured against that in *Seven Pillars,* this account has the unique quality of being simultaneously both more and less plausible. Absent the gothic cruelties described in the book, perhaps a Lawrence "not as hurt as he thought" would have had the physical wherewithal to escape. On the other hand, if Hajim had truly recognized him—this at a time when there was a 20,000-Turkish-pound bounty on Lawrence's head—it seems utterly absurd that he would leave such a prize unguarded in a hospital overnight. It's also a bit hard to imagine that a chief topic of conversation among Lawrence's captors as they set to abusing him would be of Abd el Kader's role in unmasking him.

But despite all this, there are strong indications that *something* happened in Deraa. Many of those who knew Lawrence best would report a change in his personality, an even greater remoteness, dating from around that time. It was also soon afterward that he began organizing his personal bodyguard, a detail of some fifty or sixty elite warriors who from then on would be in his almost constant company.

And as it turns out, Lawrence gave yet a third account of what had occurred in Deraa, one that suggests his experience there was very different—and in some respects, a great deal worse—from that which he told Stirling or presented to the outside world. It came in a letter to Charlotte Shaw, the wife of writer George Bernard Shaw, in 1924.

Lawrence became close friends with the Shaws after the war, with Charlotte Shaw assuming a kind of mother-confessor role in his life, or, as Lawrence put it, "the solitary woman who lets me feel at ease with her in spite of it all." Presumably in response to a question from Charlotte Shaw, he wrote, "About that night. I shouldn't tell you, because decent men don't talk about such things. I wanted to put it plain in the book and wrestled for days with my self-respect, which wouldn't, hasn't let me. For fear of being hurt, or rather to earn five minutes respite from a pain which drove me mad, I gave away the only possession we are born into the world with: our bodily integrity. It's an unforgivable matter, an irrevocable position, and it's that which has made me forswear decent living. . . . You may call this morbid, but think of the offence and the intensity of brooding over it for these years."

While rendered with his trademark obliqueness, this account suggests an altogether different picture of Deraa: that Lawrence surrendered to his attacker's advances in order to avoid being tortured—or at least to bring it to an end. If so, it not only might explain how he was able to escape—the physical torture being minimal—but why he would tell his Azraq companions "a merry tale" and swear them to secrecy, why he would make no mention of the episode to his British comrades in Aqaba, and why he would continue to dissemble about it forever after.

But if he escaped the worst of physical torture, it came at the price of a complex constellation of psychological ones. As any victim of rape or torture can attest, perhaps the most difficult aspect of the trauma to reconcile is not the pain or even the fear of the experience, but a profoundly felt, if utterly undeserved, sense of humiliation. Lawrence was apparently both raped *and* tortured. While potentially devastating to most anyone, in Lawrence's case such a trial also cut to the very core of his self-image. Since childhood, he had honed in himself the credo of stoicism, the bedrock belief that he had the ability to endure most any suffering or hardship, but now that faith had deserted him at his most desperate and vulnerable moment. Possibly further added to this—especially if the theory that Lawrence was a severely repressed homosexual is given credence—was the element of sexual self-loathing the ordeal likely inspired. Had he given in out of fear of pain or death, he probably asked himself ever afterward, or because he was secretly drawn to the act? Little wonder, then, that someone enduring such a trauma might wish to adorn its memory with staggering violence, the kind of violence that offers an absolution of guilt by making all questions of will or resistance moot.

There is another compelling reason to believe something deeply scarring occurred to Lawrence at Deraa, and something more along the lines of what he described to Charlotte Shaw than what he told Walter Stirling or wrote in *Seven Pillars*. In ten months, he would return to that railway town in Syria, and there Lawrence would commit some of his most brutal acts of the war, acts that would carry the very strong scent of vengeance.

ON THE EVENING of December 4, 1917, the leading citizenry of Beirut gathered for a banquet in honor of Djemal Pasha. "Every time I come to Beirut," Djemal began his speech, "I observe that the inhabitants are very loyal. This has filled me with affection for them. I take this opportunity of offering them my thanks for their kindness towards me."

It was a bold tack for the Syrian governor to take, since his relationship with the city had actually always been a contentious one. With Beirut long regarded as a crucible of Arab nationalism, Djemal had exiled hundreds of its citizens on the suspicion of disloyalty, and the surrounding Lebanon region had suffered disproportionately—many believed quite deliberately—in the famines that had ravaged wartime Syria. Then there was the matter of the twenty-five alleged anti-Turk conspirators, unmasked in the documents purloined from the shuttered French consulate, that Djemal had ordered hanged in the city's Place des Canons in two separate mass executions. By the time of his banquet in December 1917, Place des Canons had already been dubbed Martyrs' Square by Beirut's residents, a name it officially carries today.

Not that any of the assembled notables were likely to quibble over Djemal's generous words, considering that they had gathered that evening by way of farewell. After three tumultuous years, the volatile military man from the island of Lesbos was leaving his posts in Syria, and even if his departure was officially described as temporary, everyone in the banquet hall, including Djemal, knew this was a fiction.

As part of a reorganization recently engineered by Enver Pasha, control of the Ottoman armies in Syria had been handed over to a new German commander, General Erich von Falkenhayn. As a sop, Djemal had been named commander in chief of Syria and Western Arabia—a fine-sounding position, certainly, but more impressive if there'd been an actual army to go with it. "A sort of commander-in-chief second class," observed Djemal's private secretary, Falih Rifki. "The artillery, the machine guns, the rifles and the swords were put under the German's orders, while Djemal Pasha's share was that grand title to put over his signature.... It was like the honorary rank of pasha which we used to give to Bedouin sheikhs in the empty desert."

If calculated to offend Djemal's sense of honor, the move worked; resigning his various positions, he had announced his intention to return to Constantinople. To the degree that he blamed Enver for his downfall, Djemal appeared to exact some small revenge in his Beirut speech when he got around to mentioning the executions in the city's Place des Canons, a bit of unpleasantry that still clearly rankled some of his listeners: "It is true that some time back I hanged certain Arabs," he offered. "I did not do this of my own accord, but at the insistence of Enver Pasha."

Djemal was leaving behind a record as contradictory as the man himself. While his public vow to conquer Egypt had led to fiasco in the Sinai, he could take some credit for his army's two successful stands against the British at Gaza. He had overseen an array of ambitious modernization efforts across Syria—paved and widened city streets, electrification, new parks and mosques and municipal buildings—even as hundreds of thousands of his subjects, perhaps as many as a million, had died from starvation and disease. He had tried to ameliorate the suffering of the Armenians, at the same time that he gained a reputation as a persecutor of the region's Jews. And while his hard-line approach had tamped down any rebellious ardor among Arab nationalists in Syria—in none of its provinces had there been a significant uprising during his tenure—his kinder, gentler approach toward King Hussein in the Hejaz had badly backfired.

He was also getting out of Syria at a very good time. That autumn, Falkenhayn had struggled to bring a new elite Turkish force, the Yildirim Army Group, south for a preemptive assault on the British massing in the Sinai, but he had been beaten to the punch by Allenby, with the British smashing through the Turkish line at the end of October. In the month since, and with transiting Yildirim units still scattered over the breadth of Syria, the British had seized much of southern Palestine, and now stood poised on the outskirts of Jerusalem itself. In all of this, Djemal stood perfectly blameless.

But it also wasn't as if either Djemal or the Turkish war effort in Syria were finished just yet. Instead, and as had happened so many times over the centuries when all seemed lost for the Ottoman Empire, it was precisely at this darkest moment that a shocking turn of events had the chance to change everything.

On November 7, the very day that the Turkish army had been abandoning Gaza, Vladimir Lenin and his Bolsheviks had overthrown the Russian government of Alexander Kerensky. The following morning, the Bolsheviks released their Decree on Peace, announcing their intention to immediately withdraw from the war. All along the front, Russian forces stood down in a unilateral cease-fire. Just like that, the Ottoman Empire had seen its most implacable foe of the past two centuries simply fall away, one of the three enemy armies tearing at its frontiers suddenly go silent.

More extraordinary news had soon followed. Rifling through the overthrown government's files, the Bolsheviks found a copy of the still-secret Sykes-Picot Agreement. No document could have more confirmed the Bolsheviks' accusation that the slaughter visited on the earth over the past three years had been in the service of imperial aggrandizement, and in mid-November they published the compact for all to see. Of course, that document also played to Djemal Pasha's long-standing accusation—that British and French talk of supporting Arab independence was simply a ruse to grab Arab lands for their colonial empires—and he used the occasion of his speech in Beirut to reiterate that point to the entire Arab and Muslim world.

"The [Sykes-Picot] Agreement was a device for bringing about an Arab revolt to suit the designs of the British who, needing tools and catspaws to serve their own ends, encouraged certain Arabs to rebel by giving them mendacious promises and hoodwinking them with false hopes," Djemal said. For a long time, he told his audience, he had puzzled over why King Hussein had turned his back on his Muslim brethren; now the answer was revealed. "Eventually, the unfortunate Sherif Hussein fell into the trap laid for him by the British, allowed himself to be ensnared by their cajoleries, and committed his offence against the unity and the majesty of Islam."

But with the Western imperialist scheme thus exposed, Djemal suggested, there was still time to defeat it. Hussein could repent for his past sins by renouncing his unholy alliance. Arabs everywhere, now shown the true face of the conniving enemy, could unite to defeat them. "I am going to Constantinople, but I shall soon be back," Djemal vowed at the end of his speech. "I beg the leading inhabitants of the town to pay no attention to false rumors, and to be patient during the few remaining days of the war, so that we may reach our goal."

The following day, his Beirut speech, with its exposure of Sykes-Picot, was carried on the front page of newspapers throughout Syria and Turkey.

Djemal hadn't limited his efforts to oration. Just prior to his Beirut address, he had penned letters to Faisal ibn Hussein and to the rebels' chief military commander, and arranged for them to be delivered to Aqaba through a confidential emissary. In his letter to Faisal, Djemal rather magnanimously conceded that the Arab Revolt might be justified if it brought about a truly independent Arab government in which the "dignity and splendor of Islam" was secured. "But what sort of independence can you conceive . . . after Palestine has become an international country, as the allied governments have openly and officially declared, [and] with Syria completely under French domination, and with Iraq and the whole of Mesopotamia forming part and parcel of British possessions? And how is such a government as this going to undertake, with independence and majesty, the shaping of the destinies of Islam? Perhaps you had not foreseen these results at the outset, but I am hoping that the spectacle of the British conquering Palestine will reveal to you this truth in all its nakedness." The letter was intended as more than a scold. "If you admit this truth," Djemal concluded, "there is nothing easier than to announce a general amnesty for the Arab revolt, and reopen negotiations with a view to solving the problem in favor of Islam."

Djemal had been quite strategic in choosing the recipient of his overture. As he knew from the time they'd spent together in Damascus, Faisal was simultaneously probably the most devout and the most modern of Hussein's four sons. Djemal had also selected his words with great care, returning again and again to two: "Islam" and "independence." If he'd done so in hopes of stirring doubt in Faisal, he'd selected well.

· · ·

FOR HIS STATE visit to Jerusalem in 1899, Kaiser Wilhelm had arranged for a special entryway to be carved from the city's ancient walls. Astride a black stallion and clad in a uniform studded with medals, the German leader used this portal to enter the Old City, sacred ground to the world's Jews, Christians, and Muslims, like some latter-day conquering Crusader.

The move had proven something of a public relations black eye for Germany, and for their own celebratory entry into Jerusalem in December 1917, the British strived to keep things more low-key. Adhering to the long-distance counsel of Mark Sykes, World War I Britain's version of a political stage manager, it was decided that General Allenby would enter through one of the city's traditional gates and on foot, and that no British flags would be flown. The Allies had been handed a tremendous propaganda victory with Jerusalem's capture, Sykes pointed out, and anything that smacked of British or Christian triumphalism was a sure way to sabotage it.

Rather by chance, one of those participating in the historic procession into the Old City on that morning of December 11 was T. E. Lawrence. After his traumatic ordeal in Deraa, he had returned to Aqaba and then been summoned to Allenby's field headquarters in southern Palestine. He had made the journey fully expecting to be upbraided, perhaps even demoted, for his failure at Yarmuk, but instead found Allenby pleasantly distracted by his continuing string of battlefield victories. He was still at General Headquarters on December 9 when word came that the Turks and Germans were pulling out of Jerusalem. Lent an army uniform and the appropriate officer's "pips," he changed out of his worn Arab robes and joined in the ceremonial entry masquerading as General Clayton's staff officer. Even for a man whose Christian faith was now moribund, Lawrence found the import of that day overwhelming; for the first time in over six hundred years, a European army had returned to the cradle of Western religion, and the Middle East was never going to be the same. "For me," he later wrote, "[it] was the supreme moment of the war."

Lawrence undoubtedly felt overwhelmed for other reasons, too. It was only when he had hobbled into Aqaba in late November, racked by illness and still weakened by his ill-treatment at Deraa, that he had learned the extent of Allenby's victories in Palestine. It was also when he first learned of the Balfour Declaration, and of the Russian revolution that had brought the Bolsheviks to power. A bit closer to home, he had also been apprised of the final fall from grace of his old nemesis, Édouard Brémond.

Senior British officials had been gunning for Brémond since the previous spring; in fact, antipathy for him appeared to be one of the few points on which Lawrence and Mark Sykes fully agreed. "I am convinced that the sooner the French military mission is removed from Hejaz, the better," Sykes had written the Foreign Office back in May. "The French officers are without exception anti-Arab, and only serve to promote dissension and intrigue." In Sykes's opinion, that antagonistic tone was set by the head of the French mission, in "the deliberately perverse attitude and policy followed by Colonel Brémond."

The force of Sykes's condemnation may have actually served to keep the French colonel around that much longer. Anxious not to appear acquiescent to their ally, upon being informed of British displeasure with Brémond, Paris had replied that, coincidentally enough, they were already considering radically downscaling his Jeddah mission. Apparently to create a face-saving "decent interval" that would allow for French authorship of the idea, nothing was then done for the next six months. Playing their own role in the charade, British officials busied themselves in the meantime by debating just what honorific to bestow upon their irritant. The Most Distinguished Order of St. Michael and St. George, it was finally resolved, and Reginald Wingate had taken the opportunity of that conferral to extend to Brémond his "warm compliments and congratulations on the valuable work recently performed by the French Detachment under your command in the Hejaz."

But just because Édouard Brémond was now the holder of one of Britain's highest military commendations didn't alter the fact that, at the end of the day, he was still a Frenchman. As the dismissed colonel set sail for France—to maintain the decorous façade, he was officially taking a six-week leave—Wingate fired off a cable to a senior official at the Foreign Office. "Brémond's antecedents are known to you," he wrote, "and I think it very probable that main object of his journey is political and to canvas opinion in Paris against entente policy of Picot and Sykes. Latter should be warned."

What Brémond's departure didn't mean was an end to French maneuvering in the Middle East. Very much to the contrary. With Allenby's success in Palestine, what had previously been a hypothetical divvying up of Middle Eastern spoils between the Entente powers had suddenly turned quite real. And with tangible stakes in the game, the political intrigue was about to grow far more intense.

Lawrence got a glimpse of this on December 11 when after the ceremonial entry into Jerusalem, the senior British staff repaired to a banquet hall for lunch. As the French political agent officially attached to Allenby's army, Georges-Picot enjoyed a place of honor during the ceremony, and he evidently took that to mean the two-year-old plan he and Mark Sykes had worked out for Jerusalem's international administration remained in effect. In the banquet hall, Picot approached Allenby to announce, "And tomorrow, my dear general, I will take the necessary steps to set up civil government in the town."

In Lawrence's telling, the comment brought an awkward silence to the hall. "Salad, chicken mayonnaise and foie gras sandwiches hung in our wet mouths unmunched, while we turned to Allenby and gaped. Even he seemed for the moment at a loss." Only for a moment, though. Turning to the French political agent, Allenby explained that, as Jerusalem fell within the British military zone, the only true authority there was the military commander in chief—namely, himself.

But if the changed military situation was drawing new pressures from the French, that was only one small facet of the political troubles now facing the British. Lawrence saw this firsthand when, after the Jerusalem ceremony, he went on to Cairo. He found a city seething with rage.

Mark Sykes, apparently thinking better of his earlier opinion that the Arabs would have no objection to increased Jewish settlement in Palestine, had endeavored to keep knowledge of the Balfour Declaration in the Arab world to an absolute minimum. That effort had been an abject failure, and as news of the declaration spread among the Egyptian populace that November, dismay had quickly turned to anger. Even as British authorities tried to placate those protests, there had then come Djemal Pasha's speech in Beirut exposing the terms of the Sykes-Picot Agreement. With startling speed, and with potential consequences that might reduce Allenby's victories in Palestine to virtual insignificance, the long British campaign to win and keep the Arab world to its side was dealt a serious double blow.

As he observed the situation in Cairo, Lawrence foresaw dark days ahead; if the Balfour and Sykes-Picot revelations were stirring the normally quiescent and heavily policed Egyptian population to near revolt, what effect would they have among the Arab rebels gathered in Aqaba and their prospective allies across Syria? If secretly thankful that he'd had the foresight to inform Faisal of Sykes-Picot nine months earlier—if knowledge of that had only come now, so improvidently combined with that of the Balfour Declaration, it was hard to imagine Faisal ever trusting in Lawrence or any other Briton again—the news was certain to fuel fury among those won over by the Arab leader. No matter how committed they were to Faisal or the cause of Arab independence, it had never been far from any of these men's minds that the Hashemite leaders of the revolt might be dupes, unwitting or otherwise, of their British and French paymasters. This had been the contention of Constantinople all along, of course, and that charge had now been given both amplification and credence by Djemal Pasha's disclosures in Beirut.

In Cairo, Lawrence soon received confirmation of the box in which

Faisal was finding himself, and also learned of the potential escape hatch being offered by Djemal.

After receiving Djemal's peace-feeler letter of late November, Faisal had forwarded a copy to his father. In mid-December, Hussein had in turn passed it along to Cyril Wilson in Jeddah. Perhaps Hussein did so to show that, even now, he fully trusted in the British, or perhaps it was meant to convey a warning that in the face of British double dealing, other options were available to him. Of course, he may have simply figured the British would soon find out anyway, since Djemal had mentioned his peace overtures to the Arab rebels in his Beirut speech.

Whatever the motive, Hussein's proffer of Djemal's letter set off alarm bells in British Cairo. A few days prior, Clayton had warned Sykes that with news of Sykes-Picot and the Balfour Declaration spreading through the Arab world, it was surely only a matter of time before the Turks approached the rebels with a counteroffer; Djemal's letter was proof that this time had already come. Fortunately, in Clayton's view, neither Faisal nor Hussein had responded to the overture—they had done the proper thing and notified the British authorities—but who knew what might happen when the next Turkish offer came?

Lawrence saw matters quite differently. In fact, in Djemal Pasha's letter, he saw a unique opening for the Arab cause.

As he'd confided to George Lloyd in October, Lawrence no longer regarded himself as fighting for Great Britain, but for Arab independence. Within the upper reaches of the British military and political staff in Cairo, it was common knowledge that British emissaries had for the past several months been meeting in Switzerland with their Turkish counterparts toward forging a peace deal, and if Great Britain felt no compunction against secretly negotiating with the enemy, then why should the Arabs? To the contrary, by playing the Turkish card, by possibly extracting specific terms of settlement from them, the Arabs might then be able to turn around and wring concrete concessions from the British and French. Ultimately, by playing their cards adroitly, the Arabs might gain independence no matter who finally won the war.

Not that Lawrence chose to spell any of this out to his superiors in Cairo. Instead, he suggested that it might be in Britain's interests to ascertain just what the Turks were willing to offer the Arabs, so that the British could respond preemptively. Implausible as it might seem, this suggestion found a receptive ear in Reginald Wingate. "I have recommended King Hussein to send no official replies [to the Turks]," Wingate cabled the War Cabinet, "but Major Lawrence will consult Faisal as to whether any further confirmation of new Turkish policy could be obtained by interchange of verbal [*sic*] messages between him and Djemal."

The War Cabinet swiftly moved to scotch this proposal, but not swiftly enough; Lawrence, it turned out, had left Cairo on the same day, Christmas Eve, that Wingate had sent his cable, so that by the time the War Cabinet weighed in, he was already back in Aqaba with Faisal. Just as he had done at other critical junctures, Lawrence would now capitalize on the delay in receiving orders as an excuse to pursue his own course. That course was to encourage Faisal to enter into a dialogue with his Turkish enemies. Over the coming months, Faisal and Lawrence would establish and maintain just such a dialogue with the chief Turkish general operating on the south Syrian front.

In *Seven Pillars*, Lawrence engaged in rather labored reasoning to justify these dealings with the enemy, arguing that with the Ottoman regime increasingly riven between Islamists like Djemal Pasha and Turkish nationalists like the general, Faisal might drive a wedge between them. "By suitably guarded phrases," Lawrence wrote, "we could throw the odium of the [Arab] Revolt on [Djemal's] clerical party, and then perhaps the militarists might fall out with them." Ultimately, so this reasoning went, such a falling-out would benefit both the Arabs and the Turkish nationalists, the former to gain their independence, the latter freed up to concentrate on preserving their homeland of Anatolia.

Perhaps recognizing the thinness of this argument, Lawrence subsequently tried to put distance to his own role in the affair. Thus, the account in the 1922 so-called Oxford Text edition of *Seven Pillars*—"Faisal, with my full assistance, sent back tendentious answers to Djemal"—became Faisal acting quite on his own by 1926.

Three years later, Lawrence offered a much simpler—and more jaded—rationale for his and Faisal's actions. It came in reply to a question about those wartime contacts put to him by none other than William Yale. "All is fair in love, war, and alliances," Lawrence wrote Yale in 1929. "Poof!"

IT APPARENTLY WASN'T enough for Aaron Aaronsohn that he flagrantly violate Chaim Weizmann's gag order while in the United States. It was also necessary that Weizmann be made fully aware of it, as Aaronsohn proceeded to do in a lengthy report to the British Zionist leader on December 13, 1917. Along with a series of meetings with officials in Washington, he recounted, there had been his address to the City Club in Boston, "to which all the Jewish notables of the city were invited." This was followed by his talk at the conservative and steadfastly anti-Zionist Hebrew Union College in Cincinnati, precisely the sort of opposition bastion that Weizmann desired be avoided but where, according to Aaronsohn, he had been warmly received. "I tried to be brief—I didn't speak for more than forty minutes—and all hostility in the audience ceased."

Surely adding to the warm reception Aaronsohn received in the United States was the news of the British capture of Jerusalem on December 9. Since the beginning of the war, few events had more electrified the American public, Jews and Christians alike, and it was quickly leading to a spirited national debate over the future dispensation of the Holy Land. Nowhere was this debate more pronounced than within the Jewish community, and the early hesitation of American Zionists to embrace the Balfour Declaration was rapidly falling away.

However, Aaronsohn's charm offensive was not nearly so successful with the man Chaim Weizmann and his British supporters regarded as crucial to their American effort, Louis Brandeis. He had several cordial meetings in Washington with the Supreme Court justice, but Brandeis remained decidedly cool to the idea of an American delegation joining the Zionist Commission soon to be on its way to Palestine; this, Brandeis pointed out, would lend the appearance of official American support for Britain's Palestinian endeavor—which, of course, was precisely the British goal.

The second and more sensitive aim of the British Zionists—an American declaration of war on the Turks—was made fairly plain in a letter from Weizmann to Brandeis in mid-January. "It must be abundantly clear," Weizmann wrote, "that there is a complete coincidence of American-British-Judean interests as against Prusso-Turkish interests. . . . This is why I think that a Jewish Palestine must become a war aim for America exactly in the same way as [German-occupied] Alsace Lorraine and an independent Poland."

With that, Brandeis had evidently heard enough. As far back as April 1917, Weizmann had enlisted Brandeis to secure Woodrow Wilson's support for the Jewish homeland idea, and the Supreme Court justice had pursued that effort as far as his sense of ethics allowed. Now, not only was Weizmann asking him to lean on the president to dramatically expand the American war effort, but referring to the vague "national home for the Jewish people" noted in the Balfour Declaration as "Jewish Palestine." Brandeis finally wrote Weizmann a terse cable stating that American participation in the Zionist Commission was "now impossible." It was the beginning of a rift between two of the world's most prominent Zionist leaders that would never fully heal.

AT THE RIDGELINE, Lawrence drew up on his camel to survey the shadowed town of Tafileh in the ravine below. It was a distinctly uninviting place, and as he was soon to discover, home to a situation quite unlike any he had encountered over his sixteen months in the Arabian war theater.

It was the morning of January 20, 1918. Five days earlier, a mixed force of Bedouin warriors and a five-hundred-man unit of the Arab Legion that had been training in Aqaba had stormed into Tafileh, located in a mountain valley in southern Syria, and chased out the town's small Turkish garrison. To the north lay the Arabs' next objectives, the larger settlements of Kerak and Madeba. Lawrence had come to assist in the operations against those towns, and to then push on to the northern shore of the Dead Sea; if all went to plan, it would be there, in the vicinity of the ancient city of Jericho, that the Arab rebels would finally forge a direct land link with General Allenby's army in Jerusalem.

But as guerrilla fighters throughout history have discovered, it is one thing to conduct hit-and-run raids against the enemy, and quite another to take population centers and hold them to one's side. While modern insurgency and counterinsurgency experts have coined a term for the process—"hearts and minds"—the bare truth is there are no hearts or minds to be won. Instead, the essential focus of civilians caught in a guerrilla war zone is simply to stay alive, and they will cast their lot with whichever side best ensures that—until that side doesn't anymore, at which point the civilians will move to the other side. In this most primal of contests, appeals to nationalism or ideology are next to worthless; "allegiance" is won by providing security or instilling terror, or through some combination of the two.

In the streets of "liberated" Tafileh, Lawrence encountered a perfect illustration in miniature of this hearts-and-minds fallacy. There had been no joyous celebrations among those townspeople at being freed from the Turkish yoke or at the notion of a united Arab nation; rather, Tafileh's merchants and small farmers and shepherds saw themselves as caught between two bad choices. They regarded the marauding Bedouin warriors with equal parts fear and hatred, viewed them as little more than camel-borne bandits. If less apprehensive of the disciplined Arab Legion, they quite naturally saw this large force as a potentially calamitous drain on their meager food supplies, and had quickly hidden away whatever stores they could. Behind this was a collective fear of what would happen if the Turks retook the valley, the reprisals likely to follow, and as usually occurs in such situations, this had produced a sharp divergence of opinion over where safety best lay.

"Affairs are in rather a curious state here," Lawrence reported to Gilbert Clayton on January 22. "The local people are divided into two very bitterly opposed factions, and are therefore terrified of each other and of us. There is shooting up and down the streets every night, and general tension. We are taking steps about police, etc., which will allay this state of nerves, and I hope produce enough supplies for us to go on with."

Working against that, though, was the hoarding carried out by the villagers, a development already causing food shortages in the valley and enormous price increases in whatever was available. This, in turn, was fueling growing resentment among the populace, and growing anger among the warriors. "I'm sorry not to be able to send you proper figures of quantities of supplies here," Lawrence concluded his January 22 report, "but have been very busy since I got here in trying to find out who was for us, and where they were. The conflicts of ideas, local feuds, and party interests are so wild (this being the moment of anarchy the whole district has been longing for for years), that hardly anyone could straighten them out in a hurry."

But the situation was about to get much worse. The day after writing to Clayton, Lawrence learned that a sizable Turkish force was on its way to retake Tafileh.

By the time he reached Tafileh, Lawrence had been back in Arabia from his Jerusalem-Cairo sojourn for a full month. He'd spent that time taking stock of the Arab Revolt, conferring with Faisal in Aqaba, preparing for what was to come next. Shortly after his return, he'd joined in a foray against the Hejaz Railway aboard the newest British weapon to be introduced to the Arabian front, the Rolls-Royce armored car. While the two armored cars had inflicted only minor damage on the Turkish outpost they targeted, it was immediately apparent to all that this new weapon fundamentally changed the desert war. Now, with an absolute minimal investment of men and matériel, the British could thoroughly dominate the railway, attacking its isolated Turkish garrisons and disrupting the line almost at will. With such dominance there at last came acceptance in British military leadership of the argument Lawrence had been trying to make for nearly a year: there really was no good reason to push for the fall of Medina; better to leave those thousands of marooned enemy soldiers precisely where they were.

His preparations had also been personal. In the wake of his ordeal at Deraa, Lawrence set about organizing his own private army, or bodyguard. "I began to increase my people to a troop," he wrote, "adding such lawless men as I found, fellows whose dash had got them into trouble elsewhere." His recruitment of the "lawless" was quite deliberate and clever. Troublemakers within their own tribes, perhaps even outcasts altogether, these men would ultimately be loyal to Lawrence alone, a consideration that also explained the inclusion of the two camp miscreants, Farraj and Daud, in their number. It was a bond of personal loyalty for which the bodyguard unit would pay dearly, however; by Lawrence's estimate, nearly sixty of them would be dead before war's end.

It was with this expanded retinue that, on January 10, Lawrence had set off to join the ongoing operation at Tafileh. As he'd been informed by General Allenby's staff in Jerusalem, the British army in Palestine probably wouldn't be sufficiently rested and reequipped to embark on their next push until mid-February. In light of that delay, Lawrence and the war planners had come up with a fairly modest interim scheme for the Arab rebels. Avoiding the string of major population centers of the Syrian interior—still under Turkish control and a long way from the reach of British forces in Palestine—the rebel army would instead clear the ground in between, the Moab Plateau mountains just to the east of the Dead Sea, then forge a link with the British near Jerusalem. Capturing Tafileh had been the first objective in this campaign, and next up were the larger towns of Kerak and Madeba, but all was suddenly cast into doubt by the news that the Turks were marching on Tafileh.

If hewing to their past tactics, the Arabs would have taken this opportunity to pack up and melt away. Lawrence was enough a student of guerrilla insurgencies, however, to realize that the rules of warfare had now abruptly changed. Just as in Tafileh, the residents of Kerak and Madeba were sitting on the sidelines, waiting to cast their lot with the winner. This meant that the fate of the three towns was inextricably linked, that if Tafileh was abandoned, any chance in Kerak or Madeba was lost too. In essence, the rebels had no choice but to stand and fight.

That effort got off to a very shaky start. On the afternoon of January 24, the vanguard of the Turkish force of some one thousand soldiers sent down from Kerak entered the Tafileh valley from the Wadi Hesa gorge a few miles north of town. In quick order, they pushed the thin rebel picket line all the way back to the town's outskirts. Fortunately for the rebels, night fell before the Turks could fully press their advantage; under the cover of darkness, the commander of the Arab Legion hastily withdrew his forces all the way to the southern end of the valley. "Everybody thought we were running away," Lawrence would report to Clayton. "I think we were."

Before dawn, Lawrence ventured into the town and saw firsthand the effect of the Legion's withdrawal on the residents. "Everyone was screaming with terror, goods were being bundled out of the houses into the streets, which were packed with women and men. Mounted Arabs were galloping up and down, firing wildly into the air, and the flashes of the Turkish rifles were outlining the further cliffs of the Tafileh gorge."

Observing that a small picket force still held a bluff north of town, Lawrence urgently sent word back to the Legion commander for reinforcements and machine guns to be brought up, then hurried to the bluff himself. As morning broke, the situation for the tiny force there—perhaps thirty Arab warriors and an equal number of Tafileh residents—turned "rather difficult."

"The Turks were working through the pass and along the eastern boundary ridge of the plain," Lawrence reported, "and concentrating the fire of about fifteen machine guns on the face and flank of the rather obvious little mound we were holding. They were meanwhile correcting the fusing of their shrapnel, which had been grazing the hilltop and bursting over the plain, and were [now] beginning to sprinkle the sides and top of the hill quite freely. Our people were short of ammunition, and the loss of the position was obviously only a matter of minutes."

But the holding action on the bluff proved crucial. By the time the position was abandoned, the main Arab force had hurried forward with their machine and mountain guns to form a new line on a parallel ridge a mile and a half behind. Amid this, there occurred one of those small, seemingly insignificant deeds upon which battles are often decided. During his own dash back to safety, Lawrence had shown the presence of mind to count off his paces, and he calculated that the distance between the abandoned bluff—the position the Turks would soon occupy—and the Arabs' new defensive line was right around thirty-one hundred yards. No sooner had the main Turkish force settled upon the bluff and deployed their own heavy weaponry than they were engulfed in a storm of mortar fire from the Arabs' mountain guns.

With the Turks pinned down in the center, Lawrence drew on his knowledge of military history to conduct a classic pincer attack, dispatching small units of fighters out in a wide arc to work their way behind the unsuspecting enemy. Shortly after 3 p.m., the trap was sprung, the Arab machine gunners on the flank pouring fire into the now completely exposed Turks on the bluff. With their machine- and mountain-gun crews quickly wiped out, the Turkish troops wavered and then began a disorganized scramble for the safety of the Wadi Hesa gorge. Except there was no safety to be found there either. With all semblance of cohesion gone, throughout the evening and into the night, the fleeing Turks were set upon by Arab cavalrymen and marauding Bedouin, even mountain villagers bent on vengeance or loot. Of the thousand Turkish soldiers who marched into Tafileh, Lawrence estimated their losses at some five hundred dead and wounded, with another two hundred captured, but even this may have been on the low side; he later heard reports that no more than fifty made it back to Kerak, the rest picked off one by one in the gorge. It had come at a cost of some twenty-five Arabs killed, and perhaps three times as many wounded.

The rout at Tafileh was a classic Napoleonic-style trap, and one that would shortly win Lawrence the Distinguished Service Order medal. Yet it was an action he himself would describe as "villainous," a pointless exercise in one-upmanship. "We could have won by refusing battle, foxed them by maneuvering our center as on twenty such occasions before and since." Instead, by engaging the enemy in a conventional battle, the Arabs had lost one-sixth of their strength to casualties, making an advance on Madeba or Kerak all but impossible for the near future. "This evening," he wrote, "there was no glory left, but the terror of the broken flesh, which had been our own men, carried past us to their homes."

But at Tafileh, Lawrence would exhibit a new and unsettling trait: hatred for the enemy, an element of fury at their stupidity for having attacked him. Even if he might lament the fate of the "thousand poor Turks" who had marched into Tafileh, it was bereft of the compassion that had once marked him. Indeed, upon hearing of the Turks still being massacred in the gorge long after the battle had been won, Lawrence did nothing. "I should have been crying-sorry for the enemy," he recounted in *Seven Pillars*, "but after the angers and exertions of the battle, my mind was too tired to care to go down into that awful place and spend the night saving them."

Six months earlier, in the wake of a similarly one-sided battle at Aba el Lissan, Lawrence had ensured that the mortally wounded enemy be placed along a streambank so that they might at least have water while they died. At Tafileh, even those Turks lightly wounded were left out unattended as a fierce snowstorm came in that night; by morning, all were dead. "It was indefensible, as was the whole theory of war, but no special reproach lay on us for it. We risked our lives in the blizzard . . . to save our own fellows, and if our rule was not to lose Arabs to kill even many Turks, still less might we lose them to save Turks."

Chapter 17

Solitary Pursuits

It might be fraud or it might be farce, [but] no one should say
that I could not play it.

T. E. LAWRENCE ON HIS ROLE
IN THE ARAB REVOLT, *SEVEN PILLARS OF WISDOM*

Doggedness and a thirst for adventure had carried William Yale far
from his aristocratic origins. In 1908, those traits had taken him to
the steaming jungles of the Panama Canal Zone and, shortly after, to the
oilfields of Oklahoma and the backwaters of the Ottoman Empire. In the
autumn of 1917, they had brought him to Cairo, the locus of the Allied
war effort in the eastern Mediterranean, with the ambiguous title of special agent to the United States Department of State. That assignment also
dropped him into a new kind of jungle, a maze of different interests vying
for power in the future Middle East.

"These interests crossed and recrossed each other," Yale would write,
"creating a confused tangle of intrigues and policies which was almost
impossible to disentangle, and back of these policies and intrigues were
the interested groups in France and Great Britain: capitalistic, religious,
cultural. Added to these complications was the problem of Zionism and
Jewish desires.... No more fascinating and interesting task could be given
a man than that of attempting to understand and report upon this most
complex of problems."

Smart enough to grasp his utter unpreparedness—he was literally
the only American field intelligence officer for the entire region—Yale
quickly scoured the English-language bookstores in Cairo for histories

of the Middle East. He cultivated relationships with an array of Egyptian and émigré community leaders, and frequently dropped by the Arab Bureau offices at the Savoy Hotel for informal chats with its intelligence officers. In the time-honored tradition of both journalists and spies everywhere, he diligently put in many hours at the favored watering holes of diplomats and senior military officers; in Cairo in 1917, that most frequently meant the pleasantly appointed rooms of the Turf Club on the Nile island of Gezira.

As Yale soon discovered, the fraternizing aspect of his mission actually required minimal exertion. That's because most every player in the Cairo political swirl was only too eager to present his case to an official of the United States, the newest and, if Woodrow Wilson had his way, most influential member of the Allied military partnership. There was one notable exception, however. "The French made no effort to contact me," Yale recalled. "The formality and exclusiveness of the[ir] officials repulsed me, and a certain inherent timidity kept me from making further advances."

But if playing to his tenacious spirit, at least initially the Cairo posting offered precious little in the way of adventure. Following General Allenby's capture of Jerusalem in December, Yale sought permission from British authorities to visit the Palestine battlefront, a request denied on the grounds that only accredited military liaison officers were allowed. The real reason, Yale eventually deduced, was British concern that granting access to an American would require they do the same for their more meddlesome allies—the Italians and Greeks were constantly asking—at a time when they had their hands full in Palestine just trying to sandbag the French.

Adding to Yale's frustration in this area was the peculiarly British approach to avoiding confrontation, its officials quick to cede ground when necessary, graciously inert when it wasn't. The American special agent had an early taste of this when, shortly after the fall of Jerusalem, he learned that the British had imprisoned Zaki Bey, the city's former Ottoman military governor and the man who had been instrumental in securing Yale's escape from Palestine. In high dudgeon, Yale stormed into the offices of the relevant British officials and told them of the many favors Zaki Bey had performed for the expatriate community in Jerusalem. He also mentioned that Zaki Bey was a close friend of the former U.S. consul to Palestine, Otis Glazebrook, who in turn was close friends with Woodrow Wilson. "I told them if Zaki Bey was not released on parole, I would take the matter up with Washington and have it brought to the President's attention."

In the face of such a naked threat, the officials of most powers would have either meekly acquiesced or gotten their backs up, but the British did one better. A few days later, Yale was given Zaki Bey's release papers and "kindly requested" to deliver them personally to the prison where he was being held, thereby allowing for an emotional reunion of the two friends at the prison gates. "When the British decide to do anything," Yale noted somewhat peevishly, "they do it ungrudgingly and so gracefully that one feels under real obligation to them."

Marooned in the Egyptian capital, the thirty-year-old Yale focused his energies on trying to make sense of the multisided battle for primacy in the region. One of these struggles was of fairly long standing—the snarl of claims over the future dispensation of greater Syria—but this had now been joined, courtesy of the Balfour Declaration, by an equally acrimonious debate centered on Palestine.

Lending a certain air of unreality to these contests, as well as to Yale's earnest pondering of them, was that by the end of 1917 the Allied war effort had never looked so bleak. In the western Russian city of Brest-Litovsk, German and Russian Bolshevik negotiators were hammering out the final details of Russia's formal withdrawal from the war, and already hundreds of thousands of German soldiers had been transferred from the Eastern Front to the Western. For British and French commanders nervously watching this buildup in France, it was a sure sign the Germans were planning a massive spring offensive against their depleted armies, one intended to deliver a knockout blow to the Allies before the slowly arriving American armies could take to the field in a significant way. The Russian collapse had even emboldened the Turks, with War Minister Enver now scheming not only to recover that portion of northeastern Turkey previously occupied by the czar's armies, but also to carry his advantage into the Turkic regions of the Caucasus conquered by Russia in the nineteenth century. In light of all this, the constant bickering in Cairo over the future spoils of war seemed more than a tad premature.

Nevertheless, Yale dutifully stayed to the task before him. In each of his "Monday reports" to Leland Harrison at the State Department, he strived to bring clarity to another facet of the Middle Eastern morass by outlining the views of whatever officials or religious figures or causists he had met with during the previous week, and by mining the *Arab Bulletin* for pertinent background information. As might be expected, though, instead of clarity, these voluminous reports with their welter of opposing viewpoints tended to only render the situation more incomprehensible—or at least so it would seem judging by the utter silence emanating from Leland Harrison.

It appears this earnest search for insight also had the effect of delaying the special agent's discovery of the one simple truth to be found amid the thicket: no one else knew what was really going on either. Yale finally began to cotton to this in late December, after a meeting between General Clayton and a group of Syrian exile leaders in Cairo. To the Syrians' deepening fears that the Balfour Declaration meant a Jewish state was to be imposed in Palestine, Clayton stoutly insisted this wasn't so, that all the declaration's "national home" phrasing meant was that Jews would be allowed to emigrate, and to share politically and economically in the region's future to the same degree as everyone else. This assurance from one of the highest-ranking British officials in Egypt had a profoundly calming effect on the Syrian delegation. "On the strength of what they were told by General Clayton," Yale reported to the State Department, "the Syrians are considering the advisability of abandoning for the present their opposition to the Jews, and talk even of cooperating with the Zionists."

Except that immediately after that meeting, Yale fell into conversation with Clayton's chief deputy at the Arab Bureau, who readily confessed that neither he nor the general had any idea what the "national home" phrasing actually meant.

In seeking to unravel the Middle East, William Yale would be neither the first nor the last observer to conclude that perhaps his most accurate assessment had come at very first glance, before he had been sullied by "knowledge." As he had reported to Harrison in just his third Monday report back in November, "the truth seems to be that Downing Street has no definite policy and have given their agents no clear program to work out." As a result, those agents were adopting an "attitude of more or less sympathy with all the varied interests," or simply telling everyone what they hoped to hear.

But finally, the struggling intelligence agent stumbled upon something that seemed to clear away much of the obfuscation. It occurred in late February 1918 when, reading through a back issue of the *Arab Bulletin*, he came across an essay entitled "Syria: The Raw Material."

In just eight pages of terse and wonderfully opinionated prose, the essayist had methodically delineated the myriad fissures that divided and subdivided that country, fissures that extended beyond tribal and ethnic and religious fault lines to even produce rivalries between cities and towns. Completely shorn of wishful thinking, that dangerous proclivity of bureaucratic essayists everywhere, the writer instead painted a stark picture of the problems awaiting any outsider who might attempt to impose their will there. Of particular interest to Yale, in light of the debate then roiling Cairo, was how the writer "in a few words suggests the bitterness which exists in southern Palestine against the Zionists. This bitterness of feeling is shared alike by Moslems and Christians, and recent developments tend only to aggravate the natural hatred of the Palestinians for those Jews who come to Palestine declaring the country to be theirs."

What made this essay all the more remarkable was that it had appeared in the *Arab Bulletin* in March 1917, fully eight months before the Balfour Declaration, and, according to a prefatory note, had actually been written two years prior to that. And something else caught William Yale's eye. Its author was already known to him. It was the same man who had humiliated him at Beersheva in January 1914, and who had debriefed him in Cairo at the war's outbreak: British army major T. E. Lawrence.

In fact, without apparently realizing it, Yale had already alerted the State Department to T. E. Lawrence and his exploits. Back in November 1917, while composing a report on the history of the Arab Revolt, Yale had sufficiently picked up on stories circulating through Cairo at the time to write of "a young British officer who, with the Bedouins, organizes raids against the Hedjaz RR [railroad] and strives to win the Bedouins over to the side of the Sherif and British." In February 1918, after stumbling upon Lawrence's old report, the American intelligence agent took the unprecedented step of asking Reginald Wingate for permission to copy out the essay in its entirety for transmission to the State Department. He also resolved to meet with Lawrence the next time he passed through Cairo.

IN THE SAME week that William Yale was transmitting Lawrence's old Syria report to the State Department, Lawrence was endeavoring to have himself removed from the Syrian war theater altogether. The cause was a very costly error in judgment, blame for which could be placed squarely at Lawrence's door—or so he half hoped.

The seed had been planted a month earlier. On the eve of the battle for Tafileh, Lawrence had sent Gilbert Clayton an urgent request for £30,000 worth of gold (about $6 million in its modern equivalent) for the Arab force gathered on the Moab Plateau under the leadership of Faisal's younger brother Zeid. Without those funds, Lawrence warned, Zeid's followers would soon begin to melt away; with them, the rebels could advance north against the mountain strongholds of Kerak and Madeba, then sweep down to meet the vanguard of the British army in the Jordan valley. In one determined drive, the rebels would finally establish a direct land link to their British advisors and suppliers in Palestine, while the eastern flank of General Allenby's army would be secured against Turkish attack.

Testament to both the importance of the Moab Plateau campaign and Lawrence's reputation for punctiliousness in financial matters—he rarely exaggerated his needs—Clayton scrambled to gather up the gold in Egypt and rush it to Aqaba. A few days after the Turkish assault on Tafileh was repelled, Lawrence had personally come down to meet the gold caravan at the rebels' new forward base camp in Guweira, some thirty-five miles northeast of Aqaba. Anxious to get back to the Tafileh front as soon as possible, he had then taken as much of the gold as he and his two escorts on fleet camels could manage—about £6,000 worth—and set off ahead of the slower-moving caravan.

They rode directly into a winter blizzard, one that turned the Tafileh-Guweira run from an easy day-and-a-half jaunt into a grinding three-day ordeal. Driven by blind impatience, Lawrence abandoned his slower-moving escorts after two days and, laden down with all their gold, forged ahead alone. That proved to be a nearly fatal mistake when he and his mount became stranded in a waist-deep snowdrift, one that took hours of digging by hand to escape. Of course, the delays Lawrence experienced on his prized camel were likely to be only worse for those coming behind, putting even greater distance between him and the rest of the gold caravan.

At last reaching Tafileh on February 11, Lawrence discovered to his disgust that Zeid had done nothing in his absence to prepare for the push north. Instead, as he wrote to Clayton the next day, Hussein's youngest son had "hummed and hawed, and threw away his chance. . . . These Arabs are the most ghastly material to build into a design."

In light of that withering assessment, Lawrence's subsequent actions were close to inexplicable. Eager to scout the terrain over which the rebels would soon advance, he decided to personally conduct an extended reconnaissance of the northern countryside even as the gold caravan remained strung out along the Guweira-Tafileh path. What's more, he chose to take the only other Western officer in Tafileh, a young British lieutenant named Alec Kirkbride, with him. In departing, he put the twenty-one-year-old Zeid in charge of safeguarding the incoming gold, with instructions to "spend what was necessary for current expenses until my return."

For six days, Lawrence and Kirkbride scouted the country to the north and west, ranging as far as the eastern slopes of the Jordan valley above Jericho. When they returned to Tafileh on February 18, Lawrence was in high spirits. With the gold shipment now arrived, the campaign to clear the Moab Plateau and link up with the British at the Dead Sea appeared an easy prospect, one he estimated could be accomplished within a month. When he began outlining this to Zeid, however, he detected a peculiar discomfort in the young man's demeanor.

"But that will need a lot of money," Zeid finally interjected.

"Not at all," Lawrence replied, "our funds in hand will cover it, and more."

It was then that King Hussein's youngest son embarrassedly admitted he had already spent all the money.

Lawrence initially thought Zeid was joking, but was soon set right. As the Guweira gold caravan had drifted into Tafileh over the preceding days, Zeid's lieutenants and tribal allies, all owed back wages, had fallen upon it as if on a cash cow. Even worse, most of the gold had apparently been distributed to units that, for tribal reasons, wouldn't be participating in the push north, while those units Lawrence was counting on as his vanguard were shortchanged. "I was aghast," he recounted, "for this meant the complete ruin of my plans and hopes, the collapse of our effort to keep faith with Allenby."

He also didn't truly believe Zeid. As Lawrence soon learned, the last caravan stragglers had reached Tafileh just the day before, barely leaving time for the gold to be counted, let alone distributed. In a rage, Lawrence stormed off to his tent. "All night I thought over what could be done," he wrote, "but found a blank, and when morning came could only send word to Zeid that, if he would not return the money, I must go away."

Instead, Zeid only managed to produce a hastily scribbled "supposed" accounting of where the gold had gone. True to his word, that afternoon Lawrence saddled up his camel and, in the company of just four escorts, set out for General Allenby's headquarters in southern Palestine, one hundred miles to the west. Once there, he intended to ask to be relieved of his command, "to beg Allenby to find me some smaller part elsewhere."

If this was presented as an issue of personal honor, there was clearly another impulse at work in Lawrence. In Zeid's incompetence (or dishonesty) the young British major suddenly saw the opportunity for a kind of personal deliverance, a release from the onus of leadership that weighed so heavily upon him.

This was not at all a new burden. Five months earlier, Lawrence had confided to his friend Edward Leeds that his nerves were going and that he "was not going to last out this game much longer"—and that had been before his nearly suicidal mission to Yarmuk, his ghastly Deraa ordeal, and the hideous slaughter at Tafileh. His growing exhaustion had even registered in his most recent letter to Gilbert Clayton on the eve of the missing gold episode. "I am getting shy of adventures," he had written his superior on February 12. "I'm in an extraordinary position just now vis-à-vis the sherifs and the tribes, and sooner or later must go bust. I do my best to keep in the background but cannot, and some day everybody will combine and down me. It is impossible for a foreigner to run another people of their own free will indefinitely, and my innings has been a fairly long one."

As he would later note in *Seven Pillars*, added to this were the simple rigors and dangers of his duty. "For a year and a half I had been in motion, riding a thousand miles each month upon camels, with added nervous hours in crazy aeroplanes or rushing across country in powerful cars. In my last five actions, I had been hit, and my body so dreaded further pain that now I had to force myself under fire."

There were precious few signs this torment might soon end; much the opposite, in fact. When Lawrence had left Oxford for the war, his brother Arnold had been a fourteen-year-old schoolboy. In recent months, Lawrence had taken to counseling his brother on the skills he would need—familiarity with Arabic, the ability to drive a range of motor vehicles—if Arnold hoped to be assigned to the Middle East for his upcoming military service.

But quite beyond these burdens was the psychic toll that came with living a lie, "the rankling fraudulence which had to be my mind's habit: that pretense to lead the national uprising of another race, the daily posturing in alien dress, preaching in alien speech," upholding a promise that Lawrence increasingly realized was almost sure to be broken. In this, the slaughter at Tafileh had shorn him of the "last gloss" of wishful thinking. "To be charged against my conceit were the causeless and ineffectual deaths of those twenty Arabs and seven hundred Turks in Wadi Hesa. My will had gone, and I feared longer to be alone."

Except none of it mattered. As Lawrence discovered upon reaching Allenby's headquarters at Ramleh on February 22, not only was deliverance out of the question, but a new mission had already been planned for him. Indeed, so vital was Lawrence to this new scheme that for nearly a week an airplane had been making repeated sorties over Tafileh valley, dropping flyers ordering that he immediately make for headquarters. (The pilot, it would eventually be determined, had leafleted the wrong valley.)

True to pattern, dramatic events had occurred on the world stage during Lawrence's latest absence. While bracing for the Germans' coming offensive on the Western Front, Allied planners had desperately scoured their maps in search of some spot on the global battlefield where a preemptive thrust might distract or dilute the German military colossus building in France. In mid-February, General Allenby had been informed that task was falling to him. As soon as possible, he was to launch an all-out strike at the Syrian heartland, with Damascus as the ultimate objective. The Arab rebels would be called upon to play a crucial role in that strike, which was why headquarters had been so anxious to speak with their chief liaison to the Arabs, Major Lawrence.

But then the stakes were raised even further. In the city of Brest-Litovsk, German peace negotiators had presented their Russian counterparts with terms so staggeringly punitive that it had caused the Bolshevik delegation, led by Leon Trotsky, to pack up and go home. That breakdown in talks may have been just what Berlin was looking for; on February 18, just four days before Lawrence's arrival at Ramleh, German armies had begun steamrolling through western Russia, their advance limited only by how much ground their troops could cover in a day. So complete was the Russian collapse that on February 25 its leaders swiftly acceded to German terms even more retributive than those it had rejected a week earlier. For those Allied commanders nervously waiting on the Western Front, it meant Germany was now free to shuttle even more of its soldiers and weaponry to France, that the last small obstacle to the approaching German offensive had been removed.

Under these circumstances, the notion that Lawrence might be permitted to stand down from his crucial post over a point of honor was so risible that he apparently didn't even broach the topic with Allenby. "There was no escape for me," he recounted. "I must take up again my mantle of fraud in the East. With my certain contempt for half-measures, I took it up quickly and wrapped myself in it completely."

After a quick visit to Jerusalem to see his old friend Ronald Storrs, the city's newly appointed military governor, Lawrence continued on to Cairo. There, on March 8, he wrote a short letter home.

For many months, he had been telling his family in Oxford that he hoped to soon make use of the leave time he had accrued since 1914 to arrange a visit home. That hope was now more distant than ever. "I'm to go back [to the war front] till June at least," he wrote. "One rather expected that, I'm afraid." He went on to dimissively tell of his latest promotion and military citation, stemming from his leadership role in an action that was already coming to haunt him, the massacre at Tafileh. "They have now given me a DSO [Distinguished Service Order medal]. It's a pity all this good stuff is not sent to someone who could use it! Also apparently I'm a colonel of sorts."

During his brief stopover in Cairo, Lawrence also acceded to meet with a young American intelligence officer who was eager to speak with him.

"MAJOR LAWRENCE'S OPINIONS demand the most serious consideration," William Yale wrote Leland Harrison on March 11, "because of his intimate knowledge of the Arabs and the importance of the work he is engaged in. . . . Speaking Arabic fluently, traveling, living and working among the Bedouins, he has a knowledge of the sentiments and feelings of the Arab tribes that probably no other westerner has. His knowledge of the true condition of affairs existing at the present time among the Arabs should be more accurate than that of any other person."

It marked the third time that Yale and Lawrence had crossed paths. In their last encounter in the autumn of 1914, the newly minted British intelligence officer had pumped Yale for details on Turkish troop movements and supply lines in southern Palestine. Now it was William Yale who was the inquiring intelligence agent, Lawrence on the receiving end of a battery of questions related to the state of affairs in Syria.

Long accustomed to the opacity of British officials, Yale was clearly startled by Lawrence's candor. It enabled the special agent to report back to the State Department that "the British forces in Palestine would soon commence an offensive from which excellent results are expected." Even more remarkable, Lawrence provided Yale with almost precise details on the Arab rebels' military objectives in that coming offensive, even pinpointing the spot in the Syrian interior where he hoped to forge a link between the Arabs and Allenby's forces.

When the conversation turned to the political, Lawrence was just as forthright. As Yale reported, "Lawrence states the Arabs have no faith in the word of England and of France, and that they believe only such territory as they are able to secure by [their own] force of arms will belong to them." In Lawrence's judgment, the Arabs' inherent distrust of their Western allies had taken on new depth with the Balfour Declaration. "He characterizes it as a dangerous policy and speaks of the activities permitted the Zionist in Egypt and in Palestine as being unwise and foolhardy." Should the British go any further in their support of the Zionists, Lawrence warned, it could quickly bring about the ruin of the Arab nationalist movement—or at least its end in any way beneficial to the Allies. With his long experience in the region, he dismissed the sunny vision of a man like Mark Sykes and his imagining of a Jewish nation gradually forming in the face of grudging Arab acceptance; in one of Lawrence's most prescient comments, he allowed that "if a Jewish state is to be created in Palestine, it will have to be done by force of arms and maintained by force of arms amid an overwhelmingly hostile population."

For a British military officer to so openly disparage the policies of his own government simply wasn't done in 1918, let alone to a foreign intelligence agent, but it reflected just how powerful Lawrence had become: he was his nation's vital link to the Arab rebels in the field, no one else could fulfill that role, and because of this, he could say or do nearly anything he wished. Yet, just as at their first encounter in Beersheva, it seemed Lawrence harbored something of a hidden agenda at this meeting with Yale, an agenda masked by his disarming candor. Without showing his guiding hand, he hoped to steer Yale—and through him, the U.S. State Department—toward a policy of his choosing.

Lawrence was now keenly aware of just how little freedom of movement the Arab rebels had, that by tethering their effort directly to that of the British, the fate of both the Arab Revolt and Hussein's Hashemite dynasty had become hostage to the dictates and caprices of their vastly more powerful ally. While this had always been true to a degree—certainly the Sykes-Picot accord made plain the Arabs' junior status in the larger scheme of things—what was occurring in early 1918 was of an entirely different order of magnitude.

This was starkly illustrated by a visit Lawrence had made to Aqaba just days before his meeting with Yale. The once-sleepy port village had been so radically transformed over the previous few months as to be unrecognizable, with vast tent cities dotting the narrow coastal shelf beyond the ship-clogged harbor, towering stockpiles of supplies and war matériel everywhere. Where the British presence had once consisted of a handful of officers, there were now hundreds of Crown soldiers handling logistics, training rebel recruits, tending to the myriad needs of an encamped fighting force of thousands of warriors. Aqaba even had its own resident air force now, a fleet of Royal Flying Corps airplanes that periodically set off to bomb the Hejaz Railway and Turkish military installations inland.

The change in circumstances had also been evident in the manner of his visit. Sent to inform Faisal of Allenby's plans for the upcoming Syrian offensive, Lawrence hadn't gone to Aqaba aboard one of the slow-moving Red Sea transport ships, but as the passenger in an RFC biplane commandeered by headquarters for the purpose. In his talks with Faisal, long gone were the languorous discussions of tactics or politics over tea in the prince's tent; instead, their time together on this visit had been less an exploration of what the rebels might do in the coming offensive than a briefing by Lawrence on what they *would* do. Then, after little more than twenty-four hours on the ground in Aqaba, Lawrence had reboarded the requisitioned airplane and flown back to Cairo.

It all illustrated one of the paradoxes of power, that what the Arab Revolt had gained in importance in the eyes of its British overseers had come with a corresponding loss of autonomy. The ultimate danger of that, in Lawrence's view, was that the British were now taking their tethered Arab allies down a path that might well lead to their destruction.

From the outset, Hussein's notion of a British-sponsored pan-Arab revolt with himself as its leader had been built on very shaky ground, viewed skeptically by both Arab conservatives and progressives. To ibn-Saud, Hussein's chief rival in Arabia and the leader of the fundamentalist Wahhabist movement, the king's alliance with the British made him a toady of the Christian West (never mind that Saud was also on the British payroll). At the same time, the more cosmopolitan Arabs of Syria had felt little in common with the Bedouin "primitives" riding out of the Hejaz. These were problems to deal with down the road, once the war was over, but with the Balfour Declaration the road had rushed up to meet Hussein.

Taken aback by the furious Arab reaction to that declaration, the British had put great pressure on their principal Arab ally to come out in its support. This Hussein had done, tepidly, but instead of calming the Arab waters, the move had served to strengthen Arab opposition to Hussein. In early January, David Hogarth, Lawrence's old mentor and now the "acting director" of the Arab Bureau—the title was little more than an honorific, true authority lay elsewhere—had called upon Hussein in hopes of finally clarifying the boundaries of a postwar Arab nation. Instead, he had found a king who only wished to talk of the growing threat he now faced from ibn-Saud and his Wahhabists. Simultaneously, Arab nationalists in Egypt and Syria had adopted ibn-Saud's toady language in deriding Hussein's accommodation with the Zionists. Just how badly this British scheme had backfired was evident in an alarming letter Reginald Wingate received from Hussein in early February. As Wingate reported, "[Hussein] refers to the contingency of suicide as [an] alternative to political bankruptcy.... The phraseology is vague, but the Sherif of Mecca appears to be affected by apprehensions caused by the Allies' pro-Zionist declarations."

It was at this juncture that Lawrence became ensnared. In late January, he had penned an essay for an even more restricted version of the *Arab Bulletin,* one seen by only a handful of officials, in which he'd strongly touted Faisal's base of support in Syria, while besmirching his opponents there as dupes of French or German propaganda. While the article was a fairly transparent effort to boost Faisal's claim to authority in Syria, it also helped alert those British officials grappling with the Arab fallout from Balfour that perhaps it was Faisal, not Hussein, whom they should be looking to for help—and, of course, wooing Faisal meant going through Lawrence. In early February, just days after Lawrence's article appeared, Gilbert Clayton informed Mark Sykes that "I have urged Lawrence to impress on Faisal the necessity of an entente with the Jews."

The irony of being enlisted to sell Faisal on a policy with which he himself vehemently disagreed was not lost on Lawrence, and he had only halfheartedly agreed to do so. "As for the Jews," he'd answered Clayton from Tafileh, "when I see Faisal next I'll talk to him, and the Arab attitude shall be sympathetic—for the duration of the war at least." There was a limit to how far Lawrence would go, though; as he informed Clayton, if some public declaration by Faisal was hoped for, that "is rather beyond my province."

But however much he opposed the policy, Lawrence was enough a practitioner of realpolitik to realize he had little choice in the matter; the Balfour Declaration was a fait accompli, the Arab rebels were hardly in a position to renounce their alliance with the British over it, so the chief goal now must be to limit its damage or to play it for advantage elsewhere. In this latter category, the obvious candidate was greater Syria. Lawrence could see a calculus whereby, in return for the Arab rebels ceding to Balfour, a grateful Britain would then uphold the rebels' claim to the rest of Syria against the French. The problem was, Lawrence had sufficiently lost faith in his own government to realize that this was a very risky bet.

So what other cards to play? Certainly the most radical—and perilous—was to negotiate with the Turks. In early February, Faisal had received another secret peace feeler from General Mehmet Djemal, the new commander of the Turkish Fourth Army. This missive had been a good deal more specific and accommodating than Djemal Pasha's previous letter, and Faisal had sent an equally specific, if guarded, reply. While overtly rebuffing the overture, he had also left the door open for a possible settlement if the Turks withdrew their troops from Arabia and southern Syria. This was not such a deal-breaking ultimatum as it might sound; by February 1918, the Young Turks were already looking to concentrate their military efforts on reclaiming those Turkic lands being vacated by the defeated Russians, and might be quite happy to abandon the impoverished and quarrelsome Arab regions to do so.

But before anything so drastic as cutting a deal with the Turks, there was one more potential actor who could aid the Arab cause: the Americans. This was almost certainly why Lawrence found the time to meet with William Yale in Cairo.

Since bringing his country into the war in April 1917, President Wilson had repeatedly stressed that the age of imperialism was over, that his crusade for the world to "be made safe for democracy" also meant self-determination and independence for oppressed peoples and "small nations" everywhere. It had taken his European allies some time to accept that the American president actually held to such a quaint notion, but all doubt was dispelled with Wilson's "Fourteen Points for Peace" proclamation in January 1918.

Probably more than any other single document of the twentieth century, Wilson's Fourteen Points captivated a global audience. Amid the abject and unending ruin of World War I, the American president had outlined a semi-utopian vision of how the earth was to function in the future, a radical sweeping away of the imperial structure that had held sway for millennia, in favor of all peoples enjoying the right to self-determination, a world in which patient negotiation at a "League of Nations" might make war obsolete. So profound and revolutionary was this document that it sent shock waves through *all* the imperial powers, the war-shattered citizenry of Berlin and Vienna seeing it as a potential pathway out of their misery just as much as their brethren in London and Paris and Rome. Adding to its attraction was that in simple, unambiguous language, Wilson had laid out a road map—his Fourteen Points—for how this process would begin.

The twelfth point of that proclamation was taken up with the dispensation of the Ottoman Empire. While the American president decreed that the Turkish portion of that empire should remain its own sovereign state, "the other nationalities which are now under Turkish rule should be assured an undoubted security of life and an absolutely unmolested opportunity of autonomous development." To Lawrence, as to most other objective readers, that didn't sound at all like the Sykes-Picot Agreement, nor, for that matter, like the externally imposed Balfour Declaration.

In his conversation with William Yale, Lawrence emphasized the enormous esteem in which Arabs of all stripes held the United States. Indeed, so forcefully did Lawrence hit on this note that in his summing up of their conversation for Leland Harrison, Yale noted that the main points "upon which all evidence is agreed, are the distrust of the Arabs in the good faith of England and of France; the opposition to Zionism; and the complete confidence of the Arabs in the United States."

Idle flattery had never been one of Lawrence's strong suits, and this surely wasn't the motive behind his message to the American agent. Rather, as Yale wrote, "he declares that later, if things should not turn out as well as is expected, and if there should be an imminent danger of the disaffection of the Arabs, a declaration by the United States concerning the future of the Arabs and their country would prove to be a 'trump card' to play against the Turko-German propaganda, and he feels that such a declaration would have an enormous effect upon the Arabs."

Perhaps lulled by Lawrence's candor on other matters, Yale appears to have accepted this argument at face value—or at least not pondered it too deeply. If he had, he might have realized that such an American declaration would be a far less effective tool against "Turko-German propaganda"—after all, the United States was at war with Germany, so her motives would naturally be suspect—than against the acquisitive aspirations of America's allies, Britain and France. In essence, and while obviously of far less treasonable consequence than negotiating with Turkey, Lawrence was looking to a foreign government as the vehicle by which to undermine the policies of his own.

To that end, the time Lawrence carved out of his hectic Cairo schedule to meet with William Yale would seem well spent. In the months just ahead, the State Department's special agent would increasingly urge his government to take a more active role in Middle Eastern affairs, and to stand with the Arabs against those who would subordinate them.

DURING THE SAME week that Yale and Lawrence were meeting in Cairo, on the evening of March 14, about a dozen men gathered in a state-room of SS *Canberra* as it lay to its mooring in the Italian port city of Taranto. Nine were members of a group called the Zionist Commission, while two more were British government liaisons, or "minders," tasked to both facilitate and monitor that group's work. The meeting was intended as a kind of last-minute strategy session, for in the morning the *Canberra*, a converted Australian steamship, would sail for Egypt, the starting point of the Zionist Commission's historic mission to the Middle East.

Framing the task before them was William Ormsby-Gore, the British Conservative member of Parliament who had become an ardent convert to Zionism, and who now served alongside Mark Sykes on the British War Cabinet's Near East Committee. In the four months since the Balfour Declaration's release, Arab opposition had only grown more strident. The primary goal of the commission, Ormsby-Gore explained, was to assure the leaders of both the Christian and Muslim Arab communities that they had nothing to fear from a Jewish "national home" in Palestine.

Chaim Weizmann, the head of the delegation sailing to Egypt, then bluntly laid out his "one leading principle" for the mission, "which was that until the end of the war, the Arabs were a military asset to the British government. After the war, they might become a liability." In short, now wasn't the time to be confrontational with those who opposed them. Rather, the goal was to mollify and to calm, to bide their time and look for advantage in the future.

Needless to say, this was hardly Aaron Aaronsohn's vision of their mission—but then he was only tangentially a member of the commission at all. Back in London, there had been such fierce opposition to his inclusion by some other committee members that his official status was now that of a mere adjunct "agricultural expert," and that only on the insistence of American Zionist leaders like Louis Brandeis.

Part of this resistance stemmed from the revelations about his NILI spy ring. That had sparked fierce debate within both the Zionist community and international Jewry as a whole, with many accusing the spy mastermind of having endangered the very existence of the Palestine *yeshuv* through his actions. Just as worrisome, though, was the scientist's reputation for argumentativeness, for it was hard to imagine a more exquisitely delicate diplomatic mission than that being undertaken by the passengers on the *Canberra*.

At the same time that they attempted to calm Arab fears of a Jewish takeover, the commission needed to unite the deeply fractious Jewish community in Palestine under the Zionist banner. The best, perhaps only, way to do this was to convince them of the dramatic changes soon to be coming to Palestine in the wake of the Balfour Declaration—in other words, nearly the precise opposite of what they would be telling the Arabs. In addition to these constituencies were the British military and political officials in the region. Even those favorably disposed toward the Balfour Declaration tended to view it as an extraordinary complication, a new British commitment to compete with those already made to the Arabs and the French.

In the *Canberra* stateroom, Weizmann laid out with a broad brush how this complex initiative was to proceed. Obviously, the favor of British officials would be won or lost depending on whether the Zionists made their lives less or more difficult, so the first task was to mollify the Arabs. To this end, it would be publicly and repeatedly stated by the commission—and by "commission" in this context, Chaim Weizmann was referring specifically to Chaim Weizmann—that the Zionists had no intention of trying to install a Jewish state in Palestine at the end of the war, nor did they intend to start buying up land. To the contrary, the Zionists fully supported the British authorities' recent moratorium on land sales in Palestine, and were only looking for the opportunity for those Jews who wished to do so to return to the land of their forebears, to engage in its political and economic development hand in hand with the region's other religious or ethnic communities.

This was to be the overt message, at least. As Weizmann went on to explain, Zionist organizations needed to actively encourage Jewish immigration to Palestine on a large scale, and to stockpile funds for the purchase of land once the sales moratorium was lifted. Certainly there was no backing away from the ultimate goal—the creation of a Jewish state—but nothing to gain by acknowledging it publicly.

At least initially, this complicated dance was performed to great effect. After an ecstatic welcome by the Jewish community in Alexandria— hundreds of schoolchildren lined the wharf to sing the Hebrew song "Hatikvah" ("The Hope")—the Zionist Commission continued on to an even warmer reception in Cairo. To both British officials and members of the Syrian exile community in Egypt, Weizmann stressed time and again the benign intentions of the Zionist cause. As Kincaid Cornwallis, Gilbert Clayton's deputy at the Arab Bureau, reported on April 20, the Zionist leader told a delegation of Arabs known as the Syrian Committee that "it was his ambition to see Palestine governed by some stable Government like that of Great Britain, that a Jewish Government would be fatal to his plans and that it was simply his wish to provide a home for the Jews in the Holy Land where they could live their own national life, sharing equal rights with the other inhabitants." Further, Weizmann assured his Arab listeners that the status of Muslim holy places would remain inviolate, spoke with great sympathy of the Arab Revolt against the Turks, and even suggested it was he who had pressed on the British the land-buying moratorium. "Suspicion still remains in the minds of some," Cornwallis concluded his report, "but it is tempered by the above considerations, and there is little doubt that it will gradually disappear if the Commission continues its present attitude of conciliation."

Among those with an intimate view of this charm offensive was U.S. State Department special agent William Yale. One of the Syrian Committee leaders whom Weizmann repeatedly met with in Cairo was a man named Suleiman Bey Nassif, who also happened to be one of the troika of Jerusalem businessmen who had held the oil concessions purchased by Standard Oil in 1914. Yale had stayed in close touch with Nassif since coming to Cairo, and from the exiled businessman he received a detailed account of those meetings with Weizmann. "On the whole," Yale reported to the State Department, "these conferences were a success, the Syrian leaders came away from them with the impression that the Zionists did not wish to impose a Jewish government in Palestine, and that the Jews were coming to Palestine under conditions and with ideas that they could accept."

But if the Syrians were convinced, Yale harbored doubts. For one thing, he found it odd that the Zionist Commission would soon be traveling on to Palestine, their way facilitated by the British government, while Nassif and his fellow Syrian Committee members remained barred from the region. Yale's suspicions deepened further when he had a chat with Louis Meyer, the sole American "observer" delegate to the commission.

Perhaps Meyer was another of those who didn't fully appreciate the duties of a State Department special agent, or maybe he was simply lulled by the prospect of talking to a fellow American, but he went decidedly off script in his meeting with William Yale. As Yale would recall, "Meyer told me very directly that just because Weizmann was currently disavowing any intention of creating a Jewish state in Palestine, that didn't imply that he was bound to that disavowal for the future. Instead, the ultimate goal is a Jewish nation under either British or American protection."

As he probed further, Yale ascertained that the plans for that Jewish nation were in fact quite well advanced. Indeed, within the Zionist Commission was an ongoing debate over what should become of Palestine's Arab population once nationhood had been achieved, with those arguing that "cheap Arab labor" was essential "to the growth and success of Zionism" pitted against those who foresaw the day when non-Jews would have to be expelled. In the end, Meyer opined, it came down to numbers, that "as in the [American] south the white population would never submit to a domination by the negroes, so a Jewish minority in Palestine would never submit to a domination by an Arab majority."

To the American intelligence agent, the commission increasingly appeared to be a kind of political Potemkin village, and he took at least a small measure of delight when the façade it was presenting to the world suffered its first small tear. As might have been predicted, that tear came at the hands of Aaron Aaronsohn.

Day after day in Cairo, Aaronsohn suffered in silence through the interminable meetings and speeches to which the commission was subjected, his frustration piqued just as much by the long-winded and quarrelsome Jewish delegations as those of the Arabs. One protracted session with a group of Jewish religious notables, in which Weizmann had been forced to patiently explain why Zionism was not antireligious, had almost proved too much; as Aaronsohn railed in his diary, "once again, pearls have been thrown down in front of the pigs of the community."

Unfortunately, the agronomist reached his breaking point at the worst possible time, during a meeting with Suleiman Nassif's Syrian Committee. When one of the Arabs suggested that Jewish settlers tended to be clannish and exclusively traded with their own, to the detriment of Arabs, a furious Aaronsohn rose to denounce the charge as a lie. Weizmann swiftly tried to defuse the situation, offering that while such a lamentable state of affairs might well have occurred in the past, steps would be taken to ensure it didn't in the future. But Aaronsohn's public outburst cast an understandable pall over the gathering. "It is to be hoped," Yale wryly reported to the State Department, "that Dr. Weizmann will keep Mr. Aaronsohn in the background in all the [future] dealings of the Commission with the Arabs."

Weizmann obviously thought along similar lines. At the next conference with the same Syrian Committee a few days later, Aaronsohn was nowhere to be seen.

ON THE MORNING of April 2, Lawrence and a small entourage of bodyguards set out from Guweira, bound for the Syrian interior. It was the first time Lawrence had been on a camel in over a month, and the journey quickly lifted his spirits. "The abstraction of the desert landscape cleansed me," he wrote, "and rendered my mind vacant with its superfluous greatness, a greatness achieved not by the addition of thought to its emptiness, but by its subtraction. In the weakness of earth's life was mirrored the strength of heaven, so vast, so beautiful, so strong."

Pastoral splendor aside, this trek had been made necessary by a worrisome feature on the map of Syria, one that called into question General Allenby's proposed march on Damascus. While the British army held a strong and orderly line across the breadth of central Palestine, an approximately thirty-mile span extending from the Mediterranean shore above Jaffa all the way to the Jordan River, everything east of the Jordan still lay in Turkish hands. This meant that the farther the British pushed north for Damascus, the more exposed they would become to a Turkish counterattack on their ever-lengthening eastern flank. This danger would have been vastly reduced had the Moab Plateau been seized, but, following Zeid's sabotaging of that effort, British war planners had come up with a new scheme, a preliminary operation to pave the way for the main thrust on Damascus.

In consultation with Lawrence at those headquarters meetings in late February, it had been decided that the three-thousand-man Arab army encamped in Aqaba would storm the critical railhead town of Maan, just thirty miles northeast of the Arabs' forward headquarters at Guweira. Both to mask that attack and to prevent Turkish reinforcements from being rushed to Maan, a British cavalry force would simultaneously sweep across the top of the Dead Sea, some 120 miles above Maan, to destroy critical stretches of the Hejaz Railway in the vicinity of the town of Amman. Once Maan was firmly in Arab hands, all Turkish troops to the south, including those still holding Medina, would be permanently stranded. By then turning their attention to the north, the Arab army and British auxiliary forces could quickly clear the railway of all the small Turkish outposts below Amman. If all went according to plan, the British and their Arab allies would then have a unified east-west battle line across almost the entire length of greater Syria, allowing for the push on Damascus to commence.

The role chosen for Lawrence in this roll-up operation was relatively limited, but one for which he was uniquely qualified. As other British advisors oversaw the principal engagement, the assault on Maan, he was to take a small group of rebels one hundred miles north to a valley known as Atatir. There he would join with other tribal forces to conduct "worrying" raids against the Turks around Amman in conjunction with the British cavalry raid coming from the west. With that raid tentatively scheduled for early April, Lawrence had set out from Guweira a few days ahead of time to get into place.

By April 6, his party had reached the valley of Atatir. In Lawrence's rendering, the place was like an Eden in the first burst of spring, its hills and streambanks a riot of young sawgrass and wildflowers. "Everything was growing," he wrote, "and daily the picture was fuller and brighter till the desert became like a rank water-meadow. Playful packs of winds came crossing and tumbling over one another, their wide, brief gusts surging through the grass, to lay it momentarily in swathes of dark and light satin, like young corn after the roller."

If Lawrence's high spirits and focus on the beauty surrounding him seemed a bit incongruous for a man preparing to go into battle, another detail made it even more so. Just before setting out for Atatir, he had learned that two of the men he'd left to guard the Azraq citadel had died from cold over the brutally harsh winter. One was Daud, one of the pair of camp imps Lawrence had taken on as his personal attendants six months earlier. The bearer of that news had been Daud's inseparable companion, Farraj.

"These two had been friends from childhood," Lawrence noted in *Seven Pillars*, "in eternal gaiety, working together, sleeping together, sharing every scrape and profit with the openness and honesty of perfect love. So I was not astonished to see Farraj look dark and hard of face, leaden-eyed and old, when he came to tell me that his fellow was dead, and from that day till his service ended, he made no more laughter for us. . . . The others offered themselves to comfort him, but instead he wandered restlessly, gray and silent, very much alone." Despite his grief, or perhaps because of it, Farraj had joined Lawrence on the trek north.

In Atatir, Lawrence received word from the British army—but it was not at all what he'd expected to hear. According to the plan worked out at headquarters, the mixed cavalry and infantry force, some twelve thousand men in all, was to charge up from the Jordan valley to seize the town of Salt, in the hills some ten miles west of Amman. From there, a raiding party would continue on to destroy the most vulnerable points on the Hejaz Railway—two high-spanning bridges and a tunnel—outside Amman. But with the enemy apparently tipped to their plans, the attack force had been met in Salt by entrenched units of German and Turkish soldiers, and what was envisioned as a jaunt had turned into a bloody two-day battle. When at last Salt was secured and the raiding party made for the railway at Amman, the enemy had been waiting there, too, forcing the British to turn back without achieving any of their principal objectives. But then the news grew even worse: having suffered some two thousand casualties, the British had been forced out of Salt and were now scrambling back across the Jordan with the Turks in close pursuit.

"It was thought that Jerusalem would be recovered [by the Turks]," Lawrence wrote of the ever more ominous reports he received in Atatir. "I knew enough of my countrymen to reject that possibility, but clearly things were very wrong." Worse than the physical defeat, though, was the psychological effect it was likely to have on the Arabs. "Allenby's plan had seemed modest, and that we [British] should so fall down before the Arabs was deplorable. They had never trusted us to do the great things which I had foretold." With the rout at Salt, those doubts were sure to be deepened.

With nothing left to do around Amman, Lawrence turned south with fifteen of his bodyguards to join in the ongoing assault of Maan—but the ill-starred nature of this venture wasn't over yet. The next day, in the desert outside the hamlet of Faraifra, an eight-man Turkish foot patrol was spotted haplessly trudging along the railway ahead. After their fruitless mission north, Lawrence's men begged for permission to attack the outnumbered and exposed patrol. "I thought it too trifling," he recalled, "but when they chafed, agreed."

As the Turks scurried to take cover in a railway culvert, Lawrence dispatched his men into flanking positions. Too late, he noticed Farraj; completely on his own, the young camp attendant had spurred his camel and was charging directly at the enemy. As Lawrence watched, Farraj abruptly drew his mount up beside the railway culvert; there was a shot, and then Farraj fell from view. "His camel stood unharmed by the bridge, alone," Lawrence wrote. "I could not believe that he had deliberately ridden up to them in the open and halted, yet it looked like it."

When finally Lawrence and the others reached the culvert, they found one Turkish soldier dead and Farraj horribly wounded, shot through the side. With efforts to stanch his bleeding to no avail, Farraj's companions attempted to lift him onto a camel, even as the young man begged to be left to die. The matter was rather decided when an alarm went up that a Turkish patrol of some fifty soldiers was approaching along the rails.

Knowing the hideous end the Turks often perpetrated on enemy captives, Lawrence and his bodyguards had a tacit understanding to finish off any of their number too badly wounded to travel. With Farraj, this coup de grâce task fell to Lawrence. "I knelt down beside him, holding my pistol near the ground by his head so that he should not see my purpose, but he must have guessed it, for he opened his eyes and clutched me with his harsh, scaly hand, the tiny hand of these unripe Nejd fellows. I waited a moment, and he said, 'Daud will be angry with you,' the old smile coming back so strangely to this gray shrinking face. I replied, 'salute him from me.' He returned the formal answer, 'God will give you peace,' and at last wearily closed his eyes."

After shooting Farraj, Lawrence remounted his camel, and he and his entourage fled as the first Turkish bullets came for them.

Before the day was over, there was to be one more illustration of the mercilessness of this war, and of Lawrence's growing imperviousness to it. That night, as the party camped a few miles away from Faraifra, an argument developed over who should inherit Farraj's prize camel. Lawrence settled the dispute by drawing his pistol once more and shooting the animal in the head. At dinner that night, they ate rice and the camel's butchered carcass. "Afterwards," Lawrence noted, "we slept."

BY MID-APRIL 1918, Djemal Pasha was probably feeling quite sanguine about the future. Defying the rumors of his political demise of just a few months earlier, he remained very much a force within the shadowy CUP (Committee of Union and Progress) leadership, just as respected and feared as before. There was also heartening news from the battlefield. On March 21, Germany had launched its massive offensive in France, smashing through the Allied armies before them to make the greatest territorial gains of any Western Front army since the beginning of the war. Indeed, the first wave of that offensive, code-named Michael, had only stalled because the advancing German forces had outrun their supply lines. By April 13, a second offensive, Georgette, was closing on the French coast and the vital seaports there. Suddenly it appeared Germany just might succeed in defeating Britain and France before the incoming Americans could rescue them.

And if Germany was currently experiencing great success on the Western Front battlefield, Turkey wasn't doing so badly on the Eastern. Having first reclaimed those northeastern provinces that had been occupied by Russia, in early February Turkish troops had taken advantage of the continuing power vacuum brought about by Russia's defeat to smash into Armenia. By mid-April, those troops were preparing for the next phase of operations, a sweep all the way to the shores of the Caspian Sea and the fantastically rich oilfields of Baku. Rather like Djemal Pasha himself, the Ottoman Empire had become like a strange ever-mutating organism, shorn of influence and authority in one place only to regain it in another.

Looking to the south, it could be argued that earning the displeasure of international Zionism had produced unexpected benefits for Turkey. The Balfour Declaration had won the Zionists to the British, but it had come at the price of an enraged Arab world. That had allowed Djemal and other Ottoman leaders to make appeals to a number of disenchanted Muslim and Christian leaders in Syria, and even to the chief traitor himself, King

Hussein in the Hejaz. By mid-April, there were signs that this last and most important overture was starting to bear fruit. As Djemal had learned through his intermediaries in Syria, Hussein's son Faisal had recently responded to a Turkish peace offer by setting out demands of his own. The two sides were still quite far apart, but if there was any lesson to be learned from the musical-chairs game that World War I had become, it was that everything was fluid, that what had been lost yesterday might be recovered tomorrow. All that really mattered was who won out in the end, and by April 1918 there could be no doubt that the advantage lay with the Central Powers.

This was certainly an assessment shared by Curt Prüfer, who was also in Constantinople that spring. In curious fashion, Germany's improved situation was allowing him to return to the first great conspiracy he had been involved with, one that had long looked dead but was now suddenly given new life.

For the past six months, Abbas Hilmi II, the deposed khedive of Egypt, had occupied apartments on an upper floor of the Pera Palace hotel in the city. There, he had joined that peculiar class of aristocracy to be found in most every European capital during World War I, the prince-lings and marquises and nawabs placed on ice by their imperial patrons on the off chance that they might prove useful at some point in the future. During that time, the task of keeping the former khedive entertained and feeling important had largely fallen to Curt Prüfer. In contrast to his more sober-minded duties as director of the German intelligence bureau, deal-ing with Abbas and his eclectic entourage was often more akin to baby-sitting. According to Prüfer biographer Donald McKale, "He kept Abbas Hilmi's bickering advisers, who denounced each other as 'English spies,' under surveillance, and counseled the ex-Khedive on his difficulties with his son, his three former wives, and a French mistress."

It's clear, though, that the German intelligence chief also saw Abbas Hilmi as a useful sounding board. Abbas derided the secret negotiations with Faisal Hussein as quite pointless; the Constantinople clique would never actually cede what Faisal was demanding, and Faisal surely knew it. A much better solution, the ex-khedive opined, was for himself to become ruler of Egypt and then fashion a quasi-independent Arab nation with Hussein and Faisal—one on very friendly terms with Turkey and Ger-many, Hilmi undoubtedly hastened to add.

That had been so much idle talk in the autumn of 1917, but by early 1918 what had seemed far-fetched, even delusional, took on the patina of possibility. By then, the first reliable reports of civic unrest in Egypt were reaching the outside world, with the normally quiescent population enraged by Britain's draconian martial law rule, as well as by the Balfour

Declaration and Sykes-Picot Agreement. Then, of course, had come the final collapse of Russia, the string of battlefield successes by Germany and Turkey, the increasing signs that the Arab rebels in Arabia and Syria might be looking for a way out of their alliance with the duplicitous British. For all these reasons, by that April, the idea that Abbas Hilmi II might somehow ascend to the Egyptian throne didn't seem so crazy after all—and if that happened, Curt Prüfer's patient ministrations at the Pera Palace might pay spectacular dividends for Germany.

Abbas clearly sensed his stock rising, too, so much so that he resurrected a long-cherished goal, one he had first put to Max von Oppenheim three years earlier but which had been consistently denied him. As he informed Curt Prüfer, before anything could be decided about Egypt, he needed to meet with the kaiser. Somewhat nonplussed, Prüfer said he would see what he could do.

WHEN LAWRENCE MET General Allenby for afternoon tea on May 15, both men were at a low ebb.

After his fruitless trek to Atatir, Lawrence had hurried down to join the Arab assault on the railhead town of Maan. By the time he got there on April 13, operations were already under way.

The order of battle had called for the attackers to first strike at Maan's outlying guardhouses in hopes of luring the main Turkish garrison out of its entrenched positions around the railway station. Initially the operation had proceeded as planned, with one outer-ring Turkish post after another falling to the rebels. On April 17, however, the Iraqi commander of the Arab army, tiring of the extended waiting game, overruled the counsel of his British advisors to order a frontal assault on the train depot. The approach proved just as futile at Maan as it had on a thousand other World War I battlefields. "There was nothing to do," Lawrence wrote, "but see our men volleyed out of the railway station again. The road was littered with crumpled khaki figures."

Lawrence had stayed on in the Maan area for several more days, assisting other British officers in railway destruction operations to the south, but the battle for the crucial railway town had already been decided by that futile frontal attack. While British military communiqués made much of the damage done to the Hejaz Railway below Maan—with some sixty miles of track torn up, the Turkish garrison in Medina was now stranded for good—it was a paltry achievement when measured against the offensive's objectives.

But even more dispiriting news had awaited Lawrence when he reached Allenby's headquarters in Ramleh on May 2. Over the previous six weeks, Allied forces on the Western Front had only barely withstood two massive German offensives. In anticipation of a third, Allenby had been ordered to stand to the defense and to release tens of thousands of his best frontline troops for service in France. It meant there was to be no push on Damascus, that all the losses of the previous month—the failed British cavalry raid on Salt, the disastrous frontal assault at Maan, the death of Farraj in the desert—had been for naught. To top things off, just prior to Lawrence's arrival in Ramleh, the same British cavalry commander who'd been thrown out of Salt the first time had decided to have another go; by May 2, and after another fifteen hundred casualties, the last stragglers of this fresh British defeat were drifting back across the front lines.

All of which meant that by the time of Lawrence's next visit to head-quarters and his tea with General Allenby on May 15, both men had been forced to acknowledge that the prospects of a breakthrough on the Syr-ian front were just as distant as ever—in fact, a good deal more distant, for in the interval since Lawrence's last trip to headquarters, Allenby's army had been poached a second time by the Western Front generals. All told, the Egyptian Expeditionary Force was now slated to lose some sixty thousand soldiers for service in France, about half of its frontline strength, and while London had committed to covering those losses with troops brought over from Iraq and India, it meant the Syrian front would be dormant for many months to come.

But during that tea, and amid describing the massive reorganization his army was currently undergoing, Allenby happened to mention the Imperial Camel Corps. This was an elite unit that had been sitting idle in the Sinai for the past six months, and the general now planned to convert it into a conventional horse-mounted cavalry and discard its camels.

From the very outset of the Syrian campaign, the greatest logistical hurdle facing the Arab rebels had been a shortage of both transport and riding camels, a problem that had only grown worse as the size and scope of operations expanded. Because of that shortage, supply lines were always stretched to the breaking point, proposed actions scaled back or canceled outright for lack of mounts. What's more, the frequent camel-purchasing forays of Lawrence and other British officers had depleted the available stock throughout the region, leading to extortionate prices for the few decent animals left. Now, with the proposed disbanding of the Imperial Camel Corps (ICC), some two thousand of the finest riding mounts in the entire Middle East would suddenly become available.

To Lawrence, it raised an obvious question: "What are you going to do with their camels?" he asked Allenby.

Allenby laughed. "Ask Q."

"Q" was the British quartermaster general, who explained that the camels had been promised to an incoming Indian army division for use as transport. The quartermaster general flatly rejected Lawrence's appeals, but Allenby was swayed by his argument that using these prize animals for mere transport would be a colossal waste. At dinner that evening, the commander in chief asked Lawrence how, if given the ICC mounts, he proposed to use them.

Lawrence had, of course, anticipated the question. In addition, he divined a silver lining to the British cavalry's ill-fated second attack on Salt. As a result of that failure, the Turks would now be convinced that any future British attack would probably come at that same spot—after all, repeatedly smashing up against the enemy's strongest points had become something of a British World War I tradition by now—and align their troops accordingly. With the Turks concentrating their forces in the Salt-Amman region, it would allow Lawrence, utilizing the new ICC camels from his desert hideout in Azraq, to strike behind the enemy's lines and over a wide range of targets. These included the most vital target in all of lower Syria: the railhead town of Deraa, the junction of the principal lifeline of the Turkish forces facing the British in Palestine. At the headquarters dinner table, Lawrence gave Allenby his reply: "To put a thousand men into Deraa any day you please."

While those men might not be able to permanently hold Deraa, Lawrence explained, they would certainly have time to blow up the crucial railroad bridges in Yarmuk, leaving the Turkish forces in Palestine virtually cut off from supply or reinforcement. At this, Allenby turned to the quartermaster general and shook his head in mock sadness: "Q, you lose."

With the promise of the ICC camels, Lawrence rushed back to Faisal's headquarters. The news had an electrifying effect on the warrior chieftains gathered there, for the "gift" of the two thousand thoroughbreds meant the Arabs could finally take their revolt to the far north in a substantive way. No longer would they be limited to sniping, hit-and-run attacks; by putting enough mounted fighters in the field, they could storm and hold population centers.

It also meant—and this had been a crucial aspect of Lawrence's thinking—that the Arabs might loosen the British tether. It would still be some time before the ICC camels were delivered, and then they would need to be acclimated to the harder forage of Syria, but within two or three months' time, the Arab rebels wouldn't have to rely on the actions of the British, now stalemated in Palestine. Instead, they could take their war into the Syrian heartland independently, and with that independence would come the chance to snatch Syria for themselves. It was, Lawrence wrote, "a regal gift, the gift of unlimited mobility. The Arabs could now win their war when and where they liked."

. . .

SINCE ARRIVING IN Cairo, Aaron Aaronsohn had fallen into a dark and downcast mood. Part of it may have stemmed from his marginalized role with the Zionist Commission, the unseemly manner with which he'd been relegated to the sidelines, but his return to the region after a seven-month absence also made fresh the tragedy that had befallen his NILI organization. In Cairo, he was reunited with two of his brothers, Alex and Sam, and from them he learned more details of their sister's ghastly end. Particularly enraging to the agronomist was how Sarah and the other NILI members had been essentially handed over by their own kind, the Zichron Yaakov Committee going so far as to post a bounty on the head of the NILI fugitive Joseph Lishansky. Zichron still lay well behind Turkish lines in the spring of 1918, but in contemplating his return there, Aaronsohn noted in his diary that "if I should seek revenge on all the cowards and scoundrels, there would be hardly a half dozen people with whom I could shake hands."

More than anger, though, the memory of Sarah, or Sarati, and his fallen best friend, Absalom Feinberg, seemed to act as a kind of haunting presence on the scientist, constantly intruding on his thoughts. On one occasion, for example, he had been flabbergasted to see William Ormsby-Gore put a telephone call through to Jerusalem. "To telephone from Cairo to Jerusalem!" he marveled in his diary. "If only Sarati and Absa could have lived to see that!"

This haunting only grew worse when the Zionist Commission left Egypt for Palestine at the beginning of April. Aboard the night train taking them past Gaza, a solitary Aaronsohn stood by a window to stare out at the passing countryside. Ever the agronomist, he took note of the poor state of the fields—"very little winter cereals, and of a poor quality"—while observing that nothing appeared to have really changed in his two-year absence. "Still," he noted, "we travel by train—and we are with the English! Absa, Absa, where are you? Sarati?"

But also to grow worse in Palestine was Aaronsohn's pariah status. At one banquet honoring the visiting commission, a group of local Jewish elders refused to sit with the man who had "endangered the Yishuv" through his spying activities. At several other meetings with Jewish delegations, Aaronsohn was excoriated for the alleged strong-arm tactics he had displayed in disbursing international relief funds in the early days of the war. One of the few times any gratitude was shown him came during a welcoming ceremony in the Jewish enclave of Tel Aviv in Jaffa, the same community whose purported plight he had publicized following Djemal Pasha's evacuation order. As hundreds of young members of the Maccabean Society, a Jewish civic organization, serenaded the visiting commission members, Chaim Weizmann leaned to Aaronsohn's side. "Well, Aaron," Weizmann said, "you have a great share in all this—and you paid a big price."

That moment was an anomaly, however. Weizmann's mission to Palestine was far too sensitive to allow for discord, whereas Aaronsohn was a man loath to ever turn the other cheek. After a commission member took Aaronsohn aside to urge that he bridge over a dispute he was having with one Jewish settlement delegation, the scientist haughtily replied that "to bridge it over would mean to establish social relations which are repugnant to me. If my attitude is not prudent, fine."

With Aaronsohn's feuds extending even to other commission members, Weizmann steadily pushed the agronomist further to the periphery. At times, quite literally; in the group photographs taken of the commission during their time in Palestine, Aaronsohn is usually seen standing off to one side—when included in the portraits at all. By the end of April, he had effectively parted ways to go off and work on a project of his own.

Ironically, that venture was to produce perhaps the most tangible result of the commission's trip, for by late May, Aaronsohn had completed a remarkable blueprint for agricultural development in southern Palestine. In the papers and maps he passed to Windham Deedes at the Arab Bureau was the proposal to quickly put some quarter million acres of uncultivated and "Crown" (held by the Turkish government) land under the plow to help ease the continuing wartime food shortages. Under Aaronsohn's scheme, the project would be placed under British military control, but with the farming done by Jewish settlers and funding provided by Zionist banks; the Zionist Commission pledged at least a half million pounds. In its execution, all would benefit: food would be provided to the destitute, so the Arabs would see the material advantage of an increased Jewish presence in Palestine, and the prospect of a decent life would entice more Jews to come.

Of course, once the period of military administration ended, perhaps four or five years, title to the quarter million acres would pass to the Zionists. But as Gilbert Clayton sunnily opined to the Foreign Office in voicing his support for Aaronsohn's plan, "a small favor granted to one community can easily [be] counterbalanced by similar privileges afforded to the others and thus, in the normal course of administration, gradual progress can be made without causing friction and discontent."

Even with the contribution of his land scheme, however, Aaronsohn remained an outcast with the Zionist Commission—and what held for that panel quite naturally extended to its British benefactors. At the end of May, when General Allenby held a state dinner in Jerusalem for the soon-departing commission, the only associate not invited was Aaron Aaronsohn.

. . .

To skirt orders with which he disagreed, Lawrence frequently relied on an old standby of Victorian literature: the message that goes missing or isn't delivered in time. This ruse had been denied him when it came to the British effort to force an entente between the Arab rebel leaders and the Zionists; in this sphere, Lawrence could only delay or impede at the edges. Back in February 1918, when Gilbert Clayton had ordered Lawrence to press Faisal on the matter, his subordinate had replied that he hoped to arrange a Faisal visit to Jerusalem in the near future, and "all the Jews there will report him friendly. That will probably do all you need, without public commitment, which is rather beyond my province."

For an army major to tell a brigadier general what his needs were and the limits he would go in supplying them was no more acceptable in 1918 than it is today, but Clayton apparently accepted Lawrence's response with equanimity; he surely calculated that even this partial compliance to his order was better than nothing, since there was simply no one else in the British command with Lawrence's influence on Faisal.

Lawrence changed tactics somewhat when Clayton returned to the topic in May. In light of the continuing suspicions that Chaim Weizmann and his commission were encountering among the Arab population in Palestine, Weizmann had proposed a meeting between him and Faisal. The British leadership in Palestine had heartily embraced the idea and, on May 22, Clayton sent a telegram to Lawrence in Aqaba seeking his counsel. "What arrangements do you suggest?" the general asked. "I am of opinion you should be present at interview. . . . Let us have your views on above points at an early date, please."

Lawrence certainly received the message—he was in Aqaba the following day—but there is no record of his answering. On May 24, with the timetable for Weizmann's proposed visit now firmed up—he was scheduled to sail for Aqaba in just five days—another secret cable was fired off, this time from Allenby's headquarters to the attention of the overall Aqaba base commander. "Interview would take place at Arab headquarters to which they would motor. Wire if this is convenient to Sherif Faisal and Lawrence. It is important latter should be present at interview. Urgent reply requested."

Once again, Lawrence was most certainly informed of this cable, but he still didn't respond. Instead, on May 27, with Weizmann's arrival in Aqaba imminent, he found reason to depart on another reconnaissance mission to the north, conveniently falling out of easy communication until Weizmann had come and gone.

In his absence, the meeting between Faisal and the British Zionist leader took place on the afternoon of June 4. It was an amicable and pleas-ant enough encounter, with Weizmann ostentatiously donning an Arab headdress for the occasion, even as Faisal avoided committing himself to anything of much substance, arguing that ultimate authority lay with his father in Mecca, and that matters in Syria remained far too unsettled to start getting into specifics. Still, Weizmann was very satisfied by the talk, as were British officials. As Clayton would report to the Foreign Office after receiving a detailed report of the meeting, "In my opinion, the inter-view has had excellent results in promoting mutual sympathy and under-standing between Weizmann and Faisal. Both are frank and open in their dealings, and a personal interview such as has now taken place can result in nothing but the good."

That assessment was unlikely to be shared by Lawrence, who returned to Aqaba from his reconnaissance mission on June 8, four days after the Faisal-Weizmann meeting. To him, this British-imposed con-cord could only provide more ammunition to Faisal's—and by extension Hussein's—rivals in the Arab world.

But again, there was little to do about it. The British weren't going to walk back from Balfour. Any pressure the Americans might bring to bear in pursuit of Wilson's Fourteen Points plan wouldn't come until a peace conference, their influence on Middle Eastern affairs in the meantime resting somewhere between nil and nonexistent. As for the Arabs striking out on their own, the mounts of the Imperial Camel Corps had yet to be delivered, and even when they were, it would be some time before they had sufficiently acclimated to the Syrian landscape for large-scale opera-tions. Of course, there was one more possibility: a rapprochement with the Turks. By coincidence, Faisal had received another secret message from General Mehmet Djemal just two days before Weizmann showed up in Aqaba.

In fact, Faisal's flirtation with the Turkish general was not unknown to senior British officials. Back in late March, a spy had given Reginald Wingate a copy of Faisal's note to Mehmet Djemal outlining his terms for negotiations. "It is difficult to say how much importance should be attached to this correspondence," Wingate informed the Foreign Office, "and it would be inadvisable to enquire directly from Emir Faisal as to his motives. . . . [But] it confirms my suspicion that Sharif leaders, depressed by general military situation and doubt of Allies' policies in Palestine and Syria, are putting out feelers to ascertain Turkish official opinion about future of Arab countries."

To their credit, those Foreign Office officials apprised of this news reacted with a refreshing lack of hypocrisy. After all, several pointed out, Britain was unofficially negotiating with some half dozen Turkish emissaries in Switzerland, so it would be a bit unseemly for them to take umbrage at others doing so. Instead, and at Mark Sykes's first suggestion, they set themselves to the task of neutralizing the threat in gentlemanly fashion: by bestowing Faisal with a medal. Over the next several months, a host of senior British officials weighed in on the debate over just what commendation might sufficiently impress the Arab rebel leader to ensure his loyalty.

Curiously, one of Faisal's strongest defenders had been Gilbert Clayton, who hastened to inform the Foreign Office in early April that the charge of treachery against Faisal appeared based on a misunderstanding, that the thrust of his overture to Mehmet Djemal seemed actually directed at an Arab-Turk reconciliation in the *postwar* era. Nonetheless, Clayton had urged, London should avail herself of this opportunity "to cement the Arab Alliance with Great Britain by all possible means." Those means included recognizing Faisal's authority in all territories east of the Jordan River, and compelling the French "to give an authoritative statement" relinquishing her claims to greater Syria. But perhaps Clayton's generous view of Faisal's actions wasn't so curious given his source; as Clayton noted to the Foreign Office, he had been provided this interpretation—and perhaps his list of recommendations, too—by Major T. E. Lawrence.

The precise role Lawrence played in the secret negotiations between Faisal and the Turks has never been made clear; much like the timing of his disclosure to Faisal about Sykes-Picot, Lawrence seemed to appreciate that he was on very delicate legal ground, and gave vague and contradictory answers on the matter to his early biographers. What is clear is that he saw in those negotiations a powerful potential weapon to use against his government, a reminder that should the Arabs be betrayed, they had somewhere else to go.

"At the present day," Mehmet Djemal's new letter of June 2 began, "the Ottoman government, the mightiest representative of Islam, has obtained supremacy over the greatest enemies of the Mohammedan religion. I am persuaded that I am honoring the Prophet's name by inviting His most excellent and noble grandson [Faisal] to participate in the protection of Islam for, by ensuring the supremacy of the Turkish army, a safe and happy life will be obtained for all true believers." The general had closed by proposing a meeting with Faisal in four days' time, during which "I feel sure that we shall be able to fulfill the wishes of all Arabs."

Faisal didn't take up the offer of a face-to-face meeting, but did send another reply. In that unsigned letter, he again proposed that all Turkish troops below Amman be withdrawn, and further suggested that Syria's future relationship with Turkey be modeled along the lines of the loose federation existing between Austria and Hungary. If that still left matters a bit vague, Faisal's other preconditions didn't: all Arab soldiers in the Turkish army were to be released for service in the Arab army, and "if the Arab and Turkish Armies fight side by side against the enemy, the Arab Army is to be under its own Commander." This was no longer talk of a mere rapprochement—and certainly not one in the postwar era—but rather of an Arab-Turkish military alliance against the Allies. By best evidence, Faisal sent his offer to Mehmet Djemal from Aqaba no later than June 10. For the two days preceding, he had been joined in Aqaba by T. E. Lawrence. It wasn't until that same day of June 10 that Lawrence boarded SS *Arethusa* in Aqaba harbor, bound for Cairo and more consultations with the British military hierarchy.

The mark of a master strategist is his or her utter adaptability to circumstance, the pursuit of advantage divorced from sentiment. Whether or not Lawrence had a hand in writing Faisal's latest note to Mehmet Djemal, just days later he went into conference with the man he'd managed to avoid meeting in Aqaba: Chaim Weizmann.

By all accounts, those talks were very cordial. Weizmann was certainly keyed to the fact that it was upon this mid-ranking British officer that the success or failure of his appeal to the Arab Revolt leaders largely rested. And as one gamesman to another, Lawrence was surely impressed by the Zionist leader's agility in navigating the political minefield of Palestine, the considerable success he'd had in calming Arab concerns with one set of talking points while galvanizing the Jewish population to Zionism with another. Perhaps not surprisingly, the two master strategists soon found their way to common ground.

It was a common ground rooted in mutual dependence. To gain a "national home" in Palestine, the Jews obviously needed the British to win the war, which also meant they needed to support the Arab Revolt. In his meeting with Faisal, Weizmann had offered to employ the international Zionist movement in promotion of the cause of Arab independence, and with Lawrence in Ramleh, Weizmann got more specific: that promotion could also extend to funds and military training for the Arabs to fight the Turks. For his part, Lawrence saw a potentially pivotal role the Zionists might play in a postwar Syria. As he noted in a secret June 16 report on his meeting with Weizmann, "as soon as Faisal is in possession of [greater Syria], the [landowner] effendi class, the educated class, the Christians and the foreign elements will turn against him. . . . If the British and American Jews, securely established under British colors in Palestine, chose this moment to offer to the Arab State in Syria help . . . Sherif Faisal would be compelled to accept." With that help, Faisal could "dispense with" his domestic opposition. Better yet, given the Zionists' deep-rooted suspicions of the French, Faisal would have a ready ally in neutralizing them as well.

That was all in the future, though. In the interim, Lawrence counseled the Foreign Office, the Arabs should neither seek nor accept Zionist aid, nor should Weizmann be given the meeting he urgently sought, an audience with King Hussein.

Lawrence's apparent conversion on the Zionist issue had a gladdening effect on his superiors, even if there was a marked limit to that conversion. Whether due to naiveté or studied wishful thinking, most British officials in the region who had dealt with Chaim Weizmann over the past three months had taken at face value his soothing vision of a Jewish community in Palestine living in political and economic harmony with the Arab majority. As one schemer sitting across the table from another, however, Lawrence saw through this almost immediately. As he noted in his June 16 report, "Dr. Weizmann hopes for a completely Jewish Palestine in fifty years, and a Jewish Palestine, under a British façade, for the moment."

Lawrence would only be wrong about the timetable; it was to be just thirty years until the British façade fell away and the state of Israel created, with Chaim Weizmann installed as its first president.

As HIS TIME in Cairo extended, William Yale chafed under two enduring frustrations. The first was looking for any sign that his government was actually paying attention to events in the Middle East. Every Monday since late October 1917, he had been sending his long dispatches to Leland Harrison at the State Department, and hearing nothing back save for a handful of terse cables. Even his appeals for guidance—were his reports boring his readers? did the secretary want him to pursue another line of inquiry?—were met with silence.

Yale's second frustration was more personal, his inability to gain British permission to visit the war front. In their meeting of early March, T. E. Lawrence had invited him to visit the Arab rebel base at Aqaba, but Yale's request to that end had vanished somewhere in the British bureaucratic ether. With the Zionist Commission preparing to embark on its fact-finding mission to Palestine, Yale had petitioned to accompany it, only to be told by Gilbert Clayton that "there might be some difficulty" with the plan. He had even broached the idea of attaching himself to a delegation of the American Red Cross Commission; alas, that nongovernmental organization hadn't warmed to the prospect of providing cover for an American intelligence agent. Really the only way to Palestine, Reginald Wingate patiently explained to the American embassy, was for

Yale to be classified as a military liaison officer and accredited to General Allenby's staff—which, since Yale wasn't in the military and never had been, was a diplomatic way of keeping him right where he was, sitting in Cairo.

Rather by default, then, Yale had focused his energies on what was arguably the more important task before him: getting the Wilson administration to realize what was at stake in the region. This was easier said than done, for despite Wilson's high-minded Fourteen Points proclamation, from what Yale could determine, "our government had no policy. It was fighting, ostensibly, for nebulous ideals, little realizing that events are determined not at peace conferences, but by actions during hostilities preceding the peacemaking process. . . . The 'deus ex machina' of international affairs is not he who waits to act at some dramatic crisis, but he who consistently acts in ways which are constantly determining the course of events. President Wilson and his advisors never seemed to realize this simple truism."

The bitter paradox in this situation—and the source of Yale's frustration—was that by the late spring of 1918, most of the interested parties in the Middle East were clamoring for the Americans to determine events. As early as October 1917, Reginald Wingate had floated to an American diplomat the proposition that the United States take over the "mandate" of Palestinian rule in the postwar world, an idea that had continued to gain currency at the British Foreign Office. If to rather different ends, the hope of spurring American involvement had clearly been the subtext of Lawrence's emphasis during his meeting with Yale on the Arabs' high regard for the United States. Chaim Weizmann and the Zionists made no secret that, barring a British mandate, they'd be quite happy with an American one. Even the more imperialist-minded politicians of Britain and France and Italy appeared increasingly willing to accept a broad American role in the region since, barring their gaining of new lands, the most desirable outcome was that their European "friends" not gain any either.

To Yale, however, the truly decisive factor was the burgeoning pro-American sentiment of the Arabs. While undoubtedly sparked by the promises contained in Wilson's Fourteen Points, this attitude was also a fairly logical result of contemplating the morass of claims waiting to envelop the region in the postwar era. Yale's old friend Suleiman Bey Nassif fairly typified these concerns. A moderate Arab Christian, Nassif, even as he had reconciled to an expanded Jewish presence in Syria, remained deeply suspicious of British intentions, leery of King Hussein's pan-Arab nation, and adamantly opposed to French designs. The best, perhaps only way out of this mess, Nassif explained to Yale, was for the

Americans—nonimperialist, idealistic, far enough away to be minimally irritating—to step into the breach.

Yale wholeheartedly agreed, but looking for the right button to push with the Wilson administration was a grinding task; at one point, he even tried for base economic self-interest, pointing out to Harrison that "it is a well-known fact that certain American oil interests have recently obtained from the Ottoman Government extensive properties in Palestine," one of the rare instances, presumably, when an intelligence agent was moved to inform on his own prior activities.

Finally, in late April, after months of extolling America's standing in the region to the State Department, Yale decided to act. It came after he met a man named Faris Nimr, a leader of the Syrian exile community in Cairo and the editor in chief of the hugely influential Egyptian newspaper *al-Mokattam*. As Yale explained to Leland Harrison, ever since the United States had joined the war, Nimr and a small cabal of like-minded Syrian exiles had looked to it as their homeland's potential savior. "Quietly these few men have been spreading the idea of a sort of protectorate over Syria by the United States among the Syrians in Egypt, endeavoring to do this as secretly as possible that neither the British nor the French might become aware of it. This is an idea that appeals to both Christian and to Moslem. . . . It is stated by these ardent partisans of America that all the factions and all the parties among the Syrians would not only unite on the question of aid from the United States, but would rejoice if such were possible."

While waiting for Harrison's response to this message, Yale received a bit of gladdening news from Washington on another matter. It had been decided to send a second special agent out to the Middle East, and once that man arrived in Egypt, it would be arranged for Yale to go on to Palestine. The name of his Cairo replacement, William Brewster, was very familiar to Yale; Brewster had been the Standard Oil representative in Aleppo at the same time that Yale worked for them in Jerusalem. Thus, while doubling the size of their intelligence network in the Middle East, the American government had ensured it remained within the Standard Oil recruiting pool.

With Brewster en route, Yale was hastily appointed a captain in something called "the National Army"; perhaps not wishing to appear churlish after their months of stonewalling, British authorities declined to inquire just what this curious entity might be—the official name of the American army en route to Europe was the American Expeditionary Force—and instead congratulated the American agent on his military appointment.

"As soon as Cairo tailors could make uniforms for me," Yale recounted, "I began to prepare myself to be a soldier among soldiers. I had very little military training [actually none] and knew nothing about military matters and etiquette. For days I walked the side streets of Cairo in my new uniform, practicing saluting on passing British Tommies. When they began to salute me automatically, with no smirks on their faces, I knew I was on the way to being a soldier."

It was all in preparation for an occasion the newly minted captain rather dreaded, his formal presentation to General Allenby. In mid-July, Yale and the new American consul to Egypt, Hampson Gary, took advantage of a brief home visit by Allenby to make the journey up to his office in Alexandria. "When we entered Allenby's study," Yale recalled, "I did not know whether or not to salute the General. I wondered whether I should stand at attention or sit down. The worry was needless, for General Allenby paid as much attention to me as though I was not there."

The climactic moment came when Allenby abruptly turned in Yale's direction and, in his practiced stentorian voice, boomed, "Well, Captain Yale, what are you going to do at my headquarters?"

"I am going to continue my political work, General Allenby," he replied.

Wrong answer. "Captain Yale," the general bellowed, "if the United States government wishes to send a butcher to my headquarters, that's their privilege, [but] you will remember when you are attached to my forces, you are a soldier!" Chastened, the American visitors soon beat a retreat, with Yale convinced that "Allenby had classed me, a former Standard Oil man, as one of those lower forms of life who engage in trade."

The next day, Yale boarded a troop train for Palestine and his new billet at the British army headquarters at Bir-es-Salem, about ten miles east of Jaffa. He found reserved for him there a small tent, a cot, a writing table, and a canvas washbasin and bath. Also awaiting him was that peculiar feature of the European military officer class of 1918, the batman, or personal valet. Among British officers, the most coveted batmen were Indian army soldiers drawn from units specifically trained for the task, but possibly in retaliation for his importune reply to Allenby, Yale's was a grizzled old Scotsman.

Despite the rustic nature of his new surroundings, Yale was undoubtedly pleased to be out of Cairo and away from a job that had seemed increasingly futile. Shortly before leaving for the front, he had finally heard back from the State Department in regard to the message he had sent about Faris Nimr and his cell of pro-American Syrian conspirators fully two months earlier. If not for prompt reply, his message had been deemed important enough to go up to the desk of the secretary of state himself. "Referring your report No. 28," read Secretary Lansing's cable of July 9, "continue noncommittal attitude relative American attitude towards Syria."

THE NEWS CAME to Lawrence as a jolt, but an exceedingly pleasant one. On June 18, he and Lieutenant Colonel Alan Dawnay, the new overall coordinator of operations in northern Arabia, went to General Headquarters to outline the plan for the Arabs' independent advance into Syria. They met there with General William Bartholomew, one of Allenby's chief deputies. Bartholomew listened to their presentation for a few minutes before shaking his head with a smile; as he told his visitors, they had come to Ramleh three days too late.

As Dawnay and Lawrence soon learned, what had transpired in Palestine over the previous month was one of the very rare instances in World War I when an army had been readied for combat operations *ahead* of schedule. In recent weeks, a steady flood of British and Indian army troops had arrived from Iraq and the subcontinent, taking the place of those Allenby had been forced to send on to Europe, and tremendous effort had been made in getting these troops into the line and swiftly integrated with the rest of the Egyptian Expeditionary Force. So successful had this push been that at a senior staff meeting at headquarters on June 15, it was concluded the army would be "capable of a general and sustained offensive" into the Syrian heartland as early as September.

For Lawrence, it meant there was now no reason for the Arabs to risk an unsupported advance into Syria. Instead, with Allenby's timetable closely matching that devised by Lawrence and Dawnay for the Arabs, the rebels could simply dovetail their operations with those of the EEF. Of course, timetables had a way of getting upended in the Middle East, so Lawrence was greatly relieved when on a subsequent visit to headquarters on July 11 he learned a firm launch date for the EEF offensive had been chosen: September 19.

In the interim, a political development had made the prospect of reattaching the Arabs to the British effort even more attractive. In early May, a group of seven Syrian exile leaders claiming to represent a broad spectrum of Syrian society had written an open letter demanding to know in clear and unequivocal language precisely what Great Britain and France envisioned for their nation's future. London and Paris had tried to ignore the so-called Seven Syrians letter for as long as possible, but this time international attention wouldn't allow it; the matter had finally been dropped into the laps of the two men most responsible for the enduring controversy, Mark Sykes and François Georges-Picot. After much back-and-forth, in mid-June Sykes and Picot had answered the Seven Syrians that in those lands "emancipated from Turkish control by the action of the Arabs themselves during the present war," Britain and France would "recognize the complete and sovereign independence of the Arabs inhabiting those areas and support them in their struggle for freedom."

To Lawrence, here, finally, was the reaffirming of the promise of independence that he and the Arab rebels had been seeking for so long. But the formulation also reaffirmed the caveat that Lawrence had always suspected lay beneath the surface: Arab independence was only guaranteed in those lands that the Arabs freed themselves. In light of this, the rebels had every reason to join the coming British offensive. After his consultations at headquarters on July 11, Lawrence hurried back to Cairo, and then on to Aqaba, to start planning for the long-delayed Arab advance north.

One of the first tasks before him in that regard was to finally bring to an end Faisal's long and perilous flirtation with the Turkish general Mehmet Djemal. In late July, Lawrence passed along to David Hogarth a copy of the peace offer letter that Faisal had sent to Djemal on June 10. The cover story Lawrence concocted to explain how he had come into possession of such an explosive document—he claimed to have surreptitiously obtained it from Faisal's scribe—was absurd on its face, but apparently had a sufficiently Arabian Nights flavor to pass muster with his superiors.

Oddly, in London, the most immediate effect of this fresh revelation of Faisal's perfidy was to reactivate the debate, begun several months earlier but gone a bit dormant, on exactly which high honorific should be bestowed upon him. The episode pointed out a truly bizarre aspect of early-twentieth-century Britain: amid the bloodiest war in human history, and coinciding with a period so dark that the very survival of the British Empire was at stake, more than a dozen of the most important officials of that empire found the time in their schedules to voice their opinions, often repeatedly, on which medal should be given to a thirty-three-year-old desert prince. In doing so, all had ignored the counsel of the one Briton who knew that prince best, T. E. Lawrence, and his suggestion that Faisal wasn't much interested in medals.

On the morning of August 7, 1918, Lawrence gathered with his sixty-man bodyguard on the shore at Aqaba. His preceding weeks had been a blur of frantic preparation, and there was still a tremendous amount to be done before the Arabs would be ready to launch their September attack into the Syrian heartland. For Lawrence, though, the back-base grunt work of war—of organizing supply convoys, of plotting the movement of men and weapons across maps—was at an end; that day, he and his men were setting off for the interior, and would not return until the great battle had been joined and decided.

Embarking on that journey undoubtedly also raised a haunting "what if" in Lawrence's mind. In October 1917, on the eve of the British army's first advance into Palestine, General Allenby had asked Lawrence how the Arab rebels might contribute to the assault. Fearing a slaughter of the rebels, Lawrence had kept the Arab contribution to a minimum, instead proposing his ill-fated charge against the Yarmuk bridge. How differently things might have turned out save for his hesitation at that time. If the Arabs had gone all in, this last year of crushing stasis might have been averted, the war already over; also averted, of course, would have been Deraa, Tafileh, and the deaths of Daud and Farraj.

But now was the time to atone for all that. That morning in Aqaba he told his bodyguards in their colorful robes to prepare for victory, promised the Syrians among them that they would soon be home. "So for the last time we mustered on the windy beach by the sea's edge, the sun on its brilliant waves glinting in rivalry with my flashing and changing men."

THE HEADQUARTERS OF the German army on the Western Front was a network of pleasant châteaus and stately hotels in the small Belgian resort town of Spa. It was there, on the morning of July 31, 1918, that Curt Prüfer and Abbas Hilmi II were ushered into a conference room to meet Kaiser Wilhelm II. As Prüfer recorded in his diary, Wilhelm gained "the best impression" of the deposed khedive of Egypt, and was visibly impressed by his grand plans for the reconquest of his homeland from the British. At the end of the interview, the kaiser turned to Prüfer and said, "I request that you see me next time in a free Egypt."

But if the German emperor's spirits had been buoyed by the visit, it produced a more muted reaction in his two guests. The kaiser had aged greatly during the war, and now seemed diminished, even slightly befuddled. To Prüfer, attuned to the trappings and protocol of military life, it was clear that the German emperor no longer commanded much of anything, that for all his ostentatious medals and martial bearing he was now almost as much a figurehead as Abbas Hilmi.

It was very different from what either man had expected when they'd left Constantinople on July 23. In testament to the high hopes placed on their mission, they had been seen off at the station by an official Turkish government delegation that had included Interior Minister Talaat. But then had come the long, slow journey through the heartland of the Central Powers, images of deprivation and decline everywhere. To both men, the land and its people looked utterly spent, the situation far worse than just months earlier, and it belied the optimistic pronouncements continuing to burble from the German high command and its talk of the approaching final victory.

If not before, they had surely grasped the fiction of those pronouncements once they reached Spa. On July 17, the last of the five German offensives collectively known as the *Kaiserschlacht*, or Kaiser's Battle, that had been launched on the Western Front since March had been halted. Their number reduced by 700,000 more casualties, the remnants of the German armies were now falling back toward the Hindenburg Line, a fantastically elaborate wall of defensive fortifications that ran the length of northern France and that the Germans had begun building in 1917. Not only was there to be no German "final victory," but also no foreseeable end to the war; from behind the Hindenburg, Germany might hold out indefinitely, the battle grinding on without victors or vanquished for a long time to come.

This was certainly the assessment of generals and war planners on the other side of the front. Even with the flood of American soldiers finally beginning to reach France, the most optimistic Allied strategists were talking of a breakthrough in the summer of 1919, while their more conservative colleagues foresaw the struggle continuing far beyond; some analyses had the war going well into the mid-1920s.

Yet as with nearly every other assessment among the wise men of the Entente, these estimates were to be proven wrong. After the deaths of some sixteen million around the globe, the end was coming, and with a speed few could comprehend. Improbably, that collapse would start in one of the most remote and seemingly insignificant corners of the world battlefield, the deserts of Syria.

Chapter 18

Damascus

We ordered "no prisoners," and the men obeyed.

T. E. LAWRENCE, OFFICIAL REPORT
ON EVENTS IN TAFAS, OCTOBER 1918

It was September 12, 1918. The world war had now entered its fiftieth month. In contemplating its various battlefronts on that day, Allied military and political leaders were held in a certain thrall, their growing conviction that the enemy was nearing collapse tempered by the memory of how many times they had been wrong about this in the past. On the Western Front, the Germans had now ceded the last of their gains in the Spring Offensive to regroup behind the Hindenburg Line. The first Allied test against that defensive wall, the most formidable network of fortifications ever built, was to be a joint French-American operation near the Meuse River, scheduled for the end of the month. On the Southern Front, Italian commanders, at last chastened at having suffered over 1.5 million casualties over three years of war for no gain, were working up modest plans to move against an Austro-Hungarian army that had stood on the far bank of the Piave River for nearly a year. In the Balkans, a joint army of French, Serbs, Greeks, and Britons was preparing to push against a Bulgarian army in Macedonia. With the fresh memory of millions dead, the Allies viewed these proposed thrusts as of the testing-the-waters ilk, a chance to make some incremental gains before winter shut down offensive operations until the following spring, perhaps for even longer. British prime minister Lloyd George had recently floated a proposal to delay any all-out advance against Germany until 1920, when the American army would be fully ashore in France and Allied strength might be truly over-whelming.

In this climate, people went about their lives with a sense of cautious optimism or quiet trepidation, depending on which side of the battle lines they dwelt, a budding belief that the worst war in human history was finally inching toward some kind of resolution, even if the particulars and timetable for that resolution remained as indistinct as ever.

On that September 12, Aaron Aaronsohn was on a passenger ship five days out of Southampton, bound for New York. Having returned to England from the Middle East in August, he had spent a frustrating few weeks shuttling between Paris and London trying to win support for his Palestinian land-buying scheme. That effort had been complicated by his usual sparring with Chaim Weizmann and other British Zionist leaders, and Weizmann and Mark Sykes had seen a way both to be temporarily rid of the irksome agronomist and to put him to good use by proposing that he embark on another rallying-the-troops mission to the American Jewish community. Once Aaronsohn's ship put into New York harbor, he had a full roster of meetings and talks planned that might keep him busy in the United States for months.

Curt Prüfer's summer had steadily mutated from the strange to the surreal. After arranging Abbas Hilmi's audience with the kaiser at the end of July, he had spent weeks shuttling the pretender to the Egyptian throne around the German countryside, with official meetings and banquets in the khedive's honor interspersed with stays at the country estates of princelings and countesses. In the mountain resort town of Garmisch-Partenkirchen in mid-August, the pair had met up with the kaiser's sister, Princess Viktoria von Schaumburg-Lippe, and her eclectic retinue of hangers-on, and had spent ten days in rather debauched merriment even as the news from the war front grew bleak.

"Growing intimacy with the princess and Gräfin Montgelas and Seline von Schlotheim," Prüfer noted in his diary on August 30, referring to the kaiser's sister and two courtesans in her entourage. "In the evenings, boozing, dancing and flirting, hectic room parties and the like."

It wasn't all just parlor games, though. In Abbas Hilmi, Prüfer was in the company of one of the world's most indefatigable schemers, and as the outlook for the Central Powers dimmed, the German spy chief seemed to latch onto the Egyptians' grandiose plots with a kind of anxious fervor. One involved trying to lure Abbas's son and heir, Abdel Moneim, out of Switzerland. As the ex-khedive explained, his son was a weak and mentally unstable young man with sadistic inclinations—which went a long way toward explaining his current flirtation with the British—but if Prüfer could somehow lure Abdel Moneim to Germany, his father could then arrange his marriage to the daughter of the new Ottoman sultan, thereby cementing Abbas's own claim to Egyptian rule. It was surely an indication of just how divorced from the real world Prüfer was becoming that all this struck him as both a fine and important idea, one to be taken up at the highest levels of the foreign ministry.

But if the German spymaster increasingly lived in a deluded parallel universe, it was one in which he had a great deal of company. Not only did senior foreign ministry officials urge Prüfer to proceed with the Abdel Moneim overture, but they beseeched him for help on another matter. Alerted to the conciliatory letter Faisal Hussein had written Turkish general Mehmet Djemal back in June, they now seized upon the idea of brokering a peace deal with the Arab rebels as a last-minute solution in the Middle East—a solution that perhaps would include their dear friends in the Young Turk leadership, but perhaps not. Prodded by the foreign ministry for possible intermediaries to carry Germany's own secret peacemaking initiative to Faisal, Prüfer passed along the name of a contact helpfully provided by Abbas Hilmi.

If less colorful, William Yale's late summer was also proving frustrating. By September 12, he had spent more than a month in his tent at the British General Headquarters at Bir-es-Salem, in the foothills below Jerusalem. In that time, the State Department special agent—now reconstituted as the American military attaché to the Egyptian Expeditionary Force—had learned virtually nothing from the British military command of Allenby's much-rumored coming offensive. This had not been for lack of effort; Yale had attended any number of intelligence briefings at which British officials seemed in quiet competition with each other to impart nothing of substance, and had suffered through a host of tedious senior staff dinners even less illuminating. His repeated requests to tour the British front lines were put off with one excuse after another. He was finally given a partial explanation for this by a certain Captain Hodgson, the British officer detailed to serve as minder to the foreign attachés. "I'll tell you, Yale," Hodgson revealed, "I was told to show you as little as possible, as you were a Standard Oil man."

Yet the British had also unwittingly handed Yale an opening. Testament to the low regard with which they held the foreign military attachés in general, and him in particular, they had isolated them in the same corner of Bir-es-Salem as another distasteful group of camp followers: the resident press corps. From this motley assortment of British and Australian newspaper correspondents, far less restricted in their movements than the attachés, Yale was able to glean at least something of what was being planned, enough so that by September 12 he knew "the big show" was soon to get under way. He didn't know when, let alone where, but in the growing sense of urgency that permeated General Headquarters, in the shifting of troops and matériel that the journalists reported seeing on their travels, were the unmistakable signs that Allenby's offensive was imminent.

But beyond their qualms over Yale's Standard Oil connection, General Headquarters actually had good reason for their climate of secrecy; what they were planning in Palestine constituted a very intricate ruse. In recent weeks, an array of British army units had been brought up from Palestine's coastal plain to take up positions around Jerusalem, their new tent encampments sprawling over the Judean hillsides. Amid this redeployment, Allenby had moved his forward command headquarters to Jerusalem. Simultaneously, local purchasing agents had been dispatched to different tribes in the Amman region with orders to buy up enormous amounts of forage, enough to feed the horses and camels of a large army, come late September. To the watching Turks, the conclusion was inescapable: the British offensive was coming soon, and its target was to be the same Salt-Amman region where British attacks had failed twice before. In fact, however, those new tent cities were empty, Allenby's move to Jerusalem had been a charade, and the forage-buying effort was a red herring. Rather, the British plan was to strike at the very opposite end of the line, to sweep north along the Palestinian coastal shelf and then turn inland so as to envelop the Turks from three sides.

That was only one aspect of the ruse; another was playing out on the other side of the Jordan River. For some time, a mixed force of several thousand Allied fighters—Arab tribesmen, soldiers of the Arab Northern Army, British and French advisors together with specialized artillery and armored car units—had been making their way across the Syrian desert to gather at the old citadel of Azraq. If detected by the Turks—and it was hard to see how such a large force could go unnoticed indefinitely—it would serve to further confirm that the Allied attack was coming at Amman, just fifty miles to the west of Azraq. Instead, the Azraq unit's true target lay seventy miles to the northwest, the crucial railway junction of Deraa. Moreover, this unit was to act as the pivotal first shock troop for the entire offensive, their goal to shut down both the Hejaz Railway and its spur line into Palestine on the eve of Allenby's attack in order to paralyze the Turkish army from behind. By September 12, the last of these shock troops had arrived in Azraq, and were met there by the two British lieutenant colonels in charge of coordinating the operation: Pierce Joyce and T. E. Lawrence.

By that date, Lawrence had already been in Azraq for nearly a week, and had taken stock of the diverse fighting force as it drifted in: warriors from a dozen Arab tribes; the British and French transport and artillery specialists; a detachment of Indian army cavalry; even a small unit of Gurkhas, the famed Nepalese soldiers with their trademark curved *khukuri* daggers. On that same morning of September 12, the final component fell into place with the arrival in Azraq of the senior Arab rebel leadership: Faisal Hussein foremost among them, but also Nuri Shalaan and Auda Abu Tayi and a host of other tribal chiefs whom Lawrence had helped bring to the cause of Arab independence over the past two years. With the vanguard of the attack force set to begin deploying the following morning, the plan was for these leaders to gather at a conclave that afternoon, during which Lawrence and Joyce would go over their various objectives.

Yet it was at precisely this juncture, on the eve of the campaign he had worked so hard to bring about, that Lawrence was suddenly plunged into a paralyzing gloom. Shortly after Hussein and the other Arab leaders arrived, he slipped out of Azraq and made for a remote mountain cleft called Ain el Essad, some eight miles away. As he recounted in *Seven Pillars*, "[I] lay there all day in my old lair among the tamarisk, where the wind in the dusty green branches played with such sounds as it made in English trees. It told me I was tired to death of these Arabs."

There had in fact been warning signs for some time that Lawrence might be headed for just such a collapse. Back in mid-July, only days after receiving confirmation of Allenby's offensive launch date—an event that *should* have put him in an ebullient mood—Lawrence had written a melancholy letter to his friend and confidant Vyvyan Richards. "I have been so violently uprooted and plunged so deeply into a job too big for me, that everything feels unreal," he told Richards. "I have dropped everything I ever did, and live only as a thief of opportunity, snatching chances of the moment when and where I see them. . . . It's a kind of foreign stage on which one plays day and night, in fancy dress, in a strange language, with the price of failure on one's head if the part is not well filled."

He had gone on to describe his admiration of the Arabs, although he now recognized that he was fundamentally apart from them, an eternal stranger. He wrote of the words he carried in his mind—peace, silence, rest—"like a lighted window in the dark," but then questioned what good a lighted window was anyway. As was often the case when Lawrence wrote from the heart, he closed by denigrating what he had written, calling it "an idiot letter" born of his contrarian nature. "[I] still remain always unsatisfied. I hate being in front and I hate being back, and I don't like responsibility and I don't obey orders. Altogether no good just now. A long quiet, like a purge, and then a contemplation and decision of future roads, that is what is to look forward to."

But if his letter to Richards spoke to physical and spiritual exhaustion, it was compounded by the guilt he felt in having "profitably shammed" his Arab comrades for two years—and this guilt had recently grown worse. In early August, while planning for the Azraq operation, Lawrence had again met with Nuri Shalaan, the warlord of the powerful Rualla tribe he had first tried to woo to the Sherifian cause a year before by suggesting the chieftain believe the most recent promises Great Britain had made to the Arabs. At their August meeting, Shalaan had at last fully committed his tribe to the rebel side, although in the disclosures since their previous meeting—the Balfour Declaration, the Sykes-Picot Agreement—he surely knew his British suitor had been less than forthright. If exactly why remains elusive, it is clear both from Lawrence's memoir and comments he made to his early biographers that the deception he had perpetrated on Shalaan weighed more heavily on his conscience than any other.

Then, right before setting out for Azraq, there had been an incident that caused Lawrence to question the very purpose of his "crusade" for the Arabs. In late August, just as the main Arab army was preparing to leave the Aqaba region for the north, King Hussein had elected to pick a bitter and rather public fight with Faisal, all but accusing him of disloyalty. For nearly a week, the angry cables had passed between father and son, during which the rebel advance ground to a halt, the entire Syrian offensive cast into doubt as the clock ticked away. Lawrence had finally patched together a rapprochement—intercepting one of Hussein's cables, he had scissored off its angry second half, only passing along to Faisal the apologetic-sounding first half—but that all his plans had been nearly sabotaged by the man he was ostensibly fighting for left a bitterness that would never fully go away.

But it seems something else was also working on Lawrence that day in Ain el Essad, a very recent and devastating personal blow. By all evidence, it was during his stay in Azraq that he first learned of the death of Dahoum, his young companion at Carchemish, the apparent victim of a typhus epidemic that had swept northern Syria some time before. To a profound degree—and to a depth Lawrence himself may not have fully realized—he had come to personify the war in his own mind in the form of Dahoum; it was for that young Syrian boy and his future that the Arabs needed to be free. Now Dahoum was dead, and with him had gone so much of what had animated Lawrence to the fight. Although he would never reveal the identity of the mysterious "S.A." to whom *Seven Pillars* is dedicated—Dahoum's real name was Salim Ali—the first stanzas of the book's prefatory poem strongly suggest both the timing of when Lawrence learned of Dahoum's death and the effect it had upon him:

I loved you, so I drew these tides of men into my hands
    And wrote my will across the sky in stars
To earn you Freedom, the seven pillared worthy house,
    That your eyes might be shining for me when we came.

Death seemed my servant on the road, till we were near
    And saw you waiting
When you smiled, and in sorrowful envy [death] outran me
    And took you apart: into his quietness.

Despite his grief, Lawrence had given too much of himself, and asked too much of the Arabs, to pull away at the climax of their long campaign. He would write of his mood on September 12 that "today it came to me with finality that my patience as regards the false position I had been led into was finished. A week [more], two weeks, three, and I would insist upon relief. My nerve had broken, and I would be lucky if the ruin of it could be hidden so long." With that, he rose from his "lair" at Ain el Essad and made his way back to the gathered warriors at Azraq, now just hours away from their first strikes against the enemy.

By coincidence, that same day, a top-secret report was being sent to the U.S. military intelligence office in London, outlining the collapse of morale among the Arab rebels fighting with the British. "It is reported that the Syrians who are with Emir Faisal in the Aqaba region," the September 12 report stated, "are entirely disaffected and that there are many dissensions." One reason, apparently, was the rebels' woeful incompetence on the battlefield. "In spite of the support of the British, the Arabs of Arabia have shown their incapacity to organize or make war.... The entire Arab situation appears to be in a great muddle."

The report's author was the military intelligence bureau's chief correspondent in the Middle East, attaché William Yale. With that dispatch he was establishing a tradition of fundamentally misreading the situation in the Middle East that his successors in the American intelligence community would rigorously maintain for the next ninety-five years.

IT HAD A certain boys'-lark quality to it, a not uncommon experience in war when all the advantages and few of the risks reside with one's own side. Leaving Azraq on the morning of September 14, Lawrence spent the better part of a week careening through the desert around Deraa in a Rolls-Royce armored car, blowing up bridges and tearing up railway tracks, dodging ineffective enemy air attacks, skirmishing with the occasional unlucky Turkish foot patrol.

The ease with which he was able to do so could be largely credited to the success of the ruse concocted at Allenby's headquarters. With the Turks massed around Amman in anticipation of the presumed attack there, the Azraq strike force had nearly free rein to pursue its goals: the severing of the Hejaz Railway to the north and south of Deraa, as well as of the vital western spur leading into Palestine. The ultimate goal, of course, was to accomplish all this before Allenby's offensive got under way on September 19.

As Lawrence discovered when he caught up to the main raiding party, however, a first attempt on the southern railway link had gone awry through simple bad luck. Now quite sold on the efficacy of mechanized war in the desert, he decided to make a personal go of it, setting out for the southern railroad with just two armored cars and two "tenders," or large sedans. He found his target on the morning of September 16 in the form of a lightly defended bridge in the middle of nowhere, "a pleasant little work, eighty feet long and fifteen feet high." A particular point of pride for Lawrence was the new technique he and his colleagues used in setting their explosives, one that left the bridge "scientifically shattered" but still standing; Turkish repair crews would now have the time-consuming task of dismantling the wreckage before they could start to rebuild.

That job complete, Lawrence rejoined the main Arab force as it fell upon the railway north of Deraa the following morning. Encountering little resistance, the thousand-odd warriors quickly took control of a nearly ten-mile stretch of track, enabling the demolition teams to begin placing their mines. The action had the effect of lifting Lawrence from the dark mood that had stalked him in Azraq; his primary orders from headquarters had been to isolate Deraa, and "I could hardly believe our fortune, hardly believe that our word to Allenby was fulfilled so simply and so soon."

This left only the western spur leading into Palestine, and on that same afternoon of September 17, an Arab force stormed a railway station a few miles to the west of Deraa; in short order, they had ransacked the terminal and put to the torch all that couldn't be carried off. But Lawrence had grander plans. Leading a small band farther west, he hoped to blow up the Yarmuk gorge bridges that had eluded his destruction a year before. Once again, though, he was to be thwarted, this time by the presence of a train filled with German and Turkish troops coming up from Palestine.

Still, as Lawrence turned back to rejoin the main rebel force the next day, he had every reason to feel pleased with the "work" that had been done: the main Turkish telegraph link to Palestine was now cut, all three railway spans sufficiently damaged that repair would take days, if not weeks. There was still more mayhem to be accomplished—on that same afternoon of September 18, he would see to the blowing up of another bridge, the seventy-ninth of his career—but the Azraq vanguard had achieved most every objective asked of it in prelude to Allenby's offensive, now just hours away.

By prior arrangement, a Royal Flying Corps plane was scheduled to put into Azraq on the morning of September 21, bringing reports of how the offensive in Palestine was faring. Anxious for news, Lawrence raced back to the desert fortress the day before. Nearing a state of complete collapse—he'd barely slept since setting out from Azraq six days earlier—he found an empty cot in the encampment's field hospital and fell into an exhausted slumber.

YALE'S FIRST CLUE came when he stepped into his assigned mess hall for dinner on September 18: the journalists were gone. The next clue was when he walked down to the motor pool compound: all the vehicles were gone, too. A junior British officer bravely explained that they had all been dispatched to various parts of the front in prelude to the coming offensive; apparently, none had been detailed for Yale or the one other military attaché remaining, an Italian major named de Sambouy.

"I was irritated and perplexed," Yale wrote. "What should a military attaché do? Ought I to demand transportation to the front, or should I accept the lame excuse given us? Why shouldn't Sambouy do something? He was a regular army officer who had been in the war since 1915. I went to bed annoyed with myself and the British."

His sleep was to be interrupted. At 4:45 a.m. on the morning of September 19, Yale was wrenched awake by "a terrific roar that seemed to shake the whole world." As one, nearly five hundred British artillery guns had commenced shelling the Turkish line all along the Palestinian front.

By the time he rose and dressed, Yale had resolved what to do. Striding into a general's office, he announced that he was on his way to breakfast, and that if there wasn't a car waiting for him when he emerged, he would send a cable to Washington announcing that he was being held captive by the British. His Italian counterpart was aghast at his temerity, but when the pair emerged from the mess hall a short time later, they found a Ford Model T awaiting them with a former London cabdriver at the wheel.

They made that morning for a bluff overlooking the Plain of Sharon, from which, they were told, they could view one section of the battlefield. Finding a group of British officers already ensconced in the ruins of an old Crusader castle, the two attachés joined them, training their binoculars on the action two or three miles to the north. It was Yale's first experience observing combat, and he found it decidedly underwhelming. "Infrequent bursts of [artillery] shells [coming from] back of us on the plateau, white puffs of riflery on the hills in front of us, the intermittent rat-tat-tat of machine guns and, from time to time, lines of men who could scarcely be distinguished against the gray blankness of the limestone hills. It was nowhere near as thrilling as the sham battles I had watched as a boy at Van Cortland Park. For us, the day was long and monotonous. No one seemed to know what was happening; certainly, I had no idea of whether the British or the Turks were winning."

New to war, the American attaché couldn't appreciate that he was actually experiencing the very essence of the traditional battlefield, that amid the engulfing chaos even senior field commanders usually had only the vaguest sense of what was happening—and then often only on the ground directly before them. But the ever-resourceful Yale saw a means around this. Returning to General Headquarters that evening, he parlayed his attaché status into gaining admittance to the main telegraph room. There he discovered stacks of cables coming in from every corner of the front, dispatches that when plotted on a map gave him a grasp of the overall campaign available only to Allenby and his most senior advisors. This knowledge stood him in very good stead the following day when, having ventured to a new part of the front, Yale found himself briefing a British brigadier general on what was occurring elsewhere.

"This helped me to feel less awkward amongst the military," he recalled, "and I even began to regain the confidence in myself which had been badly shaken when first I was thrown in among professional soldiers."

For the first two days of the offensive, Yale had the luxury of observing war from a comfortable remove, the combatants appearing as so many scurrying ants in the distance. That ended on September 21, when he and his Model T companions journeyed up a mountain road leading to the town of Nablus in the Samaria foothills. The day before, a fleeing Turkish formation had made for Nablus up that same road, and there they had been found by the bombs and machine guns of swarming British warplanes.

"The Turks had no way of fighting back," Yale recounted. "There was no shelter to run to, and no way of surrendering. The results were tragic. . . . For a few miles, the road was lined with bloated corpses, swelling to the bursting point under the hot rays of the sun."

One image in particular stuck in Yale's memory, a stretch of the road where an old Roman aqueduct crossed the valley. Here, scores of Turkish soldiers had hugged the stone walls of the aqueduct as protection against the strafing British warplanes—only to fall victim when the planes circled back to attack from the other direction. The dead men lay in a neat single-file line along the entire length of the aqueduct, looking "for all the world," Yale would recall, "like a row of tin soldiers toppled over."

THE NEWS WAS staggering. When the RFC plane touched down at Azraq on the morning of September 21, its pilot told of a British sweep up the Palestinian coast that had simply steamrolled whatever scant Turkish resistance stood in its path. A few weeks earlier, General Headquarters had talked of an advance that might take them as far as the city of Nablus, forty miles north of Jerusalem; now, in a matter of just two days, the British vanguard was already far above Nablus, and thousands of enemy soldiers had thrown down their weapons in surrender. The note of triumph was evident in the letter General Allenby had sent to Azraq for Faisal. "Already the Turkish Army in Syria has suffered a defeat from which it can scarcely recover," it read. "It rests upon us now, by the redoubled energy of our [joint] attacks, to turn defeat into destruction."

More details were provided in a letter Alan Dawnay had sent to Lieutenant Colonel Joyce. By the previous evening, the British cavalry had already begun turning inland from their charge up the coast, leaving the enemy units in Palestine in imminent danger of being encircled. "The whole Turkish army is in the net," Dawnay exulted, "and every bolt-hole closed except, possibly, that east of the Jordan by way of the Yarmuk valley. If the Arabs can close this, too—and close it in time—then not a man or gun or wagon ought to escape. Some victory!"

As Lawrence plainly put it in *Seven Pillars*, "the face of our war was changed."

Also changed, naturally, were the prior battle plans drawn up for the Azraq force, the pace of events now rendering them obsolete. That afternoon, Lawrence boarded the RFC plane for its return to Palestine and an urgent meeting with General Allenby's staff.

As Lawrence learned at headquarters, and as Allenby had alluded in his note to Faisal, the goal now was not to defeat the Turkish army—that had already been achieved—but to destroy it completely. To that end, even as the left flank of the British army continued its northern advance, three other columns were to cut east across the Jordan River in order to roll up the inland Syrian towns along the Hejaz Railway and, ultimately, close on Damascus. The linchpin was, as always, Deraa, the one spot where all the Turkish units fleeing east from Palestine and all those still to the south might converge and perhaps sufficiently regroup to make a stand. To forestall that, headquarters impressed on Lawrence, there was one thing the Arabs must do—permanently sever the rail line south of Deraa—and one thing they absolutely must *not* do: make a dash for Damascus.

This latter point had already been stressed in Alan Dawnay's letter to Joyce in Azraq (with Joyce temporarily away, Lawrence had opened and read it). "Use all your restraining influence," Dawnay had ordered Joyce, "and get Lawrence to do the same, to prevent Faisal from any act of rashness in the north. . . . The situation is completely in our hands to mold now, so Faisal need have no fear of being carted, provided he will trust us and be patient. Only let him no on account move north without first consulting General Allenby—that would be the fatal error."

British concern was quite understandable. For nearly two years, Lawrence had been counseling Faisal that the only sure way for the Arabs to stake claim to Damascus was to get there first; this assertion had appeared to be further confirmed by Mark Sykes's recent open letter to the "Seven Syrians." As a result, the temptation for Faisal to drop the Deraa operations and make a dash for Damascus might prove an irresistible one. During Lawrence's brief sojourn at headquarters, Allenby's senior advisors repeatedly emphasized that Arab loyalty at this crucial juncture would be well compensated—apparently even implying that Faisal would be allowed to establish a government in Damascus.

Armed with these assurances, and with the Arabs' new orders of battle in hand, Lawrence flew back to Azraq the next morning. Over the following two days, a host of Arab bands, along with British armored car units, descended on the Hejaz Railway below Deraa to render it damaged beyond repair for the foreseeable future. Already, however, the worry that the retreating Turkish armies might recover enough to make a stand in Deraa seemed far-fetched; the enemy was now in full and panicked rout, their soldiers so stunned by the speed of events that they could think of little more than personal escape. Indeed, so rapid was the Turkish disintegration that by September 25, Lawrence was able to report to headquarters that there were probably only four thousand Turkish soldiers left in all the inland garrison towns below Deraa, most of the rest having passed through Deraa and kept on going in the direction of Damascus.

But in keeping with the broadened goal of destroying the Turkish army utterly, Lawrence saw an opportunity; if Deraa wasn't to be a Turkish rallying point, it could now be turned into a killing field. As he tersely commented in his September 25 report in describing the enemy units trying to reach Damascus, "I want to stop that."

To do so, on the twenty-sixth he directed a number of the Arab warriors to make for a small village in the foothills just twelve miles northwest of Deraa called Sheikh Saad. From there, the rebels would enjoy a commanding view of what was transpiring both in Deraa and on the road to Damascus, and also be able to monitor any retreating Turkish units coming up out of the Yarmuk gorge from Palestine.

Lawrence soon had reason to congratulate himself on the move. That same afternoon, scouts spotted a small mixed German and Turkish force coming up the Yarmuk road, "hopeless but carefree, marching at ease, thinking themselves fifty miles from any war." Walking heedlessly into a hastily prepared Arab ambush, the unit was soon overwhelmed. As Lawrence noted, "Sheikh Saad was paying soon, and well."

That was just a foretaste. The next morning, and with a British army now coming up the Yarmuk, the Turks remaining in and around Deraa prepared to abandon their positions as well. Word reached Lawrence that some four thousand enemy soldiers were about to set out from Deraa on the main Damascus road, while another two thousand were pulling out of a nearby town. This latter column was taking an overland shortcut that would bring them through the village of Tafas, just six miles below Sheikh Saad. As Lawrence drily commented in *Seven Pillars*, "The nearer two thousand seemed more our size."

ON THE AFTERNOON of September 23, the Mediterranean city of Haifa was captured from the Turks by an Indian army cavalry unit. Arriving that evening, William Yale arranged for lodging in a private home, then decided to take a stroll through the city's deserted old quarter.

At the start of World War I, most all the warring powers had horse-mounted cavalry that still carried lances as part of their complement of weaponry. By 1918, nearly all such cavalries had discarded the lance as anachronistic in the age of the machine gun and warplane, but not so the Indian army. That afternoon, they had employed it to deadly effect in the narrow back streets of Haifa's old quarter, running down and impaling terrified Turkish soldiers as they tried to flee. Everywhere Yale walked lay the dead.

"In the silent lonely streets," he recalled, "under a brilliant moon, the bodies of these Turkish soldiers seemed strangely out of place, for the peace and calm of an Oriental night covered this part of the city."

But it takes remarkably little time for the average person to become desensitized to the horror of war, and in this William Yale was to prove no exception. The following day, only his sixth on the battlefield, he and Major de Sambouy were driving down the Palestine coastal road when they began passing column after column of Turkish prisoners being marched off to internment camps. In their wake were scores of prisoners who had collapsed, too exhausted or ill to go on. Of these men being left behind to die in the sun, neither their comrades nor their Indian captors took any notice, and neither did Yale or his traveling companion. "It was not our affair and we had a long day's journey ahead of us," he would write. "It never occurred to me that we were heartlessly callous and unconcerned. We didn't even think of stopping to take an extra passenger or two."

THEY CAME UPON the first survivors hiding in the tall grass of a meadow just outside Tafas. Traumatized and speaking in hushed whispers, the villagers told of the atrocities the Turkish soldiers had begun perpetrating immediately upon entering Tafas just an hour before. Continuing on, Lawrence and the Arab vanguard soon found evidence of this; here and there, bodies lay amid the meadow grass, "embracing the ground in the close way of corpses."

Suddenly, a little girl of three or four popped into view, her smock drenched in blood from a gash by her neck. "The child ran a few steps," Lawrence recalled, "then stood and cried to us in a tone of astonishing strength (all else being very silent), 'Don't hit me, Baba.' " A moment later, the girl collapsed, presumably dead.

None of this prepared for the scene in Tafas's streets. Everywhere were bodies, many hideously mutilated, girls and women obviously raped before their dispatch. In particular, Lawrence was to remember the sight of a naked pregnant woman, bent over a low wall and grotesquely impaled by a saw bayonet; around her lay some twenty others, "variously killed, but set out in accord with an obscene taste."

By bad coincidence, one of the tribal sheikhs who had accompanied Lawrence during the previous two weeks and who now rode alongside him was Talal el Hareidhin, the headman of Tafas. As Lawrence would recount in his official report of the incident, at the sight of his ruined village, Talal "gave a horrible cry, wrapped his headcloth about his face, put spurs to his horse and, rocking in the saddle, galloped at full speed into the midst of the retiring [Turkish] column and fell, himself and his mare, riddled with machine gun bullets among their lance points."

In consultation with Auda Abu Tayi, who had also ridden into Tafas that morning, Lawrence commanded his lieutenants that no prisoners should be taken—or, as he put it more eloquently in *Seven Pillars*, " 'the best of you brings me the most Turkish dead.' "

What ensued over that long day of September 27 was a merciless and one-sided slaughter. Quite quickly, the attacking Arabs separated the fleeing Turkish column of two thousand into three isolated sections, then set to annihilating them one by one; any Turkish or German soldier who fell out wounded or tried to surrender was swiftly cut down. Soon the pursuing Arabs were joined by villagers along the way, eager to strike against their oppressors of the past four years—and perhaps just as eager to strip their bodies of valuables. Even by the standards of massacre, this one took on an especially macabre edge. "There lay on us a madness," Lawrence recounted in *Seven Pillars*, "born of the horror of Tafas or of its story, so that we killed and killed, even blowing in the heads of the fallen and of the animals, as though their death and running blood could slake the agony in our brains."

It grew worse. By chance, one of the Arab reserve columns had missed the "no quarter" order, and when a doubling-back Lawrence came upon this unit just before nightfall, he found they had taken some 250 Turkish and German soldiers captive. According to his *Seven Pillars* account, Lawrence was "not unwilling" to let this group live, until he was led over to a dying Arab warrior gruesomely pinioned to the ground by German bayonets, "like a collected insect." As Lawrence would state in his official report, written just days after the incident, "then we turned our Hotchkiss [machine gun] on the prisoners and made an end of them, they saying nothing."

All night and into the following days the slaughter went on, the panicked and exhausted prey becoming divided into smaller and smaller groups until they were quite defenseless against their attackers, a fortunate few taken prisoner, many more summarily put to death. By the time the last stragglers approached the outskirts of Damascus two days later, the estimated six thousand Turkish and German soldiers who had set out from the Deraa area on September 27 had been reduced to fewer than two thousand.

Lawrence didn't partake of this further massacre. Instead, late that night, he turned back for his command post in Sheikh Saad and then, at dawn, made for the town of his past torments: Deraa. By his account in *Seven Pillars*, the time he spent there was rather anticlimactic, especially when placed against the horrific events of Tafas. An Arab force had swept into Deraa the previous afternoon and, after rounding up those few Turkish soldiers who remained, spent the interim in the time-honored tradition of looting and pillaging. In quick order, Lawrence managed to stem the anarchy, placing armed guards over what remained of the railyard and its worksheds and helping with the appointment of a governor and police force. Indeed, by Lawrence's telling, the greatest challenge he faced in Deraa that day was heading off the bellicose ambitions of General George Barrow, the commander of the British army that had just finished its climb out of the Yarmuk gorge.

In *Seven Pillars*, Barrow comes off as a distinctly buffoonish figure, one whose comeuppance began the moment Lawrence came out of Deraa on the western road to greet him. To the general's plan of imposing calm in the town by posting pickets throughout, Lawrence "explained gently" that calm had already been established by the newly appointed Arab governor. When Barrow then insisted his men take possession of the Deraa railway station, Lawrence assented, but with the rather haughty request that the British not interfere with the railroad's functioning, since the Arabs had already cleared the line and were readying a train for travel. "Barrow," Lawrence wrote, "who had come in thinking of [the Arabs] as a conquered people, though dazed at my calm assumption that he was my guest, had no option but to follow the lead of such assurance." With the general thus sufficiently humbled, Lawrence recounted, "soon we got on well."

But this was not at all the way George Barrow would remember the situation in Deraa that day. As he would relate in his own memoir, "The whole place was indescribably filthy, defiled and littered with smoldering cinders and the soiled leavings of loot. Turks, some dead and some dying, lay about the railway station or sat propped against the houses. Those still living gazed at us with eyes that begged for a little of the mercy which it was hopeless for them to ask of the Arabs."

But this was trivial compared with what Barrow's men found when they entered the Turkish hospital train that had been stranded in Deraa station, a scene he would describe, with considerable hyperbole, as "far exceeding in its savagery anything that has been known in the conflicts between nations during the past 120 years." According to Barrow, "Arab soldiers were going through the train, tearing off the clothing of the groaning and stricken Turks, regardless of gaping wounds and broken limbs, and cutting their victims' throats. . . . It was a sight that no average civilized human being could bear unmoved." In Barrow's telling, when he angrily ordered Lawrence to remove the Arabs from the train, he was met with a refusal and the explanation that this was the Arabs' "idea of war."

"It is not our idea of war," Barrow countered, "and if you can't remove them, I will." At this, Lawrence allegedly washed his hands of the matter, telling the general he would take no responsibility for what might happen next. Summoning his own men, Barrow cleared the ambulance train and brought the killing to a stop.

Taken together, the events in Tafas and Deraa encapsulate the difficulty in getting at the full truth of the "Lawrence myth"—or even to isolate which facet of that myth is the most credible. In Lawrence's *Seven Pillars* description of Tafas, the skeptical reader might find some moments just a little too cinematic to be fully believed—the stirring war cry that the charging Talal delivered just before he was gunned down, the accusing gaze the bayonet-pinioned Arab warrior cast toward his German and Turkish tormentors with his dying breath—especially since those moments are absent from Lawrence's official report. There is also his uncomfortably keen eye for the grisly detail, reminiscent of the passage

describing his torture in Deraa the year before, that edges toward pru-
rience and war pornography. To add a different wrinkle, after the war,
several of Lawrence's British comrades in the September 1918 offensive
would stoutly maintain that he never issued a "no quarter" command, let
alone ordered the execution of prisoners once taken, even though Lawrence plainly stated as much in both his memoir and official report.

The Deraa ambulance train story underscores this difficulty in
reverse. As shockingly candid as Lawrence was in describing his actions
at Tafas, in neither *Seven Pillars* nor in his official report did he even mention the train incident—yet it's hard to imagine George Barrow, a very
"proper" career military officer, simply making up such an account. If the
incident did in fact occur, the simplest explanation for its omission is that
Lawrence wished to avoid casting the Arab rebels in a bad light—except
that there are any number of other places in *Seven Pillars* and his wartime reports where their conduct is shown in equally bad light. And if,
for whatever reason, Lawrence did consciously choose to avoid telling the
story, then why go out of his way in *Seven Pillars* to disparage the reputation of the one man, Barrow, best positioned to publicize it? Of course, to
all this there may be a simpler, if more disturbing, explanation: that amid
the wanton slaughter of those last days in September, Lawrence merely
found the ambulance train incident too trifling to mention.

Lawrence stayed on in Deraa in order to meet with Faisal, who came
over from Azraq the following day. By then, Allenby's stricture against
the Arabs making for Damascus had been lifted in light of the Turkish
army's total collapse—in fact, he had ordered all EEF units to stay out
of the Syrian capital so that their Arab allies might have the honor of
entering first—and Lawrence and Faisal discussed plans for establishing
a provisional government there. Then, in the very early morning hours of
September 30, Lawrence and his sometime driver of recent days, Major
Walter Stirling, set off north in the Rolls-Royce sedan they had dubbed
the "Blue Mist." They drove through a landscape littered with the corpses
of men and animals, some of those who had perished in the Turks' desperate flight. By that evening, they had reached a ridge overlooking Damascus, a promontory already crowded with Arab and EEF units poised to
advance into the city at first light.

During that night of waiting, Stirling watched as Lawrence sank
into a mood of deep despondency. To the junior officer, it seemed quite
incomprehensible—"we were on the eve of our entry into Damascus,"
Stirling wrote, "and in sight of the final act which was to crown all [Law-
rence's] efforts with success"—and he finally asked his companion what
was the matter. "Ever since we took Deraa," Lawrence replied, "the end
has been inevitable. Now the zest has gone, and the interest."

. . .

SOMEWHERE ALONG THAT ridge outside Damascus, William Yale and the Italian military attaché were also camped that night, wrapped in blankets on the ground beside their Model T as they tried to catch a few hours' sleep. Shortly after midnight, they were ripped from their slumber by a tremendous explosion; to the north, an enormous cloud of smoke and flame rose above Damascus, the countryside for miles around illuminated in its intense glow. "God Almighty," Yale said, "the Turks have blown up Damascus." That first great explosion was followed by many smaller ones throughout the night, geysers of flame and bursting shells arcing across the sky.

At dawn, Yale saw that his fears were misplaced, that Damascus still stood; the Turks and Germans had only been blowing up their ammunition and fuel storage depots before they fled the city.

Quite by chance, Yale and de Sambouy had camped that night beside the same band of journalists who had disappeared on them at General Headquarters on the eve of the offensive, and for some time that morning the reunited campmates discussed among themselves whether it might be safe to venture down into Damascus. The matter was rather decided when Yale, having briefly gone in search of water for coffee, returned to discover that the journalists had ditched them once again. "Where a correspondent goes," he told de Sambouy, "an attaché can go." Jumping in the Model T, they made for the city.

They were plunged into a riotous celebration. In the streets, joyous crowds of Damascenes sang and danced and beat on drums, and as Arab warriors on horses and camels fired their rifles into the air, women on overhead balconies showered them all with rose petals. The deeper the attachés ventured toward the city center, the more delirious the scenes became. "Pandemonium reigned," Yale recalled. "I, who had lived nearly three years in Palestine under the strain and in fear of the Turks, could share the madness of the Arabs with the added exhilaration of being one of the host of deliverers. . . . We were invited into people's homes and had wines and sweetmeats urged upon us. It was a wild hectic day, the like of which a man is fortunate to experience but once in a lifetime."

Lawrence was also experiencing the madness of Damascus that day, if to much weightier effect. Far earlier than the journalists or the attachés, he and Stirling had set off for the city in the "Blue Mist," only to be detained for several hours by an Indian army guard suspicious of their Arab headdresses. The delay nearly proved disastrous, for when Lawrence finally reached Damascus city hall, the gathering point for the Arab rebel leaders coming into the city, he discovered something of a coup in progress.

As Faisal's lieutenants at city hall had set to establishing a provisional government that morning, they had been joined by two men who claimed to have already done so the night before; what's more, these interlopers maintained, they were King Hussein's rightful representatives in Damascus. Lawrence knew the two men well: they were Abd el Kader, the Algerian traitor who had nearly gotten him killed at Yarmuk, and his brother, Mohammed Said. Within a few minutes, the brothers and their followers left city hall, but in hindsight probably wished they hadn't. In their absence, Lawrence summarily dismissed their claim to authority and appointed another man, Shukri Pasha el-Ayubi, as the interim Damascus military governor.

Lawrence's timing was impeccable for, just minutes later, General Henry Chauvel, the Australian commander of the EEF's Desert Mounted Corps, showed up at city hall. As the first senior EEF commander to enter Damascus, Chauvel was under instructions from Allenby to find the *wali*, the Turkish-appointed governor, and ask him to temporarily continue running the city. Instead, at city hall Chauvel was met by Lawrence, who quickly led him to Shukri Pasha. "I understood that this official was the *Wali*," Chauvel subsequently reported to Allenby, "and I issued him instructions through Lt. Col. Lawrence to carry on the civil administration of the city, and informed him that I would find any military guards and police that he required." Quite completing this sleight of hand, Chauvel then asked Lawrence "to assist in these matters, because I had no Political Officer at the moment at my disposal."

What it meant was that in one deft move, Lawrence had established the legitimacy of his personally chosen Arab "government" in the eyes of the EEF military authorities. It also meant that for the next crucial few days, he would be the de facto ruler of Damascus, able to draw on EEF troops if needed, able to direct the Arabs through the "office" of the military governor as required.

His first order of business was to neutralize the continuing threat posed by Abd el Kader and Mohammed Said. Summoning the brothers to city hall, he informed them that their government had been abolished, and named a number of Faisal loyalists to positions of authority in its place. After a tense confrontation that almost led to knifeplay, Lawrence recounted, "Mohammed Said and Abd el Kader then went away, breathing vengeance against me as a Christian." Shortly afterward, Lawrence had EEF troops called out to quell looting that was occurring in several parts of the city.

Late that afternoon, with some degree of calm restored and Faisal loyalists now in control, Lawrence dropped by Chauvel's office to allow that perhaps there'd been some misunderstanding at their earlier meeting, that Shukri Pasha was not in fact the Damascus *wali*, but rather Lawrence's own very recent appointee. But if this was couched as a clarification, Lawrence was also presenting Chauvel with a dare; with Damascus still a very tense place, the general could either accept the current arrangement or come up with his own idea and risk the consequences. Henry Chauvel already disliked Lawrence, but apparently disliked the prospect of urban insurrection even more; that evening, Lawrence was able to send his own cable off to Allenby's headquarters announcing that Chauvel "agrees with my carrying on with the town administration until further instructions."

This he proceeded to do for the next two days, and with a curious marriage of munificence to severity. Even with looting persisting in certain quarters, municipal work crews were set to restoring the city's electrical system and waterworks. Garbage was collected, a fire brigade organized, food distributed to the destitute, at the same time that new disturbances in the city center—purportedly the result of another power bid by Abd el Kader and his brother—necessitated a firmer hand. "We called out the Arab troops," Lawrence blandly noted in his official report, "put Hotchkiss [machine guns] round the central square, and imposed peace in three hours after inflicting about twenty casualties."

Given their very different roles, it's not surprising that the paths of T. E. Lawrence and William Yale intersected just once during those tumultuous days in Damascus. It's also understandable, given the weight of issues he was dealing with, that Lawrence would have no memory of their meeting; Yale sought him out in order to complain about the looting of some shops owned by American citizens. Yet the two would ultimately be joined by a shared experience in Damascus. It was a place of such unspeakable horror that both would be forever scarred by it, a place known simply as "the Turkish hospital."

ON THE MORNING of October 2, an Australian officer approached William Yale in the lobby of his Damascus hotel to ask if he had seen "the Turkish hospital." Not familiar with the site, Yale was given directions to a compound near the railway station, and he and Major de Sambouy soon made for it.

It was actually a Turkish army barracks fronted by a large parade ground. Once past the two Australian sentries at the front gate, Yale recalled, "we crossed the vacant parade ground without seeing a person, climbed the steps and entered what was a charnel house."

The Turks had converted the barracks into a makeshift military hospital, but had abandoned it on September 29 amid their general exodus from the city, leaving behind some eight hundred wounded or diseased men. In the intervening three days, those men had been set upon by Arab marauders who had stripped the place bare of food and medicine, even tossing many of the invalids onto the floor in their search for concealed valuables. Other than posting sentries at the front gate, the Australian detachment that had pitched camp nearby had done nothing for the desperate and dying patients, neglecting even to bring them water.

"The floors were slimy with human offal," Yale recounted, "hundreds of men lay in small soiled hospital cots everywhere. The dead, the wounded, the sick [were] lying side by side in their own filth, save for the corpses on the floor and those who, writhing in agony, had fallen off their cots. . . . Most of them suffered in silence; some moaned, others cried to us pitifully, their tragic eyes filled with terror, following us as we walked the length of the room."

Somehow compounding the horror, in a small alcove above the main floor Yale and de Sambouy found three nurse-orderlies mutely sitting about a table drinking coffee. "My impression was that they were badly frightened, hopeless beings who, faced with a horrible and impossible situation, had lost all capacity to act. They sat drinking coffee in a hell beyond the ken of one's imagination." Seeing enough, the attachés fled the barracks building and set out in search of someone in authority—although just what constituted authority that day in Damascus was not completely clear.

T. E. Lawrence learned of the Turkish hospital that same afternoon, and also made for it. He found a scene very much as Yale described, although, in his more accomplished hand, the macabre details would be far more graphically rendered: rats had gnawed "wet red galleries" into the bodies of the dead, many of which "were already swollen twice or thrice life-width, their fat heads laughing with black mouth. . . . Of others the softer parts were fallen in. A few had burst open, and were liquescent with decay."

Venturing deep into the room, Lawrence charted a path between the dead and dying, "holding my white skirts about me [so as] not to dip my bare feet in their puddled running, when suddenly I heard a sigh." Turning, he met the gaze of a still-living man, who whispered, "*Aman, aman* (pity)." That call was quickly joined by others, and then by a "brown waver" as some of the men tried to raise beseeching hands—"a thin fluttering like withered leaves"—before they fell back again. "No one of them had strength to speak," Lawrence recalled, "but there was something which made me laugh at their whispering in unison, as if by command."

In Lawrence's telling, he immediately took command of the hideous situation. Finding a group of Turkish doctors idly sitting in an upstairs room, he ordered them down to the sick ward. Refused help from the adjacent Australian encampment, he instead had Arab troops bring food and water, then press-ganged a group of Turkish prisoners to dig a mass grave for the dead. Even here, though, Lawrence couldn't resist the gruesome detail. "The trench was small for them," he noted of the men being buried, "but so fluid was the mass that each newcomer, when tipped in, fell softly, just jellying out the edges of the pile a little with his weight."

In his own effort to address the tragedy at the Turkish hospital, Yale eventually tracked down the recently arrived Gilbert Clayton. Over the course of their dealings in Cairo, Yale had developed a keen distaste for the brigadier general, finding him a cold and hard man, and nothing in Clayton's manner at their meeting on the night of October 2 changed that view. After hearing out the attaché's impassioned plea for something to be done, Clayton calmly said, "Yale, you're not a military man." Seeing the rage building in Yale's eyes, he then added, "You need not be offended; I'm not a soldier either."

So deeply did the Turkish hospital incident affect Lawrence and Yale that it would dominate the one dialogue they were to have in the postwar era, an exchange of letters in 1929. While Yale's initiating letter has been lost, he clearly pressed Lawrence for details on the subject, considering that fully a third of Lawrence's handwritten reply—some four hundred words—was devoted to explaining his own actions at the hospital. The episode would also figure prominently in both men's memoirs and, in the process, offer an intriguing glimpse into their very different personalities.

For William Yale, the guilt he felt over the Turkish hospital was to make for perhaps the most heartfelt and anguished passage in his manuscript. "Nothing I did during the whole war period do I regret so deeply and with such shame as my failure to use my position wisely and calmly to alleviate the atrocious suffering of those eight hundred men. May their curses be upon my head." But self-recrimination was never one of Yale's strong suits, and after just two more sentences, he'd settled on a new culprit to blame. "I lay this horror at the door of European imperialism, to be added to the multitude of crimes already committed in its name."

As might be expected, Lawrence's description in *Seven Pillars*, in addition to being far more visceral, was also—perhaps unconsciously—far more self-revelatory. By that account, Lawrence returned to the hospital the next day to find conditions vastly improved as a result of his efforts, only to be confronted by an irate Australian major. Clad in his Arab robes, Lawrence didn't bother to identify himself as a lieutenant colonel, even when the junior officer demanded to know who was in charge of the still-ghastly scene. When Lawrence acknowledged he was in charge, the Australian major spat "bloody brute," slapped Lawrence across the face, and stormed off.

If that is a rather peculiar passage to appear on the penultimate page of a 660-page book that has as its subtitle "A Triumph," there is also something about the moment that somehow rings a bit false; as with some of the Tafas details, it feels just a little too neat, too much of a stage-play coda. Yet, fictional or not, that major's slap served a great function, for it left Lawrence "more ashamed than angry, for in my heart I felt he was right, and that anyone who pushed through to success a rebellion of the weak against their masters must come out of it so stained in estimation that, afterward, nothing in the world would make him feel clean."

For the remainder of his life, Lawrence was to feel stained by what he had seen and done during the war, and in his struggle to ever "feel clean" again, repeatedly looked to self-abnegation and violence against himself—violence far worse than a major's slap—as recompense for his sins.

THE MEETING TOOK place in a second-floor stateroom of the finest hotel in Damascus, the Victoria, on the afternoon of October 3. Just eight men were present: on the British side, Generals Allenby and Chauvel, together with their chiefs of staff; on the Arab side, Faisal ibn Hussein, his chief of staff, Nuri Said, and Sherif Nasir of Medina. Acting as intermediary and interpreter was T. E. Lawrence. Despite its profound importance—in that stateroom much of the future history, and tragedy, of the Middle East was to be set in motion—no official record was kept.

General Allenby had arrived in the Syrian capital just hours earlier. Never the most patient of men, he was in a particularly cantankerous mood that day. With his offensive still ongoing—his vanguard was continuing a relentless pursuit of the Turks as they fled north—he'd been forced to take time away from his martial duties to sort out the increasingly nettlesome political situation in Damascus. As a result, when informed that Faisal, arriving on a three o'clock train from Deraa, would be slow in reaching the Victoria on account of his planned triumphal entry into the city on horseback, Allenby had thundered, "Triumphal entry be damned," and ordered Faisal to be brought to the hotel at once.

Although the general may not have been fully aware of it—or more likely was too distracted to care—the astounding initial success of his Palestinian offensive had caused the French government to frantically reassert their claims to Syria as codified in the Sykes-Picot Agreement; on September 23, the British government had largely acquiesced to their demands. The result was that two days later Allenby received a set of instructions from the Foreign Office so obtuse as to be nearly nonsensical. After stating that "the British Government adhere to their declared policy with regard to Syria, namely that should it fall into the sphere of interest of any European Power, that Power should be France," the September 25 instructions reminded Allenby that under the terms of Sykes-Picot, "you will notice that France and Britain undertake to uphold jointly the independence of any Arab State that may be set up in Area (A)"—meaning Syria. From these two seemingly opposed clauses arose an appropriately muddled proposed course of action, that "if General Allenby advances to Damascus, it would be most desirable that, in conformity with the Anglo-French Agreement of 1916 he should, if possible, work through an Arab administration by means of a French liaison."

With London apparently deciding these instructions weren't sufficiently baffling, they were followed on October 1 by a second set that rather settled the matter. Now Allenby was told that since "the belligerent status of the Arabs fighting for the liberation of their territories from Turkish rule" had been recognized by the Allied powers, "the regions so liberated [by the Arabs] should properly be treated as Allied territory enjoying the status of an independent State (or confederation of States) of friendly Arabs." A sudden burst of clarity, perhaps, except this statement was followed by the curious rider that should "the Arab authorities [in Syria] request the assistance or advice of European functionaries, we are bound under the Anglo-French Agreement to let these be French." In essence, it appeared Sykes-Picot was being invoked to annul and uphold the accord simultaneously, the intent changing from one sentence to the next.

In first hearing of this hash at the Victoria Hotel, Lawrence undoubtedly felt a note of alarm. It was his understanding that Sykes-Picot was a dead letter, and had been for quite some time; for it to return to the conversation now for any purpose was ominous. On the positive side, Allenby's instructions explicitly recognized the Arab claim to Syrian independence, and since Faisal had no intention of asking for European assistance or advice—that had been the whole point of establishing an interim government—it surely meant the rider about a French liaison officer was moot.

But matters were about to take a very ugly turn—or rather, a series of ugly turns. As recounted by General Chauvel, Allenby announced that Faisal actually didn't have any choice in the matter, that France was to be the "protecting power" of Syria. Additionally, even though Faisal, as his father's representative, "was to have the administration of Syria"—albeit "under French guidance and financial backing"—that administration didn't extend to either Palestine or Lebanon, but "would include the hinterland of Syria only." "Hinterland" was truly the operative word since, as Faisal was further informed, the boundaries of Lebanon had now been demarcated as the entire Mediterranean coastline from Palestine to the Gulf of Alexandretta, making Syria a landlocked nation. As a final insult, Allenby told Faisal that he would be immediately assigned a French liaison officer, "who would work for the present with Lawrence, who would be expected to give him every assistance."

Both Faisal and Lawrence were stunned. As Chauvel recounted, Faisal fiercely argued that it was his understanding "from the advisor whom Allenby had sent him"—meaning Lawrence—that in return for ceding Palestine, "the Arabs were to have the whole of Syria, including the Lebanon." Furthermore, he flatly refused to have a French liaison officer attached to him, "or to recognize French guidance in any way."

At this tense impasse, Allenby turned to Lawrence. "But did you not tell him that the French were to have the Protectorate over Syria?"

"No, sir," Lawrence responded, according to Chauvel, "I know nothing about it."

"But you knew definitely that he, Faisal, was to have nothing to do with the Lebanon?" Allenby persisted.

"No, sir," Lawrence replied, "I did not."

Allenby tried to defuse the situation by offering that these were only temporary measures, that all would be resolved at the great postwar peace conference being planned, but Faisal would have none of it; he knew full well that temporary measures in such circumstances had a tendency to become permanent ones. It left the British commander with only military rank to fall back on. Allenby reminded Faisal that, technically, both he and the Arab Northern Army remained under his overall command; as a result, the rebel leader had no choice but to obey orders.

After perhaps an hour, a shaken Faisal Hussein left the Victoria Hotel, to be greeted, ironically, by an enormous crowd of supporters. Lawrence did not accompany him. Instead, he stayed behind in the hotel stateroom to make a request of General Allenby.

THE DAM HAD burst. Through the rest of October, the EEF and their Arab allies pursued the remnants of the Turkish armies north, swiftly overwhelming whatever rearguard resistance the enemy could offer. It wasn't until the end of the month that Turkish general Mustafa Kemal, the future Kemal Ataturk, finally managed to establish a new defensive line at the very edge of the Turkish Anatolian heartland. By then, though, all of Syria was gone and the Constantinople regime was suing for peace. That culminated in the Armistice of Mudros on October 31; at just about the same time, the fallen Three Pashas—Djemal, Enver, and Talaat—slipped aboard a German torpedo boat and made their escape across the Black Sea.

But it wasn't just the Turkish dam that had burst. In one of the more peculiar chain reactions in history, given that their military efforts had been largely autonomous, all the Central Powers had come to their breaking points at precisely the same moment, and all now fell together—Bulgaria at the end of September, and then Turkey and Austro-Hungary in the span of a mere six days. As might be expected, Germany held out the longest, but only by the matter of a week. With their vaunted Hindenburg Line overrun in a half dozen places and their soldiers surrendering en masse, in the early morning hours of November 11, German negotiators met with their Allied counterparts in a railroad car in a French forest to sign papers of armistice, scheduled to take effect at 11 a.m. that same day. In a fittingly obscene finale to this most senseless of wars, a number of Western Front units continued to fight right up until that eleventh hour was struck, with the result that some four thousand more soldiers died on the last morning of the war.

Curt Prüfer had observed much of this staggering cascade of events from the vantage point of Switzerland, to which he had crossed in late September. Even as all fell down around him, the German spymaster had continued with his scheme to try to woo the wayward eldest son of Abbas Hilmi back into the Central Powers' fold, the keystone, in some inscrutable way, toward forging a German-Turkish-Egyptian alliance that might yet ride to triumph in the Middle East. A mentally unstable sadist Abdel Moneim may well have been, but he still had enough wits about him in October 1918 to realize that his German suitor's scheme was ludicrous. At the end of that month, an empty-handed Prüfer crossed back over to Germany, just in time to witness the final fall of his beloved Fatherland.

For a time, Aaron Aaronsohn had also been a distant observer of the events of that autumn—in his case, from the even farther remove of the United States. In mid-October, however, with the downfall of the Central Powers clearly imminent, he hurried aboard a passenger ship in New York for the return to England. Once Turkey and Germany capitulated, Aaronsohn knew, all attention would turn to the international peace conference being planned in Paris, and he was determined to make his presence there known, to press for the promises given to the Zionists in the Balfour Declaration.

By contrast, William Yale experienced the climax of the war first-hand. Through October, he followed the victorious British army north through Syria, and was in Aleppo when news of the German armistice came. Afterward, he made his way back to Cairo, not at all sure what his future held. Reluctant to go home, but with little to do in Egypt, he fixated on trying to get himself attached in some capacity to the American delegation at the upcoming Paris Peace Conference. "I feverishly wrote report after report," he recounted, "hoping that through them I could persuade someone to order me to Paris. My reports grew poorer and poorer."

That decline in quality apparently did the trick, for in late December Yale received a cable ordering him to the French capital. He was to report there to the American Commission to Negotiate Peace, to serve as their "expert on Arabian affairs." As Yale would write in a moment of rare modesty, "the title flabbergasted me."

Paradoxically, of the various spies and intelligence agents who had parried with one another across the Middle East over the previous few years, the one most completely removed from events at the war's close was T. E. Lawrence. He had ensured that on the afternoon of October 3, in the second-floor stateroom of the Victoria Hotel in Damascus.

Once Faisal had left that room after his meeting with Allenby, Lawrence had turned to the general and requested to be given leave. Apparently, Allenby initially assumed it was a request for a few days' rest—that was easy enough to arrange and certainly well deserved—but Lawrence clarified that he wanted to leave altogether, to go home to England. At first, Allenby flatly refused; the Syrian campaign was still a very active one, it relied greatly on British officers whom the Arabs trusted, and they trusted no one more than Lieutenant Colonel Lawrence.

According to Henry Chauvel, Lawrence then raised the stakes considerably by telling Allenby "that he would not work with a French Liaison officer, and that he was due for leave and thought he had better take it now and go off to England." Whether in anger at Lawrence's insubordination or in respect at his sense of honor—the accounts of Chauvel and Lawrence differ on this—Allenby finally relented. "Yes," he told Lawrence, "I think you had."

Since late 1916, Lawrence had waged a quiet war against his own government, and now he had lost. What would soon become clear, however, was that he intended to continue that fight off the battlefield, in the conference halls and meeting rooms of peacetime Paris. He may have asked to leave Damascus out of exhaustion, but it was also to prepare for the next round in the struggle for Arab independence.

The following afternoon, Lawrence was conducted out of Damascus. He was leaving the city he had invoked as a battle cry for two years. One hundred and fifty miles to the northeast of Damascus lay Jerablus, the place where he had spent the happiest days of his life. To Damascus or Jerablus, Lawrence would never return.

Epilogue

Paris

Blast the Lawrence side of things. He was a cad I've killed.

T. E. SHAW, ALIAS OF T. E. LAWRENCE,
TO H. C. ARMSTRONG, OCTOBER 6, 1924

Everything T. E. Lawrence had fought for, schemed for, arguably betrayed his country for, turned to ashes in a single five-minute conversation between the prime ministers of Great Britain and France. In London on the morning of December 1, 1918, David Lloyd George took aside a visiting Georges Clemenceau and bluntly outlined just what Britain wanted in the Middle East: Iraq and Palestine. In tacit exchange, although Lloyd George would always deny it, France would have free rein in Syria. It was a proposed "solution" to the spoils-of-war contest that had strained British and French relations ever since they had cast their covetous eyes toward the Middle East, and that had now taken on great urgency; with the Great War finally over and the Paris Peace Conference about to begin, it was vital that Britain and France present a unified front against the American president, Woodrow Wilson, with his high-minded talk of a "peace without victory" and the rights of oppressed peoples to self-determination. Faced with this imminent American threat, Clemenceau quickly acceded to Lloyd George's proposal.

In essence, the two imperial victors had not only affirmed the basic structure of the Sykes-Picot Agreement but gone beyond it, giving themselves more and the Arabs even less. But in the time-honored tradition of

European secret deals, it was to be a while before anyone outside the British and French prime ministers' closest circles would have any knowledge of that extraordinary accord. Certainly T. E. Lawrence had no intimation of it.

What followed in Paris was a yearlong shadow play that first raised hopes of a new era in relations between nations, Woodrow Wilson's vaunted "new world order," only to degenerate into backroom deals, vengeful treaties, and arbitrary borders. Many books, foremost among them Margaret MacMillan's definitive *Paris 1919*, have been written about the Paris Peace Conference and the immensely complicated maneuverings of great powers and nationalist supplicants. As far as the Middle East was concerned, the byzantine machinations meant, in the end, virtually nothing. "The Great Loot," the carving up of the carcass of the Ottoman Empire, would now come to pass.

Not that Lawrence did not try mightily to advance the Arab cause. Acting as Faisal's counselor during the Paris talks, he constantly floated schemes to give them control of the lands they had fought so fiercely for, while he also lobbied senior British statesmen and wrote passionate editorials in the Arabs' defense. But Lawrence's usefulness to the British government had ended. In an exquisite irony, at precisely the same time he was becoming a household name in Britain—an estimated one million Britons, including the king and queen, would flock to see Lowell Thomas's lecture show "With Allenby in Palestine, and Lawrence in Arabia"—government officials were penning memos calling Lawrence "a malign influence," and "to a large extent responsible for our troubles with the French over Syria." Finally, he was simply stripped of his credentials at Paris and barred from assisting Faisal in the talks. Lawrence had lost the peace.

There was at least one extraordinary aspect of Lawrence's diplomatic efforts, however, that bears emphasis. Having long known that control of the Palestine portion of Syria was lost to the Arabs, Lawrence and Faisal sought an ally to affirm their nationalist aspirations for the rest of it. They found such an ally in Chaim Weizmann. By the close of 1918, the Zionists had strong patrons in both the British and American governments, but what made those governments nervous was the continuing—in fact, growing—hostility of the Palestinian Arab population to the Zionists' goals. So what if Hashemite support for the Zionist program in Palestine could be traded for Zionist support of an independent Arab Syria? Over the course of that December, Lawrence, Faisal, and Weizmann worked out the details for such a mutually beneficial relationship, culminating in a joint proclamation on the eve of the Paris Peace Conference.

In that proclamation, Faisal and Weizmann announced their intention to work together in Paris, and in recognition of each other's claims. Surely the most controversial of the nine articles of the Faisal-Weizmann Agreement was the fourth: "All necessary measures shall be taken to encourage and stimulate immigration of Jews into Palestine on a large scale." To this document, Faisal—or more likely, Lawrence—had inserted a key closing proviso. The agreement was only valid so long as Syrian independence was achieved; barring that, it was null and void.

Yet in their desperation to find a supporting partner at the peace conference, Lawrence and Faisal had chosen to ignore several crucial details. While the Faisal-Weizmann Agreement offered a fairly detailed outline for the administration of Palestine, nowhere did it specify what Palestine actually consisted of. Further, in reaching his accord with Weizmann, Faisal had quite flagrantly turned his back on the doctrine of self-determination for Palestine, placing him in a weakened—some would say hypocritical—position in invoking that same doctrine for the rest of Syria. Most troublesome, Chaim Weizmann had recently made public just what he and other Zionists envisioned as the future status of Palestine. "The establishment of a National Home for the Jewish people," he had announced in mid-November, "is understood to mean that the country of Palestine should be placed under such political, economic and moral conditions as will favor the increase of the Jewish population, so that in accordance with the principle of democracy, it may ultimately develop into a Jewish Commonwealth."

By going into partnership with the Zionists under such circumstances, Faisal had just handed his more conservative Arab and Muslim rivals a powerful weapon to use against him. One who would soon wield that weapon to devastating effect was King Hussein's chief rival in Arabia, ibn-Saud, and his fundamentalist Wahhabist followers.

IN THE LAST sentence of his memoir, William Yale referred to the Paris Peace Conference as "the prologue of the 20th century tragedy." Yale served as an expert on Middle Eastern affairs to the American delegation in Paris and, like Lawrence, put forth great efforts to achieve a sustainable peace in the region. As with his British counterpart, with whom he sometimes aligned himself, these efforts were thwarted at every turn.

Yale placed much of the blame on his own government. To him, the grand enterprise in Paris seemed a rather perfect reflection of Woodrow Wilson's peculiar blend of idealism and arrogance. In the American president's almost comic fondness for tidy enumerated lists—his "Fourteen Points" had been followed by his "Four Principles," his "Four Ends," and finally his "Five Particulars"—was the hint of a simplistic mind-set, as if solving the world's myriad messy problems was merely a matter of isolating them into their component parts and applying quasi-mathematical principles. Nowhere was this more problematic than when it came to Wilson's cherished and oft-cited notion of "self-determination." While the phrase certainly sounded good, in the mashed-together cultures of Europe and the Middle East of the early twentieth century, where faith and ethnicity and nationalism were all exerting tremendous and often opposing pulls, just whose claim to self-determination was to win out over others? London and Paris had repeatedly warned Wilson on the dangers of opening up this Pandora's box, but there had never been any indication that the president was listening.

To William Yale's mind, all of this was actually symptomatic of perhaps the greatest paradox underlying the American role at the Paris Peace Conference: Woodrow Wilson's grand vision of a new world order rested on a bedrock of profound ignorance. That was made clear on the very day Yale arrived in Paris and met with his new supervisor, William Westermann, and the other members of the American delegation's Middle Eastern research section. Granted, the Middle East was a lesser American concern at the peace conference since the United States hadn't gone to war with Turkey, but it still struck Yale that Westermann, a classics professor from the University of Wisconsin, might have rounded up a panel with at least some familiarity with the region. Instead, they included a specialist in Latin American studies, an American Indian historian, a scholar on the Crusades, and two Persian linguistics professors.

The picture was completed when Yale was handed a briefing book on Syria, a 107-page compendium of historic, economic, and political data that was serving as the principal guide in formulating American policy in the region. The *Report on the Desires of the Syrians* didn't require a lot of study on Yale's part; almost all the citations in those sections dealing with events since 1914 were drawn from a single source, a State Department special agent in Cairo named William Yale.

Several times Yale saw opportunities for championing the cause of Arab self-determination, but they always slipped away on the tide of American inaction. At a meeting with Faisal in mid-February 1919, Yale was taken aback when the Arab leader bluntly proposed an American mandate in Syria, vastly preferring the supposedly disinterested Americans to the French. By then, however, Yale had already been with the American delegation in Paris long enough to realize that, virtuous principles aside, the Wilson administration was more interested in dictating solutions to the rest of the world than in assuming any responsibility of its own. And there was another problem, one that may not have been readily apparent to non-Americans. Its brief burst of international involvement notwithstanding, the United States was already showing signs of sliding back into an isolationist spirit, with Wilson and his Republican opponents who dominated in Congress increasingly at loggerheads. What it meant for all those in Paris looking to the United States for leadership was that time was not on their side, that the longer things dragged on, the less likely the Americans would have the ability or even the interest to do much at all. Very quickly, for Yale and others in the American Middle Eastern division, there came the deeply dispiriting sense that matters were slipping away. "We fought over boundary lines as if the destiny of the world depended upon it," Yale recalled of that time. "We fumed and fussed because Wilson and [his chief advisor Edward] House seemed to pay no attention to what we were doing. It all seemed strangely academic and futile to me."

As the peace conference extended, the folly of Yale's mission would only grow increasingly absurd. In the late spring of 1919, he was appointed to an American fact-finding committee, the King-Crane Commission, which, in pursuit of Wilson's self-determination principle, was dispatched to determine the desires of the former denizens of the Ottoman world, "to take a plebiscite," in Yale's skeptical view, "of a vast sprawling empire of 30,000,000 inhabitants." Unsurprisingly, after a tour of two months, and scores of meetings in Turkey, Syria, Lebanon, and Palestine, the message the commission had heard in each place was unequivocal: the vast majority of people wanted either independence or the Americans. In light of this, the commission came up with a sweeping set of recommendations that placed the United States at the forefront of administering a solution to the Middle Eastern puzzle. That solution, however, did not at all resemble what had already been secretly agreed to by the British and the French, nor what the Wilson administration was willing to take on. At least here, the administration was prepared to act with great dispatch; the King-Crane reports were swiftly locked away in a safe, not to be seen or read by the outside world for the next three years.

Returning to Europe from that mission in the fall of 1919, Yale would make one last attempt to salvage the situation in Syria, enlisting Lawrence's support for what became known as the Yale Plan. With the plan drawing support from senior British statesmen, it briefly appeared the coming showdown between the Arabs and French in Syria might be averted. But Yale was essentially acting in a freelance capacity, and once senior American officials learned of it, his plan was quickly scuttled. On November 1, 1919, British troops who had occupied Syria until a final settlement was reached began to withdraw. On that same day, French troops began moving in. Days later, Yale resigned from the American peace delegation in disgust and sailed back to New York.

T. E. Lawrence lost hope at about the same time. As his mother would relate to a biographer, her son slipped into a state of "extreme depression and nervous exhaustion" that autumn, and during visits home he "would sometimes sit the entire morning between breakfast and lunch in the same position, without moving, and with the same expression on his face."

PART OF THE enduring fascination with T. E. Lawrence's story is the series of painful "what if?" questions it raises, a pondering over what the world lost when he lost. What would have happened if, in 1918, the Arabs had been able to create the greater Arab nation that many so desperately sought, and which they believed had been promised them? How different would the Middle East look today if the early Zionists in postwar Palestine had been able to negotiate with a man like Faisal Hussein, who had talked of "the racial kinship and ancient bonds" that existed between Jew and Arab? And what of the Americans? Today, it scarcely seems conceivable that there was a time when the Arab and Muslim worlds were clamoring *for* American intervention in their lands; what might have happened if the United States had risen to the opportunity presented at the end of World War I?

In all probability, not quite the golden age some might imagine. As Lawrence himself frequently stated, the notion of a true pan-Arab nation was always something of a mirage, the differences between its radically varied cultures far greater than what united them. Perhaps such a fractious and vast nation could have endured for a time through sheer lack of strong central control, much as under the Ottomans' old system, but advances in technology and communication would almost certainly have soon brought these disparate cultures and peoples into conflict. Similarly, there were never going to be truly harmonious relations between the Jews and the Arabs in Palestine, given that Arab resistance to an expanded Jewish presence long preceded the Balfour Declaration and took little notice of Faisal's moderation; indeed, the one postwar Arab leader who would try to reach an accommodation with Israel, Faisal's brother Abdullah, would be assassinated by a Palestinian gunman for his troubles. As for American occupying troops being hailed as liberators, that surely would have been short-lived too, ending when those troops were drawn into policing local conflicts they little understood, with the inevitable choosing of sides this entails. Even if it somehow managed to avoid those treacherous straits, the United States would certainly have shed its image as "the one disinterested party" as it steadily became an imperial power in its own right.

All that said, it's hard to imagine that any of this could possibly have produced a sadder history than what has actually transpired over the past century, a catalog of war, religious strife, and brutal dictatorships that has haunted not just the Middle East but the entire world. That sad history began from almost the moment the negotiators in Paris packed their bags and declared their mission complete, leaving in their wake "a porcelain peace."

Denied Lawrence's assistance in the autumn of 1919, a desperate Faisal was forced to accept the few crumbs of compromise the French were willing to throw his way in Syria. When Faisal returned to Damascus, however, he found himself denounced as a traitor for selling the nation out to the European imperialists. Harnessing this popular rage, Faisal renounced his deal with the French and in March 1920 staged something of a palace coup by declaring himself king of Syria. That act, in conjunction with the San Remo conference the following month at which Great Britain and France formalized their partition of the region—Britain taking Iraq and a "greater" Palestine that included a broad swath east of the Jordan River, or Transjordan, France the rest of Syria—set Faisal on a collision course with the French. That collision came in July; after a brief and one-sided battle on the outskirts of Damascus, the French ousted Faisal and cast him into exile. By the close of 1920, the French at last had much of their *Syrie intégrale* (with the exception of the British mandate in Palestine and Transjordan), but they now faced a populace seething with rage. They also now confronted an external threat; in the deserts of Transjordan, Faisal's brother Abdullah was massing his followers with the intention of marching on Damascus.

But whatever problems the French had at the end of 1920 were dwarfed by those of the British. In Palestine, tensions between Zionist immigrants and the resident Arab population had escalated into bloodshed. In Arabia, ibn-Saud was once again pushing to oust King Hussein. The worst crisis point was in Iraq. The previous year, Lawrence had predicted full-scale revolt against British rule there by March 1920 "if we don't mend our ways," but he had been off by two months; by the time the May rebellion in Iraq was put down, some one thousand British and nine thousand natives were dead. As Lawrence would explain in his 1929 letter to William Yale, at Paris, Great Britain and France had taken the discredited Sykes-Picot Agreement and fashioned something even worse; how much worse was evidenced by the myriad fires that had spread across the region almost immediately.

To combat these crises, in December 1920 Lloyd George turned to a man who had become something of a pariah in British ruling circles, former first lord of the admiralty, Winston Churchill. One of Churchill's first acts upon assuming the position of Colonial Office secretary was to enlist the help of another recent outcast, former lieutenant colonel T. E. Lawrence.

At least initially, Lawrence had little interest in rejoining the fray. Immersed in writing his memoirs, and undoubtedly still smarting over his shabby treatment by Lloyd George's government the previous year, he told Churchill he was too busy and that he had left politics behind. He only relented when the new colonial secretary assured him that he would have a virtually free hand in helping fundamentally reshape the British portion of the Middle Eastern chessboard at the upcoming Cairo Conference. As a result, the Cairo deliberations were little more than a formality, with Lawrence and Churchill having worked out ahead of time, as Lawrence told a biographer, "not only [the] questions the Conference would consider, but decisions they would reach."

Iraq was now to be consolidated and recognized as an Arab kingdom, with Faisal placed on the throne. In Arabia, the British upheld Hussein's claim to rule in the Hejaz, while simultaneously upholding ibn-Saud's authority in the Arabian interior. Surely the most novel idea to come out of Cairo was the plan designed to stay Abdullah from attacking the French in Syria. At the close of the conference, Lawrence journeyed to Abdullah's base camp in Amman and convinced the truculent Arab leader to first try to establish a government in the Transjordan region of Britain's Palestine mandate. To Lawrence's great surprise—and perhaps to Abdullah's as well—this most indolent of Hussein's four sons actually proved to be a remarkably good administrator; in the near future, Transjordan was to be officially detached from the rest of Palestine and made an independent Arab kingdom—today's Jordan—with Abdullah as its ruler. By the time Lawrence returned to England in the autumn of 1921, his one-year service to the Colonial Office nearly over, he had quite literally become the unseen kingmaker of the Middle East.

But if all this brought a measure of stability to the center of the old Ottoman Empire map, it did little to improve matters to the north and south. There, the situation remained uncertain and bloody for some time to come.

In Anatolia, the former Turkish general Mustafa Kemal, the hero of Gallipoli, had refused to accept the dismemberment of Turkey as outlined by the Allies. Over a four-year period, he led his army of Turkish nationalists into battle against all those who would claim a piece of the Turkish heartland, before finally establishing the modern-day borders of Turkey in 1923. France's turn in this round robin of war came in the autumn of 1921 when Kemal, soon to become better known as Ataturk, turned his attention to the French troops occupying the Cilicia region.

Quickly routed, the French armies in Cilicia beat a hasty retreat back into Syria under the leadership of their commander, the unlucky Édouard Brémond.

At the same time, a bewildering arc of war extended from the Caucasus all the way to Afghanistan as various nationalist groups, Russian Reds and Whites, and remnants of the Young Turks battled for primacy, forming and reforming alliances with such dizzying regularity as to defy both logic and comprehension. Among the prominent aspirants in this crucible were both Enver and Djemal Pasha, and it was no more surprising than anything else going on in the region that Djemal Pasha should turn up in Kabul in the winter of 1921 as a military advisor to the king of Afghanistan.

And then, far to the south, it was King Hussein's turn. With the British having long since tired of his mercurial rule and refusal to accept the political realities of the Middle East—in 1921, Lawrence had spent a maddening two months in Jeddah futilely trying to get Hussein to accept the Cairo Conference accords—he was all but defenseless when ibn-Saud and his Wahhabist warriors finally closed on Mecca in late 1924. Hustled to the coast and then onto a British destroyer, Hussein was first taken to exile in Cyprus, before finally joining his son Abdullah in his new capital of Amman, Jordan. The deposed king, who had once dreamt of a pan-Arab nation extending from Mecca to Baghdad, died there in 1931 at the age of seventy-six.

From there, matters simply turned worse for the West. By the 1930s, the British faced a quagmire in the Palestine mandate they had schemed so hard to obtain, first a full-scale Arab revolt fueled by increasing Jewish immigration into the region, joined after World War II by attacks from Jewish guerrillas who saw the British occupiers as the last roadblock toward the creation of Israel. In 1946, the war-exhausted French were forced to give up their cherished *Syrie intégrale*, but not before carving out a new nation, Lebanon, from its territory; within three years, Syria's pro-Western democratic government would be ousted in a military coup, and the convoluted governing structure imposed by the French in Lebanon would set the country on the path to civil war. In 1952, British control of Egypt ended when their puppet king was overthrown by Gamal Abdel Nasser and his nationalist Free Officers Movement, followed six years later by a military coup in Iraq by like-minded junior officers that ended the pro-Western monarchy established by Faisal. By the 1960s, with the era of European imperialism drawing to its unceremonious close, the Middle East resembled the shambles the colonial powers were leaving behind in other parts of the globe, but with one crucial difference: because of oil, the region had now become the most strategically vital corner on earth, and the West couldn't walk away from the mess it had helped create there even if it wanted to. What has transpired there over the past half century is, of course, familiar to all: four wars between the Arabs and Israelis; a ten-year civil war in Lebanon and a twenty-year one in Yemen; the slaughter of ethnic minorities in Syria and Iraq; four decades of state-sponsored terrorism; convulsions of religious extremism; four major American military interventions and a host of smaller ones; and for the Arab people, until very recently, a virtually unbroken string of cruel and/or kleptocratic dictatorships stretching from Tunisia to Iraq that left the great majority impoverished and disenfranchised.

Certainly, blame for all this doesn't rest solely with the terrible decisions that were made at the end of World War I, but it was then that one particularly toxic seed was planted. Ever since, Arab society has tended to define itself less by what it aspires to become than by what it is opposed to: colonialism, Zionism, Western imperialism in its many forms. This culture of opposition has been manipulated—indeed, feverishly nurtured—by generations of Arab dictators intent on channeling their people's anger away from their own misrule in favor of the external threat, whether it is "the great Satan" or the "illegitimate Zionist entity" or Western music playing on the streets of Cairo. This is also why the so-called Arab Spring movement of today represents such a potentially transformative moment in the history of the Middle East. For the first time since 1918, the "Arab street" is having a say in its own future, and however many roadblocks are thrown in its way, an element of civic participation and personal freedom is being spawned that likely can never be boxed back up. To the degree that genuine democracy and self-determination does take hold—and in a region that has been politically and intellectually stunted for so long, it's easy to only focus on the short-term chaos—the Arab world might finally embark upon the path envisioned for it by Lawrence and a handful of other dreamers a century ago.

MARK SYKES, the man whose name has become synonymous with the disastrous policies the West pursued in the Middle East after World War I, didn't live to see their effect. Having swiftly gone from indispensable fix-it man to scapegoat in the eyes of the British Foreign Office for his coauthorship of the detested Sykes-Picot Agreement, in the autumn of 1918 Sykes embarked on an extended tour of the postwar Middle East. His diminished stature hadn't engendered a bout of modesty, however; as he informed the Foreign Office in proposing his trip, along with calming Arab-Jewish tensions in Palestine, he intended to help reorganize the Allied political and military infrastructure in Syria, cajole the British Indian regime in Iraq into adopting a more progressive, postimperial mien, and "assist in promoting good relations between Arabs and French."

For two months, Sykes and his small entourage crisscrossed the region, each day filled with an exhausting schedule of events. But even this most vainglorious of men must have seen that in the Middle East, just as in London, his sway was vastly reduced. In Damascus, Sykes called on Gilbert Clayton, once an attentive listener to his various initiatives, only to encounter a pronounced mulishness. Unknown to Sykes, Clayton had recently received advice from an official in London on how to handle his visitor. "Don't take Mark at his own valuation," the official had cautioned. "His shares are unsaleable here and he has been sent out (at his own request) to get him away."

Yet as humbling as this journey was, it seemed to spark in Sykes a genuine reappraisal of his views on the Middle East. In January 1919, as he wrote up an "appreciation" of his just-completed trip, he allowed that both Britain and France had been quite wrong in their approach in the region. In a line he could have lifted from Lawrence's *Twenty-Seven Articles*, he now suggested that "whoever takes over Syria ought to realize that to have a purely native administration running things badly, but with prospects of improvement, represents more real progress than having a European staff doing things properly, but [with] the natives learning nothing." It was a remarkable evolution in thinking in the man who three years earlier had coauthored what would turn out to be the last great compact in the service of European imperialism.

But it was too late. By the time Sykes showed up at the Paris Peace Conference in early February, his British colleagues were less interested in any evolution of his thinking than in extricating themselves from the agreement that bore his name. In the close quarters of Paris, the scorn with which they regarded Sykes took on an element of bullying. "I said something to him about the agreement," Lloyd George would recall in his memoirs, "and at once saw how I had cut him. I am sorry. I wish I had said nothing. I blame myself. He did his best."

But perhaps the prime minister's contrition stemmed from what soon followed. On the evening of February 10, Sykes took to bed early, complaining of feeling run-down. By the next morning, he couldn't stand. Doctors quickly diagnosed Spanish influenza, and for the next five days he lingered in great pain in his hotel room, tended to by his wife, Edith, herself ill with the disease. Sykes finally succumbed on the evening of February 16, one month short of his fortieth birthday.

· · ·

AARON AARONSOHN ALSO did not live to see his plans come into being. He too was at Paris, and much as with the Zionist Commission in 1918, had been led to believe that he would assume a leadership role in the Zionist delegation to the peace conference, only to find himself relegated to the sidelines at the last minute. As he thundered in his diary on January 16, 1919, after learning that the senior Zionist leadership was about to meet in London for a strategy session, "Chaim [Weizmann] said to me incidentally, 'you are coming to London also, aren't you?' 'For what?' I replied. 'To receive further insults? Many thanks.' I wrote that I was sick and tired of remaining in the false position of a mistress who is loved in the privacy of one's room, but not recognized before the world."

Just as he had threatened to do many times with the Zionist Commission, Aaronsohn resolved to quit Paris altogether, and was only stayed when the Zionist leadership that had so recently snubbed him contritely beseeched his help in drawing the proposed boundary map for Palestine. "I hate the way they work," Aaronsohn jotted afterward in his diary with a note of put-upon triumph. "Give important missions to people and at the last minute realize nothing was done because they didn't let experts do it." The map Aaronsohn drew up was a Zionist's dream, one that, if adopted, would have extended the borders of Palestine to the outskirts of Damascus, not so much making Palestine an enclave alongside a greater Syria than transforming Syria into a virtual rump state of a greater Palestine.

On the morning of May 15, 1919, Aaronsohn was preparing to return to Paris and the peace conference after a quick visit to London. At Kenley airfield south of London, however, he discovered his flight had been delayed due to thick ground fog. By 11:30, he was just about to give up and return to London when, amid a partial clearing of the skies, the pilot of a much smaller plane, a two-seater de Havilland making a mail run to Paris, offered to give him a lift. At about 1 p.m., a French fishing boat captain working the waters off the Calais coast heard a plane flying low overhead, invisible in the thick fog, then the sound of a crash. Searching through the mist, the fisherman found scattered mail floating on the calm sea, but nothing else. Neither the body of the de Havilland pilot nor of Aaron Aaronsohn was ever recovered. Since by rabbinical law a funeral can't be held without a body, on the evening of May 17 Aaronsohn's friends and colleagues gathered in Paris for an "observance" of his life and contribution to the Zionist cause.

As for Aaronsohn's colleague and sometime adversary in the Zionist cause, Chaim Weizmann, he would not only live to see the creation of the state of Israel, but serve as its first president until his death in 1952. He was joined in postwar Palestine by his rebellious younger sister Minna. For her services to the Central Powers war effort, Minna was included in a prisoner exchange between Germany and Russia in the last days of World War I. Managing yet another escape, this time from the chaos of postwar Germany, she returned to Jerusalem, where she worked for the health service of the Zionist women's organization, Hadassah.

Djemal Pasha continued his adventurous life in the postwar era, if only briefly. Having escaped from Constantinople along with his two co-pashas, Talaat and Enver, aboard a German torpedo boat in the last days of the war, Djemal wandered the battlegrounds of Central Asia, falling in and out of alliances with a bewildering array of factions. His luck finally ran out in July 1922 when he and an aide were gunned down in the streets of Tbilisi, Georgia. Claiming credit for the assassination was a shadowy Armenian nationalist organization that had vowed to liquidate those responsible for the Armenian slaughters of 1915–16, and which had earlier assassinated Talaat Pasha in Berlin. The following month, Enver, the last of the Three Pashas and Djemal's coadventurer in the Caucasus, also passed from the scene, shot in a Russian Red Army ambush in Tajikistan.

IN HIS ROLE as one of America's Middle Eastern experts at the Paris Peace Conference, William Yale did not limit his attention to the matter of peace in the region. At the same time, and perhaps mindful that one day he would have to find a new job, he sought to quietly promote the interests of his former employer, Standard Oil of New York, with the American delegation. Between President Wilson's stout defense of the "Open Door" free trade policy and a series of events that had occurred in Palestine in the summer of 1918, Yale had a good pretext for doing so.

While serving as the American military liaison at Allenby's headquarters that summer, Yale had been summoned by General Arthur Money, the British chief administrator of Palestine, who demanded that he hand over Socony's Palestine oilfield maps. When Yale refused, protesting that Money should take up the issue with Standard headquarters, the general opted for the simpler course of breaking into the old Socony office in Jerusalem and taking them. In a series of memoranda to the American peace delegates, Yale darkly warned of where these strong-arm tactics might lead, especially if the oil-hungry British were allowed free rein in their mandate territories of Palestine and Iraq. Those delegates were duly alarmed; largely at Yale's instigation, the American campaign to force the British to honor Socony's Palestine concessions would become a major source of friction between the two countries for the next several years.

Except that Socony was apparently playing something of a shell game in Palestine, fiercely fighting to protect its "strike" at Kornub in order to establish a precedent for demanding equal access to the known oilfields in British-controlled Iraq. When that access was finally ceded in 1924, Standard Oil abruptly dropped all its concessions in Palestine. Scurrying into the breach, a British oil company hastily conducted its own tests at Kornub, only to find what Yale's geologist partner, Rudolf McGovern, had found in 1914: iron tailings. Despite the periodic release of optimistic industry reports to the contrary, no commercially viable oil deposits have ever been found at Kornub.

After quitting the Paris Peace Conference in disgust in late 1919, Yale returned to the United States with hopes of being rehired by Socony. Whether due to his past impolitic remarks in the halls of 26 Broadway or because he had become too high profile in the ongoing oil battles with Britain, that effort failed. With his family's fortune long since dwindled away and jobs scarce in the deepening American postwar recession, Yale signed on with an American trading firm and went back to Cairo. On the way, he stopped off in England and married Edith Hanna, a British nurse he had met in Jerusalem before the war.

For several years, Yale juggled a number of different part-time positions in Cairo, even as he continued to prospect for oil on his own. By May 1922, he felt he'd made a strike on the British-controlled Farasan Island off the coast of Yemen. As he told a senior Socony official, the British were keeping the oil find a secret, but if a Socony geologist was sent out, Yale knew a way for them to sneak onto the island. When that offer wasn't pursued, Yale returned to the United States, where he took up the unlikely vocation of chicken farmer in rural New Hampshire as he worked toward getting his master's degree in education. By 1928, he had been hired by the University of New Hampshire as an assistant professor of history.

A prodigious if not particularly gifted writer, Yale supplemented his professor's income with articles and essays about the Middle East. These efforts gradually achieved wider recognition—he published in both the *Atlantic Monthly* and the *Christian Science Monitor*—which led to visiting lectureships and invitations to university symposia. Just as when he had lived in the region, Yale's views on the Middle East oscillated wildly over the years, so that his 1923 call for a campaign to "smash the debasing tyranny of Islamism, which for centuries has corrupted the minds and souls and bodies of countless millions of Orientals," was neatly offset by a later screed against "the exploitive nature of Jewish nationalistic imperialism," which he charged was modeled on the "German fascist pattern."

Despite such rhetoric, Yale was sufficiently well regarded as an expert in the field to be appointed to the State Department's Office of Postwar Planning as a Middle Eastern specialist during World War II. That position, in turn, led to his appointment as an assistant secretary to the Committee on Trusteeship at the first postwar United Nations conference in San Francisco in 1945. Yale's particular area of focus was on the proposed political realignment of the Arab world through a dismantling of the discredited colonial mandate system in favor of U.N. trusteeship. It must have felt very much like déjà vu, for, just as with the King-Crane Commission of twenty-six years earlier, none of the committee's recommendations for the Middle East would be acted upon.

Returned to civilian life, Yale resumed teaching history at the University of New Hampshire, and then at Boston University until his retirement in 1967. He died in a nursing home in Derry, New Hampshire, in February 1975, at the age of eighty-seven.

FROM THE OTHER side of the Middle Eastern intelligence battlefield, Curt Prüfer had a rather more colorful postwar career. Indeed, while no individual can truly personify the history of a nation, it would be hard to find a more remarkable exemplar through which to view events in Germany between the two world wars.

In 1919, Prüfer was quickly drawn to one of the most poisonous myths to take root in defeated Germany, the so-called stab-in-the-back conspiracy. According to this myth, Germany hadn't lost the war on the battlefield, but rather had been betrayed from within. Chief among these internal traitors were Germany's liberal political parties—in a case of astoundingly poor timing, a coalition of leftist parties took control of the government just two days before the armistice—and international Jewry, seduced by the promises of the Balfour Declaration into throwing their allegiance to the Allied cause. It was a myth ultimately put to devastating use by Adolf Hitler, but it found an adherent in Curt Prüfer far earlier; according to biographer Donald McKale, even as the impoverished Prüfer accepted financial support from a Jewish foreign ministry coworker in the lean early postwar years, he railed against the Jews in his diary with growing vehemence.

In fact, though, due to the unfinished business of the Paris Peace Conference, a strong argument could be made that Germany hadn't truly been defeated at all; instead, the Allies had created perhaps the best possible breeding ground for future conflict by simultaneously burdening their former enemy with crushing war reparation debts and leaving her ruling apparatus largely intact. It enabled German officials, Curt Prüfer among them, to quickly begin rebuilding the alliances and networks of influence that had helped lead to war to begin with. One of Prüfer's first tasks for the foreign ministry in the postwar era was to help a number of Germany's former partners in the Middle East—Egyptian nationalists, leaders of the

Young Turk movement, pro-German Arabs—to escape retribution and resettle within the former Central Powers. Of course, this meant Germany now had a recruitment pool of malcontents for fomenting unrest in the future.

Even before the war was over, Prüfer had seen a new way forward for that campaign, if only Germany learned from its past mistakes. "Our propaganda suffered," he wrote the foreign ministry on November 2, 1918, "because during the war we wanted to make up in urgency what we had neglected in peace.... With weepy accusations against our enemies, with longwinded recitals on our success, and inwardly untrue protestations of friendship for Islam, we tried to win sympathy from people who stood far from us spiritually." The next time around, Prüfer urged, Germany "must seek less to educate, than to please."

Amid the musical-chairs politics of the postwar Middle East, Prüfer soon had opportunity to get back into the mischief-making game. In the autumn of 1921, he was linked to a new scheme by the ever-determined Abbas Hilmi to overthrow the British regime in Egypt. A few months later, Prüfer was in Rome visiting with Chaim Weizmann. If aware that his visitor had once seduced his younger sister into spying for Germany, Weizmann apparently had bigger things on his mind; as he opined to Prüfer, since the French were clearly to blame for the British backing away from the idea of a Jewish state in Palestine, the Zionists and Germans now needed to work together against France. It was an idea with which the virulently anti-Semitic but ever opportunistic Prüfer undoubtedly heartily concurred. For these and other activities, the British government finally put Prüfer on an enemies blacklist, with the MI5 security agency maintaining an investigative file on him that would never be closed.

By the late 1920s, though, a certain equilibrium had settled into Prüfer's life. Having divorced his long-estranged first wife, the American Frances Pinkham, he married a much younger German woman who in 1930 bore him a son. He also continued to rise through the foreign ministry ranks, eventually becoming deputy director of its vitally important Abteilung (Department) III, the division dealing with both Anglo-American and Middle Eastern affairs. He was still in that position when Adolf Hitler came to power in July 1933.

Even though he shared Hitler's dream of a resurgent Germany, Prüfer, like many German conservatives, initially viewed the upstart Nazis as useful fools, rough-around-the-edges hooligans who could be utilized but controlled by the more respectable establishment. By 1936, Prüfer had sufficiently recovered from that misapprehension and his initial distaste to become personnel director of Hitler's foreign ministry and, a year later, to officially join the Nazi Party. In September 1939, with Germany having just ignited World War II with its invasion of Poland, Prüfer left for South America to serve as Hitler's ambassador to Brazil.

His three years in Brazil marked a kind of personal high point. At last Prüfer had achieved the status within the German diplomatic community that he had sought as far back as 1911. What's more, by developing a close friendship with Brazil's dictator, he helped forestall that immensely rich country from joining the war on the side of the Allies despite a treaty commitment with the Americans to do so. But alas, old habits die hard. In the summer of 1942, Prüfer was directly linked to a German espionage ring operating in Brazil and ordered from the country. If disappointed by this turn of events, the ambassador could at least be pleased by the timing; just five days after he and his family sailed for home, Brazil joined the Allies in the war and a warrant was issued for his arrest (he was eventually sentenced in absentia to twenty-five years for espionage).

Curiously trusting for a propaganda expert, Prüfer had apparently accepted Nazi pronouncements about imminent victory at face value, so he was shocked to return to a Europe where the war was turning inexorably against Germany. For a year, he stuck it out in Berlin, even as he moved his wife and child to a home he had bought in a smaller city to escape the incessant Allied air raids. "All this is terrible for me to witness," he wrote in July 1943, "not only because I have always been a person who is very attached to his homeland and always will be, but also because I was sincerely converted to some of the beautiful ideas of National Socialism."

Beautiful ideas aside, this natural-born survivor also had the instinct to find a way out. In September 1943, Prüfer led his family across the border into neutral Switzerland, where, much as in 1918, he remained until Germany's fall. The difference between his return in 1918 and that of 1945 was that this time the Allies weren't going to allow German militarists another reprise. The home Prüfer had purchased in Baden Baden, it turned out, had been confiscated from a Jewish family, and was taken away from him. The former ambassador was also put through the American "de-nazification" investigation process, where he was cleared of war crimes even as many of his immediate superiors in the foreign ministry were sent to Nuremberg. The British might have had more desire to catch up to the man who had been their nemesis for three decades, but they too lost interest when in October 1945 it was reported the always frail Prüfer was either dead or dying of tuberculosis.

But maybe not quite. Three years later, a sharp-eyed British intelligence officer in New Delhi noted a curious little item in the *Daily Telegraph* of India relating to the future training of Indian diplomats at Delhi

University. "Students will be under the supervision of Dr. Pruffer," the article noted, "a former German diplomat who left his country on the advent of the Nazi regime."

From a bit of sleuthing, it was eventually determined that the anti-Nazi "Pruffer" and the pro-Nazi Prüfer were one and the same. Much as had occurred in Cairo nearly forty years earlier, the British moved to deny Prüfer his coveted academic position, and he eventually returned to Germany. He finally died there—for real this time—in early 1959, at the age of seventy-seven. In a fitting irony, his only child, Olaf, with whom the failed former Oriental scholar had long been estranged, would eventually immigrate to the United States and become a renowned archaeologist.

OF ALL THE spies and intelligence agents who dueled with each another in the Middle East during World War I, the one most determined to divorce himself from the region in its aftermath was T. E. Lawrence. As he wrote a friend during his 1921 service for Winston Churchill at the Colonial Office, "the Arabs are like a page I have turned over, and sequels are rotten things."

In early 1922, with that service ending, Lawrence petitioned the head of the Royal Air Force for permission to join the force. There were several curious details to this request. Due both to his celebrity and former military rank, Lawrence might easily have entered the RAF as a senior officer, but instead he specifically requested to come in "with the ranks," meaning as an ordinary private. Also, he was no longer T. E. Lawrence; as he informed the RAF chief, his new name was John Hume Ross.

Making his petition especially puzzling was that Lawrence had always been openly contemptuous of military culture. As he would write in *Seven Pillars*, the military uniform "walled its bearers from ordinary life, was sign that they had sold their wills and bodies to the State, and contracted themselves into a service not the less abject for that its beginning was voluntary. . . . The soldier assigned his owner the twenty-four hours' use of his body, and sole conduct of his mind and passions."

But perhaps it was not so puzzling after all. In Arabia, Lawrence had exerted life-and-death control over thousands, had cobbled together a cause and an army as he went along. All the while, he had been tormented by a sense of his own fraudulence, the awareness that the men who fought and died at his side were almost certain to be betrayed in the end. As he would suggest in *Seven Pillars*, and state quite explicitly in letters to friends, after Arabia he never wanted to be in a position of responsibility again.

Joined to this was a desire for anonymity, to leave behind who and what he had been. Lawrence displayed this desire most overtly in the decision to change his name—first to John Hume Ross and then to Thomas Edward Shaw—but it took more subtle form, a kind of psychological washing of the hands. In the one very short mention of the Cairo Conference in *Seven Pillars*, Lawrence wrote that Churchill "made straight all the tangle" in the Middle East, fulfilling Britain's promises to the Arabs "in letter and spirit (where humanly possible) without sacrificing any interest of our Empire or any interest of the peoples concerned." Knowing the full extent of those promises, and writing at a time when his cherished Syria remained under French control, Lawrence couldn't possibly have believed his own assertion. Similarly, considering all that is contained in its pages, it's very hard to regard the subtitle to *Seven Pillars*—"A Triumph"—as anything but self-mockery.

Yet putting paid to all that had occurred so as to no longer have to think about it may well have been a matter of personal survival. What's sadly evident in many of Lawrence's postwar letters to friends, as well as in comments he made to his contemporary biographers, is that he suffered from many of the symptoms of what was known at the time as "shell shock," and what is today referred to as post-traumatic stress disorder (PTSD). Over the remainder of his life, Lawrence suffered from recurrent nightmares, endured severe bouts of depression—several of which included the contemplation of suicide—and gradually cut himself off from many of his former friends amid an intense desire to be alone.

He may have been particularly primed for this continuing torment by his own actions on the battlefield. As a boy, he had been obsessed with the tales of King Arthur's court and the chivalric code, had dreamed of leading a heroic life. In the reality of war, however, Lawrence had seen men blown to bits, often by his own handiwork, had left wounded behind to die, and had ordered prisoners to be killed. Just as any thoughtful person before or after him, what Lawrence had discovered on the battlefield was that while moments of heroism might certainly occur, the cumulative experience of war, its day-in, day-out brutalization, was utterly antithetical to the notion of leading a heroic life.

Also indicative of Lawrence's craving for anonymity were the circumstances of the publication of *Seven Pillars of Wisdom*. In 1922, he had handprinted just eight copies of his wartime memoir for close friends, but as word of the book spread, Lawrence was urged to release it publicly. His compromise was to produce a slightly abridged two-hundred-copy run of *Seven Pillars* in 1926, along with a vastly shorter mass-market version, *Revolt in the Desert*. The books might have made Lawrence wealthy, but he donated all royalties from the hugely successful *Revolt in the Desert* to an RAF charity, and refused to publish another edition of *Seven Pillars* during his lifetime.

While publicly denigrating his work as a trifle, Lawrence confided to a friend the secret hope that his memoir might join the canon of the very best of English literature. In this, he was to be disappointed. In truth, *Seven Pillars* is a fabulously uneven book, its occasional soaring lyricism and startling psychological insights all too often subsumed by long disquisitions on topography and a riot of local place names and fleeting characters likely to leave the reader struggling. Despite the glowing and insistent plaudits of many—certainly Lawrence deserves great credit for being one of the first modern writers to present an unflinching look at the grotesqueness of war—*Seven Pillars* remains one of those books that, as even an admiring critic acknowledges, "is more often praised than read."

After his first attempt at disappearing into the RAF as "Airman Ross" failed—he was quickly unmasked by the British press—Lawrence joined the Royal Tank Corps under the name of T. E. Shaw, then quietly transferred back into the RAF in 1925. For the next decade, he occupied a succession of lowly positions within the air corps—for nearly a year he served as a simple base clerk at a remote RAF base in India—while also engaging his mechanical bent with work on a new generation of high-speed military rescue boats. In 1929, he bought a tiny cottage in rural Dorset, Clouds Hill, just a mile from the Bovington Camp where he had served in the Tank Corps, and this became his refuge from a still-clamoring public and press. While he continued to write—in 1928, Lawrence penned an account of his postwar military service, *The Mint,* followed by a translation of Homer's *Odyssey*—the bulk of his time was devoted to his decidedly prosaic military duties, with off hours spent riding his beloved Brough motorcycle through the English countryside or voraciously reading at Clouds Hill. Despite the assertion of some biographers that this period in Lawrence's life was also highly productive and interesting, it is hard to escape the image of a sad and reclusive man, his circle of friends and acquaintances steadily dwindling to a mere handful, and many of these only maintained by the occasional quick note from Lawrence explaining why he couldn't see them. "Please apologize humbly for me to Mrs. S.F. [Newcombe]," he wrote Stewart Newcombe in February 1929, after apparently failing to show for a scheduled visit. "Something has gone wrong with the works, and I can't wind myself up to meet people."

One who insisted on a face-to-face meeting was Faisal Hussein. During a state visit to England in 1925, the now king of Iraq and Lawrence attended a luncheon at a politician's estate. It proved a rather awkward gathering, with the two old comrades in arms seeming to have little to say to each other, and Lawrence discomfited by their host's constant invocation of "the good old days." "I've changed," Lawrence wrote his confidante, Charlotte Shaw, afterward, "and the Lawrence who used to go about and be friendly and familiar with that sort of people is dead. He's worse than dead. He is a stranger I once knew."

During another state visit, in 1933, King Faisal had to lean on his contacts in the British military to all but order "Private Shaw" to a meeting.

By early 1935, Lawrence resolved to leave the RAF, even as he dreaded the long and unstructured days that lay ahead of him. His apprehensions proved quite accurate. As he wrote to a friend on May 6 from Clouds Hill, just two months into his retirement, "at present the feeling is mere bewilderment. I imagine leaves must feel like this after they have fallen from their tree and until they die. Let's hope that will not be my continuing state."

It would not be. Precisely a week later, on the morning of May 13, Lawrence rode his motorcycle to Bovington Camp to send a telegram. On his return, just a few hundred yards from Clouds Hill, he swerved to avoid two bicycling boys on the narrow road. Clipping the back tire of one of the bicycles, he lost control of the motorcycle and crashed, striking his head on the asphalt. Suffering from massive brain injuries, Lawrence lingered in a coma at the Bovington Camp hospital for six days, before finally dying early on the morning of May 19, 1935. He was forty-six.

Among the pallbearers at his funeral were his old friends Ronald Storrs and Stewart Newcombe, while those in attendance included Winston Churchill and the poet Siegfried Sassoon. For the occasion, King George V sent a message to Lawrence's surviving younger brother, Arnold. "Your brother's name will live in history, and the King gratefully recognizes his distinguished services to his country."

Churchill's eulogy was rather more loquacious: "I deem him one of the greatest beings alive in our time. I do not see his like elsewhere. I fear whatever our need we shall never see his like again."

It's easy to read in Churchill's last sentence an allusion to the new danger that by 1935 was already building over Europe: the rise of Nazi Germany. If Churchill imagined, however, that a living Lawrence might have played a signal role in meeting that danger, he was surely mistaken. As Lawrence himself had been trying to tell the world for many years, the blue-eyed "warrior of the desert" had passed from the scene long before, lost to the first great cataclysm of the twentieth century.

Acknowledgments

The broad scope of this book required research in some twenty different governmental archives or private collections on three continents. It would have been an utterly impossible task without the very able group of historians and researchers who assisted me in various aspects. These include Tara Fitzgerald, Claire Flack, Lars Luedicke, Frederic Maxwell, Andrea Minarcek, Kevin Morrow, Eamonn O'Neill, and Anna Van Lenten. Of these I must especially thank Kevin Morrow, who not only undertook research trips to California and Israel on my behalf, but also oversaw the collection, organization, and translation of both French and German archive material; I'm sure I would still be quite at sea with this project without his help.

I would also like to thank the curators and administrators of the various archives and private collections that I sought assistance from over the course of this project, all of whom were unfailingly helpful and generous with both their time and advice. While these are just a fraction of all those who helped me, I'd particularly like to thank Debbie Usher at the Middle East Centre, St. Antony's College, Oxford; Liz Gray, David Pfeiffer, and Eric Van Slander at the National Archives and Records Administration, Washington, D.C.; Marion Freudenthal and Ilonit Levy at the NILI Museum, Zichron Yaakov; Alex Rankin at Boston University; Carol Leadenham at the Hoover Institution, Stanford University; and Lynsey Robertson at the Churchill Archives Centre, Cambridge University. I must also single out Howard Diamond and the staff of the National Climatic Data Center at the National Oceanic and Atmospheric Administration, who made it something of a personal crusade to pinpoint when a sandstorm was likely to have struck Beersheva in early January 1914.

While it was my intention in this book to consult original source material as much as possible, there are two authors to whom I feel especially indebted. My research on Curt Prüfer would have taken infinitely longer—and, in fact, would have still been incomplete—without the pioneering work of Professor Donald McKale at Clemson University, and his two seminal books, *Curt Prüfer* and *War by Revolution*. I also want to thank Professor McKale for taking the time to read an early version of the book, and for his very helpful comments. Second, the author of any book in which T. E. Lawrence is a significant presence must acknowledge the trailblazing achievements of Jeremy Wilson in his authorized biography, *Lawrence of Arabia*. While I respectfully disagree with Mr. Wilson on several aspects of Lawrence's actions in Arabia, I am deeply indebted to the astounding amount of scholarly research he has done on Lawrence, which has greatly aided all of us who have followed in his wake.

I also benefited from a small group of advance readers on this project, some of whom read for historical accuracy and others for more stylistic concerns. In the first category, in addition to Donald McKale, I want to sincerely thank Roberto Mazza at Northern Illinois University and Thomas Goltz at Montana State University, both of whom were extremely generous with their time and deeply insightful with their suggestions. In the latter category, I wish to thank my friends Michael Fields, Wilson Van Law, and Seth McDowell for valiantly struggling through a problematic early draft of the book, and most especially Frances Shaw, who, without complaint, suffered through several more. Also in this category I must include my wonderful agent and dear friend, Sloan Harris, at International Creative Management Partners, a man who always knows how to ride that delicate line of simultaneously providing encouragement and cracking the whip.

Finally, while I can't recall this being the case for any other book I've written, I still remember the precise moment when the genesis of this one occurred: during a dinner conversation with my very good friend and editor, Bill Thomas, in the winter of 2008. I think we both instantly knew this was the book I needed to write—in fact, had been working toward writing for most of my journalistic career—and even if I have occasionally cursed Bill's name since then whilst in the midst of writing or research difficulties, I'm eternally grateful for the enthusiasm, patience, and diligence he's shown these past years in bringing the idea to fruition. I would also like to thank all the staff of Doubleday for tolerating my semi-permanent presence in their offices for several months while finishing the book's fact-checking and copyediting, especially Melissa Danaczko and Coralie

Hunter for their unstinting helpfulness in dealing with both my researching idiosyncrasies and computer illiteracy.

And last, I want to thank all the friends and family members who have been so tolerant of my canceled meetings, unreturned phone calls, and general absence of the past five years. With the book now done, I propose to be a much more attentive friend and relative going forward.

Notes

While I have drawn from a very wide variety of archival and secondary materials in this book, a few sources specifically related to the book's principal subjects proved especially valuable. As far as archival material is concerned, these are the diaries of Aaron Aaronsohn (NILI Museum and Archives, Israel); the diaries of Curt Prüfer (Hoover Institution, Stanford University); the unpublished memoir of William Yale (Boston University); and the World War I–era records of the British Foreign and War Offices (National Archives, Kew, England). Since some of those records were declassified within the past decade, for certain aspects of the book I had the opportunity to draw on material not previously available.

In addition, I am indebted to Donald McKale for his biography *Curt Prüfer: German Diplomat from the Kaiser to Hitler*, which is one of the few sources of material for Curt Prüfer's early life. With regard to T. E. Lawrence, John Mack's *A Prince of Our Disorder: The Life of T. E. Lawrence* is the most incisive psychological portrait ever drawn of the man. Most of all, I owe a tremendous debt of gratitude to Jeremy Wilson and his authorized biography, *Lawrence of Arabia*; due to Wilson's exhaustive research, his work remains the starting point for all serious Lawrence scholarship.

I also relied on a number of other primary and secondary materials for historical background on specific aspects in the book—for example, prewar Germany—and I have noted in corresponding endnotes those sources that I found particularly useful.

Abbreviations Used in Notes

BU—William Yale Papers, Boston University.

GLLD—George Lloyd Papers, Churchill College.

HO—Hoover Institution, Stanford University.

MSP—Mark Sykes Papers, Middle East Centre, St. Antony's College.

NARA—National Archives (U.S.).

PAAA—Political Archives of the German Foreign Ministry, Berlin (Politisches Archiv des Auswärtigen Amtes).

PRO—National Archives (formerly Public Records Office) (UK):

    PRO-ADM—Admiralty Records.

    PRO-CAB—British Cabinet Records.

    PRO-KV—Security Service Records.

    PRO-FO—Foreign Office Records.

    PRO-WO—War Office Records.

SADD—Sudan Archives, University of Durham.

UNH—William Yale Collection, University of New Hampshire.

UT—T. E. Lawrence Collection, University of Texas.

YU—William Yale Collection, Yale University.

ZY—NILI Museum and Archives, Zichron Ya'aqov, Israel.

Introduction

1   **On the morning:** Lawrence's official rank at this time was actually lieutenant colonel, but several weeks earlier he had been temporarily given full colonel status so as to facilitate his speedy return to Great Britain. As a result, from October 1918 onward, he was frequently referred to in official correspondence as "Colonel Lawrence."

2   **"I have some presents":** Lawrence to Liddell Hart, notes on interview of July 29, 1933, p. 2; UT Folder 1, File 1.

2   **As a boy:** Lawrence, *Seven Pillars*, p. 562.

3   **In subsequent years:** Lord Stamfordham, King's Private Secretary, to Lawrence (Shaw), January 1 and 17, 1928: A. W. Lawrence, *Letters to T. E. Lawrence*, pp. 184–86. See also Graves, *Lawrence and the Arabs*, pp. 392–93, and Churchill in A. W. Lawrence, *T. E. Lawrence by his Friends* (1937), 193–94.

4   **"a sideshow":** Lawrence, *Seven Pillars*, p. 274.

Chapter 1: Playboys in the Holy Land

9   **"I consider this new crisis":** Djemal Pasha, quoted in Aksakal, *The Ottoman Road to War*, p. 19.

10   **By dawn, the winds:** Yale, *It Takes So Long*, chapter 1, p. 10; BU Box 7, Folder 7.

10   **Now that the *khamsin* had passed:** Yale wrote several different, and slightly conflicting, accounts of his first meeting with T. E. Lawrence, including in his memoir, *It Takes So Long*. The most detailed, and the source for most information here, is his article "T. E. Lawrence: Scholar, Soldier, Statesman, Diplomat" (undated, but presumably written shortly after Lawrence's 1935 death); BU Box 6, Folder 1.

12   **The previous day:** Yale, *The Reminiscences of William Yale*, p. 7; Columbia University, Oral History Research Office, 1973.

13   **Fluent in Arabic:** McKale, *War by Revolution*, p. 22, n. 18.

Chapter 2: A Very Unusual Type

17 **A Very Unusual Type:** Many of the details on T. E. Lawrence's childhood and early years are drawn from the two most definitive books on the topic, John Mack's *A Prince of Our Disorder*, and Jeremy Wilson's *Lawrence of Arabia*; William Yale provided information about his childhood and youth in the "Prelude" to *It Takes So Long*, his unpublished memoir. For this period in Curt Prüfer's life, Donald McKale's *Curt Prüfer* is almost quite literally the only source available, his material drawn from interviews he conducted with Prüfer's son, Olaf, since deceased.

17 **"Can you make room":** Hogarth to Petrie, July 10, 1911, as cited by Wilson, *Lawrence of Arabia*, p. 85.

17 **"I think it time":** Lawrence, *The Home Letters*, p. 23.

18 **"We had a very happy childhood":** Robert Lawrence quoted in A. W. Lawrence, *T. E. Lawrence by His Friends* (1954 edition), p. 31.

19 **There, the couple assumed:** The genesis of the Lawrence family name was actually a good deal more complicated, for as T. E. Lawrence learned from his mother in 1919, she too had been born illegitimate. The name appearing on her birth certificate was Sarah Junner, and she had only adopted the Lawrence surname, that of her presumed father, as a teenager. This casualness with surnames might also help explain the apparent ease with which T. E. later assumed aliases of his own, trading in Thomas Edward Lawrence for John Hume Ross, and then Ross for Thomas Edward Shaw.

20 **"You can imagine":** Thomas (Chapman) Lawrence (undated); Bodleian MS Eng C 6740.

20 **He kept the information:** Lawrence to Charlotte Shaw, April 14, 1927, cited by Mack, *A Prince of Our Disorder*, p. 26.

20 **This wasn't the:** E. F. Hall in A. W. Lawrence, *T. E. Lawrence by His Friends* (1954 edition), pp. 44–45.

21 **"He was unlike":** H. R. Hall, as quoted in Wilson, *Lawrence of Arabia*, p. 25.

21 **These were not mere spankings:** Mack, *A Prince of Our Disorder*, p. 33.

22 **"I bathed today":** Lawrence, *The Home Letters*, pp. 65–66.

23 **"Well," Lawrence said:** Hogarth to Robert Graves, as quoted in Graves, *Lawrence and the Arabs*, p. 18.

23 **"The distances":** Doughty to Lawrence, February 3, 1909, in A. W. Lawrence, *Letters to T. E. Lawrence*, p. 37.

27 **"It is rather amusing":** Lawrence, *The Home Letters*, p. 106.

27 **"This is a glorious country":** Ibid., p. 103.

27 **"I will have such difficulty":** Ibid., p. 105.

28 **Tellingly, considering the schoolyard taunts:** McKale, *Curt Prüfer*, pp. 5; 152; 193–94 n. 5; 233 n. 28.

28 **But in contrast:** For the history of prewar Germany and the Wilhelmine era, I have primarily consulted Fischer, *Germany's Aims in the First World War*; Macdonogh, *The Last Kaiser*; and Cecil, *Wilhelm II*, vols. 1 and 2.

30 **Two years later:** Prüfer, *Personalbogen*, October 24, 1944; NARA T120, Roll 2539, Frame E309975.

31 **"The galleries and benches":** As translated by Olaf Prüfer in "Notes on My Father," unpublished memoir used by permission of Trina Prüfer.

31 **That winter, he:** Details on Prüfer's relationship with Frances Prüfer (née Pinkham) are at: NARA RG165, Entry 67, Box 379, File PF25794, Attachment 8.

33 **"Really, this country":** Lawrence, *The Home Letters*, p. 218.

34 **"the gospel of bareness":** Lawrence to Richards, July 15, 1918, in Garnett, *The Letters of T. E. Lawrence*, p. 239.

34 **"an interesting character":** Lawrence, *The Home Letters*, pp. 173–74.

34 **This passion also:** For the history of the Ottoman Empire and the rise of the Committee of Union and Progress, I have primarily consulted Aksakal, *The Ottoman Road to War in 1914*; Kent, *The Great Powers and the End of the Ottoman Empire*; and Shaw, *History of the Ottoman Empire and Modern Turkey*, vols. 1 and 2.

35   **In other European:** Lowther to Hardinge, May 29, 1910, as cited by Yapp, *The Making of the Modern Near East*, pp. 183–84.

37   **The adventurer finally set up:** Cecil, *The German Diplomatic Service*, p. 102.

37   **"Every autumn":** McMeekin, *The Berlin-Baghdad Express*, p. 25.

38   **Forwarded some of Oppenheim's:** Ibid., p. 22.

39   **In early 1909:** McKale, *War by Revolution*, p. 22.

39   **"I seem to have been":** Lawrence, *The Home Letters*, p. 217.

40   **"He was such a horrible person":** Ibid., p. 225.

42   **Just what that ideal:** For the history of Standard Oil and its breakup, see Chernow, *Titan*, and Yergin, *The Prize*.

43   **"My mind was":** Yale, *It Takes So Long*, chapter 1, p. 1.

44   **"You must not think":** Lawrence, *The Home Letters*, p. 447.

Chapter 3: Another and Another Nice Thing

45   **"Always my soul":** Lawrence, *Seven Pillars*, p. 277.

45   **"Then we took":** Lawrence, *The Home Letters*, p. 275.

46   **"I have got":** Lawrence to V. Richards, in Garnett, *The Letters of T. E. Lawrence*, pp. 160–61.

48   **And while William Yale:** Yale, *It Takes So Long*, undated early drafts, BU Box 8.

49   **"There." J. C. Hill:** Yale, *The Reminiscences of William Yale*, p. 6, Columbia University, Oral History Research Office, 1973.

49   **"from now on":** As cited by Florence, *Lawrence and Aaronsohn*, p. 91.

50   **Rather than make:** For details on Aaronsohn's childhood and early life, I have relied extensively on Florence, *Lawrence and Aaronsohn*, and Engle, *The Nili Spies*.

52   **While the notion of a return:** For the early history of Zionism, I have primarily drawn from Laqueur, *A History of Zionism*; O'Brien, *The Siege*; and Sachar, *A History of Israel*.

53   **"Before long":** Florence, *Lawrence and Aaronsohn*, pp. 90–91.

54   **Both the most likely:** Aaronsohn to Mack, "Aaron's Confession," October 9, 1916, p. 8, ZY.

54   **"he was like fire":** Lawrence, *Seven Pillars*, p. 239.

55   **"I expected to":** Newcombe in A. W. Lawrence, *T. E. Lawrence by His Friends* (1937 edition), p. 105.

55   **"We are obviously":** Lawrence, *The Home Letters*, p. 280.

56   **It was this ruse:** The most detailed account of the military and political motives behind the Zin expedition is in Moscrop's *Measuring Jerusalem*, chapter 8.

57   **"The Palestine Fund":** Lawrence, *The Home Letters*, p. 282.

59   **Most alarming to:** *Note Confidentielle*, Government of Egypt to the President of the Council of Ministers, November 11, 1911; PRO-FO 371/1114, File 44628.

59   **"unsuitable":** British government correspondence and reports related to the Prüfer khedival library dispute can be found in PRO-FO 371/1114, File 44628.

60   **"I am absolutely":** As cited by Cecil, *The German Diplomatic Service*, p. 102.

62   **"I photographed":** Lawrence to Leeds, February 28, 1914, in Garnett, *The Letters of T. E. Lawrence*, p. 165.

63   **"I learnt that":** Lawrence, *The Home Letters*, p. 287.

63   **Upon parting ways:** William Yale's account of the Kornub oil expedition is largely drawn from Yale, *It Takes So Long*, chapter 2.

64   **Caught up in:** British government correspondence related to the Socony-Palestine concession issue is held in PRO-FO 371/2124. See also Edelman to Secretary of State, April 10, 1914; NARA M353, Roll 67, document 867.6363/4.

66   **The bulk of:** Lawrence to Flecker, "Monday [June 1914]," in Garnett, *The Letters of T. E. Lawrence*, p. 171. While Lawrence did not specify on which Monday in June he was writing, it can be deduced that it was June 29 by a June 1 letter he wrote to his family from Carchemish. Discussing his upcoming journey home, Lawrence wrote that "you may look for me about the 25th. or so."

Chapter 4: To the Last Million

68   **"Sir: I have the honor":** Hollis to Lansing, November 9, 1914; NARA M353, Roll 6, Decimal 867.00/713.

69   **"It will not end":** Magnus, *Kitchener,* pp. 283–84.

70   **Over the next four years:** Stevenson, *1914–1918,* p. 54.

70   **in just a two-year span:** Keegan, *The First World War,* p. 7; J. Vallin, "La Mortalité par génération en France depuis 1899 [Mortality by Generation in France Since 1899]," *Travaux et Documents,* Cahier no. 63 (Paris: Presses Universitaires de France).

70   **"cannot be considered severe":** Haig, diary entry of July 2, 1916, as cited in Gilbert, *The Somme,* p. 93.

71   **Under orders from Kitchener:** Lawrence to Liddell Hart, in Graves and Hart, *T. E. Lawrence: Letters to His Biographers,* Pt. 2, p. 90.

71   **In early September:** Ibid.

72   **"short, cleansing thunderstorm":** As quoted in Fischer, *War of Illusions,* p. 542.

72   **"I am writing":** Lawrence to Rieder, September 18, 1914, in Garnett, *The Letters of T. E. Lawrence,* p. 185.

72   **If Lawrence hadn't:** William Yale's account of life in Jerusalem in late 1914 is largely drawn from Yale, *It Takes So Long,* chapter 2.

73   **Invoking a state:** NARA RG84, Entry 448, Volume 14.

76   **"preserve Ottoman neutrality":** Beaumont to Gray, August 3, 1913, File 35857, No. 605; and Tewfik Pasha to Grey, August 4, 1914, File 35844, No. 598, in Gooch & Temperly, *British Documents on the Origins of the War,* Vol. XI.

76   **Already by mid-September:** An excellent and fairly nonbiased account of the war tensions in Syria is to be found in the consulate diary maintained by the American consul in Damascus, John Dye; NARA RG84, Entry 350, Volume 101. An understandably more biased account is Alex Aaronsohn's *With the Turks in Palestine.*

77   **indeed, at the time of the accord's signing:** The secrecy of the Turkish-German alliance was zealously maintained by both sides. On July 29, 1914, while the secret pact with Enver was still being negotiated, General Liman von Sanders, the commander of the German military mission to Turkey, petitioned for permission to return to Germany in the event of war. Shown Sander's telegram, Kaiser Wilhelm noted in the margin, "Must stay there and also foment war and revolt against England. Doesn't he yet know of the intended alliance, under which he is to be Commander in Chief?!"

78   **In mid-August, the kaiser:** Oppenheim to Bethmann-Hollweg, August 18, 1914; NARA T137, Roll 143, Frames 16–21, Der Weltkrieg no. 11, Band 1.

78   **Even if he remained dubious:** Prüfer, *Diary,* September 8, 1914; HO.

79   **At these meetings:** Oppenheim to Bethmann-Hollweg, August 18, 1914; NARA T137, Roll 143, Frames 16–21, Der Weltkrieg no. 11, Band 1.

79   **"the handsomest man":** *New York Times,* April 20, 1915.

79   **"A man of stone":** Prüfer, *Diary,* September 7, 1914; HO.

79   **The Turkish war minister:** *Interrogation of Robert Mors,* October 10, 1914, pp. 4–5; PRO-FO 371/1972, File 66271.

80 "Even without [Turkey joining the] war": Mallet to Grey, September 15, 1914; PRO-FO 371/1970, f. 8.

80 "laughed at [the] idea": Mallet to Grey, October 6, 1914; PRO-FO 371/1970, f. 93.

80 "Because once I found": *Interrogation of Robert Mors*, October 10, 1914, p. 5; PRO-FO 371/1972, File 66271.

80 For his central role: McKale, *Curt Prüfer*, p. 31.

81 As Lawrence quipped: Lawrence to "Friend," in Garnett, *The Letters of T. E. Lawrence*, p. 188.

82 "I want to talk": Lawrence to Liddell Hart, August 1, 1933, in Graves and Hart, *T. E. Lawrence: Letters to His Biographers*, Pt. 2, p. 141.

82 "Turkey seems": Lawrence to Fontana, October 19, 1914, in Garnett, *The Letters of T. E. Lawrence*, p. 187.

83 "Now it's Cairo": Lawrence to Fontana, December 4, 1914, in ibid., p. 189.

83 "Aaron Aaronsohn watched": Florence, *Lawrence and Aaronsohn*, p. 119.

83 "to the delight of the street boys": Aaronsohn, *Present Economic and Political Conditions in Palestine*, p. 6, early 1917; PRO-FO 882/14, f. 328.

84 "were destroyed by": Aaronsohn (anonymous), "Syria: Economic and Political Conditions," *Arab Bulletin* no. 33 (December 4, 1916): 505.

84 Within days of Turkey joining: Kayali, *Arabs and Young Turks*, pp. 187–88.

84 Of course, this fatwa: Djemal Pasha, *Memories of a Turkish Statesman*, p. 204.

84 "generously forbidding": Aaronsohn (anonymous), "The Jewish Colonies," *Arab Bulletin*, no. 64 (September 27, 1917): 391.

85 It wasn't until the same commander: Alex Aaronsohn, "Saifna Ahmar, Ya Sultan!" *The Atlantic Monthly*, July 1916, Vol. 118.

85 For many of the Jewish émigrés: A number of historians have asserted that Djemal Pasha ordered the 1914–15 expulsion of Jews from Palestine as part of a general campaign to destroy the Jewish community, and none have made this assertion more forcefully than David Fromkin. On pp. 210–11 of *A Peace to End All Peace*, Fromkin contends that Djemal "took violent action against the Jewish settlers. Influenced by a bitterly anti-Zionist Ottoman official named Beha-ed-din, Djemal moved to destroy the Zionist settlements and ordered the expulsion of all foreign Jews—which is to say, most of Jewish Palestine." In fact, Djemal's December 1914 expulsion edict applied only to the citizens of belligerent nations, the same policy adopted by other warring nations at the outbreak of World War I, and was then soon amended to exempt British and French Jews. Furthermore, those "belligerent" Jews in Palestine slated for expulsion, chiefly Russian Jews, were given the choice of staying if they assumed Ottoman citizenship, an option unique to the Ottoman Empire. As a result of this comparatively lenient treatment and the many loopholes it provided, only a fraction of the estimated 85,000 Jews residing in prewar Palestine left or were forced from the territory, and certainly not the "most of Jewish Palestine" of Fromkin's estimation.

86 "I am always watched": Aaronsohn to Rosenwald, January 21, 1915; NARA RG84, Entry 58, Volume 378, Decimal 800.

87 "Woolley looks after": Brown, *The Letters of T. E. Lawrence*, p. 69.

88 "Jerusalem is a dirty town": Lawrence, "Syria: The Raw Material," written early 1915, *Arab Bulletin* no. 44 (March 12, 1917).

88 "to everyone on board ship": Yale, *It Takes So Long*, chapter 3, p. 1.

89 He also confirmed: Military Censor, *Statement of W. M. Yale*, November 17, 1914; PRO-WO 157/688.

90 "When he secured": Yale, *T. E. Lawrence: Scholar, Soldier, Statesman, Diplomat* (undated but 1935); BU Box 6, Folder 1.

90 With their Hebron road: Lawrence (unsigned and undated), handwritten notes on interview of William Yale; PRO-WO 158/689.

91 "Whenever he shook your hand": Morgenthau, *Ambassador Morgenthau's Story*, p. 120.

92   "gay, debonair, interested": Bliss, "Djemal Pasha: A Portrait," in *The Nineteenth Century and After*, vol. 86 (New York: Leonard Scott, July–December 1919), p. 1151.

92   "He had the ambition": Ibid., p. 1153.

93   "Never shall I forget": Djemal Pasha, *Memories of a Turkish Statesman*, pp. 141–42.

93   "And here is the only road": Ibid., p. 143.

94   "undoubtedly the carefully": Prüfer to Oppenheim, December 31, 1914; PAAA, Roll 21128, Der Weltkrieg no. 11g, Band 6.

Chapter 5: A Despicable Mess

95   "So far as Syria": Lawrence, *The Home Letters*, p. 303.

95   From his knowledge: Intelligence Department "Note," January 3, 1915; PRO-FO 371/2480, f. 137.

98   Understandably, the British : Details on the *Doris*-Alexandretta affair were related in a series of reports from U.S. consul J. B. Jackson, Aleppo, to U.S. Secretary of State Lansing, between December 22, 1914, and January 14, 1915; NARA RG84, Entry 81, Box 12, Decimal 820.

99   "We have been informed": Untitled Intelligence Department report advocating landing at Alexandretta, January 5, 1915; SADD Clayton Papers, File 694/3/7, p. 3.

99   "Our particular job": Lawrence to Hogarth, January 15, 1915, in Garnett, *The Letters of T. E. Lawrence*, p. 191.

99   "Everyone was absolutely": Djemal Pasha, *Memories of a Turkish Statesman*, p. 154.

100   "I used to talk": Ibid., pp. 154–55.

101   "I confess": Prüfer, *Diary*, January 26, 1915; HO.

101   "The enemy cruisers": Ibid., January 30, 1915.

101   As it was, the approximately: Erickson, *Ordered to Die*, p. 71.

101   "Despite all our agitation": Prüfer to von Wangenheim and Oppenheim, February 9, 1915; NARA T137, Roll 23, Frame 862.

102   "The holy war": Prüfer to Oppenheim, February 9, 1915; NARA T137, Roll 23, Frame 868.

103   Instead, the war strategists: For a detailed description of the Alexandretta-Dardanelles debate in the British government, see Gottlieb, *Studies in Secret Diplomacy*, pp. 77–87.

104   Even the most pessimistic: M.O.2 report, "Expedition to Alexandretta," January 11, 1915, p. 2; PRO-WO 106/1570.

104   "Taking the Turkish Army": P. P. Graves, "Report on Turkish Military Preparations and Political Intrigues Having an Attack on Egypt as Their Object," November 10, 1914; PRO-FO 371/1970, f. 187.

105   "So far as Syria": Lawrence to parents, February 20, 1915, in Lawrence, *The Home Letters*, p. 303.

105   As the Allied fleet: Gottlieb, *Studies in Secret Diplomacy*, p. 109.

105   "Can you get someone": Lawrence to Hogarth, March 18, 1915, in Garnett, *The Letters of T. E. Lawrence*, pp. 193–94.

106   Sure enough, at about 2 p.m.: Hickey, *Gallipoli*, p. 72.

107   In various geological: Manuel, *Realities of American-Palestine Relations*, p. 267. Also, "Mines and Quarries of Palestine in 1921 by the Geological Adviser,"; NARA M353, Roll 87, document 867N.63/1.

107   Just prior to Yale's return: Cole, director of Socony, to Under-Secretary of State Polk, September 18, 1919; UNH Box 2.

107   The answer: A half-million more: Cole, director of Socony, to Under-Secretary of State Polk, May 5, 1919; NARA RG59, Central Decimal File, 1920–1929, document 467.11st25/31.

107   It had no intention: Yale, *It Takes So Long*, chapter 4, p. 3, and pp. 24–25.

108   To this end: Ibid., chapter 3, p. 12, and chapter 4, p. 3.

109 "Silence!": Lewis, "An Ottoman Officer in Palestine, 1914–1918," in Kushner, *Palestine in the Late Ottoman Period*, p. 404.

109 "I now can grant": Bliss, "Djemal Pasha: A Portrait," in *The Nineteenth Century and After*, vol. 86 (New York: Leonard Scott, July–December 1919), p. 1156.

109 "Upon peeking out": Ballobar, *Jerusalem in World War I*, p. 55.

110 They told of entire orchards: While perhaps an exaggeration, Alex Aaronsohm claimed to have personally witnessed "Arab babies, left by their mothers in the shade of some tree, whose faces had been devoured by the oncoming swarms of locusts before their screams had been heard." Alex Aaronsohn, *With the Turks in Palestine*, p. 51.

110 "Your Excellency": As quoted by Florence, *Lawrence and Aaronsohn*, p. 129; Engle, *The Nili Spies*, p. 45.

110 If any petty officials: Engle, *The Nili Spies*, p. 60.

112 The result had been: For details on the history of Hussein–Young Turk relations, see Antonius, *The Arab Awakening*, pp. 125–58; Baker, *King Husain and the Kingdom of Hejaz*, pp. 12–45; Kayali, *Arabs and Young Turks*, pp. 144–73.

113 "English through and through": Prüfer to Oppenheim, November 3, 1914; NARA T137, Roll 23, Frame 213.

114 Instead, the wily old emir: Prüfer to Metternich, January 22, 1916; NARA T130, Roll 457, Turkei 65, Band 38.

115 "We had no literary": Storrs, *Memoirs*, p. 202.

116 "I found myself": Ibid., p. 135.

116 "Tell Storrs to send": Kitchener to Consul-General, Cairo, September 24, 1914; PRO-FO 141/460.

116 "immediate followers": Antonius, *The Arab Awakening*, p. 132.

116 "Great Britain will guarantee": Draft of letter from Kitchener to Sherif Abdalla, November 1914; PRO-FO 141/460.

118 "The Med-Ex came": Lawrence to Hogarth, April 20, 1915, in Garnett, *The Letters of T. E. Lawrence*, p. 196.

118 Most shocking of all: Ibid., p. 197.

119 Incredibly, it seems: As noted by Guinn in *British Strategy and Politics*, p. 70, "This drastic change in policy of what now became the Dardanelles *campaign*—from primarily naval to exclusively military—had been decided on the spot in a matter of moments without the strain of taking thought."

119 "Arabian affairs have": Lawrence to Hogarth, April 26, 1915, in Garnett, *The Letters of T. E. Lawrence*, p. 198.

119 At about 6:15: The initial Gallipoli landings of April 25, 1915, have been written about many times, most notably in the books of Alan Moorehead and Peter Hart, both entitled *Gallipoli*. From a standpoint of military science, perhaps the most authoritative account is to be found in Robin Prior's *Gallipoli: The End of the Myth*.

120 "the sea near": Weldon, *Hard Lying*, pp. 68–69.

121 Having learned of Hussein's: For details on Faisal's 1915 journey to Damascus and Constantinople, see Dawn, *From Ottomanism to Arabism*, pp. 26–31; Tauber, *The Arab Movements in World War I*, pp. 57–67.

Chapter 6: The Keepers of Secrets

124 "You know, men": Lawrence, *The Home Letters*, p. 304.

124 "We edit a daily": Lawrence to Bell, April 18, 1915, in Brown, *The Letters of T. E. Lawrence*, p. 71.

125 So a new assault: Prüfer to von Wangenheim, February 9, 1915; NARA T137, Roll 23, Frame 862.

126   "bitter, practical experience": Prüfer to (illegible), February 24, 1915; NARA T137, Roll 24, Frame 390.

126   It had been in Jerusalem: The early connections between Prüfer and Minna Weizmann are described in McKale, *Curt Prüfer*, p. 42.

126   "my dear Fanny": See Prüfer, *Diary*, October 26, 1914; January 27, 1915; May 5 and June 25, 1916; HO.

127   "people who can": Prüfer to Djemal Pasha, March 1, 1915; NARA T137, Roll 24, Frames 271–73; PAAA, Roll 21131, Der Weltkrieg no. 11g, Band 9.

127   "will try to steal": Ibid.

127   While Rothschild made: Cohn, "Report," July 16, 1915; NARA T137, Roll 24, Frame 697.

128   "She revealed": Steinbach to Ziemke, August 3, 1915; NARA T137, Roll 24, Frame 779.

128   That lineage may: McKale, *Curt Prüfer*, p. 203 n. 18.

129   "Curt Prüfer is indispensable": Von Wangenheim to Bethmann-Hollweg, in cover letter, March 3, 1915; NARA T137, Roll 23, Frame 862.

129   By most accounts, Frank: See Lawrence, *The Home Letters of T. E. Lawrence and His Brothers*, pp. 653–720.

129   "I haven't written": Lawrence to family, June 4, 1915; Bodleian MS Eng C 6740.

130   "Poor Dear Mother": Lawrence to Sarah Lawrence, undated; Bodleian MS Eng C 6740.

131   In an emotional address: Dawn, *From Ottomanism to Arabism*, p. 30; Djemal Pasha, *Memories of a Turkish Statesman*, p. 213.

131   The most recent bout: Lewy, *The Armenian Massacres in Ottoman Turkey*, p. 28. The number of Armenians killed in the so-called Hamidian Massacres is a topic of enduring historical dispute, with estimates ranging from a low of thirteen thousand by the Turkish government to a high of three hundred thousand by some Armenian historians. Probably most reliable is Lewy's figure of between fifty and eighty thousand.

132   "revolutionary and political": As cited by Lewy, ibid., p. 151.

132   "these new crimes": US Department of State telegram to US Embassy, Constantinople, May 29, 1915; NARA M353, Roll 43, document 867.4016/67.

132   "authorized and compelled": As cited by Lewy, *The Armenian Massacres in Ottoman Turkey*, p. 153.

132   by best estimate: The most authoritative history on the 1915–16 Armenian tragedy is Lewy, *The Armenian Massacres in Ottoman Turkey*.

132   The consensus among: As Armenian historian Vanakh Dadrian notes in *The Key Elements in the Turkish Denial of the Armenian Genocide*, p. 54, "It should be recognized in this respect that not only IVth Army Commander Cemal [*sic*] in Syria and Palestine, but also IIIrd Army Commander Vehib Pasha in eastern Turkey, despite their strong ties to the Ittihad Party, refused to embrace the secret genocidal agenda of the party's top leadership and whenever they could they tried to resist and discourage the attendant massacres."

132   Reiterating a March decree: As cited by Lewy, *The Armenian Massacres in Ottoman Turkey*, p. 197. See also Metternich to Bethmann-Hollweg, December 9, 1915; NARA T139, Roll 463, Band 40.

133   By September: Lewy, *The Armenian Massacres in Ottoman Turkey*, p. 192.

133   "the Arabs did not speak": Aaronsohn, *Diary*, April 1, 1915, ZY.

134   In a particularly outrageous case: Ibid., April 27, 1915.

135   "I have lived among": Quoted in Gorni, *Zionism and the Arabs*, p. 56.

135   "Our worst enemy": Quoted in Engle, *The Nili Spies*, p. 47.

136   The trip down had: William Yale's account of his 1915 journey to Jerusalem and his meeting with Djemal Pasha is in Yale, *It Takes So Long*, chapter 4.

139   "numerous humanitarian services": *New York Times*, July 29, 1915.

139   "I wonder when": Lawrence to Will Lawrence, July 7, 1915; Bodleian MS Eng C 6740.

140 His name was Mohammed al-Faroki: Due to the pivotal role he played in shaping British policy in the Near East in 1915–16, Mohammed al-Faroki remains one of the more enigmatic figures to emerge from the period. Since he is believed to have been killed in 1922 during a tribal war in Iraq, many of the questions surrounding him are likely to stay unanswered.

New attention was focused on Faroki by David Fromkin in his 1989 book *A Peace to End All Peace*, in which Fromkin repeatedly refers to the "hoax" that Faroki perpetrated, and the extraordinary effect his actions had on world events. To wit, "not only the McMahon letters, but also—and more importantly—the negotiations with France, Russia, and later Italy that ultimately resulted in the Sykes-Picot-Sazanov Agreement and subsequent Allied secret treaty understandings were among the results of Lieutenant al-Faruqi's [*sic*] hoax."

If this gives Faroki more credit than is probably his due, Fromkin also never specifies just what his alleged hoax consisted of. Instead, his charge appears to center on two broad points: that Faroki exaggerated his position in al-Ahd to both the British and Emir Hussein in order to maneuver himself into an intermediary role; and that he lied about the strength and ability of al-Ahd and al-Fatat to stage a large-scale revolt in Syria. In essence, Fromkin alleges, Faroki sold the British on a false bill of goods that he couldn't possibly deliver.

But when taking as a starting point that Faroki was an ardent Arab nationalist who was deeply suspicious of the Western colonial powers, it's hard to see how either of these accusations rise to the level of a "hoax." While Faroki almost certainly exaggerated the strength and capability of the Syrian would-be rebels in order to exact greater concessions from the British, in a time of war did this make him a fraud or a good negotiator?

This is much more than a question of labels or semantics, however. In Fromkin's view, because of Faroki's hoax, the agreement Hussein reached with the British via the McMahon-Hussein Correspondence was purchased with counterfeit coin (p. 186). To wit (p. 219), "The [British] Arab Bureau believed that the [Arab] uprising would draw support throughout the Moslem and Arabic-speaking worlds. Most important of all, it believed that the revolt would draw support from what the British believed to be a largely Arabic-speaking Ottoman army . . . In the event, the Arab revolt for which Hussein hoped never took place. No Arabic units of the Ottoman army came over to Hussein. No political or military figures of the Ottoman Empire defected to him and the Allies. The powerful secret military organization that al-Faruqi [*sic*] had promised would rally to Hussein failed to make itself known."

The problem with Fromkin's thesis is that, by the time of the Arab revolt in June 1916, neither the British nor Hussein believed anything of the sort. As Hussein informed McMahon four months prior, the Syrian wing of the prospective revolt had been severely weakened due to "the tyrannies of the [Turkish] government there," which had left "only a few" of the "persons upon whom they [the conspirators] could depend." Not only does Fromkin make no mention of this famous warning from Hussein, he also fails to note that the British had fully taken this news into account. As Gilbert Clayton, the head of military intelligence in Egypt, wrote in an April 22, 1916, memorandum (PRO-FO 882/4, f. 92–3), "the Sherif [Hussein] allows that Syria is useless for revolutionary purposes." In light of this development, Clayton noted in the same memorandum, "High Commissioner [McMahon] feels very strongly that at present the Sherif should be advised to confine himself to securing the Railway, and clearing the Turks out of the Hedjaz."

In short, far from being blindsided by the limited scope of the Arab revolt, British authorities had known well ahead of time exactly what they were—and were not—getting by supporting it; in fact, it was they who had urged its limited scope.

140 Testament to the importance: Hamilton to Kitchener, August 25, 1915; PRO-FO 371/2490.

140 Once Gallipoli started: In addition to Ian Hamilton's report of August 25, Faroki's testimony is detailed in Clayton to McMahon, October 11, 1915; PRO-FO 371/2486, f. 223–28; Faroki's own statement, entitled " 'A' Statement of Sherif El Ferugi"; PRO-FO 371/2486, f. 229–38; and in "Notes on Captain X," and "Statement of Captain X," September 12, 1915, Intelligence Department, War Office, Cairo; PRO-FO 882/2.

142   **"far more than he":** Storrs, "Memorandum," August 19, 1915; PRO-FO 371/2486, f. 150.

142   **"reserve to themselves":** Cited in Antonius, *The Arab Awakening*, pp. 414–15.

143   **A week later:** Florence, *Lawrence and Aaronsohn*, p. 172.

145   **"There is going to be":** Lawrence, *The Home Letters*, p. 310.

146   **"Things are boiling":** As quoted by Wilson, *Lawrence*, p. 223.

146   **a French liaison officer:** Ibid, p. 224.

146   **"French public opinion":** Panouse to Robertson, November 13, 1915; reprinted in PRO-WO 33/747, p. 811.

147   **By acquiescing:** Liddell Hart, *Colonel Lawrence: The Man Behind the Legend*, p. 38.

147   **"I didn't go say goodbye":** Lawrence to Sarah Lawrence, undated; Bodleian MS Eng C 6740.

148   **"I'm writing":** Lawrence, *The Home Letters*, pp. 310–11.

Chapter 7: Treachery

149   **"It seems to me":** Macdonogh to Nicolson, January 7, 1916; PRO-FO 882/16.

149   **"and partly because":** Lawrence to Leeds, November 16, 1915, in Brown, *The Letters of T. E. Lawrence*, pp. 78–79.

150   **A few smaller points:** The precise nature of the agreement reached between Emir Hussein and the British government in the so-called McMahon-Hussein Correspondence remains one of the most contentious points of Middle Eastern history. Through countless books on the subject, historians of all stripes have managed to squeeze from these brief letters an interpretation neatly suited to their thesis or political bias.

For many, a chief starting point has been to emphasize the often awkward grammatical structure of the letters—an archaic floridness on the part of Emir Hussein, a carefully calculated obtuseness on the part of Henry McMahon—to suggest that radically divergent interpretations can be drawn, and that no deliberate deception was committed by the British. Indeed, by focusing on McMahon's carefully inserted modifiers, a number of historians, most notably Isaiah Friedman, Elie Kedourie, and David Fromkin, have put forward the assertion that the British didn't actually promise Hussein anything at all. Without such a promise, so this line of argument goes, Britain was at perfect liberty to enter into its subsequent compact on the Middle East with its European allies through the so-called Sykes-Picot Agreement.

This argument, however, falters under the weight of both common sense and contemporary evidence. For any impartial observer supplied with a map of the region and the few minutes necessary to read the full McMahon-Hussein Correspondence, it becomes manifestly obvious just what Emir Hussein believed he was agreeing to. What's more, the actions of the British government at the time make clear that it too believed promises had been made to Hussein, and that those promises were undercut by Sykes-Picot. That is evidenced by their zealous efforts to keep the Sykes-Picot Agreement a secret from Hussein for nearly two years, a conspiracy of silence that undoubtedly would have continued if the agreement's existence hadn't been revealed by Russia's Bolshevik government.

154   **That estimate was initially:** Sykes to Cox, undated but late November 1915; PRO-FO 882/2.

154   **It was not a pretty:** Sykes to General E. C. Callwell, Director of Military Operations, War Office, August 2, 1915; PRO-FO 882/13, f. 367–71.

155   **"the imaginative advocate":** Lawrence, *Seven Pillars*, p. 58.

156   **"aptitude for treason":** Prüfer to Djemal Pasha, December 5, 1915; PAAA, Roll 21138, Der Weltkrieg no. 11g, Band 16.

157   "At the slightest indiscretion": Metternich to Bethmann-Hollweg, December 23, 1915; PAAA, Roll 21138, Der Weltkrieg no. 11g, Band 16.

159   Sarah fainted away: Aaronsohn, "Addendum to 'Report of an inhabitant of Athlit, Mount Carmel, Syria,' " undated but November 1916; PRO-FO 371/2783.

160   The one precondition: Engle, *The Nili Spies*, pp. 62–64; Florence, *Lawrence and Aaronsohn*, p. 205. Engle, Florence, and other Aaronsohn biographers have rendered this incident in rather more dire terms, alleging that Feinberg was tortured in Beersheva and faced imminent threat of execution in Jerusalem. Aaronsohn's diary for the period would seem to contradict this, however, considering that he noted learning of Feinberg's detention from a telegram Feinberg himself sent from Beersheva on December 29. Further, Aaronsohn's subsequent diary entries indicate little sense of urgency in resolving Feinberg's predicament, nor does the fact that Aaronsohn waited for two weeks after learning of it to make his appeal to Djemal Pasha.

161   It wasn't until a reply: Chamberlain to Hardinge, October 22, 1915; PRO-FO 371/2486, f. 254.

162   In other words: The French "escape clause" in McMahon's October 24 letter to Hussein was carefully constructed at the senior levels of the British government, as evidenced by correspondence between McMahon and the Foreign Office in PRO-FO 371/2486, f. 204–8.

162   That the French: Tanenbaum, *France and the Arab Middle East*, p. 8.

162   British officials expressed: "Results of second meeting of Committee to discuss Arab question and Syria," November 23, 1915; PRO-FO 882/2, f. 156–60.

163   Rather than be part: Sykes and Picot joint memorandum, "Arab Question," January 5, 1916; PRO-FO 371/2767. Of all the controversies that continue to surround the McMahon-Hussein Correspondence, perhaps the most specious is the assertion that the territory of Palestine was specifically excluded from the proposed independent Arab nation, and that Hussein was fully aware of this. The chief proponent of this assertion has been Isaiah Friedman in his frequently cited books *The Question of Palestine* and *Palestine: A Twice-Promised Land?*, with his claims echoed by Fromkin in *A Peace to End All Peace*.

The foundation for this assertion rests with one of the "modifications" McMahon proposed in his crucial letter of October 24, 1915, to Hussein, in which he wrote that the "portions of Syria lying to the west of the districts of Damascus, Homs, Hama and Aleppo cannot be said to be purely Arab, and should be excluded from the limits demanded [for an independent Arab nation]." With that as a starting point, Friedman goes on to list the many opportunities Hussein had after October 24 to raise an objection to the exclusion of Palestine, but consistently failed to do so. As he writes in *The Question of Palestine* (p. 90), "On receipt of McMahon's letter of 24 October, Hussein argued that Mesopotamia and the vilayets of Beirut and Aleppo 'are Arab and should therefore be under Muslim Government,' though significantly he refrained from placing Palestine in the same category. Again on 1 January 1916 he reminded the High Commissioner that after the conclusion of the war he would claim 'Beirut and its coastal regions' but made no mention of the sanjak of Jerusalem." From such omissions on Hussein's part, Friedman concludes, Hussein had clearly tacitly ceded control of Palestine in his dialogue with McMahon.

Except the first problem with this thesis is that no portion of Palestine lies "to the west of the districts of Damascus, Homs, Hama and Aleppo." Instead, that designation corresponds *roughly*—roughly because it's unclear exactly what McMahon meant by "districts"—to modern-day Lebanon and the coastal areas of modern-day Syria; Palestine/Israel lies well to the south. An even larger problem is that, over the course of his correspondence with Hussein, McMahon carefully specified each region that he was seeking "modifications" for, and at no time did he ever mention Palestine. As for why Hussein himself never raised the issue of Palestine with McMahon, Friedman and other proponents of this thesis seem determined to avoid the most obvious explanation: since Palestine fell outside of the exclusion zone McMahon had described, and since McMahon had never included it in his "modifications," there was simply nothing to discuss?

163   **As T. E. Lawrence:** Lawrence to Liddell Hart, notes from interview, undated; UT, Folder 1, File 1.

164   **"if properly handled":** Lawrence, "The Politics of Mecca," forwarded by McMahon to Grey, February 7, 1916; PRO-FO 371/2771, f. 151–56.

165   **"essentially a trivial":** As quoted in Wilson, *Lawrence of Arabia*, p. 249.

165   **"with all the narrow minded":** Ibid.

165   **"and if it prevailed":** Lawrence, "The Politics of Mecca," p. 1; PRO-FO 371/2771, f. 152.

166   **the 36th Indian Infantry Brigade:** Millar, *Death of an Army*, pp. 204–5.

168   **army of twelve thousand:** There is a considerable disparity in historical sources over the size of the Kut garrison, with numbers ranging between nine and twelve thousand. This disparity is explained by the inclusion or omission of so-called camp followers the estimates—the number of actual soldiers was closer to the lower estimate—but since the camp followers would share in their grim fate, it seems appropriate to include them.

168   **Perhaps in recognition of his uneven achievements:** For details on the battle of Dujaila, and Aylmer's actions, see PRO-WO 158/668, f. 75–127.

168   **"My dear Cox":** McMahon to Cox, March 20, 1916, as quoted by Wilson, *Lawrence of Arabia*, p. 259.

169   **after the war:** A. W. Lawrence, *T. E. Lawrence by his Friends* (1937 edition), p. 301.

170   **"undesirable and inconvenient":** Lake to Secretary of State (India), March 30, 1916; PRO-FO 371/2768, f. 36.

170   **"My general information":** Robertson to Lake, March 16, 1916; PRO-WO 158/669, no. 197.

171   **It had all the trappings:** William Yale's account of life in wartime Jerusalem is largely drawn from Yale, *It Takes So Long*, chapters 4 and 5.

173   **despite "his harmless appearance":** Ballobar, *Jerusalem in World War I*, p. 75.

174   **"[Djemal] says":** Edelman to Socony, Constantinople, March 29, 1916; NARA RG 84, Entry 350, Volume 30, Decimal 300—general.

176   **"I studied his face":** Yale, *It Takes So Long*, chapter 5, pp. 7–8.

176   **"At a dance":** Herbert, *Mons, Kut and Anzac*, p. 232.

177   **"Townshend's guns":** Herbert diary, as quoted by Wilson, *Lawrence*, p. 272. In the published version (Herbert: *Mons, Kut and Anzac*, p. 228), the sentence was changed to "We have got very little to bargain with as far as the Turks are concerned, practically only the exchange of prisoners."

178   **"Perhaps one of our [Turkish] men":** Herbert, *Mons, Kut and Anzac*, p. 234.

178   **"they gave us a most excellent dinner":** Lawrence, *The Home Letters*, p. 324.

178   **With most put to work:** While postwar British governments were meticulous in tabulating the number of British soldiers at Kut who had died in captivity—1755 out of 2592, according to Crowley (*Kut 1916*, p. 253)—they were far less with their Indian counterparts, or even in repatriating those who had survived. According to Millar (*Death of an Army*, p. 284), Indian survivors of Kut continued to show up in their native villages, having somehow managed their own passage home, as late as 1924.

178   **In a testament to the element:** Nash, *Chitral Charlie*, pp. 274–79.

179   **"Effendim":** Djemal Pasha, *Memories of a Turkish Statesman*, p. 216.

179   **"I should also draw":** Ibid., pp. 216–17.

182   **"By brute force":** Lawrence, *Seven Pillars*, p. 59.

182   **"British generals":** Ibid., p. 386.

182   **"We pay for":** Ibid., p. 25.

183   **So thoroughly did the censors:** This is to be found in the Wingate Papers at Durham University, in File W/137/7.

184   **It was the signal:** Baker, *King Husain and the Kingdom of Hejaz*, pp. 98–99. Baker gives the revolt start date as June 10.

Chapter 8: The Battle Joined

187 **"The Hejaz war"**: T. E. Lawrence, *"Military Notes,"* November 3, 1916; PRO-FO 882/5, f. 63.

187 **"A detonation about equal"**: Unless otherwise noted, all of Storrs's observations and quotes related to the October 1916 Jeddah trip are taken from his "Extract from Diary" (PRO-FO 882/5, f. 22–38) or from his partially reproduced personal diary in Storrs, *Memoirs*, pp. 186–95.

187 **On his two earlier passages:** Barr, *Setting the Desert on Fire*, pp. 9–10.

188 **"To the most honoured"**: Unless otherwise noted, all of Storrs's observations and quotes related to his June 1916 visit to Arabia are drawn from his untitled report to High Commissioner McMahon, June 10, 1916 (PRO-FO 371/2773), or from his partially reproduced personal diary in Storrs, *Memoirs*, pp. 169–76.

189 **Lending all this momentous activity:** Storrs, *Memoirs*, p. 176.

190 **In that case:** While Murray's resistance to assisting the Arab Revolt was of long standing, he expressed it most forcefully at a meeting of senior British military staff in Ismailia, Egypt, on September 12, 1916 (PRO-FO 882/4, f. 338–47).

191 **Indeed, well into the autumn:** Wilson to Arab Bureau, October 10, 1916; PRO-FO 882/5, f. 8–9. Also Clayton to Wingate, October 12, 1916; PRO-FO 882/5, f. 12–14.

192 **"it was quickly apparent"**: Storrs, *Memoirs*, p. 203.

192 **"I took every opportunity"**: Lawrence, *Seven Pillars*, p. 63.

193 **In just this way:** While it is technically true that Lawrence went to Jeddah in no official capacity, Gilbert Clayton worked behind the scenes to have him accompany Storrs so that, jointly, they could return with "a good appreciation of the situation" in Arabia (Clayton to Wingate, October 9, 1916; SADD Wingate Papers, W/141/3/35). This, in turn, was tied to Clayton's efforts to have Lawrence transferred back to the Arab Bureau.

193 **"the heat of Arabia"**: Much of Lawrence's account of his October 1916 journey to Arabia is drawn from Lawrence, *Seven Pillars*, book 1, chapters 8–16, pp. 65–108.

193 **"totally unsuited"**: Storrs Papers, Pembroke College, Cambridge, as cited by Barr, *Setting the Desert on Fire*, p. 65.

193 **In fact, the chief reason:** Ibid.

195 **"in a state of admiration"**: Storrs, *Memoirs*, p. 189.

195 **"playing for effect"**: Lawrence, *Seven Pillars*, p. 67.

196 **"The un-French absence"**: Storrs, *Memoirs*, p. 190.

197 **Promotion came steadily:** Porte, Lt. Col. Remi, "General Édouard Brémond (1868–1948)," *Cahiers du CESAT* (bulletin of the College of Higher Learning of the Army of France), issue 15 (March 2009).

197 **"a practicing light"**: Lawrence, *Seven Pillars*, p. 111.

198 **Accompanying a group:** Details on Brémond's mission to Egypt and the Hejaz are found in PRO-FO 882/5, f. 299–306, and PRO-FO 371/2779, File 152849.

198 **Should Medina fall:** Lawrence memorandum for Clayton, November 17, 1916 (SADD Clayton Papers, 694/4/42). Also Brémond to Defrance, October 16, 1917, as cited by Wilson, *Lawrence of Arabia*, p. 309.

199 **Incredibly, this information:** Brémond received his first intimation of this via a cable from Field Marshal Joffre on November 27, 1916, as reproduced in Brémond, *Le Hedjaz dans la Guerre Mondiale*, p. 97.

199 **"Very few Turkish"**: Storrs, *Memoirs*, p. 204.

202 **"Is fond of riding"**: Lawrence, *The Sherifs*, October 27, 1916; PRO-FO 882/5, f. 40.

202 **"His manner was dignified"**: Lawrence, *Seven Pillars*, p. 76.

202 **"if Faisal should"**: Ibid., p. 77.

203 **"Each hill and valley"**: Ibid., p. 83.

204 **To Lawrence, it underscored:** Lawrence made oblique reference to these previously unknown water sources in his contemporaneous reports, "Feisal's Operations," October 30, 1916, and "Military Notes," November 3, 1916; PRO-FO 882/5, f. 47–8, and f. 63.

Chapter 9: The Man Who Would Be Kingmaker

207 "[Faisal] is hot tempered": Lawrence, *The Sherifs*, October 27, 1916; PRO-FO 882/5, f. 41.

209 By arguing for this: Wilson, *Notes on the Military Situation in the Hedjaz*, September 11, 1916; PRO-FO 882/4, f. 329.

210 "a man who can't stand the racket": Minutes of Conference held at Commander-in-Chief's Residence, Ismailia, September 12, 1916; PRO-FO 882/4, f. 333.

211 Noticing Lawrence had: Boyle, *My Naval Life*, p. 99.

211 "Red-haired men": Lawrence, *Seven Pillars*, p. 143.

213 Wingate fired off: Wingate to Foreign Office, November 2, 1916; PRO-WO 158/603.

213 As for just what size: *Arabian Report* no. 16 (November 2, 1916); PRO-CAB 17/177, p. 2. Also, Wilson to Arab Bureau, November 1, 1916; PRO-WO 158/603, f. 49A.

214 "proves that Rabegh": Parker to Arab Bureau, November 2, 1916; PRO-WO 158/603, f. 17b.

215 "[Faisal] talks a lot": Brémond report, January 2, 1917, as quoted by Tanenbaum, *France and the Arab Middle East*, p. 19.

216 "full of German stuff": Aaronsohn, *Diary*, October 25, 1916; ZY.

217 That effort badly backfired: Katz, *The Aaronsohn Saga*, p. 6.

217 "The game is in play": Aaronsohn, *Diary*, October 25, 1916; ZY.

217 In Copenhagen, he: Engle, *The Nili Spies*, p. 77.

218 "Nobody can say": Aaronsohn "confession" to Julius Mack, October 9, 1916, pp. 12–13; ZY.

219 "If I were with the British": Thomson, *My Experiences at Scotland Yard*, pp. 225–26, and *The Scene Changes*, pp. 387–88.

219 "Here, I had the good": Aaronsohn to Alex and Rivka Aaronsohn, October 28, 1916; ZY.

221 "It was not easy": Lawrence, *Seven Pillars*, p. 57.

222 "moral and material": Wingate to Clayton, November 7, 1916; PRO-WO 158/603, f. 79A.

222 "they cannot provide": French Embassy (London) to Foreign Office, November 8, 1916, as quoted by Wilson, *Lawrence of Arabia*, p. 325.

222 The sirdar further: Wingate to Robertson, November 12, 1916, as repeated by Wingate to Murray, November 18, 1916; PRO-WO 158/627, f. 10A, p. 4.

223 "They are our very good": Lawrence, Report, November 17, 1916; PRO-WO 106/1511, f. 34–36.

224 "They say, 'Above' ": Ibid.

225 In a fit of pique: Parker to Wingate, July 6, 1916; SADD Wingate Papers, W/138/3/69.

226 "There is no good": Minutes of Conference held at Commander-in-Chief's Residence, Ismailia, September 12, 1916; PRO-FO 882/4, f. 333.

226 "I was astonished": Lawrence, *Seven Pillars*, p. 112.

226 "I have just seen": Murray to Wingate, November 17, 1916; PRO-WO 158/627, f. 7A.

227 "said to have an intimate": Robertson, *The Occupation of El Arish*, November 19, 1916; PRO-WO 106/1511, f. 34.

227 "Captain Lawrence's statement": Sykes, Appreciation of Arabian Report, No. XVIII, November 20, 1916; PRO-CAB 17/177.

227 "whom I knew to be": Cited by Wilson, *Lawrence*, pp. 327–28.

227 "They began to be": Lawrence, *Seven Pillars*, p. 112.

228 "there is apparently lack": Robertson to Murray, November 22, 1916; PRO-WO 158/604, f. 75A.

228 **"I have always taken"**: Murray to Robertson, November 23, 1916; PRO-WO 158/604, f. 76A.

228 **"If I brooded continually"**: Aaronsohn, *Diary*, November 11, 1916; ZY.

229 **"Of course we do not"**: W.T.I.D., *Report of Inhabitant of Athlit*, November 2, 1916; PRO-FO 371/2783.

229 **"I was probably too"**: Aaronsohn, *Diary*, November 24, 1916; ZY.

230 **In March 1915**: Schneer, *The Balfour Declaration*, pp. 135–45.

231 **"Arab Christians and Moslems alike"**: Sykes to Buchanan, March 14, 1916; PRO-FO 371/2767, File 938.

231 **"I regret complicated"**: Ibid.

231 **"obliterate from his"**: Edward Grey notes on Sykes's cable to Buchanan, March 15, 1916; PRO-FO 371/2767, File 938.

231 **"If Rabbi Gaster"**: Adelson, *Mark Sykes*, p. 213.

232 **"it would be reasonable"**: Friedman, *The Question of Palestine*, p. 122.

232 **"FitzMaurice is"**: Aaronsohn, *Diary*, October 30, 1916; ZY.

233 **"Pending Newcombe's arrival"**: Wingate to Clayton, November 11, 1916; PRO-WO 158/604, f. 18A.

233 **"The already known state of mind"**: Joffre to Brémond, November 27, 1916, as cited by Brémond, *Le Hedjaz dans la Guerre Mondiale*, p. 97.

233 **Perhaps calculating**: Clayton to Wingate, November 23, 1916; SADD Wingate Papers, 143/6/44.

233 **"I have no doubt"**: Wingate to Wilson, November 23, 1916; SADD Wingate Papers, 143/6/54.

234 **"Lawrence wants kicking"**: Wilson to Clayton, November 22, 1916; SADD Clayton Papers, 470/5/7.

234 **"I urged my complete"**: Lawrence, *Seven Pillars*, p. 114.

Chapter 10: Neatly in the Void

235 **"The situation is so"**: Lawrence to K. C. Cornwallis, December 12, 1916; PRO-WO 882/6, f. 25A.

235 **"the flame-lit smoke"**: Lawrence, *Seven Pillars*, p. 118.

235 **"There were hundreds"**: Ibid.

236 **He'd conveyed his**: Lawrence, *Faisal's Operations*, October 30, 1916; PRO-FO 882/5, f. 43.

237 **"I had better preface"**: Lawrence to Clayton, December 5, 1916; PRO-FO 882/6, f. 6 .

237 **In his October reports**: Lawrence, *Military Notes: Possibilities*, November 3, 1916; PRO-FO 882/5, f. 57.

237 **"Their real sphere is"**: Lawrence, *Faisal's Operations*, October 30, 1916; PRO-FO 882/5, f. 44.

238 **"don't use any of"**: Lawrence to Clayton, December 5, 1916; PRO-FO 882/6, f. 8.

238 **"The Arabs, outside"**: Lawrence to Clayton, undated but December 11, 1916; PRO-FO 882/6, f. 123.

238 **Without British troops**: Wilson to Clayton, December 12, 1916; PRO-WO 158/604, f. 206A.

239 **a "good dinner"**: Ballobar, *Jerusalem in World War I*, p. 98.

239 **Tiring of his propaganda**: Metternich to German Foreign Ministry, May 2, 1916; NARA T137, Roll 25, Frame 384.

239 **"With all their war"**: Prüfer, *Vertraulich*, August 6, 1915; NARA T137, Roll 24, Frames 790–97.

240 **There seemed to be**: Prüfer, *Diary*, May 8 and 14, 1916; HO.

240 **"I rightly warned"**: Ibid., June 9, 1916.

240   "The situation in Arabia": Ibid., July 8, 1916.

241   "I am unwell": Ibid., May 13, 1916.

241   After several weeks': Nadolny to German Embassy/Constantinople, October 27, 1916; PAAA, Roll 21142, Der Weltkrieg no. 11g adh., Band 1.

241   As he complained in cables: Prüfer to Central Office of German Foreign Ministry, January 22, 1917; PAAA, Roll 21142, Der Weltkrieg no. 11g adh., Band 1.

241   Having thus far failed: McKale, *Curt Prüfer*, pp. 50–51.

243   "I can see no alternative": Wingate to Foreign Office and Murray, December 14, 1916; PRO-WO 158/604, f. 211A.

245   There, and with far more: Lawrence first described the tempo of life in Faisal's camp in his October 30, 1916, report, "Feisal's Operations"; PRO-FO 882/5, f. 42–51. This served as the basis of his description in *Seven Pillars*, Book 1, Chapters 14 and 15, and book 2, chapter 19.

246   "I heard [Faisal]": Lawrence to Clayton, December 5, 1916; PRO-FO 882/6, f. 7.

247   "One of the things": Lawrence to Clayton, December 5, 1916; PRO-FO 882/6, f. 6.

247   "I regard myself as": Lawrence to Clayton, December 11, 1916; PRO-FO 882/6, f 122.

247   "If I am to stay here": Lawrence to K. C. Cornwallis, December 27, 1917; PRO-FO 882/5, f. 25A.

248   "the present time": Loytved-Hardegg to unknown addressee, May 6, 1916; NARA T139, Roll 457.

248   A notable exception: In July 1915, a Major Rochus Schmidt complained that at the same time Djemal took great offense at emissaries of the Imperial Colonial Office wearing German uniforms while in Syria, he afforded "excellent treatment of English and French civilian detainees, who are guaranteed a large measure of freedom on his order." NARA T137, Reel 139, Frame 79.

248   To the cloistered faithful: Vester, *Our Jerusalem*, pp. 243–54.

248   Similarly, Howard Bliss: Bliss to Edelman, March 11, 1917; NARA RG84, Entry 306, Volume 34.

249   "not to discuss Ottoman": Edelman to Elkus, January 20, 1917; NARA, ibid.

249   Despite the steadily worsening: Much of William Yale's account of life in wartime Jerusalem is taken from Yale, *It Takes So Long*, chapters 5 and 6.

250   "Faisal in front": Lawrence to Wilson, January 8, 1917; PRO-FO 882/6, f. 127–28.

251   "I wish I had not": Lawrence, *The Home Letters*, p. 333.

251   "So I miss you": Brown, *The Letters of T. E. Lawrence*, p. 102.

251   During his long: Much of Aaronsohn's account of his early days in wartime Cairo is drawn from his *Diary*, December 1916 to January 1917; ZY.

252   "not only very intelligent": Aaronsohn, *Diary*, December 14, 1916; ZY.

252   "Until now": Aaronsohn, *Diary*, December 16, 1916; ZY.

254   "for autonomy": "Jewish Colonies in Palestine," *Arab Bulletin* (January 19, 1917): p. 35.

254   "in charge of the Intelligence": Aaronsohn, *Diary*, January 24, 1917; ZY.

255   "So Absa, the brave": Ibid., January 26, 1917; ZY.

256   "So our brave Knight": Ibid., January 30, 1917; ZY.

256   "He called me out": Lawrence, *Seven Pillars*, p. 152.

257   "sanitary reasons": Wemyss report to Secretary of the Admiralty, January 30, 1917; PRO-ADM 137/548, f. 114–15.

257   "ransacked from roof": Bray, *Arab Bulletin* no. 41 (February 6, 1917): p. 68.

257   "The garrison was called": Lawrence to Wilson, December 19, 1916; PRO-FO 882/6, f. 49.

257   "is easily frightened": J. C. Watson, report, January 11, 1917; PRO-WO 158/605, p. 4.

258   "it is not known": Vickery, *Memorandum on the General Situation in Arabia*, February 2, 1917; PRO-FO 882/6, f. 152.

258   "is most anxious": Wilson to Arab Bureau, Cairo, January 25, 1917; PRO-FO 141/736.

Chapter 11: A Mist of Deceits

259 **"A man might clearly"**: Lawrence, *Seven Pillars* (Oxford), chapter 51.

260 **With all, he presented**: Lawrence, "Faisal's Order of March," *Arab Bulletin* no. 41 (February 6, 1917): 66.

260 **"The circle of Arab"**: Lawrence, *Seven Pillars*, p. 167.

260 **"At the Arab Bureau"**: Aaronsohn, *Diary*, February 1, 1917; ZY.

261 **British officers examining**: Lloyd to Wingate, November 24, 1916; GLLD 9/8.

261 **In fact, Brémond had**: Minutes of Conference held at Commander-in-Chief's office, September 5, 1916; SADD Clayton Papers, 694/4/8–11.

262 **In addition to touting**: Pearson to Clayton, undated; PRO-WO 158/627, f. 108A.

262 **"In reply to your letter"**: Murray to Wingate, January 22, 1917; PRO-WO 158/627, f. 113A.

263 **A heedless move**: Cited by Wilson, *Lawrence of Arabia*, p. 294 n. 47.

263 **"You can confidentially inform"**: Wingate to Pearson, January 24, 1917; PRO-WO 158/627, f. 114A.

264 **"Faisal afterwards told"**: Newcombe to Wilson, February 4, 1917; GLLD 9/9.

264 **"[Brémond] called to felicitate"**: Lawrence, *Seven Pillars*, p. 167.

264 **Indeed, by Lawrence's**: Ibid., p. 168.

265 **"Now I had not warned"**: Lawrence, *Seven Pillars* (Oxford), chapter 30.

265 **"It seemed we would"**: Yale's account of his February 1917 meeting with Djemal Pasha, and subsequent departure from Palestine, is drawn from Yale, *It Takes So Long*, chapter 6.

268 **Even Gilbert Clayton**: Clayton "Appreciation" of Aqaba landing, January 1917; SADD Clayton Papers, 694/5/17–21.

270 **Yet at some point**: In his authorized biography *Lawrence of Arabia*, Jeremy Wilson makes an extremely convincing case that Lawrence probably imparted details of Sykes-Picot to Faisal within the first few days of his return to Wejh in February 1917. Given Wilson's meticulous research in coming to this conclusion, it's curious why he then concludes that Lawrence's motive in doing so was to "deal with the French question once and for all."

As evidenced by the Rabegh episode, French military overtures in the Middle East were wholly dependent on the support—or lack thereof—of their more powerful ally in the region, Great Britain. Besides, at the time of Lawrence's return to Wejh in early February 1917, Faisal's deep distrust of Colonel Brémond was already well established. Consequently, the notion that Lawrence disclosed Sykes-Picot to Faisal out of concern over French intrigues or influence is puzzling. Instead, the most logical explanation is that Lawrence meant to thwart the one power that truly had the capacity to betray the Arabs: Great Britain.

Nevertheless, successive sympathetic Lawrence biographers have accepted this anti-French motive in explaining Lawrence's disclosure. Taking matters a step further, Wilson even asserts that Lawrence made this disclosure because "in the long run it would surely serve Britain's interests best." Perhaps in Lawrence's conception of Britain's interests, but most certainly not that of the British government at the time.

271 **"[Brémond] ended his talk"**: Lawrence, *Seven Pillars*, p. 168.

271 **"I had dreamed"**: Ibid., p. 661.

272 **"to reply to the guns"**: Lawrence, *Diary*, February 18, 1917; PRO-FO 882/6, f. 180.

272 **"to retire from"**: Lawrence, *Seven Pillars*, p. 169.

272 **"I am still of the opinion"**: Joyce to Wilson, April 1, 1917; PRO-FO 882/6, f. 227.

272 **"inestimable value"**: Pearson to Clayton, March 4, 1917; PRO-FO 882/6, f. 194.

273 **"The news horrified"**: Stitt, *A Prince of Arabia*, pp. 177–78.

274 **With his usual propensity**: Wilson, *Lawrence of Arabia*, p. 379.

275 **"In spite of General Clayton's"**: Lawrence to Wilson, as cited by Wilson, *Lawrence of Arabia*, p. 380.

275 **"rose, as ever"**: Lawrence, *Seven Pillars*, p. 177.

275 **"I think the weak point"**: Lawrence to Wilson, as cited by Wilson, *Lawrence of Arabia*, p. 380.

276 **"when the more difficult"**: Lawrence, *Seven Pillars*, p. 180.

276 **"An account of profit"**: Ibid., p. 176.

277 **"He went on calling"**: Ibid., pp. 181–82.

278 **"the Eternal One"**: 1 Samuel 15:29, as translated in ZY Archives.

278 **Reginald Wingate was**: Wingate to Balfour, February 7, 1917; PRO-FO 371/3049, File 41442.

279 **"extortionate parasite"**: *Personalities of South Syria: North Palestine*, May 1917; PRO-FO 371/3051.

279 **"The attitude of the Jews"**: Aaronsohn, *Present Economic and Political Conditions in Palestine*, pp. 20–21; PRO-FO 882/14, f. 342–43.

280 **"General Clayton listened"**: Aaronsohn, *Diary*, April 3, 1917; ZY.

280 **At sunset on March 28**: T. E. Lawrence's account of his journey to Abdullah's camp, the attack on Aba el Naam, and his ruminations on guerrilla warfare are drawn from Lawrence, *Seven Pillars*, book 3, chapters 32–36, pp. 183–215.

281 **"graciously permitted"**: Lawrence, *Seven Pillars*, p. 216.

284 **"The Turk was harmless"**: Ibid., p. 225.

285 **With the Turks put on**: In the absence of evidence pinpointing when Lawrence came up with the Aqaba-by-land scheme, most biographers have concluded he did so in early February 1917, and that he shared the idea with Faisal at that time as a way to dissuade him from the Aqaba-by-sea plan urged by Brémond and others. On closer examination, this conclusion seems unlikely.

Lawrence's idea for taking Aqaba was such a radical departure from anything previously considered, and if successful would so dramatically alter the political chessboard in Arabia, that implementing it surely would have become his overriding goal once he'd conceived of it. If that had occurred in February, it's hard to imagine why he would have then removed himself from Faisal's camp for the thirty-seven days he spent going to and from Abdullah's camp in Wadi Ais.

Similarly, had Faisal known of an inland plan in February, it's hardly credible that he would have then thrown aside Lawrence's counsel and resumed his support for a British-assisted coastal attack on Aqaba, as he did in early March, and again in early April. Although Lawrence may have offered Faisal vague palliatives in February over how Aqaba might best be taken to secure the Arabs' move north, it almost certainly wasn't until the two men were reunited in Wejh in mid-April that the inland plan took tangible form.

285 **"I was very sorry"**: Faisal to Lawrence, undated but notated "about the end of March," 1917; PRO-FO 882/6, f. 18A.

Chapter 12: An Audacious Scheme

286 **"So far as all ranks"**: Dobell, as cited by Keogh, *Suez to Aleppo*, p. 102.

287 **"a fit partner for"**: Wilson, War Message to Congress, April 2, 1917.

287 **"You beat us at communiqués"**: Moore, *The Mounted Riflemen in Sinai and Palestine*, p. 67.

288 **"He has married"**: Lawrence, "The Howeitat and their Chiefs," *Arab Bulletin* no. 57 (July 24, 1917): 309–10.

289 **"Faisal always listened"**: Lawrence to Liddell Hart, October 31, 1933; Graves and Hart, *T. E. Lawrence: Letters to His Biographers*, Pt. 2, pp. 188–89.

290 **"The move to Aqaba"**: Clayton directive of March 8, 1917, with copies to Wingate, C. Wilson, and Lawrence; PRO-FO 686/6, f. 46.

290 **"The occupation of Aqaba"**: Clayton to Wingate, May 29, 1917; PRO-FO 882/6, f. 388.

291 **"After a moment I knew"**: Lawrence, *Seven Pillars*, p. 222.

291 **"Of course it is impossible":** Lyndon Bell to Lloyd, March 17, 1917; GLLD 9/3.

292 **"a venerable and":** Sykes to Wingate, February 22, 1917; PRO-FO 882/16, f. 58.

292 **"it does not appear":** Foreign Office to Wingate, March 14, 1917; SADD Wingate Papers, 145/3/38.

293 **"obliterate" the thought:** Grey to Buchanan, ambassador to Russia, March 16, 1916; PRO-FO 371/2767, Registry 49669.

294 **These discussions had:** Adelson, *Mark Sykes*, p. 220.

294 **"a Jewish State in":** As quoted by Friedman, *The Question of Palestine*, p. 130.

295 **"offering to make War Office":** Adelson, *Mark Sykes*, pp. 220–21.

295 **"the French have no":** As quoted by Friedman, *The Question of Palestine*, p. 131.

297 **After initially giving:** Hardegg to Glazebrook, April 2, 1917; NARA RG84, Entry 448, Volume 3.

298 **Even if she had bowed:** The best English-language source on the life of Sarah Aaronsohn is Engle, *The Nili Spies*.

299 **One measure of her steeliness:** Florence, *Lawrence and Aaronsohn*, p. 287.

299 **According to Sarah:** Aaronsohn, *Diary*, April 19, 1917; ZY.

300 **"I said I considered":** Ibid., March 12, 1917.

300 **"Main difficulty":** Sykes to War Office, April 30, 1917; PRO-FO 371/3053, f. 191–93.

301 **He quickly dispatched:** As Aaronsohn noted in his diary on April 27, 1917, "I went to see [Wyndham] Deedes and told him that Sir Mark [Sykes] wanted me to submit the telegrams announcing the sacking of Jewish Jaffa through him."

301 **In writing on the plight:** Aaronsohn, "Addendum to 'Report of an inhabitant of Athlit,'" undated but November 1916; PRO-FO 371/2783.

302 **"Aaron Aaronsohn asks me":** Sykes to Graham, April 28, 1917; PRO-FO 371/3055.

302 **"It is with profound":** *Jewish Chronicle* (London), May 4, 1917; PRO-FO 371/3055.

302 **Over the next few days:** See PRO-FO 371/3055, File 87895.

302 **In the case of the British:** Oliphant, minutes to "Jews in Palestine," May 4, 1917; PRO-FO 371/3055, File 87895.

302 **"I think we ought to use":** Ormsby-Gore to Sykes, May 8, 1917; MSP-47, p. 4.

303 **"During Passover":** Wingate to Foreign Office, May 11, 1917; PRO-FO 371/3055.

303 **"Djemal Pasha Blamed":** *New York Times*, June 3, 1917.

303 **After initially refusing:** One of the most interesting documents related to the Jaffa evacuation was a report written by Heinrich Brode, the German consul in Jerusalem, to Richard von Kuhlmann, the new German ambassador, on April 5, 1917. Sensitive to any governmental actions that might alienate the Jewish population in Palestine, Brode had taken his concerns about the Jaffa evacuation order to Djemal Pasha. At their meeting, Djemal clarified that those Jaffa Jews involved in agriculture could stay on, while those being evacuated could proceed to Jerusalem if they wished, a destination denied "Ottomans." Brode to Kuhlmann, April 5, 1917; NARA T120, Roll 4333, Turkei 195, Band 12, Frames K178502–8.

303 **These assertions were seconded:** Turkish Legation to the Netherlands, May 24, 1917; PRO-FO 371/3055. Also, Alvarado to Hardinge, June 8, 1917; PRO-FO 371/3055.

304 **To lend further authority:** Deedes to Egypt High Commissioner's Office, Cairo, June 1, 1917; PRO-FO 141/805.

304 **"Turkish atrocities":** Aaronsohn to Sulzberger, June 2, 1917; PRO-FO 141/805.

304 **"In many ways":** Report to the Minister of Foreign Affairs of Sweden, August 25, 1917; NARA RG84, Entry 58, Volume 399.

304 **"grossly exaggerated":** Townley to Balfour, August 10, 1917; PRO-FO 371/3055.

304 **Even Aaron Aaronsohn:** Aaronsohn, "The Evacuation Menace," undated but late July 1917; PRO-FO 141/805.

305 **Of even greater import:** Lawrence to Wilson, Intelligence Memo, undated but circa April 21, 1917; PRO-FO 686/6, f. 88.

306   "a highly mobile": Lawrence, *Seven Pillars*, p. 224.

306   "Everyone was too busy": Ibid., p. 225.

306   "Auda is to travel": Wilson to Clayton, "Note on the Proposed Military Plan of Operations of the Arab Armies," May 1, 1917; PRO-FO 882/6, f. 351.

306   "The element I would": Lawrence, *Seven Pillars*, p. 226.

308   "We now have a chance": Wilson to Clayton, March 21, 1917; PRO-FO 882/12, f. 199–201.

308   When Wilson forwarded: Wingate to Foreign Office, April 27, 1917; MSP-41d.

309   "On 2nd May": Sykes to Wingate, May 5, 1917; MSP-41d.

Chapter 13: Aqaba

311   "Never doubt Great Britain's": As related by Wilson to Clayton, May 24, 1917; PRO-FO 882/16, f. 113.

311   "His Sherifial Majesty": Wingate to Wilson, July 20, 1917; PRO-FO 882/7, f. 35.

311   Now it required: Lawrence's account of his journey to and capture of Aqaba is drawn from *Seven Pillars*, book 4, chapters 39–44, pp. 227–312.

314   After a tense three-hour: Sykes to Wingate, May 23, 1917; MSP-41b, p. 3; slightly different version in PRO-FO 371/3054, f. 329.

315   "Monsieur Picot received": Sykes to Wingate, May 23, 1917; MSP-41b, p. 5; slightly different version in PRO-FO 371/3054, f. 330.

315   Even those senior officials: Tanenbaum, *France and the Arab Middle East, 1914–1920*, pp. 17–18.

315   "Although Sykes and Picot": Wilson to Clayton, May 25, 1917; PRO-FO 882/16, p. 5.

316   "[Hussein] stated to Faisal": Newcombe, "Note" on Sykes-Picot meeting with King Hussein, May 20, 1917; GLLD 9/9.

317   The only way Hussein: Despite Sykes's repeated assertions to the contrary, there is ample evidence that he didn't disclose the terms of the Sykes-Picot Agreement to King Hussein at their May 1917 meetings. Well into 1918, Cyril Wilson and other British officers in conference with Hussein consistently reported that the king had no knowledge of the partitions of the Arab "nation" called for in that agreement, but instead continued to believe that the far more generous framework specified in the McMahon-Hussein Correspondence remained in effect. To cite only the example discussed here, it's exceedingly hard to imagine that Hussein would have agreed to the Baghdad-Lebanon formulation had he known beforehand of the proposed dispensation of Baghdad province as specified in Sykes-Picot. As Tanenbaum (*France and the Arab Middle East*, p. 17) points out: "It did not make sense for a leader of a rebellion to ask an outside power to annex the territory for which he was fighting and hoped to rule."

317   In their back-and-forth: McMahon to Hussein, October 24, 1915, as cited by Antonius, *The Arab Awakening*, p. 420.

317   "for a short time": Report by Political Intelligence Department, Foreign Office, "Memorandum on British Commitments to King Husein [*sic*]," December 1918; PRO-FO 882/13, p. 7, f. 225.

318   "he knows that Sir Mark": "Note by Sheikh Fuad El Khatib taken down by Lt Col Newcombe," undated but May 1917, p. 3; PRO-FO 882/16, f. 133.

318   "If we are not going to see": Wilson to Clayton, May 24, 1917; PRO-FO 882/16, f. 111.

319   "we are deeply grateful": Faisal Hussein, "To All Our Brethren—The Syrian Arabs," trans. May 28, 1917; SADD Wingate Papers, 145/7/89.

319   "I do not attach very": Clayton to Sykes, July 30, 1917; SADD Clayton Papers, 693/12/30.

319   "short statement of fact": Wilson to Symes, June 20, 1917; PRO-FO 882/16, f. 127. Many historians contend that it was King Hussein and Faisal, not Mark Sykes, who dissembled about the substance of their meetings in May 1917. In *The Question of Palestine*, Isaiah Fried-

man wholeheartedly accepts Sykes's version, asserting (p. 206) that at their preliminary, early May meeting, "Feisal's misgivings were set at rest by Sykes's explanation of the Anglo-French Agreement . . . The interview with Hussein on 5 May went off equally well." Sykes's only fault, in Friedman's view, was a failure to make a personal record of his and Picot's subsequent talks with Hussein. "For this omission," he writes, "Sykes had to pay the penalty when a year later, to his surprise, Hussein feigned ignorance of the Anglo-French Agreement and pretended to have learned of it first from Djemal Pasha's Damascus speech . . . "

Not only Hussein's protestations, but Sykes's own actions, belie this contention. On May 12, 1917, just one week after his first meeting with Hussein, Sykes attended a high-level strategy meeting at Reginald Wingate's Cairo office. At that meeting, Sykes described in detail the agreement he and Picot had reached with the Cairo-based Syrian "delegates" nearly three weeks earlier, but made no mention of the vastly more important accord he had supposedly reached with Hussein just days prior. One reason may have been that this May 12 conference was attended by Colonel Cyril Wilson, the official British liaison to Hussein, and a person uniquely positioned to refute such an assertion.

As for the subsequent meetings Sykes and Picot held with Hussein, it's difficult to discern any possible motive for two career military officers, Stewart Newcombe and Cyril Wilson, whose missions in the Hejaz would have been made markedly easier if Sykes's account of those meetings were true, to so vehemently refute it.

319   "The whole question": Symes to Wilson, June 26, 1917; PRO-FO 882/16, f. 129–30.

321   As for Faisal: Wilson to Clayton, May 20, 1917; SADD Wingate Papers, 145/7/36.

321   "They saw in me": Lawrence, *Seven Pillars*, pp. 25–26.

322   "Can't stand another day": Lawrence as quoted by Wilson, *Lawrence*, p. 410 n. 40.

322   "Clayton. I've decided": Ibid., p. 410 n. 41.

322   Lawrence's northern: Lawrence, *Seven Pillars* (Oxford), chapter 51.

323   "Very old, livid": Lawrence, *Seven Pillars*, p. 546.

323   "I saw that with my answer": Lawrence, *Seven Pillars* (Oxford), chapter 51.

324   "In other words": Lawrence, *Seven Pillars*, p. 26.

324   In debriefings: In his debriefing of July 6, 1917, in London, Samuel Edelman, the U.S. consul in Damascus, reported a 25 percent desertion rate among Anatolian Turkish soldiers brought to Syria, a rate surely surpassed by less loyal elements of the empire; PRO-FO 371/3050.

324   The more perceptive: See PRO-FO 371/3050, File 47710.

325   The spare diary: Prüfer, *Diary*, May 21–July 18, 1917; HO.

325   As he reported to: Prüfer to Mittwoch, April 12, 1917; NARA T149, Roll 365, Frame 399.

326   "the High Command has": Engle, *The Nili Spies*, p. 129.

330   Now, in mid-June 1917: The account of William Yale's 1917 return to the United States is drawn from Yale, *It Takes So Long*, chapter 7.

332   The situation was even worse: Yale, "Palestine–Syria Situation," to U.S. State Department, June 27, 1917; NARA 763.72/13450.

332   "the disposition of": Yale to Secretary of State Lansing, June 30, 1917; YU Box 2/Folder 48.

335   "no guns, no base": Lawrence, *Seven Pillars*, p. 306. For an account of the battle at Aba el Lissan, see also Lawrence, "The Occupation of Akaba," undated; PRO-FO 882/7, f. 63–68.

336   Their reports noted: See field reports of Herbert Garland, May 1917; PRO-FO 686/6.

337   "It is somewhat difficult": Dawnay, "Notes on Faisal's Proposed Advance Northward," May 29, 1917; PRO-WO 158/606, f. 43A.

337   By the time Clayton penned: Clayton to Director of Military Intelligence (London), July 5, 1917; PRO-FO 882/7, f. 1.

337   "The enemy had never": Lawrence, *Seven Pillars*, p. 310.

Chapter 14: Hubris

341 "Do not try to do": Lawrence, *Twenty-Seven Articles*, August 1917; PRO-FO 882/7, f. 93–97.

341 "nothing has occurred": Clayton to Military Intelligence Director (London), July 11, 1917; PRO-FO 882/7, f. 18–23.

342 Ironically, some of: Lawrence's account of his return to Cairo and his first meeting with Allenby is to be found in *Seven Pillars*, book 5, chapters 55 and 56, pp. 317–22.

343 "considerably enhanced": Wingate to Robertson, July 14, 1917; PRO-WO 374/41077.

344 On the opposite side: Wilson, *Lawrence of Arabia*, p. 422.

344 "there is little hope": Lawrence to Clayton, July 10, 1917; PRO-FO 882/16, f. 249.

345 To make use of: Allenby to Robertson, July 16, 1917; PRO-WO 158/634, f. 4A.

346 "The advantages offered": Allenby to Robertson, July 19, 1917; PRO-WO 158/634, f.10A.

347 "A slave brought up": Lawrence, *Twenty-Seven Articles*, August 1917; PRO-FO 882/7, f. 93–97.

347 "are no good": Aaronsohn, *Diary*, July 1, 1917; ZY.

348 "I no longer had": Ibid., July 2, 1917.

348 his local "representative": Sykes to Graham, May 5, 1917; MSP-41a.

348 So vague had his: Clayton to Sykes, June 22, 1917; PRO-FO 371/3058, f. 156.

349 This the German government: Cecil to Hardinge, June 13, 1917; PRO-FO 371/3058, f. 145.

349 "There can be no doubt": Cecil to Hardinge, June 13, 1917; PRO-FO 371/3058, f. 146–48.

350 "very much inclined": Aaronsohn, *Diary*, July 17, 1917; ZY.

350 "I gather": Wingate to Graham, July 23, 1917; PRO-FO 371/3083, f. 55.

351 In his discussions with Generals: As Clayton wrote to Sykes after interviewing Lawrence in Cairo, "Faisal's name is one to conjure with. . . . Already he is accepted in practically all of the [Syrian] districts through which Lawrence passed." Clayton, July 22, 1917; PRO-FO 882/16, f. 145.

351 "Aqaba had been taken": Lawrence, *Seven Pillars*, p. 323.

352 As Lawrence explained: Wilson to Clayton, July 29, 1917; PRO-FO 882/7, f. 48.

352 A surprised Wilson: Newcombe quickly tired of his rearguard duties and transferred back to Cairo. He was captured by the Turks in early November 1917 during the EEF offensive in southern Palestine.

353 "The main points": Lawrence, "Report on meeting King Hussein," July 30, 1917; PRO-FO 371/3054, f. 372–73.

353 While he was still in Jeddah: Macindoe for Clayton to Military Intelligence Director, July 28, 1917; PRO-WO 141/668, p. 5.

353 "They were anxious": Lawrence, *Seven Pillars*, p. 326.

354 "absolutely satisfactory": Wilson to Arab Bureau (Cairo), August 6, 1917; PRO-WO 158/634, f. 25A.

354 "Since [British] Egypt kept": Lawrence, *Seven Pillars*, p. 327.

354 This Yale did: Yale, "Palestine-Syrian Situation," with addendum, July 10, 1917; PRO-FO 371/3050.

355 "with view to subsequent": Foreign Office to Spring-Rice, July 25, 1917; PRO-FO 371/3057.

355 "he was positively": Yardley, *American Black Chamber*, p. 172.

356 "the collection and examination": Department of State, "History of the Bureau of Diplomatic Security of the United States Department of State," 2011. www.state.gov/documents/organization/176705.pdf.

356 **"[Yale] is to keep us informed":** Harrison to Gunther (American embassy, London), August 30, 1917; NARA RG59, Box 1047.

357 **"I lacked a historical":** Yale, *It Takes So Long*, chapter 8, pp. 10–11.

358 **"We are glad":** Aaronsohn, "The Jewish Colonies," *Arab Bulletin* no. 64 (September 27, 1917): 389–91.

358 **"It was an interview":** Aaronsohn, *Diary*, August 12, 1917; ZY.

359 **"It might help matters":** Wingate to Balfour, August 20, 1917; PRO-FO 371/3053, f. 384.

360 **stop her "activities":** Engle, *The Nili Spies*, pp. 152–54.

360 **Their cavalier manner:** The cavalier attitude of the British toward the well-being of their intelligence assets was amply reflected in *Hard Lying*, the memoir of the *Managem* captain, Lewen Weldon. As Weldon noted on p. 195, "We were on the whole extraordinarily lucky with our 'agents.' I don't think more than seven were actually captured. Six of these were hanged and one had his head cut off."

361 **"I don't think that any":** Lawrence to Clayton, August 27, 1917; PRO-FO 882/7, f. 88–92.

362 **"colonialism is madness":** Sykes to Clayton, July 22, 1917; MSP-69.

362 **"the Anglo-French-Arab":** Sykes memorandum, "On Mr. Nicholson's [*sic*] Note Regarding Our Commitments," July 18, 1917; MSP-66.

362 **Over time, a growing consensus:** Curzon to Hardinge, August 23, 1917; PRO-FO 371/3044, f. 299.

362 **"the opinion of Sir Mark":** Nicolson précis for Balfour, July 11, 1917; PRO-FO 371/3044, f. 286–93.

363 **"Hitherto the work":** Sykes to Drummond, July 20, 1917; MSP-68.

363 **"Lawrence's move":** Sykes to Clayton, July 22, 1917; MSP-69.

364 **"What have you promised":** Lawrence to Sykes, September 7, 1917; SADD Clayton Papers, 693/11/3–8.

364 **"It is in fact dead":** Clayton to Lawrence, September 20, 1917; SADD Clayton Papers, 693/11/9–12.

365 **"to all intents and":** Yale, *Diary*, September 8, 1917; YU Box 2, Folder 2.

365 **"This Jewish chemist":** Ibid., September 12, 1917; YU Box 2, Folder 2.

367 **"swept off the top":** Lawrence, *Seven Pillars*, p. 367.

368 **"towards some rough country":** Lawrence to Clayton, September 23, 1917; PRO-FO 882/4, f. 71.

368 **"seized my feet":** Lawrence, *Seven Pillars*, p. 369.

368 **"The conditions were":** Lawrence to Clayton, September 23, 1917; PRO-FO 882/4, f. 71.

369 **"I hope this sounds":** Lawrence to Stirling, September 25, 1917; UT, Folder 6, File 7.

369 **"I hope when the nightmare":** Lawrence to Leeds, September 24, 1917, in Garnett, *The Letters of T. E. Lawrence*, p. 238.

Chapter 15: To the Flame

370 **"I only hope and trust":** As quoted by Wilson, *Lawrence of Arabia*, p. 455.

370 **"He listened very":** Aaronsohn to Alex Aaronsohn, October 1917; YU, Box 2, Folder 11.

371 **"does not wish to see":** Yale, *Diary*, September 25, 1917; YU Box 2, Folder 2.

372 **"Pascal," he wrote:** Aaronsohn to Alex Aaronsohn, October 1917; YU, Box 2, Folder 11.

374 **In his more bitter:** Clayton to Joyce, October 24, 1917; PRO-FO 882/7, f. 175; Joyce memo, undated; PRO-WO 158/634. See also Wilson, *Lawrence of Arabia*, pp. 447–48.

375 **After the operation:** Lawrence, *Seven Pillars*, pp. 387–89.

375 **"almost indispensable":** Clayton to Wingate, November 13, 1916; SADD Wingate Papers, 143/2/190.

376 **By then, the *Managem*:** Florence, *Lawrence and Aaronsohn*, pp. 298–99.

376 **Sure enough, rumors soon began circulating:** Sheffy, *British Military Intelligence in the Palestine Campaign*, p. 162; Engle, *The Nili Spies*, pp. 167–68.

377 **"Today we don't want":** Florence, *Lawrence and Aaronsohn*, p. 303.

377 **"I want to be":** Engle, *The Nili Spies*, pp. 186–87.

377 **As a result:** German warnings to the Turks over the treatment of Jews continued even after the NILI spy ring was broken, with German ambassador Bernstorff counseling Talaat Pasha to "not let a single case of Jewish espionage blow up into a full-fledged persecution of Jews." Bernstorff to Foreign Ministry for Warburg, October 26, 1917; NARA T120, Roll 4334, Frame K179639.

378 **Those spies had been:** See Sheffy, *British Military Intelligence in the Palestine Campaign*, p. 162 nn. 77 and 78.

378 **"For those who had long":** Florence, *Lawrence and Aaronsohn*, p. 326.

379 **By that afternoon:** Engle, *The Nili Spies*, p. 202. Hunted by both Turkish authorities and Jewish vigilante squads, Joseph Lishansky finally ran out of luck on October 20, when he was captured outside Jerusalem. Along with Naaman Belkind he was convicted of treason, and in December 1917 both men were publicly hanged in Damascus.

379 **For four days, she lingered:** There is a wide divergence among published accounts on both the duration of the NILI raid on Zichron Yaakov, and on how long Sarah Aaronsohn survived after shooting herself. The latter question would seem to be resolved by the testimony of the doctor summoned after the shooting, who stated it was October 5, and by the two German nuns who attended Sarah, who stated she died on October 9.

379 **"We are doing our best":** Engle, *The Nili Spies*, p. 191.

380 **"He is not well":** Hogarth to Ormsby-Gore, October 26, 1917; PRO-FO 371/3054, f. 388.

380 **"I'm not going":** Lawrence to Leeds, September 24, 1917, in Garnett, *The Letters of T. E. Lawrence*, p. 238.

380 **His comprehensive report:** See various George Lloyd reports on Hejaz economy and political situation, Autumn 1916, in GLLD 9/8.

381 **"I think I could be":** Lloyd to Clayton, September 30, 1917; GLLD 9/13.

381 **"Lawrence is quite fit":** Lloyd to Clayton, October 20, 1917; GLLD 9/13.

382 **"He has a lion's heart":** Clayton to Lloyd, October 25, 1917; GLLD 9/10.

383 **"The view up the pass":** Lloyd, "Diary of Journey with T.E.L. to El Jaffer," October 24, 1917; GLLD 9/11.

384 **Should Lawrence become:** Lawrence, *Seven Pillars*, pp. 421–23.

384 **"To them he is Lawrence":** Lloyd to Clayton, November 5, 1917; GLLD 9/10.

385 **Lawrence was surely:** Liddell Hart, *Colonel Lawrence*, pp. 193–94.

385 **If Brémond was wrong:** Prüfer to Oppenheim, November 3, 1914; NARA T137, Roll 23, Frame 213.

385 **"L not working":** Lloyd, notes from travels, undated but late October 1917; GLLD 9/10. In his authorized biography of Lawrence, Jeremy Wilson incorrectly transcribed a crucial point in George Lloyd's handwritten note, rendering Lloyd's original "HMG" (an abbreviation for His Majesty's Government) as "Allied." As a result, his quote from Lloyd inaccurately reads, "Lawrence not working for Allies but for Sherif." Obviously, this error lends a very different meaning to that Lloyd intended—and to what Lawrence presumably said—but it is an error that has been repeated by many of those Lawrence biographers who have sought wherever possible to attribute Lawrence's acts of official disobedience as directed against Allied (i.e., French) actions rather than against the British government.

385 **"He would like me":** Lloyd, "Diary of Journey with T.E.L. to El Jaffer," October 28, 1917; GLLD 9/11.

386 **"otherwise"** . . . **"his independent activities":** Knabenshue to U.S. Secretary of State, October 23, 1917; NARA RG59, Box 1047, 111.70Y1/3.

386 **Indeed, just days before:** Ibid., November 4, 1917; NARA M353, Box 6, Frame 0827.

386 **In defending his:** Hoover (U.S. Consul, São Paulo, Brazil) to U.S. Secretary of State, August 21, 1917; NARA M367, Roll 217, document 763.72112.5321.

387 **"The information the British":** Yale, *It Takes So Long*, chapter 8, pp. 18–19.

388 **And even if British:** Yale, *It Takes So Long*, margin note, chapter 7, p. 21.

388 **"Dr. Weizmann":** Weizmann, *Trial and Error*, p. 208.

388 **"His Majesty's Government":** As reproduced on frontispiece by Stein, *The Balfour Declaration*.

389 **"I am very anxious":** Clayton to Lloyd, November 12, 1917; GLLD 9/10.

390 **To the great good fortune:** Lawrence's account of the Minifir train attack is in *Seven Pillars*, book 6, chapters 77 and 78, pp. 425–34.

391 **"To me"** . . . **"an unnecessary action":** Lawrence, *Seven Pillars*, p. 163.

Chapter 16: A Gathering Fury

392 **"With reference to":** Syrian Committee of Egypt, November 14, 1917; YU, Box 3, Folder 8.

392 **"The British Authorities":** Yale to Harrison, December 17, 1917; YU, Box 2, Folder 11.

393 **"He hesitated to":** Lawrence, *Seven Pillars*, p. 435.

394 **"It was icy cold":** Ibid., p. 439.

394 **"The carrying out":** Weizmann to Aaronsohn, November 16, 1917, reproduced in Friedman, *Zionist Commission*, pp. 19–20.

395 **"The old man":** Aaronsohn, *Diary*, November 16, 1917; ZY.

396 **"provided it can":** House to Drummond, September 11, 1917; PRO-FO 371/3083, f. 107.

396 **"asks that no mention":** Wiseman to Drummond, October 16, 1917; PRO-FO 371/3083, f. 106.

396 **"help our United States":** Weizmann to Aaronsohn, November 16, 1917, reproduced in Friedman, *Zionist Commission*, pp. 19–20.

397 **His brother's cable:** Verrier, ed., *Agents of Empire*, p. 295. While accurate about the fate of Sarah Aaronsohn, the cable was in error on other aspects. The elderly Ephraim Aaronsohn survived his imprisonment in Damascus and was subsequently released, while Belkind wasn't executed until December 14.

397 **"The sacrifice is":** Aaronsohn, *Diary*, December 1, 1917; ZY.

398 **It's unlikely that":** Lawrence's account of his torture at Deraa is in *Seven Pillars*, book 6, chapter 80, pp. 441–47.

400 **"pale and obviously":** Mack, *A Prince of Our Disorder*, p. 233.

400 **"fitter and better":** As quoted by James, *The Golden Warrior*, p. 214 n. 17.

400 **"by virtue of Abd el Kader's":** Lawrence to Stirling, June 29, 1919; UT (copy) Folder 6, File 7.

401 **"About that night":** As quoted by Brown, *The Letters of T. E. Lawrence*, pp. 261–62.

402 **"Every time I come to Beirut":** Agent 92C, "Syrian Politics," December 9, 1917; PRO-WO 106/1420.

403 **"A sort of commander-in-chief":** Lewis, "An Ottoman Officer," in Kushner, *Palestine in the Late Ottoman Period*, p. 413.

403 **"It is true that some time":** Agent 92C, "Syrian Politics," December 9, 1917; PRO-WO 106/1420.

404 **On November 7:** As Russia still used the Julian instead of the Gregorian calendar at the time, the date is remembered in Russia as October 25—hence the "October Revolution."

404 **"The [Sykes-Picot] Agreement":** As quoted in Antonius, *The Arab Awakening*, p. 255.

405 **"I am going to Constantinople":** Agent 92C, "Syrian Politics," December 9, 1917; PRO-WO 106/1420.

405 **"But what sort of independence"**: Ahmed Djemal Pasha to Faisal (undated), translated and sent from Wingate to Balfour, December 25, 1917; PRO-PRO 30/30/10 f. 67.

406 **"[it] was the supreme moment"**: Lawrence, *Seven Pillars*, p. 453.

407 **"The French officers"**: Sykes to Graham, May 5, 1917; MSP-41d.

407 **Anxious not to appear:** Foreign Office to Wingate, May 29, 1917; SADD Wingate Papers, 145/7/114–15.

407 **"warm compliments"**: Wilson to Brémond, September 21, 1917; PRO-FO 371/3051.

407 **"Brémond's antecedents"**: Wingate to Graham, December 10, 1917; PRO-FO 371/3051.

408 **"Salad, chicken mayonnaise"**: Lawrence, *Seven Pillars*, p. 455.

409 **A few days prior:** Clayton to Sykes, November 28, 1917; PRO-FO 371/3054, f. 393.

409 **"I have recommended King Hussein"**: Wingate to War Cabinet, December 24, 1917; PRO-FO 371/3062.

410 **The War Cabinet swiftly moved:** Minutes to "Turkish Intrigues in Arabia," December 26, 1917; PRO-FO 371/3062, File 243033.

410 **Over the coming months:** Great historical confusion has arisen from the fact that there were two Turkish leaders in Syria known by the honorific Djemal Pasha. These were Ahmed Djemal Pasha (also sometimes denoted as "the Greater"), the Syrian governor-general, and Mehmet Djemal Pasha (sometimes denoted as *Kucuk*, or "the Lesser"). Not at all helping matters, Mehmet Djemal adopted the Djemal Pasha honorific upon assuming command of the Turkish Fourth Army in early 1918, the same command that Ahmed Djemal had just vacated. T. E. Lawrence further added to this confusion by frequently referring to "Djemal Pasha" in *Seven Pillars*, without specifying whether he was talking about Ahmed or Mehmet.

As a result, most histories of the period mistakenly conjoin the two men as one, and thereby state that Faisal Hussein maintained a secret correspondence with Ahmed Djemal into the summer of 1918. In actuality, while Ahmed Djemal initiated the Turkish overture to Faisal in November 1917, all communication between them appears to have ended with Ahmed's recall to Constantinople the following month; Faisal's subsequent correspondence was with Mehmet Djemal.

Also, in both *Seven Pillars* and statements he made to his contemporary biographers, Lawrence claimed that Faisal maintained a separate negotiating correspondence with Turkish general Mustafa Kemal, the future Kemal Ataturk. While that may have been the case, I have found no documentary evidence to support this claim.

410 **"By suitably guarded phrases"**: Lawrence, *Seven Pillars* (Oxford), chapter 115.

410 **Thus, the account in the 1922:** Lawrence, *Seven Pillars* (Oxford), chapter 115, and Lawrence, *Seven Pillars* (1926), p. 554.

410 **"All is fair"**: Lawrence to Yale, October 22, 1929; YU, Box 1, Folder 4. Curiously, Lawrence asserted to Yale that he had played no authorial role in Faisal's correspondence with Mehmet Djemal, claiming that he learned of it and read the various exchanges "unbeknownst" to Faisal. This is contradicted both by statements Lawrence made to others, and by his own account in *Seven Pillars*.

410 **It was also necessary:** Aaronsohn to Weizmann, December 13, 1917; ZY.

411 **"It must be abundantly"**: Weizmann to Brandeis, January 14, 1918; PRO-FO 371/3394, f. 423.

411 **"now impossible"**: British government White Paper, "Notes on Zionism," Part 2. Communications of the Zionist Organization II, January–March 1918; April 19, 1918, p. 11; PRO-FO 371/4171, f. 99.

412 **"Affairs are in rather"**: Lawrence to Clayton, January 22, 1918; PRO-FO 882/7, f. 251–53.

413 **"I began to increase"**: Lawrence, *Seven Pillars*, p. 462.

414 **"Everybody thought"**: Lawrence to Clayton, January 26, 1918; PRO-FO 882/7, f. 254–58.

415 **It had come at a cost:** Lawrence, *Seven Pillars*, p. 482.

Chapter 17: Solitary Pursuits

417 "It might be fraud": Lawrence, *Seven Pillars*, p. 503.

417 "These interests crossed": William Yale's personal account of his intelligence work in Cairo in 1917–18 is drawn from Yale, *It Takes So Long*, chapter 8.

420 "On the strength of what": Yale to Harrison, December 24, 1917; YU, Box 2, Folder 12.

420 "the truth seems": Yale to Harrison, November 12, 1917; YU, Box 2, Folder 6.

420 "in a few words suggests": Yale to Harrison, February 25, 1918; YU, Box 2, Folder 19.

421 "a young British officer": Yale to Harrison, November 4, 1917; YU, Box 2, Folder 5.

421 Without those funds: Lawrence to Clayton, January 22, 1918; PRO-FO 882/7, f. 251–52.

422 "hummed and hawed": Lawrence to Clayton, February 12, 1918; PRO-FO 882/7, f. 267.

422 "spend what was necessary": Lawrence's account of his confrontation with Zeid in Tafileh and his subsequent actions is drawn from *Seven Pillars*, book 7, chapter 90, pp. 499–502.

423 "I am getting shy": Lawrence to Clayton, February 12, 1918; PRO-FO 882/7, f. 268.

424 In recent months: Lawrence, *The Home Letters*, p. 341.

424 "To be charged against": Lawrence, *Seven Pillars*, p. 502.

425 "There was no escape": Ibid., p. 503.

425 "I'm to go back": Lawrence, *The Home Letters*, p. 348.

425 "Major Lawrence's opinions": Yale to Harrison, March 11, 1918; YU, Box 2, Folder 21.

428 Instead, he had found a king: David Hogarth, "Report on Mission to Jeddah," January 15, 1918; PRO-FO 882/13 f. 35–40.

428 "[Hussein] refers to": Wingate to Foreign Office, February 19, 1918; PRO-FO 3713380, f. 473.

428 In late January, he had penned: Lawrence, "Syrian Cross Currents," *Arab Bulletin Supplementary Papers*, February 1, 1918; PRO-FO 882/14.

428 "I have urged Lawrence": Clayton to Sykes, February 4, 1918; PRO-FO 371/3398.

428 "As for the Jews": Lawrence to Clayton, February 12, 1918; PRO-FO 882/7.

429 While overtly rebuffing: Wingate to Foreign Office, April 8, 1918; PRO-FO 371/3403, f. 372.

430 "upon which all evidence": Yale to Harrison, March 11, 1918; YU, Box 2, Folder 21.

431 "one leading principle": British government White Paper, "Notes on Zionism," Part 3. The Zionist Commission in Palestine; February 6, 1919, pp. 16–17; PRO-FO 371/4171, f. 102.

432 Certainly there was no: British government White Paper, "Notes on Zionism," Part 3. The Zionist Commission in Palestine; February 6, 1919, pp. 14–21; PRO-FO 371/4171, f. 100–104.

433 "it was his ambition": Cornwallis to Symes, April 20, 1918; PRO-FO 882/14, f. 358–59.

433 "On the whole": Yale to Harrison, April 8, 1918; YU, Box 2, Folder 25.

434 "cheap Arab labor": Yale to Harrison, March 25, 1918; YU, Box 2, Folder 23.

434 "as in the [American]": Yale to Harrison, June 10, 1918; YU, Box 2, Folder 34.

434 "once again, pearls": Aaronsohn, *Diary*, April 1, 1918; ZY.

434 "It is to be hoped": Yale to Harrison, April 8, 1918; YU, Box 2, Folder 25.

434 "The abstraction of": Lawrence's account of the expedition to Atatir, and of the deaths of "Daud" and "Farraj" (Ali and Othman), are drawn from *Seven Pillars*, book 8, chapters 112–113, pp. 507–17.

436 But then the news: Wavell, *The Palestine Campaigns*, pp. 173–84.

439 "He kept Abbas": McKale, *Curt Prüfer*, p. 54.

439 A much better solution: Bernstorff to von Hertling, July 19, 1918; PAAA, Roll 22348, Turkei 47, Band 7.

440 Abbas clearly sensed: Oppenheim to Jagow, February 23, 1915; PAAA, Roll 21129, Der Weltkrieg no. 11g, Band 7.

440 "There was nothing to do": Lawrence, *Seven Pillars*, p. 520.

440 **While British military communiqués:** Dawnay to EEF Headquarters, May 1, 1918; PRO-FO 882/7, f. 277–86.

441 **Now, with the proposed:** Lawrence, *Seven Pillars*, pp. 526–27.

442 **"a regal gift":** Ibid., p. 527.

443 **"if I should seek revenge":** Aaronsohn, *Diary*, March 21, 1918; ZY.

443 **"very little winter cereals":** Ibid., April 4, 1918.

444 **"Well, Aaron":** Ibid., April 6, 1918.

444 **"to bridge it over":** Ibid., April 20, 1918.

444 **Ironically, that venture:** Clayton to British Secretary of State for Foreign Affairs, June 16, 1918; PRO-FO 371/803, pp. 5–7.

444 **"a small favor":** Ibid., pp. 4–5.

445 **"all the Jews there":** Lawrence to Clayton, February 12, 1918; PRO-FO 882/7, f. 268.

445 **"What arrangements":** Clayton to Lawrence, May 22, 1918; PRO-FO 141/688.

445 **"Interview would take place":** General Headquarters to Commandant Akaba, May 24, 1918; PRO-WO 95/4370, App A.

446 **"In my opinion, the interview":** Clayton to Foreign Office, June 12, 1918; PRO-FO 141/688.

446 **"It is difficult to say":** Wingate to Foreign Office, March 23, 1918; PRO-FO 371/3403, f. 359.

447 **Over the next several months:** For the protracted debate within the Foreign Office on what medal to bestow on Faisal Hussein, see PRO-FO 371/3403, File 53608.

447 **"to cement the Arab Alliance":** Clayton to Foreign Office, April 2, 1918; PRO-FO 371/3403, f. 364–66.

447 **"At the present day":** Mehmet Djemal to Faisal (translator unknown), June 2, 1918; PRO-WO 158/634, f. 137.

448 **"if the Arab and Turkish":** Hogarth, memorandum attached to "The Arab Question," August 9, 1918; PRO-FO 371/3381, f. 113.

448 **For the two days preceding:** Lawrence, *Seven Pillars*, Appendix II.

448 **"as soon as Faisal is in possession":** Lawrence, "Note," June 16, 1918; PRO-FO 141/688.

449 **"there might be some difficulty":** Yale to Harrison, March 25, 1918; YU, Box 2, Folder 23.

449 **Really the only way to Palestine:** Gary to U.S. Secretary of State, May 30, 1918; NARA RG59, Box 1047, 111.70Y.

450 **"our government had no policy":** William Yale's account of his intelligence-gathering activities in Cairo in the spring and summer of 1918 is drawn from Yale, *It Takes So Long*, chapter 8.

451 **"it is a well-known fact":** Yale to Harrison, July 1, 1918; YU, Box 2, Folder 35.

451 **"Quietly these few men":** Yale to Harrison, April 29, 1918; YU, Box 2, Folder 28, pp. 10–11.

452 **"Referring your report No. 28":** U.S. Secretary of State Lansing to Yale, July 9, 1918; NARA RG59, Box 1047, 111.70Y.

453 **"capable of a general":** Lawrence, *Seven Pillars*, p. 534.

454 **"emancipated from Turkish":** Foreign Office to Wingate, June 11, 1918; PRO-FO 371/3381, f. 35–36. In fact, this was a rare case of Lawrence's cynicism failing him. As would be revealed at the Paris Peace Conference, Mark Sykes had very carefully phrased his "Seven Syrians" letter so that the promise of independence for lands freed by the "Arabs themselves during the present war" could be interpreted as only applying to those lands freed at the time of writing. By this sleight-of-hand construction, most of greater Syria could be excluded.

454 **The cover story Lawrence:** Hogarth, memorandum attached to "The Arab Question," August 9, 1918; PRO-FO 371/3381, f. 113. Either this did not end Faisal's overtures to the Ottoman government, or the Germans were not informed of the severing; even into early September

1918, senior German diplomats and military officers wrote of the urgent need to make peace with Faisal.

454   **In doing so, all had ignored:** Clayton to Foreign Office, May 3, 1918; PRO-FO 371/3403, f. 384.

455   **"So for the last time we mustered":** Lawrence, *Seven Pillars*, p. 544.

455   **"I request that you see me":** Prüfer, *Diary,* July 31, 1918; HO.

Chapter 18: Damascus

457   **"We ordered 'no prisoners' ":** Lawrence, "The Destruction of the 4th. Army," October 1918; PRO-WO 882/7, f. 360.

457   **British prime minister:** Gilbert, *First World War,* p. 452.

458   **"Growing intimacy with":** Prüfer, *Diary,* August 30, 1918; HO.

459   **It was surely an indication:** Prüfer to AA, September 3, 1918; NARA T137, Roll 138, Frames 329–30.

459   **"I'll tell you, Yale":** Yale, *It Takes So Long,* chapter 8, p. 30.

461   **"[I] lay there all day":** Lawrence, *Seven Pillars*, p. 586.

461   **"I have been so violently":** Garnett, *The Letters of T. E. Lawrence,* p. 244.

462   **If exactly why remains:** As in *Seven Pillars*, Lawrence was peculiarly circumspect with both Robert Graves and Basil Liddell Hart about his meeting with Nuri Shalaan in August 1918, only allowing that it tormented him deeply. When Graves pressed on the matter, Lawrence replied, "There was a particular and very horrible reason (not published) for my distress at this moment" (Graves and Liddell Hart, *T. E. Lawrence: Letters to His Biographers,* Pt. 1, p. 103). Similarly, when Liddell Hart asked the nature of the pledge that Lawrence apparently made to Shalaan, Lawrence replied, "Prefer not to reveal." (UT Folder 1, File 1.)

462   **Lawrence had finally patched:** Lawrence, *Seven Pillars*, p. 579.

463   **"today it came to me":** Ibid., p. 586.

463   **"It is reported that the Syrians":** Yale to U.S. Director of Military Intelligence, September 12, 1918; YU, Box 2, Folder 39.

464   **"a pleasant little work":** Lawrence's account of the September 1918 offensive in Syria is drawn from *Seven Pillars*, book 10, chapters 107–12, pp. 581–660.

465   **"I was irritated":** William Yale's recollections of the September 1918 British offensive in Syria are drawn from Yale, *It Takes So Long,* chapter 9.

467   **"Already the Turkish Army":** As quoted by Wilson, *Lawrence of Arabia,* p. 549.

467   **"The whole Turkish army":** Ibid.

467   **To forestall that:** Bartholomew to Joyce, September 21, 1918; PRO-WO 157/738.

468   **During Lawrence's brief:** Wilson, *Lawrence of Arabia,* p. 555.

468   **Indeed, so rapid was:** Lawrence to Dawnay, September 25, 1918; PRO-WO 157/738.

469   **"hopeless but carefree":** Lawrence, *Seven Pillars*, pp. 628–29.

470   **"gave a horrible cry":** Lawrence, "The Destruction of the 4th. Army," October 1918; PRO-WO 882/7, f. 360.

471   **"then we turned our Hotchkiss":** Ibid.

472   **"The whole place was indescribably":** Barrow, *The Fire of Life,* pp. 209–12.

473   **To add a different wrinkle:** An interesting discussion of the Tafas incident, and of the attempt by some of Lawrence's army colleagues to defend his reputation against Lawrence himself, can be found in Mack, *A Prince of Our Disorder,* pp. 234–40.

473   **"we were on the eve":** Stirling, *Safety Last,* pp. 93–94.

475   **"I understood that":** Wilson, *Lawrence of Arabia,* p. 563.

476   **"agrees with my carrying on":** Lawrence to General Headquarters, October 1, 1918; PRO-WO 157/738.

476 **"We called out the Arab":** Lawrence, "The Destruction of the 4th. Army," October 1918; PRO-WO 882/7, f. 364.

477 **"wet red galleries":** Lawrence, *Seven Pillars*, p. 656.

479 **"Triumphal entry":** Chauvel, "Notes," as cited by Hill, *Chauvel of the Light Horse*, p. 184.

479 **"the British Government":** CIGS to Allenby, September 25, 1918; PRO-FO 371/3383, f. 489–92.

480 **"the belligerent status":** War Office to General Headquarters, Egypt, October 1, 1918; PRO-FO 371/3383, f. 498–99.

481 **"who would work for":** Chauvel, "Notes," as cited by Hill, *Chauvel of the Light Horse*, p. 184.

482 **"I feverishly wrote report":** Yale, *It Takes So Long*, chapter 10, p. 3.

483 **"that he would not work":** Chauvel, "Notes," as cited by Hill, *Chauvel of the Light Horse*, p. 185.

Epilogue: Paris

485 **"Blast the Lawrence":** Lawrence to Armstrong, October 6, 1914; UT, Folder 2, File 6.

486 **"a malign influence":** Arthur Hirtzel to Curzon, June 19, 1919; PRO-FO 371/4149, f. 149A.

486 **"to a large extent responsible":** Clark-Kerr, quoted by Wilson, *Lawrence of Arabia*, p. 617.

487 **"All necessary measures":** The Weizmann-Faisal Agreement, January 3, 1919, as reproduced in Friedman, *Tension in Palestine*, pp. 157–61.

487 **"The establishment of a National":** Weizmann, "Proposals Relating to the Establishment of a Jewish National Home in Palestine," November 19, 1918; PRO-FO 371/3385.

488 **Instead, they included:** Gelfand, *The Inquiry*, pp. 60–62.

488 **The *Report on the Desires*:** E. H. Byrne, *Report on the Desires of the Syrians*, October 7, 1918; YU Box 4, Folder 23.

489 **"We fought over boundary":** Yale, *It Takes So Long*, chapter 10, p. 6.

490 **"extreme depression":** Garnett, *The Letters of T. E. Lawrence*, p. 294.

490 **"the racial kinship":** The Weizmann-Faisal Agreement, January 3, 1919, as reproduced in Friedman, *Tension in Palestine*, pp. 157–61.

492 **"not only [the] questions":** Lawrence to Liddell Hart, Graves and Liddell Hart, *T. E. Lawrence: Letters to His Biographers*, Pt. 2, p. 143.

495 **"assist in promoting":** Sykes, memorandum, October 15, 1918; PRO-FO 371/3413.

495 **"Don't take Mark":** Hogarth to Clayton, quoted by Adelson, *Mark Sykes*, p. 281.

495 **"whoever takes over Syria":** Sykes, as quoted by Adelson, Ibid., p. 289.

495 **"I said something to him":** Lloyd George, as quoted by Wilson, *Lawrence of Arabia*, p. 609.

496 **"Chaim [Weizmann] said":** Aaronsohn, *Diary*, January 16, 1919; ZY.

496 **"I hate the way":** Aaronsohn, as quoted by Florence, *Lawrence and Aaronsohn*, p. 406.

497 **In a series of memoranda:** For details on the U.S.-UK oil concession controversy of 1919–1924, see DeNovo, *American Interests and Policies in the Middle East*, pp. 167–209; Fanning, *Foreign Oil and the Free World*, chapter 5; Shwadran, *The Middle East, Oil and the Great Powers*, pp. 403–9; and PRO-FO 141/456, File 6522.

498 **Scurrying into the breach:** Suleiman Nassif to Yale, March 24, 1924; BU Box 15, Folder 6.

498 **As he told a senior:** Yale to Birch Helms (Socony), May 5, 1922; BU Box 15, Folder 5.

498 **"smash the debasing tyranny":** Yale, "Islam Versus Christianity," *North American Review*, February 1923; BU Box 11.

498 **"the exploitive nature":** Yale, letter to *Free World*, August 1942; BU Box 1, Folder 9.

499 It was a myth: McKale, *Curt Prüfer*, p. 59.

500 "Our propaganda suffered": Prüfer to Otto Gunther von Wesendonck, German Foreign Ministry, November 2, 1918; NARA T136, Roll 94, Frame 21.

500 For these and other activities: PRO-KV 2/3114.

501 "All this is terrible": Prüfer, as quoted by McKale, *Curt Prüfer*, p. 177.

502 "Students will be": From Prüfer's MI5 Security Service file, PRO-KV 2/3114.

502 "the Arabs are like a page": Lawrence to Graves, May 21, 1912; Graves and Liddell Hart, *T. E. Lawrence: Letters to His Biographers*, Pt. 1, p. 15.

502 "walled its bearers": Lawrence, *Seven Pillars*, p. 641.

503 "made straight all": Ibid., p. 276.

504 "is more often praised": Meyers, *The Wounded Spirit*, p. 11.

504 "Please apologize": Lawrence to Newcombe, February 28, 1929; UT Folder 5, File 2.

505 "I've changed": Lawrence to Charlotte Shaw, as cited in Brown, *The Letters of T. E. Lawrence*, p. 290.

505 "at present": Lawrence to Rogers, as cited in Brown, *The Letters of T. E. Lawrence*, p. 536.

505 "Your brother's name": King George V to A. W. Lawrence, *Times* (London), May 21, 1935.

505 "I deem him": Churchill, quoted in A. W. Lawrence, *T. E. Lawrence by His Friends* (1954 edition), p. 202.

Bibliography

Books and Articles

Aaronsohn, Alex. *With the Turks in Palestine*. Boston: Houghton Mifflin, 1916.

Abbas, Hilmi. *The Last Khedive of Egypt: Memoirs of Abbas Hilmi II,* translated and edited by Amira Sonbol. Reading, UK: Ithaca Press, 1998.

Abdullah, King. *Memoirs of King Abdullah of Transjordan*. Edited by Philip Graves. London: Jonathan Cape, 1950.

Adelson, Roger. *Mark Sykes: Portrait of an Amateur*. London: Jonathan Cape, 1975.

Ahmad, Feroz. *The Young Turks: The Committee of Union and Progress in Turkish Politics*. Oxford: Clarendon Press, 1969.

———. "Great Britain's Relations with the Young Turks, 1908–1914." *Middle Eastern Studies* 2 (1966): 302–29.

Aksakal, Mustafa. *The Ottoman Road to War in 1914*. Cambridge: Cambridge University Press, 2008.

Aldington, Richard. *Lawrence of Arabia: A Biographical Inquiry*. Chicago: Henry Regnery Company, 1955.

Allen, Malcolm Dennis. "The Medievalism of T. E. Lawrence." PhD diss., Pennsylvania State University, 1983.

Allen, Richard. *Imperialism and Nationalism in the Fertile Crescent*. Boulder, CO: Westview Press, 1984.

Andelman, David. *A Shattered Peace: Versailles 1919 and the Price We Pay Today*. Hoboken, NJ: Wiley, 2008.

Antonius, George. *The Arab Awakening*. New York: J. B. Lippincott, 1939.

Asher, Michael. *Lawrence: The Uncrowned King of Arabia*. Woodstock, NY: Overlook Press, 1999.

Baker, Leonard. *Brandeis and Frankfurter: A Dual Biography*. New York: Harper & Row, 1984.

Baker, Randall. *King Husain and the Kingdom of Hejaz*. New York: Oleander Press, 1979.

Ballobar, Antonio de la Cierva. *Jerusalem in World War I: The Palestine Diary of a European Diplomat*. Translated and edited by Roberto Mazza. New York: Tauris, 2011.

Barker, A. J. *The Neglected War: Mesopotamia, 1914–1918*. London: Faber, 1967.

————. *Townshend of Kut: A Biography of Major-General Sir Charles Townshend*. London: Cassell, 1967.

Barnard, Harry. *The Forging of an American Jew: The Life and Times of Judge Julian W. Mack*. New York: Herzl Press, 1974.

Barr, James. *Setting the Desert on Fire: T. E. Lawrence and Britain's Secret War in Arabia, 1916–1918*. New York: W. W. Norton, 2009.

Barrow, George. *The Fire of Life*. London: Hutchinson, 1943.

Bayliss, Gwyn. *Chronology of the Great War*. London: Greenhill Books, 1988.

Beraud-Villars, Jean. *T. E. Lawrence, or the Search for the Absolute*. London: Sidgwick & Jackson, 1958.

Berghahn, Volker R. *Germany and the Approach of War, 1914*. New York: St. Martin's Press, 1973.

Bernstorff, Johann Heinrich von. *Memoirs of Count Bernstorff*. New York: Random House, 1936.

Bertrand-Cadi, Jean-Yves. *Le Colonel Cherif Cadi: Serviteur de l'Islam et de la République*. [Colonel Sharif Cadi: Servant of Islam and the Republic] Paris: Maisonneuve & Larose, 2005.

Birdwood, William Riddell. *Nuri as-Said: A Study in Arab Leadership*. London: Cassell & Company, 1959.

Bond, Brian. *The First World War and British Military History*. Oxford: Clarendon Press, 1991.

Bonsal, Stephen. *Suitors and Supplicants: The Little Nations at Versailles*. New York: Prentice Hall, 1946.

Boyle, William. *My Naval Life*. London: Hutchinson, 1942.

Bray, Norman. *Shifting Sands*. London: Unicorn Press, 1934.

Brémond, Édouard. *Le Hedjaz dans la Guerre Mondiale* [The Hejaz in the World War]. Paris: Payot, 1931.

Brent, Peter. *T. E. Lawrence*. New York: G. P. Putnam's Sons, 1975.

Brown, Malcolm. *Lawrence of Arabia: The Life, the Legend*. New York: Thames & Hudson, 2005.

————. *The Letters of T. E. Lawrence*. London: Oxford University Press, 1991.

————, ed. *T. E. Lawrence in War and Peace: An Anthology of the Military Writings of Lawrence of Arabia*. London: Greenhill Books, 2005.

Bruner, Robert, and Sean Carr. *The Panic of 1907: Lessons Learned from the Market's Perfect Storm*. New York: John Wiley & Sons, 2007.

Bullock, David. *Allenby's War*. London: Blandford Press, 1988.

Carter, Miranda. *George, Nicholas and Wilhelm: Three Royal Cousins and the Road to World War I*. New York: Alfred A. Knopf, 2010.

Cecil, Lamar. *The German Diplomatic Service, 1871–1914*. Princeton: Princeton University Press, 1976.

————. *Wilhelm II*. Vol. 1, *Prince and Emperor, 1859–1900*. Chapel Hill: University of North Carolina Press, 1989.

Chaliand, Gerard, and Yves Ternon. *The Armenians: From Genocide to Resistance*. London: Zed Press, 1983.

Chernow, Ron. *Titan: The Life of John D. Rockefeller*. New York: Vintage, 2004.

Churchill, Winston. *Great Contemporaries*. New York: Norton, 1991.

Clayton, Gilbert. *An Arabian Diary*. Berkeley: University of California Press, 1969.

Crowley, Patrick. *Kut 1916: Courage and Failure in Iraq.* Stroud, UK: History Press, 2009.

Crutwell, C. R. *A History of the Great War.* Oxford: Clarendon Press, 1934.

Dadrian, Vahakn. *The Key Elements in the Turkish Denial of the Armenian Genocide: A Case Study of Distortion and Falsification.* Toronto: Zoryan Institute, 1999.

Davidson, Lawrence. *America's Palestine: Popular and Official Perceptions from Balfour to Israeli Statehood.* Gainesville: University Press of Florida, 2001.

Davis, Moshe. *With Eyes Toward Zion.* Vol. 2. New York: Praeger, 1986.

Dawn, C. Ernest. *From Ottomanism to Arabism: Essays on the Origins of Arab Nationalism.* Urbana: University of Illinois Press, 1973.

DeNovo, John. *American Interests and Policies in the Middle East, 1900–1939.* Minneapolis: University of Minnesota Press, 1963.

———. "The Movement for an Aggressive American Oil Policy Abroad, 1918–1920." *American Historical Review* 61, no. 4 (July 1956).

Divine, Donna Robinson. *Politics and Society in Ottoman Palestine: The Arab Struggle for Survival and Power.* Boulder, CO: Lynne Rienner, 1994.

Djemal Pasha, Ahmet. *Memories of a Turkish Statesman, 1913–1919.* New York: Doran, 1922.

Earle, Edward Mead. *Turkey, the Great Powers and the Baghdad Railway: A Study in Imperialism.* New York: Russell & Russell, 1966.

Emin, Ahmed. *Turkey in the World War.* New Haven, CT: Yale University Press, 1930.

Engle, Anita. *The Nili Spies.* London: Hogarth Press, 1959.

Erickson, Edward. *Ordered to Die: A History of the Ottoman Army in the First World War.* Westport, CT: Greenwood Press, 2001.

Evans, Laurence. *United States Policy and the Partition of Turkey, 1914–1924.* Baltimore: Johns Hopkins University Press, 1965.

Fanning, Leonard. *Foreign Oil and the Free World.* New York: McGraw-Hill, 1954.

Fischer, Fritz. *Germany's Aims in the First World War.* New York: W. W. Norton, 1967.

———. *War of Illusions: German Policies from 1911 to 1914.* London: Chatto & Windus, 1975.

Fischer, Louis. *Oil Imperialism: The International Struggle for Petroleum.* New York: International, 1926.

Florence, Ronald. *Lawrence and Aaronsohn: T. E. Lawrence, Aaron Aaronsohn and the Seeds of the Arab-Israeli Conflict.* New York: Viking, 2007.

Frankfurter, Felix. *Felix Frankfurter Reminisces.* New York: Reynal, 1960.

Friedman, Isaiah. *The Question of Palestine, 1914–1918.* London: Routledge & Kegan Paul, 1973.

——— *Palestine: A Twice-Promised Land?* New Brunswick, NJ: Transaction Publishers, 2000.

———, ed. *Germany, Turkey and Zionism, 1897–1918.* The Rise of Israel, vol. 4. New York: Garland Publishing, 1987.

———, ed. *The Zionist Commission in Palestine.* The Rise of Israel, vol. 9. New York: Garland Publishing, 1987.

———, ed. *Tension in Palestine: Peacemaking in Paris, 1919.* The Rise of Israel, vol. 10. New York: Garland Publishing, 1987.

Fromkin, David. *A Peace to End All Peace: Creating the Modern Middle East, 1914–1922.* New York: Holt, 1989.

Gardner, Brian. *Allenby*. London: Cassell, 1965.

Garnett, David. *The Essential T. E. Lawrence*. London: Jonathan Cape, 1951.

———, ed. *The Letters of T. E. Lawrence*. New York: Doubleday Doran, 1939.

Gelfand, Lawrence. *The Inquiry: American Preparations for Peace, 1917–1919*. New Haven, CT: Yale University Press, 1963.

Gelvin, James. *Divided Loyalties: Nationalism and Mass Politics in Syria at the Close of Empire*. Berkeley: University of California Press, 1998.

Gershoni, Israel. *Middle East Historiographies: Narrating the Twentieth Century*. Seattle: University of Washington Press, 2006.

Gilbert, Martin. *Exile and Return: The Struggle for a Jewish Homeland*. Philadelphia: Lippincott, 1978.

———. *The First World War: A Complete History*. New York: Holt, 1994.

———. *The Somme*. New York: Holt, 2006.

Gokay, Bulent. *A Clash of Empires: Turkey Between Russian Bolshevism and British Imperialism*. London: Tauris, 1997.

Goldstone, Patricia. *Aaronsohn's Maps*. Orlando, FL: Harcourt, 2007.

Gooch, G. P., and Temperley, eds. *British Documents on the Origins of the War, 1898–1914*. London: His Majesty's Stationery Office, 1926.

Gorni, Yosef. *Zionism and the Arabs, 1882–1948: A Study of Ideology*. New York: Oxford University Press, 1987.

Gottlieb, W. W. *Studies in Secret Diplomacy During the First World War*. London: George Allen & Unwin, 1957.

Grainger, John D. *The Battle for Palestine, 1917*. Woodbridge, UK: Boydell, 2006.

Graves, Robert. *Lawrence and the Arabs*. New York: Paragon House, 1991.

Graves, Robert, and Basil Liddell Hart. *T. E. Lawrence: Letters to His Biographers*. London: Cassell, 1963.

Greaves, Adrian. *Lawrence of Arabia: Mirage of a Desert War*. London: Weidenfeld & Nicolson, 2007.

Guinn, Paul. *British Strategy and Politics, 1914–1918*. Oxford: Clarendon Press, 1965.

Haas, Jacob de. *Louis D. Brandeis*. New York: Bloch, 1929.

Halkin, Hillel. *A Strange Death: A Story Originating in Espionage, Betrayal and Vengeance in a Village in Old Palestine*. New York: PublicAffairs, 2005.

Halpern, Ben. *A Clash of Heroes: Brandeis, Weizmann, and American Zionism*. New York: Oxford University Press, 1987.

Hanioglu, Sukru. *A Brief History of the Late Ottoman Period*. Princeton, NJ: Princeton University Press, 2008.

———. *Young Turks in Opposition*. New York: Oxford University Press, 1995.

Hart, Peter. *Gallipoli*. New York: Oxford University Press, 2011.

Heller, Joseph. *British Policy Towards the Ottoman Empire, 1908–1914*. London: Frank Cass, 1983.

Herbert, Aubrey. *Mons, Kut and Anzac*. London: E. Arnold, 1919.

Hickey, Michael. *Gallipoli*. London: John Murray, 1995.

Hill, A. J. *Chauvel of the Light Horse*. Melbourne, AU: Melbourne University Press, 1978.

Hillgruber, Andreas. *Germany and the Two World Wars*. Translated by William C. Kirby. Cambridge, MA: Harvard University Press, 1981.

Holt, P. M. *Egypt and the Fertile Crescent, 1516–1922.* Ithaca, NY: Cornell University Press, 1966.

Hopkirk, Peter. *Like Hidden Fire: The Plot to Bring Down the British Empire.* New York: Kodansha, 1994.

Hopwood, Derek. *Tales of Empire: The British in the Middle East, 1880–1952.* London: Tauris, 1989.

Hourani, Albert. *The Emergence of the Modern Middle East.* Oxford, UK: Macmillan, 1981.

Howard, Harry N. *The King-Crane Commission: An American Inquiry in the Middle East.* Beirut: Khayat, 1963.

Hughes, Matthew. *Allenby and British Strategy in the Middle East, 1917–1919.* London: Frank Cass, 1999.

Hyde, Montgomery. *Solitary in the Ranks.* London: Constable, 1977.

James, Lawrence. *The Golden Warrior: The Life and Legend of Lawrence of Arabia.* New York: Marlow & Company, 1994.

Karsh, Efraim. *Empires of the Sand: The Struggle for Mastery in the Middle East, 1789–1923.* Cambridge, MA: Harvard University Press, 1999.

Katz, Shmuel. *The Aaronsohn Saga.* Jerusalem: Gefen, 2007.

Kayali, Hasan. *Arabs and Young Turks: Ottomanism, Arabism and Islamism in the Ottoman Empire, 1908–1918.* Berkeley: University of California Press, 1997.

Kedourie, Elie. *England and the Middle East: The Destruction of the Ottoman Empire, 1914–1921.* London: Mansell, 1987.

Keegan, John. *The First World War.* New York: Vintage, 2000.

Kent, Marian. *The Great Powers and the End of the Ottoman Empire.* London: George Allen & Unwin, 1984.

Keogh, E. G. *Suez to Aleppo.* Melbourne, AU: Wilke & Company, 1955.

Khalidi, Rashid, ed. *The Origins of Arab Nationalism.* New York: Columbia University Press, 1991.

Kinross, John. *Ataturk.* New York: William Morrow and Co., 1965.

———. *The Ottoman Centuries.* New York: Morrow, 1977.

Kirkbride, Alec. *An Awakening: The Arab Campaign, 1917–1918.* Saudi Arabia: University Press of Arabia, 1971.

Knee, Stewart. "The King-Crane Commission of 1919: The Articulation of Political Anti-Zionism." *American Jewish Archives* 29, no. 1 (1977): 22–53.

Knightley, Phillip, and Colin Simpson. *The Secret Lives of Lawrence of Arabia.* London: Literary Guild, 1969.

Knowlton, Evelyn, and George Gibb. *History of Standard Oil Company: Resurgent Years, 1911–1927.* New York: Harper & Row, 1956.

Kushner, David, ed. *Palestine in the Late Ottoman Period.* Jerusalem: Yad Izhak Ben-Zvi, 1986.

Laqueur, Walter. *A History of Zionism.* New York: Schocken, 2003.

Lares, J. M. *T. E. Lawrence, la France et les Français* [T. E. Lawrence, France and the French]. Paris: Sorbonne, 1980.

Lawrence, A. W., ed. *T. E. Lawrence by His Friends.* London: Jonathan Cape, 1937.

Lawrence, A. W., ed. *T. E. Lawrence by His Friends.* London: Jonathan Cape, 1954.

———, ed. *Letters to T. E. Lawrence.* London: Jonathan Cape, 1962.

Lawrence, T. E. *Crusader Castles.* Oxford: Clarendon, 1988.

———. *The Home Letters of T. E. Lawrence and His Brothers.* New York: Macmillan, 1954.

————. *Secret Despatches from Arabia*. London: Bellew, 1991.

————. *The Mint*. London: Jonathan Cape, 1973.

————. *Oriental Assembly*. Edited by Arnold Lawrence. London: Williams & Norgate, 1939.

————. *Seven Pillars of Wisdom: A Triumph* (1922 "Oxford" text). Blacksburg, VA: Wilder Press, 2011.

————. *Seven Pillars of Wisdom: A Triumph*. New York: Anchor, 1991.

————. *Revolt in the Desert*. Ware, UK: Wordsworth, 1997.

LeClerc, Christophe. *Avec T. E. Lawrence in Arabie* [With T. E. Lawrence in Arabia]. Paris: L'Harmattan, 1998.

Lewis, Geoffrey. "An Ottoman Officer in Palestine, 1914–1918." In David Kushner, ed., *Palestine in the Late Ottoman Period*. Jerusalem: Yad Izhak Ben-Zvi, 1986.

Lewy, Guenter. *The Armenian Massacres in Ottoman Turkey*. Salt Lake City, UT: University of Utah Press, 2005.

Liddell Hart, Basil H. *Colonel Lawrence: The Man Behind the Legend*. New York: Halcyon House, 1937.

————. *The Real War, 1914–1918*. Boston: Little, Brown, 1930.

Link, Arthur S., ed., *The Papers of Woodrow Wilson*. Princeton, NJ: Princeton University Press, 1980.

Lloyd George, David. *Memoirs of the Peace Conference*. New Haven, CT: Yale University Press, 1939.

Lockman, J. N. *Scattered Tracks on the Lawrence Trail: Twelve Essays on T. E. Lawrence*. Whitmore Lake, MI: Falcon Books, 1996.

Longrigg, Stephen. *Oil in the Middle East: Its Discovery and Development*. London: Oxford University Press, 1955.

Macdonogh, Giles. *The Last Kaiser: The Life of Wilhelm II*. New York: St. Martin's Press, 2001.

Mack, John E. *A Prince of Our Disorder: The Life of T. E. Lawrence*. Boston: Little, Brown, 1976.

Magnus, Philip. *Kitchener: Portrait of an Imperialist*. New York: Dutton, 1959.

Mango, Andrew. *Ataturk*. London: John Murray, 1999.

McKale, Donald. *Curt Prüfer: German Diplomat from the Kaiser to Hitler*. Kent, OH: Kent State University Press, 1987.

————. *War by Revolution: Germany and Great Britain in the Middle East in the Era of World War I*. Kent, OH: Kent State University Press, 1998.

McMeekin, Sean. *The Berlin-Baghdad Express*. Cambridge, MA: Harvard University Press, 2010.

MacMillan, Margaret. *Paris 1919: Six Months That Changed the World*. New York: Random House, 2002.

MacMunn, George, and Cyril Falls. *Military Operations in Egypt and Palestine; History of the Great War*. London: His Majesty's Stationery Office, 1928.

Mandel, Neville. *The Arabs and Zionism Before World War I*. Berkeley: University of California Press, 1976.

Manuel, Frank Edward. *The Realities of American-Palestine Relations*. Washington, DC: Public-Affairs Press, 1949.

Massey, W. T. *Allenby's Final Triumph*. London: Constable, 1920.

Meinertzhagen, Richard. *Middle East Diary, 1917–1956*. London: Cresset Press, 1960.

Melka, R. L. "Max Freiherr von Oppenheim: Sixty Years of Scholarship and Political Intrigue in the Middle East." *Middle Eastern Studies* 9, no. 1 (January 1973): 81–93.

Meyers, Jeffrey. *T. E. Lawrence: A Bibliography*. New York: Garland, 1974.

———. *The Wounded Spirit: A Study of "Seven Pillars of Wisdom."* London: Macmillan, 1989.

Millar, Ronald. *Death of an Army: The Siege of Kut, 1915–1916*. New York: Houghton Mifflin, 1970.

Monroe, Elizabeth. *Britain's Moment in the Middle East, 1914–1956*. London: Chatto & Windus, 1981.

Moore, Briscoe. *The Mounted Riflemen in Sinai and Palestine: The Story of New Zealand's Crusaders*. Auckland: Whitcombe & Tombs, 1920.

Moorehead, Alan. *Gallipoli*. New York: Perennial Classics, 2002.

Morgenthau, Henry. *Ambassador Morgenthau's Story*. New York: Doubleday, Page & Co., 1918.

Morris, Benny. *Righteous Victims: A History of the Zionist-Arab Conflict, 1881–1999*. London: John Murray, 2000.

Morris, James. *The Hashemite Kings*. New York: Pantheon, 1959.

Moscrop, John James. *Measuring Jerusalem: The Palestine Exploration Fund and British Interests in the Holy Land*. New York: Leicester University Press, 2000.

Mousa, Suleiman. *T. E. Lawrence: An Arab View*. Translated by Albert Boutros. London: Oxford University Press, 1966.

Murphy, David. *The Arab Revolt, 1916–1918: Lawrence Sets Arabia Ablaze*. London: Osprey, 2008.

Nash, N. S. *Chitral Charlie: The Life and Times of a Victorian Soldier*. Barnsley, UK: Pen & Sword Books, 2010.

Nevakivi, Jukka. *Britain, France and the Arab Middle East, 1914–1920*. London: Athlone Press, 1969.

Nogales, Rafael de. *Four Years Beneath the Crescent*. New York: Charles Scribner's Sons, 1926.

Nutting, Anthony. *Lawrence of Arabia: The Man and the Motive*. London: Hollis & Carter, 1961.

O'Brien, Conor Cruise. *The Siege: The Saga of Israel and Zionism*. New York: Simon & Schuster, 1986.

O'Brien, Philip M. *T. E. Lawrence: A Bibliography*. New Castle, DE: Oak Knoll Press, 2000.

Ocampo, Victoria. *338171 T.E. (Lawrence of Arabia)*. New York: Dutton, 1963.

Orlans, Harold. *T. E. Lawrence: Biography of a Broken Hero*. Jefferson, NC: McFarland & Co., 2002.

Palmer, Alan. *The Kaiser: Warlord of the Second Reich*. London: Weidenfeld & Nicolson, 1978.

Phillips, Harlan B. *Felix Frankfurter Reminisces*. New York: Reynal & Co., 1960.

Renton, James. *The Zionist Masquerade: The Birth of the Anglo-Zionist Alliance, 1914–1918*. London: Palgrave Macmillan, 2007.

Richards, Vyvyan. *Portrait of T. E. Lawrence: The Lawrence of "Seven Pillars of Wisdom."* London: Jonathan Cape, 1936.

Rohl, John. *The Kaiser and His Court*. Cambridge: Cambridge University Press, 1994.

Rose, Norman. *Chaim Weizmann: A Biography*. London, Weidenfeld and Nicolson, 1987.

Sachar, Howard Morley. *A History of Israel: From the Rise of Zionism to Our Time*. New York: Alfred A. Knopf, 2007.

Sanders, Liman von. *Five Years in Turkey*. Annapolis, MD: United States Naval Institute Press, 1927.

Sanders, Ronald. *The High Walls of Jerusalem: A History of the Balfour Declaration and the Birth of the British Mandate for Palestine*. New York: Holt, Rinehart & Winston, 1983.

Satia, Priya. *Spies in Arabia: The Great War and the Cultural Foundations of Britain's Covert Empire in the Middle East.* Oxford: Oxford University Press, 2008.

Schama, Simon. *Two Rothschilds and the Land of Israel.* New York: Alfred A. Knopf, 1978.

Schilcher, L. Schatkowski. "The Famine of 1915–1918 in Greater Syria." In *Problems of the Modern Middle East in Historical Perspective,* edited by John Spagnolo, pp. 229–58. Reading, UK: Ithaca Press, 1992.

Schneer, Jonathan. *The Balfour Declaration: The Origins of the Arab-Israeli Conflict.* New York: Random House, 2012.

Seidt, Hans-Ulrich. "From Palestine to the Caucasus: Oskar Niedermayer and Germany's Middle Eastern Strategy in 1918." *German Studies Review* 24, no. 1 (February 2001): 1–18.

Shaw, Stanford. *History of the Ottoman Empire and Modern Turkey.* Vols. 1 and 2. Cambridge: Cambridge University Press, 1976.

Sheffy, Yigal. *British Military Intelligence in the Palestine Campaign.* London: Frank Cass, 1998.

Shotwell, James Thomas. *At the Paris Peace Conference.* New York: Macmillan, 1937.

Shwadran, Benjamin. *The Middle East, Oil and the Great Powers.* New York: Praeger, 1955.

Spagnolo, J. P. "French Influence in Syria Prior to World War I: The Functional Weakness of Imperialism." *Middle East Journal* 23, no. 1 (1969): 44–62.

Steed, Wickham. *Through Thirty Years, 1892–1922: A Personal Narrative.* New York: Doubleday, 1925.

Stein, Leonard. *The Balfour Declaration.* London: Valentine, Mitchell & Co., 1961.

Stevenson, David. *1914–1918: The History of the First World War.* New York: Penguin, 2004.

Stewart, Desmond. *T. E. Lawrence.* London: Paladin, 1979.

Stirling, W. F. *Safety Last.* London: Hollis & Carter, 1953.

Stitt, George. *A Prince of Arabia: The Emir Shereef Ali Haider.* London: George Allen & Unwin, 1948.

Storrs, Ronald. *Orientations: The Memoirs of Sir Ronald Storrs.* New York: G. P. Putnam's Sons, 1937.

Sutherland, James Kay. *The Adventures of an Armenian Boy.* Ann Arbor, MI: Ann Arbor Press, 1964.

Symes, Stewart. *Tour of Duty.* London: Collins, 1946.

Tabachnik, Stephen. *T. E. Lawrence: An Encyclopedia.* Westport, CT: Greenwood Press, 2004.

———. *The T. E. Lawrence Puzzle.* Athens: University of Georgia Press, 2012.

Tabachnik, Stephen, and Christopher Matheson. *Images of T. E. Lawrence.* London: Jonathan Cape, 1988.

Tanenbaum, Jan Karl. *France and the Arab Middle East, 1914–1920.* Philadelphia: American Philosophical Society, 1978.

Tauber, Eliezer. *The Arab Movements in World War I.* London: Frank Cass, 1993.

Taylor, A. J. P. *Bismarck: The Man and the Statesman.* New York: Vintage, 1967.

———. *The Struggle for the Mastery of Europe, 1848–1918.* Oxford: Clarendon Press, 1954.

Teichmann, Gabriele, and Gisela Volger. *Faszination: Max Von Oppenheim.* Cologne: Dumont, 2001.

Thomas, Lowell. *With Lawrence in Arabia.* New York: Century, 1924.

Thomson, Basil. *My Experiences at Scotland Yard.* New York: A. L. Burt, 1926.

———. *Queer People.* London: Hodder & Stoughton, 1922.

———. *The Scene Changes.* New York: Doubleday, Doran & Co., 1937.

Tibawi, Abdul Latif. *Anglo-Arab Relations and the Question of Palestine, 1914–1921.* London: Luzac, 1978.

Townshend, Charles. *When God Made Hell: The British Invasion of Mesopotamia and the Creation of Iraq.* New York: Faber & Faber, 2010.

Toynbee, Arnold. *Acquaintances.* London: Oxford University Press, 1967.

Trumpener, Ulrich. *Germany and the Ottoman Empire, 1914–1918.* Princeton, NJ: Princeton University Press, 1968.

Tuchman, Barbara. *The Guns of August.* New York: Ballantine, 2004.

Tuohy, Ferdinand. *The Secret Corps: A Tale of "Intelligence" on All Fronts.* New York: Seltzer, 1920.

Turfan, M. Naim. *Rise of the Young Turks: Politics, the Military and the Ottoman Collapse.* New York: Tauris, 2000.

Urofsky, Melvin. *Louis D. Brandeis.* New York: Pantheon, 2009.

Verrier, Anthony, ed. *Agents of Empire: Brigadier Walter Gribbon, Aaron Aaronsohn and the NILI Ring.* Washington: Brassey's, 1995.

Vester, Bertha Spafford. *Our Jerusalem: An American Family in the Holy City, 1881–1949.* New York: Doubleday, 1950.

Wavell, Archibald. *Allenby: A Study in Greatness.* London: Harrap & Co., 1941.

———. *The Palestine Campaigns.* London: Constable, 1968.

Weber, Frank. *Eagles on the Crescent: Germany, Austria and the Diplomacy of the Turkish Alliance.* Ithaca, NY: Cornell University Press, 1970.

Weintraub, Stanley, and Rodelle Weintraub. *Private Shaw and Public Shaw.* London: Jonathan Cape, 1963.

Weizmann, Chaim. *Trial and Error: The Autobiography of Chaim Weizmann.* New York: Harper, 1949.

Weldon, Lewen. *Hard Lying.* London: Jenkins, 1925.

Westrate, Bruce. *The Arab Bureau: British Policy in the Middle East, 1916–1920.* University Park: Pennsylvania State University Press, 1992.

Wilson, Arnold. *Loyalties: Mesopotamia, 1914–1917.* Oxford: Oxford University Press, 1930.

———. *Loyalties: Mesopotamia 1917–1920.* London: Humphrey Milford, 1931.

Wilson, Jeremy. *Lawrence of Arabia: The Authorized Biography of T. E. Lawrence.* New York: Atheneum, 1990.

Wilson, Mary C. *King Abdullah, Britain and the Making of Jordan.* Cambridge: Cambridge University Press, 1987.

Winstone, H. V. F. *The Illicit Adventure: The Story of Political and Military Intelligence in the Middle East from 1898 to 1926.* London: Jonathan Cape, 1982.

———. *Woolley of Ur: The Life of Sir Leonard Woolley.* London: Secker & Warburg, 1990.

Woolley, C. Leonard. *Dead Towns and Living Men.* London: Lutterworth Press, 1954.

Woolley, C. Leonard, and T. E. Lawrence. *The Wilderness of Zin.* New York: Charles Scribner's Sons, 1936.

Wrench, Evelyn. *Struggle, 1914–1920.* London: Nicholson & Watson, 1935.

Yale, William. *The Near East: A Modern History.* Ann Arbor: University of Michigan Press, 1958.

———. *It Takes So Long.* Howard Gotlieb Archival Research Center, Boston University, Box 7, Folder 7.

———. *The Reminiscences of William Yale.* New York: Oral History Research Office, Columbia University.

———. "T. E. Lawrence: Scholar, Soldier, Statesman, Diplomat." Undated article, probably 1935. Boston: Howard Gotlieb Archival Research Center, Boston University, Box 6, Folder 1.

Yapp, M. E. *The Making of the Modern Near East, 1792–1923.* New York: Longman, 1987.

Yardley, Herbert D. *The American Black Chamber.* Annapolis, MD: United States Naval Institute Press, 1931.

Yardley, Michael. *T. E. Lawrence: A Biography.* New York: Stein & Day, 1987.

Yergin, Daniel. *The Prize: The Epic Quest for Oil, Money and Power.* New York: Free Press, 2008.

Zeine, Zeine N. *The Emergence of Arab Nationalism.* Delmar, NY: Caravan, 1973.

Archives and Collections

Aaron Aaronsohn Papers. NILI Museum and Archives, Zichron Ya'aqov, Israel.

Gilbert Clayton & Reginald Wingate Papers. Sudan Archives, University of Durham, Durham, England.

T. E. Lawrence Collection. Harry Ransom Humanities Research Center, University of Texas, Austin.

T. E. Lawrence Papers. Bodleian Library, Oxford, England.

George Lloyd Papers. Churchill College, Cambridge, England.

National Archives (UK, formerly Public Records Office), Kew, England.

National Archives (U.S.), Washington, DC.

Oral History Research Office. Columbia University, New York, NY.

Political Archives of the German Foreign Ministry, Berlin, Germany.

Curt Max Prüfer Papers. Hoover Institution, Stanford University, Palo Alto, CA.

Mark Sykes Papers. Middle East Centre. St. Antony's College, Oxford, England.

William Yale Collection. Howard Gotlieb Archival Research Center, Boston University.

William Yale Collection. Milne Special Collections, University of New Hampshire, Durham.

William Yale Papers. House Collection (M658), Yale University Library, New Haven, CT.

Index

Aaronsohn, Aaron, 16, 287, 379, 434
  as agronomist, 15, 50, 51–53, 86, 110, 216, 217, 431, 443–44
  at Arab Bureau, 252–56, 260, 348–50, 357, 444
  "arrest" of, 216–17
  background and role of, 15, 50–51
  and Balfour Declaration, 388
  British inertia as frustrating to, 228–29, 251–53
  character and personality of, 49–50
  death of, 496
  Djemal Pasha and, 91, 110–11, 133–34, 156, 160, 180–81, 522n
  on expulsions from Jaffa, 298–305
  family of, 359–60
  Lawrence and, 357–60, 363–64
  locust plague and, 110–11, 131, 133–36, 159–60, 180
  NILI spy network of, 347–50, 359–60
  pariah status with Zionist Commission, 443–44
  at Paris Peace Conference, 482, 496
  and ruination caused by Ottoman entry into the war, 83–86
  spy network of, 135–36, 143–44, 158–60, 180–81, 216–20, 228–29, 232, 251–56, 277–80, 326–27, 347–50, 370, 443, 522n
  Sykes and, 220, 229–32, 294–96, 300–304, 348, 371–72
  U.S. missions of, 51–52, 394–98, 410–11, 458, 482
  Weizmann and, 394–98, 411, 458
  Yale and, 366, 370–72

Aaronsohn, Alex, 85, 134, 136, 143–44, 219, 256, 360, 371, 372, 379–80, 443
Aaronsohn, Ephraim, 86, 378, 397, 536n
Aaronsohn, Rivka, 134–35, 136, 144, 219, 298
Aaronsohn, Sam, 397, 443
Aaronsohn, Sarah, 159, 298
  character and personality of, 298
  death of, 379, 397, 443, 535n, 536n
  as head of NILI spy network, 256, 298–99, 326–27, 376–79
Aaronsohn, Zvi, 378
Aaronsohn family, 75–77
Aba el Lissan, massacre of Turkish battalion at, 333–35 Aba el Naam, 280–83, 287
  attack on Turkish garrison at, 328
Abbas Hilmi II, khedive of Egypt, 38–39, 58, 382–83, 430–31, 455–56, 458–59, 482, 500
Abd el Kader, 381, 383–85, 389, 400–401, 475–76
Abd el Karim, 256
Abdullah ibn-Hussein, 112, 115–16, 123, 188–89, 194–96, 199–202, 205, 209, 236, 261, 491–92, 520n
  attempt to reach accommodation with Israel by, 490
  British waffling criticized by, 194–95
  character and personality of, 195–96
  Jordan ruled by, 492, 493
  Lawrence's mission to camp of, 275–77, 280–81, 286, 289–90
aerial reconnaissance, 100, 243
Afghanistan, 79, 493
Africa, 239
  European imperialism in, 29, 69

About the Author

Scott Anderson is a veteran war correspondent who has reported from Lebanon, Northern Ireland, Chechnya, Israel, Sudan, Bosnia, El Salvador, and many other war-torn countries. He is a frequent contributor to the *New York Times Magazine* and *Vanity Fair,* and his work has also appeared in *Esquire, Harper's Magazine,* and *Outside.* He is the author of the novels *Moonlight Hotel* and *Triage* and the nonfiction books *The Man Who Tried to Save the World, War Zones,* and *Inside the League,* the last two coauthored with his brother Jon Lee Anderson.

THE SYRIAN THEATER

MEDITERRANEAN SEA

Beirut

LEBANON

Damascus

SYRIA

SEA OF GALILEE

Haifa

Afuleh

YARMUK GORGE

Tafas

Athlit

Deraa

Zichron Yaakov

PALESTINE

JORDAN RIVER

Minifir

Nablus

Salt

Jaffa

Amman

Azraq

Jericho

Jerusalem

Madeba

Hebron

DEAD SEA

Gaza

Beersheva

Kerak

Tafileh

Bair

Jefer

Maan

Guweira

Aqaba

Mudowarra